**PRINCIPLES OF
PSYCHOPATHOLOGY**

McGraw-Hill Series
in Psychology

Consulting Editors

NORMAN GARMEZY

HARRY F. HARLOW

LYLE V. JONES

HAROLD W. STEVENSON

McGRAW-HILL BOOK COMPANY

New York   St. Louis   San Francisco   Toronto   London   Sydney

PRINCIPLES OF
PSYCHOPATHOLOGY

An Experimental Approach

BRENDAN A. MAHER

Professor of Psychology   University of Wisconsin

PRINCIPLES OF PSYCHOPATHOLOGY

39610

789101112 HDBP 7543210

FOR MY PARENTS,
THOMAS FRANCIS AND AGNES MAHER

PREFACE

Psychopathology is a part of behavioral science. An understanding of the phenomena of disordered behavior depends, fundamentally, upon an understanding of the principles of ordered behavior. When turning for the first time to the study of psychopathology, it is therefore unnecessary for the reader to acquire new concepts. He may proceed effectively with those principles that have been worked out in the experimental laboratory and the natural habitat, and to which he has already been exposed in his earlier studies.

Many sciences have contributed to our knowledge of these principles; psychology, biology, biochemistry, genetics, sociology, and anthropology are among the foremost. In this book, the problems of psychopathology are approached from the base provided by these sciences. Impatience to find answers to the pressing human problems of psychopathology has impelled some to abandon the laborious (and frequently fruitless) business of systematic investigation in favor of the comforts of authority or the self-assurances of personal conviction. When we do this, we merely delay progress on the serious matters at hand.

Much of this is obvious. Surprisingly, however, the presentation of the material of abnormal psychology to the university student has not tended to reflect these methods and principles. Many college courses are conceived in terms that owe little to behavioral science and much to the metaphors of psychoanalysis and to the case histories of descriptive psychiatry. The transition to the study of psychopathology from courses in social psychology, experimental psychology, and the other subfields of undergraduate concentration in psychology, should be natural and systematic. Often it is not. In the writer's experience, many students have expressed surprise (and dismay) at the discovery that their mastery of the principles of general psychology stands them in little stead when they turn to the literature of the behavior disorders.

In the past two or three decades there has been, however, a considerable expansion in scientific research in psychopathology. This expansion has come about mainly from the serious application of the principles of experimental psychology to problems of disordered behavior, and from the major developments in biopsychology—especially in the physiology of consciousness, and in biochemistry.

This book is written with the belief that in these new directions lies the major hope for advancement in our knowledge of psychopathology. In them lies also the hope of the patient for relief from his sufferings. At the present time, our answers to the urgent questions of psychopathology are tentative; they often amount to confessions of ignorance. The problems to which we seek answers are fascinating; the goals of the search are crucial. Unravelling the subtle relationships between psychological and biological factors in the behavior disorders is one of the most challenging tasks of science in our time.

With these beliefs, the writer has organized the book so as to present (a) the problems of definition that must be faced when beginning the study of psychopathology; (b) a brief summary of the central psychological and biological concepts that are germane to this study; and (c) the hypotheses and findings that have emerged from scientific inquiry. Because of this organization, the writer has used case histories sparingly, but has covered research findings in some detail. The distribution of emphasis within the book reflects the emergence of research findings. Under the general rubric of the schizophrenias comes the vast bulk of hospital diagnoses. Thus four chapters are devoted to the problems of schizophrenia (where the research effort has been both large and fruitful) whereas little attention has been paid to the affective disorders. No attention at all has been paid to rare or exotic syndromes.

Theoretical analyses are offered where the data appear to warrant them; they are eschewed where the data do not. Central questions are presented whenever possible; not all of them are answerable. It is hoped that the student will gain, however, some understanding of the manner in which psychopathologists work, of the questions that are engaging their attention, and of the progress they have made to date.

In writing this book, the author has come to owe much to the generosity of many colleagues. Portions of the manuscript were read and criticised by Solomon Feldman, Harry Harlow, Frederick Kanfer, Albert Marston, David McClelland, Barry McLaughlin, Walter Mischel, Charles Noblin, Lee Sechrest, Norman Watt, and Robert White. Particular help came from Irving Gottesman, both in suggestions and in the provision of data gathered by himself and James Shields. Detailed and invaluable criticism of the penultimate draft of the manuscript was given by Norman Garmezy, to whose insights and care the writer is greatly indebted. Material, drawings, and photographs were provided by W. H. Davidson, Mildred Dubitzky, John Fredericksen, David Howe, Ogden Lindsley, and Thomas Mulholland.

Teodoro Allyon, Joseph Brady, Loren Chapman, Robert Heath, Robert Malmo, David Shakow, and Julius Wishner generously provided complete copies of their reported research and permissions to quote from them at length. The writer wishes also to express his gratitude for the patient and careful help that he received in the preparation of the manuscript, from Judith Boelkins, Imogene Bowers, Mary Gutmann, Patricia Hall, Verlyn Thiessen, Marilyn Spiegel, Helen Sullivan, and Kathy Sylva.

In addition to the many authors and publishers who have kindly granted permission to quote from their works, and are identified in the text by the bibliographic citation, I wish to acknowledge specifically the permission granted for the following quotations.

The *American Journal of Psychiatry* for permission to quote material cited on pages 331–332 from Heath, Martens, Leach, Cohen and Angel (1957); Grune & Stratton, Inc. for permission to reprint Figure 11-2 on page 282, from *Psychopathology and the education of the brain-injured child;* the material on pages 285–286 is taken from pages 330–331 of *Inhibition and choice* by Solomon Diamond, Richard S. Balvin, and Florence Rand Diamond, copyright © 1963 by Solomon Diamond, Richard S. Balvin, and Florence Rand Diamond, and is reprinted by permission of Harper & Row, Publishers. Brandt & Brandt, and Fritz Peters gave permission to print the excerpt from *The World Next Door,* Farrar, Straus & Company, copyright © 1949 by Fritz Peters, cited on page 309. *Psychiatry* and the copyright holders, the William Alanson White Foundation, gave permission for the extract from Eugene Meyer and Lino Covi, "The experience of depersonalization: a written report by a patient," quoted on pages 308–309. Mrs. James W. Papez (Pearl Papez) who made the illustration shown in Figure 13-8, originally appearing in the *Journal of Nervous and Mental Diseases,* 1949, granted permission for its reproduction here.

Brendan A. Maher

CONTENTS

**PRINCIPLES OF
PSYCHOPATHOLOGY**

INTRODUCTION

Psychopathology is the science of deviant behavior. It is scientific in two senses. First, the psychopathologist wishes to arrive at *general principles or laws* that will enable him to account for many different kinds of behavior deviation. This distinguishes his activities from those of the clinician insofar as the latter is concerned with the diagnosis and treatment of a particular individual. Secondly, the psychopathologist depends upon the *scientific method* for the gathering and ordering of information that will provide a basis for developing general laws of pathological behavior. As we shall see later in this book, the scientific method is characterized by an emphasis upon the gathering of quantifiable observations of phenomena under conditions that permit a high degree of precision and control of the situation in which they occur. Here again the psychopathologist differs from the clinician in the extent and kind of evidence that he demands before drawing conclusions about a problem. This difference need not be because of some dispute about the principles of evidence, but because of the pressure placed upon the clinician to take practical action upon whatever data he has at hand.

At the risk of oversimplifying matters a little, we might remark that the psychopathologist is largely and properly engaged in research, in theorizing, and in publication of his findings, whereas the clinician is more extensively engaged in the care of people whose behavior is deviant. Research commonly extends over long periods of time and demands repeated observations before conclusions may be regarded as reliable. Clinical work, on the other hand, usually calls for immediate and urgent solutions to the problems presented by an individual patient. Sometimes this means that the clinician must fill in the gaps in scientific knowledge by using his best judgment in each case on the basis of his past experience. Inevitably this involves some risk of error. As systematic knowledge of psychopathology becomes available, the margin of error diminishes. Indeed, it is the diminution of this error factor which constitutes a major goal of psychopathological research.

While many psychologists may prefer to engage more or less exclusively in either clinical or research activities, there is no necessary contradiction between the two functions. Clinical experience is the ground from which research hypotheses spring. Scientific psychopathology is the basis upon which sound clinical practice develops. Without a constant footing in the daily realities of deviant behavior, psychopathological research is likely to become sterile and scholastic. By the same token, clinical activities which are unrelated to basic principles of human behavior become eccentric and esoteric.

The preceding remarks are simple statements of the obvious. Nevertheless, much confusion arises when comparisons are made between the clinical method and the experimental method, a confusion which seems, to some extent, to be based upon the notion that these two methods are rivals or competitors for a position of ideological supremacy in the understanding of deviant behavior. Both procedures have their advantages and limitations, which are discussed in detail in Chapter 5. It suffices to say here that we shall take the position that any dichotomy between clinical and research activities is invalid. In this book we shall be concerned mainly with the findings of research investigators, not with the intention of slighting the contributions from clinical workers, but with the conviction that the proper function of this book is to present knowledge in a form suitable for disciplined study. An adequate understanding of clinical procedures is best gained in a clinical situation; we shall be presenting clinical material in the following pages solely to illustrate the kinds of behavior deviation with which psychopathologists have been concerned. Now that our position on this point has been made clear, we may turn to matters of definition.

DEFINITIONS

Deviant

Perhaps the most vexing definitional problem which faces the psychopathologist is that of defining "deviant," "abnormal," or "maladjusted." Many different criteria are applied to distinguish deviant from normal behavior.

Personal Distress. One criterion for defining a person as psychologically deviant is the fact that the person himself expresses feelings of distress or unhappiness. If this distress is sufficiently intense that the individual seeks professional help to alleviate it, he has thereby classified himself as suffering from psychological disorder even though his overt behavior may not strike a casual observer as in any way unusual. Example 1-1 may serve to illustrate this point.

As this case proceeded, much other material became available that is not relevant to the initial character of the definition. The point of interest here is that the client did not show any overt behaviors which might strike the observer as pathological, and there would have been little reason for any spectator to suggest that she was in need of treatment for a psychological disorder.

Disabling Behavior Tendencies. A second criterion may refer to the presence of patterns of behavior that tend to handicap or disable the person in the performance of everyday functions. Some of the more common instances of these would include classic "neurotic symptoms" such as phobic responses, obsessions, and compulsions; less clear-cut examples might involve excessively hostile, passive, or dependent behavior, or any patterns of adjustment that create diffi-

EXAMPLE 1-1

A thirty-two-year-old woman sought professional help in solving certain problems which were causing her considerable unhappiness. At the time of referral she was employed as an office supervisor in a private company in a large city. She complained of feeling continually frustrated and tense, insecure about the future, and troubled about the direction which her life seemed to be taking. As the consultation proceeded, it became apparent that her daily efficiency was not notably impaired by her anxieties—she had recently been promoted to the position of supervisor over several other employees—nor did she exhibit any peculiarities of overt behavior which might be regarded as deviant or abnormal. Later on it emerged that she had formed a sexual relationship with a married man somewhat older than she who was employed in the same office. This had proceeded to the point that they were sharing an apartment in a nearby town, she living there permanently while he spent many nights there, giving his wife the excuse that a business trip had taken him out of town. She showed no evidences of anxiety or guilt over the nature of this relationship, but was consciously worried about the long-term instability of it.

culty for the individual in his daily life. These behaviors may or may not be accompanied by conscious distress on the part of the person concerned. They are regarded as pathological because they appear to be creating new difficulties for the individual when other more adequate responses seem to be available. However, the patterns of response which psychologists describe in this way are frequently unaccompanied by any serious distortion of the perception of reality; neither are they usually sufficiently deviant or socially dangerous to require that the

person be treated in an institution. Although gross descriptive terms may be quite misleading, it is common to refer to behavior of this kind as *neurotic*. A more complex discussion of the concept of neurosis is given later in this chapter.

In Example 1-2 we can see that the patient's fear was not based upon any frightening experience that he had had; it was largely irrational—accidents do happen on the highway and in airplanes, but probability of death or injury in a railroad accident is extremely slight; and it was a handicap to

EXAMPLE 1-2

A forty-five-year-old married man came for outpatient psychiatric treatment to a private psychiatrist. He referred himself, but under some pressure from his employer, after having taken several months of sick leave. The patient was a regional sales manager for a large investment trust company, and his duties required much traveling. Some months previously he had developed strong fears of all kinds of transportation, finding it impossible to go to an airport or railroad station or get into a car without becoming anxious and nauseated. There had been no obvious incident or accident which had been related to this fear, but its onset seemed to date shortly after he had been informed that he was being considered for the position of national sales manager in the company. As his services were valued by his employers, he was given sick leave "to get over" his fears, on the presumption that they were due to overwork. As time passed with no improvement, he was asked to seek psychiatric help or be relegated to a position of less responsibility which would not require traveling. Apart from these fears, the patient had no other complaints at the time of the initial interview.

the patient by its effect upon his prospects for promotion and also upon his ability to retain his current position.

Poor Reality Contact. A third criterion refers to the extent to which a person appears to be out of *contact with reality*. Evidence for poor contact with reality comes from behavior which seems inappropriate to the person's environment. Thus the hospital patient who is replying to a "conversation" when there is no one else in the room, or who does not respond to questions and other stimulation in his immediate environment, would represent a rather gross instance of poor reality contact. A subtler version of poor reality contact is provided by the person who appears to be aware of the presence or absence of stimuli in his environment, but interprets them in unusual and seemingly irrational ways. The patient in a hospital who attacks a ward attendant because the latter is a "spy" sent by enemies would exemplify this. Sometimes the patient may not act upon his suspicions quite so dramatically. It may take much skillful questioning to discover the deviant interpretations that the patient is making about his world. A more comprehensive analysis of this concept appears later in this chapter.

Statistical Infrequency. Any response may be deviant in the sense that it is not the one made by most people under the circumstances. In the Western world it would probably be uncommon for anyone to refuse a gift of money, abandon a successful financial career for a life of contemplation, report himself to the police for a minor undetected offense, or hold the belief that the earth is flat. Rare though these actions may be, they are not unknown. When they do occur we may perhaps describe them as eccentric, but it is doubtful whether we would call them pathological. The fact that a certain course of action is not typical of the members of a society does not, in itself, lead to the conclusion that the few people who follow it are suffering from a psychological ailment. We note that the forms of behavior that are likely to be tolerated as merely eccentric are not usually regarded as injurious to the interests of society. In another society they may not be tolerated, but may be defined as either pathological or criminal. Thus many religious sects which are tolerated with some amusement in the United States are regarded as dangerous and are prohibited in Spain and Latin America. While it is obvious that pathological behavior is statistically less frequent than normal behavior, sheer infre-

EXAMPLE 1-3

A nineteen-year-old student in a state university was referred to the student health service by his dormitory counselor. During the initial interview the student produced a file folder in which he had accumulated a series of diagrams similar to those used by a football coach to plan plays. The football in the diagram was marked with the student's name, the players on one side being marked Plato, Socrates, Buddha, Christ, and so forth, while their opponents were labeled Einstein, Galileo, Newton, and so forth. The incident which had precipitated the referral was that the student (according to his own account) had been wandering late at night in the football stadium trying to hide from the forces which were pressing on him, and had sought the protection of the dormitory counselor on his return to his room. To the health service clinician he confided that he was working to develop a "one-man flying machine" which would enable him to escape from further dangers at any time. Until this was completed he planned to carry a shotgun as a means of protection.

The student was hospitalized shortly after this interview, loss of reality contact, in this case, being sufficiently marked to lead to his being classified as *psychotic*.

quency of a response does not necessarily justify our defining it as pathological.

Summary. In brief, we might conclude that the term *deviant* applies to behavior which appears inappropriate and handicapping to the person, which is marked by strong feelings of distress or unhappiness, or which is determined by lack of contact with the realities of the environment. Behavior that meets any of these criteria may be statistically infrequent, but this does not justify the conclusion that infrequency is useful as a criterion of pathology.

Behavior

Any response made by a person, whether it be a motor movement or a verbal statement, is *behavior*. We are, in the very nature of things, unable to observe one another's conscious experience; we may hear someone *describe* his feelings or perceptions, but his description in words or gestures is all that we can ourselves observe. These are the data available to the psychopathologist, and these form the basis for his theories. In order to bring system into his observations, the behavioral scientist frequently finds it advantageous to develop concepts that represent inferences from behavioral data. These concepts may be labeled as "emotions," "feelings," "drives," and so forth, but are not themselves directly observable. It is not necessary for the behavioral scientist to adopt the naïve position of denying conscious experience by explaining it away in terms of subvocal speech or translating it into changes in electrical states of the nervous system. The definition which we have given at the beginning of this paragraph does not intend any denial of conscious experience; it does intend to press the point that these experiences are not available to scientific observers as primary data. In fact, the correlations that have been obtained between verbal report, other overt behavior, and physiological measures are sufficiently coherent that the use of concepts of con-

scious experience is extremely important to the psychopathologist.

A second issue which arises is whether or not all organic responses are to be regarded as behavior. Is the heartbeat a response? Is the activity of the digestive system a pattern of behavior? Psychopathologists frequently study these events, and we shall find observations about bodily functioning being recorded in many of the research studies discussed in this book. However, the pathology of bodily functioning is not in itself of interest to the psychopathologist. He is concerned with the operation of bodily systems (*a*) insofar as they are related to behavior that is deviant in terms of the criteria already enumerated and (*b*) where bodily pathology seems to have been determined by psychological factors. Thus we shall not include deviation of the functioning of bodily systems in our definition of psychopathology, even though we shall study it wherever it helps our understanding of behavioral deviations.

CONCEPTS OF NEUROSIS AND PSYCHOSIS

In the previous discussion of pathology of behavior we made passing reference to the concepts of neurosis and psychosis. We should now consider this distinction in more detail.

Many kinds of deviant behavior appear to be exaggerations of normal response patterns. The repressions of the hysteric, the disorganization of the acutely anxious patient, seem to be extensions, albeit damaging ones, of the responses that we see in ourselves and others every day. Distressing as these problems are, they are less crucial than the problem of the severely disturbed hospitalized patient. Throughout the world, millions of human beings pass large periods of their adult lives confined to mental hospitals. Their psychopathology does not always present itself as obvious extensions of neurotic behavior. Often, indeed, the behavior seems discontinuous with that of normal people. The patient sitting in a catatonic stupor, the patient eating his own excrement or tearing his clothing to shreds— such people do not seem to be just one more step along a continuum from normalcy through neurosis. Clinicians and psychopathologists have recognized this and have been concerned to discriminate a logical basis for this distinction. At the present time, the distinction is usually referred to in terms of the difference between *neurotic* and *psychotic* behavior.

Psychosis is a concept used readily by psychopathologists; the definition of it, however, is far from precise. The rest of this chapter considers the manner in which the concept is defined—both implicitly and overtly—and the kinds of correlated distinctions that seem to go along with it.

Implicit Definition: Loss of Reality Contact

In clinical usage, it is common to regard loss of *reality contact* as the key difference between pathological patterns described as psychotic and those classed as neurotic. While the concept of reality contact is difficult to define by explicit operations, we may regard it as referring to the normal processes by which external (or internal) stimuli are perceived and adaptive responses to them produced. It also includes the thinking and conscious processes that occur in the stimulus-response chain.

Sensory-Perceptual Anomalies. When a patient is *responding to stimuli which are not present to observers,* he may be regarded as having lost contact with reality. Reality, in this case, is defined by the consensus of other observers present. Thus, if a patient replies to a remark made to him by a voice which nobody else present can hear, we assume that there is no physical stimulus of a voice and that the patient is not responding to reality as the majority perceive it. Hallucinations, which are by definition perceptions of events having no external reality, are psychotic. Now, as we shall see in later discussions, hallucinations may occur under circumstances that would not lead us to assume psychosis on the part of the perceiver. Sensory deprivation as well as certain drug and fatigue effects may induce behavior indicative of hallucinations; we tend to reject them as signs of psychosis mainly because we are able to assign another antecedent to them.

Sometimes the sensory or perceptual symptoms may be distortions of stimuli that are present. Colors may appear to be unusually bright, objects may appear to be flat and lacking in depth, sounds may seem to be unusually, even painfully, intense. Again, the patient may complain of sensations emanating from his own body that the observer could not reasonably test against some stimulus reality. Complaints that the body "feels hollow" or that there are "electrical vibrations shooting through the intestine" may be made. Here we tend to reject the complaint as "unreal" because it is couched in terms that are at odds with what we know about human bodily functions.

Disorientation as to time, person, or place is another index of poor reality contact. The defining operations for this are the failures of the patient to identify himself by name correctly, for example, or to know where he is, the date or time. Remembering one's own name is traditionally the easiest act of recall for the socialized human being. Inability to recall it is regarded as pathological in the way that failure to remember the number of one's life insurance policy is not. One's name is learned and practiced to an extent that makes it highly unlikely that it could be forgotten by any of the processes that account for forgetting of more transitory events. Not knowing where one is constitutes a less telling evidence for disorientation of a pathological process. During a long and dull railroad journey, it is possible to watch the stations go by, even to read the names on the signboards, and yet not to be able to recall the name of the last one on request. Uncertainty as to time and even date are not at all rare, as anyone who has taken an ocean voyage will testify. The repetitious conditions of life in a mental hospital are such that recall of the date, the content of the most recent meal, and so forth may be quite difficult even for a staff member. Thus disorientation must be regarded as evidence of pathological loss of reality contact only under circumstances when it might not be as readily expected from nonpatients.

Thought Disorder. Deficiencies in the logical processes of thought are often cited as core aspects of psychotic pathology. We must be careful here to note that there are several criteria for thought disorder. Firstly, the term is applied when the patient draws conclusions that are logically incompatible with his premises. For example, the patient who states both that he is omnipotent and that he is being held in the hospital against his will is clearly contradicting himself. He may have a private meaning for the term "omnipotent," but within the dictionary definition of the word, he is self-contradictory. In this case, we do not need to know the "facts" about his omnipotence or his confinement in the hospital to know that his thinking is faulty. Unfortunately, as many psychological studies have shown, invalid conclusions are readily drawn by people who are not usually classified as psychotic.

A second criterion of thought disorder is the factual incorrectness of the patient's conclusions. Thus the patient who states that he is the President of the United States is regarded as psychotic because of the empirical falsity of his assertion. The rest of his beliefs may well be congruent with this statement, but we regard him as psychotic because we know that his statement is not true, and it seems to us that the patient should know it also. On the other hand, if the patient tells us that he is the "brightest man in the hospital . . . smarter than the superintendent," we may feel that he is empirically incorrect, but we might not be so inclined to query the processes by which he came to this conclusion. In the last analysis, we are making a judgment upon the tolerability of the patient's erroneous judgments.

A third criterion may be applied when the patient expresses an assertion the truth or falsity of which we cannot judge empirically. In such cases, we make our own estimates of its probability. A patient who believes that his children are plotting to kill him for his money may well be disbelieved because his inference seems to be unlikely to the clinician. Such a statement may, in fact, be true. It may also be congruent with other statements made by the patient. Nevertheless, we reject it simply because it seems improbable.

A fourth criterion refers to the observer's difficulty in comprehending the thinking of the patient because his communication is unclear. The patient who wrote "I report that in concentration and transforming around the umbilicus and also controlling the vocal cords of Auspices is the entry to this hospital" appears thought-disordered not because of the internal contradictions or empirical falsity of her statement, but because it seems meaningless by normal standards of verbal communication.

Motor Anomalies. Psychotic processes are sometimes inferred from the presence of bizarre or deviant forms of motor behavior on the part of the patient, even where there is no indication of the stimulus that might have provoked it or of the thought processes that might be mediating it. A patient who maintains a rigid posture for hours on end or who attacks a passing visitor with dangerous violence may be assumed to be psychotic on this ground alone. Implicit in this assumption is the belief that no normal stimulus and no normal thought process could lead the person to exhibit such behavior in the environment in which it occurs.

Summary. The behavior that defines psychosis in this implicit sense may be exhibited, therefore, in the receipt of stimulation, in verbal or motor responses to the environment, or in the thought processes that mediate the stimulus-response relationship.

Implicit Definitions: Autism, Primitive Logic, and Primary Process

Loss of reality contact, as the term suggests, implies some deficit or loss of normal functioning with reference to the environment. As such, it depicts the psychotic person as suffering from some loss that might be regarded as analogous to blindness, crippling, or some other handicapping deficiency. While this picture is correct up to a point, many psychopathologists have emphasized the disruption of reality contact by the positive interference of other psychological processes. While there are some degrees of difference in their meaning, the terms *autism, primitive logic,* or *primary process* are sometimes used to designate these invasive processes.

When these terms are used, it is with a certain set of beliefs about the extent to which thinking is controlled or modified by continuous external stimulation. Fantasy, as discussed in Chapter 3, arises under conditions of low external stimulation, and its content appears to be determined to a significant extent by the motive state of the subject. In fantasy, the subject envisages events and actions that are not possible in the immediate reality that surrounds him. Intense motive states influence not only fantasy, but also the perception of ambiguous objects in reality, producing distortions. However, in normal subjects there is a continuous cross-checking between fantasy and thinking on the one hand, and the realities of the environment on the other. The hostile individual may think about attacking his boss with his fists, but his actual behavior and long-term thinking are more likely to be influenced by the facts of his situation.

Where this reality testing is not in operation, then we should expect to find the individual's thinking being governed by his motivational states. While the motive states determine the *content* of the fantasy, many psychopathologists believe that this kind of thinking is characterized by a logic that differs from that ordinarily found in reality-oriented thought. This logic is regarded as *primitive* and is sometimes termed "paralogic" or "palaeologic." For many workers in this field, primitive logical processes are regarded as natural in the early cognitions of the infant, the growth of reality testing occurring as the child develops toward maturity. Reality control of thinking, then, represents an overlay of a *secondary* process upon a more elemental *primary* process. When serious disruption of reality contact occurs, the cognitions of the patient become dominated by this primary process. Language, insofar as it reflects this kind of thinking, becomes almost meaningless to the listener or reader who is trying to fit it to his own normal secondary logical processes. Primary thought and language are often referred to as "autistic" or "self-determined."

Systematic descriptions of stages of development from purely primary to secondary thinking have been provided by several psychologists. A system deriving mainly from the study of pathological processes in schizophrenia has been hypothesized by Sullivan (1947). He differentiated three stages of development in conscious experience.

Sullivan's Modes of Experience. Sullivan conceived of the experience of the individual as passing from infancy to maturity through three stages or *modes*. These were the prototaxic, the parataxic, and the syntaxic, respectively. Very early infancy is assumed to consist of experience of momentary states, without any awareness of sequences as such or of relationships such as "before" or "after." There is no awareness of the self as differentiated from the rest of the environment, experience being uniform, undifferentiated, and without definite limits. This represents the *prototaxic* mode of experience.

Increasing maturity brings the child to the *parataxic* mode. Experiences are differentiated from each other but are not related in any sequential or logical fashion. Events are experienced simply as happening together or not, and their relations are seen as accidental rather than logical. Parataxic experience is presumed to be developing with early language acquisition. Verbalizations in very young children, according to Sullivan, are autistic; that is, they are highly personal, referring only to private experience and not yet subject to the consensual meaning that comes with interaction with other people.

When the child learns the common meanings of language, the social agreement on the reality to which the words refer, then he enters the *syntaxic* mode of experience in which thinking is achieved with language symbols that have social reality referents. For Sullivan, severe psychotic states are marked by the predominance of prototaxic or parataxic experience.

Piaget's Stages of Thought. Perhaps the most comprehensive of the systems for the understanding of the development of logical thinking has been proposed by Piaget. A complete account of his hypotheses requires references to many sources and an awareness of the modifications that have been made in his system over time. However, the major features are to be found in Piaget (1926, 1928, 1953) and Inhelder and Piaget (1958). The following paragraphs present the general outline of Piaget's developmental theory, omitting many of the details.

Piaget envisages four main stages of development, with the possibility of substages within them. The four stages are the *sensorimotor* stage (birth to roughly 18 months); the *preoperational* stage consisting of the *preconceptual* period (18 months to 4 years) and the *intuitive* period (4 to 7 years); the stage of *concrete operations* (7 to 11 years); and the stage of *abstract operations* (from about 11 years onward). These stages are assumed to represent partly the consequence of maturational factors, but may be speeded up or retarded by environmental or biological influences. However, in the normal course of events, and assuming a favorable environment, the child should progress through the stages as defined.

The Sensorimotor Stage. In its complete formulation, this stage includes six substages. Its main feature, however, is the development of learned control over simple bodily movements. Thus the child learns by experience that he can move his hand in terms of visual coordinates, i.e., toward a bottle or into or out of his own visual field, etc. Concurrently with this, the child develops some conception of external reality in the physical environment and his own role as a causal agent in it. Woodward (1963), summarizing Piaget, points out that by about 8 or 9 months, the child begins to behave

. . . as though events depended upon his own actions; for example, if the investigator, not visible to the child, makes a toy swing while the child is making some movement such as arching his back, the child, while looking at the toy, continues his movement even when it stops swinging, apparently in an attempt to make it swing again. (P. 305.)

By the end of the sensorimotor stage, the child is able to operate in terms of the memory of events not present to perception, and he is likely to look for causative agents for events where the origin is not visibly present. When the baby carriage moves, he looks for the source of the movement; when a sound is heard, he looks for the source but ceases to do so when one becomes evident.

The Preoperational Stage. For Piaget, the crucial development bridging the sensorimotor stage and the preoperational stage is the development of the *mental image*. While Piaget does not concern himself with the problems of neurophysiology involved in this concept, we may comment that the image is the conscious representation of a former percept, either in verbal form or other quasi-sensory mode. The occurrence of an image must be presumed to be mediated by appropriate neuroelectrical events in the brain of the subject, and it is in the manipulation of such events that thinking takes place. By means of images, the child is able to consider events and objects symbolically and to solve problems in relation to them even when they are not present to him perceptually.

During this stage, the child is learning language, or at least is learning to use some verbal labels. However, his symbolic processes have not yet evolved to the point where they stand for coherent classes of events extending beyond the limits of the particular objects experienced by the child. Thus the term "dog" may refer to the family dog—the first occasion for learning the word—and its extension to all other dogs may be fraught with some confusion for the child. Part of the confusion may be as to whether all dogs are somehow the same animal; the converse difficulty arises when the child sees the same object under different conditions (e.g., the moon) and is uncertain therefore whether there are several moons to which the same word applies. In our later discussions of schizophrenic thought, we shall see that this confusion has been detected also.

This period, the preconceptual period, gives way to the intuitive period, at least where some kinds of thinking are involved. Piaget studied the problem solving of children in the intuitive period (4 to 7 years) with problems in which it was necessary to take into account more than one factor at a time. Thus, for example, when pouring a fixed volume of water from one container into another of different diameter and height, the child would reason that the volume of water had changed as evidenced by the change in the visible water level. A correct solution involves taking into account not only the changed level of the water, but also the changed width of the container. When the child learns, through the environmental failures of intuitive thinking, to take account of more than one factor at a time, he is entering Piaget's next stage.

The Stage of Concrete Operations. When this stage is entered (Piaget places it normally at between 7 and 11 years), the child is able to reason by inference about problems from the limitations of his own immediate perceptual situation. Thus, provided that the concrete objects are there, he can use such concepts as *relative length* correctly. That is, he can range a series of sticks in order of length and can interpolate other sticks accurately into the series, realizing that the "longest" stick in a series is a matter of relative length. However, the child is much less effective when called upon to do this in purely verbal or symbolic form. An example cited by Woodward is in the inferential series $A = B$, $B = C$, hence $A = C$. When two blocks of identical size and shape are demonstrated to be of equal weight on a balance, and one of these is shown to be equal in size, shape, and weight to yet a third block, the child can correctly infer that the two blocks not yet compared directly are also equal. When this problem is presented verbally, however, the child finds it difficult to make the correct inference. Piaget thus concluded that the solution of inferential problems by manipulating words or images in the absence of the referent objects is a higher stage of development.

The Stage of Abstract Operations. From 11 years onward, the child begins to demonstrate a capacity for solving problems by symbolic manipulation, including problems that start with hypothetical or "as if" premises. Problems involving the manipulation of several factors simultaneously are also solved. The child begins to be able to perform abstract operations on operations themselves; thus he can conceive of the same data being handled by different concepts. Piaget has suggested that at about 15 years, there is a further stage of development of the capacity for abstract operations, namely, the independent verification of solutions which have been systematically derived from the original data or premises. This, as we can see, represents a kind of higher-order reality testing.

Piaget's system here provides a descriptive basis for conceptualizing thinking which progresses from extremely primitive sensorimotor operations up to complex higher-order abstract manipulation of symbols. His system has the merit that it is based upon extensive empirical observation of children and that it is sufficiently complex to handle the many subtleties of cognition that we see in normal and pathological states. Piaget does not emphasize the motivational influences in cognition, tending on the whole to present these stages as partly the inevitable consequence of learning and partly the result of maturation. We shall see, however, that cognitive aspects of psychotic behavior often include deficiency in dealing with abstractions correctly, the confusion of objects in conceptual classes, and other thinking patterns characteristic of the earlier stages in Piaget's system. Sullivan's classification, on the other hand, is greatly oversimplified and has few objective empirical referents.

Processes Involved in Implicit Definitions

While "loss of reality contact" is essentially a behavioral definition, the "primitive logic" definition suggests that a regressive *process* of some kind is operating to produce the observable behavior. At this level of analysis, the two definitions are not contradictory. If the maintenance of normal reality contact in a person is dependent upon (*a*) an adequate biological apparatus for the reception and processing of stimuli from the environment, (*b*) motivations of an intensity that is insufficient to distort perception and (*c*) the absence of any other psychological processes of a regressive character, then we might expect to find loss of reality contact when any one of these conditions is not met. Thus, certain kinds of biological pathology might produce loss of reality contact. Biological mechanisms concerned with the arousal and maintenance of attention to external stimulation would be especially important here. The elimination of external stimulation, as with drugs or sensory deprivation, would serve the same purpose. Unusual states of intense motivation—as, for example, extreme fear—might produce the effect. There could be other influences producing specific return to

primitive modes of thought even in biologically intact patients with normal intensity of motivation, although we have little basis for speculation as to what these might be.

While all this serves to give structure to the implications of the concept of reality contact, it is still inferential. It does not carry with it any obvious measurement procedures that might be used to quantify the psychotic process. In recent years, there have been several attempts to produce definable dimensions of psychosis that would permit measurement and quantitative analysis. We shall regard these as explicit definitions and describe them in the following pages.

Explicit Definitions: Efficiency

Wishner (1953, 1955, 1961) has tackled the problem of intensity of psychopathology through the development of the concept of *efficiency*. Efficiency, when applied to a machine, is a function of the amount of work done by the machine in relation to the energy put into it. Depending upon the design of the machine, more or less energy is lost in nonproductive effort, e.g., in overcoming friction, etc. Thus efficiency is also an inverse function of the amount of energy wasted by the system. Biological systems might be assessed for efficiency in terms of the amount of effort expended by the system to achieve a given goal or end product. Such assessment requires, of course, that we know what the intended goal is.

In studying the behavior of a person in terms of its efficiency in moving the individual toward a goal, it is plausible to distinguish between *focused* and *diffuse* behavior. Wishner, using these terms, then defines efficiency as some function of focused to diffuse behavior $[E = f(F/D)]$. In itself, behavioral efficiency is not a definition of psychopathology; however, Wishner believed that it would be a predictable correlate of psychopathology, with lower efficiency in severer pathologies. Being unidimensional, the measure of efficiency places neurosis and psychosis on the same continuum, thereby eschewing the notion of discontinuity accepted by some psychopathologists.

Focused and Diffuse Behavior.   Focused behavior is behavior contributing to the attainment of the goal, while diffuse behavior is not. For example, if the task involves only the movement of one hand, then random motor movements of the other would be irrelevant to task performance; hence these would be defined as diffuse. What is focused and what is diffuse depend entirely upon the demands of the task and cannot be specified without knowledge of it.

Experimental Investigations.   As a preliminary tactic in the investigation of efficiency in normals, Wishner and his students (Neibuhr, 1955; Wishner, 1961) studied the effects of *task-centered* versus *self-centered* instructions on performance in a variety of tasks. Task-centered groups were instructed to do their best in the task before them in exactly the way that the experimenter described, ignoring any other aspects of the procedure. Self-centered subjects were presented the various tasks as measures of some aspect of the subject's personality, e.g., his "neuroticism," thus directing his attention to himself rather than to the goal of the effort itself. In a simple reaction-time task, the two groups did not differ in their overt responsiveness, i.e., the actual reaction times, but did differ in their muscular effort to achieve this. Muscular effort was inferred from the muscle potentials of both the responding arm (the right arm) and the resting arm (the left arm). Activity in the responding arm is defined in this task as focused, while that in the resting arm is diffuse. The investigator (Neibuhr, 1955) found that diffuse activity was significantly higher in the self-centered group, focused activity was also higher, and the ratio F/D was considerably higher. The relevant data are provided in Figure 1-1.

Another of Wishner's students (Peastrel, 1961) applied the efficiency paradigm directly to a psychopathological population using a conditioning and generalization task. In this experiment, the subject established a conditioned GSR (galvanic skin response) to a word, the US (unconditioned stimulus) being a loud buzzer. The subject was instructed to pay particular attention to the *meanings* of the words. In a subsequent test of stimulus generalization, the subject was presented with words of the same meaning (synonyms) or with words of the same sound but different meaning (homophones). Here is an example.

CS (conditioned stimulus): *cent*
Synonym: *penny*
Homophone: *scent*

Subsequent generalization may be regarded as evidence of the extent to which the subjects were oriented to the original task—that of paying attention to the meanings. The data obtained are given in Figure 1-2. Here it can be seen that a group of normal subjects showed considerable generalization to the synonyms but little to the homophones, while schizophrenic subjects showed little generalization to the synonyms but somewhat more to the homophones.

As it now stands, the efficiency measure appears to be influenced by several possible factors. Distractibility, or deficiency in the maintenance of attention, would be a prime source of behavior that is diffuse in terms of the task instructions. Inability to comprehend task instructions would also tend to produce low levels of focused activity. As Wishner points out, the efficiency index is regarded by him as a correlate of more fundamental processes in psychopathology, but a correlate with potential fruitfulness for the problems of quantification.

Explicit Definitions: Conscious Regulation

Collier (1955, 1956) has suggested a model for the study of psychopathology based upon the assumption that consciousness plays an active role in the response pattern of an individual dealing with the environment. Consciousness is seen not as a kind of

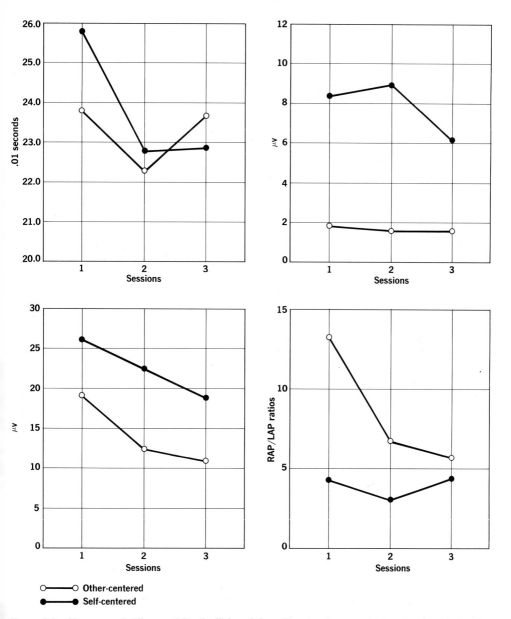

Figure 1-1. Measures of diffuse activity (inefficiency) in self-centered versus task-centered subjects. Top left, mean reaction times for three sessions; top right, mean skin potentials from the left arm during interval between ready and reaction time signals; bottom left, mean right arm preparatory skin potentials; bottom right, mean ratios of right arm preparatory potentials F to left arm preparatory potentials (D: F/D). (Neibuhr, 1955.)

passive monitoring system, but as a regulatory mechanism that serves an essential function in coordinating various needs of the individual with the realities of the external environment. Consciousness of any process, motive, etc., makes possible greater flexibility of behavior and greater possibility of mutual modification of several processes in the light of the realities of the current environment. Consciousness makes compro-

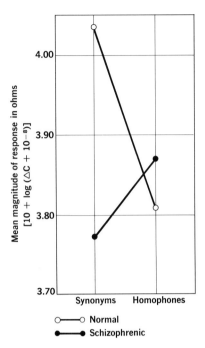

Mean magnitude of response in ohms
$[10 + \log (\Delta C + 10^{-8})]$

Synonyms   Homophones

○——○ Normal
●——● Schizophrenic

Figure 1-2. Mean GSR's to generalization test by schizophrenics and normals. (Peastrel, 1961.)

by disguising or distorting it (a secondary defense).

Stress-tolerance threshold. This is defined in terms of the amount of stress necessary to activate some particular level of the defense system of an individual.

Ego strength. The ability of the individual to accept potentially disturbing stimuli into clear consciousness and to assimilate them constructively.

Boundary permeability of the conscious field. The degree to which the conscious field is accessible to segments of experience, past or current. It is related to a variety of processes operating at any given time.

Collier himself points out that there is an unavoidable circularity about the relationship of some of these definitions to each other. Thus the definition of stress is not dependent upon a physical measure, but is in turn influenced by the stress-tolerance threshold. In fact, the observable events are (*a*) input factors such as pain and physical intensity of stimulation (*b*) physiological-psychological attributes of the subject that might contribute to stress tolerance, and (*c*) overt behavior that may be categorized as either primary or secondary defense systems. Thus, although Collier has not attempted to give clear defining operations for these concepts, it is not intrinsically impossible to do so.

Primary Defense. The essential element of the primary defense is flight, or avoidance. Where physical flight is possible, we would have the most simple kind of primary defense. For many threats, physical flight is not possible either because of limitations upon it or because the threat has no obvious location in space. When this is the case, the individual may avoid the conscious representation of the issue by restricting what is in the conscious field. Collier elaborates the dimensional nature of this restriction from minor, mild exclusions to large-scale denial operations:

For example, one who whistles in the dark or sings to avoid thinking or feeling threatened

mises between conflicting demands of the individual's needs, and it adapts the compromise to the nature of the external environment. Failure of a process or need to enter consciousness does not mean that it will not influence behavior, but that it will influence behavior without adaptation to other needs or to reality.

Collier has been concerned with consciousness and the development of pathological behaviors under stress. In order to outline his model, we must define some additional concepts as follows:

Stress. By this is meant any of a wide range of factors, physiological, physical, or psychological, that place demands upon the organism's capacity to react to a degree that is uncomfortable or threatening.

Defense system. An interrelated set of responses that protects the organism from stress either by increasing psychological distance from the threat (a primary defense), or represents a relatively mild example.* At the other extreme, deep and extensive operations of denial and repression relegate large segments of experience beyond relatively impermeable barriers from the conscious field. The tendency is illustrated by the following verbalizations often heard in a clinical situation: "This is too horrible to think about." "The best way for me to get over my war experiences is not to think about them." "Thoughts like that I keep out of my mind as far as possible." (Collier, 1956, pp. 362-363.)

However, the restriction of consciousness leads to poorer regulation of the environment generally, and the more profound the extent of this restriction, the more disorganized and ineffective behavior becomes. The end result is thus an impoverished and inadequate adaptive regulatory field. Behavior becomes dominated by motives that are as rigid as their degree of dissociation from consciousness. These are no longer organized into comprehensive, balanced patterns realistically connected to the organism's needs. Typical orientation as to self, persons, places, and time may be seriously disrupted. Hence we have some form of what has been called a psychosis.

Secondary Defense. Were the process of stress to lead always to continued movement toward further restriction of the conscious field, we would expect that pathological behavior might appear generally unidimensional, with maximum restriction representing the worst and final stage. However, Collier suggests that this movement is arrested in many instances by the develop-

* This process is aptly illuminated by J. D. Salinger's character of Les in *Franny and Zooey* as described by his wife: " 'Your *father* doesn't even like to talk about anything like this. You know that! He's worried too, naturally—I know that look on his face—but he simply will not face anything.' Mrs. Glass's mouth tightened. 'He's never faced anything as long as I've known him. He thinks anything *peculiar* or *unpleasant* will just go away if he turns on the radio and some little schnook starts *singing*.' " (Salinger, 1964, p. 82.)

ment of secondary defenses. Secondary defense systems include many of the behaviors that the psychoanalysts have thought of as defense mechanisms. Thus rationalizations, ritualistic behavior, conversion symptoms, etc., represent the operation of the secondary defense system. Repression and denial, on the other hand, are the essential elements of the primary defense. In other words, secondary defenses serve to keep the stress level low without additional restriction of consciousness.

The balance between stress and final behavior is mediated in turn by the balance between primary and secondary defenses. A diagrammatic scheme for this model is provided in Figure 1-3. In it, the x axis represents increasing increments of stress, while the y axis represents the two components of the defense system. The secondary defense component increases in ascending from the intersection of the x and y axes, while the primary component decreases accordingly; each point on the y axis thus represents some algebraic summation of the two components. Absolute threshold of tolerance for stress is defined by the line ab, stresses to the left of this line being below the threshold for the arousal of defenses. The line ac represents the point at which secondary defenses begin to break down, leaving the individual open only to extended use of primary defenses. Additional stresses will move the degree of conscious restriction toward the line ad, which represents the threshold for disorganization of psychotic proportions. Varying degrees of primary-secondary defense balance are indicated by the parameters l, m, n, o, and p. Each of these lines is drawn with a different slope, the steeper slope being assigned to the higher values of initial primary defense balance. By this, Collier means to imply that the greater the initial dominance of the primary component, the smaller is the *rate* of increase of stress necessary to produce the breakdown of the secondary component and the final frank psychosis.

Collier's model implies a continuum between normal, neurotic, and psychotic behavior, the individual being moved away

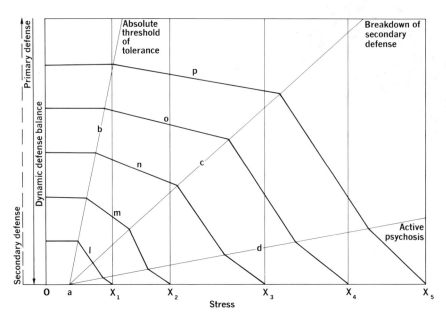

Figure 1-3. Graphic representation of the theoretical stress-defense functions. (Collier, 1956.)

from the normal end of the spectrum at a rate determined by the stress to which he is exposed and the dominance of one or the other defense system. While the dimension is continuous as to its relation to stress, it is not continuous in the behavioral characteristics that are found at various points. Thus, psychotic symptoms do not appear as exaggerated versions of neurotic behavior patterns, but rather as having qualitative differences, largely in terms of the regulatory activities of consciousness.

A Behavioral Analysis

It is possible to emphasize differences or similarities between neurotic or psychotic behavior by selection of the appropriate bases of comparison. The question of dimensionality is not a question of the nature of some "reality" about the relationships of various kinds of psychopathology, but rather reflects upon the preferred method of description. What kinds of dimensional questions might be asked about deviant behavior to which the answers might have scientific or practical importance?

If we define neurotic behavior as predominantly "learned," then we may ask whether the operation of the principles of learning can be successfully applied to the prediction or understanding of schizophrenia, manic-depressive states, or other psychotic syndromes. Should this prove to be the case, then we may argue that neurotic and psychotic behavior are continuous with each other because they are the results of the operation of the same processes.

Alternatively, we might consider the techniques that are necessary to change the behavior in the direction of normalcy. If this is possible by the application of learning principles, then we may conclude that continuity of neurosis and psychosis is present for purposes of making decisions about therapy. This conclusion is entirely plausible even though the methods used to *prevent* the development of neurotic behavior may be entirely different from those used to prevent psychotic development.

Yet again, we might emphasize the presence or absence of biological pathology in the genesis of the behavior. Biological pathology might be examined directly, i.e., we might look for demonstrable proof that psychotic patients do have physical pathologies while neurotic patients do not; or it might be studied inferentially, i.e., we might see to what extent it appears theoretically necessary to assume biological pathology to account for some of the behavior. If we wish to assume a basic discontinuity between learning effects and biological effects, then a distinction of this kind might lead us to differentiate between disorders as having a biological component versus having no biological component. Many psychopathologists hold that some such distinction exists between the neurotic and psychotic disorders.

Finally, we might emphasize the social reaction to the behavior. Thus patients are classified as in-patients or out-patients, corresponding roughly (but by no means completely) to the psychotic-neurotic distinction.

Clearly this question borders on several different problems, and it is not possible to give an unambiguous answer. It is not even clear what value an answer would have unless phrased in terms of some existing dimension of behavior. The writer takes the view that the distinction between neurotic and psychotic behavior is better handled by asking different questions about the deviant behavior displayed by any given individual.

1. What are the determinants of it in the present environment, and what biological determinants are present?
2. How may it be modified?
3. What can be done to prevent similar developments in other individuals?

Perhaps more often than not, an answer to these questions will involve knowledge of the conditions that produced the behavior originally as well as those that are presently maintaining it. Preventive measures, especially, depend upon adequate knowledge of the genesis of various patterns of deviation. Therapeutic steps may not be so dependent. The general philosophy underlying this emphasis has been well expressed by Bindra (1959) and deserves quotation here at some length.

It must be recognized once and for all that the behaviour on the basis of which we classify a person as, for example, a neurotic or an organic psychotic is not determined solely by a particular set of anxiety-related experiences or by a particular type of brain damage. As has been pointed out by so many, the functional-organic dichotomy of behaviour disorders does not correspond to facts of psychopathology. Not all those who have undergone anxiety-producing experiences become neurotics, nor do all with a certain type of brain damage show identical behavioural deviations. In the case of a compulsive neurotic, for example, though the specific compulsions could undoubtedly be shown to be related to the life experiences of the patient, a psychologist must still face the problem that not all persons with similar experiences develop the same compulsions, and, indeed, many do not develop any compulsions at all. Similarly, the various activities that characterize the general paretic do not result from brain damage alone; there is no specific type of brain damage that will cause a person to propose marriage to the ward nurse three times a day, or to walk the hospital wards wearing nothing except a hat and a cigar. Of course, since the existence of tertiary syphilitic infection in general paretics has been established, general paresis has come to be defined in terms of the syphilitic damage to brain cells. However, this happy finding, no matter how useful it may be practically, leaves unanswered the psychological question of why the general paretic behaves as he does. What I am saying is that explaining neurotic or psychotic behaviour involves more than linking it to some aetiological factor, such as particular antecedent experiences or the abnormality of brain function. The medical concept of aetiology is too narrow to cover all aspects of scientific inquiry. In analysing and explaining behaviour disorders, the psychologist faces many subtle problems which go beyond the interests of the practising clinicians.

The essential problem in developing explanations of behaviour disorders seems to reside in the interaction between habit strength, on the one hand, and on the other, the so-called aetiological factors, be they chemical, organic or experiential in origin. I employ the term "habit strength" to refer to nothing more than the degree of prepotence acquired by a particular activity. The variable of habit strength occupies a special place among the factors that control behaviour, for, as the habit strength of an activity increases, it seems to become functionally autonomous, or relatively independent of the chemical, situational, and other factors that initially controlled it. . . . Thus, what I consider to be the crucial interaction is the one between the habit strengths of the various activities that exist in an individual's repertoire and the operation of the so-called aetiological factors such as anxiety-producing experiences, brain damage, and changes in body chemistry. (Bindra, 1959, pp. 143-144.)

PLAN OF THIS BOOK

Notwithstanding its disadvantages, which are discussed later, the bulk of research on psychopathology has been performed in terms of the medical model of disease, diagnosis, and symptom. Experimental groups are usually formed from existing diagnostic categories, and insofar as these categories manage to incorporate subjects with psychological attributes in common, this approach is not wholly fruitless. This book is, therefore, organized around the major existing diagnostic categories, and the presentation of research findings is within that framework to a large extent. Where possible, a behavioral analysis of the problem and the findings is also provided. The necessary principles from behavioral science are given in the chapters immediately following. They should provide the basis upon which the reader may enter into the discussion of psychopathology in the later chapters.

SUMMARY

In this chapter we have looked at some typical illustrations of psychopathology. Examination of them points up the problems involved in defining pathology of behavior and in measuring degrees of it. Central features of a general definition of pathology include *personal distress, disabling behavior tendencies,* and *deficient reality contact.* Sta-

tistical *infrequency* was examined but rejected as not intrinsic to a definition of pathology.

With respect to the traditional distinction between neurosis and psychosis, emphasis was placed upon loss of reality contact as a criterion for differentiating between these two classes. Poor reality contact is in turn inferred from sensory-perceptual anomalies, including disorientation in time, person, or place; disorder of thought; and certain kinds of motor behavior.

Psychotic characteristics of *autism* or *primary process thinking* were examined and defined. Recent attempts at explicit definitions of psychoticism, including *lack of efficiency* and *impaired conscious regulation,* were described.

Finally, the fundamentals of a behavioral analysis were described. These will provide a framework for some later material.

SUGGESTED READINGS

1. Collier, R. Consciousness as a regulating field: theory of psychopathology. *Psychol. Rev.,* 1956, **63,** 360–369. An attempt to develop a systematic hypothesis of the role of consciousness in mediating the stress-defense symptoms of the patient.
2. Kaplan, B. (Ed.) *The inner world of mental illness.* New York: Harper & Row, 1964. A collection of autobiographical accounts of their illnesses by former patients. An excellent introduction to the substance of the psychotic experience.
3. Weinberg, H., & Hire, W. *Casebook in abnormal psychology.* New York: Knopf, 1956. A useful collection of case histories in behavior pathology with a minimum of technical terminology.

REFERENCES

Bindra, D. Experimental psychology and the problem of the behavior disorders. *Canad. J. Psychol.* 1959, **13,** 142–145.

Collier, R. M. An outline of a theory of consciousness as a regulatory field: preliminary statement. *J. Psychol.*, 1955, **40**, 269–274.

Collier, R. M. Consciousness as a regulatory field: a theory of psychopathology. *Psychol. Rev.*, 1956, **63**, 360–369.

Inhelder, Bärbel, & Piaget, J. *The growth of logical thinking.* New York: Basic Books, 1958.

Neibuhr, H. R. Muscle action potential patterns as a function of practice and task-continuing. Unpublished doctoral dissertation, Univer. of Pennsylvania, 1955.

Peastrel, A. Studies in efficiency: semantic generalization in schizophrenia. Unpublished doctoral dissertation, Univer. of Pennsylvania, 1961.

Piaget, J. *The language and thought of the child.* New York: Humanities Press, 1926.

Piaget, J. *Judgment and reasoning in the child.* New York: Harcourt, Brace, 1928.

Piaget, J. *The origin of intelligence in the child.* London: Routledge, 1953.

Salinger, J. D. *Franny and Zooey.* New York: Bantam, 1964.

Sullivan, H. S. *Conceptions of modern psychiatry.* Washington, D.C.: William A. White Psychiatric Foundation, 1947.

Wishner, J. Neurosis and tension: an exploratory study of the relationship between physiological and Rorschach measures. *J. abnorm. soc. Psychol.*, 1953, **48**, 253–260.

Wishner, J. The concept of efficiency in psychological health and psychopathology. *Psychol. Rev.*, 1955, **62**, 69–80.

Wishner, J. Efficiency: concept and measurement. Paper read at 14th Int. Congr. Appl. Psychol., Copenhagen, 1961.

Woodward, Mary. The application of Piaget's theory to research in mental deficiency. In N. Ellis (Ed.), *Handbook of Mental Deficiency.* New York: McGraw-Hill, 1963.

MODELS FOR
THE STUDY
OF PSYCHOPATHOLOGY

In approaching the study of deviant behavior, psychopathologists have had recourse to various *models* for the conceptualization of the problems that faced them. A model is, essentially, an analogy. When developing a model, the theorizer conceives of a process or structure which he believes contains the essential elements of the phenomena that he is trying to understand. The model may consist of an existing and effective theory about another class of problem, and the scientist may use this model in the hope that it will turn out to be equally valid for the solution of his own problems. In its simplest form, this consists of borrowing the terms, concepts, and laws developed from the study of another set of phenomena and applying them, as they stand, to the new problems. Application of an intact model in this way involves deciding which of the events or items in the new problems should be regarded as analogous to the categories developed in the original model. For example, if we propose to regard a certain pattern of deviant behavior as a "disease," then we are applying a *medical model* to our conceptualization of behavior. Among the many problems this entails is that of deciding which responses should be classed as "symptoms," which should be thought of as the direct and primary "disease process," and what we are doing when we try to "diagnose" the individual's "illness."

Models may be relatively miniature; they may be derived from known laws about some rather limited set of events that fall within the scope of behavioral science as a whole. Thus we may decide to see if the principles and processes that have been found useful in studying simple learning may be applied equally well to pathological behavior. This application may be either extensive—where wide ranges of deviant behavior are subsumed under the model—or may be confined to some specific kind of deviation. A major virtue of the use of a psychological model for the study of pathological behavior is that it does not create problems of fitting behavioral events into descriptive categories that were generated by other kinds of events. We already have adequate definitions of "response" and "stimulus" and do not need to worry whether they should be thought of as "symptoms" and "disease agents."

Yet a third kind of model is purely symbolic, or mathematical. Here the model consists of statements of mathematical relationships between observable events, and the theorist attempts to construct a model that will express these relationships with the greatest accuracy and fewest terms. Such models arise from experiment and do not involve reasoning by analogy from some other scientific discipline. In one sense, all sciences have an underlying mathematical model, although for the sake of communication, the scientist may prefer to use words to indicate his concepts and laws.

A model derived from another scientific theory is an analogy until it has been shown empirically to have valid application to the new data. However, in order to show this, it is necessary to use the model as a working framework for the research which may eventually demonstrate its correctness. When this is done, it ceases to be a model and becomes a theory.

Over the centuries, the problems of deviant behavior have been studied and observed from the viewpoint of several different models. We shall not go into the history of these ideas here, as they are well described elsewhere (Zilboorg & Henry, 1941). However, for many centuries deviant behavior was approached from what might be regarded as a *supernatural* model, whereby the individual was assumed to be either divine or possessed by the devil.

Granted these assumptions, then the "treatment" of the person became, necessarily, either the granting of worshipful respect or the administration of punishment to the devil within. This model has, in large part, disappeared from the thinking of psychopathologists in civilized societies. Supplanting it are several other models, which we shall now consider.

THE MEDICAL MODEL

Modern society possesses three formal institutions designed to change the behavior of its members—the school, the prison, and the mental hospital. Each of these institutions has developed a particular language and set of concepts for dealing with its own problems. The school attempts to change behavior which is called *ignorant* or *untrained,* the processes by which it seeks to bring about change are called *teaching* or *education,* and the end product is a *skilled* or *trained* person. The evidence that the process has had some effect upon behavior is derived by observing the behavior of those who have gone through it.

Prisons deal with people whose behavior is defined as *criminal* or *antisocial,* the process is called *correction* or *rehabilitation,* and the end product is ideally a *reformed* or *social* person. In general, the prison is designed to serve the purpose of correcting certain kinds of failure of the previous training, which had been provided formally by the school and informally by the family and the community. Where the failure appears to be beyond correction, custodial confinement may be used with the protection of society in mind. Both correction and custody are undertaken in ways which are publicized as unpleasant in the hope that this will serve to prevent others from criminal activity. In this sense the prison is designed to change not only the behavior of prisoners but also the behavior of society at large.

Society currently uses the model of physical illness as a basis for the terms and concepts to be applied to deviant behavior.

Such behavior is termed *pathological* and is classified on the basis of *symptoms,* classification being called *diagnosis.* Processes designed to change behavior are called *therapies* and are applied to *patients* in mental *hospitals.* If the deviant behavior ceases, the patient is described as *cured.* At the present time there are continuing and occasionally acrimonious discussions about the question of medical training as a prerequisite for engaging professionally in the activities necessary to bring about changes in deviant behavior. As we shall see, the use of medical language and concepts exercises a profound influence upon our ways of dealing with people whose behavior is deviant, as well as upon the way in which we set about doing research into the origins of their difficulties.

Public Attitudes

When we hear that a friend or acquaintance (even perhaps an enemy) is ill, we tend to respond in rather predictable ways. The patient is permitted to relinquish most of his daily responsibilities; he is treated with care and kindness by his community, and any irascibilities or discourtesies on his part are apt to be forgiven on the grounds that he is sick. All this is quite apart from the professional care which is provided by the physician; it represents a general pattern of responses which society makes toward those defined as physically ill.

Now much deviant behavior is quite bewildering, irritating, or even threatening to the observer. It is sometimes criminal and may lead to severe penalties being applied by society. Several centuries ago it was common to "treat" the deviant individual by such methods as flogging, chaining in a cell, exposure to public ridicule, and the like. In societies where a belief in demoniacal possession was current, the deviant might be put to death by burning as a witch or wizard. Reactions of this kind are representative of the effects of a *religious* or *moral* model when applied to deviant behavior. They

bear many resemblances to the present-day criminal model already described.

A major change in public attitude was achieved by the redefining of certain kinds of behavior deviation as "mental illness." Most historians would probably agree that the work of Philippe Pinel (1745-1826) was one of the earliest successful attempts to redefine deviant behavior as a type of sickness. As chief physician of the Bicêtre, a Paris hospital largely filled with people suffering from behavior disorders, Pinel inaugurated a program of minimal restraint, commenting that the inmates "are sick people whose miserable state demands all the consideration that is due to suffering humanity" (Zilboorg and Henry, 1941). While this policy was at first slow to spread, it is safe to say that the many humanitarian changes in the treatment of hospital inmates have been largely due to the introduction of medical terminology into public thinking about deviant behavior. Just how important is the medical definition may be seen by considering the outcome of a trial for homicide where the defendant pleads "guilty but insane." The activity of which he is accused is not in doubt, but the definition of it is. Should a jury decide that the behavior is properly defined as "sick," the patient goes to the hospital; should they decide that it is criminal, the prisoner may go to his death.

Scientific Optimism

Physical medicine has been remarkably successful in discovering both causes and cures for many of the physical disorders that have plagued men from time immemorial. Research of the kind that has been necessary to achieve this springs from an initial belief that causes and cures can be discovered. Diseases once classified as hopeless or incurable are even now the subject of large-scale research—research based upon the conviction that a cure can be found. By bringing deviant behavior out of the category of human wickedness into that of human illness, Pinel laid the ground for conducting research into its origins and into methods of changing it. Pinel's contribution to the welfare of his patients was not confined to the improvement of their surroundings and care. As White (1956) points out, "Of enduring importance was his introduction of the psychiatric case history and the systematic keeping of records. . . . Before his time it often happened that no one remembered when or for what cause a patient had entered the hospital. Obviously it was impossible to build up a sound knowledge of mental disorders until Pinel's custom of making records became an established practice" (pp. 9–10).

Recruitment of Personnel

Medicine has always attracted a number of dedicated people, a distinction which it shares with the other professions. Physicians, nurses, and other members of the medical profession are to a large extent self-selected by their interest in helping people in trouble. Consequently the inclusion of deviant behavior among the many problems which medicine has sought to solve has meant that professional ability and interest of a high level have been directed toward it.

Organic Orientation

One consequence of the medical model has been that research into possible organic causes and treatments for deviant behavior has been conducted as a matter of course. While many students of the behavior disorders would question that this has been wholly advantageous, nevertheless important discoveries have been made by research workers proceeding in this way. Because medical training develops a tendency on the part of the physician to seek for organic causes of the complaints which people bring to him, it seems indubitable that this kind of research approach has been facilitated by the medical definition of deviant behavior.

The advantages which have arisen from thinking of aberrant behavior as a type of

sickness are considerable. When the current state of affairs is compared with the period before Pinel, it is impossible to doubt the benefits which have accrued. However, no gain is ever made without cost, and it is appropriate at this point to consider the difficulties which have accompanied the adoption of medical concepts.

Logic of the Disease Concept

One main problem which has developed with the use of medical concepts in dealing with disordered behavior is concerned with the classification of mental "diseases." Let us consider the specific question, "Is schizophrenia a disease?" In order to answer this question sensibly, we must have a definition for the class of phenomena which we call diseases and a definition of the phenomenon "schizophrenia." Curiously enough, it is very difficult to find a clear definition of the term *disease*. If we adopt the role of a naïve inquirer and consult a dictionary, we find disease defined as "A condition of the body, or of some part or organ of the body, in which its functions are disturbed or deranged" (*Oxford Universal Dictionary*, 1955). If we adopt this definition, then our question resolves into that of deciding whether or not there is some derangement of bodily function in schizophrenia. The answer to this question is an empirical one, to be obtained by research on the biology of schizophrenia.

However, the criteria which are invoked when making a diagnosis of schizophrenia do not refer to bodily malfunctioning—they refer to certain kinds of behavior. The *diagnosis* of schizophrenia is not a matter of inferring the nature of some bodily state of the patient; it is a matter of describing his overt behavior. In the present state of knowledge it is not possible to give a clear answer to the question of a biological basis for this kind of behavior. Thus in the dictionary sense of the word, we do not know if schizophrenia should be called a disease.

Unfortunately, the picture is complicated

even more by the looseness of the definition of schizophrenia. The situation has been well described by Guertin (1961a):

> The desire to bring schizophrenia into the realm of clearly defined disease entities is a noble one; but unfortunately, investigators engaged in the task resemble dogs chasing their own tails. . . . It is generally agreed that schizophrenia is such an inclusive label that there is no single behavior symptom always present in every patient, nor does a group of schizophrenics show much uniformity in traits or symptoms. (P. 200.)

In the light of this state of affairs, our question becomes impossible to answer, even empirically, until we have a clear definition of the behavior patterns in which we are interested. Patterns of bodily symptoms which tend to occur together are known as *syndromes,* and thus this first problem in applying the medical model to behavioral disorders is that of identifying syndromes. As Eysenck (1960a) has summarized the situation:

> Before we can reasonably be asked to look for the cause of a particular dysfunction or disorder, we must have isolated, however crudely, the dysfunction or disorder in question, and we must be able to recognize it and differentiate it from other syndromes. (P. 1.)

The isolating of syndromes of behavior is basically a matter of recording the frequency with which certain kinds of deviant behavior tend to go together. While this can be done in a casual way by a clinician drawing on what he remembers or has recorded from his own experience, reliable descriptions of this kind require large-scale investigations using rather sophisticated statistical techniques in analyzing the correlations between responses. Work along this line has already been begun, e.g., by Eysenck and his colleagues (1960) and by Guertin (1952, 1961a, 1961b).

Within a disease entity, the syndrome or symptom picture represents one of a trio of features which, taken together, comprise the entity. Hence Kraepelin, quoted by Diefendorf (1921):

Judging from our experience in internal medicine, it is a fair assumption that similar disease processes will produce identical symptom pictures, identical pathological anatomy, and an identical etiology. If, therefore, we possessed a comprehensive knowledge of any one of these three fields—pathological anatomy, symptomatology, or etiology—we would at once have a uniform and standard classification of mental diseases. A similar comprehensive knowledge of either of the other two fields would give not only just as uniform and standard classifications but all these classifications would exactly coincide. *Cases of mental disease originating in the same cause must also present the same symptoms and the same pathological findings.* (P. 200; italics added.)

Current Psychiatric Classification

The importance of the disease entity concept in present-day classification is evident from the *Diagnostic and Statistical Manual of Mental Disorders* (American Psychiatric Association, 1952). It is the standard reference for current psychiatric diagnostic terminology and replaces a similar but less extreme nosology first put forward in 1933. It incorporates the clinical and diagnostic experiences of the profession during the intervening years, especially the World War II period. In this scheme, a basic distinction is made between those disorders in which "there is a disturbance of mental function resulting from, or precipitated by, a primary impairment of the function of the brain, generally due to diffuse impairment of brain tissue," and those which "are the result of a more general difficulty in adaptation of the individual, and in which any associated brain function disturbance is secondary to the psychiatric disorder" (p. 9). Each of the two major groups is broken down into more specific "disorders," which in turn identify groups of related syndromes or "reactions." The disorder known as mental deficiency, diagnosed primarily on the basis of the individual's IQ, stands outside and midway between the organic and functional groups. The full scheme, excepting mention of specific brain disorders, is presented in Box 2-1.

BOX 2-1 Diagnostic Classification of Mental Disorders

A. **Disorders caused by or associated with impairment of brain tissue function**
   1. Acute brain disorders (11)
   2. Chronic brain disorders (23)
B. **Mental deficiency**
   1. Mental deficiency, familial or hereditary
   2. Mental deficiency, idiopathic
C. **Disorders of psychogenic origin, or without clearly defined physical cause or structural change in the brain**
   1. Psychotic disorders
       Involutional psychotic reaction
       Affective reactions
          Manic-depressive reaction, manic type
          Manic-depressive reaction, depressive type
          Manic-depressive reaction, other
          Psychotic depressive reaction
       Schizophrenic reactions
          Simple type
          Hebephrenic type
          Catatonic type
          Paranoid type
          Acute and undifferentiated type
          Chronic undifferentiated type
          Schizo-affective type
          Childhood type
          Residual type
       Paranoid reactions
          Paranoia
          Paranoid state
       Other
   2. Psychophysiologic autonomic and visceral disorders
       Psychophysiologic skin reaction
       Psychophysiologic musculoskeletal reaction
       Psychophysiologic respiratory reaction
       Psychophysiologic cardiovascular reaction
       Psychophysiologic hemic and lymphatic reaction
       Psychophysiologic gastrointestinal reaction
       Psychophysiologic endocrine reaction
       Psychophysiologic nervous system reaction
       Psychophysiologic reaction of organs of special sense
   3. Psychoneurotic disorders
       Anxiety reaction
       Dissociative reaction
       Conversion reaction
       Phobic reaction
       Obsessive compulsion reaction
       Depressive reaction
       Other
   4. Personality disorders
       Personality pattern disturbance
          Inadequate personality
          Schizoid personality
          Cyclothymic personality
          Paranoid personality

Models for the Study of Psychopathology

BOX 2-1 Continued

Personality trait disturbance
    Emotionally unstable personality
    Passive-aggressive personality
    Compulsive personality
    Other
Sociopathic personality disturbance
    Antisocial reaction
    Dyssocial reaction
    Sexual deviation
    Addiction
Special symptom reactions
    Learning disturbance
    Speech disturbance
    Enuresis
    Somnambulism
    Other
5. Transient situational personality disorders
    Gross stress reaction
    Adult situational reaction
    Adjustment reaction of infancy
    Adjustment reaction of childhood
    Adjustment reaction of adolescence
    Adjustment reaction of late life

This nosology is not a taxonomy in the strict sense of the word, since no systematic principle of classification is employed. The organic disorders are classified in terms of etiology—specific pathological brain anatomy. Mental deficiency is diagnosed primarily on the basis of psychological tests. The classification of the functional disorders is based primarily on symptom syndromes and thus tends to be purely descriptive or "phenomenological." In some cases, however, there are subsidiary considerations. The differentiation of the psychoneurotic reactions from other functional disorders as well as the subdivision of these reactions is largely dictated by psychoanalytic theory. For example, the full diagnostic description of the psychoneurotic conversion reaction includes the following: "Instead of being experienced consciously, the impulse causing the anxiety is 'converted' into functional symptoms in organs or parts of the body, usually those that are mainly under voluntary control. The symptoms serve to lessen conscious (felt) anxiety and ordinarily are

symbolic of the underlying mental conflict" (p. 32). The etiology of the psychophysiologic autonomic and visceral disorders (psychosomatic disorders) is thought to be "a chronic and exaggerated state of the normal physiological expression of emotion, with the feeling, or subjective part, repressed," and this group of reactions is thus distinguished from the others. The dissociation of the symptom syndromes included under the personality disorders from other major groups is made primarily on ethical-evaluative terms.

Although the various functional reactions are seen as unsatisfactory adjustments to internal or external stresses, note that the disease entity model is implicity assumed in the nosology. The major basis of classification remains the symptom syndrome: this classificatory principle "attempts to make possible the gathering of data for future clarification of ideas concerning etiology, pathology, prognosis, and treatment in mental disorders" (p. 9). In other words, it is assumed that individuals suffering from mental disorders can be typed as "possessing one or another diseases," known through an invariant patterning of symptomatology. It is hoped that future research will uncover the antecedents as well as the prognoses of these various disease entities, with suitable treatment methods developing in the process.

While there has been striking success in defining some disease entities which have an organic etiology and pathology (e.g. paresis), the general picture with regard to the discovery of disease entities for the majority of behavior disorders is still as Cameron described it in 1944:

All current attempts at classification of functional personality disorders are unsatisfactory; this is true for the neuroses as well as the psychoses. No causal organisms have been implicated, hence we cannot fall back upon them as we can in the specific infectious diseases. There are no characteristic organic lesions, as there are in the systemic diseases; and the central nervous system exhibits no consistent changes that can be correlated with the syndromes as in neurological disorders. (P. 870.)

Thus, at the present time we have no systematic basis for regarding most of the major behavior pathologies as instances of disease.

Criticisms of Classification

We have already considered the difficulties inherent in the logic of the disease model. However, quite apart from logical problems, a major issue is the vagueness and instability of the descriptions of disease syndromes themselves. Many studies have demonstrated this unreliability. For example, Mehlman (1952) and Raines and Rohrer (1955) studied the manner in which psychiatrists used diagnostic labels with patients, and their data compelled them to conclude that there was a highly significant relationship between the kind of diagnosis that was made and the psychiatrist who made it.

Several studies have shown that clinicians diagnosing the same patient may agree with each other fairly well as to the broad category of diagnosis to apply (for example, psychotic or organic); within these categories, the specific diagnosis may be a source of much disagreement. A good illustration of this problem is provided in a study by Schmidt and Fonda (1956). Each member of a group of 426 patients, drawn from two state hospitals, was diagnosed independently by psychiatrists, using the official diagnostic nomenclature. When their agreement was computed on the basis of three broad groupings (organic, psychotic, or characterological), there was good agreement—an average of 84 per cent over all cases. When this agreement was computed for the more specific categories, the average agreement dropped to 55 per cent. The results are given in detail in Table 2–1.

Problems of this kind have led psychopathologists to criticize the classification system on several distinct grounds.

Inappropriateness of All Classifications. One criticism which has been leveled against current diagnostic categories is based upon the possibility that any system of categorization is inherently incorrect. The determinants of the behavior of any two people are so complex, according to this argument, that classifying several individuals into one group because of some similarities in their behavior will obscure the many important differences. Thus, when two patients are diagnosed in the same way because they both present delusional behavior, we are not justified in assuming any similarities other than the one which was used to put them into that particular category. As the current system of diagnostic categories clearly makes the assumption that both patients are suffering from the same "disease," it must be criticized on these grounds.

Inadequacy of Current Classification. A less sweeping criticism of present diagnostic classifications points to the inadequacies of the present system, but does not reject gross classification per se. Several writers (e.g., Jellinek, 1939; Eysenck, 1960a) point out

TABLE 2-1 Agreements between Pairs of Psychiatrists Diagnosing the Same Patients from State Hospital Populations

General diagnosis	Per cent	Specific diagnosis	Per cent
Organic	92	Acute brain syndrome	68
		Chronic brain syndrome	80
		Mental deficiency	42
Psychotic	80	Involutional	57
		Affective	35
		Schizophrenic	51
Characterological	71	Neurosis	16
		Personality pattern	8
		Personality trait	6
		Sociopathic	58

SOURCE: *Schmidt and Fonda (1956).*

that the present system tends to include many irrelevant features in defining diagnostic categories. However, what makes a particular feature relevant can only be known after it has been shown to have some relationship to the future of the patient—i.e., the prognosis or therapeutic outcome. In a word, therefore, we may wish to develop a new set of diagnostic categories based upon those characteristics of patients which are related to important predictions about their future behavior.

In Defense of Classification

Defenders of the classification system have argued that the empirical evidence of the failure of clinicians to agree upon diagnoses of patients may be attributed to insufficient care in observing the patient on the part of one or both of the diagnosticians. The fault, it is argued, lies in the professional observers rather than in the principles behind the classification scheme. It seems quite probable that, under the conditions which prevail in many state hospitals, hasty diagnoses may be made; but the great frequency of reported diagnostic disagreements from many parts of the world suggests that technical carelessness is not sufficient to explain away the data.

The most fundamental defense of classification springs from the proposition that the description and classification of phenomena are a prerequisite to the development of any science, including a science of psychopathology. Insofar as any science consists of statements about lawful relationships between events of various kinds, then it is necessary to define the events with which the law deals. Defining events in this way, is, of course, classification. To this extent, therefore, it is difficult to see the ways in which laws relating to psychopathology can be developed without some kind of classification.

Summary. We may say that there is little doubt that existing diagnostic classification seems to have had little utility for predicting the future behavior of patients, or even for identifying stable patterns of difference between the various diagnostic groupings. Furthermore, the classes as presently defined have generated considerable disagreement at the clinical level, making it impossible to use them consistently from one institution to another.

However, the answer to these difficulties seems to lie not in rejection of the principle of classification per se, but in the discovery of those features in either the present behavior or past history of individuals which will enable us to make valid predictions about their future behavior. Such features would then provide a basis for meaningful classification and the development of systematic principles for psychopathology.

Training

When we consider deviant behavior to be a disease, it is inevitable that we assume that training in physical medicine is a prerequisite for engaging in either the study of or care of the mentally ill patient. On the other hand, if we emphasize that deviant behavior is determined by the operation of the same processes that produce normal behavior, then the most appropriate prerequisite for the psychopathologist is a thorough knowledge of normal psychology. In fact, deviant behavior may occur from the operation of both physical and psychological factors, although in the former case the patient may perhaps be regarded as more suitable for treatment by a neurologist or endocrinologist than by a psychopathologist.

From the evidence currently available, it appears reasonable to identify two general classes of deviant behavior: those associated with organic disease, such as paresis, Alzheimer's disease, etc., and those where psychological variables appear to be most important, such as the character disorders, conversion hysteria, and so forth. It seems, in the light of this, that the most appropriate training for the researcher or therapist with the organically based disorders is to be obtained in medicine, within the specialties of neurology and endocrinology. For the latter group of behavior deviancies, training in psychology, sociology, measurement, and related disciplines appears to be most appropriate. Unfortunately, the effect of the medical model for behavior deviation is to emphasize the function of traditional medical training at the expense of training in the behavioral sciences.[1]

Hospital Milieu

The organization and environment created in the mental hospital are based, in large part, on those which are commonly found in general medical hospitals. Treatment is frequently regarded as something which occurs at assigned times and places in much the same way that physical therapies are administered with many organic diseases. On the other hand, if we assume that behavior of the patient is being constantly influenced by the environment in which he is living, then the proper manipulation of that environment becomes a full-time consideration. At the present, we are witnessing a transition from the traditional hospital concepts of patient environment to newer concepts based upon the notion of a "therapeutic milieu" (e.g., Maxwell Jones, 1953) and, at a less comprehensive level, the plea for halfway houses designed to bridge the gap between the hospital and the social environment to which the patient must return. These issues are discussed in detail in Chapter 16. It becomes clear, on careful examination, that the kind of environment necessary to produce improvements in deviant behavior is not that implied by the term "hospital." Even in older mental hospitals, the use of the term hospital is evidently metaphorical, because the administrative policies and general atmosphere are perceptibly different from those of medical hospitals.

The Physician-Patient Relationship

In physical medicine, the physician is cast in the role of an expert who is skilled in diagnosing disease and in applying the necessary treatment. The patient places his welfare in the physician's hands and is expected to be obedient to "doctor's orders." In many cases, the physician may judge that it is not necessary for the patient to understand the nature of his own illness, the prognosis, or the treatment. A relationship of this kind is essentially one of protector-dependent and constitutes the model for the typical interaction between physician and patient. Decisions about daily living habits are frequently taken out of the patient's hands and not returned to him until he is pronounced "cured." Deviant behavior is not readily changed within the framework of this kind

---

[1] It is quite rare for a psychiatric resident to receive formal training in the behavioral sciences.

of relationship, and much psychotherapy is oriented toward the contradictory task of inducing the patient to be responsible for his own life—a goal which may require increasing the patient's awareness of his own problems. Thus the more usual physician-patient relationship of physical medicine is often inappropriate for the task of changing deviant behavior and may even militate against it.

THE MORAL MODEL

The use of the medical model has brought with it a problem which has only recently begun to interest workers in the field of mental health. As we have seen, the use of the term "sick" to describe a person whose behavior is deviant has created a situation in which the individual is regarded as free from responsibility for his own actions in the eyes of the law. His behavior is thought to be beyond his own control in much the same way that a physically ill patient cannot voluntarily control his own fever. We have already seen how this question arises in cases of criminal proceedings. It arises even more widely when we consider the impact that psychoanalytic determinism has had upon popular thinking about individual responsibility and free will. Thus, lack of responsibility is not only attributed to those whose behavior is markedly deviant; it is inherent in the assumption that all human behavior is determined. In this respect, it becomes nonsense to talk about responsibility for behavior at all.

It is not surprising that psychopathologists view with some suspicion any attempt to attach blame to a patient for his behavior. When concepts of moral responsibility were applied to deviant behavior centuries ago, the reaction of society was to punish, more or less regardless of the effect of this upon the behavior in question. Nevertheless, the concepts of responsibility and the importance of moral issues have been reintroduced by several workers in the field in recent years, although without the concomitant implication that punishment is a logical therapy.

Ethical Problems of Living

Szasz (1960, 1961) has argued the "mythical" nature of the concept of mental illness. He points out that most behavior deviations may best be thought of as *problems in living*. "I submit," he states, "that the idea of mental illness is now being put to work to obscure certain difficulties which at present may be inherent—not that they need be unmodifiable—in the social intercourse of persons. If this is true, the concept functions as a disguise; for instead of calling attention to conflicting human needs, aspirations and values, the notion of mental illness provides an amoral and impersonal 'thing' (an 'illness') as an explanation for *problems in living*" (Szasz, 1960, p. 117.) Problems in living are regarded by Szasz as inevitable in human society because of the great stresses and strains involved in even the simplest human relationships. With increasing knowledge of the world and of his own nature, man is faced with a greater awareness of the problems which he must solve; but there is also the possibility of better technical solutions. Solving problems of human living requires the development of rational solutions; in this way, the improvement of human relationships is seen as depending upon reason, patience, and hard work rather than upon the outcomes of conventional medical therapy or psychotherapy.

For Szasz, the major goals of human life are not just those involved in biological survival, but rather those which center around the question of the meaning of life in the broader moral sense. From the point of view of the psychopathologist, this position is important not because it offers immediate possibilities for scientific development, but because it represents another aspect of the difficulties which are created by use of medical terms and concepts in the behavioral sciences.

Deviant Behavior as Sin

A somewhat similar position has been advocated by Mowrer (1960). Pointing to the more recent history of psychopathology, he has commented, "Despite some pretentious affirmations to the contrary, the fact is that psychoanalysis on which modern 'dynamic' psychiatry is largely based, is in a state of virtual collapse and imminent demise. And the tranquilizers and other forms of so-called chemotherapy are admittedly only ameliorative, not basically curative. So now, to the extent that we have accepted the 'illness' postulate, and thus been lured under the penumbra of medicine, we are in the ungraceful maneuver of 'getting out' " (p. 302).

Like Szasz, Mowrer suggests that calling deviant behavior "sickness" has a detrimental effect on man's perception of his own worth. We are left, he feels, unable to answer such questions as "Who *am* I?" "What is *my* destiny?" or "What does living *mean?*" In this light, psychopathology is described as a "living death" from a moral point of view. Any behavior which carries the individual closer to psychopathology is identified as "sin," and the fundamental process involved in psychotherapy is the individual's acceptance of his own guilt, with contrition and restitution for past behavior.

The implications of what we have called the moral model go beyond the question of the usefulness of medical terminology. Here the problem is not whether deviant behavior calls for disease concepts in our understanding of it. It is the much larger issue of reconciling scientific determinism with beliefs in the moral nature of human existence. This problem has been with us for many centuries and is relevant to all behavior, not only the psychopathological.

At the present time, the moral model does not provide a clear basis for the systematic investigation of pathological behavior, although it is not impossible that it might do so. Mowrer has commented that perhaps "our best policy is to become frankly agnostic for the time being, to admit that we know next to nothing about either the cause or correction of psychopathology and therefore ought to concentrate on *research*." It would be difficult to quarrel with this conclusion, although the present status of the moral model does not provide a ready guidepost as to the direction which research might take.

THE BEHAVIORAL MODEL

Both of the preceding models envisage the behavior of the individual as being amenable to understanding in terms that have not been directly derived from the study of behavior. This is strange, but it is not surprising. It is strange in the way that it would be strange to find the study of bridge building being conducted without benefit of the concepts and principles of physics. Bridges were being built successfully long before modern physical theory was developed, but it would be an unusual engineer who would now take the position that his activities were more effectively understood without reference to physics!

This isolation of psychopathology from the mainstream of behavioral science is attributable in part to the scientific inadequacies of medical training and in part to the ideological hegemony that has been established by the doctrines of psychoanalysis. Some considerable share of the responsibility for this neglect must fall, however, on the behaviorists themselves. With some outstanding exceptions, many behavioral scientists have actively avoided becoming involved with real human problems, dismissing them to the provinces of "applied psychology." For decades, much of the energy of behaviorism was spent in dueling over the relative merits of one theory of learning versus another.

There is, properly speaking, no single integrated "behavioral model." Rather there is a sizable body of experimental literature regarding the determinants of many kinds of human response. From this literature there has emerged a general set of principles that have gained wide acceptance because of the reliability with which they can be demonstrated. These principles may be regarded as the elements of a behavioral model, although a precise use of the term "model" might demand that we speak of *normal behavior* as the model the principles of which we wish to extend, by analogy, to pathological behavior. Let us consider the elements of the model here.

For the behavioral scientist, the behavior of living organisms may be understood as the outcome of (*a*) past learning in relation to similar situations, (*b*) current states of motivation with their influence upon both activity level and sensitivity to the environment, and (*c*) individual differences of a biological order. These individual differences may be attributed to genetic differences at a variety of levels or to other nongenetic differences in the operation of the biological systems that mediate learning, motivation, and perception. Deviant behavior may be generated by anomalies in any of these factors; particular kinds of learning experience in an otherwise intact and biologically normal individual may produce deviant responses. Biological anomalies of the systems serving attention and consciousness may produce bizarre perceptions of the environment and bizarre responses to it.

However, the study of psychopathology is envisaged by the behavioral scientist as involving the application of the principles of learning, motivation, and perception on one hand, and physiological psychology and genetics on the other. It does not involve analogizing from other disciplines except insofar as some current explanations of learning, etc., are themselves analogies. Significant progress has been made in this kind of application by Dollard and Miller (1950), Rotter (1954), Mowrer (1960), Eysenck (1960b), and Phillips (1956). Much of the material in this book is discussed from the standpoint of the behavioral scientist. The chapters immediately following this one present the most relevant principles in some detail.

THE DYNAMIC MODEL

Modern psychiatric practice reveals a curious disjunction of the disease model on the one hand, and the influence of *dynamic* theory on the other. Dynamic theory refers here to the body of doctrines developed in the main by Freud and his followers and sometimes termed, generically, *psychoanalysis*. Space does not permit a complex discussion of all aspects of the various derivatives of psychoanalysis, and we shall confine ourselves to the major features.

As the term "dynamic" implies, one of the fundamental aspects of the model is the assumption that behavior results from the various kinds of equilibria that may be attained by *energy systems* within the individual. These energies are assumed to be the product of drives—fundamentally instinctual—in the individual. When the operation of the energy system is unhindered by any other system, then it leads to certain kinds of predictable behavior. Blockage of this by conflicting energy systems or by outside obstacles serves to prevent direct behavioral expression. The blockage, in turn, leads the energy to produce some other kind of behavior that might be conceived of as a resultant of the various forces operating at the time. Such behavior may be more or less satisfying, but would be regarded as pathological if it met any of the criteria listed in the previous chapter.

Along with the dynamic aspects of the theory are the so-called "topographic" features. These are the assumptions of *unconscious, preconscious,* and *conscious* processes, implying the location or placement of processes in such a way that they are differentially available to conscious awareness on the part of the individual himself. Processes may be classified as "unconscious" or not in terms of the readiness with which the subject recognizes their influence on his own behavior.

Yet a third feature of this model is the concept of the *mental apparatus*. The apparatus comprises, among other features, the well-known notions of super-ego, ego, and id. For a brief summary description of this, we may turn to Fairbarn (1952).

The well-known theory which he [Freud] eventually formulated was to the effect that, towards the end of early childhood, it becomes possible to distinguish three parts of the mind—viz. the id, the ego and the superego. The id was conceived by Freud as representing the original instinctive endowment of the individual and as constituting the source of the impulse. The ego was conceived as a structure developed on the basis of experience for regulating instinctive activity in such a way as to promote adjustment to outer reality. The superego has been described by Freud as "a deposit left by the earliest object-choices of the id"; and since the child's first libidinal objects are parental figures, the superego resolves itself into an internal representative of these figures. The parental figures themselves are, of course, external objects; but according to Freud's conception, the super-ego arises in consequence of the child's establishing a representative of these figures inside his own psyche under the pressure of his need for them. . . . (P. 123.)

It is not clear from the writings of psychoanalysts whether or not the mental apparatus is a purely conceptual matter or whether it is based upon some suppositions about human neurophysiology. Thus Freeman (1958) comments that the mental apparatus "was conceived by Freud as an entirely psychological construct. It was not tied to anatomical sites or physiological substrates." On the other hand, according to Frenkel-Brunswik (1957, p. 163), "Freud readily acknowledges that a 'rough correlation of the mental apparatus to anatomy . . . exists.' If, so far, every attempt to establish a localization of his constructs has miscarried, *the present imperfect state of the biological sciences must be held responsible*" (italics added).

Processes which are of primary interest to behavioral scientists, such as learning, perception, memory, judgment, and the like, are classified by the dynamic psychologist as *ego functions*. Development of these functions in the person may be explained as the outcome of the interaction between the primary instincts and the pressures of reality. This development is a matter of theoretical discussion within the ranks of psychoanalysis. Schilder (1942) suggested that perception, for example, develops independently of drive dynamics, even though it may be influenced by them. Later, Hartmann (1951) suggested that a number of ego functions such as perception, control of mobility, and memory have independent beginnings within the ego, do not arise because of conflict between bodily needs and the environment, and are themselves independent of bodily needs. Although they follow their own laws of maturation, they do become involved with dynamic conflicts later and may be influenced by them.

On the whole, psychoanalysts have been little interested in the processes by which learning and perception are governed except in those cases where the ego functions are notably deviant, as in hallucinations, amnesias, and the like. These they explain in terms of motivational or dynamic variables related to the instinctual needs of the patient; they show minimal concern with explanations derived from the study of normal perception.

Dynamic theory is also described by its adherents as *genetic*. By this is meant that the theory makes several assumptions about the central importance of certain bodily functions from birth through infancy. Thus stimulation of the mouth (oral) and the anus (anal) and the development of pleasure in genital stimulation are assumed to be the central foci of motivational development in early life. A further assumption is that the occurrence of frustrations or other crucial experiences in relation to these stages produces an arrest of motivational development at the current stage. Thus the individual may become "fixated" at one of these levels. Such fixations are thought to have significance in determining the general personality development of the individual and in influencing the subsequent features of deviant behavior, should it appear.

One of the more crucial concepts within the genetic structure of psychoanalysis is the concept of *regression*. When the satisfaction of a drive is frustrated in some way, a substitute form of behavior will develop. In general terms, the appearance of this new response is an instance of the general phenomenon of *displacement*. However, if the new substitute response is one that was appropriate to an earlier stage of normal development, then the individual is said to have "regressed." Thus, a person who is unsuccessful, for one reason or another, in forming a satisfactory heterosexual adult relationship may begin to overeat, regressing from the genital stage of adult adjustment to the earlier oral stage.

A comprehensive discussion of dynamic theory is not possible here; the foregoing is, of course, a mere sketch of the major features. The reader is referred to the writings of the psychoanalysts for more elaborate exposition. However, certain aspects of this general theoretical position must be discussed in order that we can understand the difficulties which arise when we try to apply it meaningfully to the science of psychopathology.

Problems in Dynamic Theory

In any science, we must distinguish between observation and inference. *Observations* are necessarily communicable and referable to elementary characteristics of the event observed. A student has to be taught what is a single cell viewed under the microscope; but he is taught by communication using terms he already understands. He can be told, "It is the round thing, stained blue, mottled, with the dark spot in the middle and divided off from the other cells by a thin dark wall around the edge." None of these terms is technical. Later he will learn to use words like "nucleus" and "granules," but each of these is referable to primary terms also. He will learn to distinguish different types of cells and develop special words for each one;

but each of these differences is also referable to primary descriptions. If it were not so, there would be no way to teach or to get observer agreement. Observation does not depend upon the theory that will be built up around the observations; the *inferences* that may be made from them will both generate the theory and will later tend to be made as a consequence of the observer's holding the theory.

Dynamic theorists have commonly failed to comprehend the distinction between inference and observation. Let us take an example:

"The little boy," writes Main (1958), "who babbles tenderly to himself as he soaps himself in his bath does so because he has taken into himself his tender soaping mother" (pp. 3–4).

Obviously a writer who refers to a child having "taken into himself his tender soaping mother" has not made an *observation;* he has made an *inference*, albeit couched in metaphorical terms. He has inferred some process which he prefers to describe as "taking into" from the observation of some similarity between the behavior of the child and the behavior of the mother. Main, however, appears to be completely unaware of this distinction but goes on to say:

"The process of projection and introjection in the *infant* which are inferred from clinical work are of course easily observable in the *child*" (pp. 3–4).

Considerations of meaning make it clear that the language of dynamic psychology is largely figurative. The data available to the psychoanalyst are the same as those available to any other kind of psychologist, namely the words and actions of people and the characteristics of the environments in which they occur. The psychoanalyst may use these data to infer the presence of some inner state in the individual, but he has no way to observe this state directly. Unless this kind of inference is to be merely a superficial verbal exercise, it must lead to some prediction about the future behavior of the person and/or the history of events which brought the state about. Predictions of this kind can be made and tested only when the events and behaviors predicted are defined in such a way that observers can agree that they are present.

A third difficulty with the dynamic model is the *absence of quantification.* Not only must observations have objective referents; they must permit measurement. If we cannot assign units to the "energy" systems adduced to account for behavior, then we have no possible basis for predicting any given behavior under any set of circumstances. Instinctual energy has been described as comparable to a fluid which is discharged from a container by consummation of a drive, which increases in pressure with the passage of time and which, when one channel of discharge is obstructed, will tend to discharge through whatever other channels may be available. Every response is seen as requiring—as using up—some quanta of energy. However, no means exist or seem to be contemplated for measuring such concepts as "quantum," "pressure," or rate of "discharge," etc. Without such measures, it is impossible to predict the future behavior of an individual.

The concept of psychic energy is essentially a picturesque fiction which explains everything but predicts nothing. Its antecedents are unknown, its properties are unquantified, but its behavioral consequences are unlimited. It is a concept which supplies us with many possibilities for dramatic language in describing behavior pathology; it offers little or no prospect of the development of scientific laws for predicting it.

Of the many ramifications of the dynamic model, perhaps the most fruitful for subsequent research in psychopathology has been the emphasis upon conflict as a source of maladaptive behavior. We have already seen that early experimental work from Pavlov's laboratory demonstrated the importance of certain kinds of discrimination conflict in determining experimentally "neurotic" responses. Behind the many metaphors of dynamic terminology, the same essential process exists.

Thus the role of the super-ego may be defined in terms of avoidance tendencies acquired by punishment (or the threat of it). These avoidance tendencies are cued, primarily, by stimuli provided by the person's own approach responses—the approach responses that were punished originally. Thus the conflict between super-ego and id impulses has many of the characteristics of an approach-avoidance conflict. By the same token, the conflict is exacerbated by the fact that, typically, the environment provides no ready escape. Since the approach tendency is the central stimulus, and since as such it goes with the individual, there is no easy way to escape by leaving the environment—unless it is by exchanging that environment for one in which there are no external stimuli to arouse the approach tendency.

Because there is no ready escape from this kind of conflict, the patient's maladaptive responses tend to become relatively permanent features of his behavior. Indeed, the categorization of personality types on the basis of the predominant pattern of avoidance response is quite common in the study of normal personality as well as in psychopathology. Chapter 8 will treat this subject in more detail.

At the present time, the testing of hypotheses derived from dynamic theories is hampered by the vagueness of definition of the states or processes postulated in the dynamic model. This is not to say that the model cannot be reformulated in such a way that testable hypotheses might be deduced; merely that so far, an adequate reformulation has not been made.

This reformulation, as O'Neil (1953) has pointed out, requires three steps:

First we must discover clearer means, possibly in the form of operational criteria, of distinguishing the "data" from the "impressions" in the psychoanalytic findings. Secondly, we must reformulate many psychoanalytic hypotheses in order to make their empirical reference less equivocal. Thirdly, we need to set out quite explicitly the premises, both hypothetical and empirical, and the deductive steps in arriving at explanations and predictions, and not with wisdom after the event or shrewd prognostications. (Pp. 160–161.)

A recent and sympathetic essay on the impact of dynamic psychology remarks of its present status:

Psychoanalysis, too, has its practical obstacles. The first of these is a problem which we considered earlier: the lack of a systematic theoretical literature, especially on the general psychoanalytic theory. Although this situation is to some extent being alleviated by the work of persons like Rapaport (1955, 1959) and Gill (1963), it still remains an obstacle to theoretical progress. . . . In addition, . . . there are a number of theoretical obstacles arising from the very nature of the subject matter and the field which psychoanalysis and psychology have in common. Regard for the individual's legal and moral rights is a major empirical barrier to the observation and manipulation of behavior inside and outside the laboratory. This problem also has important theoretical aspects: the effects of such trespass upon the subject, the observer, and the observation. There is, too, the "hierarchy" problem. Much experimentation lies ahead before laws of hierarchic transformation are developed which will permit adequate handling of field problems taken into the laboratory. Still another problem grows out of the fact that a large proportion of psychological phenomena occur only in the contact of one person with one or more others. The method of participant observation has been developed to deal with this problem, but the implications of this method have not yet been theoretically formulated, and the lack of such systematization has in turn retarded the theory's development. A final obstacle is that of mathematization, including quantification. (Shakow & Rapaport, 1964, pp. 195–196.)

In view of all these considerations, the dynamic model does not currently present a vehicle suitable for the conduct of precise research. Many attempts at experimental investigation of psychoanalytic propositions have been made. In one of the leading surveys of such research, Hilgard points out that, when judged by the standards of laboratory science:

Anyone who tries to give an honest appraisal of psychoanalysis as a science must be ready to admit that as it is stated it is mostly very bad science, that the bulk of the articles in its journals cannot be defended as research publications at all. Having said this, I am prepared to reassert that there is much to be learned from these writings. The task of making a science of the observations and relationships may, however, fall to others than the psychoanalysts themselves.

If psychoanalysts are themselves to make a science of their knowledge, they must be prepared to follow some of the standard rules of science. (Hilgard, 1952, p. 44.)

In this book, the concern is with the application of a laboratory-based science to the problems of psychopathology. As such, it is not possible to accept the dynamic model as a suitable point of departure. This decision should not be regarded as intending to deny the various cultural impacts of many psychoanalytic propositions, nor the remarkable perspicacity of many of the psychoanalysts' classical observations.

THE STATISTICAL MODEL

The models which we have already described have envisaged some process which is central to understanding deviant behavior. The process is perhaps hypothetical, being inferred from behavior; in one case, the process is a "disease," in another it is misplaced "energy," and in yet another, it is "moral miscalculation." We may now turn to what, for the sake of convenience, we have called the *statistical* model. Properly speaking, this represents an *approach* rather than a model, as no process or concept other than simple description and measurement is involved.

Stimulated by the unreliability of current diagnostic categories, for the reasons which have already been discussed, several psychopathologists have returned to the fundamental problem of identifying patterns of behavior which occur with sufficient frequency and regularity to provide a basis for scientific classification. However, these patterns are identified by careful measurement and statistical analysis of the data obtained. Patterns which are obtained are not assumed to represent underlying disease entities—indeed, there is no necessary assumption that they represent the results of any single process. The main requirement of this procedure is that the method of measurement be clearly defined. The mathematical-statistical techniques applied depend upon certain logical considerations which will not be discussed in detail here.

The Dimensional Approach

One approach to the classification of behavior has turned to the concept of *dimensions* of personality rather than *types* of deviant behavior. The dimensional approach, which has been especially advocated by Eysenck (1960, etc.) has used statistical analysis—especially the various forms of factor analysis—to identify a limited number of factors or dimensions which may be used to describe an individual's behavior. For example, Eysenck considers the behavior

of a person who might, in a typical hospital setting, be diagnosed as *hysteric*. Such a classification implies, as we have already noted, some single process or agent which has "caused" the hysterical pattern to appear; it implies that this person is one of a homogeneous group of persons who are all hysteric and are qualitatively distinguishable from nonhysterics; and it suggests the possibility that there may be some single appropriate method of therapy for all people diagnosed as hysteric.

With the dimensional approach, however, the patient would be described in terms of his position on certain dimensions of personality. In Eysenck's formulation, the most pertinent dimensions would be those of *neuroticism* and *introversion-extraversion*. In Figure 2-1 we may see how individuals representing the common psychiatric disease entities would be located with respect to their description in terms of these two dimensions. For a full description of pathological behavior, Eysenck has found it necessary to utilize a third dimension, which he has labeled *psychoticism*. In Figure 2-2 we have depicted the relative position of some of the common syndromes in terms of the

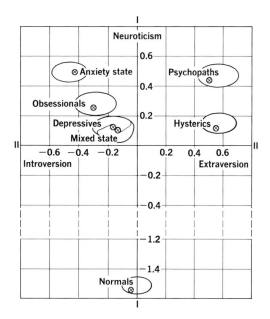

Figure 2-1. Position of one normal and six neurotic groups in two-dimensional framework determined by canonical variate analysis of objective test performances. (Eysenck, 1960a.)

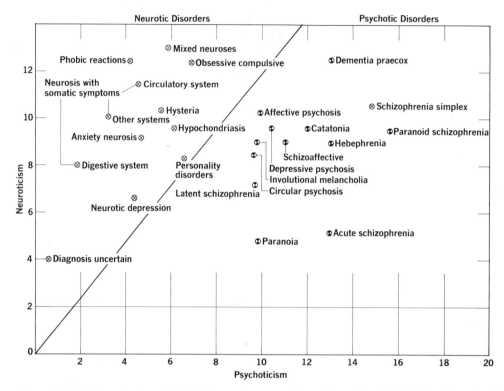

Figure 2-2. Position of various clinically diagnosed groups of neurotics and psychotics in two-dimensional framework provided by canonical variate analysis of symptom ratings. (Eysenck, 1960a.)

psychoticism and neuroticism dimensions as formulated by Eysenck.

In addition to these three major dimensions, several minor factors are used within Eysenck's dimensional model. The importance of this approach lies not in the possibility of generating dimensions along which present syndromes might be placed, but rather in providing these dimensions for the location of individual patients. Factorially derived dimensions are *continuous*. An individual's location along any of these dimensions is based upon *measurement* and not upon classification. Continuity of personality differences between individuals is more in accord with common observation than is the notion of discrete syndromes. Measurement represents an advance over classification in the development of any science. These considerations suggest that the kind of approach typified by Eysenck possesses considerably greater potentiality than any existing static classification system.

It should be remembered, however, that the factor-analytic studies which generate dimensional concepts of this kind are producing plausible dimensional descriptions—not established conclusions. The usefulness of this kind of dimensional description depends, as Eysenck has pointed out, upon the possibility of relating it to laws derived from the experimental study of behavior. If we were to imagine a descriptive study of heat, for example, we might emerge with correlations between the amount a metal plate expands, how long a given quantity of water takes to boil when placed on the plate, the painful sensation we experience when we touch it, how closely we can approach it before we feel warm air, etc. All these would represent measures of a possible dimension to be called *hot-cold,* and along which objects could be placed in continuous fashion. But this dimension is essentially descriptive and of limited value without a systematic theory of heat transfer organized into a series of appropriate laws. A statistical dimension model, in the same way, is of limited value until it has been successfully integrated into a coherent theory of the determinants of behavior.

Bearing this in mind, it may be profitable to summarize the main outlines of Eysenck's statistical dimensional model.

1. There are two main factors or dimensions in behavioral pathology; one of these is psychoticism and the other neuroticism.
2. Both of these represent continuous dimensions which extend from normalcy to severe behavior pathology. There are no clear discontinuities to suggest the presence of groups or syndromes.
3. A third factor is introversion-extraversion, which serves as an additional dimension of special importance in relation to the neuroticism factor. Its relation to psychoticism is unclear.
4. When psychoticism is considered separately, several minor dimensions emerge which are related to traditional psychiatric concepts of pathological behavior.
5. Individual persons tend to have scores on all dimensions, not on just one—a fact which gives further force to the objections against diagnoses into single syndromes.

The Typological or Type-factor Approach

Eysenck has used statistical techniques to produce continuous measurements, in sharp contrast to the syndrome classification model. Other statistically minded psychopathologists have used them to produce syndromes or behavioral patterns, but with the aim of defining the patterns with greater precision than those in the present psychiatric nosology. Here again, the statistical procedures which are used are derived from factor analysis. Ignoring the mathematical aspects of this approach, we might illustrate it by reference to Guertin (1961b). From a rating of the behavior of 49 hospitalized male schizophrenics, he derived a series of correlations between certain psychiatric symptoms. Employing a technique known as "manifest structure analysis" (du Mas, 1956), he derived five type factors representing classifications of types within the general diagnostic category of schizophrenia. Details of the types and the most important defining behaviors for each type are given in Table 2-2.

Guertin has used this kind of statistical model without any explicit suggestion that the type factors should be regarded as entities having separate etiologies and being completely homogeneous. However, it is clear that the purpose of this kind of statistical model is to produce a classificatory rather than dimensional scheme, and it is thus subject to the problems which beset all gross classifications of human behavior, whatever the precision of the measurements which preceded them. It is also clear that whereas the dimensional approach does not begin with any assumption about the validity of such psychiatric diagnoses as "schizophrenia," the type-factor approach as we have illustrated it accepts such a grouping and then attempts to identify subgroups within it.

A comprehensive and sophisticated application of the factor-analytic model has been reported by Zubin and his associates (e.g., Zubin et al., 1961). They have been concerned with the identification factors in the behavioral patterns of patients that might be related to good or poor prognosis in combination with selected forms of treatment.

Their method involved the follow-up of patients released from hospitals and on whom a variety of psychological and behavior rating measures had been obtained. Although some provocative relationships were found (e.g., patients whose performance on a perceptual task exceeded their performance on a reasoning task had a better prognosis),

TABLE 2-2 Type Factors Produced by an Application of the Statistical Approach to the Description of Schizophrenic Behavior

Type factor	Most definitive behaviors
Normal	Very aware of other patients Very cooperative No obsessive thoughts Usually relevant
Catatonic-withdrawn vs. Overexpressive	Mannerisms or gestures ⎫ Some positioning ⎬ Withdrawn Slowed movements ⎪ Place disorientation ⎭ Assertive ⎫ Generally hostile ⎬ Expressive Generally initiates conversation ⎪ Overtalkative ⎭
Paranoid	Bizarre thoughts Generally hostile Influenced by persecutors Can show hostility toward personnel
Resistive-isolation	May dislike being told what to do Underactive Social avoidance Not dependable
Anxious-dysphoric	Expresses despondency Recognizes illness Overconcerned about others' opinion Some fear of doom

SOURCE: *Guertin (1961b).*

the authors felt compelled to conclude: "We have very little to offer at the present time since we are disenchanted with the application of factor analysis or methods of correlation to predicting outcome in what is probably an unhomogeneous population" (Zubin et al., 1961, p. 202).

SUMMARY

Psychopathology includes a range of behavioral and biological phenomena that may be approached with any of several sets of assumptions. Each set of assumptions may be regarded as a *model*. A model is a more or less complicated system that has been found useful in organizing one range of phenomena and may be applied, by analogy, to the new phenomena under scrutiny.

Pathological behavior has been approached historically with *religious* models, which gave way in the eighteenth century to the *disease* model or *medical* model. The medical model has indeed had great value, especially in helping to redefine public attitudes toward deviant behavior. However, the analogy between organic disease and disordered behavior is seriously inadequate at many points.

Other models have been suggested. The *moral* model and the *statistical* model are of comparatively recent development, while the psychoanalytic *dynamic* model has a somewhat longer history.

An approach is possible that takes its origin from the laws governing behavior as established in psychological and biological laboratories. This does not involve a model, but instead regards the problems of psychopathology as integral parts of the whole range of psychobiological science.

SUGGESTED READINGS

1. Hendrick, Ives. *Facts and theories of psychoanalysis.* (2d ed. rev.) New York: Knopf, 1941. A survey of the basic theoretical structure of psychoanalytic psychology. Covers all the essential features of the dynamic model.
2. Mowrer, O. H. Sin: the lesser of two evils. *Amer. Psychologist,* 1960, **15,** 301–304. An exposition of the writer's thesis that guilt is a prime determinant of psychopathology and that the moral model is most applicable in its treatment.
3. Ritchie, A. D. *Scientific method.* Paterson, N.J.: Littlefield, Adams & Co., 1960. A simple introduction to principles of scientific investigation. Basic issues of validity of laws and methods of measurement are covered.
4. Szasz, T. The myth of mental illness. *Amer. Psychologist,* 1960, **15,** 113–118. A brief exposition of the moral model, emphasis being placed upon mental "illness" as a psychosocial and ethical problem.

REFERENCES

American Psychiatric Association. *Diagnostic and statistical manual: mental disorders.* Washington, D.C.: Author, 1952.

Cameron, N. The functional psychoses. In J. McV. Hart (Ed.), *Personality and the behavior disorders.* New York: Ronald, 1944.

Diefendorf, A. R. *Clinical psychiatry.* New York: Macmillan, 1921.

Dollard, J., & Miller, N. E. *Personality and psychotherapy.* New York: McGraw-Hill, 1950.

du Mas, F. M. *Manifest structure analysis.* Missoula, Montana: Montana State University Press, 1956.

Eysenck, H. J. Classification and the problem of diagnosis. In H. J. Eysenck (Ed.), *Handbook of abnormal psychology.* London: Sir Isaac Pitman, 1960. (a)

Eysenck, H. J. The effects of psychotherapy. In H. J. Eysenck (Ed.), *Handbook of abnormal psychology.* London: Sir Isaac Pitman, 1960. (b)

Fairbarn, W. R. D. Theoretical and experimental aspects of psychoanalysis. *Brit. J. Med. Psychol.,* 1952, **25,** 122–127.

Freeman, T. Aspects of perception in psychoanalysis and experimental psychology. *Brit. J. Med. Psychol.,* 1958, **31,** 9–13.

Frenkel-Brunswik, Else. Perspectives in psychoanalytic theory. In H. P. David & H. von Bracken (Eds.), *Perspectives in personality theory.* London: Tavistock, 1957.

Gill, M. M. Topography and systems in psychoanalytic theory. *Psychological Issues,* **3** (2). New York: Int. Univ. Press, 1963.

Guertin, W. H. An inverted factor analytic study of schizophrenia. *J. consult. Psychol.,* 1952, **16,** 371–375.

Guertin, W. H. Medical and statistical-psychological models for research in schizophrenia. *Behav. Sci.,* 1961, **6** (3), 200–204. (a)

Guertin, W. H. Empirical syndrome groupings of schizophrenic hospital admissions. *J. clin. Psychol.,* 1961, **17** (3), 268–275. (b)

Hartmann, H. Ego psychology and the problem of adaptation. In D. Rapaport (Ed.), *Organization in pathology of thought.* New York: Columbia, 1951.

Hilgard, E. R. *Psychoanalysis as science.* E. Pumpian-Mindlin (Ed.), Stanford: Stanford Univ. Press, 1952.

Jellinek, E. Some principles of psychiatric classification. *Psychiatry,* 1939, **2,** 161–165.

Jones, M. *The therapeutic community.* New York: Basic Books, 1953.

Main, T. F. Perception and ego-function. *Brit. J. Med. Psychol.,* 1958, **31,** 1–7.

Mehlman, B. The reliability of psychiatric diagnosis. *J. abnorm. soc. Psychol.,* 1952, **47,** 577–578.

Mowrer, O. H. Sin: the lesser of two evils. *Amer. Psychologist,* 1960, **15,** 301–304.

O'Neil, W. H. The relation of clinical and experimental methods in psychology. *Brit. J. Med. Psychol.,* 1953, **26,** 158–162.

Phillips, E. L. *Psychotherapy: a modern theory and practice*. Englewood Cliffs, N.J.: Prentice-Hall, 1956.

Raines, G. N., & Rohrer, J. H. The operational matrix of psychiatric practice, I: consistency and variability in interview impressions of different psychiatrists. *Amer. J. Psychiat.*, 1955, **110**, 721–733.

Rapaport, D. The development and the concepts of psychoanalytic ego psychology. Twelve seminars given at the Western New England Institute for Psychoanalysis. Multilithed. 1955.

Rapaport, D. The structure of psychoanalytic theory: a systematizing attempt. In S. Koch (Ed.), *Psychology: a study of a science,* vol. 3: Formulations of the person and the social context. New York: McGraw-Hill, 1959. Pp. 55–183. Also in *Psychological issues,* **2** (2). New York: Int. Univ. Press, 1960.

Rotter, J. B. *Social learning and clinical psychology*. Englewood Cliffs, N.J.: Prentice-Hall, 1954.

Schilder, P. *Mind, perception and thought in their constructive aspects*. New York: Columbia, 1942.

Schmidt, H. O., & Fonda, C. P. The reliability of psychiatric diagnosis: a new look. *J. abnorm. soc. Psychol.,* 1956, **52,** 262–267.

Shakow, D., & Rapaport, D. *The influence of Freud on American psychology*. New York: Int. Univ. Press, 1964.

Szasz, T. S. The myth of mental illness. *Amer. Psychologist,* 1960, **15,** 113–118.

Szasz, T. S. The uses of naming and the origin of the myth of mental illness. *Amer. Psychologist,* 1961, **16** (2), 59–65.

White, R. W. *The abnormal personality*. (2d Ed.) New York: Ronald, 1956.

Zilboorg, G., & Henry, G. W. *A history of medical psychology*. New York: Norton, 1941.

Zubin, J., Sutton, S., Salzinger, K., Burdock, E. I., & Perez, D. A biometric approach to prognosis in schizophrenia. In P. H. Hoch and J. Zubin (Eds.), *Comparative epidemiology in the mental disorders.* New York: Grune and Stratton, 1961.

3 PSYCHOLOGICAL CONCEPTS IN PSYCHOPATHOLOGY

This chapter presents some account of the more important psychological concepts that are relevant to the understanding of experimental psychopathology. It should not be surprising that the major emphasis is on concepts most commonly used in experimental psychology, especially those related to *learning, motivation,* and *perception.* Research in these areas has advanced to a level that is considerably more sophisticated than much that has been done so far within a purely clinical framework, and the prospects for a fruitful union of the experimental method with clinically significant problems seem encouraging.

LEARNING: CONDITIONING

Definitions of *learning* are numerous. In this book we shall define learning as *the process which changes the probability that a given response will be elicited by a given stimulus.* Having defined learning as a process in this way, we can recognize that the investigation of learning is largely directed to discovering the environmental influences which affect it and the biological variables which may modify it. On the whole, the majority of learning theorists have paid less attention to biological variables than they have to environmental ones, and our body of scientific knowledge is consequently more advanced with regard to the effects of the latter. Indifference to biological processes and their effects upon behavior is most plausible when the investigator is fairly sure that he is dealing with biologically normal behavior. We may proceed as though the organism is "empty" when we know that it is full but intact. Psychopathologists, on the other hand, may make no such assumption unless they are bent on futility. Behavioral consequences of biological aberration are of great significance in psychopathology and are so treated in the chapters which follow. However, since simplicity will be better served by considering environmental variables separately from biological ones, discussion of the latter is deferred to the next chapter. Let us now turn to examine the influence of environmental variables upon the learning process.

Technical Terms in Conditioning

For practical purposes the simplest example of learning is the acquisition by a subject of a *conditioned response* (CR). In what is called *classical conditioning,* a stimulus which already has the power to elicit a response is presented in contiguity with another stimulus which does not yet have this power. Repeated presentations of these two stimuli in contiguity eventually lead to a situation where the formerly neutral stimulus will now elicit the response when it is presented alone. The response remains essentially the same—the occurrence of learning is demonstrated by the fact that the probability that it would occur to the neutral stimulus was originally zero. Following the conditioning procedure, it has been raised to some positive level of probability.

Certain technical terms are used to describe this process. The stimulus which originally elicits the response is referred to as the *unconditioned stimulus* (US) and the response, when made to it, is an *unconditioned response* (UR). The previously neutral stimulus is described as the *conditioned stimulus* (CS) and the response, when made to the CS alone, is called the *conditioned response* (CR). An example of this procedure would be provided by the acquisi-

tion of a conditioned eyeblink response. A puff of air, delivered to the eye, will elicit an eyeblink. At this point the air puff is the US and the eyeblink the UR. If the delivery of the air puff is preceded by a short audible sound stimulus, and if this sequence of stimuli is repeated sufficiently often, the sound will elicit the eyeblink response. Now the sound is a CS, and the eyeblink response to the CS is a CR.

Learning may be demonstrated by a different sequence of events in a procedure generally known as *operant conditioning.* This refers to the procedure wherein a reinforcing stimulus is presented to the subject whenever he makes a given response. The response in question is not being elicited by the reinforcing stimulus, the latter usually being concealed until after the desired response has occurred. Conditioning is defined as having been established when the rate of occurrence of the reinforced response increases in the situation. For some purposes we may wish to use increases in the speed of responding or in the magnitude of the response.

The best-known illustration of experimental operant conditioning is the acquisition of a bar-pressing response by a rat (or a key-pecking response by a pigeon) in an apparatus which is constructed so as to deliver food when the bar is pressed. This kind of apparatus is usually called an "operant-conditioning chamber"—or more colloquially, a "Skinner box," referring to the major contribution of B. F. Skinner to our understanding of operant conditioning. A typical operant-conditioning chamber is illustrated in Figure 3-1.

More specific developments of the operant-conditioning technique involve the use of special schedules of reinforcement, whereby the response is not reinforced each time it is made. Schedules may include reinforcement of a predetermined percentage of the responses made, of responses made only in the presence of some special stimulus such as a light, or of responses made during specified time intervals. Much work has gone into the study of effects of different schedules of rein-

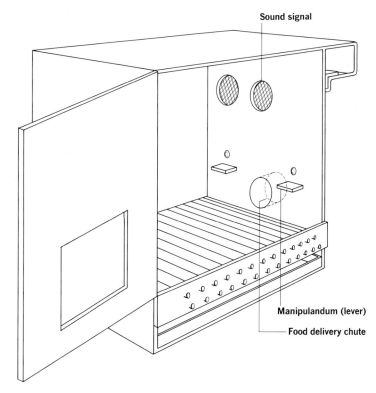

Figure 3-1. Operant-conditioning chamber of the kind used in laboratory procedures.

forcement, but we cannot discuss them in detail here.

Extinction

After establishing a conditioned response, we may proceed to *extinguish* it; that is to say, we may reduce its rate, speed, or magnitude by eliminating the reinforcement related to the response. In the case of classical conditioning, for example, we may establish a CR of salivation to a bell (CS) by presenting the CS in contiguity with food (US). When the CR has been well established, we may extinguish it by giving repeated presentations of the bell alone, never pairing it again with food. The salivation response will begin to diminish in magnitude and frequency and will eventually extinguish.

Extinction of operant conditioning is achieved by removing the reinforcement entirely so that the conditioned response is never followed by reinforcement. Here again we will find a slowing down of the rate of responding until it is extinguished. We should note, however, that the attainment of complete extinction of a previously conditioned response is a questionable phenomenon. When a response has been extinguished, and is then neither elicited nor emitted for a period of time away from the conditioning environment, the return of the subject to the conditioning environment will be accompanied by the reappearance of the response at higher strength than that which it had at the end of the extinction procedure. This reappearance of a conditioned response that had been apparently extinguished is called *spontaneous recovery,* and the phenomenon is of considerable importance in the application of learning theory to human behavior.

Counterconditioning

If for some reason we wish to extinguish a certain response which has been conditioned, we may use both the procedure of extinction and that of *counterconditioning*. Counterconditioning consists simply of the reinforcing of a new response which is incompatible with the one which it is desired to extinguish. As we shall see later on, certain aspects of psychotherapy may be regarded as instances of the counterconditioning of new and more adaptive responses to take the place of the undesirable pathological behaviors which have brought the patient into treatment.

Reinforcement

Of all the concepts which are crucial to the understanding of learning, that of *reinforcement* is perhaps the most central. It is, at the same time, the most troublesome to define. As a beginning, let us turn to Verplanck (1957). He defines reinforcement as "the operation of presenting to the animal in operant conditioning, after it has made a response (and therefore contingent on its occurrence), a reinforcing stimulus or of withdrawing a negative reinforcing stimulus," and "in classical conditioning, the operation of presenting, contiguously in time, a conditioned stimulus and an unconditioned stimulus" (p. 25).

The problem of this definition is that we do not know what will be a reinforcement until learning has occurred. Commonsense observation has led to the assumption that food is a reinforcing stimulus to a hungry subject, or that reduction of pain is a reinforcement to almost any living organism. Most of the time this assumption is supported, i.e., animals learn responses which are reinforced by food or by pain reduction, etc. However, at the present time, there is no adequate definition of reinforcement that is independent of observation of learning. In effect, any consequence of a response that will occur again under like conditions is a reinforcement. If this change is one of increasing the probability, then it is a *positive* reinforcement; if it is a change to a lower probability, then it is a *negative* reinforcement.

Animal experimentation makes major use of *biological* or *primary* reinforcements. Typical biological reinforcers include food for a hungry animal, water for a thirsty animal, sexual activity after a period of deprivation, and removal of excessive heat, cold, painful stimulation, etc., from the environment. These reinforcements are classed together as primary because they appear to be effective for any animal in a given species without training.

By and large, in Western society much behavior does not appear to be supported by direct primary reinforcers. Social reinforcers, such as the acquisition of success, prestige, acceptance by others, and the like, appear to be responsible for much social learning which takes place. Likewise, social punishment, failure, and rejection seem to act as negative reinforcers. Social learning theorists have suggested many lists of social reinforcers. We shall not be concerned here with these lists, except to note that among them have been included such events as the acquisition of material wealth, the construction of objects or of systems, praise, prestige, friendship, pity, and so on.

Theoretical interest attaches to the question of whether social reinforcers are acquired on the basis of experience with primary reinforcers, or whether some of them at least are as fundamental to human behavior as the primary biological reinforcers. From a practical point of view this distinction is of less importance. Adult behavior may be so greatly determined by the occurrence of social reinforcers that the origin of these reinforcers may be irrelevant to the problem of the extinction or change of specific behaviors.

Secondary Reinforcement

Stimuli which are present and contiguous with the delivery of a reinforcer may, after a number of such presentations, acquire the power to act as reinforcers for the response in the absence of the original reinforcer. When this state of affairs has been reached, the stimuli in question are described as *secondary reinforcers*. It is clear that the development of a secondary reinforcer may sometimes be accidental. Contiguities between situational stimuli and existing reinforcers may occur in an unlimited number of ways, leading to the establishment of the situational stimuli as secondary reinforcers. There may be no "logical" or obvious connection between the secondary reinforcer and the response when they occur together at some much later time.

Stimulus Generalization

Once a response has been conditioned to a particular CS, it will also be evoked by any other stimulus which has some similarity to that CS. Similarity of one stimulus to another is a rather complicated matter. Any physical characteristic of a stimulus might vary—size, color, shape, brightness, etc., in visual stimuli; pitch, loudness, etc., in an auditory stimulus. Where the variation is measurable in physical units, such as inches, lumens, decibels, frequency in cycles per second, and so forth, we speak of *primary stimulus generalization*. An illustration of a curve or gradient of primary stimulus generalization is given in Figure 3-2.

Questions of theoretical interest have been raised about the shape of the gradient of stimulus generalization, but we may here concern ourselves only with the observation that with decreasing similarity to the original CS, other stimuli evoke the response with decreasing strength, probability, and speed. By the same token, the extinction of the response is more rapid when extinction is established with a generalization stimulus than it is when extinction procedures use the original CS.

Generalization of Extinction

We may establish a response to a particular CS and then proceed to extinguish it to a similar generalized stimulus. After some measure of extinction has been achieved with the generalized CS, we may once more present the original CS and will find that the response to it has been weakened by the intervening extinction process. This phenomenon is referred to as the *generalization of extinction*. Apart from its interest for learning theorists, the procedure is of some importance in understanding clinical techniques involved in the extinction of pathological behavior. Under many circumstances it may be tactically more practicable to attempt extinction in a situation where it is likely to be most feasible—i.e., in a generalization situation, before attempting extinction in the situation which is most central to the subject's behavior.

Figure 3-2. A stimulus generalization gradient. (From Guttman and Kalish, 1958.)

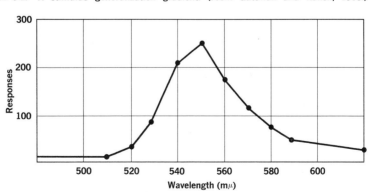

Semantic Generalization

Much human behavior is verbal. Human social, interpersonal behavior is predominantly verbal. Consequently the significant stimuli and responses are spoken or written words, the physical attributes of which are much less important than the symbolic meanings that they have acquired. Similarity between words may exist on the basis of meaning rather than on the basis of the number and order of letters which they have in common. Experiments by Lacey and Smith (1954) and Lacey, Smith, and Green (1955) demonstrate that the establishment of conditioned responses of the autonomic system to a stimulus word "cow" also generalized to other rural words such as "corn" and "tractor" when these were presented to the subject. Here, presumably, the basis of generalization was the rural connotation of the words.

There is some reason to believe that the dimensions of semantic generalization change in the period of childhood and the transition to adulthood. Reiss (1946), for example, established a conditioned GSR to words and found that stimulus generalization was most apparent to homophones (words of the same sound but with different spelling and meaning) between the ages of 7 and 9; for antonyms (words of opposite meaning) for the age range 10 to 12; and for synonyms between 14 and 20 years.

Partial Reinforcement Effect

When a response is learned under conditions in which the CS is not always accompanied by the US, an interesting and paradoxical effect is obtained. The response learned under these conditions is harder to extinguish than one which is learned under conditions of 100 per cent reinforcement. To this phenomenon is given the name *partial reinforcement effect* (PRE). Sophisticated theoretical explanations have been developed to account for this effect, and sophisticated experiments have been made to discover the limits within which it occurs. None of these

will be discussed here, but we may note that the existence of PRE suggests that learned behaviors may be kept at fairly high strengths if an occasional reinforcement is provided. It is not necessary for CS-US contiguities to be consistent or frequent in order for an established CR to be maintained. In fact, the PRE indicates that behaviors which were acquired under conditions of partial reinforcement will be relatively difficult to eliminate.

LEARNING: AVOIDANCE LEARNING

Responses which are conditioned to stimuli associated with a painful US exhibit certain features which make it necessary to treat avoidance learning as a somewhat special problem. Let us consider some concepts first.

Avoidance Response

In establishing an *avoidance response,* we pair a CS with a painful US (in the experimental laboratory, the latter is typically a painful electric shock) under conditions in which the subject can avoid receiving the shock at all provided that he makes a predetermined response when the CS appears. Technical steps usually involve the response being one which will break the shock circuit before the shock is delivered, as for example by pressing a bar, or the response may involve the movement of the subject from the region where the shock will occur. In either case, the response is said to be learned when the subject is able to successfully avoid shock a significantly large number of times.

Escape Responses

A different procedure is one in which the subject is not able to avoid the shock completely but may terminate it, after it starts, by some predetermined response. The main difference between the *escape* and avoidance situations is that in the former the US is always applied, whereas in the latter it never appears once the response has been learned.

Conditioned Emotional Response

A third type of conditioning to painful stimulation is one in which the CS is paired with the US and in which there is no way in which the US may be avoided or terminated. Under these conditions, the subject's response represents the UR typical of the species in the presence of unavoidable pain and has been termed an "emotional" response. After sufficient conditioning trials, the CS alone will evoke the pattern of response elicited by the US. When produced by the CS alone, it may be termed the *conditioned emotional response* or CER. Clearly the CER will be quite variable from one kind of organism to another, and will also be influenced by the manner and site of delivery of the US. In the case of the laboratory rat, for example, delivery of shock across a grid floor on which the subject is placed commonly elicits a pattern of reponses which includes immobility or "freezing" to the floor, defecation and urination, and flattening of the ears as the major components.

From these three procedures, we may now turn to the theoretical explanations and problems which the phenomena of avoidance learning have created.

Learned Fear

One explanation of avoidance learning is that the painful stimulation produces both pain and fear (Miller, 1948)—*fear* being a term for a group of responses which accompany pain but are independent of them, in the sense that they can be elicited when no pain is present. A complete description of the fear responses might be difficult to provide, but we may note that many of them would be functions of the visceral nervous system and would include increases in heart rate, respiration, perspiration, and generalized muscular tension. Miller suggested that the effect of pairing a CS with a painful

US was to produce a conditioned fear response such that the onset of the CS would then produce the pattern of fear responses— a process very similar to the conditioned emotional response.

A second aspect of this explanation is that the termination of fear is a reinforcer and that any response which terminates fear will be acquired. Many experiments have demonstrated that once a subject has developed a conditioned fear response to a stimulus, he will learn further responses the only reinforcement of which is that they remove the CS and thus presumably terminate the fear. Removal of the CS in such a case is clearly acting as a secondary reinforcer in much the same way that the presence of the CS may act in learning based on positive reinforcements. Particular importance attaches to this phenomenon, because it illustrates the fact that an individual may develop many responses which serve to avoid a CS, responses which may not have occurred at all in the presence of the US.

Extinction of Avoidance Responses

During the previous discussion of extinction, we noted that the essential step in extinguishing a response is to present the CS without the US, so that the response is made but is not followed by reinforcement. Unreinforced responses then diminish in strength and extinguish. Avoidance learning presents a rather unusual problem in this respect, as the avoidance response—by definition—ensures that the US is not experienced. Speaking colloquially, we might say that the subject doesn't stay around to find out whether or not there is going to be a painful stimulus. Thus the very nature of avoidance behavior is such that extinction is difficult to achieve unless special techniques are involved. Inasmuch as it is necessary that the subject be given repeated trials in which the CS is not accompanied by the US, it is necessary that the avoidance response not be permitted to occur. In a word, the subject must be induced or compelled to undergo the extinction process.

Limits of Extinction of Avoidance Responses.
Every clinical psychologist knows from experience that the removal of pathological behaviors based upon fear is an extremely difficult task. Many forms of pathological behavior receive punishment from society, in the form of social rejection, contempt, and the like. Psychological symptoms are obviously the occasion of much distress to the patient himself. In the light of this we ask ourselves, "Why does someone persist in behavior which is receiving no positive reinforcement and is, indeed, being punished?" There seems to be every reason why symptoms should extinguish without the need for special procedures. This phenomenon has been called *the neurotic paradox* (Mowrer and Ullman, 1945).

The resolution of the paradox is comparatively straightforward. Provided that we are dealing with symptomatic behavior which is being reinforced by avoiding exposure to fear-producing situations, all the conditions necessary to the maintenance of the symptom are present, and present in sufficient degree to outweigh the effects of such social punishment as the symptom is receiving. In order to extinguish symptoms which are being reinforced by removing the patient from fear-producing stimuli, we must prevent the symptoms from serving this purpose. Provided that we can keep the patient in contact with the feared situation long enough and often enough for him to learn that the feared danger (the US) will not occur, extinction *should* take place.

Unfortunately the problem is much less simple than that. We have touched upon the possible nature of the fear response itself and have suggested that the reduction of it constitutes the reinforcement which maintains avoidance behavior. Visceral responses, of the kind which are commonly thought to constitute the major features of the fear response, have considerably longer latencies than many avoidance responses which are supposed to be based on them. In a word, much experimental avoidance behavior has been shown to occur so rapidly after the CS appears that the fear response could not

have had time to develop (Solomon & Wynne, 1953, 1954). If the avoidance response terminates the fear stimulus, then some of the major components of the fear response will not occur in the presence of that stimulus, and it will thus be difficult to extinguish the fear response.

Conservation and Partial Irreversibility of Anxiety. From the foregoing we might summarize the situation by saying that since the speed with which motor avoidance responses may be made is greater than the speed with which visceral components of fear can occur to the same stimulus, there is an inherent physiological reason for the difficulties experienced in extinguishing avoidance behavior. In the case of human behavior, we all are probably familiar with the situation where a sudden emergency while driving on the highway produces a rapid, skilled reaction of swerving from the path of danger—but may be followed some seconds after the danger is over by a very unpleasant experience of fear or distress. The important point here is that we recognize that avoidant behavior may occur without any conscious feeling of fear on the part of the individual. This feeling may come later. If the avoidance response is well learned, it may never come at all. As a descriptive term for the fact that fear tends to be saved from extinction by the speed of the avoidance response, Solomon and Wynne have suggested the phrase *the principle of anxiety conservation.*

So far, so good. However, in the nature of things some avoidance responses may be delayed by random variations in the circumstances in which they are elicited. Thus, from time to time, the response may be made slowly enough for the fear response to develop. When this happens often enough and the US does not occur, the process of extinction should begin, and in the long run responses should become slower, extinction be hastened even further, and so on. Yet where the original US was an intense traumatic stimulus, ultimate extinction of the avoidance response seems to be very rare. Solomon and Wynne have suggested that fear reactions of this kind may be impossible to extinguish completely. Thus for this hypothesis they have offered the principle of *partial irreversibility* of fear responses.

Generalization of Avoidance Responses

Just as other kinds of conditioned responses are elicited by stimuli which are somewhat similar to the original CS, so avoidance responses will occur to generalized stimuli. No special concepts are necessary here. However, some questions have been raised regarding the probability that the gradient of stimulus generalization for avoidance responses may be steeper than that for positively reinforced responses when the two are acquired and compared in similar situations. The rationale behind this suggestion is rather complex. Is is dealt with in our discussion of conflict in a later chapter.

Punishment and the Suppression of Behavior

The child who raids the cookie jar may find that this response leads to punishment. If this were the only and regular result of his behavior, we should expect that he would develop avoidance behaviors of some kind toward cookie jars, parents, or other stimuli which were regularly associated with the punishment. Common sense indicates that this is not the case and that punishment of this kind does not eliminate the behavior for which it is given. We must recognize that the effect of punishment upon behavior which is being independently reinforced is different from the effect of punishment upon behavior which is not being reinforced. The child who is burned by a hot radiator is likely to stay away from it indefinitely, because the response of touching the radiator has not been positively reinforced in any way. On the other hand, the response of raiding the cookie jar is likely to be reinforced at least some of the time, unless the child has an unusually alert mother! The

effect of punishment under such circumstances is to suppress the response when the stimuli associated with punishment are present, but it is likely that the response will occur when these stimuli are absent. When his mother is in the room, the child will stay away from the cookies; when she is absent he will go ahead with his depredations. Thus the effect of the conditioned stimuli for punishment is to *suppress* the behavior, not to eliminate or extinguish it.

A simple laboratory demonstration is illustrated in Figure 3-3. In this experiment a hungry rat has learned the operant response of pressing a bar to obtain food. After the response has been acquired, the animal maintains the bar-pressing response at a fairly stable rate. Then the experimenter proceeds to deliver punishment (electric shock) preceded by a light, which acts as a conditioned stimulus. The effect of the shock is to produce the CER of freezing in the rat, and this effectively prevents the occurrence of the bar-pressing response. After the ex-

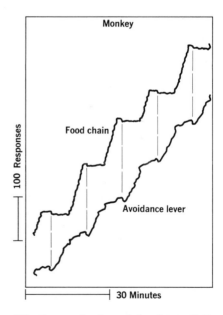

Figure 3-3. Suppression in a chain of operant responses. When a warning signal for punishment is on, the responding for food is suppressed while the animal makes an avoidant response. The vertical broken lines indicate the onset of the warning stimulus. (From Sidman, 1958.)

Psychological Concepts in Psychopathology

perimenter gives a number of these punishments, he eliminates the shock but presents the CS from time to time. In this final stage of the demonstration, the animal will not press the bar while the CS is present, but it soon returns to its normal rate of pressing when the CS is absent. We may describe this situation as one in which the CS *suppresses* the bar pressing but does not extinguish it.

We should note that the suppression of ongoing behavior may be achieved by delivering punishment which is in no way contingent upon the subject's responses (as in the experiment just described) or by punishing the response if it is made when some warning stimulus is present (as in the example of the child and the cookie jar).

VERBAL LEARNING

Some psychologists have paid particular attention to the processes by which people acquire verbal responses—an area of investigation which is of prime importance in human behavior. Generally speaking, this kind of work has followed two main approaches. One is the study of verbal rote learning, and the other is the study of the manner in which language is acquired in a social setting. For convenience we shall consider these separately.

Rote Learning

In a typical rote-learning situation, the individual is given a list or series of items which he is required to memorize in such a way that he can recall them on demand. The form which this response acquisition must take depends upon the experiment, but two common tasks have been used widely. In the first the subject is called upon to rote-learn a series of words, syllables, or symbols in the order in which they are presented. A second kind of task involves the learning of items in pairs, so that when presented with the first member of a pair, the subject will respond with the second member.

By the time a subject enters an experiment on verbal rote learning, he has already acquired a considerable repertoire of verbal learning. The effects of this previous learning would be to contaminate the experimental procedures. One standard method of controlling it is to use meaningless verbal symbols in such experiments; nonsense syllables are the most frequently employed.

Most of the problems which are investigated in verbal learning studies have obvious parallels in the conditioning procedures described above. Thus, questions regarding the effects of practice or number of trials, the spacing between trials, and so forth are directly analogous to the same questions which we have asked regarding the acquisition of a classically conditioned response. However, psychologists exploring this area have been particularly interested in the problem of *transfer* in verbal learning, and we should examine this concept.

Transfer

When we learn one set of responses to a series of stimuli (or one response to a single stimulus), we may find that the learning has some effect upon the manner in which we will acquire new responses to other stimuli. This problem, the effect of existing learning upon the acquisition of new learning, is called the problem of transfer. These effects may be *positive,* i.e., the new learning is acquired sooner because of the effects of past learning; or they may be *negative,* where the new learning is more difficult by virtue of past learning.

Inhibition

In a transfer situation, we may find that the retention of either or both of the two learning tasks has been impaired by the other. Thus, if a subject learns task A and then learns task B, the recall of either A or B might be less adequate than would be the case if only one task had been learned. When the learning of a second task interferes with the retention of a previously learned task, we speak of the process of *retroactive inhibition,* while the detrimental effect of the prior learning of the first task upon the retention of the second is referred to as *proactive inhibition.*

Reactive Inhibition

The concepts described in the previous paragraph should be distinguished from the concept of *reactive inhibition.* When a subject has repeated a particular response a number of times, a slowing up of both the rate and the magnitude of the response may begin to develop. This decrement in behavior is sometimes ascribed to a process termed reactive inhibition, which in turn is thought to be dependent upon the amount of effort involved in making the response, the number of times the response has been made, and the interval which has elapsed since the previous occurrence of the response.

Although this term was developed originally as a rather technical concept within behavior theory, it has particular interest in experimental psychopathology because some attempts have been made to apply it to the understanding of the behavior of schizophrenic patients.

Forgetting

Verbal material is particularly suitable for the study of forgetting, because the use of serial lists or lists of paired associates permits the quantification of retention with more precision than does the use of single stimulus-response connections. The problem of forgetting has intrigued psychologists for many years, and several hypotheses have been put forward to account for the common observation that as time passes, we find it hard to recall events when we try to do so. For practical purposes we may make an initial distinction between forgetting and experimental extinction in that experimental extinction is deliberately produced by the technique of presenting the CS unaccompanied by the US for a number of times, whereas forgetting *appears* to be largely influenced by the passage of time since the response was last performed. However, many important variables do affect the rate of forgetting, and we should consider them here.

Unpleasantness of the Experience. Psychoanalytic theories of forgetting have emphasized the active effect of the unpleasantness of an experience upon the ability to recall it. This position suggests that unpleasant experiences are less amenable to recall than pleasant ones. Several experimental studies have been conducted on this point (e.g., Jersild, 1931; O'Kelly & Steckle, 1940). The best interpretation of the results, however, may require that we attend to the question of self-esteem rather than sheer pleasantness itself. For example, Gordon (1925) found that there was no difference in retention between material associated with pleasant and unpleasant odors. The more plausible way of looking at this problem is to consider pleasantness and unpleasantness in terms of the self-concept of the individual.

Self-esteem. Incidents which reflect adversely upon the self-esteem of a person are likely to be forgotten, whereas those which reflect favorably are likely to be remembered. In a word, we remember our successes and forget our failures. The importance of self-esteem in determining what will be remembered is clear from studies by Eriksen (1954), Glixman (1949), and Rosenzweig (1933). Their data indicate that when subjects are required to recall tasks of which some were incomplete and others were completed, they recall the incomplete tasks more easily than they recall complete tasks *when success or failure on the task was presented to them as irrelevant to their abilities.* On the other hand, when ability to complete a task in the allotted time was presented to the subject as an important measure of his abilities, the results were reversed: he forgot the uncompleted tasks and remembered the completed ones.

Compatibility with Value System. A person's evaluation of himself is a part of his larger system of attitudes toward the world and people around him. We have already noted that events which are incompatible with his attitude toward himself are likely to be forgotten. In the larger sphere, the same principle seems to hold true. Retention of material which is incompatible with the subject's attitudes on the topic is poorer than retention of material with which the subject agrees. There are certain important questions about these findings which should be noted. It seems likely that an individual will have had much more prior learning of material with which he agrees, because he will have been more exposed to it and interested in it. Thus in experiments of this kind it is difficult to assume that the task material is all equally unfamiliar to the subject.

Competing Responses. The social world does not always reinforce the same response to the same stimulus with experimental regularity. New responses to old stimuli are frequently required, and the learning of new responses interferes with the retention of the old ones. The principle is essentially that of retroactive inhibition, but some psychologists have preferred to refer to this cause of forgetting as *reproductive interference.*

Changed Cues. Just as a human environment may not reinforce the same response with consistency, the environment tends not to repeat stimuli in exactly the same way each time. Unlike the pigeon in the Skinner box, the human is likely to find that no situation facing him ever repeats itself exactly in all details. If the changes in a situation are sufficiently great, they may interfere with the production of the previously learned response. It will be "forgotten" because the stimuli necessary to elicit it are not present.

Passage of Time. We have deferred to the end the most popular explanation of forgetting in the eyes of the man in the street. This view is that we forget events because it is a long *time* since they occurred or since we last had occasion to recall them. Experimental investigation of this belief has taken the form of studying the loss in retention over time when the time was (*a*) spent in normal daily activity and (*b*) spent sleeping. The results of this kind of study show clearly that the loss after time spent sleeping is considerably less than that which occurs after the same amount of time spent in normal waking activities. A comparison of these two conditions is given in Figure 3-4. From these data we are strongly impelled to conclude that passage of time by itself is not important in forgetting, but that the nature of the activity which occurs during that time is.

Clearly there are many variables which influence the retention of learned material. Forgetting may be determined by any or many of these acting together. At the present time there is no unitary theory of forgetting, and most work is still devoted to clarifying empirically the nature of the relationship between forgetting and various aspects of the learning process.

In the field of psychopathology, however, prominence has been given to the Freudian notion that forgetting is always determined by the psychological significance of the forgotten event. Material which is forgotten is regarded as stored "in the unconscious," to be recovered by suitable techniques practiced by the therapist. Let us therefore consider the concept of the unconscious determination of behavior within the framework of the general learning theory.

LEARNING AND AWARENESS

Some psychologists object to the application of learning principles to human behavior because it seems probable that there are crucial differences between the manner in which animals develop behavior and the way in which humans do so. Differences of a serious kind may well exist because of (*a*) the major importance of verbal behavior

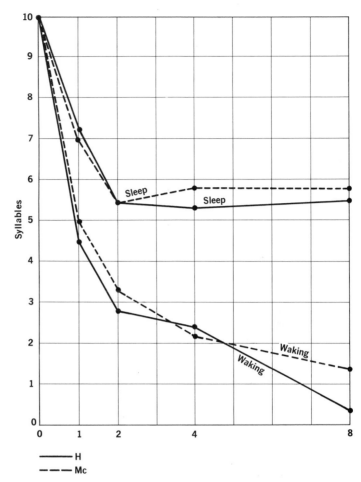

Figure 3-4. Average number of syllables reproduced by each O after the various time-intervals of sleep and waking. (Jenkins and Dallenbach, 1924, as corrected by Dallenbach, 1963.)

in human activity and (*b*) the complexity of the central nervous system in the human being.

At the outset we shall consider the phenomenon of *conscious awareness* in the human being and its relationship to verbal behavior. The problem of nervous system differences is taken up in a later chapter.

The Concept of the Unconscious

Psychoanalytic terms have so seeped into popular speech that their definitions have become obscured. One of the most popular of these is the term "unconscious." We speak of behavior being motivated unconsciously and of memories being "buried" in the unconscious, and we use it in many other metaphorical ways. Whatever the use, however, the central implication of the notion of unconscious phenomena is that behavior is occurring under the influence of determinants that the person himself is not able to identify. The evidence that an individual is not able to identify these determinants is the fact that he cannot describe them verbally.

When the individual is not able to identify the stimuli which are eliciting his own behavior, then the problem of what these stimuli are becomes one which is amenable to solution by behavioral inferences made by an observer. Thus a person may state that he sometimes becomes aggressive or destructive for reasons which are unclear to him—and may describe this behavior as something over which he has no control, something which happens "on impulse." An observer, noting the behavior, may be able to recognize that it always occurs whenever a certain kind of stimulus is present, such as an attack upon the individual's occupational competence, or so forth. If the correlation between this kind of stimulus and the behavior is sufficiently high, the observer may conclude that one is a determinant of the other even though the subject has failed to make a similar observation about his own behavior.

Sometimes the individual may be able to "explain" his behavior, but may offer a different explanation each time it happens. Thus he may say that he became aggressive the first time because he wasn't feeling well, the second time because he was trying to reform the critic, and yet another time because he had been upset by some other incident. Here the observer may be able to offer one consistent explanation for several repetitions of the behavior while the subject offers many different ones. The observer may prefer his single explanation to those of the subject because his is more parsimonious and consistent.

Both of the examples above have one thing in common. In both cases the subject's verbalizations about his own behavior differ from the conclusions of the psychologist observer.

The validity of hypotheses of this kind rests, in the long run, upon the ability to use them accurately to predict future behavior. Unless the observer turns out to be a better predictor of the subject's aggressive behavior than the subject is himself, there is no good reason to accord more validity to the observer's hypothesis. If the observer is also a psychotherapist he may, in the course of working with the patient, offer his own explanation of the patient's behavior for the latter's consideration. The patient may either reject or accept it, or may suggest modifications. If the patient accepts it, we have a situation where two people now agree on a hypothesis which explains the behavior of one of them. This agreement, of course, confers no validity upon the hypothesis—it may simply be a testimony to the persuasiveness of the therapist. It is most important to note that the fact that a patient "accepts" the therapist's hypothesis about his own behavior is utterly irrelevant to the validity of this hypothesis.

Within the framework of behavior theory, then, the important questions we may ask are:

1. Is it possible for human learning to take place without the subject being able to verbalize what has been learned? and

2. If so, what conditions are necessary to produce this?

Let us consider the empirical answers to these questions.

Learning without Verbal Accompaniment

The first line of evidence which we should consider is the occurrence of learning in infants who have not yet learned. There are numerous studies in the experimental literature reporting the successful conditioning of infants. Morgan and Morgan (1944) established a conditioned eyeblink in infants as young as 66 days of age, and other investigators have conditioned sucking responses to a buzzer, etc. It is self-evident that this learning is unconscious in the sense in which we have defined it. It is also quite likely that responses which are learned before language develops may remain unconscious for a long period after language develops—perhaps indefinitely.

A second source of evidence comes from studies in which behavior was acquired by human adults but without awareness of what was being learned. One interesting demonstration of this has been reported by Greenspoon (1955). He instructed his subjects to say as many words as they could think of, excluding phrases or sentences. Whenever a subject mentioned a plural word, the experimenter responded with an approving "mmm-hmm." For the control subjects no response was made by the experimenter. Under these conditions the use of plural words by the experimental subjects increased by more than 100 per cent after 25 minutes of reinforcement. The frequency of plural words in the control group did not show this effect. Greenspoon reports that none of his subjects was aware of the fact that plural words were being reinforced by the experimenter.

This effect, sometimes referred to colloquially as the "Greenspoon effect," has been reported by other experimenters in many different conditions. A rather more direct evidence of this kind of learning is given by Cieutat (1959) in a demonstration in which a fellow student was socially punished for excessive talking.

Thirdly, we may note that many experimenters have successfully conditioned responses which are not available to the awareness of the subject anyway. The pupillary response—the contraction of the size of the pupil when the light striking it increases—has been conditioned to other stimuli although there is no way for the subject to be aware of the response which he is making. Likewise, changes in the electrical resistance of the skin (the GSR) have been conditioned, as well as certain changes in the electrical rhythms of the brain. None of these responses is available to the awareness of the person who is making them.

Space does not permit a complete survey of all the experimental literature bearing on the phenomena of learning without awareness.[1] Although there are many methodological questions that are important in evaluating the experimental data which have been obtained, we may conclude that there is a strong body of evidence that learning does take place without awareness in many situations. Thus it should not be surprising

to find in everyday life that many forms of behavior are produced regularly by people who are not directly aware of the circumstances under which the behaviors were learned, or even aware that they behave in these consistent ways. Explanations of these behaviors do not demand that we assume that the person once was aware or conscious of the determinants of his own actions and has since repressed them!

Learning of Avoidant Cognitive Responses

Our own behavior is often accompanied by verbal conversation directed at ourselves. In the behavior of children, this conversation may be conducted aloud as a kind of running commentary upon the child's own actions. "I must wash my hands and get my shoes and then I can go out to play," may accompany all the actions described as the child carries them out. Later the audible talking may drop out, but much private conversation may be carried on which is not audible. It is not necessary to assume that the vocal apparatus is used in this conversation, and indeed this talking to ourselves is what most people would call "thinking." Thinking, or talking to ourselves, about events or behaviors of our own which led to punishment may well serve as conditioned stimuli for fear in exactly the same manner that an externally controlled CS does. If the thought had preceded the behavior which was punished, it is all the more likely that the thought will acquire the power to act as a CS for the fear generated by the punishment. Thus, in our illustration of the child and the cookie jar, if the punishment following the taking of the cookies is both regular and intense, the very thought of cookies may evoke the fear which the sight of the parent does. In fact, all the responses which were being made by the child, and all stimuli present just before the punishment, may acquire this fear-producing property. In an extreme case of this kind, for example, the awareness of hunger might provoke fear because the child was hungry when punished.

We have already seen that animals and

[1] For a fuller review of this problem, the reader is referred to Adams (1957).

people will learn responses which serve to avoid the conditioned stimuli for fear. In the case of the fear-arousing *thoughts,* the only possible avoidance responses available are (*a*) not to think at all—i.e., to become unconscious, or (*b*) to think about something else—to do for oneself what a tactful hostess will do when a conversation is threatening to become disruptive, namely to "change the subject." Distasteful topics may be handled in the way typified by Scarlett O'Hara in *Gone with the Wind*—"I'll think about that tomorrow." Changing the topic of one's thoughts will be accompanied by a reduction in the anxiety produced by the previous train of thought, and this response of "thinking of something else" will thus be reinforced.

For this response to be completely effective in preventing anxiety from occurring, it would be necessary for the person to make it whenever any chain of thought develops which has even a remote probability of leading in the direction of the anxiety-producing topic. The more anxiety-arousing the crucial topic is, the more widespread we would expect the range of avoidance to be.

Avoidance of this kind might not, in itself, create any special problems for the person concerned. In its own way, it might be likened to the avoidance of the radiator by the burned child. Unless there is a vital reason why the child should be close to a radiator, his fear of them would not create any significant handicap in his daily living. However, if the situation is such that the person is continually brought into contact with stimuli which will lead him toward thinking of the feared topic, or if thinking about the topic has been positively reinforced as well as punished, a much more difficult state of affairs arises.

Thinking as a Punishable Response

In Western cultures at least, some behavior is punished by parents not only because the behavior itself is unacceptable, but also because the behavior is regarded as evidence of an immoral mind. The adolescent who is found in possession of pornographic material is likely to be punished by his parents not only for the illegality of his behavior but also for having a "dirty mind." When he is punished for this, he is likely to be told that he is being punished for having "bad thoughts" as much, if not more, than for his overt behavior. In this way the punishment is made contingent upon the way he is *thinking* rather than on what he is doing. Prohibitions against sexual thoughts are likely to be exercised even more severely against girls than against boys, and we should expect that avoidance of thoughts on sexual topics—and guilt when thinking about them—would be considerably more marked in Western women than men.

Hostile or aggressive behavior will tend to meet a similar fate. Verbal expressions of hatred for another are often punished in this way, with accompanying admonitions that it is bad to feel hatred, quite apart from the act of expressing it. Here again the sanctions against such thoughts by girls are somewhat more severe than those against boys. The extent to which these thoughts are punished, and the severity of the punishment given, depend to a large extent upon the class and culture in which the person is living. Punishment of both sexuality and aggression is most marked in the middle classes in Western Europe and North America and is less evident in the low-income groups in these areas. All in all, we should expect to find that the extent to which anxiety is generated by thinking about these topics will vary according to sex, class, and culture, as well as individual family attitudes.

Internal and External Stimuli

In our analysis of avoidance behaviors so far, we have identified the avoidance of external stimuli which are CSs for anxiety and the avoidance of internal "thought" stimuli which are also CSs for anxiety. Except in some extremely severe cases of psychopathology, the thinking behavior of an individual is subject to continual stimulation by external happenings. The photograph of a lover may prompt thoughts of past times together; hearing a familiar voice may stimulate thoughts of an appointment to be kept with the speaker, and so forth. If a particular external stimulus tends to evoke an anxiety-producing train of thought, then the person may seek not only to think about something else, but may learn to avoid the external situation which is responsible for these thoughts. In this way it is quite possible that avoidance behavior will develop to external stimuli by generalization which is mediated by the thinking process—even though the external stimulus was never directly associated with the original anxiety-producing experience.

Extinction of Avoidance of Thinking

As we have already seen, the extinction of avoidance behavior is a very complicated matter. In order to extinguish motor avoidance responses, we must both prevent the response from occurring and also reward some other response in its place. As the response of not thinking about a particular topic is extremely hard for an observer (therapist) to detect, the techniques required for extinction are correspondingly difficult. The inference that a certain topic of conversation is anxiety-arousing for a subject is made by observing his behavior when the topic is introduced. If he appears to be unusually reluctant to respond to discussion of this topic, he can be reprimanded (and thus punished) for his avoidance behavior—he can be told that it is evidence of unacceptable resistance to the observer. If the avoidance behavior is part and parcel of some serious problem of adjustment for which the subject is seeking help, he can be told that no help can be effectively given unless he abandons his avoidance tactics. Under these circumstances it is possible that the subject will come closer to discussion of the feared topic, and every occasion on which he does can be rewarded by the observer's approval, thereby increasing the probability that this response will occur again.

From the foregoing it will be evident that for extinction of this kind of avoidance behavior to take place, there must be some powerful incentive which will prevent the subject from leaving the extinction situation completely. Where the incentive is lacking, the extinction of the avoidance behavior will be difficult and perhaps impossible. As we shall see later in the book, attempts to change certain kinds of avoidant behavior are often fruitless for just this reason.

The Unconscious: A General Summary

From our discussion of forgetting, of learning without awareness, and of the avoidance of thinking about feared topics, we can see that much human behavior is carried out under conditions in which the person is not able to verbalize readily about the determinants of his own actions. He may never have known what they are because he acquired them under conditions in which verbalization was at a minimum. He may at one time have been able to verbalize them, but both the verbalization and the covert thinking about them have become an occasion for avoidance behavior. When the determinants seem clear to an observer, it is tempting to conclude that the subject "really knows" what they are but has actively "buried" his knowledge of them in some remote recess of his being. Metaphorical thinking of this kind is valuable for dramatic or literary purposes but has no place in science. Responses which a person is unable to make do not have a covert existence somewhere else. When a memory is "repressed," what we mean is that the stimuli which we are presenting in an attempt to elicit recall have failed to do so; it also implies that we believe that some configurations of stimuli could elicit it. When we find the effective conditions for recall, it is unnecessary for us to conclude triumphantly that the memory was there all the time. The only way in which statements of this kind can be made scientifically is when they are intended to refer to some physiological alteration in the organism brought about by the relevant experience. Physiological changes of this kind may continue to be "there" whether or not we have found the correct stimulus for eliciting the recall of the events related to them.

It would be presumptuous to pretend that experimental investigations have given us a clear empirical account of the conditions under which behavior without awareness develops. A tremendous amount of work is yet to be done, and most of what we have said here should be taken as a point of view rather than a summary of established laws or principles.

MOTIVATION AND THE CONCEPT OF DRIVE

When demonstrating that a dog has been conditioned to salivate at the sound of a bell, the experimenter must ensure beforehand that the dog is hungry. If this condition is not present, then all other conditioned stimuli which have effectively elicited the response in the past will now fail to do so. The study of motivation is primarily concerned with discovering the principles by which certain conditions of this kind control the appearance of behavior. Students of motivation have developed certain concepts and hypotheses in their work, and we consider them briefly in this section.

Primary Motive States

The survival of a living organism depends upon the availability of certain things in the environment such as food, water, shelter, escape from injury, rest, and so forth. When the conditions which produce these are not present, specific bodily processes occur in the individual labeled with such terms as "hunger," "thirst," "cold," "pain," "fatigue," and so on. These bodily changes are definable and measurable in purely physiological ways, and it would be possible to decide that a subject was "hungry" physiologically without asking him or watching his behavior. Characteristically these processes may vary in intensity, so that the physiological results of 4 hours of hunger will

differ from the consequences of 24 hours of hunger.

As these processes begin to operate, the behavior of the organism undergoes certain changes, the precise nature of the changes being dependent upon the bodily process in question and the length of time it has been developing. In the ordinary course of events, these behaviors will serve to change the environment in such a way that the necessary object (food, water, and so on) becomes available. When this object has acted upon the organism, the bodily process will terminate, and with it the behavior patterns which accompanied it.

One of the most important features of this process is that the bodily changes are not readily acquired or modified by learning. They are inherent in the structure of the living organism, and in some cases a failure to find the necessary support in the environment will lead to the destruction of the organism. A second important aspect of these *primary motive states* is that the behavior which they initiate is only minimally dependent upon environmental stimuli present at the time. The hungry man will start looking for food no matter where he is at the time and no matter how unfamiliar the environment is to him. By the same token, when he has eaten and is no longer hungry, the sight and smell of food cooking will fail to produce food-seeking responses. In a word, a vital stimulus element in eliciting this behavior is the internal bodily state of the subject.

While this bodily state is a necessary precondition for the chain of behavior to begin, the actual sequence of responses which it initiates is readily subject to modification by learning. If we consider the behavior of a hungry traveler in an unfamiliar town, we may find that he engages in searching behavior until he sees a restaurant and that he then begins to move toward it. As he does so, his speed of walking may increase as he gets nearer to the restaurant. In this event the intensity of his behavior has been modified by the proximity of the external stimulus rather than by any sudden increase in the bodily processes of hunger. Thus the characteristics which hunger-motivated responses display will depend upon (a) the state of the bodily processes, (b) previous learning about the conditioned stimuli associated with eating, and (c) changes in the proximity, intensity, or magnitude of these.

Some of these characteristics will be considered in detail elsewhere. In the meantime let us turn to the concept of learned motives.

Secondary Motive States

In middle-class Western society much, if not most, behavior seems to be motivated by states which are not primary. Many men work for money, prestige, a sense of social worth, a feeling of personal accomplishment, etc. The fact that the money which they earn will buy their food is largely irrelevant to our understanding of their behavior. Men work whether they are hungry or not, and they often continue to work long after all their primary needs have been satisfied. Putting it more simply, we may say that much behavior seems to occur without any correlated change in bodily state which we might identify as a motive.

As far as we can tell, the stimuli necessary to initiate this behavior are to be found in the environment rather than in the physiology of the subject. Competitive behavior seems to be stimulated by the presence of someone to compete with; acquisitive behavior by the presence of objects to be acquired; and so on.

There are several conflicting views within psychology regarding the manner in which stimuli acquire the power to elicit chains of behavior in this way. One hypothesis is that the stimuli have gained power because of their previous association with a primary reward. This argument supposes that stimuli associated with an object which acts as a reinforcer for behavior motivated by a primary motive state will acquire general reinforcing properties. The subject will therefore learn responses in which the chief reward is simply the appearance of these conditioned stimuli. An illustration would be

the role of a child's mother as a general conditioned stimulus for primary reinforcements. Inasmuch as the mother is likely to be physically present whenever the child is being fed; whenever wet, cold clothing is being removed; and whenever bedtime is in the offing, she becomes a CS for many different kinds of primary reinforcement. Eventually, so this argument runs, the presence of the mother per se becomes reinforcing, and the child will now learn many responses for which the only reinforcement is the presence of the mother.

Thus such behavior patterns as "seeking approval" are presumed to be based fundamentally upon primary motives such as hunger and thirst. Granted this assumption, we can see how very specific motives—e.g., the motivation to achieve academically— may in turn develop as part of the motive of seeking approval. When we recognize the wide range of stimuli which may become conditioned stimuli for primary reinforcements, we can accept the possibility that vast ranges of social behavior might develop in this way.

However, a major problem of this position is that it is almost entirely a post hoc explanation of observed events. It is difficult to demonstrate clearly that secondary motives do not develop from primary motives —and equally difficult to prove that they do. Additionally, the force of this explanation has been weakened somewhat by the demonstration that some motive states which were traditionally regarded as secondary or learned now appear to be as fundamental as any more obvious primary state. Specifically, the motive of *curiosity* or *seeking stimulus change* appears to possess the properties of a primary motive. The achievement of *competence* appears to be another, and the need for physical signs of *affection* (e.g., handling, fondling) also seems to be a candidate.

In a practical sense the problem of how adults acquired the motives which appear to guide their behavior is not of major importance. The distinction between primary and secondary motives is of concern only insofar as there are differences in the way these motives influence behavior. We have already noted one such difference, namely that secondary motives appear to depend upon the presence of certain external stimuli to arouse them. A second distinction has been made by Miller (1959). He hypothesizes that the gradient of stimulus generalization for learning based upon secondary motives falls away more rapidly than that for responses learned on the basis of primary motives. Miller and Dollard (1941) have also noted that secondary motives, like all learned phenomena, should be liable to extinction if the appropriate reinforcements are unavailable, and that when the secondary motive is reinforced, it should increase in strength—unlike primary motives, which are reduced in intensity by receipt of a reinforcement.

Motives and Perception

The perception of objects in the environment is likely to be influenced in two ways by the motive states which predominate at the time. Firstly, a strong motive state will lead the individual to be especially alert to any stimuli which are relevant to the goal objects for that motive. Secondly, the motive may—if sufficiently intense—produce errors in perception so that neutral or irrelevant objects are perceived as goal objects. Let us consider some experimental examples of these effects.

Motivation and Selectivity. In an ingenious experiment, Bahrick, Fitts, and Rankin (1952) studied the influence of levels of motivation upon the selectivity of attention to stimuli in the environment. They offered the hypothesis that when the incentives for responding to a stimulus field were high, the subject would tend to perceive only those aspects or stimuli which were relevant to the receipt of the incentive, whereas under lower motivation the irrelevant stimuli would also be included in the subject's perceptions. In a word, the hypothesis was that the higher the motivation, the more selectively an individual attends to relevant stimuli only.

Using money versus no money in a task which involved responding to a central stimulus while irrelevant peripheral stimuli were also displayed intermittently, they found that the high-motive group was more efficient on the central task and noticed less about the irrelevant stimulus patterns than the low-motive group—thus supporting their prediction.

Motivation and Perceptual Accuracy. Leaving the question of changes in sensitivity determined by motivational states, let us consider the effect which motivation has upon the accuracy of perception. Evidence of inaccuracies in perception would be in the form of changes, omissions, and additions to the real stimulus on the part of the perceiver.

Two psychologists, Gilchrist and Nesberg (1952), asked subjects to abstain from food or from water for periods up to 24 hours. Then the subjects entered the experiment proper. Here they were presented with an apparatus consisting essentially of a screen upon which a picture was flashed at a predetermined level of brightness for a period of 15 seconds. After a brief interval, the same picture was repeated at a different level of brightness. Now the subject was asked to operate a knob which controlled the illumination so as to change the brightness to equal that used on the first exposure. Some of the pictures were of food (steaks, fried chicken, etc.) and others were of liquids (ice water, juice, milk). A third group of pictures was simply of homogeneous colors.

The results may be summarized briefly by stating that the objects related to motive state of the subjects, i.e., food pictures for the hungry group and liquid pictures for the thirsty group, were most often illuminated to a level which was brighter than that at which they were originally shown. The general effect is shown in Figure 3-5. Here we have a good illustration of the way in which the motivation of the subject influences his estimation of the characteristics of a rewarding stimulus. It is interesting to note that

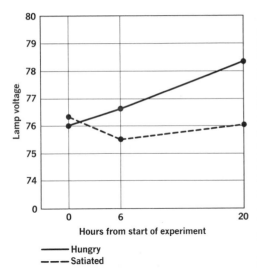

Figure 3-5. **Mean lamp voltage matches of the hungry and satiated groups as a function of time from the start of the experiment. (Gilchrist and Nesberg, 1952.)**

none of the subjects was aware that he had been erring in this consistent way; all felt instead that they had been performing with equal accuracy on all test pictures. In general we can see that the effect of increasing the strength of a motive state is to render the person more sensitive to any stimuli which are relevant to the objects of his motivation, and also to produce a tendency to distort the perception of stimuli in order to make them more congruent with his current motives.

Perceptual Defense.   During our discussion of forgetting earlier in this chapter, we noted that unpleasant events tend to be forgotten—that aversion to a certain stimulus interferes with the accurate recall of it. There is some evidence that aversive stimuli are less likely to be perceived in the first place, and this evidence has led to the development of the concept of *perceptual defense.* Perceptual defense is essentially a special instance of the tendency to distort perception of external stimuli so as to fit the current motives of the subject. In this case, however, the motive is avoidance of an aversive object rather than attainment of a desired one.

Differences in the accuracy of perception are most likely to be found under conditions in which complete accuracy is not likely because of the manner in which the stimulus is displayed. Therefore most experiments on perceptual defense have employed the method of tachistoscopic recognition. The tachistoscope is a device which will present visual stimuli for very short intervals of time, e.g., hundredths of a second. If we find that some classes of stimuli require much longer exposure before they are recognized than others do, we may wish to conclude that there is some process at work which is militating against perception of the former class. Thus the usual evidence for perceptual defense is in the form of longer time intervals required to recognize anxiety-producing stimuli than the intervals required for neutral stimuli.

An interesting demonstration of perceptual defense is provided by an experiment conducted by Eriksen and Browne (1956). A group of subjects was given the task of solving a series of anagrams under conditions which prevented them from succeeding and in which the failure was accentuated by the visible success of other "subjects" (who were accomplices of the experimenter). Later the solutions to the anagrams were announced to the subjects. In the final stage of the experiment these words and a set of neutral words were projected tachistoscopically, and the number of exposures necessary before the subjects recognized the word were recorded. The results indicated that the anagram words, having been associated with failure, were less readily recognized than the neutral words.[2]

Rigidity.   In any environment at a given time there are an infinite number of stimuli or stimulus patterns to which an individual might respond. Many of them are stimuli for definite kinds of response because of the

[2] This is a simplified account of the problem, as certain personality variables are important in influencing the phenomenon. A fuller account is presented in Chapter 8.

effects of past learning. Having seen that high levels of motivation produce a narrowing of perceptual selectivity, so that only a few stimuli are attended to, we should expect to find a concomitant narrowing of the range of responses exhibited in the situation. Sometimes we may find that the responses elicited by the present stimuli are no longer appropriate—they no longer bring the individual into contact with the object of his motive state. For efficient behavior it may be necessary for the person to turn to new responses, perhaps to responses which have little past history of reinforcement in the present environment.

A man who has developed a set of responses to women on the basis of his experiences with his mother may generalize them to his wife—and find that they are ineffective. In the ordinary way his experiences with his wife will bring about new learning, and more appropriate behavior will develop. Under certain conditions, however, the extinction of the generalized responses and the acquisition of the new ones may be unusually difficult. One of these conditions is the existence of especially intense motivations for the rewards formerly provided by the mother. Apparent inability to acquire new responses when old ones are inadequate has been termed *rigidity,* and we can see that rigidity might be expected of anyone who is highly motivated to respond in the presence of the stimuli to which his available responses are inappropriate. An experimental illustration may be of value here.

Maher (1957) administered verbal and mathematical problems to two groups of students. One of these groups had been informed that their performance would be taken into account in determining their grade in a course, whereas the others were told that they were simply participating in order to establish norms for the performance of the test items. The test items were designed so that the first part of the series was soluble by one kind of response only, whereas the second part included items which were soluble by either the original response or a new and shorter procedure. Rigidity was measured by the number of problems in the second series which were solved by the more complicated route before the subject perceived the availability of the new simpler solution. Rigidity scores were significantly higher in the highly motivated group, suggesting that the more intense the motivation, the less easily a person will perceive and acquire a new stimulus-response relationship.

Motivation and Efficiency. Looking back over the material in the preceding paragraphs, we notice that when motivation is low or absent, responses to stimuli are unlikely to occur. When motivation is very high, we may expect simple responses to occur with great magnitude and probability. The nature of this relationship is shown in

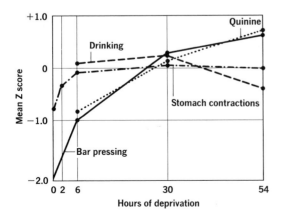

Figure 3-6. Comparison of four measures of "hunger": (1) the volume of enriched milk drunk by rats before satiation; (2) the amount of quinine required to stop drinking; (3) the rate of bar pressing reinforced by food on a variable-interval schedule, and (4) the sum of excursions of the record of stomach contractions measured from a balloon permanently implanted on the end of a plastic fistula. (Miller, 1956.)

Figure 3-6. When the behavior which is required is complex and adaptive—calling for frequent changes in response to changing stimulus elements—the performance curve is of a different order. As the strength and probability of a simple response increases with increasing motivation, the likelihood of a person perceiving stimulus changes and adapting his behavior accordingly is reduced. *Where behavior efficiency is defined as responding adaptively to stimulus change,* then increasing motive strength will be accompanied by decreasingly adaptive behavior and thus by loss of efficiency. This relationship is illustrated in schematic form in Figure 3-7.

Of importance here is the concept of *arousal,* described in detail in Chapter 4. Any increase in motivation brings about certain changes in bodily processes over and above those which are specific to the motive state. This is the case whether the increase in motivation is due to internal bodily changes, such as those which occur in hunger, or is due to some change in the nature of the external stimulation impinging upon the person. Extreme states of arousal —such as those which are seen in panic reactions—are accompanied by much additional muscular activity and the appearance of responses which may be utterly inappropriate to the task at hand. Activity of this kind would necessarily be "diffuse" in Wishner's terminology (see Chapter 1), and thus we should expect a decline in efficiency when arousal is unusually high. Combat infantry in action may be assumed to be in an unusually high state of arousal. Under these conditions it has been estimated (Marshall, 1947) that only one-third of soldiers who are ordered to fire actually do so, and not all of these do so effectively. The presumed relationship between bodily changes in arousal and behavioral efficiency in arousal is illustrated in Figure 4-17 (see Chapter 4). Increasing hunger motivation was achieved by increasing the hours of food deprivation in rats. With longer deprivation there was a constant increase in the animal's heart rate. Up to 48 hours of

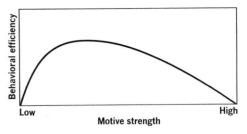

Figure 3-7. Curve of rise and fall of behavioral efficiency with increasing drive.

deprivation, the rate of bar pressing also increased, but beyond this point the bar pressing dropped off again. This inverted U curve for motivation-efficiency relationships is consistent with the observations which we have already made in this section of the chapter.

Motives as Aversive Stimuli

We have described how primary motive states are determined by bodily processes, e.g., hunger states. We have seen how the person becomes selectively attentive to food stimuli as hunger increases and how his behavior becomes correspondingly more food-seeking. We have also seen how stimuli associated with punishment become conditioned stimuli for avoidance responses, including the response of thinking about other topics than those which the stimulus evokes. If the behavior which led to punishment occurred under the influence of a primary motive state, we should expect the bodily processes of the primary motive state to become conditioned stimuli for avoidance also. For example, consider an animal which has learned to approach a given stimulus when hungry and there to receive food. Now we punish the animal when it reaches the stimulus, and punish it repeatedly and severely. Many aspects of the situation should then become conditioned stimuli for avoidance. Thus the physical appearance of the stimulus, the response of approaching it, and the bodily change associated with hunger should develop the power to evoke avoidance behavior. The complex response patterns which these developments will produce are discussed in the chapter devoted to conflict (Chapter 6).

Motivation and Fantasy

So far we have considered the effects of motive states upon motor behavior—overt behavior which is open for observation. Of great importance in the understanding of psychopathology is human fantasy behavior. By fantasy we refer to the chains of thought and imagery which occur frequently in the human and which are relatively free from immediate influence by stimuli in the external environment. Dreaming during sleep would be the best example of fantasy almost entirely free from direct control by the external environment. Much fantasy occurs during waking, however. It is most likely to take place when the external environment is stable, monotonous, and free from intense physical stimulation.

The effects of external stimulation being minimal, we must turn to other variables to account for the content of fantasy. One of the major sources of influence seems to be the motivational state of the person. The following illustrations show how motivation acts to determine fantasy.

Primary Motives and Fantasy. Atkinson and McClelland (1948) studied the kinds of imaginative stories produced by hungry subjects in response to a series of pictures. Some of these pictures had food-relevant elements in them (i.e., a picture of a restaurant and a picture of two men with a piece of meat) while others did not. Stories told by the subjects were scored for the presence or absence of references to food, food deprivation, eating, etc. While the data were somewhat complex, the general nature of the results is shown in Figure 3-8. As the number of hours of hunger increased, the frequency of fantasies related to food deprivation also increased, while the references to eating (goal activity) decreased.

At a more clinical level, Frankl (1959) has described the experiences of starving prisoners in German concentration camps:

What did the prisoner dream about most frequently? Of bread, cake, cigarettes and nice

Figure 3-8. Percentage of S's showing selected food-related story characteristics as function of increasing hunger. (Atkinson and McClelland, 1948.)

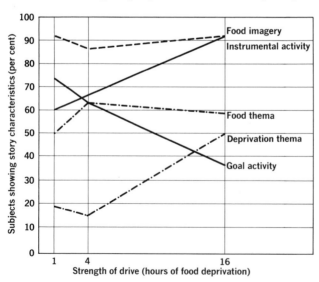

warm baths. The lack of having these simple desires satisfied led him to seek wish-fulfillment in dreams. . . .

Because of the high degree of undernourishment which prisoners suffered, it was natural that the desire for food was the major primitive instinct around which mental life centered. Let us observe the majority of prisoners when they happened to work near each other and were, for once, not closely watched. They would immediately start discussing food. One fellow would ask another working next to him in the ditch what his favorite dishes were. Then they would exchange recipes and plan the menu for the day when they would have a reunion—a day in the distant future when they would be liberated and returned home. (Pp. 27–28.)

While the way in which hunger affects the content of fantasy (i.e., whether or not it consistently produces fantasies of deprivation or dreams of eating) may be in question, there seems to be little doubt that it produces fantasies largely relevant to the hunger state in one way or another.

Secondary Motives and Fantasy. Investigation of secondary motive states and their influence upon fantasy involves a minor change in technique. Motive states of this kind depend, as we have seen, upon external stimulation for their arousal. Thus a typical experimental comparison involves the study of aroused versus nonaroused subjects in terms of their fantasy productions.

A good illustration of this procedure is reported by Veroff (1957) in his investigation of the arousal of the *need for power* and its consequences for fantasy concerning power activities. In brief, the experiment involved the comparison of two groups of university students in terms of the stories which they produced about five pictures. One group consisted of 34 men who were candidates for office in college elections, and they were examined in the interval which elapsed between closing the polls and announcing the results of the balloting. This situation may be legitimately regarded as one in which external events have aroused the power motive to an unusual degree. As a nonaroused control, a similar number of undergraduate men were tested; these subjects were not candidates for any elective office and were examined after having been told that the main purpose of their participation was to secure normative data.

The results of this investigation indicated that aroused power motivation was associated with a greater appearance of power fantasies. Thus the relationship between the strength of motive and the nature of fantasy response is similar to that already discovered for primary motives.

Fantasy and the Reduction of Motive Strength. One possible difference between primary and secondary motives and their effects upon fantasy is in the manner in which fantasy may in turn affect the motive. Feshbach (1955), for example, showed that when aggression was aroused in subjects by insulting them, the extent to which they would behave aggressively toward the insulter could be reduced by allowing an intervening period in which aggressive fantasies could occur. If this period was occupied by activities which prevented aggressive fantasying, the subjects showed more overt aggression toward the insulter when they were given the opportunity.

Now as far as we know, fantasies of eating do not reduce the intensity of hunger —although the experiment does not seem to have been made that would confirm this. Certainly it is difficult to see how the biological determinants of hunger motivation could be significantly affected by fantasy. Granting this, then the drive-reducing properties of fantasy may be confined to secondary motive states. As the evidence available from experiments is sparse, we may wish to limit this conclusion even further and simply content ourselves with noting that aggressive fantasies seem to reduce the potentiality for later aggressive behavior. Whether this is so for other secondary motives is an unanswered question.

Sensation

In the study of differences between psychopathological and normal subjects, some attention has been given to differences in sensitivity to external stimulation. For clearer understanding of what is involved in this kind of investigation, we should discuss briefly some of the elementary concepts and terms used in the study of sensation.

The Absolute Threshold. Any stimulus can be varied in terms of its intensity. Lights may differ in brightness, sounds in loudness, and so on. That part of psychology which is referred to as psychophysics is largely concerned with the quantitative relationship between the physical properties of stimuli and the responses which they elicit. One of the fundamental values of a stimulus is the lowest intensity at which it can be identified by the subject. Thus we may wish to study the lowest intensity of light which can be identified as a light by a human subject, and will find that certain very low values may be measurable by an appropriate instrument but cannot be detected by the human observer. The lowest value at which an identification can be made is referred to as the *absolute threshold*. In more precise terms, the absolute threshold is the value of a stimulus which marks the transition between response and no response on the part of an organism.

Differential Thresholds. Once we have moved above the absolute threshold, we may be concerned with the ability of the organism to detect a change in the physical value of a stimulus. The smallest change to which the organism is capable of responding is the *differential threshold*. This difference is often called the *just noticeable difference* (or jnd). Complex mathematical problems arise in the relationship between the magnitude of physical change necessary to produce a changed response and the perceived or judged magnitude of the change by the subject. We shall not discuss these here. However, we might mention that there are some indications that jnd units for increases in *intensity* of a stimulus follow different laws than those governing the relationship of jnd units for changes in stimulus *quality*, e.g., the pitch of a note (Stevens, 1951).

Equality. The problem of psychophysical *equality* has been described as that of discovering what two different stimuli produce the same response. Earlier in this chapter we described a study (page 62) in which the investigators required subjects to equate one stimulus with another in terms of the brightness of illumination. We saw that the significance of the stimulus altered the judgment of equality. This would be an example of the use of the concept of psychophysical equality in the experimental situation.

Many of the observations made by psychophysiologists produce measurements of sensory processes which are closely parallel to measurements made directly upon physiological mechanisms in the sensory system. Psychophysics thus represents an area of psychology which has many implications for biology, and in which theories of sensory function frequently involve biological processes as the basic explanatory level. Disorders in sensory systems may be detected by psychological measurement, but there is an underlying assumption that the psychophysical evidence is to be interpreted as an indication of some organic pathology in the sensory system.

Judgments of the attributes of stimuli are highly amenable to influence by nonbiological variables. People with intact sensory systems show considerable variation in the way in which they judge external stimuli, and much of this variation may be accounted for by investigation of psychological influences. Our previous discussion of motivation has already suggested what some of these influences might be. Let us now consider other important findings in the general area of perception.

Perception

Experience and Perceptual Accuracy. As we have seen, there is evidence that motivational factors present in the perceiver influence the probability that a stimulus will be recognized and also influence the kinds of distortions which may occur perceptually. Another potent variable is that of frequency of exposure to the stimulus in question before the recognition is required. Solomon and Postman (1952), for example, demonstrated very clearly that tachistoscopic recognition of nonsense words was readily aided by providing prior experience with the words. This relationship is shown in Figure 3-9. The threshold for recognition of words which had been previously presented to the subject 25 times was much lower than that for words which had been shown 1, 2, 5, or 10 times.

Discussing these findings, the authors comment:

> The results shown in Figure [3-9] provide a theoretical bridge between learning theory and perception theory. Let us assume that, by differentially exercising pronounceable words in this experiment, we have established associations of differential strength between the visually presented verbal stimulus and the response of reading or saying the word. The strength of this association is measured by the duration or intensity of the stimulus exposure necessary for a correct verbal report.

> Given a population of associations, the one which has been exercised most frequently will have the greatest probability of being elicited to other, like associations. How will this fact influence S's responses in a tachistoscopic situation? When a stimulus pattern is presented at short durations or at low illumination intensities, only fragments of the total stimulus are "effective." Such a stimulus fragment may be considered to represent a point on the generalization dimension of stimulus patterns capable of eliciting the correct verbal response. (Solomon & Postman, 1952, p. 199.)

Their analysis is developed by pointing out that the subject's perceptions are in the form of guesses about total stimuli from information about only some parts of them. Therefore the effect of prior experience with a stimulus is to make it increasingly likely that observations of some fragment of it will lead to the perception of the total stimulus. In this sense, perception may be thought of as involving a continuous process of predicting or guessing about the total attributes of the surrounding environment from sampling only parts of it.

Constancy. In the ordinary course of events we tend to perceive objects as we have learned them to be, rather than as they might appear at the specific moment of perception. Thus the white object is still perceived as white even in low illumination —illumination under which it is "really" gray. In the same way, large buildings on the distant horizon are still perceived as large even though in fact they are occupying a very small portion of the visual field. Perceived brightness, color, and size thus tend to remain relatively constant, determined largely by the stable physical characteristics of the object rather than by the

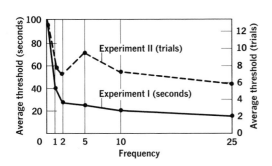

Figure 3-9. Average recognition thresholds for core-words of different frequencies. (Solomon and Postman, 1952.)

local circumstances under which they are occurring. This perceptual phenomenon is referred to as *constancy* and may be regarded as a consequence of the influence of large numbers of past experiences with the object concerned. For example, we learn that a dinner plate is circular even though we often see it at angles at which it is elliptical. Experimental investigations of the perception of disks lying flat show that the observer is likely to judge the shape of the object somewhere between the true circle which it is and the flat ellipse which may be the shape of the image striking the eye.

In this way we see that perceptual judgments about objects are influenced both by the specific attributes of the stimulus as it is now impinging upon the sense organ and by the attributes which we have learned it possesses. Effective behavior in the environment requires, in fact, that we do just this. Responses which are made entirely to stimuli in the form in which they are occurring at the moment would often be inappropriate. It is important, for example, that our judgments about the height, distance, weight, size, and shape of objects around us be reliably stable if we are to interact with them effectively. The possibility that some deficit in the perceptual constancies may be present in psychopathology is discussed in a later chapter. However, we can readily see that maladaptive behavior would occur in the event that there was a serious impairment in constancy of judgments of stimuli.

Perceptual Effects of Sensory Deprivation.

As we have just seen, perceptual phenomena are, in the ordinary way, a kind of compromise between the external stimulation impinging directly upon the sense organs and the knowledge which the individual has about the general characteristics of the objects in the environment. We may expect to find that when the external environment is particularly devoid of cues as to the stable characteristics which it might have, then distortions and peculiarities of perception may occur. Interesting experimental demonstrations of this effect have been reported several times. Let us turn to a description of such a situation given by Bexton, Heron, and Scott (1954).

In their experiment the subjects, 22 male college students, were confined in lighted cubicles through a whole day with time out only for eating and going to the toilet. While in a cubicle, a subject wore translucent goggles which permitted the entry of light but prevented the perception of patterns. An arrangement of gloves and cardboard cuffs prevented him from receiving much tactual stimulation, and the cubicle was partially soundproof, thereby limiting auditory stimulation. Each subject was alone in his cubicle but was in frequent communication with the experimenter by means of an arrangement of microphone and earphone.

Among the results described by the investigators were visual hallucinations—fluctuation and drifting of objects in the visual field. There were also experiences of cognitive difficulty, i.e., difficulty in performing arithmetic problems, and peculiar bodily sensations. One subject reported, "My mind seemed to be a ball of cotton wool floating about my body."

In further work it was found that subjects who returned to a normal environment following sensory deprivation noted distortions in the perception of objects in the visual field. These included "fluctuation, drifting and swirling of objects and surfaces," distortion of shapes, lines, and edges, accentuation of afterimages, and excessive brightness and saturation of color.

Here again the similarity between these effects and certain psychopathological symptoms is quite striking. The perceptual mechanisms of the human being appear to be especially susceptible to impairment, and impairment of them appears to be quite common in certain forms of behavior disorder. The later sections of this book discuss in detail several investigations which have been directed specifically toward the question of perception in pathology.

SUMMARY

In this chapter we have attempted to provide a brief summary of some of the mental concepts and terms in psychology. We have confined ourselves to the areas of learning, motivation, and perception, and our purpose has been to provide a basis for the better understanding of certain experimental work which is reported from time to time in the book.

However, we have seen that motivational states, especially anxiety, have profound effects upon the perception of environmental stimuli and upon the performance of learned responses. Fantasy and thinking have been considered, and it has been possible to treat them as responses governed by the same principles that control more visible motor behavior. Many of these motivational effects are of a kind that parallels the symptoms of various psychopathologies, involving as they do the occurrence of maladaptive or deviant behavior.

Denial of perceptions, difficulty in recall, failure in making adequate discriminations between different stimuli are all examples of these effects. In the space available to us it has not been possible to do more than identify the central issues, and many of the theoretical subtleties have been ignored. For the reader who is interested in a more detailed study of these topics, a brief list of books is appended which will provide a more complete introduction.

SUGGESTED READINGS

1. Beardslee, D. C., & Wertheimer, M. *Readings in perception.* Princeton, N.J.: Van Nostrand, 1958. A helpful collection of readings covering a wide variety of topics in the general area of perception.
2. Dollard, J., & Miller, N. E. *Personality and psychotherapy.* New York: McGraw-Hill, 1950. One of the few systematic attempts to apply learning theory to the understanding of social and psychopathological behavior.
3. Kimble, G. A. *Hilgard and Marquis' conditioning and learning.* (2d ed.) New York: Appleton-Century-Crofts, 1961. A good standard text on the current state of the psychology of learning.
4. Young, P. T. *The motivation of behavior.* (2d ed.) New York: Wiley, 1961. A thorough survey of the research data available in the study of motivation.

REFERENCES

Adams, J. K. Laboratory studies of behavior without awareness. *Psychol. Bull.,* 1957, **54**, 393–405.

Atkinson, J. W., & McClelland, D. C. The projective expression of needs. II: The effect of different intensities of the hunger drive on thematic apperception. *J. exp. Psychol.,* 1948, **38**, 643–658.

Bahrick, H. P., Fitts, P. M., & Rankin, R. E. Effects of incentives upon reactions to peripheral stimuli. *J. exp. Psychol.,* 1952, **44**, 400–406.

Bexton, W. H., Heron, W., & Scott, T. H. Effects of decreased variation in the sensory environment. *Canad. J. Psychol.,* 1954, **109**, 70–76.

Cieutat, V. J. Surreptitious modification of verbal behavior during class discussion. *Psychol. Rep.,* 1959, **5**, 648.

Dallenbach, K. M. Tables vs. graphs as means of presenting experimental results. *Am. J. Psychol.,* 1963, **76**, 700–702.

Eriksen, C. W. Psychological defenses and "ego strength" in the recall of completed and incompleted tasks. *J. abnorm. soc. Psychol.,* 1954, **49**, 45–50.

Eriksen, C. W., & Browne, T. An experimental and theoretical analysis of perceptual defense. *J. abnorm. soc. Psychol.,* 1956, **52**, 224–230.

Feshbach, S. The drive reduction function of fantasy behavior. *J. abnorm. soc. Psychol.,* 1955, **50**, 3–11.

Frankl, V. *Man's search for meaning: an introduction to logotherapy.* Boston: Beacon, 1959, 1962.

Gilchrist, J. C., & Nesberg, L. S. Need and perceptual change in need-related objects. *J. exp. Psychol.,* 1952, **44,** 369–376.

Glixman, A. F. Recall of completed and incompleted activities under varying degrees of stress. *J. exp. Psychol.,* 1949, **39,** 281–295.

Gordon, Kate. Recollection of pleasant and unpleasant odors. *J. exp. Psychol.,* 1925, **8,** 225–239.

Greenspoon, J. The reinforcing effect of two spoken sounds on the frequency of two responses. *Amer. J. Psychol.,* 1955, **68,** 409–416.

Guttman, N., & Kalish, H. Experiments in discrimination. *Sci. Amer.,* 1958, **198,** 77–82.

Jenkins, J. G., & Dallenbach, K. M. Oblivescence during sleep and waking. *Amer. J. Psychol.,* 1924, **35,** 605–612.

Jersild, A. T. A note on the pleasures and unpleasures of college men and women. *J. abnorm. soc. Psychol.,* 1931, **26,** 91–93.

Lacey, J. I., & Smith, R. L. Conditioning and generalization of unconscious anxiety. *Science,* 1954, **120,** 1045–1052.

Lacey, J. I., Smith, R. L., & Green, A. Use of conditioned autonomic responses in the study of anxiety. *Psychosom. Med.,* 1955, **42,** 208–217.

Maher, B. A. Personality, problem-solving and the Einstellung-effect. *J. abnorm. soc. Psychol.,* 1957, **54,** 70–74.

Marshall, S. L. A. *Men against fire: the problem of battle command in future war.* Washington: Combat Forces Press, 1947.

Miller, N. E. Studies of fear as an acquirable drive. I: Fear as motivation and fear reduction as reinforcement in the learning of new responses. *J. exp. Psychol.,* 1948, **38,** 89–101.

Miller, N. E. Effects of drugs on motivation: the value of using a variety of measures. *Ann. N.Y. Acad. Sci.,* 1956, **65,** 318–333.

Miller, N. E. Liberalization of basic S-R concepts: extensions to conflict behavior, motivation and social learning. In S. Koch (Ed.), *Psychology: a study of a science,* vol. 2. New York: McGraw-Hill, 1959. Pp. 196–292.

Miller, N. E., & Dollard, J. C. *Social learning and imitation.* New Haven: Yale Univer. Press, 1941.

Morgan, J. J. B., & Morgan, S. S. Infant learning as a developmental index. *J. genet. Psychol.,* 1944, **68,** 281–289.

Mowrer, O. H. & Ullman, A. D. Time as a determinant in integrative learning. *Psychol. Rev.,* 1945, **52,** 61–90.

O'Kelly, L. I. & Steckle, L. C. The forgetting of pleasant and unpleasant experiences. *Amer. J. Psychol.,* 1940, **53,** 432–434.

Reiss, B. F. Genetic changes in semantic conditioning. *J. exp. Psychol.,* 1946, **36,** 143–152.

Rosenzweig, S. The recall of finished and unfinished tasks as affected by the purpose with which they were performed. *Psychol. Bull.,* 1933, **30,** 698.

Sidman, M. *Tactics of scientific research.* New York: Basic Books, 1958.

Solomon, R. L., & Postman, L. E. Frequency of usage as a determinant of recognition thresholds for words. *J. exp. Psychol.,* 1952, **43,** 195–201.

Solomon, R. L., & Wynne, L. C. Traumatic avoidance learning: acquisition in normal dogs. *Psychol. Monogr.,* 1953, **67,** No. 4 (Whole No. 354).

Solomon, R. L., & Wynne, L. C. Traumatic avoidance learning: the principles of anxiety conservation and partial irreversibility. *Psychol. Rev.,* 1954, **61,** 353–385.

Stevens, S. S. Mathematics: measurement and psychophysics. In S. S. Stevens (Ed.), *Handbook of experimental psychology.* New York: Wiley, 1951.

Veroff, J. Development and validation of a projective measure of power motivation. *J. abnorm. soc. Psychol.,* 1957, **54,** 1–8.

Verplanck, W. S. A glossary of some terms used in the objective science of behavior. *Psychol. Rev.,* 1957, **64** (supplement).

4 BIOLOGICAL CONCEPTS IN PSYCHOPATHOLOGY

Living organisms are not empty. While some psychologists have developed theories of a limited kind that do not take account of biological factors, the problems of psychopathology require that we consider any and all information that may help us understand the genesis of disordered behavior. Pathological behavior is frequently observed in people and animals known to have suffered damage to some bodily system. Exposure to prolonged anxiety or trauma is known to cause marked changes in the bodily functioning of the individual, sometimes leading to organic disease. The interplay of effects between the environment and the biology of the patient is continuous and complex; it is not possible to make complete sense out of the phenomena of behavior pathology without careful attention to this reciprocal action. Consequently, we shall turn, at this point, to consider some biological concepts that have become significant in psychopathological research. Of necessity our discussion is far from complete, and the reader might wish to study further the sources cited at the end of the chapter.

THE BIOLOGY OF STRESS: THE ENDOCRINE SYSTEM

Let us now consider the effects of stressful, dangerous, or fear-provoking stimuli upon bodily reactions. For the sake of convenience, we shall examine two general classes of bodily response: (1) the responses of the endocrine

73

system known as the pituitary-adrenal axis, and (2) the responses of the visceral nervous system.

The endocrine system consists of series of glands which produce chemical products known as *hormones*. Hormones are typically released into the bloodstream, and once in circulation, they selectively affect bodily "targets" elsewhere. The initial release of the hormone by an endocrine gland may be triggered by the activity of another hormone and/or by direct nervous stimulation of the gland. Very small amounts of hormone may have marked effects upon bodily activity. Hormones may act together to produce certain results, or some combinations may antagonize or counteract each other. The major endocrine glands, their hormones, and the chief effects of these hormones are given in Table 4-1. The location of the glands is shown in Figure 4-1.

Particular importance is attached to the

T A B L E   4 - 1   Principal Hormones and Their Major Functions

Gland	Hormone	Major functions
Anterior pituitary	Thyrotrophic (TTH)	Stimulates thyroid secretion
	Adrenocorticotrophic (ACTH)	Stimulates secretion of some hormones of adrenal cortex
	Lactogenic (prolactin)	Stimulates milk secretion by mammary glands
	Luteinizing (LH)	Development of interstitial cells of testis and ovary, and corpus luteum
	Follicle-stimulating (FSH)	Development of spermatogenic tissue in male and follicle in female
	Growth (STH)	Stimulates growth
Posterior pituitary	Oxytocin	Excites nonstriated muscles especially of uterus; excites mammary glands
	Vasopressin	Produces rise in blood pressure
	Antidiuretic	Prevents loss of water through kidney
Thyroid	Thyroxin	Influences metabolic rate
Parathyroid	Parathormone	Maintains calcium and phosphorous balance in blood
Islet cells	Insulin	Necessary for utilization of blood sugar
Adrenal cortex	Cortical Steroids	Increased carbohydrate metabolism, sodium retention and potassium loss; some androgenic and estrogenic effects
Adrenal medulla	Epinephrine Norepinephrine	Increased sugar output by liver, stimulate most SNS end organs (differentially)
Ovary	Estrogen	Produces female primary and secondary sex characteristics
	Progesterone	Prepares uterus for implantation of embryo
Testis	Androgen (Testosterone)	Sexual arousal; produces primary and secondary sex characteristics

SOURCE: *Wenger, Jones, & Jones (1956).*

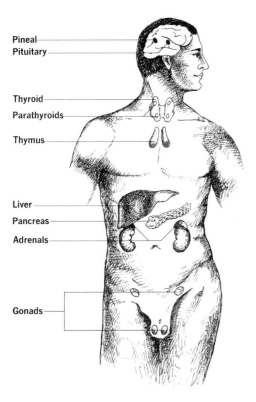

Pineal
Pituitary

Thyroid
Parathyroids

Thymus

Liver
Pancreas

Adrenals

Gonads

Figure 4-1. The names and positions in the body of the endocrine, or ductless, glands that secrete hormones.

activities of the *pituitary gland* (or *hypophysis*). It is divided into three components, the *anterior, intermediate,* and *posterior.* The anterior pituitary secretes a number of hormones known as *trophic* hormones because their action is to seek out other glands and stimulate them to produce their own secretions. Thus, the thyrotrophic hormone acts to stimulate the activity of the thyroid gland. Because of its importance in producing activity in other glands, the pituitary has sometimes been described as the "master gland" of the system. Adrenocorticotrophic hormone (ACTH), secreted by the anterior pituitary, stimulates the activity of the adrenal cortex, a sequence of events that is of great importance in understanding the reaction of the body to stress. The total interaction of these two glands is often symbolized by the term *pituitary-adrenal*

axis which refers to its functional relationship.

The adrenal glands are also of prime interest in the study of behavioral pathology, because so many of their activities are significant in the response of the body to psychologically threatening stimuli. Adrenal cortical activity is stimulated by ACTH, as we have already seen. Activity of the *adrenal medulla,* however, is produced largely by stimulation from the sympathetic nervous system. Sympathetic nervous activity is, in turn, responsive to environmental emergencies or threats, and thus we have a sequence of events in which such threats lead directly to an increased secretion of epinephrine into the bloodstream and thereafter to many physiological changes in the individual.

With this brief description in mind, we can now turn to consider the effects of stress on the activity of the pituitary-adrenal axis.

THE BIOLOGY OF STRESS: THE PITUITARY-ADRENAL AXIS

One of the most used and least accurately defined terms in the language of psychopathology is *stress.* States of fear, prolonged physical effort, prolonged uncertainty, and exposure to unusual extremes of heat, cold, noise, poor diet, lack of sleep, and so forth are commonly referred to as "stressful." Attempts to define these stimuli in such a way that we can recognize a stressor by its characteristics have not been successful. Considerable headway with the problem has been made, however, by several scientists who have studied the general effects upon the body of a variety of stressful agents. Thus, the stressor is defined by the effects it *produces* rather than by any intrinsic characteristics. Foremost among those who have studied this problem is Hans Selyé of the University of Montreal. With his colleagues he has developed a systematic theory of the general effects of stressors upon bodily functions, a theory which has been of great importance in the study of psychosomatic disorders and pathological conditions generally. The pattern of effects that he describes has been termed the *general adaptation syndrome* (GAS) (Selyé, 1957).

The General Adaptation Syndrome

When a particular stressor acts on the body —as, for example, when there is a local injury to part of the body—one result is that the anterior area of the pituitary gland secretes adrenocorticotrophic hormone. Once in the bloodstream, this hormone activates the adrenal glands to secrete further substances known as *corticoids*. These corticoids, which are produced by the adrenal *cortex,* have specific functions in dealing with the local effects of the stressor. The corticoids are of two general types:

1. Mineralocorticoids or prophlogistic corticoids (P-C's) stimulate the proliferative ability and reactivity of connecting tissue; they enhance the "inflammatory potential." Thus, they help to put up a strong barricade of connective tissue by which the body is protected against further invasion by the pathogenic stressor agent. Examples are *desoxycorticosterone* (DOC) and *aldosterone.*
2. Under ordinary conditions, ACTH stimulates the adrenal much more effectively to secrete glucocorticoids or antiphlogistic corticoids (A-C's). These inhibit the ability of the body to put up granulomatous barricades in the path of the invader; in fact, they cause involution of connective tissue with a pronounced depression of the inflammatory potential. Thus, they can suppress inflammation, but by the same token, they open the way to the spreading of infection. Examples of A-C's are *cortisol* and *cortisone.*

The Temporal Sequence of Adaptation

When a stressor is applied for a period of time, the stress reactions of the body undergo certain ordered changes. The GAS thus has certain definable phases, three in all. In temporal order these are known as the *alarm reaction,* the *stage of resistance,* and the *stage of exhaustion.* During the alarm reaction, a stressor generates high corticoid production throughout the body, irrespective of the site of the actual stress. This reaction gives way to the stage of resistance, where the body's defensive activity is confined to the local region of stress. Should the stress be prolonged sufficiently, the local defensive reactions start to become exhausted, leading the body once again to produce A-C's. As we have seen, the production of A-C's tends to inhibit local defensive reactions.

The transition through these stages at the local site of stress is known as the *local adaptation syndrome.* The changing nature of the local stress response is indicated in Figure 4-2. The GAS proceeds through the same triphasic sequence, but in the stage of general exhaustion we are dealing with a much more serious state of affairs. Prolonged exhaustion under severe stress may lead to the death of the organism.

Inspection of Figure 4-2 will show that there are several points in the chain of events at which some failure of reaction might occur. In the first place, there might be some failure of the pituitary to react to the stressor, i.e., an inadequate production of ACTH might fail to stimulate the production of corticoids by the adrenal cortex if the latter is defective. Secondly, a normally acting pituitary may fail to stimulate a pathologically defective adrenal cortex. Thirdly, even if the adrenal cortex is functioning normally, the bodily reactions to the corticoids might be deficient at some other level.

Conversely, we can see that the stress reaction might be produced in the body by the direct introduction of ACTH or of the corticoids. Stress generates several products in the blood and the urine of the subject, as well as causing other bodily changes. Measurement of these is one of the techniques used to study the effects of stressful situations upon other kinds of behavior. We should be familiar with these measures in order to understand the meaning of various experimental findings that will be discussed.

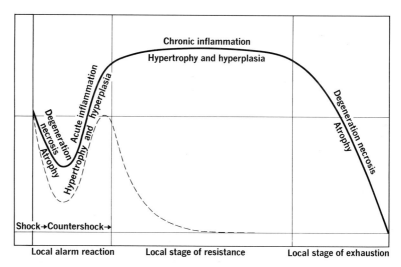

Figure 4-2. Schematic drawing illustrating the characteristic changes in morphologic structure and topical resistance, as they occur during the three stages of the LAS. The heavy line represents "specific resistance," the interrupted line resistance to additional stresses. (After Selyé and co-workers, 1950.)

Measures of Stress Response

The adrenal corticoids produced under stress are metabolized in the body and produce certain metabolites. Among the most important of these for measurement purposes are the corticosteroids. Also widely used to gauge stress response are measures of the number of eosinophils in the blood and measures of the amount of ascorbic acid in the adrenals.

Corticosteroids. The two major kinds of product in the steroid group are known as *17-ketosteroids* and *17-hydroxycorticosteroids* (17-OH-CS). The production of these steroid substances is influenced by other variables, as well as by the activity of the adrenal cortex. For example, the output of 17-ketosteroids is partly determined by the metabolism of testosterone, a hormone that is unrelated to the stress response. However, for practical purposes, the level of both of these steroids is sufficiently sensitive to stress effects that changes in the levels may be used to define the presence of a stress response. As might be expected from our description of the stress response, stress brings about an increase in both of these steroid groups. As we shall see shortly, there is also some evidence that relaxation is accompanied by reduction below the normal daily level.

Evidence has been advanced to suggest that the initial stage of stress involves a much greater increase in the production of 17-OH-CS than of 17-ketosteroids. As the condition of stress endures, the ratio changes, with a more pronounced output of 17-ketosteroids.

Eosinophils. Circulating in the blood at any time are a number of cells known as *eosinophils*. When a stressor impinges on the organism, there is evidence that the quantity of eosinophils undergoes some measurable changes. Precise understanding of the nature and form of these changes is still lacking, but there seems to be little doubt that the initial effect is a reduction in the number of circulating eosinophils. When the stress is prolonged for some time, this reduction gives way to a change in the other direction, the count of circulating eosinophils going up. It seems possible that there would be a series of cyclical changes

T A B L E 4 - 2 Effects of Various Natural-habitat Stresses on Military Subjects and Controls

Group	Eosinophils per mm³				17- hydroxycorticosteroids micrograms per hour			
	N	M	SD	p*	N	M	SD	p*
Fire	6	164.5	142	*ns*	4	643.25	276	<.05
CBR	15	133.5	109	*ns*	15	507.60	180	<.05
Artillery	15	209.8	240	*ns*	11	520.27	138	<.05
Control	11	305.8	351		6	364.00	48	

* *Mean difference from control group. N = number of cases; M = mean value for group; SD = standard deviation (a measure of the spread of individual scores around the mean); p = probability of such differences occurring by chance.*
SOURCE: *Berkun, Bialek, Kern, and Yagi (1962).*

of this kind if measurements were taken over a long period of time (McDonald, Yagi, & Stockton, 1961).

Adrenal Ascorbic Acid (AAA). Much evidence has been gathered from animal studies to indicate that one feature of the stress response is a drop in the amount of ascorbic acid in the adrenals. This depletion of *adrenal ascorbic acid* (AAA) is thus available as a measure of the extent to which the organism has responded to the stress. Assaying the AAA depletion in an animal involves removing the adrenals (and therefore destroying the animal), a procedure which is feasible for certain kinds of research but renders the measure inappropriate for studies in which poststress behavior is to be studied also.

Several other responses have been used in addition to the three just described. Indeed, any response which is produced by activity of the pituitary-adrenal axis may be studied in relation to stressor effects. However, most of the major research that has been done on experimentally induced stress has used one or more of the measures that we have already discussed.

Experimental Studies of Stress

Many experiments have been performed to study the effects of stress upon bodily reactions. One of the most dramatic series of investigations was reported by Berkun,

Bialek, Kern, and Yagi (1962). Using inexperienced soldiers as subjects, they arranged a series of psychologically stressful situations. In one study the subjects were aboard a plane on an apparently routine flight, when an emergency was simulated so that the subjects believed they were to make a crash landing in the ocean. In another study the soldier subject believed that he had been responsible for an accident to another man and was required to repair a telephone before he could use it to call for help. At various stages in these experiments, measures of adrenal-pituitary activity were taken. The output of urinary 17-hydroxycorticosteroids (17-OH-CS) and the eosinophil counts for subjects under several different degrees of stress showed a relatively consistent relationship between these responses and the presence or absence of stress. These data are given in Table 4-2.

An interesting aspect of the 17-OH-CS response has been studied by Handlon (1962). Normal subjects were shown two kinds of motion picture. One group of films was selected to be arousing or stressful, namely *Ox Bow Incident, High Noon,* and *A Walk in the Sun.* The other group was chosen for being "bland" or relaxing. These were Walt Disney nature study films and were intended simply to provide control stimuli for comparison with the arousing films. Surprisingly, the effect of the *bland* movies in lowering the 17-OH-CS count was much more evident than the power of the arousing movies to raise it. Figure 4-3 shows the changes brought about by exposure to the two types of film and compares them with the changes in a control group who saw no films at all. Subjects were asked to report their emotional mood as it changed during the pictures, and we can see from the figure that these changes are in line with those in the 17-OH-CS count.

Turning from the 17-OH-CS count to the excretion of 17-ketosteroids, we find that much research has been reported to confirm the power of stressors such as fatigue, battle stresses, pursuitmeter performance with anoxia, and so forth. The effects of stresses of differing degrees of intensity upon 17-ketosteroid excretion are shown in Figure 4-4. While there are fluctuations in the relationship between steroid output and the subject's rating of his distress in the situation, the general form of it is comparatively clear.

Individual Differences in Stress Resistance

Although it is quite possible to show the effect of stressors upon the resting rate of the measures already described, the in-dividual effects are quite variable. Some subjects respond much more than others to stressors of the same physical intensity. The level of stress required to produce a response is, therefore, variable among people. Because resistance and responsiveness to stress are important factors in the genesis of psychosomatic disorders, it is important to know what is responsible for the differences between people in their reactions to stress. Experimental alteration in resistance to stress is not very feasible with human subjects, but much work has been done with animals.

One of the guiding hypotheses behind a large part of this work is that experiences of stress during early infancy may have a critical effect upon the way in which stress-resistance mechanisms will operate later in life. The hypothesis has been tested by subjecting infant animals to various kinds of stressors at different periods in infancy and then measuring their resistance to stress during adult maturity. Typical of the procedures and findings of this kind of research is the work of Levine and his associates (e.g., Levine, 1959; Levine & Lewis, 1958). Infant rats are manipulated by a technique that involves simply taking the animal from

Figure 4-3. Effects of "bland" versus "arousing" movies on biological and psychological measures. (Adapted from Handlon, 1962.)

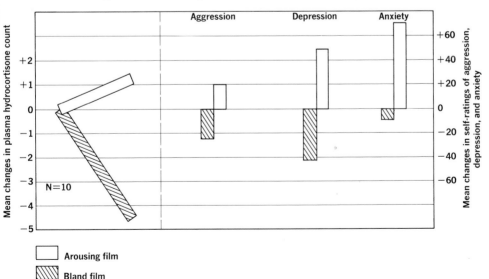

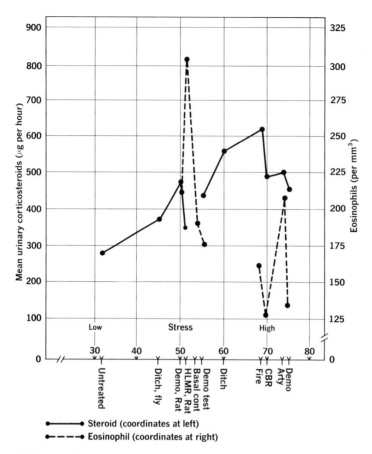

Figure 4-4. Mean physiological response in each situation, as a function of the intensity of stress. (Berkun et al., 1962.)

the nest, placing it in a small compartment for a few minutes, and then returning it to the nest. The stimulation provided by this method is at first sight rather trivial, but the data indicate that the effects it produces are comparable to much more violent kinds of stress, such as electric shock or vigorous vibration.

Manipulation of this kind leads to more rapid growth and development of the infant. Body hair and eye-opening appear sooner, while the myelination of the central nervous system occurs significantly earlier. In addition to the acceleration of development in this way, other studies show that response to stress in adulthood is much greater in the manipulated animal. For example, the

quantity of circulating corticosteroids produced by electric shock to the feet of the adult rat differs as a consequence of the presence or absence of manipulation in infancy. These effects are shown in Figure 4-5.

Comparison of the stress reactions of manipulated and nonmanipulated animals has led Levine to several conclusions. The manipulated animal is much more reactive to noxious stressors (shock, extreme cold, etc.), but relatively unresponsive to unthreatening changes in the environment. On the other hand, the nonmanipulated animal is sluggish in reaction to noxious stress, but more reactive to simple environmental change than the manipulated animal. So far, the effects of manipulation in infancy seem

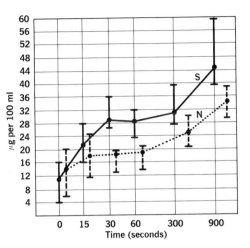

Figure 4-5. **Circulating corticosteroids following an electric shock in stimulated (S) and nonstimulated (N) rats. The zero time is the control value without shock. The circles represent the means of the groups; the bars indicate the range. (Levine, 1963.)**

to be beneficial in preparing the animal to react appropriately to real threat. However, the benefit depends upon the intensity of the manipulation used. Optimal levels of infantile stimulation probably exist, and excessive early stress may produce changes that are detrimental to later responsiveness to stress.

Stress Resistance and Psychosomatic Disorders

Exposure to prolonged stress may bring about irreversible changes in the functioning of certain bodily systems. Since there are many different kinds of stressors, it is possible that the detrimental effects of any one of them may impair the power of the patient to resist other kinds of stressors. Thus, a person who has been subjected to extreme anxiety for a long period of time may be unable to resist stress from wounds or illness in the usual way. We have already noted the bodily changes in the immediate or alarm stage of stress. However, prolonged stress may produce changes of a much more complicated type. Pathological overresponsiveness and pathological insensitivity to stress are both possible.

The precise manner in which prolonged stress leads to a particular organic disorder is still far from clear. Where the stressor is itself some kind of organic damage, such as a burn or a wound, the resultant chronic consequences may be regarded as part of the total medical picture. However, as we shall see in detail in Chapter 10, the manner in which psychological stressors produce later organic disorders is one of the major concerns of the psychopathologist. These disorders, the *psychosomatic* disorders, may be interpreted in terms of the stress-resistance hypothesis already discussed here.

An interesting experimental illustration of the genesis of a psychosomatic disorder has been provided by Porter, Brady, Conrad, Mason, Galambos, & Rioch (1958). Monkeys were subjected to a series of experimental behavioral conditioning procedures, being restrained in a holding apparatus for the purpose. Conditioning procedures included schedules in which punishing electric shock was delivered to the animal, both with and without the possibility of avoiding it. Of the 19 monkeys used in this study, 11 died or became moribund and had to be killed after 2 to 17 weeks of experimental study. Generally speaking, these animals appeared quite normal during the experimental period and gave no visible sign of illness until 12 to 72 hours before death. All the 11 monkeys showed organic pathology of a gastrointestinal kind. Gastric hemorrhage and erosion, chronic ulceration of the duodenum, and chronic colitis were observed. The investigators were properly cautious in presenting their results, but pointed out the significance of psychological stress in producing disease processes which are not known to occur spontaneously in monkeys and which bear striking resemblance to human diseases.

Summary

We have seen how a variety of stressors produces the same syndrome of alarm and resistance in living organisms, especially the syndrome of changes in the level of operation of the pituitary-adrenal axis. Individual differences in this response are quite marked, and experimental work with animals suggests that early experiences may be important in influencing these differences. The significance of prolonged stress for the later development of psychosomatic disorders has also been considered.

THE BIOLOGY OF STRESS: THE AUTONOMIC NERVOUS SYSTEM

Earlier in this chapter we mentioned the effects of stress upon the activity of the adrenal medulla and the general importance of the functions of the autonomic nervous system. We shall now consider these in detail. First it should be noted that some recent investigators have preferred the term "visceral nervous system"; but in this book we shall retain the term "autonomic" in order to avoid confusions that might arise from a change in terminology.

General Structure of the Autonomic Nervous System

The visceral organs of the body, including vascular and glandular structures, are supplied with nerves which activate them. These nerves, called *efferent* or *motor* nerves, collectively form the autonomic nervous system.[1] Cell bodies of these nerves are generally located in ganglia that lie outside the spinal cord and are parallel to it. Thus the typical nerve leaves the spinal cord and synapses in a ganglion. At the ganglion, another neuron receives the impulse, carries it directly to the visceral organ, and activates the organ. The ganglia are located in several places. Two long chains run parallel and

[1] There is a difference of usage here also, as the term "autonomic nervous system" is sometimes used to include both motor and sensory nerves. In this chapter we shall retain the usage of Kuntz (1945), who points out that visceral afferent neurons which terminate in the cerebrospinal ganglia without interruption in the autonomic ganglia may not be regarded as constituents of autonomic nerves.

close to the spinal cord and are known as the *sympathetic trunk*. Other ganglia are found in a *plexus* or network of nerve fibers, most of which are located in the abdominal cavity. A third group of ganglia are located directly near the organ which is to be activated. However, regardless of where the ganglion is located, the connection between the spinal cord and the viscera is always interrupted by one synapse, and this occurs in a ganglion. Using this fact as a basis for description, we can identify a *preganglionic* fiber leading from the cord to the ganglion and a *postganglionic* fiber leading from the ganglion to the viscera. This is an important distinction, as will appear presently.

Ignoring certain complexities of anatomy, we may separate the autonomic system into (a) the craniosacral division and (b) the thoracolumbar division. Craniosacral nerves emerge in the 3d, 7th, 9th, 10th, and 11th cranial nerves and in the 2d, 3d, and 4th sacral nerves. The thoracolumbar division includes nerves which emerge in the thoracic and upper lumbar nerves.

The thoracolumbar division has more commonly been called the *sympathetic* division, while the craniosacral division has been called the *parasympathetic* division. Most visceral structures receive fibers from both the sympathetic and the parasympathetic system. Very often these two systems have antagonistic effects, as for example, in the innervation of the iris of the eye. The iris has two sets of muscles, one of which contracts the pupil and is activated by the parasympathetic system, and the other of which dilates the pupil and is controlled by sympathetic innervation. Thus, the continually changing size of the pupil is a result of the changing balance between the two kinds of nervous activity. A simplified diagram of the supply of autonomic nerves to the viscera is provided in Figure 4-6.

Chemical Properties of Nerve Transmission

From both pre- and post-ganglionic neurons, chemical substances are released when a nerve impulse reaches the end of the fiber.

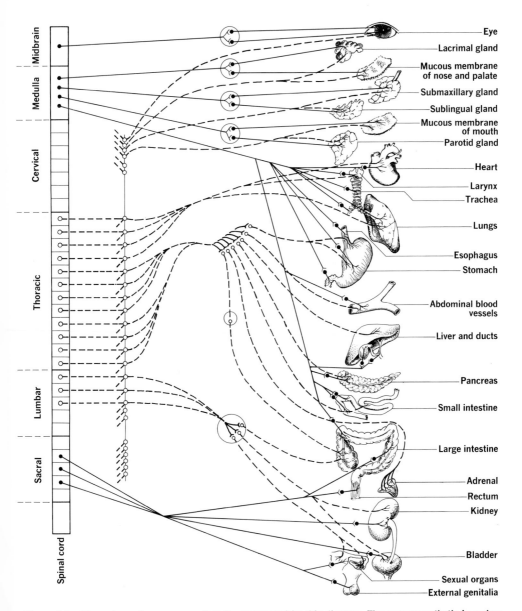

Figure 4-6. The autonomic nervous system is represented by this diagram. The parasympathetic branches, arising from the brain and sacral vertebrae, are indicated by black lines; the sympathetic branches, arising from the thoracic and lumbar vertebrae, by broken lines. (Funkenstein, 1955.)

Generally speaking, all preganglionic fibers release a substance known as *acetylcholine*. Sympathetic postganglionic fibers release *noradrenalin;* parasympathetic postganglionic fibers release acetylcholine. This chemical difference does not correspond completely to the anatomical division between the cranio-sacral and thoracolumbar systems. For instance, the thoracolumbar supply to the human sweat glands is completely mediated by acetylcholine in both the pre- and postganglionic fibers. For general purposes of discussion, however, we can consider the basic functional divisions as being thoracolumbar-sympathetic-adrenergic on the one hand, and craniosacral-parasympathetic-cholinergic on the other.

The Adrenal Medulla

From the adrenal medulla, one of the endocrine glands, three substances are secreted: *adrenalin, noradrenalin,* and *dopamine.* These three substances are referred to as *catecholamines,* and we shall be mainly concerned with the first two of them. In addition to their production by the adrenal medulla, we have seen that noradrenalin is produced by the sympathetic nerves. Both adrenalin and noradrenalin have also been found in urine and in blood. We can see that the sources and locations of these hormones are quite complex. We shall demonstrate shortly the differing effects that they are believed to have upon emotional behavior.

Examination of the structure of the tissue of the adrenal medulla reveals that it is composed of modified postganglionic sympathetic nerve cells. The catecholamines are stored in small particles in the cells and are released into the bloodstream when the splanchnic nerve leading to the adrenal medulla is stimulated. Activity of the splanchnic nerve is mediated by acetylcholine, and the same effect may be produced by giving a short injection of the substance methacholine or *mecholyl* (acetyl-β-methyl-choline). Immediately following this injection there is an initial fall in blood pressure, which is followed by a return to normal levels. However, there is a good deal of individual variability in this effect, and it has been developed by Funkenstein, Greenblatt, Rool, & Solomon (1949) as a method of testing the characteristic response of a subject's autonomic system.

The Mecholyl Test. The standard procedure for the administration of mecholyl is to inject a small quantity of the drug into the muscles of the arm and to record blood pressure and heart rate for about 15 to 20 minutes. While there are marked differences in the manner in which subjects respond to

this drug, Gellhorn has described three major types of reaction:

1. The blood pressure falls only slightly and briefly, returning to the base line after 3 to 5 minutes and then rising above the base line.

2. The blood pressure falls from 15 to 25 millimeters of mercury and then returns to the base line after about 5 to 8 minutes.

3. The blood pressure falls even more than in reaction 2 above and does not return to the base line within 15 minutes (Gellhorn & Loofbourrow, 1963).

With increasing age, there is a tendency for people to move from the first to the third type of reaction, i.e., to show less sympathetic activity after the mecholyl has been injected. The significance of the mecholyl test in relation to particular patterns of behavior disorder will be discussed later at various points.

The Catecholamines and Emotion

Several lines of research have suggested that the effects of adrenalin and noradrenalin may be related to the experiences of anxiety and anger respectively. When a subject is given adrenalin and then mecholyl, there is a large fall in blood pressure, as in Gellhorn's reaction 3. However, if the subject has received noradrenalin before the mecholyl, then there is only a slight fall in blood pressure. From this observation it might be argued that the response of a normal subject to the mecholyl test will indicate whether there is an adrenalin or a noradrenalin dominance in the typical response of his adrenal medulla. Pursuing this line of reasoning, Funkenstein, King, & Drolette (1953) report that young men faced with a stress situation responded either by overt anger, self-blame for their inadequacy, or simple anxiety. Those who exhibited open anger (Funkenstein referred to this as *anger-out*) showed a noradrenalin pattern to mecholyl injection, whereas those who revealed self-blame (*anger-in*) or anxiety revealed an adrenalin pattern of reaction on the mecholyl test.

A very similar line of evidence comes from an investigation by Ax (1953) in which he led subjects to believe that they might receive an electric shock from defective wiring of a circuit. Those who reacted with anger produced a noradrenalin reaction, while those who responded with fear showed an adrenalin reaction. Data of this kind suggest that there are hormonal differences in the two states of emotion, anger and fear; it also suggests that there are individual differences in the typical hormonal reaction to threat and therefore in the accompanying emotion. Experiments that have attempted to demonstrate the reverse proposition—that injections of one or the other of the catecholamines can generate the appropriate emotional experience—have not been reliably successful. Emotional experiences must be regarded as the correlates of very complicated patterns of bodily activity, invoking mechanisms that are much more subtle than simple hormonal processes.

Bodily Consequences of Sympathetic Activity

We have already seen that the activities of the sympathetic and parasympathetic divisions of the autonomic nervous system are generally antagonistic. In anger or fear the predominant activity is sympathetic and is mediated by adrenalin or noradrenalin. Ignoring the specific differences in the effects of these catecholamines, we may briefly review the general bodily changes that occur with sympathetic activity. These are summarized in Table 4-3. Also provided in the table are the related and often antagonistic functions served by the parasympathetic division of the autonomic nervous system.

POLYGRAPHIC MEASUREMENT

Direct assay of hormonal or nervous system activity is not readily feasible in the intact normal subject. Even where it is possible to take blood specimens, the procedures involved in taking them are likely to produce some emotional reaction. Furthermore, the time that must elapse between taking such a sample and completing the analysis of it is an obstacle to the continuous observation of bodily states during different kinds of external stimulation. Because of this, research investigators have for many years used an indirect measure of different aspects of bodily activity, namely the polygraphic recording of the electrical side effects produced by this bodily activity.

The polygraph consists of a series of devices that are responsive to the movement of various parts of the body or that detect electrical changes accompanying the move-

TABLE 4-3 Parasympathetic and Sympathetic Nervous System Functions

Organ	Response	Sympathetic effect	Parasympathetic effect
Heart	Rate	Increases	Lowers
Lungs	Dilate	Facilitates	Inhibits
Blood vessels at periphery	Constriction	Facilitates	Inhibits
Sweat glands	Secrete	Facilitates	Inhibits
Eyes	Iris	Dilates	Contracts
Lacrymal glands	Weeping	Inhibits	Facilitates
Salivary glands	Salivation	Inhibits	Facilitates
Gastrointestinal tract	Peristalsis	Inhibits	Facilitates
Glands in stomach	Secretion of acid, pepsin, and mucus	Inhibits	Facilitates

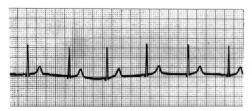

Figure 4-7. Heartbeat (EKG) as monitored by the polygraphic method.

ments. Each of these devices relays the signals of the changing activity that are first amplified considerably and then used to deflect a pen across a moving paper chart. Typical measures taken, and their normal characteristics, are as follows.

The Electrocardiogram (EKG)

As the heart beats, the muscular contractions involved produce a certain standard sequence of electrical activity that may be detected by placing electrodes on the body surface near the heart. The typical normal sequence is shown in Figure 4-7. From one peak to another on the record represents one beat of the heart, and the rate at which the individual's heart is beating may, in turn, be recorded as an additional but separate aspect of the activity of the heart. The latter measure is recorded by a *cardiotachometer;* it can also be computed by simply measuring the time between each beat on the electrocardiogram directly.

The Electromyogram (EMG)

Activation of a muscle produces electrical changes that may also be recorded in a manner much the same as that used in the EKG. Unlike the EKG, however, the frequency or rate of the wave produced by muscular activity is quite variable and can reach very high frequencies. A typical EMG record demonstrates periodic bursts of activity when a muscle is activated, with low-frequency changes when a muscle is relatively relaxed.

The Plethysmogram

The volume of blood at the periphery of the body changes with autonomic activity, as we have already seen. Blood volume measures are also recorded polygraphically with a plethysmograph. As we might expect, these changes take place slowly compared with the changes in muscle and heart potential, and the typical record is one of slow, irregular fluctuations.

The Galvanic Skin Response (GSR)

With fear, there is increased activity of the sweat glands located near the surface of the body. When an electrode is placed on the body and put in circuit with a galvanometer, any change in the resistance at the electrode will produce a deflection of the galvanometer. Sweating will reduce resistance on skin surfaces, and thus if we place the electrode on the palm of the hand, we are likely to get a fairly responsive measure of palmar perspiration by recording these changes in resistance. This kind of response has been called the *galvanic skin response* (GSR) and the *psychogalvanic reflex* (PGR). Here again, we should expect to find slow, irregular changes in response to external stimulation, such as the record shown in Figure 4-8.

Blood Pressure

Our earlier discussion of the mecholyl test indicated the usefulness of measurement of blood pressure changes in studying autonomic functions. Blood pressure is typically measured with an instrument called a *sphygmomanometer,* and here again we may maintain a continuous record of changes in pressure by polygraphic means.

Other Measures

Other measures that are taken include *skin temperature* (which itself reflects changes in blood volume at the surface of the body) and *heart rate* or pulse rate. For different

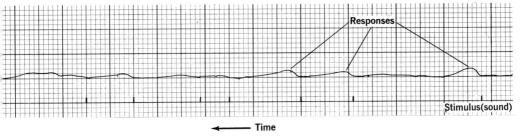

Figure 4-8. GSR responses in normal subject to random loud sound stimuli.

purposes these measures may be taken at various parts of the body.

Telemetry

Polygraphy has one rather serious limitation. The apparatus is static, and the subject is restricted in his movements by the electrodes and direct wires that lead to the amplification system. This means that the investigator is confined to the study of stresses or situations that may be produced in the laboratory. Necessarily, many of these differ from the kind of stresses that occur naturally in the daily life of the individual. We are, therefore, compelled to assume that the response patterns noted in the laboratory are representative of those that would appear in the face of more typical and realistic stresses.

One solution to the problem is provided by the use of a radio link between the electrode and the amplifier in lieu of the usual wire. This kind of system is referred to as *radiotelemetry*. The subject wears a miniature radio transmitter, the signal from which is modulated by the biological events at the electrode—such as the EKG. A radio receiver nearby converts the signal into a conventional display by relaying it to a standard chart such as that used in the polygraph. The final record of the response is similar to one obtained in the usual way (see Figure 4-9), while the subject may carry the transmitter in an inconspicuous manner for long periods of time (Figure 4-10).

Figure 4-9. Comparison of direct recording of EKG and radio-transmitted (telemetered) recording.

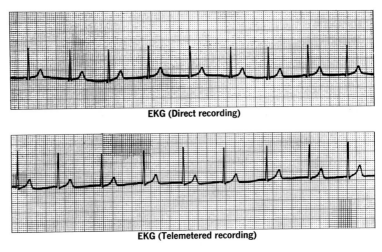

EKG (Direct recording)

EKG (Telemetered recording)

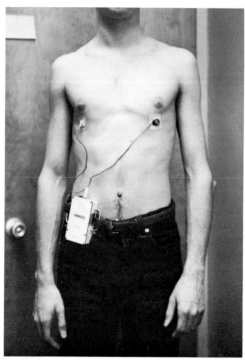

Figure 4-10.   Method of attaching and wearing telemeter transmitter.

Some limitations are inherent in measurement by telemetry. For practical purposes it is difficult to monitor more than one kind of autonomic response at a time without the use of very costly and elaborate equipment. Thus it is not easy to study *patterns* of response, but simply the changes in a single response. Also, while it is true that the system permits the investigator to move the subject out of the laboratory, the effective range of most miniature transmitters is less than 600 feet, which imposes some limitations upon the experiment. Finally, the interpretation of telemetric data requires that the investigator record the behavior and environment of the subject at the time the signal was being transmitted. In the natural habitat this cannot be done with the same degree of accuracy and completeness that we find in the laboratory.

Nevertheless, the technique of radiotelemetry opens up a wide area of investigation that had been closed to study by previous methods. We may expect to find its use increasing in the near future.

Autonomic Response Specificity

Much work has been done toward discovering principles that will permit the interpretation of polygraphic records for psychological purposes. Several possibilities have been considered. One might hope to find that particular kinds of emotional states are associated with distinct patterns of polygraphic data, so that by examining the record the investigator might deduce the state of the subject at the time the record was obtained. Alternatively, we might find that distinct patterns of response were produced by particular external stimulation, regardless of the emotional state of the subject. All in all, neither of these approaches has been supported to any significant extent. Instead, the upshot of these investigations has been to suggest that each person has a characteristic pattern of autonomic response. *Autonomic response specificity* is the term that has been applied to this phenomenon by workers in the field, especially by Lacey and his colleagues of the Fels Research Institute (Lacey, 1950; Lacey, Bateman, & VanLehn, 1953). A good description of the principle is provided by this group:

The autonomic nervous system does indeed respond to experimentally imposed stress "as a whole" in the sense that all autonomically innervated structures seem to be activated, usually in the direction of apparent sympathetic dominance. But it does not respond "as a whole" in the sense that all autonomically innervated structures exhibit equal increments or decrements of function. Striking intra-individual difference in the degree of activation of different physiological functions are found when the different reactions are expressed in equivalent units. (Lacey, Bateman, & VanLehn, 1953, p. 8.)

Measurement of Response Specificity. When a subject produces autonomic responses to stress, or to any kind of stimulus, there are two ways in which we might evaluate the level of the response. First, we may measure the absolute level reached by a particular response, i.e., we may report that the heart rate reached a maximum of 105. Second, we may consider to what extent the value obtained represents a deviation from the average response of the normal population. Both of these measures may be evaluated sensibly by taking into account the initial value of the measure when the subject was at rest; a gain of 10 heartbeats per minute may have a different meaning when the initial value was 70 than when it was 95.

One solution to the problems raised by these considerations has been to standardize the measures from different autonomic systems so that the mean value of a measure is always 50 and the standard deviation is 10 units. Accomplishing this with absolute stress levels of a response is a fairly simple task requiring mainly that the experimenter have data on the normal heart rate, skin resistance, etc., for a large population of subjects.

To achieve the same kind of standardization of scores when they are calculated as percentage changes from the base line is a little more complicated, as there is reason to believe that the base-line value of an autonomic measure influences the extent to which it can be changed by stress. The most obvious problem would arise with a subject who was already responding nearly at the "ceiling" for some response and who had little further room to increase it. We shall ignore the mathematics of the problem except to state that by allowing suitable corrections for this kind of correlation, the experimenter can compute T scores of a kind essentially similar to those for absolute levels. In Lacey's terminology, the absolute levels attained following stress are labeled *autonomic tension* scores, while the relative changes are termed *autonomic lability* scores.

The Law of Initial Values. Wilder (1957) has proposed that the relationship between the initial value of the functioning of a physiological system and its response to stimulation is such that the lower the initial value, the greater will be the response. He believes that this principle will operate except at the extreme levels, where a reversal may be found, thus producing a paradoxical effect. Application of this principle, sometimes called the *law of initial values,* to autonomic functioning would lead us to predict that the lower the base line of a measure in the resting state, the greater will be the response when stress is applied. As yet, there has been little in the way of systematic testing of this principle—more appropriately called a hypothesis rather than a law—but in one study of its application to autonomic functioning, it was found to be supported when the measure was of GSR but not supported when the measures were of heart rate and respiration rate (Kaelbling,

King, Achenbach, Branson, & Pasamanick, 1960).

Empirical Findings. Eighty-five male college students were exposed to four stressors in an investigation conducted by Lacey et al. (1953). Palmar conductance (a measure of sweat gland activity), heart rate, and heart-rate variability were recorded for all subjects during each of the stressor applications. With this kind of measurement, the investigators defined a subject as having "maximum specificity" if he responded at a peak level in the same measure during each of the four stresses; "high specificity" if he produced peak reactivity in one measure three times and in another the fourth time; "low specificity" if he produced a peak response in one measure for two of the stresses and in a different measure for the other two stresses; and "minimum specificity" if peak reactivity occurred in all three measures over the four stresses.

These possible combinations might take place in some subjects simply on the basis of random association of responses. However, the actual data gained in the research showed that specificity of response occurred more than twice as often as chance expectancy would predict. Detailed analysis of the results led the investigators to conclude that for a given set of autonomic measures, individuals tend to respond with a pattern of autonomic activation in which maximal activation occurs in the same physiological function whatever the stress. Likewise, there is a strong tendency for the entire pattern of autonomic activation to be reproduced from stress to stress.

Response Specificity and Psychopathology. So far we have considered evidence from the mecholyl test and from polygraphy all suggesting that there are stable individual differences in the way in which people respond autonomically. Because of the great frequency with which psychiatric patients present somatic complaints, we may turn logically to consider the extent to which these complaints reflect their own bodily responses to stress. One of the best-known investigations of this question was conducted by Malmo and Shagass (1949). Groups of patients were presented with painful experimental stimuli. Those patients whose psychiatric picture included complaints of headache or related symptoms showed more muscular than cardiovascular responses to the pain. Another group of patients having cardiovascular symptoms showed more heart-rate changes than muscular responses to the experimental stimulation.

Further investigation by these researchers (Malmo & Shagass, 1952) produced evidence that patients who were diagnosed as neurotic differed from normal controls in their blood pressure response to stress. When the normal subjects were exposed to stressful situations (pain-heat stimulation, rapid discrimination task, and a mirror drawing task), there was the expected rise in blood pressure followed by a leveling off or decline as the stress continued. The psychiatric group, however, showed a continuing rise. This suggested to the authors that in these patients there might be a basic deficiency in some regulatory mechanism that normally operates to check an excessive rise in blood pressure. Figure 4-11 illustrates the difference in blood pressure response of the two groups.

Psychosomatic disorders present the kind of problem for which this method of analysis has particular importance. Where there is a definite malfunction of a bodily system or organ, and where this follows on prolonged exposure to stress, there is considerable value in developing knowledge of the manner in which individual responses to stress are determined. This issue is discussed in detail in Chapter 10 on psychosomatic disorders.

ELECTROENCEPHALOGRAPHY

When electrodes are attached to the scalp of a human subject, it is possible to record current of fluctuating voltage. When this is amplified and connected to a chart and pen-

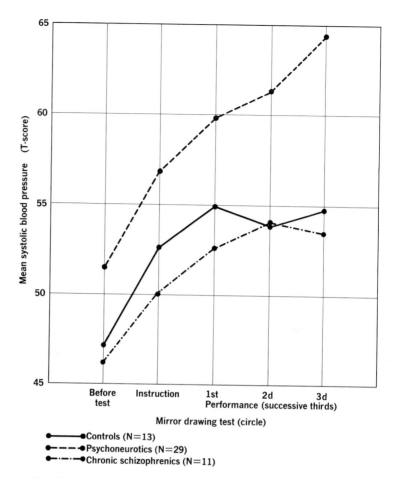

Figure 4-11. Mean blood pressure during second mirror drawing test. Note continuous rise in curve for psychoneurotics. (Malmo & Shagass, 1952.)

writer, the current produces movements of the pen that appear as waves on the moving chart. The discovery of this phenomenon is credited to Hans Berger in 1924,[2] and the wave discovered was referred to as the Berger rhythm. Since that time, the development of methods of detecting and recording electrical rhythms in the brain has proceeded rapidly, and the technique is termed *electroencephalography* (EEG).

While the use of surface electrodes is standard practice in clinical electroencephalography, research investigators may from time to time use electrodes that are directly in contact with nervous tissue. Direct placement of electrodes in the brain or the brainstem is not uncommon when animals are being studied, and it is also used in some instances when human patients are undergoing brain surgery. Characteristic wave patterns are found, depending upon the placement and type of the electrode. Various forms of brain pathology also produce deviant rhythms, and these may be used as an aid to diagnosis in clinical neurology. The broad group of brain

[2] Schwab (1951) reports that these waves had been observed in 1918 by a medical student at Harvard, but had been ignored at that time.

dysfunctions that is termed "epilepsy" is of particular interest in clinical EEG, as the dysfunctions are associated with a tendency to produce certain kinds of atypical waves.

In normal subjects the two main frequencies found are the *alpha* rhythm and the *beta* rhythm. Alpha waves are of a frequency between 8 and 13 cycles per second, while beta waves are in the range of 14 to 25 cps. Other frequencies that are sometimes identified are *delta* (0.5 to 3.5 cps), *theta* (4 to 7 cps), and *gamma* (26 cps and higher). Alpha rhythms are ordinarily found when electrodes are placed in the occipital and parietal areas, while beta frequency is found in the frontal and central areas. Alpha frequency is readily blocked or eliminated by certain kinds of external stimulation, especially visual stimulation. It may also be blocked by certain kinds of conscious activity, but the conditions under which this blocking occurs are not as yet clearly established.

Alpha Blocking and Attention

Alpha rhythm is found in the occipital and parietal areas when the subject is relaxed, at rest, and with eyes closed. When an external stimulus, especially a bright light, impinges upon him, the subject's EEG response is marked by alpha blocking. The occurrence of alpha blocking may be regarded as defining *attention* or *arousal* on the subject's part; it is correlated with conscious awareness of the stimulus. With repeated presentation, the same stimulus will lose the power to block the alpha rhythm. This phenomenon is known as *adaptation*.

Alpha blocking has been established as a conditioned response. Jasper and Shagass (1941), for example, used a light as the unconditioned stimulus and a sound as the conditioned stimulus. The light effectively blocked the alpha rhythm of the subject, whereas the sound alone did not. After pairing sound and light, the former being presented for 10 seconds before the light came on, the experimenters succeeded in establishing alpha blocking as a conditioned response to the sound alone.

Alpha Blocking and Feedback Loops

Mulholland (1962) has devised an ingenious technique, which is based upon the principle of the *feedback loop*, for the study of alpha blocking. The principle is quite simple. When alpha frequency is being recorded from the EEG, it activates a switch that is built into the recording circuit. This in turn switches on a lamp placed to shine in the subject's eyes. A light shining in the eyes, as we have seen, blocks the alpha frequency, and so the lamp is switched off. When the lamp goes off, alpha returns, the lamp goes on once more, and the cycle repeats itself. However, after the lamp has been switched on and off several times, adaptation begins to develop, so that alpha ceases to be blocked by the light. Now the light remains on for longer periods and finally remains on more or less continuously. The transition from brief bursts of alpha and the blocking effect of the light to the prolonged periods of alpha after the light ceases to block it is shown in Figure 4-12.

Using this technique, Mulholland has studied *internal gradients* of attention. Once adaptation has been established, the subject is asked to count light flashes up to a predetermined number—for example, from the first to the fifteenth. As the light flashes come closer to fifteen, the subject's attention to the task appears to increase in a gradient fashion. The effect of increasing attention is to block alpha and thereby to terminate the light. Thus, the closer the light exposures come to fifteen, the briefer and more widely spaced they are. When duration and spacing are measured and plotted, a gradient effect is produced.

This procedure offers interesting insights into the manner in which attention may be determined by variables other than those produced purely by the external environment. It also offers a way in which we may study the problem of the learning of an

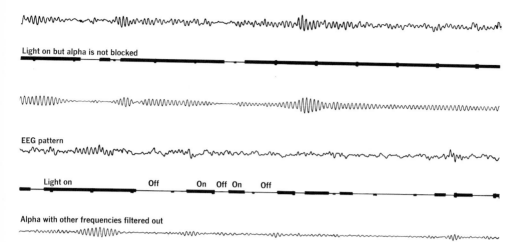

Light on but alpha is not blocked

EEG pattern

Light on   Off   On Off On   Off

Alpha with other frequencies filtered out

Figure 4-12. Blocking of alpha frequency by onset of light. System adapts to light which produces less blocking as time passes. Chart should be read from left to right, first sessions at the bottom and the final adaptation effects at the top.

attention response. Reference has been made to the phenomenon of conditioned attention (as defined by conditioned alpha blocking). Operant conditioning of attention is also possible. Certain kinds of activity, e.g., "mental arithmetic," will produce alpha blocking; in the feedback loop the subject may be reinforced for producing an attention response by the switching off of the lamp. Informal investigations of this possibility by Fowles (1962) show that subjects will produce longer and longer periods of attention when they are instructed to do so and when the lamp provides information about the effectiveness of their attempts.

Sleeping, Attention, and EEG

So far we have been concerned with the comparatively limited range of attention that we find in the waking state. Alpha frequencies are seen in relaxed wakefulness and beta waves in alertness. Increased alertness, up to a state of excitement, is accompanied by a loss of the wave shape in the EEG trace. This flattening is known as *desynchronization.* Looking at the EEG in states of decreasing attention, we find that in deep sleep there are large, low-frequency waves. In lighter states of sleep the waves become

more rapid and more shallow, shifting in this way to the alpha frequency in the relaxed waking state. The various frequencies found between deep sleep and desynchronization are given in Figure 4-13.

Psychopathology and EEG

Success in discovering relationships between brain injury and deviant EEG patterns, especially in the area of the epilepsies, raised hopes that similar relationships might be found between EEG phenomena and psychopathological states. In the gross sense, these investigations were based on the implicit belief that pathological behavior is determined by some dysfunction of the central nervous system. While the findings pertinent to different patterns of behavior pathology are discussed in the relevant chapters later in the book, we should note one or two general problems at this point.

Increased frequency and lowered amplitude of wave are, as we have seen, typical of a state of alertness. Any normal individual facing situational tension will produce this kind of frequency, and it is therefore to be expected in a patient who is chronically anxious or tense. Anxiety or tension is to be found in many patterns of psychopathology,

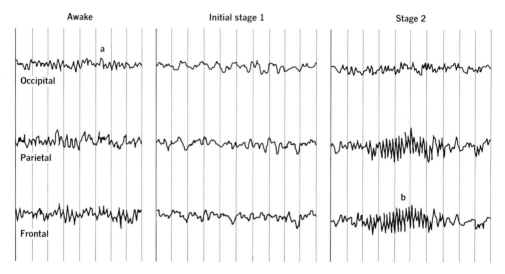

Figure 4-13. EEG frequencies between relaxation and deep sleep. In the first stage a resting subject shows the typical alpha pattern (a). With the onset of sleep (initial stage 1) a slowing is seen, moving to the deepest stage (stage 4). During deeper sleep the bursts of "sleep spindles" (b) are seen.

and thus this kind of EEG record is widely observed in many patients, both neurotic and psychotic.

Psychotic patients in a mental hospital tend, on the whole, to come from the lower socioeconomic strata of a community. Poorer physical health is more commonly found in the same population, and we should expect to find a higher incidence of almost any kind of bodily disorder than we find in a comparable group of people from higher economic levels. A sheer count of the number of EEG anomalies (including epilepsies) in a mental hospital population should, therefore, reveal a higher frequency of them than that found in the community at large.

Drugs affect the type of EEG trace that is to be found in the human. With the increasing use of tranquilizing drugs in hospital populations, a further complication is introduced into this kind of research. Likewise, metabolic changes associated with prolonged exposure to hospital diet and general hospital environment may interfere with straightforward interpretation of brain rhythms.

Bearing these factors in mind, we find that the data from *clinical* EEG is as yet of little use in diagnosing psychopathology. Hill (1950) has commented, "At present the practical value of electroencephalography for the psychiatrist is to enable him to know more about the organic cerebral disorder and little else." Techniques of deep electrode placement have, however, proved fruitful in conducting research into problems of attention and general emotional mechanisms in psychopathology, and it is in this context that the greatest progress may be made.

Brain Pathology and EEG

Any deviant wave form may be a basis for suspecting the presence of brain pathology in the subject. Certain kinds of cerebral malfunction are correlated with certain specific EEG phenomena, but there are many instances where the organic pathology produces abnormal EEG tracings of a nonspecific kind. Equally important is the fact that deviant or atypical EEG patterns are found in a percentage of the normal population. Thus the diagnosis of brain pathology from EEG alone is a rather uncertain procedure subject to some perceptible margin of error.

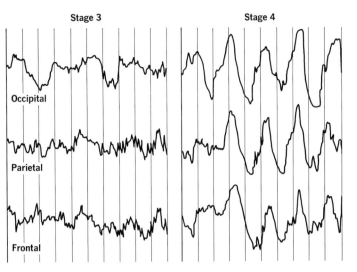

Stage 3   Stage 4

Occipital

Parietal

Frontal

We have already mentioned the emphasis that has been placed on EEG in the diagnosis of epilepsy. To complete our discussion of this topic, let us mention the better-known varieties of EEG abnormalcy. There are many possible variations of the normal rhythms of the EEG. Classification systems are not completely standardized either, but one of the more widely used is that developed at the Harvard Medical School by Gibbs, Gibbs, and Lennox (1943), sometimes called the "Harvard group." Four major categories of frequencies are used in this classification:

1. Paroxysmal. This includes five categories of pattern found in conjunction with epileptic seizures:
   a. Petit mal
   b. Petit mal variant
   c. Grand mal
   d. Spikes
   e. Psychomotor
2. Normal. Frequencies in the alpha and beta wave bands.
3. Slow.   S.1.   Theta activity
          S.2.   Delta activity
4. Fast.   F.1.   Activity of 14 to 20 cps
        F.2.   Activity of higher frequency than beta

Among the paroxysmal group, all but the spike frequency are named for their association with particular clinical types of epileptic seizure. Spike frequencies are seen in many kinds of epileptic record, but are also found in a variety of other anomalies. Like the slow- and fast-activity groups, the spike is generally regarded as evidence of some dysfunction, but is not specific to any one kind of pathology or to any one kind of behavioral manifestation. These frequencies are illustrated in Figure 4-14.

PUPILLOGRAPHY

An additional insight into the balance of the divisions of the autonomic nervous system may be obtained by studying the rate at which the pupil of the eye dilates and contracts under appropriate stimulation. When the intensity of illumination falling on the eye is increased, the pupil contracts—a response that is mediated largely by cholinergic activity. Reduction of light intensity results in pupillary dilation—an adrenergic response. By using controlled light intensities, it is possible to photograph the size of the pupil at different time intervals during either dilation or contraction and thus to

Brain Wave Patterns

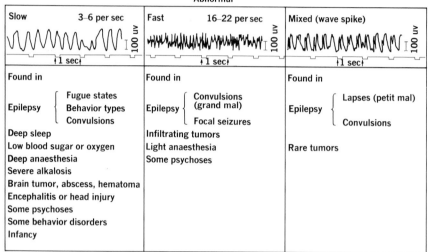

Normal		
Slow 9–11 per sec 100 uv ↑1 sec↑	Fast 18–24 per sec 100 uv ↑1 sec↑	Mixed type 100 uv ↑1 sec↑

Abnormal		
Slow 3–6 per sec 100 uv ↑1 sec↑	Fast 16–22 per sec 100 uv ↑1 sec↑	Mixed (wave spike) 100 uv ↑1 sec↑
Found in Epilepsy { Fugue states / Behavior types / Convulsions Deep sleep Low blood sugar or oxygen Deep anaesthesia Severe alkalosis Brain tumor, abscess, hematoma Encephalitis or head injury Some psychoses Some behavior disorders Infancy	**Found in** Epilepsy { Convulsions (grand mal) / Focal seizures Infiltrating tumors Light anaesthesia Some psychoses	**Found in** Epilepsy { Lapses (petit mal) / Convulsions Rare tumors

Figure 4-14. Summary table of the most frequent normal (alpha, beta, and mixed) and abnormal (slow, fast, and mixed) frequencies in the electroencephalogram. (Schwab, 1951.)

plot the rate at which these responses are occurring. From these data, individuals may then be compared with the norm for their age as to the rate of response. Over- or under-activity of the two divisions of the system may be identified and used as a basis for diagnosing pathology in one or both of them. Figure 4-15 shows typical pupil films obtained with this technique. In our later discussion of the biology of schizophrenia, we shall study some of the results that have been secured with pupillography.

AROUSAL AND ACTIVATION

When a stimulus impinges upon an individual, it has two kinds of effect. One of these is the *arousal* or *activation* of the subject; the other is the guiding or selective effect that the stimulus has upon the response that is made to it. The guiding effect

is contingent to a large extent upon past learning in relation to the stimulus. On the other hand, the more general effect of arousal is common to all stimuli and represents a nonspecific consequence of stimulation per se.

All states of activity of an organism might be graded along a dimension from complete

Figure 4-15. Sequence of dilation of human pupil under reduction of light stimulation. A pupillography measure. (Courtesy of Mildred Dubitzky.)

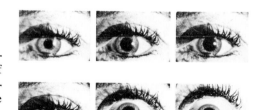

rest to maximum arousal. Deep sleep would thus constitute the lowest end of the arousal continuum, and the more aroused states would progress through light sleep up to wakefulness and then through various stages of tension and excitement. Arousal, as we are using it here, refers to a biological state of a living organism. While there are many correlations between the physiological measures of arousal and overt measures of behavior, these are not perfect. Consequently, we must emphasize that arousal is a *state* of the organism, and that the state of arousal is not always directly reflected in overt behavior. It is quite possible for a person to be highly aroused but be inactive from the viewpoint of an observer.

Measures of Arousal

Different investigators have tended to emphasize different measures of arousal. However, there is general acceptance of three measures:

1. Desynchronization of the EEG. We have already seen that when a stimulus occurs while a subject is producing alpha frequency in the EEG record, this frequency is blocked and gives way to beta waves. These beta waves are considerably less synchronized than the alpha frequency, i.e., they do not have the same regularity and smoothness that we find in alpha. For one group of investigators this *desynchronization* is a standard measure of arousal (e.g., Lindsley, 1959). As we shall see later, desynchronization may be obtained by stimulating certain parts of the central nervous system and may be eliminated by destroying these parts.

2. Palmar conductance. Measures of the electrical conductance of the surface of the palm of the hand indicate the amount of activity of sweat glands in that area. Palmar conductance is thus one of the measures related to similar techniques for recording skin resistance and skin potential.

3. Muscle tension. Muscular tension

has also been used as a measure of arousal, the recording being made in the manner described previously in the section on polygraphy.

While these three measures have been the major ones employed, the use of other signs of autonomic activity has been reported from time to time.[3] It will be apparent that the measures used to define arousal overlap considerably with those that have been used to define responses to stress. Indeed, the introduction of the concept of arousal would have nothing to offer the psychologist if it were simply another term to describe the pattern of bodily responses to external stimulation. Of much greater interest, however, is the relationship that has been demonstrated between measures of arousal and measures of behavior.

Arousal and Behavior

When talking about the relationship between stimulation and responses, we have confined ourselves so far to discussions of the effects of learning. Motivation has been discussed in terms of specific drives or needs, attributable to internal or external stimulation and determining what kinds of stimuli will be attended to in the environment. With the concept of arousal, we turn to consider the relationship between responses and a general state of the organism. In the sleeping state we find that measures of arousal and measures of organized overt behavior are both low. When we begin to increase the level of arousal of an organism, we find an increase in the efficiency of its behavior. "Efficiency" is not a simple question of the intensity of a response or the amount of sheer activity that we find in the subject. If we require a subject to respond as quickly as possible to the appearance of a light by pressing a button, the speed with which this is done is the measure of efficiency. If we

[3] An excellent summary of these is available in Bindra (1959).

require a complicated discrimination between many different kinds of lights, and speed of response is not essential, then the lack of error is our measure of efficiency. "Level of performance" is often used in lieu of "efficiency" as a descriptive term, and for our purposes here the two are interchangeable.

One of the simplest and clearest illustrations of the relationship between arousal and level of performance is provided in a study described by Malmo (1959) already mentioned in Chapter 3. As the experimental logic of this relationship is important in understanding the arousal concept, we shall describe it here. Rats which were deprived of water were tested for heart rate at different degrees of deprivation. The results were quite straightforward: As the amount of thirst increased, the heart rate of the animals increased. Using heart rate as a measure of arousal, the experimenters thus established the connection between the arousing condition (thirst) and a physiological measure of the arousal state (heart rate). Meantime the animals were placed in an operant chamber and received water by depressing a bar in the chamber—a standard operant situation. With increasing thirst, the rate of bar pressing went up, as we would naturally expect. This increase was observed up to 48 hours of deprivation; but at higher levels of thirst, the rate began to drop again. Thus although heart rate showed maximum arousal, response rate showed a decline. Figure 4-16 shows this relationship graphically.

In an experiment of this kind, there is the obvious possibility that high levels of thirst produce physical weakness in the animal and that this accounts for the decline in response rate. Control for this problem was provided by spacing each deprivation session between several days of ad lib. drinking. Further, the experimenters noted that there was little

Figure 4-16. Data from Belanger and Feldman showing curve of heart rate and bar pressing as a function of deprivation. (Cited by Malmo, 1959.)

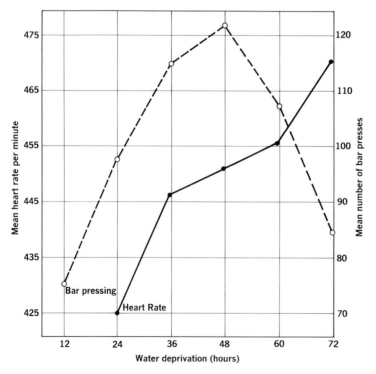

difference in weight across the various degrees of thirst.

The relationship between degree of stimulation, extent of arousal, and level of performance shown in Figure 4-16 is central to the concept of arousal as it relates to behavior. Workers in this field refer to it as an inverted-U curve, and it appears in many experiments and under many different conditions.

Arousal and Psychopathology

Detailed discussion of the relationships between arousal and behavior pathology is provided in later chapters. At this point it is interesting to note that much behavior pathology, especially of the severe kind, is marked by apathy, withdrawal, and general unresponsiveness to the outer environment. Venables and Wing (1962) studied the relationship of arousal (measured by skin potential) and behavioral withdrawal in chronic schizophrenics and found a close correlation in the expected direction. This is shown in Figure 13-8 (see Chapter 13). The curve presented there may be regarded as equivalent to the "low thirst" segment of the curve shown in Figure 4-16.

Central Arousal Mechanisms

When diverse stimuli have some effects in common, we are not surprised to find that they are "processed" by some common system within the organism. The very observation of the nonspecific arousing properties of so many different kinds of events leads us to look for some unitary structure or system which is affected the same way by all stimuli. Evidence now available suggests that the most likely candidate for this role is a complex group of structures within the central nervous system, known collectively as the *reticular activating system* (RAS). This system may be divided into two functional parts, one of which is called the *ascending* reticular activating system (ARAS). Stimuli received by the sense receptors of the subject not only are channeled to the appropriate sensory area of the brain but also have an additional route to the ARAS. While the structure of the ARAS is extremely complex, the main structures are the reticular formation of the medial brainstem, and parts of the hypothalamus and thalamus. Once received by this system, impulses are directed widely to all parts of the cortex. When they are received by the cortex, their function seems to be not to provide information about the specific stimulus which initiated the arousal (that information is discriminated at the primary sensory area), but more simply to keep the cortex active.

The second division of the reticular activating system is the *descending* system. Descending fibers in this system appear to inhibit or prevent incoming sensory impulses from getting to the sensory areas of the cortex. Several electrophysiologists have repeatedly demonstrated that in a condition of arousal produced by an external stimulus, sensory impulses from other kinds of stimulation are prevented from reaching the cortex. Loosely speaking, we might state that the effect of the descending components of the reticular system is to "damp down" other stimuli and thus facilitate selective attention to the initial arousal stimulus.

A schematic version of the operation of the reticular activating system is given in Figure 4-17.

Pathology and the RAS

Any tissue may become pathologically inactive or hyperactive. Accidental injury, pathological growths, toxic or infectious invasions, and so on may disrupt the normal functioning of an organ system. Should this happen to any of the structures included in the RAS, we can see that the resulting deviant behavior might include any gradation between pathologically low arousal to pathologically high arousal. Experimental evidence on this point has been presented by Lindsley (1959). He reports that lesions in the ARAS abolish the activation pattern of the EEG and are accompanied by lowered levels of motor activity. By the same token, electrical

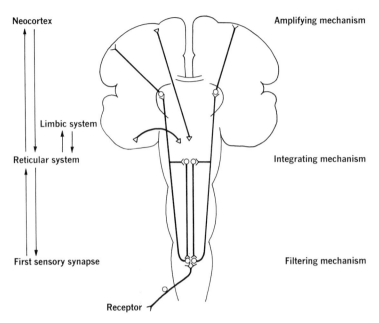

Neocortex

Limbic system

Reticular system

First sensory synapse

Receptor

Amplifying mechanism

Integrating mechanism

Filtering mechanism

Figure 4-17. Schematic representation of some of the main neuronal circuits involved in the transmission and integration of sensory impulses. (From Hernandez-Péon, 1961.)

stimulation of these areas produces the activation pattern of the EEG. Fuster (1958) adds evidence to the picture by showing that mild stimulation produces improved accuracy and speed of visual discrimination but that stronger stimulation is accompanied by slower reaction times and more errors.

In view of these phenomena, we can conclude that where behavior pathology is characterized by marked apathy, hyperactivity, or difficulties in the arousal and maintenance of attention, there is some reason to investigate the possibility that organic damage to the reticular system is involved. Equally obviously, the data presented at various points previously indicate that failure of a stimulus to produce arousal may well occur as a result of learning. A response of "tuning out" environmental stimuli is quite possible and would represent a logical extension of the processes involved in avoidance learning at the motor level.

Many arousal stimuli are internal. These include a range of events from autonomic sensory impulses to images and thoughts

presumably occurring at the cortical level. Intense preoccupation with thoughts and inner stimuli generally should lead to the kind of damping out of external stimulation that we described in our account of the functions of the descending reticular system. The normal person who is concentrating upon some mental activity is often oblivious to things happening around him—the extreme being the caricature of the absent-minded professor. Conversely, the student trying to work on a problem requiring concentrated mental activity may find that a loud radio blaring in the room prevents him from thinking effectively. We can see, therefore, that while a patient who is unresponsive to the events that are happening around him may be suffering from some organic disruption of the arousal mechanisms, he may on the other hand be intensely aroused by inner stimuli which are effectively making it impossible for him to attend to the external environment. Biological and psychological mechanisms may, and probably do, interact in many severe behavior disorders. The mode of operation of arousal that has been described gives a good example of how such interaction may take place.

A Summary Scheme of the Arousal-Behavior Relationship

We may describe the arousal-behavior relationship in the form of several propositions:

1. Internal and/or external stimulation produces a biological condition of arousal. The minimum level of arousal is deep sleep, and with continuous increase of arousal several measures may be made. Three main types are measures of EEG, autonomic responses, and muscle tension.

2. Beginning with low levels of arousal, increments are associated with improvements in level of performance up to a maximum, after which further arousal leads to a deterioration in performance.

3. In a condition of high arousal generated by a given source of stimulation, the organism is relatively insensitive to other sources of stimulation.

4. Central to the physiology of arousal is the reticular activating system. Direct stimulation, destruction, or inactivation of the RAS may lead to disruption in the power of other stimuli to produce arousal. Similar temporary effects may be produced by the action of some drugs.

5. There are individual differences in level of arousal and in the pattern of responses to arousing stimuli. The origin of these differences is unclear, but may involve genetic factors and/or organic pathologies.

6. Thresholds for arousal may be altered by learning, although we lack good empirical evidence on this point.

SUMMARY

In this chapter we have considered some fundamental patterns of biological reaction to stimulation and stress. Their relation to behavior, both normal and pathological, has also been examined. Although we have presented a simple account of some major

response systems, the reader will appreciate the enormous complexity with which all these systems may interact with each other and with external stimuli. This very complexity, which makes for great ranges of adaptive behavior, brings with it numerous possibilities for the development of malfunction. Many of these will be described later, especially in Chapters 13 and 17.

SUGGESTED READINGS

1. Bindra, D. *Motivation: a systematic reinterpretation.* New York: Ronald, 1959. This is a brief but significant and systematic application of concepts of arousal and activation to questions of the psychology of motivation. Chapter 8 is especially relevant to our discussion here.

2. Gellhorn, E., & Loofbourrow, G. N. *Emotions and emotional disorders.* New York: Hoeber-Harper, 1963. A detailed account of the physiology of emotional behavior, with special reference to psychopathology.

3. Selyé, H. *The stress of life.* London: Longmans, 1957. A simplified and relatively nontechnical account of the mechanisms of the general adaptation syndrome.

4. Sourkes, T. *Biochemistry of mental disease.* New York: Hoeber-Harper, 1962. A rather specialized textbook giving wide coverage to all the major biochemical problems and factors in the study of psychopathology.

REFERENCES

Ax, A. F. The physiological differentiation between fear and anger in humans. *Psychosom. Med.,* 1953, **15**, 433–442.

Berkun, M., Bialek, H., Kern, R., & Yagi, K. Experimental studies of psychological stress in man. *Psychol. Monog.,* 1962, **76**, 534.

Bindra, D. *Motivation: a systematic reinterpretation.* New York: Ronald Press, 1959.

Fowles, D. *Personal communication.* 1962.

Funkenstein, D. The physiology of fear and anger. *Science,* 1955, **192,** 74–76.

Funkenstein, D. H., Greenblatt, M., Rool, S., & Solomon, H. C. Psychophysiological study of mentally ill patients. II: Changes in the reactions to epinephrine and melcholyl after electric shock treatment. *Amer. J. Psychiat.,* 1949, **106,** 116–121.

Funkenstein, D. H., King, S. H., & Drolette, M. The experimental evocation of stress. *Symposium on Stress,* Army Medical Graduate School, Washington, D.C. 1953.

Fuster, J. M. Subcortical effects of stimulation of brain stem on tachistoscopic perception. *Science,* 1958, **127,** 150.

Gellhorn, E., and Loofbourrow, G. N. *Emotions and emotional disorders.* New York: Hoeber-Harper, 1963.

Gibbs, F. A., Gibbs, A. L., & Lennox, W. G. Electroencephalographic classification of epileptic patients and control subjects. *Arch. Neurol. Psychiat.,* 1943, **50,** 111–128.

Handlon, J. H. Hormonal activity and individual responses to stresses and easements in everyday living. In N. Greenfield & R. Roessler (Eds.), *Physiological correlates of psychological disorder.* Madison, Wis.: Univer. of Wisconsin Press, 1962.

Hill, D. Psychiatry. In D. Hill and G. Parr (Eds.), *Electroencephalography.* New York: Macmillan, 1950.

Jasper, H. H., & Shagass, C. Conditioning the occipital Alpha rhythm in man. *J. Exp. Psychol.,* 1941, **28,** 373–388.

Kaelbling, R., King., F. A., Achenbach, K., Branson, R., & Pasamanick, B. Reliability of autonomic responses. *Psychol. Rep.,* 1960, **6,** 143–163.

Kuntz, A. *The autonomic nervous system.* 3d Ed.) Philadelphia: Lea & Febiger, 1945.

Lacey, J. I. Individual differences in somatic response patterns. *J. comp. physiol. Psychol.,* 1950, **43,** 338–350.

Lacey, J. I., Bateman, D. E., & VanLehn, R. Autonomic response specificity. *Psychosom. Med.,* 1953, **15,** 10–21.

Levine, S. Emotionality and aggressive behavior in the mouse as a function of infantile experience. *J. genetic Psychol.,* 1959, **94,** 77–83.

Levine, S., & Lewis, G. W. Critical period for effects of infantile experience on maturation of stress response. *Science,* 1958, **129,** 42–43.

Lindsley, D. B. Psychophysiology and motivation. In M. R. Jones (Ed.), *Nebraska symposium on motivation.* Lincoln, Nebr.: Univer. of Nebraska Press, 1959.

McDonald, R. D., Yagi, K., & Stockton, E. Human eosinophil response to acute physical exertion. *Psychosom. Med.,* 1961, **23,** 63.

Malmo, R. B. Activation: a neuropsychological dimension. *Psychol. Rev.,* 1959, **66,** 367–386.

Malmo, R. B., & Shagass, C. Physiological study of symptom mechanisms in psychiatric patients under stress. *Psychosom. Med.,* 1949, **11,** 25–29.

Malmo, R. B., & Shagass, C. Studies of blood pressure in psychiatric patients under stress. *Psychosom. Med.,* 1952, **14,** 82–93.

Mulholland, T. *The electroencephalogram as an experimental tool in the study of internal attention gradients.* Paper presented to the N.Y. Academy of Sciences, New York City, March, 1962.

Porter, R. W., Brady, J. V., Conrad, D., Mason, J. W., Galambos, R., & Rioch, D. Mck. Some experimental observations on gastrointestinal lesions in behaviorally conditioned monkeys. *Psychosom. Med.,* 1958, **20,** 379–394.

Schwab, R. S. *Electroencephalography in clinical practice.* Philadelphia: Saunders, 1951.

Selyé, H. *The stress of life.* London: Longmans, 1957.

Venables, P. H., & Wing, J. K. Level of arousal and the subclassification of schizophrenia. *Arch. gen. Psychiat.,* 1962, **7,** 114–119.

Wenger, M. A., Jones, F. N., & Jones, M. H. *Physiological psychology.* New York: Holt, 1956.

Wilder, T. The law of initial value in neurology and psychiatry. *J. nerv. ment. Dis.,* 1957, **125,** 73–86.

5 RESEARCH METHODS IN PSYCHOPATHOLOGY

Research investigations into problems of psychopathology proceed in many different ways. Over the years the methods and techniques which have been used have developed to the point that it is possible to recognize certain common tactics and to consider their advantages and their limitations. Many factors influence an investigator in making his decision as to the research method which he applies to a particular problem. Practical considerations such as the availability of subjects, apparatus, time, and money often seem to play a major—and perhaps unfortunate—part in determining the form which a research study takes. The nature of the hypothesis to be tested should determine the procedure which is used. However, the difficulties of conducting research in a clinical setting are often formidable, and sometimes they seem to limit the kind of hypothesis which is investigated.

Let us first consider some fundamental problems which are met in drawing conclusions from research investigations. Then we can proceed to examine specific technical procedures.

SOME LOGICAL PROBLEMS IN RESEARCH

Exploration versus Hypothesis Testing

Our initial distinction between two general approaches to research is that between research which tests *deductive* hypotheses, and research which is designed for preliminary *exploratory* purposes. In the former case, the investigator states his hypothesis in precise, specific terms before proceeding with the experiment. His hypothesis is, in essence, a prediction about the kind of results he will get. It usually is deduced from some more general body of theory, and when the hypothesis is not confirmed by experimental results, it necessitates some change in the theory.

A very simple example of this is to be seen in a recent study by Chapman (1961). He investigated the hypothesis that psychotic behavior is related to the phases of the moon. In its general form this hypothesis has been widely held in common or folklore usage for many generations and it accounts for the original choice of the term "lunatic" to describe the psychopathological patient. From this belief we may deduce that measures of the phases of the moon should be correlated with measures of overt psychotic behavior. This deduction represents the specific hypothesis which is to be tested. Chapman's data indicate that there is no significant relationship between the two events, and the hypothesis thus fails to receive support.

The overwhelming majority of research investigations conform to this practice of testing deductive hypotheses—so much so that Hebb (1958) has been moved to protest:

Our current sophistication with respect to the design of experiments, statistically speaking, is a brilliant development of method without which we would be much better off. Hypothesis testing, and the compulsion on graduate students to present their thesis plans in such terms, is naive and a barrier to research. . . . No research gets done by the man who must do only the experiments that are beyond criticism.

These propositions may be overstated, but they are not entirely ridiculous. There are schools in which research cannot begin until the student has a plausible hypothesis to test. This is unwise for it rules out the study which starts with the question, "What would happen if I did so and so?" or with the feeling or hunch that there is something of interest to be found out in some particular area. A fertile investigation is more likely to end up with a hypothesis in testable form than to begin with one. The hypothesis, of course, can then be tested; I do not mean to deny that this is part of research. (Pp. 463–464.)

These remarks point up clearly the difference between research activities which are concerned with testing hypotheses and those which are conducted without a clear hypothesis but rather to explore problems and develop hypotheses. As a matter of fact, the difference between the two approaches is a matter of degree of precision and a question of how explicitly the investigator holds his hypothesis. When he decides to do something "to see what will happen," we may assume that he has some feeling that what he is doing will produce some noticeable result. Feelings or hunches may be regarded as loosely held hypotheses. The difference lies in the fact that in exploratory research, the investigator is more likely to observe everything which happens in his experiment, because he has not committed himself to recording only certain data.

Determinants versus Correlates

Another distinction which we must make is between research which attempts to answer such questions as "What is the effect of A?" and research which attempts to answer the question "What is the cause of B?" The logic of the first kind of research is relatively clear. The experimenter defines A, manipulates it in some way, and then looks for effects which were not present before A was introduced. This is the logic of experiments which seek to discover the effects of a particular kind of therapy upon pathological behavior or the effects of a drug upon some bodily function. Provided that adequate controls have been exercised to eliminate factors other than A which might be confusing the results, it is possible for the experiment to demonstrate a relationship between A and some effect (B). If repeated experiment confirms this finding, then we have a relationship which may be stated as a law governing the relationship between A and B, with A being a determinant of B.

In the second kind of research, however, the experimenter is faced with a rather difficult logical problem. If he discovers that B may be a consequence or effect of A in his experiment, he cannot conclude that every time we observe B it must have been produced by A. It is quite possible that B may be produced by a wide range of different factors of which A was only one. Human behavior represents the kind of phenomena which are particularly likely to arise from many different determinants, and thus this problem is especially acute in research into psychopathology. Drawing the conclusion that B is always produced by A is a logical fallacy which is known technically as *affirming the consequent.*

Research of the kind which asks "What is the cause of B?" is largely *correlational* in design, even though a superficial examination of the statistical procedures which are used might not suggest this to us. When we demonstrate that a group of patients differs from a group of nonpatient controls on some task or response, we have reported a correlation between one variable (patient versus nonpatient status) and another (the task performance). If we have established in the laboratory that brain injury leads to the same kind of performance as that shown by our patient group, we have demonstrated the possibility that our patients may be brain-injured. We have not proved it, and with this kind of design there is no way to prove it. However, every additional correlation which fits in with the hypothesis of brain injury may serve to increase our confidence in the possibility, and may increase our willingness to risk affirming the consequent.

As Sidman (1960) has pointed out, "Few

students in the elementary logic course have been told that affirming the consequent, despite its logical fallaciousness, is very nearly the life blood of science," for if we can show that every time we get B we also get other effects known to be produced by A, we increase our confidence in the hypothesis that B is an effect of A only. In the very nature of things, many of the important determinants of human behavior are not easily manipulated—for instance, the manner in which parents treat their children, or the accidental happening of distressing experiences. We may attempt to create these events in miniature form by using laboratory analogues—a procedure which is discussed later in this chapter. But when we turn to the human in his natural social environment, we are forced to draw our conclusions by accumulating evidence which will increase confidence in the *probability* that we have correctly identified the origin of the behaviors we are studying.

While this kind of evidence may never meet satisfactory criteria for proof in the way that laboratory investigations might, it nevertheless adds to our knowledge and provides a basis for deriving rational methods of treatment. In the final analysis, this is its major justification.

We may now consider particular tactics of research currently available to the psychopathologist.

Experimental Analogues

In its simplest form the *experimental analogue* involves the creation under controlled conditions of an event which is similar to a naturally occurring phenomenon, where our ultimate interest is in the natural phenomenon itself. Thus, if we are interested in hallucinations, we may seek to produce hallucinations in otherwise normal subjects under circumstances of considerable experimental control and precision. On the other hand, we may be interested not so much in artificially producing a particular kind of behavior, but in observing any of the effects of a certain kind of environment upon behavior. In this case we seek to create the desired environment either exactly or with some degree of similarity. We use the term experimental analogue here to indicate that we are studying phenomena which are deemed to be analogous to the focus of our ultimate inquiry. In this way we distinguish our investigations from those which observe the natural event directly. Let us first turn to the procedures which seek to produce behavior analogues.

Behavior Analogues. The most important purpose of procedures which are designed to produce specified kinds of behavior is that of generating hypotheses about the probable etiology of the behavior in the natural environment. If we can demonstrate, for example, that a particular drug will produce psychotic-like behavior in a normal person, we are in the logical position of having shown that a certain antecedent (the drug) produces a certain consequence (the psychotic behavior). We have not demonstrated that the same psychotic behavior in any individual must therefore be attributed to the presence of some organic process like that created by the action of the drug. However, the demonstration of the effects of the drug justifies us in looking for evidence of some such organic process in psychotic patients. Thus, we may say that the chief value of the analogue was in pointing up a hypothesis worth investigating by other means.

Before we can accept the hypothesis as valuable, two precautions are necessary. First, we must be satisfied that the psychotic behavior produced by the drug is the same as that which we observe in psychotic patients. Bearing in mind that the behavior of psychotic patients differs from one patient to another in many details, even though the gross diagnosis of all of them may be identical, we are concerned only that our experimentally produced behavior be psychotic in certain essential features. This in turn requires that the investigator define what the essential features are. As we have seen in an earlier chapter, this is by no means easy

to do, since there is considerable lack of agreement among psychopathologists themselves on the matter of definition of psychotic syndromes. Where the investigator is confining his studies to more specific forms of behavior or symptoms, such as hallucinations rather than psychoses, the problem of definition is considerably simpler.

The second precaution is that we must know the characteristics of the antecedent which we used to produce the behavior. If we do not understand the nature of the organic action of the drug, we emerge from the study without a testable hypothesis about the organic processes which might be operating in psychotic patients. Where the antecedent was a special kind of environment rather than a drug or similar organically operating agent, the same principle applies. Investigations of fearful or anxious behavior, for example, may use laboratory-produced conflicts to generate the desired symptoms. From such studies it is only possible to arrive at hypotheses about conflicts in the natural environment when the investigator has defined the features which a situation must have in order to be classed as a conflict.

Behavior analogues of this kind should not be confused with research techniques where the aim of the investigation is to study some characteristics of the behavior itself. Pathological behavior may be produced under experimental control so that the investigator can observe and measure some aspects of the behavior without having to wait for a patient to exhibit it spontaneously. Although superficially similar to the analogue method, this procedure should be distinguished from it because of the difference in purposes.

Situation Analogues. Clinical or other naturalistic observations of pathological behavior may suggest an etiological hypothesis to the astute clinician. For example, he might become impressed by what appear to be certain similarities in the life histories of patients who exhibit similar symptoms. Or he might develop a hypothesis from study of a single case only. Whatever its origin, the hypothesis may ultimately be formulated as a statement that certain antecedent conditions seem to be sufficient to lead to a specified kind of pathological behavior. Hypotheses of this kind may be investigated in several ways. Practical problems often make it difficult, if not impossible, to create the necessary antecedents in the natural social environment of normal people. One possibility is to create the necessary environment in some brief miniature form in a research setting. If we then note the reliability between the environment which we have created and the occurrence of the behavior, our hypothesis receives support. Our confidence in the hypothesis is, however, dependent upon the success with which our brief miniature situation meets the definition of the antecedent which had been noted clinically, and upon the extent to which the laboratory behavior of the subject resembles that of the original clinical patients.

It will be readily apparent that the chief difference between behavior analogues and situation analogues as we have described them is that in the case of behavior analogues, the reverse sequence applies.

Subject Analogues. A third approach to the creation of laboratory analogues of psychopathology is in the use of animals. The basic assumption underlying the use of animals in psychopathological research is that it is possible to generalize from animal to human behavior (although we should note that comparative psychologists have a legitimate interest in unusual behavior in animals as a branch of knowledge in its own right). Many students of human (and animal) behavior will not grant this assumption. The objections are many. Harlow (1953) has commented that "the results from the investigation of simple behavior may be very informative about even simpler behavior but very seldom are they informative about behavior of greater complexity." Pointing to the differences between human beings, who possess language, and animals,

which do not, Hilgard (1948) remarked, "A price is always paid for the convenience of a given approach to a problem. The price to be paid for overmuch experimentation with animals is to neglect the fact that human subjects are brighter, are able to use language—and probably learn differently because of these advances over lower animals" (p. 329).

The essence of these objections is clear. Man is a more complex organism than the animal, and the possession of language makes the complexity one not only of degree but of kind. Where animal data are advanced as "proof" of hypotheses about human psychopathology, then the foregoing objections seem to be irrefutable. Granting this, the justification for animal studies in relation to problems of human behavior has been stated simply by Hebb and Thompson (1954):

"Finding that a psychotic behaves in a certain way does not prove anything about normal persons, but no one would argue from this that clinical studies have not helped in our understanding of the normal. In principle the study of animals has exactly the same status . . . animal experiments may clarify a human problem without 'proving' anything. It may draw attention to facets of human behavior one has not noticed; it may point to a troublemaking but implicit assumption; it may suggest a new principle of behavior. . . . But in all these cases, the relevance of animal work is strictly dependent on whether, when applied to man, it does clarify the human problem" (Hebb & Thompson, 1954, pp. 532–533).

We might summarize the situation by stating that while animal experiments cannot themselves confirm hypotheses about human behavior, their usefulness in clarifying problems makes them valuable as a research tactic.

A more troublesome problem encountered in using animals is the greater difficulty in producing adequate behavior and situation analogues. It is not at all certain that anything akin to human schizophrenic behavior can be detected in lower animals, or that physical punishment of a rat with electric shock is analogous to a mother scolding a child. One partial solution lies in seeking analogies at a more general level than that of specific symptomatic behavior. We can produce behavior in a laboratory animal which is perceptibly deviant or abnormal in a gross sense, and we may want to compare this with human behavior classified also in such broad terms as "abnormal" or "pathological." More precise analogies are difficult to create.

Summary. The experimental analogue has an important place in the array of tactics available to the researcher in any behavioral field. We may agree with Cowen (1961) in remarking that the major potential contributions of the analogue method are "(a) more rigorous control of extraneous variables, (b) greater refinement of experimental design and (c) greater breadth and precision of measurement of relevant critical functions." The limitations of the analogue method have already been described and may be recapitulated briefly as (1) the difficulty of ensuring that the analogue— either subject, situation, or behavior—shares the essential characteristics of the natural event, and (2) the ultimate necessity of confirming hypotheses in the natural environment.[1]

Clinical Investigation

Some methods of investigation in psychopathology are referred to as *clinical* methods, or as *the clinical method* when considered

[1] We are concerned here only with the *tactical* use of the experimental analogue in the study of psychopathology. Philosophers of science have pointed out that the question whether two objects or phenomena are analogous is empirical. Keynes (1921), for example, has remarked that when the same law is true for several objects or phenomena, then these objects may be said to be analogous with respect to the law concerned. Thus it may not be possible to conclude that an experimental analogue is a valid one until the naturally occurring events have also been measured and shown to obey the same laws.

collectively. The definition of clinical method is somewhat vague, and we shall therefore attempt to identify certain separate procedures which may be loosely classified as clinical. We must recognize, however, that there is a lack of precision in our terms.

Casual Clinical Observation. A clinician dealing with a particular patient may be struck by the fact that the patient's life history possessed some unusual features. He may wonder whether there is a connection between the patient's present behavior and these earlier events in his life. When another patient comes along with the same kinds of behavior, the clinician may decide to see if he can find evidence of the same kind of life history. If he does not find this evidence, he may lose interest in his earlier hunch; if he does find it, he may become more attached to his original hypothesis. Should he find this relationship in several more patients, he may become convinced that his hypothesis is correct and that for his purposes it has now been confirmed. Apart from using this hypothesis in his daily clinical activities, our clinician may publish his conclusion as a general principle or minor "law" of psychopathology.

This kind of observation has a long tradition behind it in the field of psychopathology. In its preliminary stages it is identical with the procedure of natural observation which has led to the development of hypotheses in every branch of science. As a method of *confirming* hypotheses, it has several serious defects. The most serious problem is that of objectivity on the part of the observer. It is of prime importance that the techniques used to evaluate the patient's past history be of a kind that would produce the same results if used by another clinician. It is also vitally important that the techniques do not vary from one patient to another and that the material obtained from the patient is not reinterpreted by the clinician simply to fit the data to the hypothesis. Data may, of course, be interpreted, recoded, or transformed in any systematic fashion, provided that all data obtained from all patients treated in the same way.

Exactly the same cautions apply to the evaluation of the patient's current behavior. As an additional control it is usually necessary that the clinician who observes and rates the behavior of the patient not be informed beforehand of the patient's history, a precaution which eliminates the risk that such knowledge might bias his observations. Control of bias in this way usually means that the clinician who takes the case history data is not involved in the behavior observation. When these precautions are adopted, however, it is obvious that we have departed from the procedure of *casual* clinical observation and are now engaged in some form of *controlled* clinical observation.

A second problem which arises from clinical observation is that we are limited to observing correlated events with no guarantee that there is any causal relationship between them. As we have seen in the discussion of experimental analogues, the experimental method permits the investigator to manipulate the environment in predetermined ways and to determine the effect of these manipulations upon the subject's behavior. In clinical observation we are limited to observing relationships between the patient's present behavior and his statements about his past experiences and environment. The status of such relationships as laws within a psychological theory is a complex problem which lies beyond the scope of the present discussion. A thorough presentation of the issues is available elsewhere (Spence, 1944). Suffice it to say at this point that correlational laws are generally shadowed with the possibility that the event which is presumed to be the determinant of the behavior may be mainly a consequence of some undiscovered determinant responsible for both of the events which we have correlated.

Controlled Clinical Investigation. Hypotheses generated by casual clinical observation may be developed further by clinical observation and measurement under controlled conditions. An initial step in proceeding from casual to controlled observation involves the *operationalizing* of the hypothesis. A casually formed hypothesis may be stated in some form such as "All depressive patients have a history of excessive early emphasis upon moral values." Before this hypothesis can be submitted to investigation under conditions of control, it is necessary that we define precisely what we mean by "depressive," "excessive early emphasis," and "moral values." The definitions must be both explicit and stated in such a fashion that someone else could repeat the observations with high reliability. We may decide that depressive behavior can be catalogued in some way, and thus our definition may develop into a checklist or rating list which records the presence or absence of many specific kinds of response in the patient. Identical steps would be taken with respect to the other terms in the hypothesis, so that someone reading over the case history could identify whether or not the patient met the defined requirements for a history of excessive early emphasis upon moral values.

Armed with these definitions, the investigator can now proceed to record the behavior of patients and to codify their case histories in order to determine empirically the extent of the hypothesized relationship. The most common design of this kind of research involves the comparison of the experimental group (the group about which our hypothesis was formed) with one or more control groups. The control group is selected for its similarity to the experimental group in every respect except the presence of the pathology under study. Thus, such variables as age, education, sex, intelligence, socioeconomic status, etc., are commonly considered when the groups are equated. It is equally important that certain other variables be controlled, especially those which may be correlated with the pathology, such as hospitalization. Behavior and case history analyses of the control group members proceed in identical manner to those used with the experimental group. As an additional control against observer bias, the observers or raters are usually unaware of which group a patient belongs to until all the ratings and measurements have been made.

Finally, the observed relationship between history and behavior in the experimental group is compared with that found in the control group. If it is greater in the experimental group than in the control group, according to some criterion of acceptable statistical significance, the hypothesis may be substantiated. If the hypothesis simply stated a relationship, then the demonstration of the relationship confirms it. On the other hand, if the hypothesis identified the early experience as being the *determinant* of the pathology, the hypothesis is not yet confirmed, although it may be regarded as more plausible by virtue of the results of the investigation.

Curiously enough, the criticisms of this method have come with almost equal vigor from the clinical and experimental wings of psychology. From the clinical practitioner comes the complaint that explicit definitions of pathological behavior are usually too narrow and superficial, lacking the full meaning of the concepts with which he finds it convenient to work. Meehl (1954) describes this position in his reference to the clinician who, when asked for the evidence of some diagnostic predictive or postdictive statement he has just made about a patient, "states simply that he feels intuitively that such-and-such is the case. 'My third ear tells me . . .' or 'I don't know, but I feel very strongly about this patient that. . . .' 'He gives me kind of a schizy feeling.' " In a word, the hypothetical clinician may argue that he really cannot make his own definitions explicit, and that if he is compelled to do so they will necessarily fail to communicate adequately the nature of his "intuitive" definitions. The position is tantamount to asserting that, in the very nature of things, it will be impossible to arrive at a systematic understanding of pathological behavior because the essentials are revealed only to a clairvoyant clinician with uncommunicable talents.

Experimental psychologists, who in their own investigations have achieved remarkable degrees of direct control of environmental variables, sometimes object to controlled clinical observation on the grounds that it is impossible to get sufficient control of the relevant variables to justify drawing firm conclusions. Many individual studies have indeed been performed and reported which suffer from serious methodological weaknesses, especially in the matter of equating the experimental and control groups. However, errors of this kind do not compel us to conclude that control is inherently impossible, but merely that it is difficult.

In spite of these criticisms, the method of controlled clinical observation is one of the most frequent research tactics of the experimentally minded clinician. It will feature prominently in our later accounts of research which has been conducted into problems of psychopathology.

The Idiographic-Nomothetic Controversy

Following the lead of Allport (1937), some clinical psychopathologists have argued for a distinction between *idiographic* and *nomothetic* methods in the study of personality. Originally the distinction was proposed by the philosopher Windelband (1904). He suggested that there is a basic difference between the intellectual foundations of the social sciences and the natural sciences, the distinction being based upon the kind of knowledge gained within the two areas. As we shall see shortly, the distinction is to a large extent artificial, but when originally proposed it included several general propositions about the idiographic method:

1. The idiographic method aims at formulating laws or principles that will enable us to predict the behavior of a particular individual, even though the same principles may be invalid for some other individual. **2.** Where such prediction is not possible, the idiographic method seeks to develop a set of explanatory principles for *understanding* the behavior of the personality—this being differentiated from the goal of predicting it.

3. Intuition is regarded as a form of knowledge in its own right, having equal significance to that obtained by empirical methods.

Many other implications have been drawn by idiographically minded psychopathologists. One of the major ones is that since each new case is unique, the attempt to apply principles which had utility in a previous similar case will lead to confusion. In this sense the idiographic psychologist is, presumably, facing the necessity of discovering new laws for each person, and also of realizing that his conclusions have no value for work with any other person.

Let us look at some examples of idiographic and nomothetic methods.

Nomothetic All students who have had no mathematics background fail physics.
Smith has had no mathematics courses. Hence he will fail physics.

While the prediction is about a particular individual—Smith—it is based directly upon a general nomothetic proposition that has been demonstrated, presumably empirically.

Idiographic Judging by the content of the play *Hamlet,* William Shakespeare had problems relating to the Oedipal situation.

From this kind of statement, which is an inference from limited sampling of specific behavior, it is difficult to know what to predict about Shakespeare. We might predict (*a*) that if we find out some facts about his personal history, they will reveal other behaviors which are indicative of Oedipal problems, or (*b*) that if we look at his other plays, we shall see mother-son relations depicted in a way which is congruent with the Oedipal hypothesis. However, before we can even formulate the notion of an Oedipus problem, it must have been defined by similar behaviors seen in other people. Clearly, we have simply applied a nomothetic statement to a particular case—Shakespeare—in a manner that does not differ logically from the previous statement about Smith.

Careful consideration of this kind of distinction suggests that the difference is not one of logic, but of the specificity of the prediction that is being made. Let us consider the statement "When a goal response is frustrated, the subject becomes aggressive." This principle is stated in general terms, i.e., it does not specify what kind of aggressive behavior will occur when a particular goal response is frustrated in a particular way. If I know a certain person well, I may have observed that frustration generates bad language on his part, while his neighbor reacts with physical violence. Both of these responses are in line with the basic principle, but with additional observations I have been enabled to make a prediction about the specific kinds of aggressive action that will be elicited. Likewise, if I know that a person is hungry and is given food, he will eat it. If he is given a choice of foods, I do not know what he will eat unless I have more information about the person and his tastes. My prediction may also be much more accurate if I happen to know that this person has been punished in the past for eating so that when hungry, he shows conflict responses, not simple eating. But this observation is essentially nomothetic also—namely, that when the same response has been rewarded and punished, conflict will be seen. Close knowledge of the particular case in which a prediction is to be made permits more accurate selection of the nomothetic principles that should be applied and more specific predictions of the nature of the response that will be made. It does not involve the derivation of new principles, nor could it lead to principles that would be invalid when applied to another case, provided that the new case was truly identical in all important respects to the first.

For instance, if I happen to begin the study of hunger by observing the man who becomes conflicted in the presence of food, then I might advance the "law" that hunger produces conflict. When I test this on the next case, I find that no conflict occurs. Now I can respond to this difficulty by concluding (*a*) that all people are unique and thus we must construct new sets of laws for each one, or (*b*) that there is some crucial difference between the two cases and that I will be able to amend my "law" to be more specific when I have found out what this difference is.

The idiographic method serves exactly the same purpose as the clinical method—namely, to provide the material upon which hypotheses may be developed for later testing. When the hypothesis is not confirmed in the next case, then the appropriate response is to advance new hypotheses capable of accounting for both observations, and to proceed to test them. To conclude that the initial hypothesis is somehow correct and that it may be upheld while a new hypothesis is found which is applicable only to the second case is simply sloppy thinking.

On the positive side, the chief value of the idiographic method is in applied work. It may be very necessary to know whether a particular patient will respond to frustration with physical violence or with sarcasm. General propositions that he will respond with aggression may be valid but valueless at this point. In order to build a bridge over a certain river, we must know the details of the soil mechanics, water flow, prevailing winds, topography, traffic usage, availability of labor and materials, and so on. When we consider all these, the total picture might not be like any other bridge that has ever been built. Nevertheless, none of the principles or assumptions that go into the final decisions could be made in contradiction to the laws of physics, economics, and the like.

In the study of psychopathology, the greatest need is for nomothetic principles. Idiographic applications will probably be more impressive when they are shown to rest on firm nomothetic bases, not when they are applied simply because they have convinced the user of their elegance and of his own sensitivity.

Cluster Analysis

The method of controlled clinical observation described in the preceding paragraphs is, as we have seen, essentially correlational. That is, it ultimately produces evidence of a correlation (or lack of correlation) between two sets of events, one of these being the clinical aspects of the patient's behavior and the other being some previous experiences which the patient has had. However, we have noted the necessity of a prior definition of the behavior with which we are concerned. Such a definition may be given rather arbitrarily by the researcher and may arise largely from his own experience. Whether or not certain patterns of behavior occur together in patients, or in people generally, is itself a matter for empirical research. In practical terms, the investigator may wish to know if patients who hallucinate also tend to be delusional; do hallucinations and delusions constitute a syndrome? If so, what other symptoms are included in the syndrome?

Brief reflection on this problem will indicate that the questions which have been asked are questions about correlations. The specimen questions which we have used may be rephrased as "Are symptoms A and B correlated?" Thus, we find a body of research procedures which are devoted mainly to discovering correlations of this kind, with the ultimate intention of identifying several basic patterns of pathological behavior.[2] Each pattern would include highly correlated symptomatic behaviors and would have little correlational overlap with other patterns. Several different statistical procedures are available for this kind of analysis, but for the sake of convenience we may classify them all as methods of *cluster analysis,* or the analysis of behaviors which tend to occur in correlated clusters.

Objectivity in recording the behaviors which are to be correlated with each other

[2] For more detailed accounts of these methods the reader is referred to du Mas (1956), McQuitty (1959), or Guertin (1961).

is the major requirement in this kind of investigation. The investigator may have no specific hypothesis in view when he collects his data, other than the very general hypothesis that some kind of consistent clusters will be found. His observations may be extended to include material about the patients which is not readily seen in their spontaneous behavior. He might record responses to a psychological test, physiological measures, and so forth. Out of these data there may emerge one or more discernible clusters. Inspection of these clusters may then lead to hypotheses about their probable origins, or the future course of development (or prognosis) and suitable methods for changing the undesirable behavioral components of the clusters. Hypotheses which are developed in this way are, of course, matters for separate investigation by other methods.

Experimental Psychology

Psychopathologists have taken many of their research techniques from the experimental psychological laboratory. Specifically, they have applied those methods which involve placing the subject in a stimulus situation which is under the control of the experimenter and measuring the subject's responses in a quantitative fashion. One feature of the experimental laboratory has been missing from the work of experimental psychopathologists. They generally confine their research to the comparison of responses produced by different groups of patients, where the differences between the groups existed prior to the experiment. In contrast, many laboratory studies within the field of experimental psychology commence with subjects who are similar and then attempt to generate differences between them within the laboratory itself. Provided that all the necessary controls have been exercised, the experimental psychologist is in a position to describe the determinants of the behavioral differences which he produced between his groups of subjects in the laboratory. Experimental psychopathologists, on the other

hand, are dealing with groups of subjects who differ from each other, where the determinants of these differences were operating long before the subjects entered the experiment. Often the purpose of the psychopathologist's laboratory experiment is to test a deduction made from a hypothesis about the determinants of the differences between the groups.

Generally speaking, laboratory studies of pathological subjects that employ techniques taken from experimental psychology are directed toward the testing of certain kinds of problems. Some of these are examined below.

Related Nonpathological Behaviors. Starting with clinical observation, the psychopathologist may develop a hypothesis about the motivational state of a certain class of patients. For example, it may appear plausible that autistic behavior in certain schizophrenic patients represents a way of avoiding social interaction. Social interaction is thus hypothesized to be threatening to the patient. From this we might predict that the schizophrenic patient will respond differently to some social stimuli than will the nonschizophrenic. In the laboratory these stimuli are presented and the responses of the pathological group compared with those of the controls to see if the prediction is confirmed. If it is, then we have discovered another behavior which is correlated with clinical schizophrenic behavior patterns. The laboratory behavior might, however, be regarded as nonpathological in that it has no maladaptive or bizarre features in itself.

The chief advantage of this kind of research is that, apart from providing an empirical correlation, it has rendered more plausible a hypothesis which refers to pathological behaviors as aspects of a total pattern of determinants; and these determinants are open to investigation in more controlled circumstances. To use the example of the previous paragraph, we might find support for the belief that the major determinants of schizophrenic behavior are motives to avoid social stimuli. As we can study avoidant behavior in normal subjects under conditions of control, we increase the justification for applying the results of such experiments to understanding schizophrenic behavior. Thus the long-run effect of our psychopathological research is to bring a pattern of responses called "schizophrenia" under the broader domain of "avoidant" behavior and to enable us to understand pathological behavior with the aid of general psychological laws. Many illustrations of this kind of research approach are reported in Chapter 14.

Related Pathological Behaviors. The determinants of certain kinds of pathological behaviors are well known. Organically produced disorders are examples of this. Some investigators consider the possibility that other patterns of behavior pathology may also be organically determined although the nature of the organic process is not apparent. One approach to this question is to demonstrate in the psychological laboratory that although the gross clinical pictures may not be similar, patients with a known organic condition produce some responses which resemble those of patients suffering from the as yet unexplained disorder. In order for this demonstration to support the hypothesis, it is necessary that the response which is examined be one which has already been shown to differentiate between patients with known organic pathology and patients known to be free of it. If the demonstration can be made, it lends support to the notion that the unexplained disorder is a special case of an organic disorder. The study of Saucer and Deabler (1956), reported in Chapter 14, provides an illustration of this procedure.

Response to Treatment Conditions. Perhaps the most clear-cut application of the methods of experimental psychology to problems of psychopathology is in the study of the outcomes of methods of treatment. Here, the experimenter compares the effects of one or more treatment methods with each other, or with the effect of no treatment, upon patients who all presented the same pretreatment behaviors. The patients are assigned randomly to treatments much as an experimental psychologist assigns his subjects to various laboratory conditions. Changes in posttreatment behavior are then compared to determine the consequences of the therapy. Systematic changes which appear permit us to conclude that the therapy was a determinant and not just a correlate of the behavior change—provided that all the usual controls for other effects have been exercised. These controls include control over the behavior of the therapist in order to make sure that the treatments which we assign to our patients really do differ between the groups and do not differ within any one group. In contrast to the conclusions possible in the other approaches which have been described, conclusions which emerge from these studies are not in the form of correlations.

The major problems in research on therapy are technical rather than logical. Ensuring adequate control over the therapeutic conditions is extremely difficult, and by the same token it is not easy to ensure that patients assigned to different therapies are equated on all the relevant variables. Robbins and Wallerstein (1959) have provided a succinct outline of the variables which require either measurement, control, or manipulation in research on psychotherapy. They may be summarized as follows:

1. *Patient variables.* The ways in which patients entering therapy may differ from each other are probably infinite. However, a gross classification of them could include:
   a. Sex, age
   b. Behavioral symptoms or responses
   c. Nature of conflicts; determinants of behavior
   d. Methods of dealing with conflict problems
   e. Resources — intelligence, education, etc.

f. Motivations for treatment—fee paid, secondary gain from being a patient

g. Environmental factors outside therapy —reactions of family, physical health, etc.

2. *Treatment variables*

a. Major technical aspects; method used, e.g., suggestion, manipulation, clarification, etc. The theoretical orientation of the therapist

b. Topics raised in therapy, past history, dream and fantasy material, behavior during therapy sessions, etc.

c. Goals in therapy—changing behavior, reducing distress, etc.

d. Coincidental events in patient's life outside therapy

e. Method of termination; causes of termination in therapy

3. *Environmental variables*

a. Background—religion, cultural influences, etc.

b. Pattern of relationships in family, at work, etc.

c. Marital and sexual relationships

d. Living arrangements—financial, space, and other problems

e. Occupation—status, stability, leisure time, etc.

f. Recreational activities, hobbies, community interests

g. Handicaps of physical ability or appearance

The above list is rather more suggestive than complete, but it may help to illustrate the enormous complexity of factors which must be taken into account when research in psychotherapy is designed. Many of the variables are hard if not impossible to control. This is especially true in the case of the environmental factors listed.

Where control is not possible, the experimenter is faced with the problem of measuring each factor. This brings with it the necessity of ensuring that the method of measurement is reliably free from bias on the part of the observer who is doing the

measuring. For many reasons the therapist himself is not well suited to play the part of observer, and thus this kind of research usually takes the form of independent assessment of improvement, behavior in therapy, and the like. For a thorough discussion of methods of this type, the reader is referred to Rubinstein and Parloff (1959).

Experimental Treatments. Some investigations of response to treatment are concerned with the effects of treatments which were developed from studies of changes in normal behavior rather than from clinical observation. From the framework of general learning theory, we may wish to study the effects of particular kinds of reinforcement upon the intensity of the frequency of overt psychotic responses. The research design for this kind of investigation does not differ logically from any other already described above, and presents no special problems.

From the foregoing, it will be clear that simple reports of the number of patients described as "cured" or "improved" following a particular course of treatment are of no scientific value in themselves and cannot be regarded as contributions to our knowledge of psychopathology. Reports of this kind may, however, serve to generate hypotheses about the possibility that the treatment is significantly better than no treatment. Such hypotheses may then be tested in more adequate fashion.

Before going on to consider biological methods in the study of psychopathology, see Box 5-1 for a summary of the tactics available to researchers in both clinical and experimental psychopathology.

Biological Methods

For some patterns of pathological behavior, definite biological factors have been isolated. Illustrations of these are to be found in our description of the toxic psychoses, paresis, and other organic syndromes. Success in discovering biological bases for behavior

Method	Data source	Measure	Product
Casual clinical observation	Single case, or a few un-selected cases of a phe-nomenon	Unquantified description	Crude hypothesis
Controlled clinical observation	Pathological group and one or more control groups, behaving in nat-ural setting	Coded and quanti-fied behavior rat-ings	Correlational conclusion; strengthened and more precise hypothesis
Related behaviors (pathological and nonpath-ological)	Laboratory investigations of responses to controlled situations, in pathological and control groups	Quantified measures of responses	Same as above
Experimental analogue	Subjects, situations, and re-sponses regarded as ana-logues to psychopatho-logical instances	Same as above	Antecedent-consequent re-lationship established for laboratory analogue; hy-pothesis developed for psychopathological phe-nomenon
Treatment investigation	Behavior during and after treatment	Behavior measures during treatment; pre- and post-treatment behavior comparisons	Antecedent-consequent re-lationships for therapy variables established

pathology has encouraged investigators to continue the search for similar origins in other behavior pathologies. Research of this kind utilizes several tactical approaches which we shall consider here.

Discovery of Organic Pathology. One of the more obvious approaches for the bio-logical researcher is to seek for some causative physical agent, following the same tactics that are common in medical research generally. The investigator may be guided by some specific hypothesis about the organic origins of the psychopathology or may simply investigate a very large number of physiological systems in his patients in the hope of turning up differences between patients and nonpatients in some of them. In general, the problems which are met in this kind of research do not differ logically from those encountered in psychological research of an experimental kind. It is, for example, equally necessary for the investiga-

tor to ensure that his patients and his con-trols differ only with regard to psycho-pathology and do not differ also with regard to such variables as age, duration of hospi-talization, frequency of other physical dis-abilities or diseases, and so forth.

However, the biological investigator may, within certain limits, validate his conclusions in a manner which is not normally available to the psychologist. Where the initial in-vestigation leads the biologist to isolate a substance present in his patients but not in his controls, he may hypothesize that this substance is the determinant of the patho-logical condition—and may predict that if the substance is introduced into a normal subject, the latter will exhibit symptoms similar to those found in patients. If this turns out to be the case, the hypothesis would gain considerable support. Finally, it may be possible to eliminate the pathogen from the patient by physical means (drugs, surgery, or other procedures). Should this be followed by disappearance of the behavioral symptoms, the hypothesis would be supported with relatively little margin of doubt.

Sometimes the investigator may study the effect of the pathogen upon the behavior of animals. In this case, the aim is to observe the occurrence of patterns of response in the animals which may be analogous to the pathological behavior of the human patient. At this point it is clear that we are again dealing with an experimental analogue, which brings with it the problem of recognizing behavior in the animal subject which can legitimately be regarded as analogous to that of the human. In practice, most investigations of this kind are limited to demonstrating the occurrence of some disorganization in the animal's behavior, regardless of its similarity to human pathological behavior.

Investigation of Therapeutic Processes. Physical or somatic therapies for pathological behavior may develop accidentally, or *nonrationally*. That is to say, clinical observation may indicate that the therapy is effective, while the therapist may not yet have discovered the manner in which the therapy achieves its effects. Beginning with this kind of phenomenon, the researcher may first attempt to discover the way in which the therapy affects the bodily processes of the patient. Once this is understood, it can provide the basis for hypothesizing about organic etiologies for the disorder. These hypotheses can then in turn be investigated in the manner described in the preceding paragraphs.

A good example of this procedure is to be seen in the historical development of *electroconvulsive therapy* (ECT). At the present time there is no agreement on the manner in which the shock and subsequent coma produce improvement in depressed patients. However, a considerable number of hypotheses have been offered, each tending to emphasize some aspect of the organic changes brought about by the shock. Thus Kalinowsky and Hoch (1949) report that

Stief, on the basis of histopathological examinations, formulated the hypothesis that convulsive therapy produces spasms in the brain capillaries which eliminate diseased nerve cells—and thus bring about a reaction in pathological behavior. Here we can see that a hypothesis about the operation of the shock treatment generates another hypothesis about the *origins* of the disorder. In this case the new hypothesis—that the pathological behavior is determined by the presence of diseased neurons—has not been well supported by evidence from histological studies of the brains of patients.

Physiological Psychology. One of the major interests of some psychologists is the discovery of the relationships between bodily functions and behavior in the normal organism. This area of investigation and the body of knowledge which has been developed from it is usually referred to as *physiological psychology*. While there are many techniques available to the physiological psychologist, they tend to possess certain common characteristics.

1. Deactivation techniques. In order to study the part which is played by a particular organ or system, the investigator may render it inactive either permanently or temporarily while noting the changes in behavior which follow his operations. Destruction of parts of the nervous system, temporary immobilization of muscle groups, and tissue changes brought about pharmaceutically would all represent instances of this kind of research approach.

2. Direct stimulation techniques. Another method used in physiological psychology involves the application of direct stimulation to tissue by electrical, mechanical, or chemical means. In this approach, the experimenter usually does not wish to destroy the tissue which he is stimulating. Behavior changes are recorded concomitantly and conclusions drawn about the normal functions of the stimulated area.

3. Environmental stimulation. A third approach seeks to discover changes in bodily functions or tissue structure following from exposure of the animal to certain kinds of stimulation in the environment. The type of stimulation which is investigated may range from radiation to systematic handling by a human being. More often than not, the investigator will measure not only the bodily changes which may follow from this stimulation, but also behavioral changes, thus opening the possibility of relating bodily functions to behavior in terms of their common origin in the environment.

Experiments of these kinds frequently report behavior changes which appear to resemble those found in psychopathology. By the same token, other investigators report changes in behavior which appear as "therapeutic" improvements in the responses of the subject. In either event, data from research in physiological psychology are another source of hypotheses about the possible organic origins of pathological behavior in humans. For obvious reasons, the overwhelming mass of information already gained in physiological psychology has been acquired from the study of animals. Consequently, these studies hold the status of experimental analogues when we attempt to apply their results to an understanding of human behavior. At the bodily level, however, the analogue is somewhat easier to support than at the behavioral level. Generalizations from animal physiology to human physiology, especially when the animals are mammals, have been made very successfully in biological and medical research. At the behavioral level, the analogues are complicated by all the problems discussed in detail at the beginning of this chapter.

The General Organic Hypothesis

All the biological methods and tactics which we have examined so far have been concerned with identifying an organic determinant or correlate of pathological behavior. The goal of the researcher has been to dis-

cover with some precision the nature of the *specific* physiological factors which appear to be related to the behavioral symptoms. In this way, the purpose of the research is essentially similar to that of medical research generally.

In addition to this kind of approach, however, there is a sizable research effort devoted to a much more general problem concerning the organic origins of certain behavior pathologies. Instead of attempting to answer the question, "What, if any, are the organic origins of behavior?" it is concerned with the question, "Is behavior X organic in origin?" Provided that the answer to this question is affirmative, the question of the specific organic factors may then be raised. A brief examination of this general organic hypothesis shows us that the question may be stated more concretely: "Does behavior X show features which have been found characteristic of the behavior of patients with known organic damage?" In practice, the kind of "known organic damage" with which the comparison is usually made is "brain damage," or damage to the central nervous system.

Bearing in mind the enormous investment of effort which any serious research demands, we may notice the advantages of this kind of research. If we can demonstrate that the behavior of schizophrenic patients is very similar to that of brain-damaged patients in many respects, then we may feel more optimistic about the possibilities of discovering a specific organic etiology. Likewise, we may look with more confidence for a somatic therapy for the condition. Unfortunately, there are many methodological problems to be faced in making our preliminary comparisons, and we should consider them here.

Validity of the Organic Diagnosis. How do we know that our group of patients with "brain damage" do have damaged brain tissue? The ultimate proof can be obtained only by looking at the brain tissue of the patient, either during some neurosurgical procedure or by autopsy. Most studies of the kind we are describing are not conducted under circumstances which permit either of these checks to be made. Instead, the diagnosis of brain damage is made on the strength of certain signs or indicators present in the patient. These signs may be in the form of neurological symptoms, such as an abnormal electroencephalogram (EEG), loss of reflexes, and so forth. Frequently, the signs are behavioral in a grosser fashion, and may include responses on psychological tests, evidences of certain kinds of memory loss, difficulties in enunciating clearly in speech, and many others.

Now it is clear that when we are using these signs to diagnose organic damage, our diagnosis is based on inference from behavior. The diagnosis will be only as accurate as the signs are. For example, many people present abnormal EEG records but are not found to have more direct evidence of brain injury. In fact, many neurological and behavioral signs are less than perfectly correlated with demonstrable evidence of brain injury. This naturally introduces an element of doubt whenever we are comparing schizophrenic patients and patients who have been diagnosed in this way as brain-injured.

General versus Specific Behaviors. The term "brain-injured" or "organic" covers an extremely diverse range of tissue pathologies. A brain-injured patient may be suffering from a localized bullet wound to the head, a spreading tumor, or the diffuse changes which come with conditions such as cerebro-arteriosclerosis. The consequences of these varied conditions are such that, on the whole, no two brain-injured patients can be said to be identical. An additional complication is provided by the fact that the behavior of a person who suffers organic damage is significantly affected by the behavior patterns which she showed before the injury— another factor which will differ from patient to patient. Finally, we may note that many of the behaviors we see in the brain-injured

individual represent his attempts to cope with the problems created by his handicap. As such they are not primary consequences of the injury and should be distinguished from them.

Because of these problems, when similarities are found between the brain-injured and some other group, it is difficult to interpret them as evidence of organicity in the comparison group. In practice it is usual to compare the brain-injured and the psychopathological groups in conjunction with a control group of non-brain-injured, non-psychopathological subjects. Where the data support the conclusion that the brain-injured and psychopathological groups differ from each other, this kind of control may be adequate. However, when the results indicate similarities between the two groups and differences between both of them and the controls, it is not possible to decide whether the similarities are due to the fact that both groups are "organic," that both groups present behavior pathologies, that both groups are adjusting to the handicap, or that both groups are hospitalized. Thus, appropriate controls should include subjects who are psychopathological in some respect, patients who are suffering from some other kind of handicap (such as being crippled, etc.), and patients who have been hospitalized for equal lengths of time.

It will also be evident that the similarities which may be found are likely to be of a very general, gross kind, unless the brain-injured group includes only patients with highly similar kinds of tissue pathology.[3] Such homogeneity tends to be the exception in recent research reports, and we must be

[3] More typically, investigations of this kind confine their selection to rather broad categories of brain damage. Thus Chapman (1960) grouped together 41 patients of whom 13 were diagnosed as suffering from cerebral vascular disorder, 6 from alcoholism, 6 from multiple sclerosis with cerebral disorder, 3 from brain tumor, 2 from head injury, 1 from Huntington's chorea, 1 from syphilitic paresis, and 9 from unspecified cerebral damage.

cognizant of the limitation when evaluating data obtained from such comparisons.

Primitive versus Complex Behaviors. Many investigators have been struck by the apparent resemblance between the behavior of psychotic patients and the behavior of children. This kind of observation has led them to speculate that psychopathological responses may represent some kind of reversion or *regression* to more primitive forms of behavior. Because the central nervous system is not fully developed in the young child, it appears plausible that psychopathological patients might be compared both to normal children and to patients whose central nervous system is known to have suffered destruction. The behavior of all three is then regarded as exemplifying the functioning of a primitive nervous system. In this sense, children may be regarded as "organic" by definition for the purposes of comparisons.

Adults differ from children in many ways; differences in the maturity of the nervous system represent only one of these. Differences in experience and in demands and pressures of the environment are among the more prominent of the others. Thus, studies which demonstrate that the behavior of a psychopathological group is like that of a group of normal children may justify the conclusion that the patients are "childlike" in their behavior—or "primitive," if the investigator prefers the term. They do not make it possible to draw firm conclusions about the organic factors which may be operating to produce resemblances between children and psychotics.

Psychopharmacological Methods

Students of behavior have long been interested in the effects of drugs on both human and animal responses. However, the last decades have seen a tremendous increase in interest in drug-behavior relationships, due perhaps in the main to the development of new compounds of psychological importance. The growth in interest

has been of such magnitude that the term *psychopharmacology* has been coined to identify this area within pharmacology generally.

The kinds of questions which psychopharmacologists attempt to answer may be itemized as follows:

1. What are the behavioral effects of a given chemical compound in both animals and man? How are these effects altered by such factors as size of dose, type of subject, conditions of the experiment, and so forth?
2. What is the manner of action of the drug within the body of the subject, including such processes as metabolism, nervous system changes, etc.?
3. What are the limitations (such as toxicity, undesirable side effects, addiction, etc.) upon the use of the drug for therapeutic purposes?

In searching for answers to these questions, investigators have developed an awareness of special problems which they face, and have devised solutions to some of them. We shall now discuss these in some detail.

Drug-Behavior Relationships. At first sight, the basic design of an experiment might appear to be quite simple. The investigator might administer the drug to one group of subjects and compare their subsequent behavior with that of a group which has not had the drug. Several technical questions arise, however, in this kind of experiment.

Subjects. Obtaining subjects for experiments in which drugs are used presents certain difficulties. Hospital patients are not necessarily the most suitable subjects even though they may be readily available. Psychotic patients may be poorly motivated, and their behavior may be sufficiently disorganized or their perceptions sufficiently inaccurate that measurement of responses becomes difficult. Some investigators have turned to prison groups in an attempt to find subjects who are not psychologically disturbed. Even here the subjects are apt to be atypical of the normal population, and it is questionable whether or not we can apply results obtained from them to an understanding of normal behavior.

Volunteer subjects have also been used, but some investigators have found that volunteers often include numbers of people who have severe psychological problems (Lasagna & von Felsinger, 1954). Because the effects of drugs have been found to vary according to differences in personality before the experiment begins (e.g., Lindemann & Malamud, 1934; Hollister, Traub, & Beckman, 1956), the presence of psychopathology in many subjects is likely to produce effects which obscure the more fundamental actions of the drug.

Obviously there is no simple solution to these problems. The investigator is confined mainly to trying to eliminate deviant subjects from his groups before the experiment begins, and trying to motivate his subjects adequately during it.

Research with animal subjects is not free from similar problems. Current recommendations of the National Institutes of Mental Health (1961) point out that it is unwise to assume that results found with one species will be applicable to another. Strain differences within a species also represent a source of variability in drug-behavior relationships, as do factors such as sex, age, body weight, and physical health.

Suggestion and the Placebo Effect. Many investigators have found that subjects will respond to the administration of a drug in accordance with what they believe the drug will do to them. Their behavior then confirms the investigator's hypothesis about the drug, although the drug itself may have had no pharmacological effect at all. This is the effect of suggestion, either suggestion by the experimenter (usually unwitting on his part) or suggestion from other sources such as hospital gossip, etc. In the majority of experiments, suggestion operates so as to produce spurious effects rather than to mask real effects (Rosenthal & Frank, 1956).

This problem is of sufficient magnitude that it is now customary to control for it by using a *placebo* group. A placebo is a substance which is pharmacologically inert but which is given to the subject in such a way that he does not know whether he is getting the placebo or the drug. In general medical practice, placebos are given with the express intention of producing improvement in the patient's condition by suggestion, and they are often given with explicit predictions that the patient will get better. Many do.

In research, the placebo is given without attempts to suggest its effects to the patient, the purpose being to permit the experimenter to measure the effects of suggestion from other sources. Such suggestion is presumably operating equally on the drug group and the placebo group. When the experiment calls for an observer to rate the behavior of the subject, the observer may also be influenced by his expectations about the effect of the drug. This factor of observer bias is not unique to experiments which use drugs—we have already mentioned it in our discussion of controlled clinical observation. To eliminate it in psychopharmacological studies, the observer is usually kept in ignorance of whether or not a subject has had the placebo or the drug. This control technique, whereby neither the subjects nor the observers know which group is which, is called the *double-blind* procedure.

Kurland (1960) has also pointed out the problem which is created by the presence of side effects in some drugs. For example, if a tranquilizing compound is being studied with regard to its power to reduce anxiety, we may not be interested in the fact that it also produces a general slowing down of responsiveness to all stimuli. However, the subject and the observer may soon recognize this and therefore be able to distinguish the drug group from the placebo group on this basis. One method of dealing with the problem is to use a placebo compound which will mimic the side effects. Such a compound would not be pharmacologically inert, and for it Kurland has proposed the term *positive placebo* to distinguish it from the inert or negative placebo.

Dosage Level. Drug effects usually vary depending on the dosage of the drug which is given. If we wish to obtain a clear answer to questions about drug effects, it is important that we give many different dosages and note the effects associated with each. Apart from plotting these effects, we may be interested in discovering *threshold values* of dosage and *interaction effects.* By a threshold value we mean the minimum dosage of a drug which is necessary to produce some particular behavioral or physiological response. Gross response measures such as the threshold for sedation with dosages of drugs like amobarbital and alcohol have been studied extensively by several investigators (Kawi, 1958; Shagass, 1960), with results which suggest that personality differences between subjects are important in determining the effects of drug dosage upon response.

Some drug effects appear only in conjunction with particular experimental conditions. The drug may then be said to *interact* with specific circumstances in the experimental setup to produce effects which would not otherwise be present. Our previous remarks that the effects produced by a drug are influenced by the personality of the subject refer to drug-subject interactions. An illustration of such an interaction is given in Figure 5-1, where we see that a 100-milligram dosage rate of chlorpromazine produces no difference in accuracy of tachistoscopic recognition between normal and schizophrenic subjects. With a 200-milligram dosage rate, the schizophrenic subjects make significantly fewer errors in recognition than do the normal subjects. Here we have an interaction between dosage level and subject pathology producing a significant difference in error responses.

Dosage Sequences. Repeated administration of a drug, or of any somatic treatment, may produce changes which differ from those following a single dose. Immediate short-term effects of a drug are usually termed the *acute* effects, whereas the long-

Figure 5-1. Comparison between schizophrenic and normal subjects after acute administration of chlorpromazine and secobarbital on tachistoscopic threshold. (Kornetsky et al., 1959.)

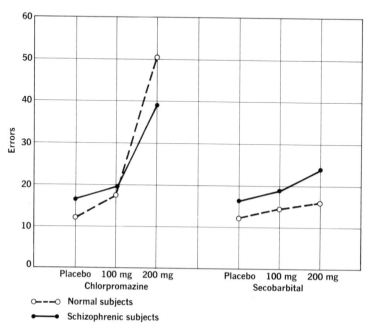

term effects of repeated dosages are referred to as the *chronic* effects.

Acute effects may themselves change as the time following the administration of the drug increases. Generally speaking, the concentration of a drug in the blood or any other place where it acts diminishes in proportion to the amount of the drug present. As the drug undergoes chemical change, its power to bring about behavioral changes may either decrease or increase. Thus we need to take measures during the postadministration period to ensure proper observation of the drug's activity.

Chronic effects are likely to be influenced both by the total number of administrations given and by the frequency with which they are given. On the whole, the effects obtained with long intervals between administrations tend to be more stable than those obtained after an equivalent number of closely spaced doses.

Method of Administration. The manner in which a drug is administered may vary in many ways. The form of solution in which the drug is prepared—as, for example, a water (aqueous) solution versus an alcohol solution—may affect the action. Variations may arise as a consequence of the route by which the drug is administered. Common routes are described in Table 5-1.

All in all, we can see that considerable refinement of method is necessary in planning research into drug-behavior relationships, and it will not surprise us to find that many experimental studies appear to provide contradictory answers to the same question because of the uncontrolled effects of the factors described here.

Drug-Body Relationships. An adequate account of the tactics involved in discovering the manner in which a drug acts in the body is beyond the scope of this book. We will consider only the major procedures so as to provide a simple background with which the reader may be able to approach the study of more technical writing. Primary problems in the pharmacology of psycho-active drugs include the identification of the *site of action* and the discovery of drug-produced changes in physiological responses. Basic observational procedures may be summarized as follows.

Analysis of Nervous System Changes. Doses of a drug may be administered and measures made of nervous system characteristics, such as rate of transmission of an impulse along the fiber, changes in the substances released at the synapse (e.g., sympathin or acetylcholine), changes in the EEG in the drugged patient, or changes in sensory threshold for stimulation.

Analysis of Changes in Body Fluids and Tissues. Estimates may be made of the manner in which drugs are metabolized and the time this takes by analyzing samples of body fluids for the presence of the drug. Blood and urine are among the more common fluids studied. Blood samples may be taken from different locations in the body to assist in determining the routes by which the drug is absorbed. A somewhat more refined technique involves the use of *isotopically labeled* versions of the drug. Radioactive samples of the drug are introduced into the animal, the subsequent dispersion of the sample being more easily detected by appropriate techniques.

Essentially similar procedures are used in the analysis of body tissues taken from subjects which have received the drug. For obvious reasons the procedure of taking tissue samples is easier with animals than with human subjects, whereas fluid samples are taken from humans without difficulty.

Microinjection Techniques. Recent developments in the design of apparatus have permitted the injection of small quantities of drugs into selected organs or sites within the body, thereby making it possible to observe the direct action of the drug on particular bodily systems. A major advantage of this technique is that the drug can reach the selected site without going through the modifications which might occur if it

TABLE 5-1 Common Routes of Administration of Drugs

Route	Advantages	Disadvantages
Oral (by mouth)	Natural route. Least traumatic. May be given with food. Not necessary to handle the subject.	Uncertainty of absorption. May be altered during digestion. Dosage quantity per unit of time difficult to control.
Subcutaneous (injection under skin)	Quick and easy technique. Little trauma.	Slow absorption.* Some risk of irritation or infection with repeated injections of this kind.
Intramuscular (injection into muscle)	Drug quickly absorbed.* May be used with drug solutions too irritating for subcutaneous route (e.g., oil solutions).	Mildly traumatic. Some risk of accidental occlusion of blood vessels. Dosage volume requires critical control.
Intraperitoneal (injection into abdominal cavity)	Rapid absorption.* Easily administered. May be used with insoluble drugs.	Mildly traumatic. Risk of severe infection with some animals.
Intravenous (directly into a vein by injection)	Immediate effect. No uncertainty of absorption. Possible to administer dosage determined by some response—e.g., sedation. Possible to terminate drug action when desired (e.g., when experiment is completed) and thus minimize unwanted aftereffects.	Demands more skill in technique. Sterile procedures are necessary. Can be traumatic (e.g., when vein is inaccessible). Sight of blood is anxiety-arousing in human subjects. Many drug solutions are incompatible with blood elements. Toxic and circulatory side effects possible.

* *Whether or not speed of absorption is regarded as an advantage depends, of course, upon the purpose of the research. In general, rapid absorption is required for most psychopharmacological studies.*
SOURCE: *National Institutes of Mental Health (1961).*

were introduced in a more conventional way, such as by mouth.

Chemical Structure. Analysis of the structure of a molecule of a drug may lead to hypotheses about its mode of action and place of action within the body. If the drug shows some structural similarity to a substance normally present in the body, the hypothesis may be that the drug occupies the bodily locations normally occupied by the substance, substituting for the latter and performing its normal function. Woolley and Shaw (1954), for example, suggested that the drug LSD (lysergic acid diethylamide)

is sufficiently like the brain substance serotonin that it would occupy those areas of the brain which normally act as receptors for serotonin. However, it would not perform the same functions as serotonin, and hence there would be behavioral changes— in this case of a rather severe and bizarre kind. They used the model of a lock and a key: LSD could be pushed into the same "lock" as serotonin, but could not open it.

Other hypotheses suggest that similarities of structure of this kind may mean that the introduction of the drug acts to produce an *excess functioning* of the normal substance. Thus LSD might be regarded as doing the same thing as serotonin, and when introduced into the body may bring about a condition similar to an excess of serotonin.

A third class of hypothesis arises from the fact that some drugs are *antagonistic* to certain naturally produced bodily substances, combining with them to form new products and thereby creating a deficiency of the normal substance.

In any event, we can see that the major value of structural analysis of drugs lies in the power to generate hypotheses about the action of the drug in the body—hypotheses which can then be tested by physiological experiment.

GENETIC METHODS

Over the years many authorities in the field of psychopathology have been interested in discovering a genetic or hereditary origin for various behavior disturbances. This interest has been maintained by the successful identification of genetic factors in many forms of deviant behavior, notably in the area of mental retardation. Following are some of the simpler principles involved in behavior genetics.

Chromosomes and Genes

The simplest unit in heredity is the *gene*. Whether or not such an entity exists is a matter of current dispute, considerable scepticism about the usefulness of the notion of the gene having been voiced by many Russian investigators (cf. Turbin, 1959). However, we shall not pursue this dispute here but shall merely state that genes are generally presumed to occupy a site or locus along a *chromosome*. Man has 23 pairs of chromosomes and a total of genes estimated to range between 2,000 and 50,000 (Stern, 1960). During reproduction one member of each pair of chromosomes from the male unites with one member of each pair from the female, thus forming 23 new pairs in the offspring. The pairing of chromosomes is random, so that there is a very large number of possible combinations in the offspring of any pair of parents—somewhat over eight million.

Chromosomal Anomalies

Much progress has been made in recent genetic research because of the development of better methods of identifying chromosomes. In particular the development of the *karyotype*, or photograph of chromosomes, has rendered possible the investigation of chromosomal anomalies in a variety of disorders. The 23 pairs of chromosomes inherited by the offspring are classified as *sex chromosomes* (2 in number) or *autosomes* (22 pairs). At a meeting in Denver in 1960, an international uniform method of classification was accepted for the autosomes, each pair being identified by a sequence number. When photographed in sequential order, the resulting karyotype permits comparisons between normal and deviant chromosomal compositions. Figure 5-2 shows the karyotype of a normal human subject, with positions shown on the Denver system.

In 1959 a group of French workers (Lejeune et al., 1959) discovered a small extra chromosome in three cases of Down's syndrome (a variety of mental deficiency once named "mongolism"). The extra chromosome was at position 21. Other workers have confirmed this finding, and there is now considerable interest in the identification of typical chromosomal anomalies for other disorders.

Major Genes and Polygenes

Current genetic theory distinguishes between *major genes* and *polygenes*. The former are regarded as responsible for certain characteristics of development by themselves, whereas polygenes are presumed to have cumulative effects which are quantitatively the same from one to another. As an illustration of the effects of a major gene, we may turn to the transmission of Huntington's chorea. The parent with a gene for Huntington's chorea will, on a probability

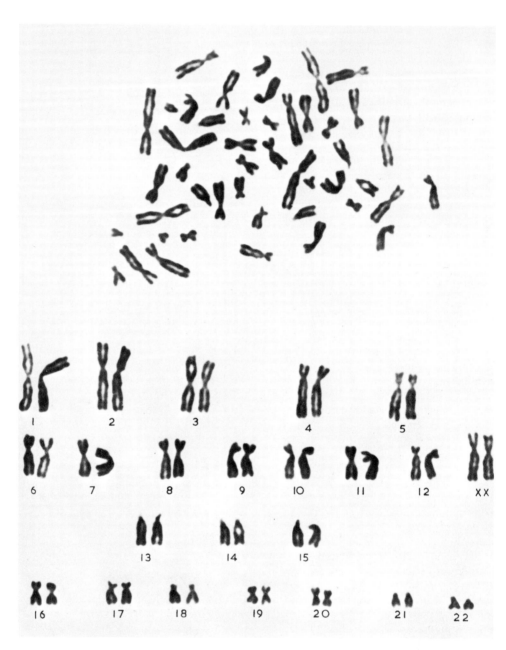

Figure 5-2. Normal human female chromosome pattern. (Courtesy of Prof. W. M. Davidson.)

basis, give the gene for the disease to one-half of his offspring. These children will receive a normal gene from the other parent, but will develop the disease because the gene for it will dominate the normal gene with which it is paired. In a case such as this, the pathological gene is referred to as *dominant,* while the normal gene would be termed *recessive.* Many pathological genes are presumed to be recessive, and would not lead to appearance of the characteristic except in the case of the offspring of parents who both carry the gene. In this case we would expect one-fourth of the offspring to exhibit the characteristic, this being the proportion in whom we could expect the pairing of both recessive genes to occur randomly.

However, much pathological behavior is not of the all-or-none variety which we see in the case of Huntington's chorea, but may range with many gradations between non-existence and presence to a severe degree. The same is true for many human physical traits, such as height, hair color, etc. To account for these characteristics, it appears plausible to assume the presence of poly-genes which may combine cumulatively to determine the degree of the characteristic which appears in the offspring. The method of combination and addition is assumed to be the same as that for major genes, but the large number of genes of equivalent value for any given trait permits a larger number of gradations in the offspring.

Gottesman (1963), in his hypothetical application of the polygene model in the inheritance of intelligence, has given us a good illustration of the processes presumed to be operating in polygenic inheritance.

An illustration of the principles of polygenic inheritance may be seen in the explanatory power of a simple two loci model. . . . First let us assume that intelligence, as measured in some objective fashion, is controlled by two independent loci, each with one or the other of two alleles: A^1 and A^2 at one locus and B^1 and B^2 at the other. Our hypothetical parents would be from two pure lines homozygous as follows: $A^1 A^1 B^1 B^1$ and $A^2 A^2 B^2 B^2$. We will call the former the dull parent and the latter the bright one. The higher intelligence of the brighter parent is considered to be associated with the additive action of A^2 and B^2 alleles, and we further assume, in this simplified model, that the substitution of a "2" for any "1" type allele leads to equal enhancement of the phenotypically measured IQ. It follows that an $A^1 A^2$ combination will be intermediate in intelligence to $A^1 A^1$ and $A^2 A^2$.

We move now to the first generation children who can only have the genotype $A^1 A^2 B^1 B^2$ since each can only receive one kind of gamete from each parent for each of the two loci. Independent assortment in the gametes produced by the first generation (usually denoted F_1) will lead to the formation of four different kinds—$A^1 B^1$, $A^1 B^2$, $A^2 B^1$, and $A^2 B^2$. When these combine at fertilization in all the possible different ways, the offspring in this second generation fall into five different phenotypic classes defined by having zero to four intelligence enhancing alleles:

		$A^1 A^1 B^2 B^2$
	$A^1 A^1 B^1 B^2$	$A^1 A^2 B^1 B^2$
$A^1 A^1 B^1 B^1$	$A^1 A^2 B^1 B^1$	$A^2 A^2 B^1 B^1$
class 0	**class 1**	**class 2**

$A^1 A^2 B^2 B^2$	
$A^2 A^2 B^1 B^2$	$A^2 A^2 B^2 B^2$
class 3	**class 4**

This simple two locus model, with a limited number of assumptions, accounts for five phenotypic classes which we could label, left to right, retarded, dull normal, average, bright average, and superior. Of course this is artificial since there is a continuous distribution of discriminable phenotypes for intelligence, i.e., an IQ score of 81 is different from one of 80 or 82. However, by increasing the posited number of loci, we rapidly approach the standard Gaussian curve since we are really dealing with the expansion of the binomial expression $(\frac{1}{2} + \frac{1}{2})^{2n}$ where n equals the number of loci. Remembering that this model, up to now, makes no provision for environmental contributions to variation, we can point out that such a provision with, at the most, 12 loci or gene pairs posited, can easily fit the observed distributions of IQ. Theoretically, then, we are forced to deal with the effects of a minute number of the total possible 50,000 genes. (Gottesman, 1963, pp. 262–263.)

Research Methods

After this brief introduction to some of the terminology of genetics, we turn to a consideration of research methods used in the genetics of psychopathology.

The Twin Method. The method par excellence for genetic research is based upon the investigation of the behavior of twins. *Identical* or monozygous twins are twins born from the splitting of a single fertilized cell, and the genetic constitution of both children is therefore identical. *Fraternal* or dizygous twins are born of separately fertilized ova and are thus no more likely to have the same genetic constitution than any pair of children born at different times of the same parents. We have already seen that this possibility is less than 1 in 8 million. However, fraternal twins provide better controls than nontwin siblings because they share some things in common, such as age, birth order, and so on.

Any dissimilarity observed between identical twins with respect to a certain behavior or trait must be due to the action of the environment. The extent of a similarity may be determined by both heredity and environmental commonality. To have an estimate of the influence of environment, we may examine the resemblances between fraternal twins from comparable environments. For a characteristic in which the resemblance between identical twins is greater than the resemblance between fraternal twins, we may wish to hypothesize that heredity plays a part in determining its development. The estimation of how great a part in determining behavioral characteristics is played by heredity is a more complex matter.

Twins Raised Apart. Another use of twins involves the observation of identical twins who have been separated early in life and raised in different environments. Remaining similarities between the subjects which exceed those found between nontwins similarly separated might be attributed to the greater genetic commonality on the part of the identicals, giving support to the notion that the traits in which resemblances are found have genetic limitations. The discovery of twins raised apart is not easy and requires a wide search through the population (e.g., Shields, 1958).

Nontwin Comparisons. For a trait which is wholly determined by heredity, we would expect a perfect similarity, or *concordance,* between identical twins, and for other relatives the concordances would be as follows. Parent-child pairs, fraternal twins, and nontwin siblings should reveal 50 per cent concordance rates. Between a subject and his grandparents, grandchildren, uncles, aunts, and nephews or nieces, there should be a concordance of 25 per cent, and between a subject and his first cousins, a concordance of 12½ per cent. The significance of such concordance rates when they are obtained empirically depends upon the base rate for the trait in the population at large. Thus, if we discover that 12½ per cent of the entire population suffers from a certain disease, a concordance rate of the same figure between first cousins would not indicate any special importance of a hereditary factor.

If we find that with increasing closeness of relationship we get higher concordance rates for a trait, we may be more inclined to suspect a genetic factor. This suspicion is justified, however, upon the supposition that the environments of the subjects do not increase in resemblance in the same way. Unfortunately this supposition is usually not valid except in the case of the twin comparisons already mentioned.

Pedigree or Breeding Studies. In the laboratory it is possible for the geneticist to breed animals selectively to determine the genetic origins of a given trait through many generations. Studies of human genetics depend upon the tracing of the generations which emerge through the normal process of mating in society. Such studies are naturally subject to many sources of uncontrolled variance, but certain kinds of mating have special interest for the student of psychopathology. Shields and Slater (1961) report an investigation of 355 psychiatric patients who were the offspring of consanguineous marriages. They found that the frequency of a schizophrenic diagnosis was significantly greater in this group than in a control population of psychiatric outpatients of normal marriages. Other diagnoses were not differently distributed between the two groups.

Another method of studying human mating is the observation of the children where both parents present psychopathology. The frequency of psychotic development in this group of offspring is compared with the frequencies found in children of marriages where only one parent was psychotic, and with the frequencies in children of normal parents. This technique carries with it the problem that children born of psychotic parents or of one psychotic parent are not being exposed to a normal environment in the home. The greater incidence of psychosis reported from such studies (e.g., Elsässer, 1952) may reflect the influence of environment as much as of heredity.

The earliest pedigree studies typically attempted to trace the frequency of pathology in all the generations of a given family. The difficulties inherent in this approach are many. Reports of pathological behavior derived from the studies of old records are subject to many kinds of observer error; diagnostic criteria for psychopathology have changed over the past century; studies of this kind usually focus upon striking cases of repeated pathology in several generations without reference to control families where the pathological behavior did not reappear; and after one or two generations, the offspring are being raised in increasingly unfavorable environments.

Inability to manipulate the major variable —the gene—or to identify its presence until the trait has appeared overtly in the offspring constitute serious difficulties in the genetic approach to psychopathology. Nevertheless, the success of geneticists in demonstrating hereditary factors in animal behavior and the strongly supportive evidence from several studies of twins and families make it necessary to give serious consideration to genetics in any examination of psychopathology.

EPIDEMIOLOGY AND POPULATION SURVEYS

Some clues to the determinants of psychopathology may be gained by the study of the distribution of pathology between social classes; between racial, ethnic, and religious groups; between age groups; between sexes; and in terms of geographical location. Many of these divisions overlap. Ethnic origin of immigrant groups is closely related to religious and socioeconomic group membership, and the influence of these variables needs to be separated. However, the basic method involved is essentially the same for all such surveys of psychopathology.

The task of the investigator is to secure a full accounting of the per unit frequency of psychopathology within a given population. These frequencies may then be compared within various groups of the population with a view of discovering group differences of significant proportions. Variations of this method occur when changes in frequency in one group over a time period are compared with similar changes in other groups. Once these frequencies have been obtained, they may provide hypotheses about the determinants of psychopathological behavior. Hypotheses derived in this way may then be tested more directly by measurement and observation of the variables which are presumed to be important.

While the survey method is comparatively straightforward from a logical point of view, there are some problems to be encountered in its application.

Diagnostic Criteria

The same behavior on the part of one man may be regarded as amusing or eccentric, while in another it may lead to his hospitalization. Many types of deviant behavior may be tolerated in a rural community which would not be permitted in an urban community. Minor theft by a wealthy man may lead to his being advised to seek psychiatric help; the same offense by a poor man may land him in prison. Instances of the divergent bases upon which the same behavior may be diagnosed can be multiplied, but they will only serve to repeat the point that surveys of populations based upon diagnostic categories of psychopathology are subject to several kinds of systematic bias. The investigator has no ready way to eliminate such bias when interpreting his statistics, but he may seek to identify it as far as this is possible.

Paradoxically, the presence of a high rate of psychopathology of all kinds in a given region or group may reflect the high level of efficiency in detection and diagnosis in the psychiatric services available to that population, rather than being purely a symptom of poor mental health in the group itself.

Sampling

Apart from inconsistencies in diagnosis and detection, the survey method may suffer from sampling biases in the survey itself. Upper socioeconomic groups may tend to seek psychiatric care on an outpatient or private-office basis and may thereby be underrepresented in statistics which are compiled from hospital admissions. Thus, even where the criteria for diagnosis within a city hospital system are consistent, and all figures are made available, many cases of psychopathology may never be recorded at all. Where the survey is made on only a sample of institutions or people within the population concerned, the risk of sampling error is naturally increased.

In spite of these problems, the population survey has proved a useful and fruitful technique in the study of psychopathology, as we shall see in later chapters.

S U M M A R Y

In this chapter we have considered the methodologies that are used in the study of psychopathology. They are drawn from a wide range of scientific disciplines, including pharmacology, physiology, and genetics, as well as experimental and clinical psychology. We have made an initial distinction between research that is aimed at *testing an explicit hypothesis* and research that is *exploratory* in nature. These kinds of research differ mainly in the degree of precision with which the investigator wishes to observe the phenomena under scrutiny. Typically, research passes from the exploratory stage (which usually ends with the production of a precise hypothesis) to the hypothesis-testing stage, whence, hopefully, it will emerge with a reliable conclusion.

Depending upon the circumstances under which the investigator can control important variables, his conclusion may be in the form of statements about *determinants* or about *correlates* of the pathological phenomenon. With the major exception of studies of therapy, methods for the discovery of determinants of psychopathology are rare. Nevertheless, by amassing findings about correlates, we can increase the confidence with which we begin to take practical action on the basis of correlational research.

Another approach to this problem is the use of *experimental analogues*. Here the investigator produces in the laboratory a state of affairs that he believes to be analogous to the psychopathology that he observes in the natural habitat. These analogues may be produced by the selection of *analogous subjects* (often animals or normal college students), *analogous stimuli* (laboratory threat, for example), and *analogous behaviors* (such as the forgetting of learned responses as an analogue of "repression"). Analogues serve to sharpen the investigators' definition of the problem but require validating in the natural habitat before we can accept their results as definitive.

However our conclusions are reached, we have seen that the fundamental aim of research in psychopathology is to arrive at general or *nomothetic* principles. Although some psychologists have argued for the establishing of laws that would apply only to the single case—*idiographic* laws—we have suggested here that they are essentially instances of the application of nomothetic principles.

Strategic goals of research in psychopathology often include: (a) the attempt to bring a certain kind of psychopathological syndrome under the rubric of a broader psychological concept, such as trying to demonstrate that schizophrenic autism is a subtype of avoidance behavior, or (b) the attempt to bring one syndrome under the general rubric of another, where the etiology of the latter is better understood than that of the former. Research that tries to show similarities between schizophrenic behavior and that of the brain-injured is sometimes of this type.

Turning to biological methods, we have seen that a large variety of technical controls is necessary to ensure interpretable results. Drug studies require careful consideration of dosage amount and sequences, route of administration, drug interactions, and the like. Responses to drugs may be measured behaviorally, neurophysiologically, and biochemically. In the area of genetics we have seen the necessity of turning to sophisticated polygenetic models to account for complex behaviors. The uses of twin control methods, kinship samples, and pedigree studies were discussed.

Clearly, we have not been able to give detailed attention to all the important variables in any of the methods that were discussed, but the brief descriptions that are given should provide a basis for understanding the research findings to be discussed in later chapters. For more comprehensive accounts of various methods, the reader is referred to the list of suggested readings below.

SUGGESTED READINGS

1. Fuller, J. L., & Thompson, W. R. *Behavior genetics.* New York: Wiley, 1960. An excellent basic text on the genetic method in the study of behavior.

2. Hollingshead, A. B., & Redlich, F. C. *Social class and mental illness: a community study.* New York: Wiley, 1958. A now classic study of psychopathology distributions in social classes in an urban area.

3. Holt, R. R. Experimental methods in clinical psychology. In B. B. Wolman (Ed.), *Handbook of clinical psychology.* New York: McGraw-Hill, 1965. A very thorough discussion of research methods and problems arising from clinical questions. Topics covered range from issues of subject privacy and experimenter-subject relationships to scaling and coding techniques in projective research.

4. Rubinstein, E. A., & Parloff, M. B. (Eds.). *Research in psychotherapy.* Washington, D.C.: American Psychological Association, 1959. A comprehensive symposium volume on logical and methodological problems in research on psychotherapy.

5. Sidman, M. *Tactics of scientific research.* New York: Basic Books, 1960. A concise account of the logic and tactics of experimental psychology from an operant-conditioning viewpoint. It does not cover many techniques commonly used in experimental psychology, however.

6. Uhr, L., & Miller, J. G. (Eds.). *Drugs and behavior.* New York: Wiley, 1960. Part I of this volume gives a good account of problems of research and interpretation in psychopharmacological research.

7. United States Public Health Service. *Behavioral research in preclinical psychopharmacology.* Psychopharmacology Service Center Bulletin, U.S.P.H.S. Washington, D.C., September, 1961. A brief but concise presentation of the central issues of research design and technique in behavioral psychopharmacology. Critical independent variables are identified and their effects discussed. Measurement of dependent variables is described.

REFERENCES

Allport, G. W. *Personality: a psychological interpretation.* New York: Holt, 1937.

Chapman, L. J. Confusion of figurative and literal usages of words by schizophrenics and brain damaged patients. *J. abnorm. soc. Psychol.,* 1960, **60,** 412–416.

Chapman, L. J. A search for lunacy. *J. nerv. ment. Dis.,* 1961, **132,** 171–174.

Cowen, E. L. The experimental analogue: an approach to research in psychotherapy. *Psychol. Rep.,* 1961, **8,** 9–10.

du Mas, F. M. *Manifest structure analysis.* Missoula, Mont.: Montana State Univer. Press, 1956.

Elsässer, G. *Die Nachkommen Geisteskranker Elternpaare.* Stuttgart: Thieme, 1952.

Gottesman, I. I. Genetic aspects of intelligent behavior. In N. Ellis (Ed.), *Handbook of mental deficiency.* New York: McGraw-Hill, 1963.

Guertin, W. H. Medical and statistical-psychological models for research in schizophrenia. *Behavioral Sci.,* 1961, **6,** 200–204.

Harlow, H. F. Mice, monkeys, men and motives. *Psychol. Rev.,* 1953, **60,** 23–32.

Hebb, D. O. Alice in wonderland or psychology among the biological sciences. In H. F. Harlow & C. N. Woolsey (Eds.), *Biological and biochemical bases of behavior.* Madison, Wis.: Univer. of Wisconsin Press, 1958.

Hebb, D. O., & Thompson, W. R. The social significance of animal studies. In G. Lindzey (Ed.), *Handbook of social psychology.* Vol. 1. Cambridge, Mass.: Addison-Wesley, 1954.

Hilgard, E. R. *Theories of learning.* New York: Appleton-Century-Crofts, 1948.

Hollister, L. E., Traub, L., & Beckman, W. G. Psychiatric uses of reserpine or chlorpromazine: results of double-bind studies. In N. S. Kline (Ed.), *Psychopharmacology.* Washington, D.C.: Amer. Ass. Adv. Sci., 1956, pp. 65–74.

Kalinowsky, L. B., & Hoch, P. M. *Shock treatment and other somatic procedures.* New York: Grune and Stratton, 1949.

Kawi, A. The sedation threshold. *Arch. neurol. Psychiat.,* 1958, **80,** 232–236.

Keynes, J. M. *Treatise on probability.* London: Macmillan, 1921.

Kornetsky, C., Pettit, M., Wynne, R., & Evarts, E. V. A comparison of the psychological effects of chlorpromazine and secobarbital in schizophrenics. *J. ment. Sci.,* 1959, **105,** 190–199.

Kurland, A. A. Placebo effect. In L. Uhr & J. G. Miller (Eds.), *Drugs and behavior.* New York: Wiley, 1960.

Lasagna, L., & von Felsinger, J. M. The volunteer subject in research. *Science,* 1954, **120,** 359–361.

Lejeune, J., Turpin, R., & Gautier, M. Le mongolisme, premier example d'aberration autosomique humaine. *Ann. Genetique,* 1959, **2,** 41–49.

Lindemann, E., & Malamud, W. Experimental analysis of the psychopathological effects of the intoxicating drugs. *Amer. J. Psychiat.,* 1934, **90,** 853–879.

McQuitty, L. L. Differential validity in some pattern analytic methods. In B. M. Bass & I. A. Berg (Eds.), *Objective approaches to personality assessment.* Princeton, N.J.: Van Nostrand, 1959.

Meehl, P. *Clinical versus statistical prediction.* Minneapolis: Univer. of Minnesota Press, 1954.

National Institutes of Mental Health. *Behavioral research in preclinical psychopharmacology.* Psychopharmacology Service Center Bulletin, Bethesda, Md., 1961.

Robbins, L. L., & Wallerstein, R. S. The research strategy and tactics of the psychotherapy research project of the Menninger Foundation and the problem of controls. In E. A. Rubinstein & M. B. Parloff (Eds.), *Research in psychotherapy.* Washington, D.C.: American Psychological Association, 1959.

Rosenthal, D., & Frank, J. D. Psychotherapy and the placebo effect. *Psychol. Bull.,* 1956, **53,** 294–302.

Rubinstein, E. A., & Parloff, M. B. (Eds.). *Research in psychotherapy*. Washington, D.C.: American Psychological Association, 1959.

Saucer, R. T., & Deabler, H. L. Perception of apparent motion in organics and schizophrenics. *J. consult. Psychol.,* 1956, **20,** 385–389.

Shagass, C. Drug thresholds as indicators of personality and affect. In L. Uhr & J. G. Miller (Eds.), *Drugs and behavior.* New York: Wiley, 1960.

Shields, J. Twins brought up apart. *Eugenics Rev.,* 1958, **50,** 115–123.

Shields, J., & Slater, E. Heredity and psychological abnormality. In H. J. Eysenck (Ed.), *Handbook of abnormal psychology.* New York: Basic Books, 1961.

Sidman, M. *Tactics of scientific research.* New York: Basic Books, 1960.

Spence, K. W. The nature of theory construction in contemporary psychology. *Psychol. Rev.,* 1944, **51,** 47–68.

Stern, C. *Principles of human genetics.* (2d Ed.) San Francisco: Freeman, 1960.

Turbin, N. V. Philosophical problems in contemporary genetics. In Russian Scientific Trans. Program., N.I.H., *The Central Nervous System and Behavior.* Bethesda, Md., 1959.

Windelband, W. *Geschichte und Naturwisserschaft.* (3d Ed.) Strasbourg: Heitz, 1904.

Woolley, D. W., & Shaw, E. A biochemical and pharmacological suggestion about certain mental disorders. *Science,* 1954, **119,** 587.

APPLICATION 6
OF PSYCHOLOGICAL
CONCEPTS: CONFLICT

Equipped with the principles and concepts outlined in the preceding chapter, we now turn to consider their application to the phenomena of behavior pathology. The use of experimental psychological techniques in the study of deviant behavior is a matter of comparatively recent history. At the theoretical level, it has depended heavily upon the concepts of *frustration* and *conflict*.

THE EXPERIMENTAL NEUROSIS

Origin

For some years, experimental psychopathologists have been interested in the phenomenon of what has been loosely called *experimental neurosis*. The earliest evidence of scientific interest in the phenomenon is in the descriptions (Pavlov, 1928) of a now classic experiment by Shenger-Krestovnikova in Pavlov's laboratory. In this experiment a dog was conditioned to salivate whenever a circular stimulus was present, and reinforcement was withheld whenever an ellipse was substituted. Predictably, the dog learned to discriminate between the circle and the ellipse, salivating in the presence of the former but not in the presence of the latter. When a stimulus was presented which was more circular than the ellipse, but more elliptical than the circle (the ratio of the two axes of the stimulus being 9:8), the dog developed a breakdown of discrimination and began to struggle and howl.

Pavlov's explanation of this effect was couched in terms of a hypothetical state of equilibrium between excitation and inhibition on the cortex. He remarked, "Our experiments on dogs give us the right to consider these changes which we produce—the chronic deviation of the higher nervous activity from the normal—as pure neuroses, and some light can be thrown on their origin" (Pavlov, 1928, p. 348).

It should be noted in passing that after the discrimination had broken down at the difficult ratio of 9:8, discrimination at simpler ratios was also disturbed. The breakdown of discrimination appeared to generalize to other discriminations which had previously been made without difficulty.

Many other investigators followed up this problem. A tabular summary of their procedures, subjects, etc., is given in Box 6-1 from a representative sample of such investigations. Inspection of this box suggests that the presence or absence of restraint in the experimental setup is an important factor in determining whether or not behavioral abnormalities occur. The possible theoretical significance of this will be discussed later.

Symptoms

A wide list of deviant responses has been reported from the studies already mentioned. Pavlov referred to muscle tremor, and rage reactions, while other investigators have mentioned hyperexcitability and restlessness, deviations in breathing and in heart rate, immobility, falling asleep, extremely fast reaction time to external stimulation together with increased magnitude of response, motor tics, sexual disabilities, "hallucinatory" responses [i.e., making eating responses to nonexistent food (Masserman & Pechtel, 1953)], and several others.

The readiness with which we can describe these behaviors in language that has developed from the description of human deviant behavior indicates the striking nature of the analogy these investigators feel they have found. Not all the researchers who have engaged in this work believe that the analogy between the experimental neurosis and human behavior disorders is entirely adequate. Furthermore, the method of argument from analogy is surrounded with the hazards described in Chapter 5. Granted this, we cannot fail to be impressed by the appearance of these responses in a wide range of organisms and by the reappearance of response patterns across organisms and situations.

Nearly all students of the experimental neurosis have noticed differences in the extent to which particular animals developed deviant responses. Individual differences are consistent features of these reports in terms of both the magnitude of the deviations observed and the kind of response which emerged. In the absence of any other explanation, these differences have generally been referred to temperamental factors in the animals. Pavlov, for example, distinguished between *excitatory* and *inhibitory* types of dogs on the basis of the behavior of the animals when the discrimination became difficult. He thought of both these types as subtypes of a broader dichotomy— the *stable* and *unstable* nervous systems. In the unstable organism, one or another process of excitation or inhibition was dominant, depending on whether the dog was an excitatory or inhibitory type. Beyond the historical interest of the explanation, there is little to recommend it, because the nervous system typology is purely *post hoc* in that it is necessary to observe the behavior of the dog in the experimental situation before being able to "diagnose" what kind of nervous system it has.

Neurotic Behavior and Restraint

Returning to our earlier observation that restraint seems to be a necessary precondition for the development of experimental neurosis, let us consider an experiment by Cook (1939). He compared the effects of

BOX 6-1

Investigator	Type of conditioning	Subject	CS+	CS−
Pavlov (1928): M. N. Yerofeyeva	Classical, salivation	Dog	Shock to skin	No shock
N. R. Shenger-Krestovnikova	Classical, salivation	Dog	Circle	Ellipse
Cook (1939)	Instrumental	White rat	Bright light (for food and water)	Dim light (for shock)
	Instrumental	White rat		Dim light (for shock)
Dworkin (1939)	Instrumental, consumatory motor-alimentary response	Cat, dog	Low pitch (2,700 cps)	High pitch (as low as 2,800 cps)
Anderson & Parmenter (1941)	Classical, leg flexion	Sheep, dog	Varied	Varied
Masserman (1943)	Instrumental, consumatory feeding response	Cat	Light, buzzer, or bell	Lack of CS +
Gantt (1944)	Classical	Sheep, dog	Varied	Varied
Lichtenstein (1950)	Eating in restraint	Dog	Appearance of food pellet in feeder	Appearance of food pellet
Liddell (1956)	Classical, leg flexion	Shropshire ram	Metronome at 60 beats per minute	Metronome 120–72 beats per minute

SOURCE: *John R. Frederiksen*

punishing rats while drinking but unrestrained, with the effects of the same sequence of reinforcements upon rats who were unable to escape from restraint in the apparatus. The CS for positive reinforcement was a bright light and that for punishment, a dim light. As the lights were made more and more alike in intensity, a difficult discrimination was created. The restrained rats developed the classical symptoms of experimental neurosis while the unrestrained ones did not.

Speculation about this suggests that the presence of the difficult discrimination itself is aversive or threatening to the subject. This speculation is buttressed by the frequency with which the investigators have concluded that the symptoms produced in their subjects represent in part an attempt to get out of the situation. Falling asleep or attacking the

UCS	Source of conflict	Restraint?	Behavior abnormalities observed
Food	Conflict between CR to shock and natural defense reaction to shock	Yes	Yes, limited to the laboratory.
Food	Difficult discrimination: ellipse approaches circle	Yes	Yes, limited to the laboratory.
Water, shock	Conflict of drinking and avoidance of shock	No	No
Food, shock	Delay of food-getting response combined with difficult discrimination	Yes	Yes
Food	Difficult discrimination	No (cat) Yes (dog)	Slight and transitory (cat) Yes (dog)
Shock to leg	1. Difficult discrimination 2. Experimental extinction 3. Rigid time schedule	Yes	Yes, in 7 out of 28 cases.
Food plus air blast or shock at time of feeding	Incompatible response tendencies of feeding and escape from shock or air blast	Some: cat confined to small apparatus, but able to avoid shock or blast	Yes
Varied	1. Conflict of emotions 2. Difficult discrimination 3. Change in time schedule 4. Increase in intensity of conditioned stimulus 5. Failure to follow CS+ by UCS	Yes	Yes, limited to the inside of the experimental apparatus.
Food. Shock	Food pellet in CS for both food and shock	Yes	Yes
Shock	Difficult discrimination: between 60 and 72 beats per minute	Yes	Yes, outside the laboratory as well as inside.

restraining apparatus are obvious instances. Liddell, however, went somewhat further than this, claiming that every response observed in the experimental neurosis—"in sheep, goat, pig or dog, whether positive or negative, exemplifies a refinement and elaboration or even chronic distortion of the crude fight or flight pattern" (Liddell, 1956, p. 15).

Taking stock, we may say that (a) the availability of actual escape from the difficult discrimination appears to reduce the probability of deviant behavior occurring, and (b) when deviant behavior does occur in restraint, some of the responses seem to have the characteristics of escape responses. We notice, at the same time, that the discrimination need not be between conditioned stimuli for reward and punishment. In the experiments in Pavlov's laboratory and in that reported by Dworkin (1939), no punishment is involved—merely the presence or absence of reward. Nevertheless, deviant behaviors did appear.

From these facts we may wish to conclude that the psychological state generated by a difficult discrimination is intrinsically aversive. That is to say, it is aversive quite apart from any history of punishment which may be associated with any of the stimuli present. When faced with a difficult discrimination, the subject will respond by escaping from the situation. When escape is not possible, the responses may include whatever partial escape responses are possible, but also will include those responses which commonly occur as unconditioned responses to noxious stimulation, i.e., the pattern of response usually identified as *fear*.

Neurotic Behavior and Conflict

Difficult discriminations are situations in which the stimulus pattern present has been associated with two incompatible responses. Incompatible responses may be developed either (*a*) by pairing the CS at different times with different USs, each of which produces a different UR, or (*b*) by establishing a discrimination between two different CSs on the basis of pairing with different USs, and then presenting a generalization stimulus which lies within the generalization gradients of both the CSs concerned. In some cases the stimuli conditioned to the competing responses have been clearly under the control of the experimenter; in others the stimuli evoking the response may include the internal stimuli of hunger.

A stimulus generalization analysis of the difficult discrimination task has been presented by Brown (1942). The principles involved in this analysis, which are presented in Figure 6-1, are quite simple. Here CS^1 evokes R^1 while CS^2 evokes R^2, as established by suitable prior conditioning. Both of the conditioned stimuli are in the same continuous physical dimension, e.g., one is a bright light and the other a dim light. Both of the conditioned stimuli generate gradients of stimulus generalization, and these gradients overlap for a certain part of their range. At the point designated CS^G in Figure 6-1, the stimulus CS^G should elicit both R^1 and R^2 with equal strength, thereby producing a conflict of incompatible responses and the situation of experimental neurosis. We may therefore define the basic

Figure 6-1. Generalized tendencies to make competing responses elicit conflict when the two gradients meet.

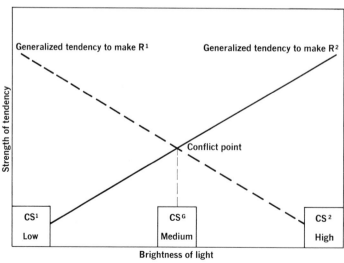

determinant of experimentally produced behavior deviations as *conflict*. Conflict may in turn be defined as *any pattern of stimulation presented to an organism which has the power to elicit two or more incompatible responses, the strengths of which are functionally equal.*[1] Conflict situations are inherently aversive and will elicit avoidance behavior if this is possible under the prevailing conditions. Where it is not possible, the pattern of responses which emerges will resemble those elicited by direct noxious stimulation.

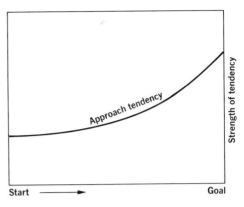

Figure 6-2. Strength of tendency to make approach response with increasing proximity to goal.

THE GRADIENT MODEL: MILLER'S THEORY

The Concept of Gradients

Experimental investigations of conflict states in recent decades have been largely influenced by the *gradient* model of conflict developed by Miller and his associates (e.g., Miller, 1959). Miller's formulations have been directly applied to the interpretation of a wide variety of human behavior, both normal and deviant. As we shall see, the phenomena which he has studied have much in common with the experimental-neurosis paradigm, but his assumptions, measurements, and deductions about conflict-produced behavior are considerably more sophisticated and rigorous than any of the work so far described.

One of the major theoretical influences in the development of Miller's model was the concept of the *goal gradient* derived by Clark L. Hull (1932). Stated simply, Hull hypothesized that when a chain of responses is terminated by reinforcement, each response in the chain is conditioned to the stimuli present at the moment of the re-

[1] The term "functionally equal" may be preferred to an assumption of absolute equality, because of the fact that stimuli which are different in absolute physical measurements may not be discriminably different to a living observer. The concept of the just noticeable difference (see Chapter 3) is applicable here.

sponse. However, those responses which occur later in the chain, i.e., closer to the point of reinforcement, are more strongly conditioned than those earlier in the chain. This hypothesis follows from the observation that the longer the interval between a response and the reinforcement for it, the weaker is the conditioning of that response to the concomitant stimuli. When the chain of responses consists of the repetition of the same response, as would be the case when an animal is simply running along a straight alley for food, then we should be able to observe a gradual increase in magnitude of the response the closer the subject gets to the food box. Increases in magnitude might take the form of greater speed in running, or greater magnitude in any generalized response if running is prevented.

This change in response strength with increasing proximity to the point of reinforcement (or *goal*) may be drawn graphically as a rising gradient which reaches its maximum height at the goal. A simple illustration of a gradient of running toward a goal in a straight alley is presented in Figure 6-2. Careful consideration of this hypothesis will make it clear that the gradient should be similar to the gradient obtained when we study the effect of delay in reinforcement upon the acquisition of a response. However, the form which the gradient might take in the case of running along a straight alley will also be a function of any consistent change in stimulus intensity which might occur as the response chain is emitted. For example, we might place a bright light over the goal, so that the strength of illumination impinging upon the animal is at a maximum at the goal and gets weaker the farther the animal is from the light source. Under these conditions we should expect to find that the gradient of stimulus generalization is also operating to produce weaker responses distant from the goal and stronger responses close to the goal.

Bearing these two processes in mind, we can proceed to the enunciation of Miller's postulates:

A. The tendency to approach a goal is stronger the nearer the subject is to it.

B. The tendency to avoid a feared stimulus is stronger the nearer the subject is to it. (Miller, 1959, p. 205.)

Postulate B is clearly a simple extension of the idea of a gradient to include avoidance learning. The two postulated gradients are termed the *gradient of approach* and the *gradient of avoidance*.

Gradients: Space and Time

Before going further with the problem of the gradient model, we should note that spatial distance is not a stimulus per se. Where some physical stimulus changes with distance, such as stimulus size, brightness, loudness, etc., then the use of space measurements is simply a crude but convenient substitute for direct measurements of the changes in stimulus strength. Where there are no changes in a physical stimulus pattern associated with changes in distance from a goal, then we should expect little or no spatial gradient per se. However, the delay-of-reinforcement gradient is inevitably produced whenever the subject is required to move through space to get to the goal. Now many human behavior chains occur in relation to goals which may be reached after some temporal period has elapsed, but which do not necessarily have any particular or

fixed relation to the person in space. Thus the individual who is anticipating a visit to the dentist with some fear may become increasingly apprehensive as the time for his appointment draws near. When his appointment is still a long time in the future, the fact that his daily round may take him physically close to the dentist's office is not likely to produce an increase in anxiety.

These considerations are important, for we shall see that whereas most of the experimental data available in support of the Miller model are obtained from animals moving in space, most of the clinical applications of the model are to human beings behaving over time.

The Relative Steepness of Gradients

Experiments with animals which had been given food at the end of the runway showed that if shock was substituted for the food on later trials, the animal would subsequently run part of the way toward the goal and then stop. To handle this phenomenon, Miller found it necessary to make a further assumption, which is stated in the form of a postulate:

C. The strength of avoidance increases more rapidly with nearness [to the goal] than does that of approach. (Miller, 1959, p. 205.)

This assumption is illustrated in Figure 6-3.

Postulate C rather neatly describes the effect of the two gradients which we assume to be operating in the case of a subject who has been both rewarded and then punished in the same situation. Two deductions follow from this postulate.

1. When a subject is placed sufficiently far from the goal, he will approach it until the two gradients are of equal height. That is to say, when the strength of the tendency to approach equals the strength of the tendency to avoid, the subject will do neither, but will remain in equilibrium at that point.

2. When a subject is placed close to the goal, he should retreat until the two gradients are in equilibrium as defined in no. 1.

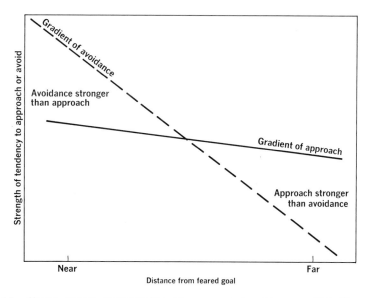

Figure 6-3. Simple graphic representation of an approach-avoidance conflict. The tendency to approach is the stronger of the two tendencies far from the goal, whereas the tendency to avoid is the stronger of the two near to the goal. Therefore, when far from the goal, the subject should tend to approach part way and then stop. In short, he should tend to remain in the region where the two gradients intersect. (Miller, 1959.)

We would note that no. 1 did not follow from the postulate; it is the empirical observation that led to the formulation of the postulate. On the other hand, no. 2 is a real deduction and may be tested when we are inquiring into the validity of this postulate.

Varieties of Conflict

Consideration of the concept of gradients and their relationship to goals indicates that several types of conflict situation might arise in the course of normal interaction with the environment.

Approach-Approach Conflict. Under some circumstances an organism might be presented with two stimuli each of which is a CS for a different response but where the conditioning in both cases was established by positive reinforcement. Should this ever occur in such a way that the tendency to respond to one was equal to the tendency to respond to the other, then a state of equilibrium would exist. Should the response

of escaping from the point of equilibrium result in bringing the individual closer in space or time to one of the goals rather than the other, then the equilibrium would be destroyed, to be replaced by the dominance of the closer goal. Consequently we should expect to find very few situations where conflict behavior, or "neurotic" behavior, was produced by an approach-approach conflict.

There may be some question as to whether or not a purely approach-approach conflict could ever be identified. Whenever the selection of one goal necessarily means the loss of the other, then the avoidance of this loss may develop avoidance gradients which complicate the analysis.

Avoidance-Avoidance Conflicts. Here we are dealing with a conflict in which the subject is placed in a situation where two aversive stimuli are present and the response of avoiding one brings him closer to the other. In a spatial conflict, avoidance of the equilibrium point will bring the subject

Application of Psychological Concepts: Conflict

physically closer to one of the aversive stimuli and will thereby increase the tendency to avoid it. This will bring the subject back to the equilibrium point, and the cycle should repeat itself. Overt behavior in such a conflict then should consist of oscillation around the equilibrium point until some new variable enters the environment to alter the relative strength of the two tendencies.

Approach-Avoidance Conflicts. In our discussion above of the relative steepness of gradients, we describe a conflict based upon a history of both reward and punishment at the same point. Whenever the responses conditioned to a stimulus are both approach and avoidant in nature, we have an approach-avoidance conflict, with the phenomenon of the partial approach response already described.

Double Approach-Avoidance Conflicts. In human conflicts it is often the case that each of the two alternatives possesses both attractive and aversive features. Thus the decision to approach one of them produces a "movement" that will begin both to increase the avoidance tendency for the stimulus approached and to reduce the avoidance tendency for the one that was not chosen. Under these circumstances, a state of equilibrium should soon be reached. Retreat from the equilibrium point involves approach toward the previously rejected option and the reaching of a new equilibrium. Thus, at least hypothetically, the individual should oscillate indefinitely between two equilibrium points.

It is more than likely that this state of affairs exists in what may seem, on the face of it, to be simple approach-approach conflicts. The decision to choose a particular career may involve giving up another one. While both careers may be attractive, i.e., free from intrinsically aversive aspects, the actual selection of one may generate distress at the seemingly irrevocable loss of the other. This fact may interfere with a straightforward pursuit of the goal first chosen and may lead to much oscillation. It is questionable whether any true approach-approach conflict occurs in human experience—other than perhaps purely trivial and momentary decisions about which necktie to wear or meal to order.

Empirical Gradients

Moving from questions of assumptions and definitions, we may consider the nature of the gradients of approach and avoidance which have been obtained experimentally. First let us study the now classic experiment of J. S. Brown (1948) in which gradients of approach and avoidance were inferred from measuring the strength of pull which rats would exert to get closer to a goal box in which they had received food or to avoid a goal box in which they had received painful electric shock. Briefly, Brown's experimental procedure involved the observation of the responses of four groups of animals. Two were avoidance groups—strong and weak, depending upon the strength of shock administered to them. Two approach groups were defined as strong or weak depending upon the hours of food deprivation under which their responses were measured. Each animal was first given a number of trials under hunger motivation, in which it ran along a straight alley to a goal box where it received food. After the running response was well established, the approach groups were treated under either 1 hour or 48 hours of deprivation. In a test trial the animal was harnessed with an arrangement of rubber bands and permitted to run toward the goal. The harness was hooked to a device which came into tension against a restraining spring, thus preventing the animal from approaching a chosen point. Prearranged points were used, each animal in the strong-approach group being tested at points 30 and 170 centimeters from the goal.

The weak-approach group was tested at only one point, the 30-centimeter location. The avoidance groups received the same initial approach training that the approach groups did and then were given additional trials under minimum hunger, on which they received shock at the goal box. Their strength of pull in the harness to avoid the goal box was recorded in the manner described. Brown's data are presented in graphic form in Figure 6-4.

Before proceeding further, it should be noted that the gradients reported by Brown are, of course, obtained from animals in either an approach or an avoidance condition. The slopes of these gradients do not indicate the effect of a history of both punishment and reward *in the same subject* unless we make an additional assumption. This assumption is that gradients obtained from studies of reward alone and of punishment alone may be summated directly to provide a combined gradient predictive of the response tendencies of individuals who experience both kinds of reinforcement.

As they stand, the data of Brown appear to provide empirical verification of Miller's postulate C—although the postulate was developed before the empirical data were in. This postulate is crucial to the Miller model, since most other deductions about conflict behavior come from it. Because of the central position postulate C occupies, we should examine the evidence with considerable care.

Critique of Brown's Experiment. Certain technical problems in Brown's experiment make it difficult to accept the interpretation that has usually been offered. Because repeated measures were used (i.e., each animal pulled twice), it is quite possible that fatigue and extinction of avoidance produced some changes in the shape of the avoidance gradient. Replicating Brown's avoidance group, Maher and Nuttall (1962) found that the animals which were first tested at the 30-centimeter point produced much weaker pulls when tested for the second time at 170 centimeters than did the animals that were tested in the reverse order. These data are shown in Figure 6-5. The effect of combining the pulls of all the animals in calculating the mean produces a spurious depression at the 170-centimeter point and thus gives greater steepness to the avoidance

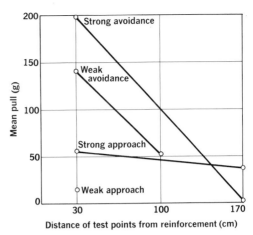

Figure 6-4. Data on strength of pull to approach and pull to avoid in the original study by Brown (1948).

gradient than would be the case if we measured it free from these effects, i.e., if we used first pulls only.

A second problem is the anchoring of gradients by using two locations only. By measuring responses of large numbers of animals, it is possible to plot the shape of a gradient at several points along the runway. This has been done for approach gradients by Smith (1960) and for avoidance by Maher and Nuttall (1962). The gradients obtained in these two studies are shown in Figures 6-6 and 6-7. Both studies produced S-shaped gradients. Smith also obtained declining gradients for hooded rats, suggesting that the shape of gradients may be significantly affected by genetic characteristics of the organism used.

Yet a third difficulty with Brown's experiment is the fact that in the strong-avoidance group, 16 of 20 animals failed to pull at all at the 170-centimeter position. Because of this, statistical evaluation of the results is severely handicapped.

Probability Gradients

In the experiments so far cited, the evidence for a decline in response tendency with increasing distance from the goal has con-

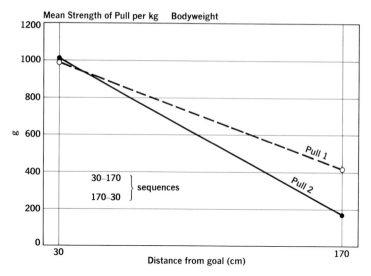

Figure 6-5. The effect of fatigue in producing steeper gradient for avoidance when repeated measures are used. (Maher and Nuttall, 1962.)

sisted of attempts to demonstrate that the *strength* of the response diminishes. Another aspect of this question relates to whether or not a measurable response will occur at all at increasing distances from the goal.

At the distant point in Brown's experiment (170 centimeters), only four animals pulled in the avoidance condition. From this we might want to conclude not only that responses decline in physical magnitude, but

Figure 6-6. Differential steepness of approach gradient obtained with differing strains of rat. (Smith, 1960.)

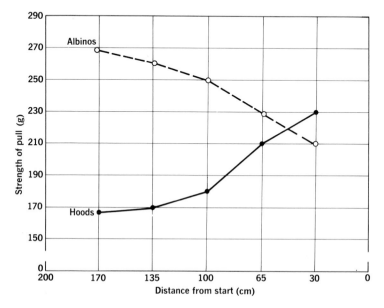

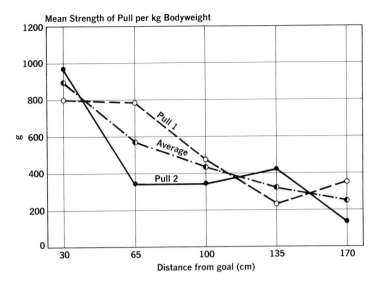

Figure 6-7. S-shaped gradient of approach when measured at several points, showing effects of averaging in producing smooth curve. (Maher & Nuttall, 1962.)

that there is a concomitant decline in the probability that they will be made at all. We have also pointed out that distance from the goal is not a stimulus per se, but is simply correlated with some other changes in the environment which occur as distance increases. Distance from the goal, then, is a stimulus generalization variable. With increasing distance we should expect to find the same phenomena which are seen when any physical stimulus attribute of a CS is changed.

Some collateral evidence on this problem is provided by Hearst (1960), who obtained separate gradients for the probability of the occurrence of a positively rewarded or an avoidance response in the presence of a CS, when different values of the CS were used for generalization testing.[2] These gradients were obtained from the same animals

[2] In Hearst's experiment the approach response and the avoidance response were not mutually incompatible, and thus his study is not necessarily descriptive of gradients obtained in conflict situations. It is cited here because of its importance in demonstrating that his gradients of stimulus generalization do not follow the pattern to be expected from Miller.

(rhesus monkeys), i.e., there were no separate groups for reward and punishment conditions. As Figure 6-8 indicates, the stimulus generalization gradient for the aversive condition was considerably flatter than that for the reward condition—an almost exact reversal of the position to be expected from the Miller postulates.

Temporal Gradients

Not many investigations of temporal gradients have been made, even though the temporal relationship of responses to reinforcement may well be fundamental to any spatial effects. Rigby (1954), however, has reported gradients of approach and avoidance obtained from rats given both reward and punishment in a temporal conflict. In this experiment the animal was restrained in the presence of a stimulus which preceded the delivery of food by a fixed period of time. Later the reward was replaced by shock. Efforts to move toward or away from the stimulus were recorded as a function of the increasing temporal proximity of the goal. These are given in Figure 6-9.

Rigby's gradients are approximately parallel, and they rise at an increasing rate as the time for reinforcement draws near. He also noted the occurrence of conflict behaviors as the time goal approached. These were reminiscent of the responses already discussed in the section on experimental neurosis. This is not surprising, of course, in view of the fact that in Rigby's study there was no way for the animal to escape from a purely time-bound event.

In the human subject, the question of temporal gradients in conflict behavior has been little studied. Epstein and Fenz (1962) measured the responses of parachute jumpers as the day for the first jump approached. They conceived of the situation as being one in which the fear of death or injury was in conflict with the desire for excitement or prestige. Their data show that as the day for the jump approached, there was an increase in an autonomic response (GSR) to words which were related to parachute jumping. The more closely related the stimulus word, the more pronounced was the GSR. This relationship itself was more evident on the day of the jump than it was when measured two weeks beforehand. Reaction times to these words were affected in the same manner, and perceptual errors also were more marked on the day of the jump than two weeks prior to it. Thus as the subject approaches the goal, measures of conflict increase in intensity. No estimates can be made from these data regarding the rela-

Figure 6-8. Generalization gradients for reward-controlled and punishment-controlled behavior. (From Hearst, 1960; copyright 1960 by the American Association for the Advancement of Science.)

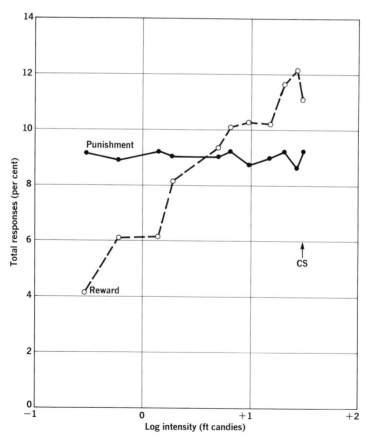

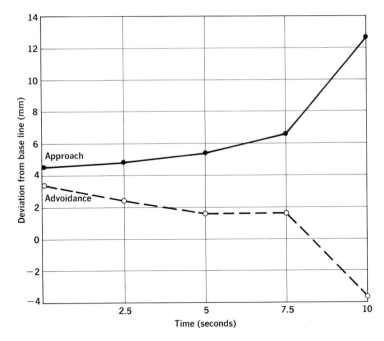

Figure 6-9. Composite approach and avoidance gradients after differentiation training. (Rigby, 1954.)

tive shape of approach and avoidance gradients over time, but it is clear that measures of conflict state change in gradient fashion as the time draws near.

Maher, Weisstein, and Sylva (1964) studied the behavior of young children when confronted with a choice between different goal objects. Facing an apparatus shown in Figure 6-10, the subject selected one of the two objects by pressing the appropriate lever which activated the clock timer. When the timer ran back to the zero point, the selected object would be delivered. Should the subject change his mind while the clock was running, he could depress the lever, which would reset the timer back to the starting point so that the cycle would begin again. In this experimental setup, it is possible to record oscillations and the time distance from the goal at which they occurred. Some of the experimental conditions involved uncertainty about the side which would deliver the most desired goal object, and others involved an uncertain choice between a desired object versus no reward at all. Observations

Figure 6-10. Apparatus for the study of temporal conflict.

made in these experiments are shown in Figure 6-11. It will be seen that the larger the number of goal objects at stake, the more oscillations were made, and that the situation which involved a risk of getting no reward at all produced the maximum number of oscillations.

If we conceive of these experiments as involving a double approach-avoidance response, we can understand why the condition with the maximum avoidance, i.e., the fear of ending up with nothing, should generate the most conflict and the greatest oscillation. It is particularly interesting that the mean point in time at which the oscillations occurred was not a constant distance from the goal but rather was a constant ratio of the total time to be run. This suggests that conflict-produced behavior in time may be determined not merely by how far away in time the threatening event is, but also by

the total time the subject must wait before it happens.

Another interesting aspect of these data is the fact that there was a wide range of oscillation responses among the children; some never oscillated, and others did so with great frequency. For example, the correlation between a child's oscillations on the risk of no reward condition and the certainty of some reward condition was .94. We might speculate that these children had already learned certain tendencies in the face of decision conflicts, and that these tendencies were operating experimental conditions themselves.

Distance from the Goal

In all the foregoing investigations, the anchoring point from which predictions are made is the goal or point of reinforcement.

Figure 6-11. Effect of increasing goal values and uncertainty on the number of oscillations in a temporal conflict. (Maher, Weisstein, & Sylva, 1964.)

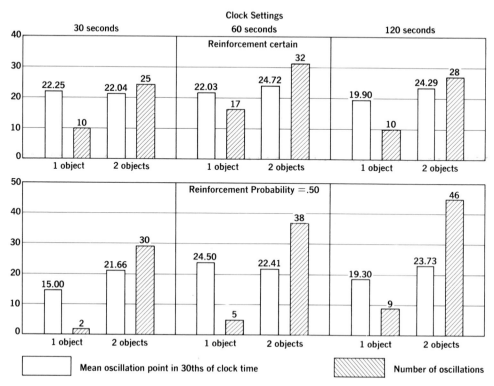

Mean oscillation point in 30ths of clock time   Number of oscillations

The heights of gradients are determined by t, and thus the intersection of conflicting gradients is also determined by it. A very simple prediction from this is that when gradients intersect at, let us say, 3 feet from the goal end of a straight alley, then the subject ought to stop running at that point, no matter how far away it was from the goal when the approach began. This prediction was tested by Maher and Noblin (1963) by the simple expedient of giving approach and avoidance training to a group of rats and then continuing to give trials in the straight alley until each S reached the trial on which its stopping point was between 33 and 39 inches from the goal box. Two subgroups of the animals were next given the subsequent trials with the start box moved back 12 and 24 inches respectively from the usual position. We would expect that all subjects would come to a stop at approximately the same distance from the goal on the next trials, irrespective of the distance from which they started.

In fact, the data clearly showed that each animal came to a stop after it had run a constant distance (see Figure 6-12). Thus, the farther away from the goal it was at the start, the farther away was its stopping point. This conclusion is difficult to reconcile with the notion that gradients are determined by

the variable of distance from the goal, and indeed these data suggest another way of looking at the problem. The alternative possibility is that the fear which leads the subject to inhibit the approach response is to a significant extent generated by the making of the approach response itself. Since, in the experiment just described, the response of running was followed by punishment, then running became a conditioned stimulus for fear. Thus the subjects all stopped after about the same distance from the start because the extent of the running response was a major determinant of the strength of fear which developed.

Problems of Gradients in the Approach-Avoidance Model

Before proceeding further, let us summarize the problems which have developed with the present form of the approach-avoidance model of conflict.

1. Experimental investigations have reported gradients in which the approach is steeper than the avoidance, or in which both are flat, or in which both slope but are parallel. Thus the implication that the avoidance gradients are necessarily steeper than approach gradients obtained in the

Figure 6-12. Inches run from the position of start point in a spatial conflict, suggesting relative unimportance of distance from the goal as a determinant of equilibrium. (Maher & Noblin, 1963.)

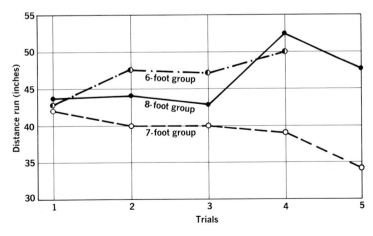

same situation is not validated by all the current data. The presence or absence of visual cues, the strain of animal used, the selection of response measure, and the elimination of repeated measures all affect the shape of the gradient.

2. There is only one study so far reported (i.e., Rigby, 1954) in which the shape of gradients for approach and avoidance were obtained from the same subjects where the approach and avoidance responses were incompatible. Observations about the relative shapes of individual gradients are only relevant to the question of the shapes of gradients in conflict situations if we assume that such gradients can be summated. Rigby's data do not support that assumption.

3. The application of spatial gradients to temporal situations involves drawing an analogy between spatial distances and time periods which gains no support from the rather scanty data available.

4. Where the influence of distance from the goal has been directly measured in a conflict situation, the data obtained seem to be more congruent with the possibility that the approach response is an important determinant of the appearance of the avoidance response.

Most of these problems arise from data concerned with individual gradients. Let us now consider the material which has been collected about the behavior of individuals in conflict situations, insofar as this is relevant to the Miller model.

Consequences of Summation of Gradients

From the simple form of the approach-avoidance model, certain deductions are necessary. One of these is that avoidance behavior should be greater the closer to the goal the subject is, when the approach and avoidance gradients have intersected somewhere behind him. In its most obvious form, this deduction would lead us to predict that a subject will avoid the goal area of an alley when prior training has created an avoidance gradient which intersects with the approach gradient somewhere in the alley. Just as the animal will run from the start to the equilibrium point, it should run from the goal back to the equilibrium point. Trapold, Miller, and Coons (1960) report that animals in such a situation more often ran *toward the goal* than away from it. Taylor and Maher (1959) report frequent observation of the response of running toward the goal by animals introduced to a situation in a presumably avoidance-dominant zone.

At the present time we lack complete data upon the behavior of subjects in the avoidance region of an approach-avoidance conflict, and much more research is necessary before we can understand it. However, what data we do have do not seem to be in accordance with the simple deductions demanded by the Miller model.

THE NEUROTIC PARADOX

Temporal Gradients and Neurotic Behavior

Early in Chapter 1 we noted that one of the criteria for defining behavior pathology is the presence of disabling behavior tendencies. These were described as behaviors which appear to be creating difficulties for the patient when more adequate responses to the situation are available. More simply, much pathological behavior persists in the face of continual social punishment, with little evidence of any offsetting reward. This phenomenon, which is mentioned briefly in Chapter 3, has been termed *the neurotic paradox*.

Many observers have been impressed by the fact that some individuals maintain behaviors which are so clearly inadequate, in the face of the ready availability of responses which should be more satisfying. This persistence of frequently punished responses has led to the formation of descriptive explanations on the part of some clinical theorists. The psychoanalytic notion of "repetition-compulsion" (Freud, 1920) represents a partial approach to this issue. Mowrer and Ullman (1945) have referred to the behavior as "paradoxical," and Dollard and Miller (1950) have termed it "stupid."

Moving from descriptive terms, let us examine the explanations of this behavior which have drawn upon the concept of reinforcement.

The Mowrer-Ullman Hypothesis

One hypothesis which has been offered (Mowrer & Ullman, 1945) points to the differences in the delay between the positive and negative consequences of neurotic behavior. If a particular response receives immediate reinforcement but the punishment is delayed, the occurrence of the response will depend not only upon whether or not the reinforcement is more significant than the punishment, but also upon the extent to which the latter is delayed. Under suitable conditions, the punishment could be quite severe but so delayed that it would be ineffective in inhibiting the response—when the response is receiving some immediate reinforcement. Thus punishment which would certainly be effective in suppressing a response if it were administered immediately after the response is made, may be ineffective if the interval between response and punishment is sufficiently great.

We can recognize three possible situations where punishment and reward are consequent upon the response.

1. The punishment and reward are both immediate, and punishment is sufficiently intense to inhibit the response. The outcome is that the response does not occur.
2. The punishment is intense, but is delayed too long to inhibit the response. However, the delay-of-punishment gradient is not zero at the time the response is made, and thus anticipatory fear is experienced immediately after the response. Renner (1962) describes this effectively in terms of the patient who says, "Whenever I do anything enjoyable I feel frightened and things end up going wrong but I don't know why, and I don't see that I can do anything about it."
3. The delay of punishment is so great that

the gradient has a zero value when the response is made. Thus the subject does not attach the experience of fear to his own behavior, since the two do not occur in contiguity. Instead his fear becomes exclusively conditioned to the punishing agent. Such an individual would continue to exhibit the punished behaviors but would not appear to be anxious about them. His position might be indicated by some statement such as "They [society] are just a bunch of killjoys. Whenever they find out you have been enjoying yourself, they try to make things hot for you."

Where the act is being reinforced by immediate anxiety reduction, and where it consists of withdrawal from or avoidance of society, then the latter social punishment will simply reinforce it further. In this case both the immediate reinforcement (anxiety reduction) and the fear of punishment will act together to produce the same responses.

Limits of the Mowrer-Ullman Hypothesis. The Mowrer-Ullman hypothesis is consistent with both the principles and the empirical findings of delay-of-reinforcement studies. However, it does have some limitations, which need to be noted.

1. Many neurotic situations seem to involve immediate punishment and later secondary gain. Thus the sophisticated observer may be compelled to recognize that the patient's symptoms are making him continually miserable and that we have to look long and far to find anything which seems like a reward or gain from his behavior. Such situations are not handled within the Mowrer-Ullman hypothesis.
2. The hypothesis does not deal with the manner in which responses, or symptoms, are developed in the first place; it deals only with the conditions under which they persist after development.

Extension of the Mowrer-Ullman Hypothesis. Renner (1962) has extended the assumptions of the Mowrer-Ullman hypothesis to include situations where the delay-of-reward gradient might be sufficiently high that under appropriate conditions an immediate punishment would be insufficient to counteract the motivational effects of the forthcoming positive reinforcement. Thus the making of the punished response would result in a net increment of reinforcement, and the likelihood of the response occurring again would be increased. Renner's extension of this hypothesis includes two assumptions:

1. When a response has been both punished and rewarded, we predict whether or not it will occur by comparing the delay-of-reinforcement gradients generated for both punishment and reward. These gradients will be altered by the actual history of delay, strength of relevant motives, and so forth. This represents a more explicit statement of what is implied in the use of the goal gradient by Miller, but is essentially in line with it.

2. The temporal gradient for punishment may be flatter than that for reward. Since this is in contradiction to the basic assumptions of the spatial model of approach-avoidance conflict, it raises some difficult questions which will require resolution.

The Neurotic Paradox Considered

Leaving aside technical questions about the shape of temporal-delay gradients, we may summarize the situation by saying that provided we know the histories of punishment, reward, and the delay of each of these in the case of a particular individual, then the occurrence of punished responses may be understood. The paradox is resolvable as long as we bear in mind that neurotically paradoxical behavior is generated by conflict—that is, by situations in which a history of punishment and reward exists for the behavior in question.

Much neurotic behavior is not paradoxical. Many of the behaviors which we label psychopathic are regarded as neurotic mainly because they involve actions which are morally reprehensible but not necessarily punishable by society. Drug addiction and homosexuality may be directly rewarding and, in the ordinary course of events, may not meet with much punishment. No obvious paradox is involved in this kind of behavior.

DISPLACEMENT

Up to this point we have seen that behavior in conflict situations may be understood by the suitable application of the concept of gradients—both gradients of stimulus generalization and gradients of delay in reinforcement. We have also seen that the exact nature of these gradients is open to considerable argument and that the available experimental data is not at all clear on several important points. However, let us postpone any further discussion of this for the time being and turn to consider some of the clinical applications of the gradient concept. One of the most interesting has been made with regard to the concept of displacement.

Displacement Defined

When an individual is prevented from carrying out some activity in relation to another object or person, he may instead carry out the same activity toward some irrelevant target. The prime example is the so-called "displaced aggression" phenomenon. A typical illustration would be a soldier who is reprimanded unjustly by a superior officer and is prevented by fear of punishment from attacking him or expressing any of the aggressive behaviors which are elicited. When a target comes along which he does not fear, such as another soldier inferior in rank, he abuses him instead. The aggression which was aroused by his superior is thus *displaced* onto the unoffending subordinate. Here the activity is essentially unchanged; it is simply displaced onto another object.

Another use of the concept of displacement refers to the fact that when a subject is prevented from engaging in one activity, he may engage in an entirely different one. Tinbergen (1951) comments as follows:

It has struck many observers that animals may, under certain circumstances, perform movements which do not belong to the motor pattern of the instinct that is activated at the moment of observation. For instance, fighting domestic cocks may suddenly pick at the ground, as if they were feeding. . . . Herring gulls, while engaged in deadly combat, may all at once pluck nesting material. (Pp. 113–114.)

Here the term "displacement" refers to appearance of a new activity, not to the shift of activity to another target. There are however, some aspects common to the explanations which have been offered for these activities.

Object Displacement and Conflict

Perhaps the most detailed analysis of object displacement has been offered by Murray and Berkun (1955). Their analysis, which elaborates some earlier work of Miller (1948), extends the notion of the gradients of approach-avoidance to include a situation in which "nearness to the goal," and the similarity of other goals to the original goal, represent two dimensions within which displacement is likely to occur. In Figure 6-13 we see the outlines of the situation.

Let us consider the behavior of an individual who is making an approach to the original goal, O. Starting at Z_0, he proceeds toward O to the point D at which the gradients of approach and avoidance are equal. At this point he may leave the field[3] and move into situation Z_1. Here the effects

[3] The question of why the subject leaves the field requires an answering assumption that equilibrium is noxious in itself and that the response of moving away from the situation is motivated by this aversiveness.

Figure 6-13. The original goal, where approach and avoidance tendencies were learned, is at point zero. The plane OXY, shows the decrement in approach and avoidance tendencies toward goals less and less similar to the original goal. The plane OYZ, shows decrements in approach and avoidance tendencies as a function of nearness to the goal. The vertical axis, OY, represents the strength of the behavioral tendency to approach or avoid a goal. (Murray & Berkun, 1955.)

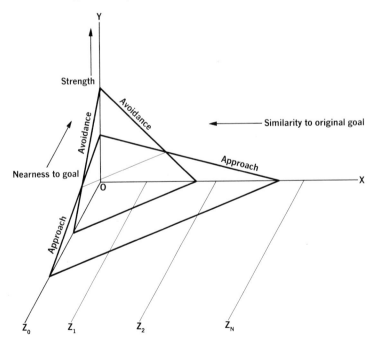

of stimulus generalization upon the two gradients are such that the avoidance gradient should have declined relatively more than the approach gradient (the gradient of generalization for avoidance being steeper than that for approach). Thus the intersection of the two gradients will be closer to the new goal and the individual will therefore approach it until the new equilibrium is reached. At this point the shift to Z_2 will occur, and so on until the point is reached at which the avoidance gradient does not intersect the approach gradient. At this point a complete approach will be made and the goal will be attained. In Figure 6-13 this would be at the line designated Z_2, since the avoidance gradient has diminished to zero somewhere between Z_1 and Z_2.

From this analysis we see that the approach behavior which was inhibited in the presence of the original goal (a) should occur in the presence of a suitably dissimilar goal, between Z_1 and Z_2, but (b) would not occur in the presence of a very dissimilar goal, e.g., Z_n, as this would be too far out on the generalization gradient to evoke either avoidance or approach responses. At this point, therefore, no displaced response will be seen.

This visual diagram of displacement is simply a convenience in expounding the nature of the model which is used in the explanation. Similarity of goal object is a rather complex concept. Target objects may be similar to some original goal in many different ways. Physical similarity, e.g., the wife who is the displacement target for responses which were originally aroused and inhibited by the subject's mother; and similarity of relationship, such as the mother who becomes dependent upon her grown daughter when dependent behavior is inhibited by her husband, would be examples of two possible dimensions.

Psychopathologists are interested in the concept of displacement for two reasons. First is the fact that displaced responses are often inappropriate to the goal to which they are made. The man who behaves toward his wife as a displacement response from a conflict in a relationship with his mother may be behaving in a way which will generate new and different problems with his wife. His behavior may be quite inadequate to the husband-wife relationship, and in this respect the behavior may be looked at as deviant.

Second, the concept of displacement is important because such a man's displaced behaviors may give the clinician a clue to the nature of the conflicts which he had with his mother, the original goal. Indeed, the notion of object displacement is commonly invoked to account for the way in which patients respond to psychotherapists, and it is crucial to some theories of therapeutic processes.

Object Displacement: Experimental Analogues

In an ingenious attempt to study an analogue of displacement based upon the three-dimensional model described in the preceding paragraphs, Murray and Berkun (1955) established an approach-avoidance conflict in rats in a straight alley which was painted a distinctive color. After this had been done, the animals were allowed access to neighboring alleys which were increasingly dissimilar in color and width to the original alley. The experimenters' prediction was that the subjects would approach progressively further along each "displacement" alley the more dissimilar it was to the original. In fact, this was the case, and the effect of stimulus generalization along a physical similarity dimension seemed to be demonstrated. Unfortunately, in their experimental procedure the location of the dissimilar alleys was such that the most similar alley was also in closest proximity to the original, and the least similar was the farthest away.

Replicating the study, Elder, Noblin, and Maher (1961) separated the effects of similarity and proximity by an apparatus which permitted several combinations of these two variables in the arrangements of the alleys (see Figure 6-14). With this precaution

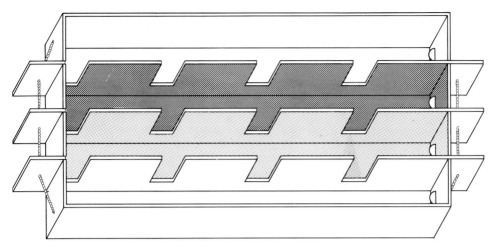

Figure 6-14. Parallel alleys for testing displacement. (Elder, Noblin, & Maher, 1961.)

taken, it was evident that physical similarity was not responsible for the displacement effect, but that proximity was. Both of these studies are experimental analogues, however, and should not be regarded as tests of the validity of the three-dimensional model itself.

Activity Displacement and Conflict

In discussing the displacement activity of animals, Tinbergen has commented that it appears to occur whenever there is (*a*) conflict of two strongly activated antagonistic drives, or (*b*) strong motivation of a drive, usually the sexual drive, together with the lack of the external stimuli necessary to release the goal responses appropriate to that drive. Characteristically, the animals showing displacement activities give the observer the impression of being highly motivated, and it is this feature that has been used by Bindra (1959) in his analysis of activity displacement. His explanation is as follows.

1. When an individual is prevented from engaging in an activity toward which he is motivated, there is an increase in his state of *arousal*. This state of arousal may be likened to a state of intense motivation and

activity. The heightened arousal lasts for some time after the inhibition of original activity.

2. In this state of arousal the activities which are most likely to occur are those which have high habit strength in the individual's repertoire of behaviors. Thus sheep prevented from escaping painful stimulation may show displacement grazing. Because grazing is a response which is practiced repeatedly by the sheep in the course of their daily activities, it is a response with considerable general habit strength. As such it is a likely response to occur in a high arousal state.

3. Which of the several strong habits in an individual's repertoire will actually occur will be determined by the other surrounding stimuli. In a complicated human social environment, there are many possibilities, and thus displacement activities might assume many forms. On the other hand, the relatively restricted range of stimuli present in an experimental apparatus makes it difficult to elicit strikingly irrelevant displacement responses.

When we apply Bindra's analysis to the case of the reprimanded soldier mentioned earlier, we note that his displacement of aggression onto his subordinate is quite predictable because this kind of behavior toward subordinates is common in a military situation anyway. In this case object displacement and activity displacement would lead to the same outcome. However, when we consider the case of a man who has been rebuked by his employer, Bindra suggests that whether or not he will later displace his aggression onto his wife will depend upon the activities for which his wife represents a stimulus. If his wife is a cue for relaxing, he may seek comfort and reassurance from her, rather than aggress toward her.

When discussing object displacement, we noticed that it might lead to deviant behavior. Exactly the same inference might be made about activity displacement. Here we would be dealing with a patient whose behavior might be quite appropriate to the surrounding stimuli but would not include the goal responses most pertinent to his motivations. The anxious patient, actively conflicted between his fear of responsibility and his desire for promotion in his work, may pace nervously up and down at home and may find himself picking up a cigarette, twiddling with the television set, and pouring himself a cup of coffee simply because the cigarette pack, television set, and coffeepot are all present in his room. His activities with each of these objects are appropriate to the object but irrelevant to his anxieties. In this sense his behavior is inadequate and ineffective.

Both of these explanations, the object displacement model and the activity displacement model, offer useful vehicles for understanding certain kinds of inappropriate behavior. They are not mutually exclusive, and it is quite possible that either mechanism may be operating in different situations. Irrespective of which analysis is the most suitable for a given sequence of behavior, we note that both of them are explicit and do not depend upon assumptions about the "draining away of energy." From either point of view, the appearance of deviant behavior is determined by the stimuli present

to the subject and the repertoire of habits which he has developed in his past experience.[4]

CONFLICT WITH PARALLEL GRADIENTS

At this point we have examined many of the problems of the gradient model of conflict and have studied its application to the phenomenon of displacement. Equipped with the data that have been presented here, we shall now turn to suggest a simpler model of conflict which may resolve some of the difficulties already encountered.

Punishment of Approach Motivation

When the hungry rat runs down the familiar alley to obtain food but is shocked instead, many stimuli are present. Quite apart from the external stimuli provided by the apparatus, there are the stimuli of hunger and the stimuli provided by the response of running. We must therefore expect that hunger and running will become conditioned stimuli for fear and that they will have an influence upon the avoidance behavior which the animal may exhibit. When an adolescent is punished for overt sexual behavior, the punishment is likely to result in a conditioned fear response not only to overt behavior but also to ~~whatever fantasies and~~ other motivational conditions were present at the time. In fact, the goal of the punishing agent is to deter the child from overt behavior by attaching the fear to the covert, preliminary stimuli.

Many classic experiments have demonstrated that animals, for example, are able to

---

[4] Tinbergen (1951) does explain displacement by reference to "surplus motivation the discharge of which through the normal paths is in some way prevented" (p. 114). Bindra has avoided this kind of language, preferring to invoke the more general concept of arousal.

discriminate their own motivational states and to use them as cues for differential responses. Noblin and Maher (1962) noted that some part of the avoidance component in an approach-avoidance conflict was reduced when the animal had the experience of the same state of hunger as when it was shocked, but had this experience outside the conflict apparatus. Nuttall (1963) likewise investigated the extent to which the avoidance component of a conflict was diminished by conducting extinction under degrees of hunger that differed from the one present when the animal had been punished. Under these conditions, animals which were extinguished under the same hunger schedule as that at which they had been punished were significantly slower to reduce avoidance than animals at other hunger levels. Once again this suggests that some part of the avoidance tendency is determined by the strength of the approach motivation. In the light of this it appears erroneous to assume that the approach motive and the avoidance motive affect only their respective gradients. There is good reason to assume that the approach motive contributes to both the approach and the avoidance tendencies.

Punishment of the Approach Response

During our previous discussion of the effect of distance from the goal, we noted that in at least one experimental study (Maher & Noblin, 1963), the stopping point in an alley was related to the distance run rather than to the point reached by that running. If we recognize that running was punished in the original avoidance training, we should expect that running acts as a conditioned stimulus for fear, which then inhibits running. Because the running response itself is largely controlled by the approach motive—i.e., the hungrier the animal, the more rapidly it runs—we see that the approach response is another mechanism by means of which the approach motive will affect the buildup of fear and the avoidance behavior associated with it.

A Parallel Gradient Model

Temporal gradients obtained by Rigby (1954) were, as we have seen, approximately parallel. These gradients were obtained from subjects that were responding after both punishment and reward experiences. Thus we are looking at gradients without having to make any assumptions about the summation of separate groups. Let us assume, for the sake of discussion, that the effect of training to both punishment and reward is to produce gradients which are essentially of the same shape and slope, their relative heights being determined by the number of rewards or punishments and the strength of drive for each of the two motives. The form of such gradients is illustrated in Figure 6-15. Let us also remember that in the classic experimental neurosis described in the opening pages of this chapter, the breakdown in the animal's behavior occurred when it became impossible to discriminate between the positive and the negative stimulus. In the Shenger-Krestovnikova study, the stimulus which produced the breakdown was actually an ellipse, but was not noticeably different from a circle insofar as the dog's power of discrimination was concerned. Thus the circle and the ellipse in question were functionally equal, although not physically so.

In Figure 6-15, we suggest that when the subject is at a point distant in space or time

Figure 6-15. Model of conflict assuming conditions of parallel gradients. (Maher, 1964.)

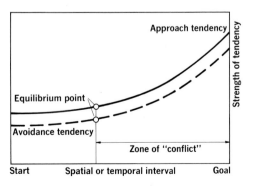

from the goal, and the approach gradient is higher than the avoidance gradient, the subject approaches the goal. With increasing nearness to the goal in space or time, the local pattern of stimulation (including the approach response and approach motives) augments both tendencies equally. Both gradients are thus increasing at the same rate. Soon a point is reached at which the pattern of stimulation is producing a strong approach response and an almost equally strong avoidance response. The relative difference between them has been reducing as their absolute heights increase. When this point of *functional equilibrium* is reached, the organism is by definition in a state of conflict and will retreat from this point, conflict states being noxious. Retreat will bring it back into the preconflict zone, i.e., the approach zone, and this will return the organism once again to the equilibrium point. Thus, in space the behavioral oscillation which is commonly observed is predictable without any further concepts being necessary.

Once the subject is in the conflict zone with no retreat available, we should expect to find a variety of behaviors occurring. Attempts to leave the field by attacking the restraints in the environment, perceptual defense against the surrounding stimuli, and activity displacement would be among the most obvious outcomes. As the goal continues to come closer, the intensity of these activities might increase. An excellent example of this is provided by Epstein and Fenz (1962):

A dog belonging to one of the authors provides an excellent illustration. The animal makes intense approach responses in the form of running and leaping towards a ball, and clearly exhibits a gradient of approach by reacting more vigorously when the ball is near than when it is far. However, if he is commanded to sit still, and the ball is made to approach the dog, a gradient of *activation* is observed in place of the gradients of approach. As the ball is brought closer, the dog becomes perceptibly more tense, his muscles

appear to bulge through his skin, and a general tremor appears. We have no doubt but that if physiological measures of activation were recorded a steep gradient of activation would be indicated. Finally, when the ball is almost touching the animal's nose, the tension becomes unbearable and the dog barks vigorously, snaps at the ball, or entirely breaks the inhibition and dashes about the room. (P. 98.)

Much the same suggestion is implicit in the work of Greenfield (1960). Using the latency of response in a conflict situation, he speculates that this will be greater (*a*) when the two competing tendencies are strong rather than weak, and (*b*) when the two responses are completely incompatible rather than partially so. The hypothetical relationship of these two variables is shown in Figure 6-16. Here we see that with two

Figure 6-16. Measures of conflict (latency of response) as a function of degree of incompatibility and strength of the conflicting responses. (Adapted from Greenfield, 1960.)

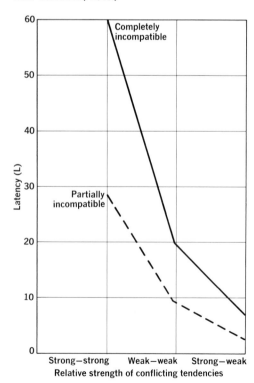

strong tendencies in conflict, the indecision (latency) measure should be greater than when two weak tendencies are in equilibrium. This would be the case where we are comparing the conflict just at the equilibrium point with that which would exist close to the goal. Both would be situations of conflict in which neither approach nor avoidance would dominate, but one would be considerably more intense than the other. The failure of animal experiments to find an avoidance-dominant zone near the goal (see the section "Consequences of Summation of Gradients") now becomes comprehensible. In a straight alley we should expect that at any point in the conflict zone, the subject will attempt to get out of the zone. There are only two directions in which an animal can move in an alley, and if its behavior is motivated toward getting away from the point at which it is, it might move either direction with equal probability. The data from the Trapold, Miller, and Coons study (1960) suggest that this is the case.

Parallel Gradient and Social Conflicts

In Western civilization, conflicts between simple biological motives, such as hunger, versus simple primary punishment, such as physical pain, are probably rather rare. Many human conflicts revolve around such issues as the desire for success, social rejection, or loss of love. Under some circumstances, the person may have had such a mixed series of results from his activities that the stimuli which arouse the motivation for success also arouse the fear of failure. Indeed, there must be some risk of failure in a situation in order for an effective performance to be defined as a success.

If the outcome—success or failure—is destined to occur at a stated time, then there may be little that the person can do to keep distance between himself and the goal. The student contemplating a forthcoming final examination cannot avoid the goal, or get out of the conflict zone. Absence from the examination does not do this, as it merely

guarantees failure! All the cues associated with the approach of the examination are equally cues for the approach and avoidance responses involved. They are cues for the activation of *learned* motives, and even within the Miller framework we should expect the gradients of tendencies based upon learned drives to have the same slope. Maher (1964) has presented a more detailed analysis of this issue.

The Conflict Zone and Psychopathology

Behavior within the conflict zone is characterized by certain features. These features are important in the genesis of pathological responses and should be considered in detail.

Changes in Physiological Functioning. When conflicting tendencies are present, we find that many autonomic functions are affected, including heart rate, respiration, galvanic skin measure of perspiration, and so forth.

Disintegration of Behavior. The appearance of fragments of the approach and avoidance responses, displacement activities, motor tremor, and the like are also in evidence. In general, we see behavior which appears to be inadequate to the demands of the conflicting motives. It neither approaches nor avoids the goal.

Escape. The one integrating process which we see in conflict is the attempt to escape from the situation. In spatial experimental conflicts, escape is possible, and when the subject is removed from the experiment the disturbances of behavior most often disappear. In the human environment, however, where it is the approach motive and its concomitant cue for fear of punishment that create the conflict, no ready escape is possible. Wherever the person goes, he carries the conflict with him. To the extent that the approach motive is aroused by external stimuli, it may be possible to reduce the conflict by seeking an environment which has few of the arousing stimuli in it. The old-fashioned recommendation of a "change of scene" as a cure for psychological symptoms is perhaps effective to some extent as long as the patient stays in the new surroundings, and as long as the new surroundings are strikingly different from his habitual environment. When he returns, however, the "cure" turns out to have been temporary, and the conflicts return in their former strength.

Where no escape is possible, and where the individual continues to live in the environment that generates the conflicting tendencies, certain behaviors may occur that serve as partial escape responses. Probably all of us exhibit some of these behaviors from time to time, but under conditions of intense and continuing conflict, these escape patterns may begin to dominate much of the person's daily life.

Partial Escape Responses

Perceptual Defense. One very simple response that may serve to reduce conflict is the response of not perceiving those stimuli that serve to arouse the approach motive. In its simplest form, this response may consist of distorting the perception of such stimuli so that they are perceived as something innocuous. In its extreme form, it may develop into functional blindness or deafness, thus obliterating perception of both the dangerous stimuli and all other stimuli as well. We see examples of this behavior in Chapter 8 in the so-called "hysterical" disorders.

Repression. Parallel to the response of not perceiving is the response of not thinking or not remembering events that are related to the arousal of the conflict. Murray's study (1959) of experimentally produced repression during a period of sleep deprivation is an excellent analogue of this process. Subjects who had been prevented from going to sleep for a period of 98 hours were compared with controls who had been permitted

to follow a normal sleep-waking schedule. "During the sleep-deprivation period, Murray points out, "the response of going to sleep was in strong conflict with a number of social pressures. The exact nature of these social pressures is not known, but they would appear to include the subject's needs to appear strong, masculine, and grown-up in comparison with his fellows and in the eyes of the staff" (p. 100).

Under these circumstances, the subjects who were conflicted regarding the response of sleeping were presented with stimulus cards depicting scenes of various kinds. Some of these were very suggestive of sleeping, while others were less so. Compared with the control group, the experimental subjects produced much *fewer* stories in which words or ideas dealing with sleep were used. Murray interprets these data as indicating that in the face of conflict, the subjects avoided any words or verbal responses that might add to the already strong physiological drive to sleep.

This study illustrates beautifully the processes by which a state of conflict might lead to the avoidance of thoughts, words, or other symbolic responses that could serve as stimuli for the approach motive. When we consider that the experimental conflict just described was of limited duration, we can understand how the same process of repression would become more intense and permanent in the case of long-continuing conflict.

Stereotyped Behaviors. The response of not thinking or not talking about some disturbing subject must, in any individual case, consist of thinking or talking about something else. When thinking about some other subject has been reinforced by its effectiveness in reducing conflict, there is an increasing probability that this topic will be used on subsequent occasions. Consequently we should expect that the topic will become increasingly common in the subject's repertoire when he is faced with a continuing conflict. When the conflict is both continuous and intense, the subject may become unable to change from the topic, and it will then begin to assume the proportions of an obsession.

Factors determining what this "safe" thought will be are manifold. Thoughts of past situations in which distress was notably absent may serve the purpose. Thus the obsessive thinking may contain references to past successes, previous times when affection or general psychological security were at a maximum. On the other hand, the topic of the thought can be largely accidental, determined by stimuli present in the environment when the avoidance of conflict-producing thoughts was first developed.

In much the same way, the person may engage in some overt activity that serves to prevent him from conflict-producing thoughts. Activities that are irrelevant and mechanical but require some degree of attention are perhaps best suited to this purpose. For example, the person who must compulsively read the license plates of every passing automobile will thereby be prevented from thinking about other things while walking or driving in the street. When he momentarily ceases this behavior, the conflict may be reactivated; thus any failure of concentration is likely to be accompanied by distress. These lapses, in turn, will reinforce the compulsive behavior and lead to an even greater strength of the tendency on subsequent occasions.

Somatic Escape. During conflict many temporary changes occur in bodily responses. Where the subject is unaware of the stimuli that are generating the conflict, he may simply experience considerable distress without being able to identify the origin of it. When this happens it is quite likely that the person may conclude he is suffering from some bodily ailment—"palpitations of the heart" or some other popular descriptive term being applied. Bodily ailments usually lead to the adoption of protective behaviors on the part of the patient, such as consulting a physician, going to bed, "taking things easy," and the like. If these protective responses happen to remove the patient from the scene of his conflict, they are thereby reinforced, and sickness may become a partial escape response to the conflict or to any future conflict that develops.

Logically we should expect that while the patient is taking care of himself and his physical "illness," the effect of escaping from the conflict should reduce the bodily symptoms. This in turn should lead to the abandonment of the protective behavior and the return of the conflict situation. Such a process would be cyclical at first, but the continual reinforcement of health-protective behaviors that would ensue should lead them to become prolonged and consistent. Ultimately these behaviors should be more or less constant, requiring only an occasional bodily symptom to maintain them. The additional positive reinforcements which are given to the physically ill—sympathy, succorance, and so on, would serve to augment this. Much of the behavior that is termed *hypochondriacal* may be understood in this light, as well as the development of other psychologically produced organic symptoms.

Specific Fears. In principle, the four types of partial escape response already described may occur without any accompanying distress on the part of the individual. Fear or distress will occur only when the behavior is omitted. However, under some circumstances an escape from a conflict situation may be achieved by the development of a specific fear that is essentially irrelevant to the conflicting tendencies themselves. An example of this, encountered by the writer, is provided by a married woman who found herself physically attracted to a man who worked in a nearby grocery store. Her previous history showed that she had been punished as a child for any evidence of sexual interest, and thus her visits to the store provoked an intense conflict. This conflict was activated frequently, as she often had occasion to go to the store. She soon developed a strong avoidance of leaving the apartment to go anywhere, and attributed her fears to "open spaces" and "traffic." These fears were effective in keeping her from shopping and thus keeping her away from the conflict that was the fundamental determinant of her behavior. Later discussion of *phobias* will consider such examples in more detail.

Summary.   We have seen how certain kinds of pathological behavior are reinforced because they serve to prevent the individual from being directly exposed to conflict-arousing stimuli—whether these are external to him, or are provided by his own thinking. Many kinds of behavior pathology are not amenable to an explanation as simple as this; and many instances that are amenable to this analysis require more detailed elaboration if we are to make sense of them. Nevertheless, the process described here is fundamental to the genesis of many deviant responses and will be invoked from time to time in later chapters.

One important aspect of partial escape responses is that they are only partially effective. The very occurrence of such behaviors tends to generate new conflicts because of the social punishments which they engender. Obsessive and compulsive behavior, for example, begins to interfere with adequate performance of many occupational and social obligations and thereby creates new problems for the person. However, because the pathological behavior now has a history of reinforcement as a method of escape, the new problems are likely to lead to an intensification of this behavior. Typically we expect to see a widening range of stimuli which will produce the pathological response and thus a progressive worsening of the individual's adjustment. These escape responses should not be thought of as static or fixed, but rather as subject to continuing amplification and change. Because their effectiveness is incomplete, they are themselves the source of further conflicts. The acquisition of more complex and more disabling responses is the most likely outcome of such processes.

EXPERIMENTAL REDUCTION OF CONFLICT

The reduction of conflict is the central problem in the extinction of behavior pathology. Even a cursory examination of the model of conflict which has been presented will reveal that several steps are possible in achieving this.

In principle, conflicts may only be reduced by reducing either the approach or avoidance tendencies to such an extent that the opposing response will occur without competition. In learning terms, it is necessary to extinguish one or the other of the approach or avoidance responses to the conflict-arousing stimuli. Extinction, as we have seen, requires that the individual be exposed to the stimulus but that his response not be reinforced. But for extinction to occur, it is necessary that the individual remain in the presence of the stimulus—and the escape response normally removes the individual before this can take place. Thus it appears to be essential that the pathological behavior which is removing the individual from the conflict be prevented from achieving this effect.

Where we are dealing with experimentally produced conflicts in animal subjects, it is a comparatively straightforward matter to eliminate responses that take the subject out of the apparatus. People living in complex social situations present a different problem, although the principles are the same in both cases. Let us consider the experimental data.

Escape Effects

Several animal studies have investigated the effect of escape upon later resistance to extinction of the avoidance component of an approach-avoidance conflict. Page (1955), Hall (1955), and Page and Hall (1953) have shown that animals restrained in an anxiety-provoking situation exhibit more rapid extinction of an escape response acquired prior to restraint than control animals without the restraint experience. Kalish (1954) has likewise shown that under similar conditions of restraint, animals will be less likely to acquire an escape response after restraint experience than animals not previously restrained. All in all, the evidence suggests that restraining a subject so that it is compelled to remain in proximity to the anxiety-arousing cues tends to reduce anxiety and avoidance, whereas permitting escape tends to prolong it.

We have already seen that escape from an approach-avoidance equilibrium is a predictable event in a conflict situation. Taylor and Maher (1959) studied the effects of combining escape and displacement upon resistance to extinction of the avoidance component of a conflict. The evidence indicated that under conditions of high anxiety, escape tended to retard extinction of the avoidance response. Under conditions of low anxiety, the effect of escape was to facilitate extinction. Thus we must note that the effects of escape may depend to a significant degree upon the level of anxiety present when the escape response is made.

Drug Effects

Anxiety is presumed to depend upon internal visceral changes in the organism. There is thus a distinct possibility that the removal or reduction of these changes by drug administration should reduce the avoidance component but leave the approach component of a conflict intact. Many studies have been performed that bear on this topic, and we shall consider only a few of them. A major consideration in such studies is our general ignorance regarding the actions of many drugs that are used. Besides interfering with the autonomic components of anxiety, they frequently have effects on motor responses, perception, and so forth. In the light of this it is difficult to be sure that the changes observed in behavior are due to any of these effects alone.

Sodium Amytal. Wartime experience showed that the drug *sodium amytal* had an effect of ameliorating combat neuroses. Miller and his colleagues (esp. Miller, 1961) have since conducted an exhaustive and systematic series of investigations designed to find out whether or not sodium amytal acted by reducing the avoidance component of an approach-avoidance conflict. Using different drives (hunger and thirst), different kinds of conflict situations (alley running, bar pressing, and the CER) and different stimuli (proprioceptive, auditory, and visual), they found that the effect of the drug was consistent. It served to reinstate the approach response when a placebo of saline solution did not. Miller comments on this finding:

The fact that so similar results appear in tests involving different cues, different responses, and different drives, makes it unlikely that the effects are specific to the peculiarities of the testing situation. The remarkable agreement in the results of the six different experiments makes it clear that the sodium amytal definitely reduced the relative strength of fear in our different conflict situations. (1961, p. 14.)

Chlorpromazine. The effects obtained with *chlorpromazine* are less striking than those obtained with sodium amytal. However, these effects transfer to the undrugged state more than do the effects of sodium amytal. The experimental evidence on this question is comparatively clear. In Figure 6-17 we see the comparative effects of the two drugs and a placebo (saline solution) in diminishing the avoidance component of a conflict (*a*) while the animal is drugged and (*b*) after the drug has been withdrawn. The relative efficacy of the drugs is reversed in the undrugged condition.

Similar results were obtained by Maher and Chapoton (1960) and Maher and Taylor (1960) comparing the effects of chlorpromazine, *thiopropazate dihydrochloride,* and placebo (distilled water). In these investigations the effect of both drugs was to produce somewhat stronger appearance of

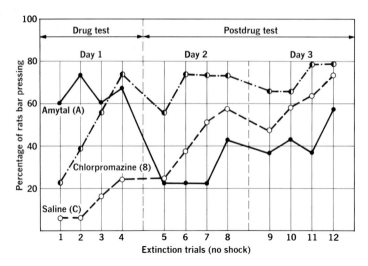

Figure 6-17. Effects of drugs upon elimination of an avoidance response and the stability of this effect after the drug has been withdrawn. Sodium amytal (A) produces many approach responses while dosage is in effect, but this gain is mostly lost when the drug is removed. Chlorpromazine (B) is effective both during drug and nondrug condition. Saline group (C) is a placebo control. (From Miller, 1961.)

the approach response than that found in the placebo group, but to show considerable generalization of this when the animals were shifted to the undrugged state.

Alcohol. One of the commonest drugs used by man to reduce fear is alcohol. Conger (1951) investigated the effects of injections of alcohol upon the strength of the avoidance tendency in a conflict. He found that there was a sharp reduction of the strength of the avoidance component but no reduction in the strength of an approach tendency. A study of related significance was reported by Masserman and Yum (1946), who found that after an experimental neurosis was induced in cats, they developed a preference for alcohol in their drinking water. This suggests that under conditions of conflict, alcohol is drive-reducing—the anxiety drive presumably being the one that is reduced.

Many other drug studies have been performed which are relevant to this problem. However, the few that have been cited at this juncture serve to indicate the manner in which drugs may change the variables operating in a conflict.

Surgical Effects

Psychosurgery, especially those procedures which involve destruction of or interference with the frontal cortex of the brain, has been assumed to reduce anxiety in the human patient. For obvious reasons there have been no experimental studies on human subjects.[5] Studies of the effects of frontal lobe ablation upon animals have produced results which do not support the view that anxiety is reduced by this procedure. Whenever avoidance behavior is defined in terms of motor movement—i.e., by immobility (Streb & Smith, 1955; Maher & McIntire, 1960) or by running away from the locus of punishment (Maher, Elder, & Noblin, 1962)—the effect of the frontal ablation is to increase locomotor activity generally, thereby making it impossible to determine whether or not anxiety has been reduced. However when a viscerally controlled response—defecation—

[5] There have been several studies in which measurements of anxiety have been made before and after psychosurgery, but none in which anxiety was manipulated as an experimental variable.

is used as an additional measure, the ablation clearly fails to remove it. A comparison of these two response measures is given in Figure 6-18. In it we see that whereas the anxiety-produced immobility is disrupted by hyperactivity,[6] the defecation response is still evoked by the CS. Thus, at this time, we must conclude that ablation has no effect upon the avoidance component of a conflict,

[6] Hyperactivity is a widely reported consequence of frontal ablation in animals, e.g., Richter and Hawkes (1939), French (1959), Maher (1955).

or upon anxiety-produced behavior generally.

Shock Effects

Another hypothesis, derived from a consideration of therapeutic approaches to human psychopathology, is that anxiety and the accompanying avoidance tendencies will be reduced by electroconvulsive shock (ECS). Poschel (1957) has reported that ECS reduces the strength of the avoidance component of a conflict, while evidence has

Figure 6-18. Failure of frontal lobe operation to remove visceral component (defecation) of avoidant pattern while eliminating the motor component (immobility). (Maher and McIntire, 1960.)

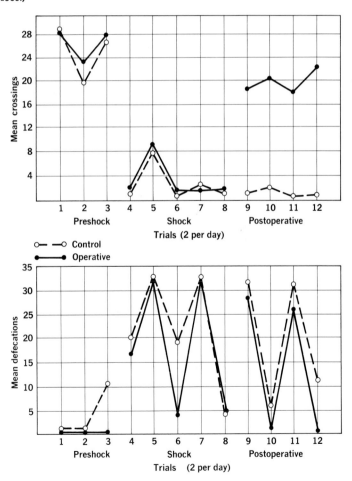

been offered to indicate that it does not reduce the strength of an approach tendency (Siegel, 1943; Brady, 1951; Hunt & Brady, 1951). However, the problem of the effects of ECS upon learned behavior is extremely complicated. It may well be that the shock provokes competing responses rather than diminishing the anxiety component (Adams & Lewis, 1962; Lewis & Adams, 1963), or that it serves to produce conditioned protective inhibition. These possibilities are discussed at length in Chapter 17.

Time Effects

Popular belief has it that given sufficient time, a person will "get over" fears or anxieties that he has acquired. Psychological analysis of this belief suggests that time is not a variable per se and that if we find the anxiety diminishing over time, it must be related to some other changes in conditions which happen to be correlated with the passage of time. Noblin and Maher (1962) have reported data which indicate that some extinction of the avoidance component of conflict is produced simply by permitting the subject to remain in its home cage for a few days. However, during this period of time the animal has the experience of food deprivation and feeding without either of these being associated with the avoidance cues of the experimental alley. Thus, it seems likely that time alone was not producing the effect, but rather the extinction of the avoidance tendency attached to the hunger stimuli. Other experimental data advanced by Miller (1961) confirm the conclusion that it is the changes in conditions rather than passage of time that accounts for the phenomenon of fear reduction which is sometimes seen.

Increasing Approach Motivation

So far we have discussed techniques that are used to reduce the avoidance tendency in a conflict. Another obvious possibility is to increase the approach tendency. As a technique, this has the disadvantage that it is likely to intensify the conflict at points increasingly nearer to the goal. Considerable increases in approach motivation may be necessary if the approach tendency is to remain clearly higher than the avoidance tendency at all points during the approach behavior.

Experimental procedures available are quite simple; they usually involve an increase in the hours of deprivation, or weight loss, that defines the strength of the approach motivation. A demonstration of this is available in the data of Nuttall (1963). Animals were trained to make an approach run along a straight alley under 25 per cent body-weight loss. After several days of approach trial for food, they received shock. Following shock, the group of animals was divided into subgroups that were extinguished at 40, 30, 25, 20, and 10 per cent weight loss and at *ad lib.* feeding. The number of trials to produce an approach goal response are shown in Figure 6-19. With increasing hunger there is a more rapid reappearance of the approach response. At the deprivation weight used in the original training (25 per cent), the reappearance of the approach response is especially rapid,

Figure 6-19. Relearning of an approach response is facilitated by increasing drive (hunger) and by the similarity of the drive level to that used in training. (Nuttall, 1963.)

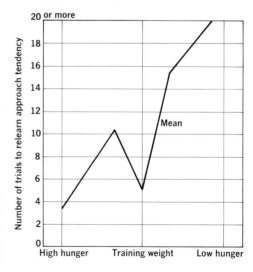

suggesting that the level of hunger involved is not only affecting the approach motive strength, but is also a discriminable stimulus for the making of the approach response.

SUMMARY

Approach-avoidance conflicts represent useful models for analyzing human behavior pathology. By the same token, the methods employed to resolve these conflicts in the psychological laboratory provide analogues for the understanding of various therapies that are applied to pathological behavior. As a matter of historical interest, we may note that many of the methods used in the laboratory were adopted from reports of the clinical application with human patients. In the last analysis, the efficacy of therapeutic techniques used with human patients must be demonstrated with studies of patients and not merely assumed by extrapolation from animal experiments. However, an understanding of the principles described in the preceding paragraphs will make it easier to consider the effects of various therapies discussed in later chapters of this book.

SUGGESTED READINGS

1. Dollard, J., & Miller, N. E. *Personality and psychotherapy.* New York: McGraw-Hill, 1950. A now classic book, presenting a systematic interpretation of many facets of behavior pathology in learning terms.
2. Kogan, N., & Wallach, M. *Risk taking: a study in cognition and personality.* New York: Holt, 1964. A detailed report of studies of cognitive processes involved in decision making. It provides a useful economic model for conflict resolution.
3. Miller, D. R., & Swanson, G. E. *Inner conflict and defense.* New York: Holt, 1960. A detailed report of a study of conflict and its resolution in preadolescents. It contains an excellent but brief account of the relationship of conflict resolution to defense mechanisms.
4. Miller, N. E. Liberalization of basic S-R concepts: extensions to conflict behavior, motivation and social learning. In S. Koch (Ed.), *Psychology: a study of a science.* Vol. 2. New York: McGraw-Hill, 1958, pp. 196–292. A full statement of the postulates, corollaries, and data of the Miller model of conflict. It also includes a comprehensive account of the conceptual steps involved in applying stimulus-response principles to human social behavior.
5. Schelling, T. C. *The strategy of conflict.* Cambridge, Mass.: Harvard, 1960. A simply written account of the application of games theory to the study of human behavior in conflict situations.
6. Yates, A. J. *Frustration and conflict.* London: Methuen, 1962. An excellent brief text dealing with various models of conflict and frustration.

REFERENCES

Adams, H. E., & Lewis, D. J. Retrograde amnesia and competing responses. *J. comp. physiol. Psychol.,* 1962, **55,** 302–305.

Anderson, O. D., & Parmenter, R. A long-term study of the experimental neurosis in the sheep and in the dog. *Psychosom. Med. Monogr.,* 1941, **2,** Nos. 3 & 4.

Bindra, D. An interpretation of the 'displacement' phenomenon. *Brit. J. Psychol.,* 1959, **50,** 263–267.

Brady, J. V. The effects of electroconvulsive shock on a conditioned emotional response; the permanence of the effect. *J. comp. physiol. Psychol.,* 1951, **44,** 507–511.

Brown, J. S. Factors determining conflict reactions in difficult discriminations. *J. exp. Psychol.,* 1942, **31,** 272–292.

Brown, J. S. Gradients of approach and avoidance responses and their relation to motivation. *J. comp. physiol. Psychol.,* 1948, **41,** 450–465.

Conger, J. J. The effects of alcohol on conflict behavior in the albino rat. *Quart. J. Stud. Alcohol,* 1951, **12,** 1–29.

Cook, S. W. The production of "experimental neurosis" in the white rat. *Psychosom. Med.,* 1939, **1.**

Dollard, J., & Miller, N. E. *Personality and Psychotherapy.* New York: McGraw-Hill, 1950.

Dworkin, S. Conditioning neuroses in dog and cat. *Psychosom. Med.,* 1939, **1,** 388–396.

Elder, T., Noblin, C. D., & Maher, B. A. The extinction of fear as a function of distance versus dissimilarity from the original conflict situation. *J. abnorm. soc. Psychol.,* 1961, **63,** 530–533.

Epstein, S., & Fenz, W. D. Theory and experiment on the measurement of approach-avoidance conflict. *J. abnorm. soc. Psychol.,* 1962, **64,** 97–112.

French, G. M. A deficit associated with hypermotility in monkeys with lesions of the dorsolateral frontal granular cortex. *J. comp. physiol. Psychol.,* 1959, **52,** 25–28.

Freud, S. *Beyond the pleasure principle* (1920). London: Hogarth, 1948.

Gantt, W. H. Experimental basis for neurotic behavior. *Psychosom. Med. Monogr.,* 1944, **3,** Nos. 3 & 4.

Greenfield, N. Summation of conflict states. *Percept. mot. Skills.,* 1960, **11,** 103–110.

Hall, J. F. Activity as a function of a restricted drinking schedule. *J. comp. physiol. Psychol.,* 1955, **48,** 265–266.

Hearst, E. Simultaneous generalization gradients for appetitive and aversive behavior. *Science,* 1960, **132,** 1769–1770.

Hull, C. L. The goal gradient hypothesis and maze learning. *Psychol. Rev.,* 1932, **39,** 25–43.

Hunt, H. F., & Brady, J. V. Some effects of electroconvulsive shock on a conditional emotional response ("anxiety"). *J. comp. physiol. Psychol.,* 1951, **44,** 88–98.

Kalish, H. I. Strength of fear as a function of the number of acquisition and extinction trials. *J. exp. Psychol.,* 1954, **47,** 1–9.

Lewis, D. J., & Adams, H. E. Retrograde amnesia from conditioned competing responses. *Science,* 1963, **141,** 516–517.

Lichtenstein, P. E. Studies of anxiety: I. The production of a feeding inhibition in dogs. *J. comp. physiol. Psychol.,* 1950, **43.** 16–29.

Liddell, H. S. *Emotional hazards in animals and man.* Springfield, Ill.: Charles C Thomas, 1956.

Maher, B. A. Anticipatory and perseverative errors following frontal lesions in the rat. *J. comp. physiol. Psychol.,* 1955, **48,** 102–105.

Maher, B. A. The application of the approach-avoidance conflict model to social behavior. *J. conflict Resolut.,* 1964, **8,** 287–291.

Maher, B. A., & Chapoton, Patsy. The comparative effects of chlorpromazine, restraint and displacement experience upon recovery from an approach-avoidance conflict. Paper read at Southeast. Psychol. Ass., Atlanta, 1960.

Maher, B. A., Elder, S. T., & Noblin, C. D. A differential investigation of avoidance reduction versus hypermotility following frontal ablation. *J. comp. physiol. Psychol.,* 1962, **55,** 449–454.

Maher, B. A., & McIntire, R. W. The extinction of the CER following frontal ablation. *J. comp. physiol. Psychol.,* 1960, **53,** 549–552.

Maher, B. A., & Noblin, C. D. Conflict equilibrium and distance from the goal: a demonstration of irrelevance. Paper read at Southeast. Psychol. Ass., Miami Beach, 1963.

Maher, B. A., & Nuttall, R. The effect of repeated measures and prior approach training upon a spatial gradient of avoidance. Paper read at Amer. Psychol. Ass., St. Louis, 1962.

Maher, B. A., & Taylor, Janet A. The effects of thiopropazatedihydrochloride upon recovery from an approach-avoidance conflict. Paper read at Midwest. Psychol. Ass., St. Louis, 1960.

Maher, B. A., Weisstein, N., & Sylva, K. The

determinants of oscillation points in a temporal decision conflict. *Psychon. Sci.,* 1964, **1,** 13–14.

Masserman, J. H. *Behavior and neurosis.* Chicago: Univer. of Chicago Press, 1943.

Masserman, J. H., & Pechtel, C. Conflict engendered neurotic and psychotic behavior in monkeys. *J. nerv. ment. Dis.,* 1953, **118,** 408–411.

Masserman, J. H., & Yum, K. S. An analysis of the influence of alcohol on experimental neuroses in cats. *Psychosom. Med.,* 1946, **8,** 36–52.

Miller, N. E. Theory and experiment relating psychoanalytic displacement to stimulus-response generalization. *J. abnorm. soc. Psychol.,* 1948, **43,** 155–178.

Miller, N. E. Liberalization of basic S-R concepts: extensions to conflict behavior, motivation and social learning. In S. Koch (Ed.), *Psychology: a study of a science.* Vol. 2. New York: McGraw-Hill, 1958.

Miller, N. E. Some recent studies of conflict behavior and drugs. *Amer. Psychologist,* 1961, **16,** 12–24.

Mowrer, O. H., & Ullman, A. D. Time as a determinant of integrative learning. *Psychol. Rev.,* 1945, **52,** 61–90.

Murray, E. J. Conflict and repression during sleep deprivation. *J. abnorm. soc. Psychol.,* 1959, **59,** 95–101.

Murray, E. J., & Berkun, M. M. Displacement as a function of conflict. *J. abnorm. soc. Psychol.,* 1955, **51,** 47–56.

Noblin, C. D., & Maher, B. A. Temporal and physical factors in avoidance reduction. *J. comp. physiol. Psychol.,* 1962, **55,** 62–65.

Nuttall, R. L. Drive generalization as a factor in approach-avoidance conflict. Unpublished doctoral dissertation, Harvard Univer., 1963.

Page, H. A. The facilitation of experimental extinction by response prevention as a function of the acquisition of a new response. *J. comp. physiol. Psychol.,* 1955, **48,** 14–16.

Page, H. A., & Hall, J. F. Experimental extinction as a function of the prevention of a response. *J. comp. physiol. Psychol.,* 1953, **46,** 33–34.

Pavlov, I. P. *Lectures on conditioned reflexes.* (trans. W. H. Gantt.) New York: International Publishers, 1928.

Poschel, B. P. H. Proactive and retroactive effects of electroconvulsive shock on approach-avoidance conflicts. *J. comp. physiol. Psychol.,* 1957, **50,** 392–396.

Renner, K. E. Temporal factors in the neurotic paradox. Unpublished manuscript, Univer. of Pennsylvania, 1962.

Richter, C. P., & Hawkes, C. D. Increased spontaneous activity and food-intake produced in rats by removal of the frontal poles of the brain. *J. neurol. Psychiat.,* 1939, **2,** 231–242.

Rigby, W. K. Approach and avoidance gradients and conflict behavior in a predominantly temporal situation. *J. comp. physiol. Psychol.,* 1954, **47,** 83–89.

Siegel, P. S. The effect of electroshock convulsions on the acquisition of a simple running response in the rat. *J. comp. physiol. Psychol.,* 1943, **36,** 61–65.

Smith, N. An empirical determination of an approach gradient. *J. comp. physiol. Psychol.,* 1960, **53,** 63–67.

Streb, J. M., & Smith, K. Frontal lobotomy and the elimination of conditioned anxiety in the rat. *J. comp. physiol. Psychol.,* 1955, **48,** 126–129.

Taylor, Janet A., & Maher, B. A. Escape and displacement experience as variables in the recovery from approach-avoidance conflict. *J. comp. physiol. Psychol.,* 1959, **52,** 586–590.

Tinbergen, N. *The study of instinct.* Fair Lawn, N.J.: Oxford, 1951.

Trapold, M. A., Miller, N. E., & Coons, E. E. All-or-none versus progressive approach in an approach-avoidance conflict. *J. comp. physiol. Psychol.,* 1960, **53,** 293–296.

APPLICATION OF PSYCHOLOGICAL CONCEPTS: ANXIETY

Anxiety is a central concept in the understanding of psychopathological behavior. We have already seen the importance of anxiety in explaining avoidance behavior in the laboratory, and we have noted that it represents a pattern of responses which occur as unconditioned reactions to painful or threatening stimuli. When these reactions develop in the presence of a stimulus which is *realistically* threatening, we tend to speak of *fear* rather than anxiety. Although the term is rather loosely defined in the literature of psychopathology, anxiety is generally used to refer to the same reaction pattern when it is made in the presence of stimuli which are not intrinsically threatening. Anxiety, then, refers to the fear response when it is made to stimuli which elicit it on the basis of past learning.

Exactly how much of the power of a stimulus to evoke the fear response is due to past learning would be very hard to decide in any clinical case. Consequently, the practical criterion by which anxiety is judged to be inappropriate or pathological is based upon what appear to be "normal" anxieties in the general population. Many people are anxious while flying: they become tense during takeoff and landing and do not relax until their flight is over and they are safely out of the plane. During flight, they may be unusually perceptive to changes in the noise of the motors, the apparent stability of the plane, the hazards of the weather, and indeed anything even slightly out of the ordinary about the flight procedure. Such anxieties are not regarded as pathological even though they may have been acquired entirely on the basis of newspaper and television accounts of plane wrecks rather than from any personal experience of hazardous flying.

Yet other people are sufficiently anxious about flying that they will not fly at all, preferring to take a train or car when a journey is necessary. But even though this anxiety is mildly incapacitating, i.e., it makes traveling less convenient than it might be, very few of us would regard the nonflyer as pathological or in need of "treatment" for his anxiety.

Our view of these anxieties would probably be different in the case of a person who experiences acute anxiety when looking at a picture of an airplane, or when hearing casual conversations about flying. We recognize that there is some danger in air travel (even though it may be minimal), but there is no danger in pictures or conversation. Consequently we would regard anxieties in the presence of the latter as deviant and to some extent pathological.

In general, then, we see that anxiety is not ordinarily regarded as deviant unless it occurs in situations in which most people do not respond with anxiety. Anxiety in the presence of open spaces, particular words or phrases, etc., is uncommon; hence such anxieties are regarded as deviant. It is important to note that insofar as the response pattern itself is concerned, pathological anxieties are not fundamentally different from those we recognize as normal. It is the circumstances under which the anxiety occurs that is critical.

CLINICAL FEATURES

The typical characteristics of the anxiety response may be described at several levels. Here are some descriptions from people who have experienced acute anxiety attacks.

Subjective Reports

1. "A knot in my stomach, a feeling of hot flashes and warmth throughout my entire body, tightening of the muscles, a lump in my throat and a constant feeling that I am going to throw up."

2. "I noticed that my hands began to sweat, my legs crumpled under me. I saw white spots floating before my eyes. I felt like getting up and running." (Sarnoff, 1957.)

Clinical Symptoms

The general symptomatology which is presented in anxiety states may be identified as follows:

1. Conscious feelings of fear, apprehension, anticipation of danger or threat, usually without any ability to identify a particular threat which might account for these feelings.

2. A miscellaneous pattern of bodily complaints including *cardiovascular symptoms* (palpitation, rapid or erratic pulse, raised blood pressure, faintness, etc.); *gastrointestinal symptoms* (nausea, loss of appetite, vomiting, diarrhea); *respiratory symptoms* (breathlessness, feelings of suffocation, rapid shallow breathing, etc.), together with other symptoms such as perspiration, frequent urination, sleeplessness, and so forth.

3. Muscular tension, including muscular tremors, hyperactivity, a low threshold for motor responses, general motor disorganization, and "clumsiness." Frequently there are complaints of muscular fatigue following the prolonged muscular tension.

4. A general feeling of disorganization or loss of control over the environment, accompanied by difficulty in thinking clearly.

Anxiety Reactions: Examples

Experiences and symptoms of the kind we have listed above may be elicited in any normal person under unusual stress. If the stress is removed, the symptoms diminish and disappear in the usual course of events. Transitory anxiety states of this kind are not uncommon. Example 7-1 may serve to illustrate the phenomenon.

Among the interesting features of this example is the close correlation between the onset of the symptoms and the assignment

EXAMPLE 7-1

Transitory Anxiety State

The patient was an Air Force pilot, aged forty-one, with 2,426 hours of flying time in conventional aircraft.

"He reported to the flight surgeon with complaints of fatigue, nervous stomach, headache, insomnia, indigestion, nervousness and cramping bowels. This symptomatology had been present for about 8 months. Its onset was related to an assignment to primary duty as a second pilot on a Military Air Transport Service transport plane. For 10 years prior to this his primary duty had been in manpower. He had flown only the minimum number of hours necessary to maintain flying status each month.

"He blamed his inability to function adequately as a transport pilot on aging, decrease in proficiency and the presence of his somatic symptomatology. Because of this he requested transfer to a primary ground job with secondary flying duties. He was removed from flight status. Upon removal from flying status the fatigue, nervous stomach, headache, insomnia, indigestion, nervousness and cramping bowels with which he presented himself to the flight surgeon cleared up completely." (Sarnoff, 1957, pp. 85–86.)

to flying duty, together with the rapid disappearance when the patient was relieved of this duty. Equally important is the fact that he was easily able to identify the source of the stress which was producing the anxiety, even though he mistook the manner of its operation.

Anxiety Following Trauma. Sometimes a person is subjected to an experience which threatens his life or safety in some dramatic way. It is not rare to find that for a period of time following this, he experiences acute anxiety with many of the overt symptoms described in the preceding paragraphs. Combat episodes, shipwreck, automobile accidents, and the like are all possible precipitators of this syndrome. For obvious reasons we are most liberally supplied with data on the effect of military trauma. Example 7-2 is an excellent illustration of traumatic anxiety.

In this case the recovery of the patient is an example of a fairly common outcome of such episodes. However, it also illustrates the principle that recovery from anxiety following trauma is very dependent upon the patient remaining in contact with the situation in which the trauma occurred. Folk wisdom has long stated that we should always remount the horse from which we

have just fallen if we are to avoid developing a marked fear of riding. Experience in both world wars convinced many clinicians that the most effective treatment of anxiety in combat troops consisted of rest and supportive psychotherapy conducted in the combat zone. Removal of the patient to a rear area appeared to have the effect of reinforcing the symptoms and increasing resistance to treatment. Kardiner (1959), writing of this problem, remarked:

In the acute phase, the therapeutic job is to prevent the soldier from capitulating and taking refuge in escape from duty. The fear and exhaustion states must be admitted by the physician, but the subject must be encouraged to believe that he has not reached a breaking point. Permitting the soldier to admit fear is a policy that has paid off well.

The first requirement is to keep the soldier within his combat unit after his first break. Kitchen duty and rest routine are excellent, combined with sedation at night. There should be four or five days of this program, followed by a return to active duty. (Pp. 253–254.)

When the person has been removed from the dangerous environment, we sometimes find that the anxiety response increases in strength. This increase may not be apparent until the person is again face to face with stimuli associated with the traumatic event. Because the anxiety response seems to have gained strength during a period of time when there were no additional stresses present, we refer to this phenomenon as *incubation.*

A more complicated situation arises when the patient is not able to identify the stimuli in the situation which are provoking the anxiety response. Under such circumstances he is aware of all the symptoms of anxiety, including the subjective feelings of apprehension, but is unable to relate them to any recognizable threat in his environment. Several possibilities are open to the patient in such a case. He may search his environment for some explanation of his anxiety and find one which is partially plausible even though really irrelevant. We may observe this in Example 7-3.

While the development of intense anxiety in the example was mainly determined by the approach of the date for the patient's return to his home, we notice that there are some other similarities between the two situations in which he experienced the anxiety attacks. In both instances he was living in comparatively confined quarters—a tent or a prison cell—and in both cases he was about to leave institutional regimentation for the independence of civilian life. The physical resemblance between his living conditions in both cases neatly illustrates the tendency for anxiety responses to become conditioned to aspects of the environment which are not directly relevant to the

basic threat which has generated them. When the environmental similarity combines with the presence of the underlying threat, the appearance of overwhelming anxiety is almost certain.

This spreading of the anxiety response to any stimulus resembling those which were associated with the feared situation is termed *generalization* and represents an example of stimulus generalization of the kind discussed in Chapter 3. It is quite possible for this generalization to take place with respect to stimuli which were only accidentally present when the original fear was experienced. Simple contiguity of the threatening stimulus with any other stimulus may give the latter the power to evoke anxiety and may permit generalization from it to other stimuli.

THEORETICAL ASPECTS

At this point let us turn from consideration of clinical instances to examine the problem of the origin of anxiety. Our question is "Why do some situations produce an anxiety response?" or, better still, "What are the characteristics of situations which produce anxiety responses?"

Several possibilities, not mutually exclusive, exist which we shall discuss in turn.

1. Anxiety represents a conditioned fear response, in that it is conditioned to stimuli which were associated at some time in the past with *painful* punishment.

EXAMPLE 7-2

Traumatic Anxiety (Traumatic Neurosis)

Flying a jet fighter aircraft at night, a 34-year-old Air Force officer lost control of his plane. Attempts at recovery failed and he finally bailed out at 500 feet. His parachute opened not more than five seconds before he hit the ground. Although he suffered only minor injuries from the fall, the patient developed considerable tension and anxiety in the months that followed the incident. He described himself as having run the gamut of emotion because of this experience. His flying proficiency decreased and his performance was especially poor when flying by instruments (which he had been doing at the time of the accident). The feelings of anxiety and tension lasted in full force for three months. Then the tension began to decline until about five months after the incident it was not noticeably different from that of any pilot. (From Sarnoff, 1957, pp. 57–60.)

Application of Psychological Concepts: Anxiety

EXAMPLE 7-3

Acute Anxiety State

A man serving a prison sentence for robbery referred himself to the prison psychiatrist a few weeks before he was due to be released. He complained that for some weeks past, he had been finding it difficult to sleep and that during the day he was bothered by feelings of unexplainable panic and tension. At night, when alone in his cell, he complained that he could hear his heart beating loudly and irregularly, that he felt suffocated and found breathing difficult. Eating had become difficult for him, as he had lost his appetite. These feelings and symptoms had become gradually worse until they reached a point where the patient sought help at the prison hospital.

Quite apart from the unpleasantness of his condition, the patient was especially upset by his inability to identify anything which had happened recently to account for these fears. On the contrary, he pointed out that he was soon to be returned to his home—a release to which he had been looking forward with anticipated relief. His wife was waiting for him and his employer had agreed to find him a job.

Further inquiry showed that the patient had had a similar episode once before. This had happened when he had been serving in the Army in India in World War II. The symptoms which he described were much the same and had developed several weeks before he was due to be returned home and released from military service. During combat duty he had had no problems of this kind, and he had attributed this episode to having no sleep for several weeks in a tent hemmed in by mosquito netting.

Prolonged treatment of the patient revealed that his marriage contained many elements which were threatening to him. In fact, the circumstances of the crime for which he was imprisoned were such that it seemed probable he committed it in order to be arrested—perhaps thereby to escape from an unbearable home environment. Imminent release from prison, like the previous imminent discharge from the Army, served to bring the patient close to a dreaded situation and thus intensify his apprehension to a degree which constituted an anxiety attack.

2. Anxiety is a response that occurs in any situation which threatens the survival of the individual. Thus loss of affection, of protection, of physical support, and the like are fundamental causes of anxiety—just as fundamental as physical pain. Any stimuli associated with these situations will, by conditioning, develop the power to elicit anxiety also.

Anxiety as a Conditioned Response to Pain

Most studies of anxiety which have been conducted in the laboratory have utilized physically painful stimulation as the unconditioned stimulus. Additional limitations have developed in the laboratory as a result of the necessity of controlling the intensity of the painful stimulus—a necessity which has led to the predominance of painful electrical stimulation as the preferred stimulus.

There seems to be no doubt that this procedure does produce learning in the following ways: (a) the pattern of responses made originally to the painful stimulus is now elicited by neutral stimuli which were paired with it, and (b) the subject will rapidly acquire those responses which effectively remove the threatening stimuli. This topic has been dealt with in greater detail in Chapter 3 and we shall not elaborate it here.

Suffice it to say that while the laboratory model of avoidance learning in human or animal subjects is in many respects adequate to account for the clinical aspects of anxiety, it is nonetheless an experimental analogue.

There is abundant evidence that the anxiety response pattern occurs in the absence of previous painful stimulation. For example, it is well established that distress responses will occur in the newborn infant when he is startled by a loud noise, or when physical support is suddenly removed. Animals display evidences of avoidance and escape behavior and other signs of distress when faced with predators, and these responses occur in the absence of any painful experience with the predator.

Perhaps the most striking evidence against the pain-anxiety argument is provided by clinical cases of congenital analgesia. This is a syndrome which consists of complete lack of sensitivity to painful stimulation, so that the patient is able to sense all other aspects of the environment but does not register pain. Apparently inherited, this disorder leads to frequent burns and injuries because the patient has not learned avoidance responses to stimuli which are painful to the normal person. However, as Kesson and Mandler (1961) point out, the patient does develop anxieties toward other nonpainful events in the same way that other people do.

In conclusion, it seems impossible to defend the hypothesis that all anxiety develops on the basis of some original painful trauma.

Anxiety as Fundamental Distress

In the approach discussed in the previous section, anxiety is seen as a response to certain external stimulating conditions. Conditioning is invoked to explain the eliciting of the anxiety response by stimuli associated with the trauma. When these stimuli are removed, the anxiety response diminishes and finally disappears. The disappearance of anxiety is presumed to be a reinforcing state of affairs, and thus responses are acquired which lead to its reduction. Kesson and Mandler (1961) have proposed that we look at this sequence of events in a different light. They have offered the term *fundamental distress* to identify certain aspects of the anxiety response which

are of special interest. Their position can best be presented by the following quotation:

It is our contention that a non-traumatic theory of the sources of anxiety can be defended and, further, that anxiety may be reduced or terminated by devices other than escape from or avoidance of threat. These alternative formulations are proposed as a supplement to, rather than substitutes for, the archetypical theories of anxiety.

The schematic model suggested here for the occurrence of anxiety—in distinction from the classical model of the organism fleeing the association of pain—is the cyclical distress of the human newborn. There may be antecedent events which could account for the crying and increased activity we recognize as distressful in the young infant—for example, food privation, shifts in temperature and so on—but *it is not necessary to specify or even to assume such a specific antecedent event.* (Kesson & Mandler, 1961, p. 399.)

Taking the distress of the human newborn as a fundamental phenomenon, i.e., as something which does not require explanation in terms of some prior determinants, they suggest that perhaps some of the specific unconditioned fears mentioned in the preceding paragraphs may be better understood as conditioned forms of fundamental distress. Distress is a condition which accompanies many other conditions of the organism. Thus the child is cold and distressed, hungry and distressed, and pained and distressed; in fact any state of need or drive may be accompanied by distress.

This model assumes, clearly, that the physical states which we call hunger, cold, pain, etc., are separable from the state which we call distress. Consequently we might expect that in any painful situation, the individual's pattern of response will include some responses which are to the pain per se and some which are evidences of distress. Likewise we would not be surprised to find that removing the pain, providing food, or providing warmth serves to eliminate the responses to the pain, hunger, or cold, and that the distress is thereby reduced.

Above and beyond this kind of distress

reduction, Kesson and Mandler propose that there may be certain responses of the organism and events in the environment which will *inhibit* distress. These *specific inhibitors* will inhibit distress regardless of the specific need, drive, or deprivation which generated it. Examples of specific inhibitors would include nonnutritive sucking in the newborn (i.e., sucking on a rubber nipple stuffed with cloth—the "pacifier"), rocking a child, the appearance of an adult face, rhythmical stimulation of various kinds, etc. So long as the specific inhibitor is being applied, the distress response is inhibited, but when it is removed the distress will return unless some new intervening state, especially sleep, has been reached.

If cyclical distress in the newborn is inhibited as it arises, the inhibitor could be removed when the peak of the cycle has passed without there being any reappearance of the distress response. By the usual processes of conditioning, any stimulus which has been associated with the action of a specific inhibitor might acquire inhibitory properties as a *secondary inhibitor*. Thus the appearance of the rocking chair might acquire some power to inhibit distress. Conversely, those stimuli which are associated with the termination of the specific inhibitor might acquire the power to produce the distress response:

Thus the phenomenon of separation anxiety seen in the young child can be understood as the interruption of well-established inhibitory sequences. The failure of the mother to appear, that is, the omission of an important inhibitor, leads to the rearrousal of distress. (Kesson & Mandler, 1961, p. 403.)

It should be clear that these proposals are not to be regarded as substituting for or contradicting the pain-anxiety theory, but rather are intended to extend the range of situations which might be operating in the production of human anxieties. At the present time, they may be regarded as provocative and plausible proposals which seem to permit the systematic interpretation of data which do not fit easily into the pain-anxiety framework.

Anxiety as Overarousal

Malmo (1957) has suggested that anxiety be considered a "disease of overarousal." By this he means that prolonged exposure to arousal stimulation may lead to a critical change in the capacity of the person to inhibit arousal. Two central concepts need to be understood in order to evaluate this explanation. The first is the concept of *arousal,* which has already been described in Chapter 4. Malmo has used measurement of autonomic activity as major indices of arousal level, particularly muscle tension measures, heart rate, and blood pressure. The second concept is that of *inhibition,* which refers to the operation of a process antagonistic to arousal. Inhibition serves to damp down or diminish arousal measures when the arousing stimulus has been removed. It is conceived of as an active process, not simply as the absence of arousal, and is presumed to be mediated by particular kinds of cells in the nervous system. In the normal state of affairs, brief elevations in the level of arousal would be followed by inhibition and the return of the arousal level to the resting state.

Prolonged exposure to arousal stimulations will, Malmo hypothesizes, lead to overuse of the inhibitory mechanisms, and ultimately they will weaken. Specifically he suggests that the inhibition is produced by a chemical transmitter, and that in prolonged anxiety this substance loses effectiveness. With these assumptions in mind we should expect that in a resting state—a state of nonarousal—there would be no necessary difference between anxious and nonanxious subjects on any of the physiological indices of arousal. Introducing an arousal stimulus would produce differences between these groups, however, for the reasons enumerated already.

Malmo makes certain related observations which are of importance here. Pathologically anxious subjects should respond with behavioral arousal to any arousing stimulus, whether or not it has any resemblance to those which generated the pathological anxiety in the first place. He cites the following statement by Cameron (1944), which illustrates the point well:

It will be noted that nearly all such patients (with anxiety states) complain that they cannot go into crowded places or into any situation where sustained efforts will be required of them. Their symptoms are made more severe by anything which elicits emotional reactions, such as altercations or participating in a discussion of illness. Nearly all find, at least at first, that their symptoms are increased by visiting their former places of employment or meeting fellow workers. In other words, their symptoms are exacerbated by anything which serves to increase tension. *Emphasis should be placed on the fact that their symptoms are elicited or intensified, not primarily by the reactivation of any conflict situation which may exist, but literally by everything in the course of the day which serves to increase tension.* [Italics added.]

A second observation of interest relates to the notion of a critical change in the inhibitory process after prolonged arousal. Following such a change, it would be expected that the person would be particularly susceptible to arousal by stimulation which would not produce arousal in a normal subject. Thus chronic or pathological anxiety would be characterized by a low threshold for arousal to comparatively minimal stimulation and an extremely slow return to a resting state. Malmo has suggested that longitudinal studies of individuals suffering from severe anxiety states should reveal differences over time of this sort.

Anxiety as a Response to Threatened Values

In the three preceding sections we have discussed anxiety as a response, or pattern of responses, determined by environmental stimuli of a relatively primitive kind—pain, hunger, and the like. Similarly, the reduction of anxiety has been described as a consequence of the removal of noxious stimulation or the introduction of specific inhibitors. All the concepts used might be applied to the understanding of animal behavior, and indeed evidence from animal behavior is frequently used to demonstrate the operation of one or another of the proposed mechanisms. However, in recent years there has developed an interest in the concept of anxiety as a response which is specifically human and occurs when the value system which gives meaning to a person's life is threatened with dissolution. This point of view has been elaborated by psychologists who work within the framework of *existential philosophy.* Anxiety, or as the existential psychologist prefers to call it, *angst*, has been described in this way by May (1959):

The existential psychiatrists emphasize the point that anxiety is an ontological characteristic of man, rooted in his very existence as such. In contradiction to practically all other approaches, they hold that anxiety is not an affect among other affects such as pleasure and sadness. It is not a reaction which may be classified with other reactions; it is always a threat to the foundation, the center of existence. It is the experiencing of the threat of non-being. . . . Anxiety is not something we "have" but something we "are." It is the subjective aspect of a being facing imminent non-being, that is, facing the dissolution of the existence of himself as a self. (P. 1354.)

This description of anxiety is offered in contradistinction to the description of fear. Fear, for the existentialist, is associated with some threat to the periphery of the person's existence, whereas anxiety is concerned with the very notion of existence itself. Thus, what we have described as anxiety in the previous definitions is regarded by the existentialist as largely conditioned fear and therefore as different from anxiety in some essential way.

We cannot here enter into all the ramifications of the existential position and the many concepts which it utilizes. Nevertheless, we should note that the position itself more or less precludes the possibility of the prediction of human behavior. Frankl (1955), for example, comments that "A real human person is not subject to rigid prediction. Existence can neither be reduced to a system nor be deduced from it" (p. 286). Unfortunately, this position, if taken seriously, would compel us to conclude that the search for laws of human behavior is bound to be barren, and would substitute so-called "understanding" for prediction.

It is, of course, obvious that recognizing the importance of the fear of nonexistence (death) or the loss of guiding values in generating human anxieties does not compel us to conclude that human behavior is unpredictable. It does, however, extend our conceptions of the range of situations in which anxieties may be developed, and thus it provides additional arguments against the pain-anxiety hypothesis.

At the present time, the existential position has not produced anything which might be regarded as scientific research. It seems inevitable that the existential psychologist will eschew the experimental method because of the necessary assumption of determinism which the experimental approach demands.

EMPIRICAL ASPECTS

We have examined some clinical instances of anxiety, we have considered some major theoretical positions regarding the origins of anxiety, and now we may turn to the findings of investigators who have studied the concomitants of anxiety under controlled conditions.

Measurement and Definition

Empirical studies of anxiety have typically used one of three methods. (1) They select subjects who demonstrate clinical evidences of anxiety, as judged by one or more observers, and compare their performance on a wide range of tasks and tests with that of subjects judged not to be anxious. The conclusions of such studies are in the form of correlational statements about clinically evident anxiety and other psychological phenomena. (2) They assume a particular position regarding the origin of anxiety and then attempt to generate anxiety in otherwise normal subjects by applying a suitable elicitor, such as pain, threat of pain, threat of failure, and so forth. Depending upon the preference of the investigator, the anxiety-producing stimulus may be called a "stress" stimulus or some other term. (3) A third method represents a combination of the two. Proceeding from some theory of anxiety, the investigator selects subjects who are anxious in terms of his definition and predicts differential responses to stress of his anxious subjects compared with nonanxious or low-anxious subjects.

Questionnaires and Ratings

Perhaps the best-known and most widely used measure of anxiety is the Taylor Manifest Anxiety Scale (MAS). This scale is a pencil and paper questionnaire consisting of 225 items, of which 50 contribute to an "anxiety" score and the remainder are irrelevant buffer items (Taylor, 1951, 1953). In the original version of the scale, a group of five clinicians selected items from the Minnesota Multiphasic Personality Inventory (MMPI) which corresponded to the description of chronic anxiety reaction given by Cameron (1947). Those items which commanded a high level of agreement from the clinicians as being indicative of manifest anxiety were used to make up an anxiety score. Typical items which met this criterion are:

"I work under a great deal of strain."
"I sweat very easily even on cool days."
"My sleep is restless and disturbed."
(Taylor, 1953.)

While the MAS was developed by Taylor as a device for selecting subjects in conditioning and learning experiments, it would be surprising if scores on the scale did not correlate with clinical observations of anxiety. Many studies have been performed to investigate correlations between MAS scores and other measures of anxiety. The results have been mixed: some illustrations are given in Table 7-1. From these we see that scores on the MAS correlate less than perfectly with many other defining measurements of anxiety. The correlations with physiological measures are significant when the latter are measures of physiological changes in stress situations, but not significant when they are measures of physiological functioning in resting or nonstressful circumstances.

As we pointed out, the MAS was not designed as a predictor of other measures of anxiety, and the correlations obtained are not directly relevant to its use in experimental investigations of the kind for which it was designed. The ranges of scores obtained on the MAS by clinical populations have been reported by Taylor (1953) and give some indication of the relationship of test performance to clinical status. This comparison is shown in Figure 7-1.

Manifest Anxiety Scores and Response Characteristics. When the MAS was first used, the major finding of interest was that subjects who obtained high scores on it demonstrated different levels of performance than low-anxiety subjects in a simple conditioning situation. Earlier classic studies had

TABLE 7-1 Correlations of Taylor Manifest Anxiety Scale with Other Anxiety Measures

Measure	Correlation of Physiological Functioning	Sig.	Source
Highest specific autonomic reaction	.599 (Male students)	.01	Mandler et al., 1961
Blink rate	−.11 (Male NP)	N.S.	Jackson & Bloomberg, 1958
Palmar sweating	−.15 (Patients)	N.S.	Jackson & Bloomberg, 1958
Palmar perspiration	.06 (Female students)	N.S.	McGuigan et al., 1959
Questionnaires			
Autonomic perception questionnaire	.410 (Males)	.01	Korchin & Heath, 1961
	.634 (Females)	.01	Korchin & Heath, 1961
Autonomic perception questionnaire	.52 (Males)	.01	Mandler, Mandler, & Uviller, 1958
Rotter sentence completion score	.573 (Male & female students)	.01	MacIntosh & Maher, 1958
Maudsley medical questionnaire	.92 (20 normals, 60 neurotic adults)	.01	Franks, 1956
Clinical ratings			
Clinical ratings of psychopathy	Sig. diff. between primary sociopaths versus neurotic sociopaths	.01	Lykken, 1957
Test signs			
Placement and size in figure drawing	Sig. diff. between high- & low- anxious female psychiatric patients	.05	Hoyt & Baron, 1959

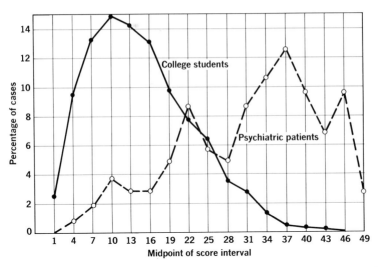

Figure 7-1. Percentages of university students and psychiatric patients receiving scores throughout the range of the Manifest Anxiety Scale. (Taylor, 1953.)

been performed by Welch and Kubis (1947). They found that conditioning of the GSR was more rapid in subjects diagnosed as pathologically anxious than in normal controls. Taylor's original experiment, comparing high- and low-anxious subjects in a conditioned eye-blink response, found that the former produced the CR significantly sooner than the latter, and were also somewhat slower to extinguish (Taylor, 1951). These results were confirmed in subsequent studies (Spence & Taylor, 1951; Spence & Farber, 1953).

In a logical extension of these findings, Spence and Taylor (1953) predicted that higher rates of conditioning should be found in neurotic and psychotic subjects. MAS scores were available from their subjects, as well as psychiatric data. In terms of the total amount of conditioning, the psychotics were significantly higher. Neurotic subjects were insignificantly higher than normals. However, when neurotic subjects were divided into those with high MAS scores versus those with low MAS scores, the predicted differences in conditioning were obtained. Generally speaking, the many studies that have been performed on this topic indicate that the MAS reliably predicts differences in conditionability when the *extreme* scores are used; overall correlations between test scores and conditioning are much less impressive.

Another aspect of this line of research has been the relationship between MAS scores and stimulus generalization. Rosenbaum (1953) investigated the effect of induced anxiety (threat of shock) upon the height and slope of a gradient of stimulus generalization. He found that high anxiety both raised the overall magnitude of response and flattened the gradient, which suggests that under high anxiety the subject's precision of discrimination is impaired.

Manifest Anxiety Scores and Complex Responses. The kinds of response involved in the research summarized in the preceding paragraphs are quite simple. Let us now consider the effects of anxiety upon complex patterns of response. The definition of a response as complex or simple may be made in terms of the number of incorrect responses that the subject has already acquired in relation to the stimuli comprising the task. Where the production of the correct response to a stimulus requires the nonappearance of other responses previously acquired to that stimulus, we shall define the stimulus-response relation as complex. Where there are few or no competing responses in the individual's past repertoire of learning, then the relation is simple. Clearly, we are dealing here with a continuum in which the major variable is the existing pattern of responses with which the person enters the task of acquiring a new S-R connection.

We have already seen that the effect of increasing motivation is to raise the probability that any response which has been learned to the stimulus will appear. Thus, the high-anxiety subjects are likely to produce competing responses in any given situation more often than low-anxiety subjects will. Competing responses, in a complex task, will generate errors wherever they occur. Thus the high-anxiety individual is likely to make a greater number of incorrect responses in a complex task than the low-anxiety individual.

An early experiment of this kind was performed by Malmo and Amsel (1948). Comparison was made between the performance of psychiatric patients with severe anxiety symptoms and normal controls on a verbal learning task. In this task, the subject was required to learn one list of nonsense syllables and then to learn a second list. Such a design generates the probability that the responses learned in the first list will produce interference errors when the second list has to be learned. Data from the Malmo and Amsel study indicate that the anxious subjects were prone to interference errors of this kind.

Using the MAS as the criterion of anxiety, Farber and Spence (1953) compared the performance of low- and high-anxious subjects on a stylus maze. The maze consisted of ten choice points with two alternatives (left versus right) at each choice point. The level of difficulty of each choice point had been previously established. Low-anxiety subjects were significantly superior to the high-anxiety subjects at every choice point but one, and an analysis of the errors revealed that their superiority varied directly

with the level of difficulty of the choice point (rank order correlation of .74). A comparison of subjects from both groups, matched for total scores, showed that while the high-anxiety subjects were worse in performance than the low-anxiety subjects at the most difficult choice points, this relationship was reversed at the easier choice points.

Maher (1956) studied the effect of anxiety level (as shown by the MAS) and shock upon the production of interference errors in a verbal learning task. The data of this investigation indicated that, as usual, high-anxious subjects produced more interference errors than low-anxious subjects. However, the presence of a shock-threat condition washed out these differences, since it appeared to degrade the performance of both high- and low-anxiety subjects to a point beyond that found in high anxiety alone. The investigator suggested that the shock-threat condition had served to push the motivation level to a "ceiling," at which differences in the MAS groupings disappeared.

Anxiety and Rigidity

When anxiety is high, existing responses are likely to be elicited to any stimulus that lies on a generalization gradient relative to the original "training" stimulus. We have already come across this phenomenon in our earlier study of the effects of drive upon stimulus generalization. Should the new generalized stimulus require a different response from the one that was originally acquired, then this high generalization gradient will interfere with the acquisition of a new response.

Let us consider the case of a young man who has been raised by a highly punitive mother and father. His response to his father has been to defer to him in all matters of opinion and to be very obedient. Obtaining employment in a business organization, he generalizes this response to the stimulus figure of his employer and behaves with passive obedience, becoming a yes-man. Unfortunately, the position demands that the employee show considerable personal initiative, and the young man finds that his employer begins to express disapproval and to criticize his work. This state of affairs should, ordinarily, lead the employee to change his behavior and to ultimately develop the responses that are likely to be rewarded. In other words, he must make a discrimination between his father and the employer, producing different responses to each of them. But receiving rebuffs from his employer is likely to increase the individual's anxiety and hence increase the likelihood that the existing response—deference—will recur. Prolonging this state of affairs may lead to the man losing his job and thus experiencing an even greater punishment.

Failure to make adequate discriminations is sometimes termed *rigidity*. People who have developed avoidance responses to a wide range of potential threats may exhibit considerable rigidity in many areas of their personal life. Later we shall note that rigidity of this kind is commonly found with individuals who exhibit obsessive-compulsive patterns of maladjustment.

In one sense, all neurotic behavior may be regarded as a type of rigidity—as a failure to adapt behavior to changing situations and as a persistence in this maladaptive activity in the face of no reward or even direct punishment. Our previous account of the effects of anxiety upon complex behavior represents a special case of this. The exact way in which anxiety produces rigidity of response is not quite clear. High states of drive narrow perception so that the individual perceives only those stimuli or stimulus aspects that are pertinent to the current drive. For him to notice other aspects, he must be in a state of relatively lower motivation. It may well be that the anxious person—such as the young man mentioned above—is literally not aware of the ways in which the employer-employee situation differs from the father-son relationship.

Rigidity may be trained without threat, by the simple expedient of rewarding consistency and punishing the response of seeking alternative solutions. Experimental evidence for this has been given by Schroder and Rotter (1952). Situational rigidity may be invoked in normal subjects by placing them under some clear threat when called upon to perform a task that intrinsically demands a wide span of perception and changes in response from one point to another. Maher (1957) required normal college students to solve a series of verbal mazes under threat of academic failure for inadequate performance. The series was so designed that the initial method of solution became incorrect partway through and a new technique was necessary. Threatened subjects were significantly slower than controls to perceive and apply this change in solution.

Pervin (1963) investigated general rigidity in a group of hospitalized neurotic patients and found that as with a group of hospitalized normal controls, there was little commonality of rigidity, since individuals revealed it on some measures but not on others. His data did tend to suggest that the neurotic pattern was related to the type of rigidity, patients with anxiety neurosis showing more motor rigidity while obsessive patients showed more rigidity on cognitive tasks.

Anxiety and Arousal

It will now be evident that many of the predictions which might be made about the effects of anxiety upon behavior could equally well be made from the model of *arousal* described in Chapter 4. The individual who is chronically anxious may be regarded as living in a state of stable high arousal. Thus his behavior will follow the inverted U curve of arousal-efficiency, but his normal starting point will be much higher up the curve than that for the low-anxious individual. In this respect, therefore, anxiety appears to possess the general properties of other motive states, both in its effect upon organized behavior and in its effect upon autonomic responses.

Semiprojective Methods: Sentence Completion

In an attempt to derive a measure of anxiety that would be based upon more spontaneous verbalizations of individuals, Renner, Maher, and Campbell (1962) developed a method of scoring a sentence completion test for the presence of anxiety statements. Here, the subject is required to complete a number of sentences for which he is given the first word or phrase. He is free to complete each sentence in any way, but the completed responses are then scored for the presence of overt expressions of anxiety using a manual of examples. Sample sentences and the score assigned them are as follows.

Stem: I regret
> ...that I am always tired and tense. (2 points)
> ...the thought of final examination week. (1 point)
> ...not having more time to do everything I want to do. (0 points)

This method has been validated against self-descriptions and against the peer reputation of the subject (obtained by gathering judgments about his general daily anxiety from associates who live with him). These correlations were .34 and .43 respectively for women and .24 and .08 for men.

Biological Measures of Anxiety

In general, the measurement of anxiety as it is defined by biological changes has depended heavily upon the polygraphic techniques described in Chapter 4. Thus, the autonomic changes associated with stress or arousal are, to a large extent, the same as those that occur when a threatening stimulus is presented to the individual. Figure 7-2 shows the polygraphic record of a normal subject who was presented at intervals with a series of pictures, some of which were selected because they were judged to be anxiety-producing by a previous group of observers. The marked responses to an aversive picture may be compared to the relatively minor changes in the record when a "bland" picture was shown. In the study in which these data were obtained, the subjects were free to eliminate (i.e. avoid) the picture at any time by switching it off. The rapid avoidance of the unpleasant picture is also evident in the record.

Chapter 4 notes that there may be some differences between the autonomic patterns found in anxiety and those found in anger, with the anger pattern perhaps being mediated by high noradrenalin reactions while anxiety may be mediated by high adrenalin reactions. Ax (1953) has suggested a somewhat different patterning of anxiety and anger. His two patterns were distinguished most clearly from each other as follows:

Anger
Increase in diastolic blood pressure
Increase in muscle tension
Increase in skin conductance
Decrease in heart rate

Anxiety
Increase in muscle tension
Increase in skin conductance
Increase in respiration

Figure 7-2. Polygraphic record of a subject's responses to threatening and bland slides. Slide 37 (lower left) evokes increased GSR (fifth trace from the top of chart) and suppression of breathing. Period of viewing is very brief. Slide 38, a bland slide, is viewed longer and does not provoke the same degree of autonomic reaction.

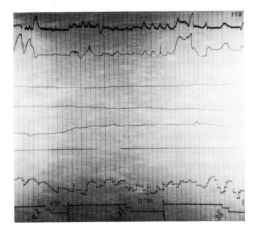

Whether or not these patterns are definitive is arguable. After a thorough survey of many studies of this general type, Martin (1961) concludes that they "are consistent with the possibility that some pattern of physiological measures may allow one to infer the magnitude of the hypothetical anxiety reaction differentially from other hypothetical states such as anger or pain" (p. 239).

From the many studies performed, the most plausible conclusions that arise appear to be that anger is accompanied by increase in diastolic blood pressure while anxiety is accompanied by increases in heart rate. Inferences about other measurable differences are much less supportable. However, it is clear that during states of emotion there are changes, largely autonomic, in bodily reactions, and that these probably vary in pattern from one person to another. Whatever the pattern, its existence plays a central role in the experience of the emotion itself, the perception of bodily changes being part and parcel of the conscious experience.

The Perception of Autonomic Feedback

It is generally agreed by psychologists that the bodily changes occurring in the face of a threatening stimulus contribute to the experience of anxiety and are themselves regarded as unpleasant. However, the extent to which people are aware of changes in their own bodily processes may vary considerably, some being very sensitive to even

TABLE 7-2 Anxiety Scale

1. Death anxiety—references to death, dying, threat of death, or anxiety about death experienced by or occurring to:
   a. self (3)*
   b. animate others (2)
   c. inanimate objects destroyed (1)
   d. denial of death anxiety (1)
2. Mutilation (castration) anxiety—references to injury, tissue, or physical damage, or anxiety about injury or threat of such experienced by or occurring to:
   a. self (3)
   b. animate others (2)
   c. inanimate objects (1)
   d. denial (1)
3. Separation anxiety—references to desertion, abandonment, ostracism, loss of support, falling, loss of love or love object, or threat of such experienced by or occurring to:
   a. self (3)
   b. animate others (2)
   c. inanimate objects (1)
   d. denial (1)

4. Guilt anxiety—references to adverse criticism, abuse, condemnation, moral disapproval, guilt, or threat of such experienced by:
   a. self (3)
   b. animate others (2)
   d. denial (1)
5. Shame anxiety—references to ridicule, inadequacy, shame, embarrassment, humiliation, overexposure of deficiencies or private details, or threat of such experienced by:
   a. self (3)
   b. animate others (2)
   d. denial (1)
6. Diffuse or nonspecific anxiety—references by word or phrase to anxiety and/or fear without distinguishing type or source of anxiety:
   a. self (3)
   b. animate others (2)
   d. denial (1)

* *Numbers in parentheses are the scores or weights.*
Notes:
1. In the above scale the reference is not scored if the speaker is the agent and the injury criticism, etc., is directed to another.
2. When "we" is used, score as "I."
3. Death, injury, abandonment, etc., may come from an external source or situation.
4. In any of above, the weight should be increased by 1 if the statement of anxiety or fear is modified to indicate that the condition is extreme or marked.

minor changes while others perceive only the most marked alterations. Variations of this kind are of obvious importance in determining the extent to which the individual feels anxious in the face of a given set of events.

Mandler, Mandler, and Uviller (1958) developed a questionnaire designed to elicit individual differences in awareness of autonomic responses, or, as they termed it, *autonomic feedback*. The questionnaire, called the Autonomic Perception Questionnaire (APQ), consisted largely of items requiring the subject to identify the frequency with which certain bodily changes occurred in states of pleasure and states of anxiety. For example, one item is, "When you feel anxious, how often are you aware of any change in your heart action?" To this question the subject responds by marking a point somewhere on a line 14.5 centimeters long, one end of which is marked "Never" and the other "Always." The items cover seven classes of bodily reaction: heart rate, perspiration, temperature changes, respiration, gastrointestinal disturbances, muscle tension, and blood pressure.

Studies of individuals under laboratory stresses showed that high scorers differed from low scorers significantly in five measures of actual autonomic reactivity: heart rate, perspiration, temperature, respiration, blood volume, and total reactivity. That is, of course, to be expected. However, the data suggest that the questionnaire does not simply reflect the actual state of reactivity

---

5. *The following is a list of words of the kind that may be scored in category 6 if the type of anxiety is not explicitly stated and in any one of the other categories if the stimulus source of the reaction is denoted. Any grammatical form of the word may be scored, whether it is an adjective, noun, adverb, or verb, and so forth. The following list is not intended to be complete but mainly to provide examples of scorable word concepts.*

adjectives	nouns	adverbs	verbs
fearful	fear	fearfully	to fear
frustrated	frustration	frustratedly	to frustrate
tense	tension	tensely	to tense
worried	worry	worriedly	to worry
shaky		shakily	to shake
desperate	desperation	desperately	to despair
agitated	agitation	agitatedly	to agitate
irritable	irritation	irritably	to irritate
trembling	tremble	trembly	to tremble
scared		scarily	to scare
dangerous	danger	dangerously	to endanger
troubled	trouble		to trouble
jittery	jitters		
panicky	panic		to panic
upset	upset		to upset
terrified	terror		to terrorize
frightened	fright	frightfully	to frighten
overwhelmed		overwhelmingly	to overwhelm
threatened	threat	threateningly	to threaten
eerie	eeriness	eeriely	
weird	weirdness	weirdly	
rattled			to rattle
anxious	anxiety	anxiously	
timid	timidity	timidly	
nervous	nerves	nervously	

SOURCE: *Gleser, Gottschalk, and Springer (1961).*

of the subject's autonomic system; the high scorers tended to overestimate their reactivity, while the low scorers tended to underestimate it. Thus, in the chain of events between the occurrence of anxiety and its perception and interpretation by the subject, there are at least two important variables: the extent of the bodily reaction and the subject's estimate of it. In the light of this we cannot expect to find high correlations between objective measures of autonomic activity and subjective report.

Measurement in the Natural Habitat

The methods so far described all involve the formal presentation of a stimulus or test item to the subject and the measurement of the subsequent response. As with all laboratory methods, there is some question about the representativeness of stimuli presented and the validity of verbal self-report. Consequently, techniques have been developed to measure anxiety in natural situations as it is revealed in behavior (both motor and verbal) and in bodily changes.

Analysis of Spontaneous Verbal Behavior. Gleser, Gottschalk, and Springer (1961) developed a coding system for the analysis of what they term "free" anxiety, in contrast to "bound" anxiety. The latter, as we have seen, is inferred from various kinds of pathological or maladaptive behavior; the former refers to manifest anxiety, i.e., where there are overt evidences of fear. However, these workers have preferred to consider verbal expressions of fear and apprehension and to omit references to physiological experiences as such. The coding system is applied to samples of speech or writing produced by an individual under open-ended conditions. Six general classifications of anxiety are included in the system, namely, anxiety about death, anxiety about mutilation, anxiety about separation, guilt anxiety, shame anxiety, and nonspecific or diffuse anxiety. Greater weight is given to expressions of these kinds of anxiety when they are directed toward the self; less weight is given

the more the target is remote or displaced. The coding system is shown in Table 7-2.

Validity studies of this coding system have indicated that total scores correlate significantly with clinical ratings of psychiatric patients (+.66) and with the Welsh A-scale of the MMPI (+.68). Other studies indicate higher anxiety scores for hypertensive patients, and regular cyclical changes in the scores of female subjects correlated with phases of the menstrual cycle.

Behavior Rating Scales. Another method of recording anxiety in the natural habitat is provided by the use of behavior rating scales. These consist of checklists in which a variety of itemized response patterns are used as bases for inferring anxiety. Different weights are assigned to particular kinds of response, depending upon the investigator's conception of their relative importance or reliability for inference.

Autonomic Responses. Two kinds of approach have been made to the study of autonomic responses under anxiety-arousing conditions. Beam (1955) studied the responses of subjects just before doctoral examinations and just before opening-night performances of plays. He found an increase in palmar sweat and in GSR conditioning during the stress situations. These measures were made under laboratory conditions—

Figure 7-3. Heart rate responses differing widely in two individuals faced with laboratory stresses do not differ so clearly when they are monitored in the natural habitat. (Maher & Howe, 1964.)

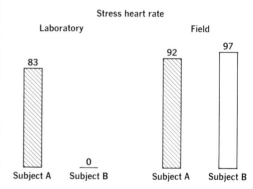

Stress heart rate

Laboratory   Field

and in anticipation of the stressful event rather than during it. However, we may assume that the data do reflect the anxiety state of the subject and are rather less subject to laboratory artifact than those obtained under conditions of experimenter-induced stress.

Maher and Howe (1964) studied the relationship of laboratory-induced stress and real stress with the aid of a radiotelemetric system. Two subjects were selected on the basis of their heart-rate response to laboratory stress, one having been totally unresponsive and the other showing marked increase in heart rate. Both of these subjects were monitored during an academic examination and at rest in their rooms. The differences in stress responsiveness that were apparent in the laboratory disappeared under the serious stress of the examinations; in the latter case both students showed very high heart rates maintained for the full hour of the examination. These data are shown in Figure 7-3. With the development of radiotelemetry the possibility of recording autonomic data during real stresses has been opened up considerably.

SUMMARY

Anxiety is best regarded as a construct, or *inferred* state of the individual. The presence and the degree of anxiety are defined by measurements of verbal behavior, motor behavior, and certain bodily changes, notably in the autonomic nervous system. Anxiety, thus defined, appears to occur whenever the subject is faced with a threatening stimulus (or a stimulus contiguous with some previous threat). Behavioral changes during anxiety lie along a dimension on which low states of anxiety appear to facilitate responses and increase behavioral efficiency, while high states of anxiety produce interfering responses and behavioral disorganization.

Measures of anxiety in the three categories above have not generally produced high correlations with each other, and many problems exist with regard to their reliability. At the present time, there is no strong evidence to warrant an empirical distinction between anxiety and any more general conception of increased drive or arousal. Measures of one are highly congruent with measures of the other, and the behavioral consequences of one are much the same as those of the other.

Many kinds of pathological behavior may be regarded as anxiety-reduction techniques —that is to say, they are patterns of response that have developed because they have been reinforced by anxiety reduction. In the next chapter we consider some of the major common patterns.

SUGGESTED READINGS

1. Martin, B. The assessment of anxiety by physiological behavioral measures. *Psychol. Bull.*, 1961, **58**, 234–255. A survey of the intercorrelations between bodily measures of anxiety and behavioral indices. A useful summary of recent data.
2. May, R. *The meaning of anxiety*. New York: Ronald, 1950. A now classic text on the definition and characteristics of anxiety from several viewpoints.
3. Taylor, Janet A. Drive theory and manifest anxiety. *Psychol. Bull.*, 1956, **53**, 303–320. A precise description of the role of anxiety as a useful construct in behavior theory, with special reference to the Manifest Anxiety Scale.

REFERENCES

Ax, A. F. The physiological differentiation between fear and anger in humans. *Psychosom. Med.*, 1953, **15**, 433–442.

Beam, J. C. Serial learning and conditioning under real life stress. *J. abnorm. soc. Psychol.*, 1955, **51**, 543–551.

Cameron, D. E. Autonomy in anxiety. *Psychiat. Quart.*, 1944, **18**, 53–60.

Cameron, N. *The psychology of the be-*

havior disorders. Boston: Houghton Mifflin, 1947.

Farber, I. E., & Spence, K. W. Complex learning and conditioning as a function of anxiety. *J. exp. Psychol.,* 1953, **45,** 120–125.

Frankl, V. E. *The doctor and the soul.* New York: Knopf, 1955.

Franks, C. Conditioning and personality: a study of normal and neurotic subjects. *J. abnorm. soc. Psychol.,* 1956, **52,** 143–150.

Gleser, G. C., Gottschalk, L. A., & Springer, K. L. An anxiety scale applicable to verbal samples. *Arch. gen. Psychiat.,* 1961, **5,** 593–605.

Hoyt, T. E., & Baron, M. R. Anxiety indices in same-sex drawings of psychiatric patients with high and low MAS scores. *J. consult. Psychol.,* 1959, **23,** 448–452.

Jackson, D. N., & Bloomberg, R. Anxiety: unitas or multiplex? *J. consult. Psychol.,* 1958, **22,** 225–227.

Kardiner, A. Traumatic neuroses of war. In S. Arieti (Ed.), *American handbook of psychiatry.* Vol. I. New York: Basic Books, 1959.

Kesson, W., & Mandler, G. Anxiety, pain and the inhibition of distress. *Psychol. Rev.,* 1961, **68,** 396–404.

Korchin, S. J., & Heath, Helen A. Somatic experience in the anxiety state: some sex and personality correlates of "autonomic feedback." *J. consult. Psychol.,* 1961, **25,** 398–404.

Lykken, D. T. A study of anxiety in the sociopathic personality. *J. abnorm. soc. Psychol.,* 1957, **55,** 6–10.

McGuigan, F. J., Calvin, A. D., & Richardson, Elizabeth C. Manifest anxiety, Palmar Perspiration Index and stylus maze learning. *Amer. J. Psychol.,* 1959, **72,** 434–438.

MacIntosh, Shirley P., & Maher, B. A. Relationship of verbal fluency to sentence-completion scores in anxious and non-anxious subjects. Paper presented to the Midwest. Psychol. Ass., Detroit, 1958.

Maher, B. A. Personality, problem solving and the *Einstellung*-effect. *J. abnorm. soc. Psychol.,* 1957, **54,** 70–74.

Maher, B. A., & Howe, D. Stress responses in the laboratory and the natural habitat. Unpublished manuscript, Harvard, 1964.

Maher, Winifred B. Manifest anxiety, shock, and stimulus-response condition as determinants of performance on a verbal learning task. Unpublished doctoral dissertation, Ohio State Univer., 1956.

Malmo, R. B. Anxiety and behavioral arousal. *Psychol. Rev.,* 1957, **64,** 276–287.

Malmo, R. B., & Amsel, P. Anxiety-produced interference in serial rote learning, with observations on rote learning after partial frontal lobectomy. *J. exp. Psychol.,* 1948, **38,** 440–454.

Mandler, A., Mandler, J. M., & Uviller, E. T. Autonomic feedback: the perception of autonomic activity. *J. abnorm. soc. Psychol.,* 1958, **56,** 367–373.

Mandler, G., Mandler, Jean M., Kremen, I., & Sholiton, R. D. The response to threat: relations among verbal and physiological indices. *Psychol. Monogr.,* 1961, **75,** whole no. 513.

Martin, B. The assessment of anxiety by physiological behavioral measures. *Psychol. Bull.,* 1961, **58,** 234–255.

May, R. The existential approach. In S. Arieti (Ed.), *American handbook of psychiatry.* Vol. II. New York: Basic Books, 1959.

Pervin, L. The need to predict and control under conditions of threat. *J. Pers.,* 1963, **31,** 570–587.

Renner, K. E., Maher, B. A., & Campbell, D. T. The validity of a method for scoring sentence completion responses for anxiety, dependency, and hostility. *J. appl. Psychol.,* 1962, **46,** 285–290.

Rosenbaum, G. Stimulus generalization as a function of experimentally induced anxiety. *J. exp. Psychol.,* 1953, **45,** 35–43.

Sarnoff, C. A. *Medical aspects of flying motivation.* Randolph Air Force Base, Texas: Air University School of Aviation Medicine, 1957.

Schroder, H. M., & Rotter, J. B. Rigidity as learned behavior. *J. exp. Psychol.*, 1952, **44,** 141–150.

Spence, K. W., & Farber, I. E. Conditioning and extinction as a function of anxiety. *J. exp. Psychol.*, 1953, **45,** 116–119.

Spence, K. W., & Taylor, Janet A. Anxiety and the strength of the UCS as determiners of the amount of eyelid conditioning. *J. exp. Psychol.*, 1951, **42,** 183–188.

Spence, K. W., & Taylor, Janet A. The relation of conditioned response strength to anxiety in normal, neurotic and psychotic subjects. *J. exp. Psychol.*, 1953, **45,** 265–272.

Taylor, Janet A. The relationship of anxiety to the conditioned eyelid response. *J. exp. Psychol.*, 1951, **41,** 81–92.

Taylor, Janet A. A personality scale of manifest anxiety. *J. abnorm. soc. Psychol.*, 1953, **48,** 285–290.

Welch, L., & Kubis, J. Conditioning PGR (psychogalvanic response) in states of pathological anxiety. *J. nerv. ment. Dis.*, 1947, **105,** 372–381.

NEUROTIC PATTERNS OF AVOIDANCE

We have already noted that when an individual is faced with a situation in which there are elements of both punishment and reward, a state of conflict is presumed to exist. Among the concomitants of conflict is anxiety, which may be due both to the proximity of the punishing aspects of the situation and to the indecision engendered by the equilibrium state per se. In this connection we have also noted that in the face of conflict, a variety of behavior patterns may develop, the main character of which is that they serve to avoid direct confrontation with the conflictful stimuli.

When this analysis is applied to human behavior, we should point out that there are some additional considerations. First is the fact that many human conflicts are engendered by the use of punishment for a forbidden *response,* and less frequently because the person is in a forbidden place. Thus the experimental observation of the conflicts produced in laboratory rats by the delivery of punishment at a specific location have only a limited application to our understanding of response-produced conflicts. The child who is punished when he behaves destructively is punished for his behavior, and this punishment is not generally limited to the behavior in a particular situation. Should the punishment be prolonged and severe, then the individual should develop anxiety whenever he observes preliminary aggressive activity on his own part.

A second consideration is that the human may develop *many* ways of avoiding an anxiety-arousing stimulus—he is not limited to simple physical avoidance. A feared stimulus may be avoided by closing one's eyes to it, by learning to attend to something else in the environment whenever the threat is present, and so on. Hence we may expect to find that intense anxiety will produce a wide range of symptomatic responses, all of which serve to avoid a threat.

If the punished response is one that is likely to be elicited by common situations (for example, aggressive responses may occur to many different kinds of attack or frustration), then the person cannot escape the conflict by changing his environment. In this sense, he is "carrying the conflict around with him." Thus, the important aspect of a response-produced conflict is that it tends to become chronic; the subject can never get completely away from the threat, and his symptomatic avoidance will be maintained for a long time.

The development of ways in which to avoid threat is not, in itself, maladaptive. In fact we must assume that adequate anxiety is necessary to survival for a living organism. Likewise, if the attractions and dangers in the conflict are actually present, then we should not be justified in considering the behavior of the person necessarily neurotic. Patterns of avoidance may be termed "neurotic" when:

1. They develop in relation to threats that are not realistically present, and/or
2. They involve avoidance to many situations that have inconsequential similarities or relationships to the original threat.

Let us consider an example. A male adult suffers from intense anxiety whenever he is in a room in which there are gardenias. His anxiety is not relieved until he manages to leave the room or can get someone else to remove the flowers. He cannot enter a florist's shop and has even come to avoid walking down the street where the neighborhood flower shop is. He is upset by pictures of gardenias and has become recently rather apprehensive about perfumes that might have a gardenia fragrance.

Upon investigation, it develops that gardenias were among the bouquets at his mother's funeral. His relationship with her had been very stormy, involving much resentment on his part at her attempts to continue domination of his life after adolescence. When she died, he experienced a mixture of both sorrow and relief, the intensity of the latter surprising him and creating strong feelings of anxiety.

While we can understand the feelings that entered into the original conflict, his avoidance of the flowers is neurotic by both of the criteria suggested above. The flower does not represent any realistic danger; his fears have spread from the physical presence of the flower to such a wide array of related places and stimuli that his daily behavior is being limited by it.

In other words, we see here the operation of exactly the same principles of avoidance learning that were presented in more basic form in Chapter 3. The psychopathologist has been interested in rather more precise understanding of the different kinds of symptom that develop and their relation to the personality of the patient. Let us first examine the major categories of avoidance response.

HYPOCHONDRIA PATTERN

From time to time we meet people who appear unusually preoccupied with the care of their health, even though there seems to be no reason for their concern. In the bathroom cabinet are many bottles of medicine and pills, their reaction to trivial aches and pains is pronounced, and they take precautions to avoid any possible threat to health, however minor. Besides this abnormal caution, there tends to be a kind of intellectual interest in health and disease, so that the patient often has a minor medical library in his home and seems to gain satisfaction from self-diagnosis. This pattern of behavior is termed *hypochondria*. In extreme instances it can seriously limit the patient's efficiency, keeping him away from work and preventing him from engaging in a wide range of recreational activities.

We have already noted that the physical changes accompanying anxiety are inherently distressing, and it is quite likely that some people interpret them as evidence of physical ill health, when the threatening stimulus that has provoked the anxiety has not been identified. By seeking medical treatment, the individual may have removed himself from the immediate vicinity of the threat, and thus the response of going to the doctor is inadvertently reinforced.

Physical illness is an acceptable reason for avoiding many kinds of responsibility, and in this sense society generally "rewards" it by providing special care and protection for the sick. Sickness in a child generally leads to additional overt affection by parents and more indulgence than might ordinarily be the case. In view of this combination of factors, it is not surprising that the hypochondriacal pattern is found in combination with many other types of neurotic avoidance response. Most psychopathologists do not regard it as a clear-cut syndrome, because of its common appearance in combination with other symptoms.

However, it is customary to distinguish between hypochondriacal concern with illness—the pattern of "enjoying ill health"—and the plethora of somatic complaints that may arise from psychotic patients. The central feature of the hypochondriacal pattern is its clear function as an *avoidance* response.

DENIAL PATTERNS

Threatening situations may be avoided by denying their existence. Denial may be achieved in several ways, some of which involve the relatively simple technique of not looking at or listening to events that are pertinent to the threat. It is a procedure that is readily observable in children. One of the writer's children had the experience of falling on a hot-air register built into the floor of a long hall. He burned his hands,

and healing took some time. For weeks afterwards, the child would not venture down the hall until one day he was seeking a favorite teddy bear. The toy was on the other side of the register, and after some preliminary indecision and distress, the problem was solved. Placing his hands firmly over his eyes to blot out the sight of it, the child walked across the register and recovered his toy.

In adults, denial may take the form of a seeming failure to recognize some aspects of the environment that are evident to everybody else. Alternatively, or additionally, it may be accompanied by marked forgetting of events or behavior, the recollection of which may be anxiety-provoking to the individual. In a previous chapter we discussed the development of cognitive avoidance patterns—the responses of "not thinking about" disturbing topics and of not noticing disturbing stimuli. Example 8-1 illustrates this kind of behavior developed to a pathological extent.

We notice in this case that the patient's behavior appears to be maintained by its effects upon other people. It served to frustrate her mother and then to control her husband. Both of these individuals were the targets of some of the patient's resentment, but in neither case did she seem to recognize or admit this. The actual circumstances under which the symptom arose originally are very unclear, and they are irrelevant to the maintenance of it in the patient's adult life. Most important in this kind of behavior, however, is the patient's continued presentation of a bland and nonaggressive social appearance and her apparently genuine ignorance of the variables in her relationship with the husband that served to exacerbate her difficulties. It is this insensitivity to important aspects of the environment and of the individual's own behavior that defines the denial pattern.

In addition to denial in this sense, such individuals also seem to behave in a manner that implicitly denies or rejects reality. This patient was approaching middle age, but she was actively denying it by adopting a

EXAMPLE 8-1

Denial with Hostile Behavior

A woman, aged forty, referred herself to a hospital clinic complaining of a variety of physical ailments. These included nausea after meals, dizziness, and difficulty during menstruation. She had already been examined by several physicians, but no physical diagnosis was made. One physician gave her tranquilizers and advised her to "relax" more. Finally she was referred to the clinic for extensive diagnostic work-up. When the results of this were uniformly negative, she was referred for outpatient consultation in the psychiatric service of the hospital.

At first she was reluctant to keep the appointment that had been made, but she finally did so. During the initial interview she repeatedly stressed that she realized many of her problems were "mental" but wanted to point out that they were not "psychiatric." The patient was seen in psychotherapy for over eighteen months, during which time the major elements of her case history became apparent.

Her parents were divorced when she was eight, leaving her mother with the patient and two younger sisters. She was called on to testify during the divorce proceedings and remembered her fear and horror about this. After the divorce, her father left the country and failed to contribute anything to the support of the family. The patient's mother went to work in a variety of menial jobs, and much of the care of the house devolved upon the patient. In the early interviews the patient affirmed her conviction that her symptoms had a physical basis; she stated that she had never suffered from vomiting at any time in her life and that her childhood had been marked by great closeness and warmth with her mother.

When she was sixteen, the patient met her husband and married him one year later. At that time he enlisted in the Navy (during World War II) and was absent for four years, except for occasional furloughs. The patient lived with her mother and sisters in a small apartment. On her husband's return to civilian life, they moved in with his mother, who had more room to accommodate them. Bickering between the patient and her mother-in-law developed almost immediately, and the husband played the part of mediator. Finally, the patient and husband found an apartment of their own, and two children were born subsequently.

The patient attributed the onset of her present troubles to her hearing that her father had died following stomach surgery. Although she had not seen him for many years, the patient was quite depressed at his death and shortly afterwards began to experience digestive difficulties which she feared presaged some similar fate for herself. Her husband, she stated, was tolerant and supportive during her fears and her continual consultation of physicians. She described her relationship with her husband as "nearly ideal," attributing many virtues to him.

With ensuing interviews, however, many new facts emerged. At one point the patient's daughter suffered from nausea, causing the family to terminate a social visit sooner than they had expected. In the patient's anger at this, she shouted to the therapist "She's just like me. . . . I used to vomit all the time when I was her age. It used to make my mother mad at me too!" Beginning with this recollection, which came as a surprise to the patient herself, she now recalled that her childhood had, in fact, been marked by considerable hostility toward her mother—whom she really blamed for the disappearance of a loved father—and that she had discovered accidentally that vomiting and general physical ailments always served to provide her with control of the situation.

Additional data developed to indicate that the patient's current symptoms had been coincident, indeed, with her learning of the death of her father, but were perhaps determined less by the character of his terminal illness than by their previous relationship to the expression of hostility toward the mother. Although they may have been stimulated by these events, the patient's symptoms now appeared to be maintained by their contemporary effects upon her husband's life. Close inquiry into the situations in which the patient had suffered her more recent bouts of nausea revealed that they invariably occurred when she was dining out socially with her husband. This had become a frequent obligation, as her husband had been elected master of his lodge and was expected to preside at a number of social meals. The inconvenient illness of the patient now compelled him to take her home in the middle of such affairs and was causing him some embarrassment in his official role. As soon as they reached home, the symptoms would subside—sometimes to the extent that the patient would then prepare a large meal for both of them and eat it with no distress. Transparent as the patient's motivations were—and they were sufficiently so that her husband had pointed this out to her several times—she strongly denied any hostility toward him, praising him lavishly in terms she had used orginally about her mother.

Under much pressure from the patient, her husband abandoned much of his own social life and was induced to take a "hard line" in his hitherto friendly relationship with the patient's mother. With this, the patient's overt symptomatology diminished dramatically, there being no recurrence over a follow-up period of 18 months.

manner of dress and cosmetics that would be more typical of a twenty-year-old. She proudly referred to the fact that she and her sixteen-year-old daughter had been mistaken for sisters.

A patient of this kind would tend to be diagnosed as suffering from "hysteria." Current nosology in psychopathology uses this term to describe patterns in which threatening experiences and events are not perceived, or if perceived, are rapidly forgotten. Insofar as a label such as hysteria implies a disease entity, it may be misleading, and we shall therefore continue to emphasize the response characteristic.

The Origins of Denial Patterns

It is a matter of considerable interest to psychopathologists to discover the factors that generate denial responses in people. Several important questions have been asked. Is denial a typical response of the individual to all threats? What are the antecedents of denial patterns, either biological or experiential? Is the verbal or behavioral denial of distress accompanied by lack of autonomic signs of disturbance? Let us examine some of the empirical evidence on these points.

Generality of Denial

Lazarus and Longo (1953) reported that subjects who recalled their personal failure in an experimental task also recalled material that was associated with a painful electric shock. At the other end of the continuum, subjects who could not recall one could not recall the other. Other experimental evidence indicates that people who recall failure in a threatening situation learn emotionally significant words as easily as neutral ones, while those who forget the incompleted tasks find learning difficult (Eriksen, 1952). These studies and others have been reviewed by Byrne (1964) and have led him to comment that they suggest "rather strongly the presence of an approach-avoidance sort of dimension with respect to threatening stimuli. It should also be noted that these behavior tendencies appear to be fairly pervasive ones in that they are identifiable in perceptual responses, responses given to projective tests, behavior in learning and memory tasks and in symptoms of maladjustment" (Byrne, 1964, p. 173).

Byrne has conceptualized a dimension of repression-sensitization, the repression end of which is characterized by slow perception of threat, denial of threat or failure, ready forgetting of distressing events, and so forth. At the sensitization end, the reverse of these behaviors is found, with unusual speed of threat recognition, better than average memory of failure and distress, etc. To measure these tendencies in individuals, Byrne developed a Repression-Sensitization Scale (R-S Scale). This consists of a questionnaire of 156 items which was derived from the MMPI—just as the Taylor MAS was—and which after suitable corrections yielded high reliabilities.

Byrne has studied repressors and sensitizers in great detail, both in terms of the generality of behaviors associated with high and low scores on the scale, and with reference to the antecedents of this kind of behavior.

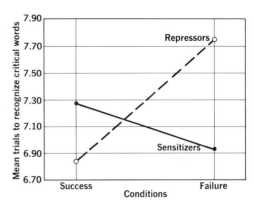

Figure 8-1. Perceptual recognition thresholds for critical words under success and failure conditions. (After Byrne, 1964.)

Byrne's Repression-Sensitization Scale

Scores on this scale have been correlated with various psychiatric clinical judgments of denial tendencies, and close agreements have been obtained. Selective forgetting of material associated with threat to self-esteem has also been reported for high repressors (Gossett, 1964). Tempone (1962) studied the perceptual responses of high and low scorers on the R-S Scale. Forty repressors and forty sensitizers were given the task of solving anagrams in company with a group of confederates of the experimenter acting as subjects. Half of each group were given failures: very few correct solutions to anagrams were obtained by them. The other half of the subjects were given success on nearly all the items. Following this, each subject had the task of recognizing words presented on a tachistoscope. The words consisted of three practice words, the eight correct anagram solutions, and eight neutral words. Repressors who had been in the failure group had significantly higher thresholds for the recognition of anagram words than repressors who had been in the success group. Thresholds for the neutral words had no relationship to the experimental manipulations. The forms of these data is shown in Figure 8-1.

Additional investigation by Byrne and Sheffield (1965) indicated that when exposed to reading sexually arousing passages from novels, both repressors and sensitizers rated themselves as being sexually aroused, but only the sensitizers rated themselves as being anxious. Byrne speculates that a possible interpretation of this finding is that the repressor is either unaware of any anxiety or is denying it. The precise interpretation is a matter of some doubt, hinging to a large extent upon whether or not the subject is reacting with anxiety some other way, i.e., producing autonomic signs of anxiety. In other words, we do not know whether or not the denier is genuinely free from any autonomic response to the disturbing stimulus (having perhaps avoided seeing it as threatening); whether he is genuinely unaware of autonomic responses which are, in fact, present; or whether he is aware but denies it when questioned.

This problem has been studied by Lazarus and Alfert (1964), who presented subjects with a distressing movie under conditions in which the threatening aspects of it were minimized or maximized. Using the R-S Scale, they found that high deniers refused to admit to distress verbally but revealed it autonomically (as measured by skin conductance during the showing of the movie), while low deniers verbalized more distress but showed less autonomically. These data suggest that the denier is not free from autonomic patterns of distress in the face of threat; they do not make clear, of course, whether the denial is verbal or whether the subject is simply unaware of the autonomic aspects of his own state.

Studies of the antecedents of repression have been conducted by Byrne and others, and have led him to tabulate certain patterns of child-rearing practice that seem to be important in determining the development of these tendencies. From several studies of parental attitudes and practices, Byrne reports findings that are a little surprising. The general tenor is shown in Table 8-1.

Inspection of these differences reveals that the repressors tend, on the whole, to perceive their parents in a favorable light and to perceive themselves as having been raised in a very healthy psychological climate. Sensitizers, on the other hand, describe their parents in terms that are psychologically unfavorable. These data do not demonstrate that the parental practices were, in fact,

determinants in the way that they are identified here. We already know what repressors, by definition, tend to forget unpleasant or threatening events in the past and that the reverse is true for the sensitizers. Thus these variables may be direct reflections of the differences in memory processes and not accurate accounts of the way in which the subjects' parents actually behaved.

In view of the implicitly maladaptive connotation of the term "repression," it is instructive to examine data on the way in which repressors and sensitizers are regarded by other people. Joy (1963) and Byrne, Golightly, and Sheffield (1965) studied the characteristics of the two ends of the dimension in terms of their correlation with other measures of personality. One of these was the California Psychological Inventory, and from this correlation Byrne concluded that repressors and sensitizers would tend to be differentially described by others as shown in Table 8-2.

The repressors here emerge as being

T A B L E 8 - 1 Descriptions of Their Parents by Repressors and Sensitizers

Repressors	Sensitizers
Males	
1. Mother permissive about sexuality	1. Mother restrictive about sexuality
2. Mother perceived as having high self-esteem	2. Mother perceived as having low self-esteem
3. Mother perceived as having high expectation of son achieving masculine role	3. Mother perceived as not having high expectation of son achieving masculine role
Females	
1. Mother strict	1. Mother permissive
2. Mother does not expect deification of parents	2. Mother does expect deification of parents
3. Feels confident in parental role	3. Does not feel confident in parental role
4. Mother perceived as accepting; as nonpunitive and not using physical punishment; and as having high self-esteem	4. Mother perceived as rejecting; punitive, including physically; and having low self-esteem.
5. Parents' relationship seen as positive	5. Parents' relationship seen as negative
6. Mother seen as consistent	6. Mother seen as inconsistent

SOURCE: *Byrne (1964).*

TABLE 8-2 Descriptions of Repressors and Sensitizers as Seen by Others

Repressors	Sensitizers
1. Active, alert, ambitious, competitive, energetic, enterprising, forward, industrious, ingenious, productive, progressive, quick, resourceful, strict and thorough in their own work and in expectations for others, and valuing work and effort for its own sake	1. Apathetic, excitable, lacking in self-direction, leisurely, overly judgmental in attitude, passive, pessimistic about their occupational futures, quiet, submissive, unambitious, and unassuming
2. Broad and varied interests, capable, clear-thinking, high value on cognitive and intellectual matters, intellectually able, intelligent, original and fluent in thought, valuing intellectual activity and intellectual achievement, verbally fluent, versatile, and well informed	2. Coarse, constricted in thought and action, conventional and stereotyped in thinking, narrow, opinionated, shallow, and shrewd
3. Calm, conscientious, deliberate, diligent, efficient, honest, inhibited, organized, patient, persistent, planful, practical, responsible, self-denying, sincere, slow, stable, thorough, and thoughtful	3. Awkward, cautious, confused, easily disorganized under stress or pressures to conform, easygoing, impulsive, insecure, lacking in self-discipline, stubborn, and uninhibited
4. Concerned with making a good impression, cooperative, helpful, informal, outgoing, sociable, and tolerant	4. Aggressive, aloof, apologetic, assertive, cool and distant in their relationships with others, defensive, detached, disbelieving and distrustful in personal and social outlook, irritable, overemphasizing personal pleasure and self-gain, overly influenced by others' reactions and opinions, retiring, self-centered, self-defensive, suggestible, suspicious, too little concerned with the needs and wants of others, and wary

SOURCE: *Byrne (1964).*

considerably better adjusted in the eyes of others, and as being behaviorally more effective. Byrne considers, in the light of this and of other findings, that the two extremes of repression and sensitization should not be regarded as two different but equally maladaptive responses to conflict. On the contrary, he points out that the data available suggest a rough linear relationship between sensitizing defenses and maladjustment, repression (within limits of the population samples that he has studied) appearing to be a more acceptable pattern of behavior in the face of threat. However,

we know that extreme instances of denial and repression result in the development of patterns of behavior which ultimately lead the individual to seek psychological help. While repression may be more satisfactory than sensitization within the confines of a normal population, it is unsatisfactory in its more extreme forms.

Drive States and Denial

So far we have described denial patterns in terms of their efficacy in reducing anxiety in the face of threatening stimuli. However, there is also evidence to suggest that the same kind of avoidance begins to appear when an individual is in a high state of positive motivation and is not able to obtain the appropriate goal of this motive. For example, Lazarus, Yousem, and Arenberg (1953) studied the perceptual consequences of food deprivation in human subjects who had gone without eating for 2, 4, or 6 hours. These subjects were shown slides tachistoscopically that depicted food objects or neutral objects. Individuals who had been deprived of food for 2 or 4 hours had significantly lower thresholds for the recognition of food slides than for the control pictures. However, with 6-hour deprivation of food, the threshold of recognition was considerably elevated. One possibility here is that when a state of drive becomes distressingly heightened, any external stimulus that might serve to intensify it is excluded from perception. Thus thoughts of "tantalizing" and desirable objects or states may be repressed because their occurrence is punishing. The response of "not thinking" about something may develop equally well whether it reduces anxiety based upon fear, or distress based upon unreduced, strong, positive motivations. We may recall the discussion in Chapter 3 of the development of food-related fantasies in subjects undergoing severe food deprivation (Atkinson & McClelland, 1948) and the observation that fantasy of consummatory activity declined markedly with increasing hunger.

Another instance of this process is provided by Murray (1959). He deprived subjects of sleep for a period of over 86 hours and at that point administered a TAT of which some pictures had obvious sleep-related content. He found that the deprived subjects showed significantly fewer sleep-story responses to these cards than did a group of undeprived controls. Of the very few sleep themes in the experimental group's stories, there were fewer goal-response items (stories of actual sleeping) than instrumental responses. This agrees closely with other experiments cited.

Murray offers an interpretation of these data along the following lines.

The Ss adjusted to this situation by avoiding those responses which would add to the already strong physiological stimulus of going to sleep. It is difficult to say to what extent this was unconscious repression, or conscious suppression. The qualitative evidence would suggest that the Ss were not aware of avoiding sleep themes on the TAT. (Murray, 1959, p. 100.)

Thus we see that repression or denial mechanisms may come into play when the acts of thinking about a particular topic, noticing stimuli related to it, or talking about it will exacerbate a drive which is either impossible to fulfill or is in conflict with other drives. Denials operate, therefore, not only to prevent awareness of obvious stress, but also to prevent awareness of pleasurable stimuli where this will intensify some conflict in relation to them. The data reported suggest that the latter is particularly true with respect to the consummatory activities, i.e., those which are most clearly associated with the reduction of the drive.

When denial patterns are not effective in preventing punishment or pain, then we should expect to find that there is a marked development of anxiety in the denier. On the other hand, the individual who is chronically aware of anxiety and has not developed denial patterns should not find this anxiety especially exacerbated by a new threat.

This proposition has been tested by Eriksen (1954). Two groups of subjects were selected: hysteric (deniers) and psychasthenic (anxious) males. Selection was made upon the basis of their scores on appropriate subdivisions of the Minnesota Multiphasic Inventory. These subjects were then divided into an avoidance- and nonavoidance-condition group respectively. Avoidance responding was established by requiring the subject to make a motor response to a stimulus—a square shape—within a given time period. If the response was too slow, then a shock was delivered.

Two squares of different size were used as generalization stimuli, and to these no shocks were given. Under the nonavoidance condition, shocks were presented in conjunction with a particular stimulus irrespective of response. In fact, the experiment was carefully programmed to ensure that all subjects received the same number of shocks regardless of condition—a control necessary to counteract the effect of frequency of punishment per se. Stimulus generalization was measured by recording avoidance responses to the other two squares—the generalization stimuli. Eriksen's data are shown in Figure 8-2.

The figure reveals clearly that higher gradients of avoidance generalization were obtained from the hysterical subjects than from the psychasthenics, supporting the prediction that when denial avoidance responses are inadequate to their function, anxiety reappears. From Eriksen's data we might glean the clue that the denier is more likely to experience *intense* anxiety than is the nondenier and that perhaps repression develops in individuals who find anxiety intolerable.

Summary

In this discussion we have seen that denial is an adaptive response that seems to occur in the face of frustration of simple drives, in the face of direct threat, and as a resolution to conflicts involving pleasurable activities with fear of unpleasant consequences (i.e., approach-avoidance conflicts). Denial itself may take the form of failure to recognize certain classes of external stimuli; failure to recall certain kinds of events, including the patient's own past behavior or experiences; and avoidance of thinking about current drive-related phenomena when these would exacerbate an unfulfillable mo-

Figure 8-2. Mean response amplitudes to the training and generalization stimuli. (Eriksen, 1964.)

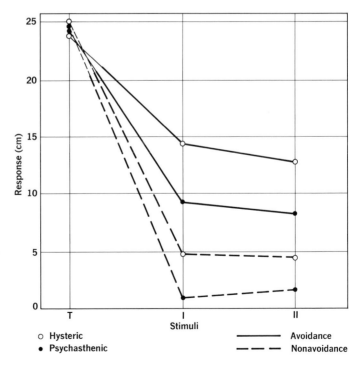

o Hysteric
• Psychasthenic

———— Avoidance
— — — Nonavoidance

Neurotic Patterns of Avoidance

tive state. When denial fails to serve its purpose, as in the case of unavoidable threat, then anxiety may appear to an even greater extent than is found in more typically anxious patients.

We have preferred to use the term "denial" here because it is descriptive of the central feature of the individual's avoidance pattern. However, common terminology in the field of psychopathology would apply the label "hysteria" to many of these behavioral elements.

REPETITIVE PATTERNS

Some individuals develop patterns of behavior in which the most striking feature is a tendency to repeat stereotyped activities—motor, verbal, or thinking. These activities become routine to a point of ritual, and the individual may experience considerable anxiety if he is prevented from bringing the chain of activity to its usual conclusion. As soon as the sequence is completed, he feels relief. However, with the passage of time his anxiety may begin to mount again, and the ritual commences its cycle.

Not uncommonly these patterns of activity have many obvious elements of socially approved behavior. Ritualistic cleanliness, with compulsive hand washing or bathing; compulsive orderliness and neatness of appearance; strict adherence to rules under circumstances in which society normally accepts some relaxation of the expected standards—all may be seen in this kind of behavior pattern. However, some patterns of this general class may have no "obvious" feature. Let us consider the boy in Example 8-2.

This patient was subsequently admitted into the hospital for prolonged observation and treatment. No clear understanding of the functional relationship of his compulsive concern with geography to his psychological difficulties ever emerged. The case serves to illustrate the fact that compulsive patterns do not necessarily exhibit obvious features of excessively moral or social behavior.

Much attention has been given, however, to those kinds of repetitive patterns that do exhibit features of social-moral themes. For example, there is the individual who repeatedly washes his hands with an apparent fear lest any trace of dirt be on them may be regarded as disobedience of a moral percept, i.e., the necessity of personal cleanliness. On the other hand, his behavior may be interpreted symbolically—hand washing

EXAMPLE 8-2
Obsessive-Compulsive Behavior in A Boy

A boy, aged seventeen years, was referred to a hospital by his parents, who had become alarmed about a gradual but marked change in his behavior over the previous six months. This patient had developed a highly elaborated ritual based upon the cardinal points of the compass. He could not sit down until he had identified the north, south, east, and west sides of the room that he had entered. When he had done so, he touched each wall in that order and then relaxed and was capable of conducting conversation on other topics. According to his parents, he would now refuse to eat his breakfast until he had been assured that food from each compass direction was on the table. Thus breakfast cereal from the North, orange juice from the South, and so forth were provided and eaten in the correct order.

Before this behavior developed, the parents described the boy as extremely interested in science, and especially geography. He had large collections of books on various scientific topics and a very large library of maps that he collected voraciously. In conversation he made frequent reference to the completeness of these collections but seemed to have little interest in their content for its own sake.

being a common symbol for the attempt to rid oneself of guilt. We see the symbolic use of this gesture in the act of Pontius Pilate when abandoning Jesus to his fate, and in the famous scene from Macbeth where Lady Macbeth tried, while sleepwalking, to remove the long-vanished traces of blood from her hands.

Because of the belief that such patterns of ritual behavior have an "atonement" quality, some psychopathologists have assumed that the prime factor in the patients' problems must include intense guilt. This belief is buttressed by the occasional observation that coupled with these apparent patterns of atonement are sometimes found *obsessive thoughts* of a strikingly antisocial nature. Sometimes these may involve intense but irrational fears on the part of the patient that he may murder his family or commit some sexual violence on an unwitting victim. Where this pattern of thinking is found with compulsive acts that are clearly moralistic and counteractive, it is not difficult to infer that the patient's fundamental difficulty is a conflict between immoral impulses and his strong social training.

One interesting feature of this kind of pattern is that both the obsessive thoughts and the compulsive acts are frequently disavowed by the patient. He regards them as almost external to himself—the thoughts appear to "impose" themselves upon his consciousness, and he may make efforts to prevent them from occurring. Likewise the compulsive acts are seen as motivated by impulses that the individual realizes are irrational but is nevertheless unable to subdue. This sense of detachment has been regarded as another process that serves to keep unacceptable thoughts at some distance from the patient. Where denial operates to prevent some patients from ever thinking hostile thoughts, this detachment acts to reduce the anxiety of other patients when the thoughts do occur.

Turning to the analysis of this kind of behavior in learning terms, we may note several important attributes of the total pattern.

1. Obsessive thoughts are usually disturbing to the patient; their occurrence generates anxiety, following which elaborate anxiety-reducing responses must be made. Inasmuch as we have preferred to regard thinking as a response, then we are confronted with a seeming paradox. The patient is responding (thinking) in a fashion that generates anxiety, and we should expect in the ordinary way that such responses would fairly quickly drop out of his repertoire. But they do not drop out, and in fact have a special quality of persistence and continuity.

2. The patient's sense of detachment requires some particular explanation, especially in relation to the obsessive-compulsive pattern.

3. Although the sequence of obsessive thought and compulsive act is common, it is far from universal. Complaints of obsessive thinking occur without any obvious evidence of accompanying compulsive atonement, and vice versa.

4. While the inference of guilt seems to follow plausibly from consideration of the atonement interpretation of compulsive rituals, it is not readily evidenced in the overt complaints of the patient. Obsessive-compulsive patients do not commonly complain of discomforting feelings of guilt.

CONFLICT ANALYSIS

When somebody engages in an action that is totally unfamiliar, he may experience a feeling that "it is not me doing it"—a feeling of being almost a spectator of his own behavior. Soldiers or sailors under fire for the first time may find that they observe their own behavior with a strong feeling of detachment. The person who wins some national contest and is suddenly thrust into the limelight, the newly bereaved person going through the funeral ceremony, the middle-aged tourist visiting a foreign country for the first time—all these people may have feelings of unreality and detachment. Emotional concomitants of grief or joy may exist without reducing the feelings of unreality that are generated by the person's own unfamiliar behavior in an unfamiliar environment.

In other words, "feelings of unreality" may not represent the success of complex processes designed to protect the person from the full implications of his own behavior. They may, much more simply, be a natural accompaniment to the performance of any unfamiliar set of responses, especially if these occur in an unfamiliar environment. From this point of view, the detachment which the obsessive patient assigns to his hostile or sexual thoughts is not necessarily evidence that they are being "isolated" for defensive purposes. It may, rather, reflect the fact that such thoughts have been extremely rare in the patient's past history. Far from being a defensive measure for dealing with the anxiety generated by the thoughts, detachment may be an inevitable by-product of their unfamiliarity.

The fact that these thoughts are unfamiliar suggests that previous expressions of hostility or sexual interest were severely punished, so that stimuli that might ordinarily elicit them elicit fear instead, which in turn results in avoidance of that kind of thinking. Obsessive thoughts might be expected to occur when the cues for punishment are notably absent—as, for example, when the patient has left home for the first time and the parents no longer supply the stimuli for avoidant thinking. In brief, any significant transition from a restrictive environment to a permissive one might be sufficient for the appearance of previously avoided thoughts when the appropriate stimuli occur to elicit them.

Equally important in the appearance of forbidden thoughts would be any intensification in the motivations associated with them. A child who has been strictly punished for sexual activities in his early years may find sexual thoughts obtruding in later adolescence when sexual motivations have a stronger biological basis—especially if he is away from home at that time. Thus we can see that the sequence of events which precedes obsessive problems is (a) strict punishment for certain kinds of behavior, (b) the avoidance of this behavior and of thoughts relevant to it, (c) the intensification of the relevant motives for this behavior and/or the removal of the inhibiting stimulus leading to (d) the appearance of unfamiliar and unacceptable thoughts. The unfamiliarity of these thoughts will generate a feeling of unreality. This state of affairs will be unpleasant and consequently will lead to the next steps in the sequence.

A careful distinction must be made between obsessive thoughts that are anxiety-arousing—such as those we have discussed so far—and obsessive or repetitive thoughts that seem to be reinforced by their properties of anxiety reduction. Since avoidance learning operates as it does, we should expect that the former may often be replaced by the latter through much the same process that "thinking about something else" follows in repression. If the anxiety generated by the unacceptable obsessive thought is very intense, then the likelihood that a rigid and stereotyped avoidance response will develop is quite high. We sometimes find patients who appear to be preoccupied with cognitive tasks of a self-imposed and ritual variety. One patient in the writer's experience complained that he felt compelled to recite the names of all the state capitals in alphabetical order, and that he became very anxious when he was momentarily unable to do so or when he lost the correct sequence. This kind of thinking is more properly regarded as an avoidance response and is of the same psychological nature as the compulsive acts mentioned already.

Reparative Responses

While some obsessive thinking may be interpreted as serving the purpose of avoidance of disturbing thinking, the overt compulsive activities that were discussed above may best be interpreted as *reparative* responses. Reparation or atonement behavior is imposed upon children frequently as a precondition of the cessation of the punishment following some forbidden act. When one child strikes another, he may be punished and told that he will not be forgiven until he has said that he "is sorry." Refusal to perform this ritual may evoke further punishment, at least in the form of withholding of forgiveness until the child has complied. Thus reparative responses are often established by a process very similar to that of operant conditioning. Deprivation will not be relieved until the desired response has been made, whereupon a reinforcement will be forthcoming. Responses of this type are often acquired very early in life, before the child could have any understanding of the communicative significance of the reparative phrase. "I'm sorry" becomes automatic following a transgression, much like "please" and "thank you."

Where the parental values have emphasized certain kinds of behavior, the relevant transgressions will become especially salient. By the same token, the appropriate reparations should become strongly established as anxiety reducers, ultimately becoming liable to occurrence whenever the child commits any transgressions—even those for which the reparation is irrelevant. Some parents place considerable emphasis upon personal cleanliness and neatness; the appearance of the child returning from play covered with dirt may provoke considerable anger that will not be appeased until the child has been cleaned, or has cleaned himself up. If this particular sequence of punishment, anxiety, and reparation is well established by repetition, then we might expect it will become a highly probable response whenever the individual is in a state of expecting punishment (i.e., a state of "guilt").

Under these circumstances the adult who is rendered anxious by the awareness of hostile thoughts may well attempt to reduce this by reparative hand washing, even though the reparation has no logical connection with the transgressive hostility. It is psychologically irrelevant to decide that the hand-washing compulsion is "symbolic" of "cleansing" of guilt. The main feature of importance is that it is a well-established anxiety reducer in the face of the anxieties generated by transgressive acts. This argument has been put forward most cogently by Aronfreed (1963):

The fact that reparative responses may have no rational relationship to the transgressions which are the stimulus for their occurrence is hardly surprising when we consider the original contingencies under which they are often reinforced. Socializing agents do not necessarily make their reinforcement of the child's reparative actions contingent upon their perception that the child comprehends the relationship between its actions and the consequences of its transgressions. Their reinforcement of the child's reparative actions is more generally contingent on whether the actions tend directly or indirectly to alleviate their own displeasure. As a result, being indiscriminately helpful or kind to others (even though they may not be those who were adversely affected by the transgression), or otherwise displaying praiseworthy behavior, may turn out to be, for some children, an effective way of minimizing both social punishment and their own internalized anxiety following a transgression, . . . (P. 72.)

Reparative Patterns and the Obsessive Character

Many psychopathologists have accepted the Freudian assumption that obsessive-compulsive patterns of behavior are, as it were, symptomatic of a more pervasive pattern of personality that has, as its core, long-established attitudes toward toilet functions. Major attributes of this personality are given as excessive cleanliness, extreme orderliness, financial stinginess, tendencies to accumulate and save petty objects, and rigidity in thinking, especially on matters of morality. Because the stinginess and saving pattern seems to have no rational connection with personal cleanliness, it has become necessary to assume that money has a symbolic signifi-cance—the tendency to "retain" money be-coming a superficial instance of the pro-founder tendency to retain feces established by harsh toilet-training practices.

Unfortunately this proposition is impos-sible to test and is thus scientifically mean-ingless. However, we might note that the list of attributes given above sounds very close to the traditional pattern of "middle-class morality" and that training in personal cleanliness might well be simply a part of a total pattern of training in many moral practices.

Sears, Maccoby, and Levin (1957) studied the child-rearing practices of over 300 mothers. Among the topics investigated was that of maternal attitude toward toilet training. They found that this attitude was correlated with other general values for the child's behavior. Mothers who were demand-ing and punitive in toilet training were also demanding and pressuring in the matter of table manners, suppression of aggression to parents, general quietness, personal orderli-ness, school performance, and obedience. Such mothers were also punitive toward childish sex play, and they strongly equated sexuality and bowel habits in a general area of modesty. Inasmuch as the bodily organs subserving both sexual and excretory func-tions are nearly identical, the close equation of the two functions is not surprising. How-ever, we do not need to suppose that one of these is symbolic of the other, but more simply that punishment in one area (bowel habits) is likely to correlate with punishment in the other (sexual display).

Parental values of this kind need not, of themselves, lead to the establishment of an obsessive pattern of behavior. Punitive en-forcement of these values is probably essen-tial if the child is to develop anxieties about transgressions of this code and if he is to experience intense anxiety when transgres-sive thoughts obtrude in later life. Training in generalized obedience is probably espe-cially pathogenic here, as it places upon the child a double "crime" whenever he breaks a rule. Thus a failure to inhibit

hostility will evoke parental punishment on two counts—first, because it is "wrong" to be hostile and second, because it is "wrong" to disobey a rule about hostility that has already been laid down.

There is no reported evidence regarding the inclusion of thrift training in this pat-tern, but it does not seem unjustified to assume that it is a likely correlate of the value system that emphasizes the other conventional virtues above described. One striking aspect of this pattern is not only the high standard of morality that is im-posed upon the child, but also the sweeping range of behaviors that are brought under the jurisdiction of the code. It is difficult to think of an important realm of behavior in which the child is free to be spontaneous. Since the child is trained in self-control in many different situations, there is a consider-able likelihood that he has been trained to be careful and nonspontaneous in general—even in circumstances that are not specifi-cally under the parental prohibition. Rigidity, inhibition, and other characteristics are thus probable in almost any area of activity that we might observe. When transgressions do occur in later life, it is inevitable that they should surprise and alarm the patient—an unexpected exhibition of uninhibited joy might well have the same effect upon him.

THE DETERMINANTS OF INDIVIDUAL NEUROTIC PATTERNS

While the root problem in neurosis is anxiety, and this anxiety appears to be chronic because of its maintenance by an approach-avoidance conflict, the various patterns of neurotic behavior have distinc-tive features. It is these features that lead the psychopathologist to be concerned with the problem of etiology. Why does one patient utilize denial, while another patient becomes obsessive? This problem is some-times referred to as the "choice of neurosis," although it is misleading to imply that any act of choice is involved in the development of the patterns.

Heredity and environment are, as usual, invoked by different workers to account for these patterns. Let us look at some of these explanations.

The Inheritance of the Neuroses

Later in this book we shall examine the proposition that certain kinds of serious psychopathology may be determined by the inheritance of specific biological deficiencies —as, for example, deficiencies in the processes of metabolism. When we consider neurotic behavior, however, the problem becomes much more complex. Genetic factors can only affect bodily structure and function, and it appears probable that they do so in relatively simple ways. Eye color, etc., appear to be determined in this way, as well as susceptibility to certain kinds of disease. While the genetic linkage to bodily structure seems fairly straightforward, the linkage between bodily structure and behavior is much less easy to demonstrate. Linkage sequences of this kind have been termed the genes-to-behavior pathway. As Gottesman (1963) has pointed out, "The genes exert their influence on behavior through their efforts at the molecular level of organization. Enzymes, hormones and neurons may be considered as the sequence of complex path markers between the genes and the aspects of behavior termed personality" (Gottesman, 1963, p. 2).

As these pathways are as yet unknown, there seems to be no direct way to test the proposition that a given pattern of neurotic behavior is determined by some deviation in hormonal balance that is in turn inherited. Consequently, what little research has been done on this problem has rested in the main upon the study of twins and the discovery of high correlations between them on measures of general personality functioning.

Empirical Studies. Shields and Slater (1961) have studied the simple incidence of neurosis in monozygotic and dizygotic twins without regard to the specific pattern of neurotic behavior displayed. They report rates of concordance of 53 per cent for

MZ twins and 25 per cent for DZ twins. Unfortunately their data do not permit any more sophisticated analysis of the behavioral components of the disorders.

Gottesman (1963) studied 34 pairs of normal MZ twins and 34 pairs of normal, same sex, DZ twins in an attempt to discover personality factors that would be specifically concordant for the MZ twins. From his investigations he concluded that neurotic patterns with a hysterical or hypochondriacal theme had little or no genetic component, while those with elements of anxiety, depression, or obsession seemed to possess a substantial genetic component.

Environmental Influences

We have already seen that repressive moral training seems to be a major factor in the subsequent development of obsessive-compulsive patterns of neurosis. If there is, as Gottesman suggests, an important genetic component in obsessive neurosis, then we must assume that the early childhood discipline is necessary but not sufficient to produce later obsessive behavior. By the same token, lack of this kind of training in a potentially obsessive individual might prevent the behavior from developing. While some psychopathologists emphasize the occurrence of a particular traumatic event in determining the development of a neurosis, there is rather more reason to assume that prolonged and consistent behavior of parents and other influential figures plays the most serious role in producing anxieties and characteristic patterns of avoidance.

SUMMARY

We can see that neurotic patterns of behavior develop in the first place from anxiety, commonly generated by parental discipline or other kinds of threatening experience in early life. Anxiety of this kind serves to precipitate neurotic patterns only when the stimuli for its occurrence are continually present in the adult life of the patient. This is very likely to be the case where the punishment was contingent upon the child's expressing certain kinds of thought or engaging in certain kinds of activity which are commonly evoked in the ordinary social habitat of the human person. A central feature of neurotic behavior is its function in keeping the patient unaware of the threatening stimuli (as in denial), in keeping him away from them physically (as in the phobias), or in attempting to avert the feared punishment when the threatening stimulus has been perceived or performed (as in compulsive reparation for forbidden obsessive thoughts).

Once established, a neurotic avoidance pattern will be elicited by any threat—even if it is irrelevant to the anxiety under which the pattern was acquired in the first place. Thus the precise conditions that established such a pattern may be of less interest than those that are maintaining it in adulthood. Liability to autonomic distress may be genetically determined—at least in part— and there appear to be stable individual differences in the extent to which people are aware of general anxiety—either autonomically or behaviorally.

SUGGESTED READINGS

1. Dollard, J., & Miller, N. E. *Personality and psychotherapy.* New York: McGraw-Hill, 1950. An analysis of many patterns of neurotic behavior in learning terms. Now a basic source for this kind of analysis. The authors essentially accept the dynamic model of the origins of neurosis but translate its terms into the language of learning theory.
2. Kutash, S. B. Psychoneuroses. In B. B. Wolman (Ed.), *Handbook of clinical psychology.* New York: McGraw-Hill, 1965. A summary account of common neurotic patterns, but presented within a conventional psychoanalytic language.
3. Mowrer, O. H. *Learning theory and personality dynamics.* New York:

Ronald, 1950. A systematic and now classic application of learning theory principles to human behavior, both normal and neurotic.
4. Rotter, J. B. *Social learning and clinical psychology.* Englewood Cliffs, N.J.: Prentice-Hall, 1954. A social learning theory with particular application to problems of the acquisition of psychopathology via reinforcement effects.

REFERENCES

Aronfreed, J. Conscience and moral value. Mimeographed manuscript, Univer. of Pennsylvania, 1963.

Atkinson, J. W. and McClelland, D. C. The projective expression of needs. II: The effect of different intensities of the hunger drive on thematic apperception. *J. exp. Psychol.,* 1948, **38,** 643–658.

Byrne, D. Repression-sensitization as a dimension of personality. In B. A. Maher (Ed.), *Progress in Experimental Personality Research.* Vol. 1. New York: Academic, 1964.

Byrne, D., Golightly, Carole, & Sheffield, J. The Repression-Sensitization Scale as a measure of adjustment: relationship with the C.P.I. *J. consult. Psychol.,* in press, 1965.

Byrne, D., & Sheffield, J. Responses to sexually arousing stimuli as a function of repressing and sensitizing defenses. *J. abnorm. Psychol.,* 1965, **70,** 114–118.

Eriksen, C. W. Defense against ego threat in memory and perception. *J. abnorm. soc. Psychol.,* 1952, **47,** 230–235.

Eriksen, C. W. Some personality correlates of stimulus generalization under stress. *J. abnorm. soc. Psychol.,* 1954, **49,** 561–565.

Gossett, J. T. An experimental demonstration of Freudian repression proper. Unpublished doctoral dissertation, Univer. of Arkansas, Fayetteville, Arkansas, 1964.

Gottesman, I. I. Heritability of personality:

a demonstration. *Psychol. Monogr.*, 1963, **77,** Whole No. 9.

Joy, V. L. Repression-sensitization, personality and interpersonal behavior. Unpublished doctoral dissertation, Univer. of Texas, Austin, Texas, 1963.

Lazarus, R. S., & Alfert, Elizabeth. Short-circuiting of threat by experimentally altering cognitive appraisal. *J. abnorm. soc. Psychol.,* 1964, **69,** 195–205.

Lazarus, R. S., & Longo, N. The consistency of psychological defenses against threat. *J. abnorm. soc. Psychol.,* 1953, **48,** 495–499.

Lazarus, R. S., Yousem, H., & Arenberg, D. Hunger and perception. *J. Pers.,* 1953, **21,** 312–328.

Murray, E. J. Conflict and repression during sleep deprivation. *J. abnorm. soc. Psychol.,* 1959, **59,** 95–101.

Sears, R. R., Maccoby, Eleanor, & Levin, H. *Patterns of child rearing.* New York: Harper & Row, 1957.

Shields, J., & Slater, E. Heredity and psychological abnormality. In H. J. Eysenck (Ed.), *Handbook of abnormal psychology.* New York: Basic Books, 1961.

Tempone, V. J. Differential thresholds of repressors and sensitizers as a function of success and failure experience. Unpublished doctoral dissertation, Univer. of Texas, Austin, Texas, 1962.

CHARACTER DISORDERS AND ANTISOCIAL BEHAVIOR

Some people behave in ways that are unacceptable to society because they violate the established law or customs of their group. When the violation is clearly a breach of the legal code, such people are likely to be tried and, if convicted, punished for their actions. On the other hand, if their behavior is not actually illegal, they may meet more subtle sanctions from their fellows, such as rejection, loss of employment, or exclusion from the social life of their environment.

Generally speaking, people in the first category are termed criminals and are dealt with by punishments including fines, imprisonment, deprivation of various rights, or death. However, illegal behavior has created problems of definition and treatment for both lawyers and psychopathologists because of the difficulties surrounding the legal emphasis upon the motivation of the accused at the time a crime was committed.

THE LEGAL CONCEPT OF CRIMINAL BEHAVIOR

A basic assumption underlying the legal interpretation of human behavior is that, with certain specified exceptions, everyone is responsible for his own behavior. This implies that where someone commits a crime, he is assumed to have been able to behave otherwise had he chosen to do so. He is regarded as having *chosen* to commit the crime, and therefore society is justified in punishing him for his behavior. In other words, the legal position compels society to believe in free will, if it is to be justified in punishing those who commit crimes. At first sight, this may all appear rather obvious. Indeed, the assumption of individual responsibility is such an integral part of our daily thinking that we may never have considered all its implications. If we do examine these propositions more closely, we shall see that the crux of the matter lies in the view that society must be *justified* in punishing the criminal—justified morally, that is.

We tend to seek justification for the punishment of criminals by arguing that we are not entitled to inflict pain on anyone unless he has chosen to render himself liable to it by an illegal act. Ordinarily we do not apply this reasoning to medical treatment of disease. Where medical treatment is painful, we justify its use by arguing that the patient would be worse off without it than with it. We argue not that he "deserves" the pain, but that it is being done for his own good. In Chapter 16 we see that some therapists treat neurotic behavior by administering painful electric shock whenever the patient performs the symptomatic act. Here the patient is being punished, in the technical sense of the word, not because his symptom is criminal, but because the punishment may cure him. For a therapist to administer a painful method of therapy does not require that he assume the patient has *chosen* to behave psychopathologically. In the same way it is quite possible to approach the legal definition of criminal behavior by assuming (*a*) that the criminal did not choose to behave as he did, but that his behavior was determined, like any other kind of behavior, and (*b*) that punishment is justified if it can be shown to be effective in changing the person's future behavior.

Unfortunately, the legal approach to criminal behavior is complicated by the fact that punishment is intended by society to serve more than one purpose. If the purpose were solely therapeutic, then the solution proposed above would be fairly satis-factory. Many legal analysts of the problem argue that an additional—and perhaps even central—purpose of punishment is to make the criminal suffer regardless of what this may do to his subsequent behavior. From their point of view a major concern is to select a punishment that will adequately balance the account with society, even though it may increase the probability that the man will engage in further crime after the punishment.

Thus the fundamental moral premise behind punishment is that society has a right to revenge itself on those who disobey its laws. The only people to whom this right does not apply are special classes of individuals who are assumed to be not completely responsible for their own actions. Classes typically exempt from responsibility are children, the mentally retarded, and people suffering from certain kinds of psychopathological conditions. Arbitrary definitions of the first two classes are easily made, using chronological age, intelligence test scores, or other numerical criteria. Once these criteria are defined, there is little ground for conceptual confusion in their practical application. The same cannot be said for the legal definition of the psychopathological states regarded as reducing the responsibility of the patient for his own criminal actions.

From a strictly deterministic point of view, no man is free to do other than what he does do in response to any specified situation. It is not possible for a psychopathologist to make sense of the question, "Was the prisoner free to have acted otherwise when he committed the crime?" Perhaps the closest approach that can be made is to ask whether or not there were some unusual circumstances surrounding the situation, such that the individual is unlikely to repeat the response again. For example, the law recognizes that a man should not be punished for driving over the speed limit when he does so at the point of a gun. Nor can he be punished for behavior that occurs when drugged, if he was drugged against his wishes. It is quite possible for a court to conclude that the person was not "free" to do other than what he did under these circumstances. A behavioral scientist, however, must take the position that the same principle applies to all behavior, where the limitations on response are imposed by the prisoner's past history rather than by external threat or physical intervention. Thus there is no valid distinction to be made between an "irresistible impulse" and any other motive that resulted in action.

Differences in "awareness" may also be irrelevant. We have seen already that conscious awareness of the form of one's own behavior does not automatically bring it under control—if it did, there would be rather fewer neurotic patients than there are. Likewise, it is unhelpful to distinguish between "intent" and "criminal intent." A man who will murder because he has a genuine conviction that God demands this of him is just as socially dangerous as one who does so because he thinks that self-interest demands it of him.

In practice, of course, the legal decision about responsibility is simply a decision about "treatment," different dispositions being reserved for those who are responsible versus those who are not. Thus when the law asks if the prisoner is responsible, the question is really, "What should we do with him?" When framed in this way, the question permits some meaningful answers by the psychopathologist. Now he can concern himself with methods of changing behavior that will reduce the probability of further crime and can make recommendations accordingly. To do this, he must study the various determinants of criminal behavior in exactly the same way as he studies the determinants of any other kind of behavior. There are limits to his possible usefulness. If the court wishes to know what treatment will satisfy a supposed public demand for retribution (whether or not such treatment will improve the prisoner), the psychopathologist is not a suitable resource. He is only of use when the question relates to techniques that will change the behavior of the prisoner.

In the rest of this chapter we present some of the findings regarding determinants of criminal and antisocial behavior, together with what is known about the effects of some kinds of treatment. In spite of the enormous social importance of the problem, it is one that psychopathologists have generally neglected, as we shall see.

The McNaghten Rules

In England, in 1843, Daniel McNaghten was tried for the murder of a man whom he believed to be Sir Robert Peel, then the Home Secretary for the British government. He committed the murder because he was "instructed" to do so by the "voice of God." As a matter of fact, the victim was a government clerk McNaghten mistook for Peel. At the trial, McNaghten was acquitted by reason of insanity. However, the difficulties attendant upon this kind of judgment were such that a committee of the judges of England was requested to present their views as to acceptable criteria for legal insanity for future general use. The essential part of their conclusion was that for a legal defense of insanity to be sustained, it must show that the defendant was laboring under such defect of reason from disease of the mind as not to know the nature and quality of the act he was doing or if he did know it that he did not know that what he was doing was wrong.

These two criteria became known as the McNaghten Rules. They dominated the legal interpretation of mental illness for many years, but in recent years some modifications have begun to evolve as a consequence of new court decisions.

The Irresistible Impulse

While analyzing the concept of responsibility we noted that, logically considered, a man may only be held responsible for his actions if he was free to behave in some other way at the time he committed the criminal offense. If a motorist is compelled to drive dangerously at the point of a gun held by a bandit, he is not liable to be punished later for driving in that way. It was not reasonably possible for him to do anything else at the time. This application of the responsibility principle was first made explicit shortly before the McNaghten case, in a judgment made in Ohio in 1834. In this case, the court held that where the accused was unable to inhibit his own action because he was driven by a pathological irresistible impulse, then a plea of insanity could be sustained. The principle advanced was that if the accused was free to forebear or to do the act he is responsible as a sane man. This principle can apply to support a defense of insanity where the McNaghten Rules would not.

The New Hampshire Rule

Recognizing the difficulties in the application of legal tests to problems of psychopathology, the Supreme Court of New Hampshire specifically rejected them in 1871. In the Jones case the court declared that symptoms or behaviors which were used as legal tests of capacity to form a criminal intent should be treated as problems of fact and not problems of law.

They are all clearly matters of evidence to be weighed by the jury upon the question whether the act was the offspring of insanity. If it was, a criminal intent did not produce it. If it was not, criminal intent did produce it and it was crime.

The effect of the New Hampshire Rule is to establish that where the criminal act is in any way symptomatic of the psychopathology, then there could be no criminal intent. In the absence of criminal intent, there can be no crime. This removes the burden placed upon the defense of showing that the mental illness was such that the accused did not know what he was doing, or did not know that it was wrong, or was not able to inhibit it.

The Durham Decision

In 1954, the United States Court of Appeals ruled that an accused is not criminally responsible if his unlawful act was the product of mental disease or of mental defect.

This ruling was made in the case of *United States versus Durham* following the conclusion of the court that the right-wrong test is inadequate, in that it does not take sufficient account of psychic realities and scientific knowledge and it is based upon one symptom and so cannot be validly applied in all circumstances. We find that the irresistible impulse test is also inadequate in that it gives no recognition to mental illness characterized by brooding and reflection.

A somewhat similar position was recommended by the British Royal Commission on Capital Punishment in 1953. The recommendation was that the McNaghten Rules be abandoned, leaving the jury to decide whether the evidence presented regarding the psychological condition of the accused was such that he should be held responsible. Again, the tendency is to shift the question of psychopathological irresponsibility from being one of law to being one of fact.

Technical Problems

Those recent decisions have gone a long way toward bringing legal practice into line with the realities of psychopathology. Some difficulties remain, but they largely reflect the inadequacies of our scientific knowledge. A diagnostic decision as to whether or not an individual is psychotic may cause disputes between presumably competent clinicians. In many court areas there tends to develop a body of clinicians who frequently find psychosis (defense clinicians) and a body of clinicians who do not find it (prosecution clinicians). This is an outgrowth of the fact that the clinical testimony presented to the jury is adduced by one side or the other, the clinician being an expert witness and liable to cross-examination by the opposing attorney. If there were as good agreement about what constitutes paranoid schizophrenia as there is about what constitutes a broken leg, there would be less opportunity for disputes of testimony to occur.

One solution that has been proposed, and adopted in some cases, is to require a report of the psychological state of the accused from a disinterested professional expert. This report is made available to the court and to both opposing attorneys. The clinician is thus in the role of *amicus curiae,* or "friend of the court," testifying neither for the prosecution nor for the defense. Many lawyers object to this procedure, arguing that any evidence submitted to the court should be open for examination and debate in order that its validity may be tested publicly.

An additional scientific difficulty is that the clinician must decide whether or not the accused was suffering from a psychopathological condition at the time the unlawful act was committed. This involves inferring a patient's clinical condition in the past from evidence that might be available in his behavior now. Even where two or more clinicians might agree that the patient is now behaving pathologically, there is still latitude for them to differ about his presumed condition at the time of the crime.

All these considerations are complicated by the fact that a successful plea of insanity is likely to lead to the hospitalization of the accused in an institution for the criminally insane. For many defense attorneys this is indistinguishable from a sentence to indefinite imprisonment. A defense attorney regards it as his duty to gain aquittal for his client, or failing that, to get the lightest possible punishment. From this position, there is no merit in pleading insanity to a charge for which the maximum punishment is a few years in prison, since the accused will be worse off if the plea succeeds than if it fails. Consequently, insanity pleas are usually made only to charges for which the punishment is likely to be death or life imprisonment. Insanity pleas are thus found most often when the charge is murder. Testimony in murder trials is given under circumstances of great public interest and often of intense indignation against the accused. By the same token, the incentive for the accused to dissemble and act the part

of insanity is very great. All these factors contribute to a state of affairs where the calm weighing of evidence is very difficult and where dispassionate jurymen are hard to find.

Under the circumstances it is hardly surprising that we find many men serving prison sentences who exhibit behaviors that are clearly pathological. They are in prison either because their psychopathology did not meet the legal definition of the court in which they were tried, or because the crime was insufficiently grave to justify making a defense of insanity.

PSYCHOPATHIC BEHAVIOR

One of the enduring problems of behavior pathology is presented by people who have been called "psychopaths" or "psychopathic personalities," or more recently, have been categorized as suffering from a "character disorder."

Clinical Description

Let us consider the major features of this kind of behavior pattern. Typically the person is of at least average intelligence. Often he is intellectually gifted and possessed of considerable social charm. From time to time he will work steadily toward normal goals in life and may do unusually well. However, this behavior is marked by spasmodic antisocial acts which may range from overt criminal offenses such as check forgery to noncriminal irresponsibility such as gambling away his paycheck and leaving no provision for his family. Sexual behavior is also likely to be immoral, although not necessarily deviant. Offenses are committed upon what appears to be a fleeting impulse with no thought of the inevitable consequences; thus car stealing, bigamy, petty theft, and so forth are not uncommon in the repertoire of the psychopath.

These antisocial acts are often accompanied by sincere expressions of regret and repentance; the individual may be able to provide a very impressive account of the way in which he has reconstructed his personality and his plans for better behavior in the future. Such people usually have good knowledge of what is regarded as ethically or morally appropriate. Interrogation on these points does not suggest any deficiency in cognitive understanding of society's expectations for the behavior of its members. In spite of this, and in spite of frequent punishments for impulsive antisocial activity, the psychopath appears not to learn anything from his own experience.

A characteristic feature of this pattern of behavior is the ability of the individual to impress others to an extent sufficient to protect him from many of the punishments which would befall a person of lesser intelligence or charm. Thus the early history of the psychopath is, in fact, one of antisocial acts followed by threat of punishments that are then successfully avoided by the use of social skill in manipulating the people involved.

However, while this is fairly typical of the *early* history of many psychopathic personalities, their adult experience usually includes many instances of punishment, some of it severe. Rather than their initial skill in avoiding punishment, it is their seeming inability to change their behavior following it that leads to a diagnosis of psychopathy.

While impulsive antisocial behavior is perhaps the prime feature of the psychopathic pattern, many writers have been impressed by the striking inability of these individuals to form lasting and genuine emotional attachments. Their personal relationships are often brief and superficial, seemingly based upon the use that may be made of the other person and not upon any real affection. Thus the psychopath of either sex may present a history of casual promiscuity in sexual relations, entering into them for temporary personal gratification more or less upon impulse.

A third feature of this pattern is the *vanity* of the individual over matters to do with his looks, social importance, and so forth. Thus the criminal psychopath may be much more concerned with whether or not the newspaper reporters have spelled his name correctly than with the fact that he has committed a crime and will suffer for it.

Example 9-1, a typical case history, illustrates these characteristics.

While a case history serves to illustrate some features of the behavior of a psychopath, we must turn elsewhere for hypotheses regarding the origin of this kind of behavior. Before doing so, we should notice that the positive attributes, such as antisocial behavior, emotional shallowness, and vanity, are accompanied by certain negative attributes. Notable among these are the absence of overt anxiety and the absence of guilt. Also, the psychopath's behavioral insensitivity to punishment requires explanation in any satisfactory account of the determinants of this pathological pattern.

Because of the central role that antisocial behavior plays in the diagnosis of the psychopath, it is necessary to distinguish this pattern from other kinds of behavior that are also accompanied by antisocial acts. We should recognize that criminal activity may arise from a variety of origins. Many inmates of prisons are serving sentences for criminal acts that were accepted and reinforced by their particular strata of society. Such a person may well feel guilt, but he would feel it most strongly if he were to report someone else's crime to the police. In others words, the prisoner may have a very definite moral code which happens to run counter to that prevailing in society's legal framework.

We also find instances where an individual commits a crime under circumstances which make it inevitable that he will be caught. Some such crimes appear to be committed from a pathological need for punishment, presumably because punishment brings some relief of anxiety that has developed for other reasons. Thus we must reiterate that the essential ingredients of our definition of the psychopath include the occurrence of antisocial behavior, the absence of guilt or anxiety about it, and the

EXAMPLE 9-1

Primary Psychopathy: A Criminal Case

The subject was a male, forty years of age, convicted of check forgery and embezzlement. He was arrested with a young woman, aged eighteen, whom he had married bigamously some months before the arrest. She was unaware of the existence of any previous marriage; the subject had already been convicted for two previous bigamous marriages and for forty other cases of passing fraudulent checks.

Some interest attaches to the circumstances of this man's arrest. He and his "wife" had obtained employment as manager and hostess of a small restaurant in a large city. The owner of the restaurant lived in another town some distance away and had arranged to call in at the end of each week to check on progress and income. Living quarters over the restaurant were provided, plus a small salary and a small commission on the weekly total of the cash register.

At the end of one week of employment, the subject took all the money (having avoided banking it nightly as he had been instructed) and departed shortly before his employer arrived. He left a series of vulgar messages scribbled on the walls, saying that he had taken the money because the salary was "too low." He found lodgings, with his wife, a few blocks away from the restaurant and made no serious effort to escape detection. The police arrested him and his wife within a few days of the offense.

During the inquiry it emerged that he had spent the past few months cashing checks in department stores at various cities. He would make out the check and send his wife in to cash it; he commented that her genuine innocence of the fact that he had no bank account made her very effective in not arousing suspicion. He did not trouble to use a false name when signing checks or when making the bigamous marriage. Nevertheless, he was astonished at the speed with which the police discovered him.

Inquiry into the man's past history revealed that he had been well educated, attending a private school for most of his elementary and high school education. His parents were in good financial circumstances and had planned for him to enter college. Unfortunately his academic record prevented this (although on examination he proved to have distinctly superior intelligence). Failing to enter college, he was employed by an insurance company as a trainee salesman and there proceeded to do very well. He was a distinguished-looking young man and an exceptionally fluent speaker.

When it appeared that he could anticipate a successful career in the insurance business, he ran into trouble because of a failure to hand in checks that had been given him by customers to pay their initial premiums. He admitted to having cashed these checks and spent the money on a variety of small items, mainly clothes and liquor. Apparently it did not occur to him that the accounting system of the company would rapidly catch up with any embezzlement of this kind. Indeed, he described this part of his history with a note of amused indignation at the failure of the company to appreciate that he had intended to pay the money later from his own salary. No legal action was taken, but he was requested to resign from his position, and his parents made good the missing money.

At this point, World War II provided him with an opportunity to escape the tedium of civilian life, and he enlisted in the Army. His social presence and educational background were such that he was rapidly transferred to Officer Candidate School, graduating as second lieutenant and thence assigned to an infantry unit. While there was no record of any unusual difficulty at OCS, he soon ran into trouble in his operational unit for a series of minor disciplinary infractions, such as missing morning parades, being drunk on duty, and smuggling women into his quarters. These incidents earned him a series of reprimands, but more serious trouble developed when he began to cash checks in the nearby town without funds in the bank to cover them.

He was tried by the civil authority, and convicted of fraud, and sentenced to a few months' imprisonment. Simultaneously, he was court-martialed and dismissed from the Army with a dishonorable discharge. Following his release from prison, his life followed a regular pattern of finding a woman to support him, either with or without marriage. The first woman to do so was, in fact, his legal wife. She owned a small flower shop and was some ten years older than he. It was her hope that he would take over the business, and again for a time he put a good deal of energy into it. Unfortunately, he soon became involved with a woman in the neighborhood and spent many nights with her, much to his wife's distress. Finally he took a large sum of money from the safe in the store and left his wife entirely, moving in with his new sexual partner. His wife never did divorce him, apparently persisting in the belief that he had been misled by the other woman and would someday come back to her. Many subsequent affairs and offenses did nothing to shake this belief.

At the trial, where he was sentenced to five years' imprisonment, he used the traditional opportunity to speak before the sentence was passed to make a long and extremely articulate speech. He pleaded for clemency toward the young woman who was being tried with him and said that for himself, he was glad to have the opportunity to repay society for his crimes. The speech included many expressions of repentance, especially for having ruined this woman's life.

inability to form close personal relationships. Some psychopathologists have referred to the anxiety-free psychopath as the *primary* psychopath, while the individual whose antisocial behavior stems from underlying conflicts is termed the *neurotic* psychopath.

Theories of Etiology

Speculations about the etiology of psychopathic behavior lead us to consider two broad possibilities. One is that the patient has suffered some biological deficiency which selectively affects the psychological processes important in the acquisition of moral behavior and emotional capacity. The other is that these processes depend upon appropriate learning conditions and that the psychopath has not been exposed to them. These twin themes of biological defect and unfavorable environment have survived through more than a century of discussion of the problem. One of the earliest hypotheses was that of Prichard (1835), a British psychopathologist who coined the term

"moral imbecile" to describe patients of this kind.

There is likewise a form of mental derangement in which the intellectual faculties appear to have sustained little or no injury, while the disorder is manifested principally or alone, in the state of feelings, temper or habits. In cases of this nature, the moral and active principles of the mind are strongly perverted or depraved; the power of self-government is lost or greatly impaired and the individual is found to be incapable, not of talking or reasoning on any subject proposed to him, but of conducting himself with decency and propriety in the business of his life. (Prichard, 1835, p. 15.)

Kraepelin (1915) developed a list of seven categories of psychopath, using the predominant symptom in each case to define the category. Thus he identified Antisocial, Eccentric, Excitable, Impulsive, Liar and Swindler, Quarrelsome, and Unstable types. Unfortunately this kind of classification led no further to understanding of the determinants of psychopathic behavior.

Kraepelin felt that the most important influences were hereditary, but provided no substantial evidence for this belief.

Psychoanalytic theorists have emphasized the importance of early emotional deprivation. Bender (1947) suggests that the major variable is:

. . . the emotional deprivation in the infantile period due to a serious break in parent-child relationships, for example, the child who has spent a considerable time in infancy or early childhood in an institution without any affectional ties, or a child who has been transferred from one foster home to another with critical breaks in the continuity of affectional patterns. The defect is in the ability to form relationships, to identify themselves with others, and, consequently, in conceptualization of intellectual, emotional and social problems and asocial or unsocial behavior. (Bender, 1947, p. 362.)

The major weakness of this kind of formulation is that it is much too vague. Many children raised in institutions and series of foster homes do not develop into psychopaths. Many diagnosed psychopaths do not have that kind of history at all; in fact it is not uncommon to find that they have been protected and indulged during childhood.

Learning and Psychopathy

No hypothesis purely in learning theory terms has yet been advanced to account for the acquisition of psychopathic behavior. This is not surprising in view of the fact that one of the most striking features of the syndrome is the inability to learn to avoid punishment. In these paragraphs we shall suggest the outlines of a learning explanation, and the next section considers the evidence for it.

On the face of it, the psychopathic patient should have no difficulty in learning. Our clinical description says that such people are often of superior intelligence and show unusual social skills. By the same token they are adept in the verbal part of ethical behavior and can recite and endorse common principles of social morality. Therefore we will begin this explanation by assuming that the patient is not, in fact, suffering from any *defect* at all. Rather we shall assume that his behavior stems predictably from a particular set of learning experiences which happen to equip him poorly for adult responsibilities.

Moral behavior in young children is produced by certain contingencies of reward and punishment for special classes of behavior. Behavior which is, by social definition, immoral is usually visited by direct punishment, which includes deprivation of the profits of the punished action. The child who steals money from his mother's purse is usually punished and has the money taken away from him. Sometimes the punishment may be forestalled or at least reduced in severity by suitable expressions of repentance and promises not to repeat the behavior. When a child is consistently able to avoid punishment in this way, the parent is reinforcing repentance behavior while extinguishing the fear of punishment that may otherwise become attached to forbidden acts. Punishing a child is not an easy task for a parent. When a child is unusually attractive or appealing in appearance and behavior, the parent may find it difficult to utter even verbal promises of punishment. Under these circumstances the stage is set for the child to learn that "being lovable" is highly likely to lead to removal of any unpleasant consequences of his own actions. In brief, the child learns to become a manipulator of other people, using charm and attractiveness to gain his ends.

Much the same kind of manipulation may serve to ensure that the child is generally indulged in other respects. He may rarely have to wait long for some desired object because his social skill will help him persuade adults to give him what he wants now. Making a child wait for something, or work in order to get it, is frequently seen by the adult as somewhat punitive or harsh, and thus the mechanisms that operate to prevent the adult from punishing the child also operate to lead him to indulge the child's wishes. Two consequences emerge from this kind of training. One is that the child gets no opportunity to learn to work and wait for long-term rewards; the other is that he does not learn to tolerate frustration.

Up to a point we might regard the child as living in a kind of paradise of immaturity. But the very same processes which teach the child that certain kinds of overt behavior will lead to gratification of his wishes also teach him that parental love is contingent upon them. He is not loved for himself, but because he is good-looking, "cute," or appealing. One of the outstanding aspects of the life history of the psychopath is the remarkable extent to which he is able to get other people to cover up for him or to bail him out of trouble. While the psychopathologist is amazed at the degree to which the patient seems indifferent to punishment, a more provocative observation is that in many clinical cases the patient is not punished much at all. His social skills and charm usually stand him in good stead for a significant part of his career.

We have hinted at the genesis of the patient's difficulties in establishing meaningful emotional relationships with other people. For fuller understanding of this, we must consider the meaning of "genuineness" in an emotional relationship. With the psychopath, the problem is that he does not seem to be able to really love anyone else. This statement is based upon the observation that when he has entered into a relationship which generally implies affection, he treats other people in such a way that they may be badly hurt by him. Thus, he hurts his parents, his wife, his friends, his sexual partners, and so forth. But he hurts them because he is actually indifferent to them, not because of a positive motive toward injuring them.

Now this kind of behavior is significant only because it is assumed that under certain circumstances, most people forgo their own wishes to avoid hurting someone else. The extent to which one is willing to forgo something is a measure of the existence of a love relationship. When we say that the psychopath does not seem to be able to love anybody, we mean that he does not seem to be able to give up some wish of his own for the sake of someone else. It is not necessary to assume that any dramatic sacrifice is involved in this definition; simple things like curbing momentary irritability, tolerating minor annoyances, and so on all represent everyday instances of genuine love.

Love is learned behavior. From our analysis in the previous paragraph we might expect that the child ordinarily learns to understand the distress of others by experiencing it himself. A child who has been protected from distress will have no basis for interpreting it in others when he sees it. By withholding punishment and frustration, the parents of our hypothetical child are preventing him from gaining the experiences he needs in order to appreciate the distress that these events cause others. In fact, his ability to amuse and please adults and to avert their displeasure is contributing to prevent him from noting that his behavior can cause distress, and that this should be avoided.

This analysis is purely speculative. Some deductions might be made from it that could be empirically tested. We should expect to find that in this kind of patient there is no inability to learn, providing that the reinforcements for a response are immediate and positive. Where the task involves learning to respond to stimuli which signal the coming of a painful event, there should be some deviance in the psychopath's performance. Because the patient has been living in a childhood environment in which he has been generally protected from punishment and fear, we should expect to find that there is little anxiety in his behavior. Likewise, he should be inferior in any performance where anxiety facilitates the response and superior in any where anxiety impairs the response. He should not lack knowledge of the current social-ethical code; in fact, in view of his repentance training, we might expect that the psychopath would be a little better than most people at verbalizing these principles.

Learning Theory and the Development of Conscience

Much work has been done on the problem of how a child develops a conscience. A systematic treatment of this question has been provided by Sears, Maccoby, and Levin (1957). They begin by defining three criteria for the presence of conscience in a child. These are *resistance to temptation, self-instruction to obey* the rules of behavior, and overt *evidence of guilt* when the child has broken the rules. When these effects are present, the authors believe that a process has occurred by which the child has "internalized" the control which was previously located in outside punishments and rewards.

The concept of "internalizing control" is essentially fictional and picturesque. Behavior is controlled by stimuli, which may occur in the environment of the child, may be provided by his own actions, or may be internal bodily responses ordinarily thought of as "emotional." Hill (1960) has given a particularly penetrating analysis of the three criteria mentioned above, from a viewpoint of current knowledge of learning. Let us examine these.

Resistance to Temptation. We say that a person demonstrates resistance to temptation when the appearance of a stimulus that ordinarily provokes an approach response fails to do so in a case where the making of the approach response is regarded as immoral by his society. For the behavior to qualify as resistance to temptation, it should also occur under circumstances in which there is no evidence that punishment will follow. In other words, the person should decline to perform the act even though it seems reasonably clear that he could get away with it. From a learning viewpoint, the most probable interpretation of this kind of behavior is that the inhibition of the approach response is controlled by some stimulus aspects of the situation that have in the past been associated with punishment. Thus while there may be, logically speaking, no obvious signal that punishment will follow the act, the past experience of our subject may be that in the presence of the approach stimuli of this kind, punishment has been delivered. Simply stated, resistance to temptation is thus an instance of avoidance learning, where cues for avoidance are provided by the stimulus for the approach response, the initial approach-response elements themselves, or the autonomic accompaniments of the approach motive that the stimulus has aroused.

The child who has been punished for stealing may be faced with the chance of stealing something under circumstances in which detection is almost impossible. He may become anxious and inhibit the response as soon as he recognizes that the object in question is desirable. Alternatively he may become anxious when he finds that he is planning how to steal it or that he has made some preliminary moves toward doing so. At which point he becomes anxious depends largely upon the point where he has typically been punished. If punishment has tended to be infrequent and long delayed, then resistance of temptation may not develop at all.

Self-instruction. Hill suggests that self-instruction to obey moral principles is learned by observation of the verbal principles enunciated by parents. In this respect the major principle adduced to account for the learning is *imitation*. Presumably a child may fail to learn this kind of self-instruction either because the principles are never verbalized to him by parents or because the conditions necessary for imitation of parents do not exist. An example would be the child who is raised in a foster home or institution which provides no single stable figure to imitate.

From our previous description we see that inability to express moral principles is not a problem for the psychopath. Quite the contrary; the patient is often well versed in the clichés of conventional morality. Consequently it seems more than likely that verbalizations of this kind have never been associated with inhibition of the deviant behavior, and that they may instead have served to prevent punishment.

Guilt. The term "guilt" includes many kinds of phenomenon. Some of these are emotional-visceral responses, and others include verbalizations of "feelings of guilt." Perhaps the most important element of the pattern is the tendency of the subject to seek punishment. On the face of it punishment should, by definition, be something that is avoided, and the behavior of seeking punishment presents a striking paradox to the simpler kinds of behavioral analysis. However, we may consider the situation in which the delivery of punishment is a precursor of the restoration of affection or other token of forgiveness. In this way, the acceptance of the punishment might be likened to the process by which an experimental subject will cross an electrified grid in order to get to the food at the other side.

There are many instances in the life of the child in which a misdemeanor is followed by scolding and the withdrawal of love until some punishment has been duly endured by him. Provided that this sequence has occurred sufficiently often, the child may learn that following the performance of some forbidden act, the quickest way to make sure that affection is not interrupted is to confess to the parent, take whatever punishment is given, and get it over with minimum delay. Following a breach of moral rule, the expectation of rejection and the concomitant seeking of punishment might be regarded as the components of what the individual would himself describe as the feeling of guilt.

We should note, at this point, that just as the commission of a crime should lead to guilt and punishment seeking, so the occurrence of unwarranted rejection may lead the victim to conclude that he must be guilty of some crime and lead him to search his memory to discover what it might be. This situation has been presented in several works of fiction, notably Kafka's *The Trial*.

When the child grows up and enters the adult world, he may break some parental prohibitions without fear of punishment, but still feel guilt. To relieve this guilt it would be necessary to confess and/or seek punishment, even by punishing himself if no substitute authority can be found. However, we should expect that as it becomes clear that no punishment is forthcoming from society for certain kinds of immoral behavior, the anticipation of punishment becomes extinguished, and a necessary ingredient of the feeling of guilt thus disappears. For most normal adults, guilt is thus likely to be maintained at an adaptive level, increasing or diminishing in some proportion to the real probabilities of punishment.

Mosher (1965) has studied the differences between subjects who show considerable guilt about sexual motives and those who show low levels of such guilt. These subjects were placed under conditions of sexual arousal and required to identify taboo words, half of each group being given cues that punishment would follow socially unacceptable responses, while the other half were reassured that this would not be the case. Subjects with high levels of guilt appeared relatively uninfluenced by the cues for the presence or absence of punishment, while the low-guilt subjects responded to these cues with significant changes in their recognition of the taboo stimuli. Thus we can see that individual differences in guilt are likely to be accompanied by differential sensitivity to external cues. Where the subject has acquired strong inhibitory tendencies toward punished responses, he appears to be relatively indifferent to the external evidences of the probability of punishment. Where these inhibitory tendencies have not been acquired, the individual is largely reliant upon external guides.

Summary. From the foregoing discussion we see that the development of guilt and other criteria of conscience hinges in large part upon the person's history of punishment for immoral behavior. Guilt is thus a particular instance of anxiety, namely, the anxiety accompanying the expectation of loss of love and other punishments for one's own acts. Based upon early parental withdrawal of love, it extends in adulthood to other close relationships and to society in general. The way in which guilt may fail to develop in relation to forbidden behavior is of considerable importance in our understanding of psychopathic behavior. We now turn to consider the application of this kind of analysis to the development of the psychopathic personality.

Empirical Evidence

Let us first consider the performance of psychopathic subjects in simple learning tasks. Fairweather (1954) studied simple rote learning in groups of subjects including psychopaths and found no inferiority of performance. Sherman (1957) studied *retroactive inhibition* in groups of normal criminals, neurotic patients, and pyschopaths. The psychopathic subjects showed better retention of meaningful and nonsense material, whether measured by relearning or recall. Discussing these results, Sherman points out that the phenomenon of forgetting is commonly interpreted in terms of the interfering effects of interpolated activities. His experimental design capitalized on this by using a retroactive inhibition method, that is, a procedure whereby the subject learns one set of material and then another interfering set. Recall and relearning of the first list are used as indexes of the extent to which the interpolated learning is interfering with retention of the original material.

Although Sherman did not take measures of anxiety from his groups, he suggests that the data are consistent with the notion that retroactive inhibition is highest in subjects who are operating under maximum motiva-

tion, and that in this case the lowest anxiety would be found in the psychopathic prisoners. Although his study cannot be regarded as a direct test of this hypothesis, it is consistent with it in that the most retroactive inhibition—and worst retention—was found in his group of neurotic subjects. Fairweather, whose study was cited above, did take a measure of anxiety (the Taylor MAS) and obtained lowest scores from his psychopathic sample, indirectly corroborating Sherman's assumption.

Of more immediate relevance to the question of psychopathic personality and learning is the evidence concerning the acquisition of behavior under conditions of negative reinforcement. As we have seen, it is the psychopathic subject's imperviousness to punishment that seems to be most crucial clinically. This has been investigated directly by Painting (1961). He studied the behavior of primary psychopathic postnarcotic drug addicts, compared with a group of neurotic patients and a like group of male college students. There were no differences between these groups in intelligence. Subjects were required to predict which of two stimuli were correct under varying conditions of predictability. Errors were punished by the loss of cigarettes from a preliminary total, and correct responses were rewarded by additional cigarettes.

Various strategies were available to the subjects, and the investigator's purpose was to detect differences in their use of these. Primary psychopaths showed considerable deterioration of performance when the task necessitated taking into account the manner in which *remote* previous responses had been reinforced, but they were superior to others when efficient performance was determined by immediate previous reinforcement. Behavior under conditions of avoidance was significantly less adaptive in the primary psychopaths than in the other groups.

An additional aspect of this study that deserves some comment is the experimental distinction between *primary* psychopaths and *neurotic* psychopaths. The distinction is one that we have already encountered earlier in this chapter. Painting's data indicate that the latter group was indistinguishable from the normal controls in this kind of task. As the distinction is essentially one between individuals who do not avoid punishment and those who do, it is not surprising that the former fail to develop adaptive responses in avoidance learning tasks.

Time Perspective. Turning for the moment from the questions of learning differences between psychopaths and other individuals, we may consider the idea that the seeming inability of the former to adapt their behavior to its probable future consequences reflects some difficulty in behaving in terms of the future at all. Thus the problem may be not only that the patient does not respond to the threat of punishment, but that he does not respond to *future* consequences of any kind—preferring immediate gratifications to future gratifications. Several experimental investigations have been reported that are pertinent to this possibility.

Brock and Del Giudice (1963) studied the behavior of 120 children from a low-income group in Pittsburgh. During the experiment, the investigator provided each child with an opportunity to steal money from her under circumstances in which detection appeared to be unlikely. Forty-nine of the children did so. All children were then tested with verbal tasks that could elicit time-oriented words and with a story production accompanied by an estimate of the time span covered by the events in the story. Comparison of the stealers and non-stealers showed highly significant differences between time-oriented choices, the stealers using fewer time words and shorter time spans in their stories. Intelligence, race, and sex differences were not significant.

Siegman (1961) studied male delinquents in an Israeli prison population and emerged with essentially similar findings: measures of time perspective showed that the delinquents had shorter future time perspectives. The delinquents also showed poorer ability in estimating brief durations of actual time that had passed, their tendency being to underestimate the speed with which time was passing.

Conditioning. One deduction made from the assumption that the primary psychopath is low in anxiety and unamenable to control by punishment is that the establishment of a conditioned response to punishment should be difficult with this kind of patient. Lykken (1957) conducted a highly systematic study of this problem. Although he preferred to use the term *sociopath,* his groups consisted of institution inmates diagnosed as primary or neurotic psychopaths, together with additional groups of controls. These subjects were given several experimental tasks, including the acquisition of a conditioned GSR to a buzzer paired with shock, the learning of an avoidance response in a "mental maze" in which certain errors would produce shock, and a variety of anxiety-scale measures.

The primary sociopaths scored significantly lower than the neurotic groups or the normals on all anxiety scales. Furthermore, they were least adaptive in the avoidance learning task. Next in adaptiveness were the neurotic psychopaths, while the controls were the most adaptive. A similar pattern was found for the GSR conditioning. Lykken concludes from these data that the primary sociopath is defective in his ability to condition the anxiety response. Franks (1956) also reports that psychopathic delinquents are slower to condition and quicker to extinguish than other groups. In this case he was using the conditioned eye-blink response already described in Chapter 7 on anxiety.

Summary. All in all, the evidence suggests that there is a behavior pattern marked by poor acquisition of a conditioned response to noxious stimulation, poor development of adaptive response in an avoidance learning task, little sign of any manifest anxiety, poor or shortened future time perspective, and a history of antisocial behavior. This pattern seems to define the diagnostic category known as the primary psychopath. Antisocial behavior is seen in other individuals either as part of a more anxiety-ridden and neurotic syndrome, or as a simple consequence of learning criminal activities by direct reinforcement in a criminal culture.

The apparent incorrigibility of the primary psychopath has led, as we have seen, to speculations that this behavior may be determined by hereditary and biological factors. Under the circumstances it is not surprising that much research has been conducted along these lines, and we shall consider it now.

Biological Aspects of Psychopathy

One of the main areas of interest to biological research into psychopathy has been the electroencephalogram. An extensive literature now exists on this topic, and we can consider here only a few of the major features of it. A typical problem has been the simple frequency of deviant EEG traces in psychopathic subjects compared with other groups. Knott and Gottlieb (1943), for example, defined *normal* EEG records as those in which no repetitive waves below 8 cps appeared. Records in which lower-frequency waves appeared in short sequences and at low voltage (i.e., in a limited number of leads) were labeled *questionable*. Where low-frequency waves occurred often and at voltages higher than the average for the record, the case was classified as *abnormal*. With these criteria, the percentages obtained are shown in Table 9-1. The trend of the data is clearly in the direction of more occurrences of low-frequency wave abnormality in the EEG records of the psychopathic group.

This kind of finding has been reported by many other investigators. In general, the form of abnormality is an excess of *theta* rhythm (4 to 7 cps, as described in Chapter 4). Paroxysmal bursts, such as those found in epilepsy, are rather infrequent in psychopathic subjects. In fact, any deviation of EEG tends to be in the form of abnormally slow rather than abnormally fast activity. A record which exemplifies this is given in Figure 9-1.

Records containing slow activity are comparatively common in young children. Indeed, Hill and Watterson (1942) have observed that the records of many psychopathic adults would be indistinguishable from those of normal young children. This similarity has raised the question whether the EEG deviations found in the psychopath may represent some slowing of the rate of maturation of central nervous system functioning. Supporting this observation is the reported decline in EEG anomalies in psychopathic subjects with increasing age. A comparison of the rate of decline found in psychopaths and that found in neurotic patients is shown in Figure 9-2. This figure reveals that the psychopathic group is much slower to lose these dysrhythmias, wide differences being evident between the ages of 21 and 40. Past the age of 40, there is a fairly pronounced drop in the incidence of EEG anomalies in psychopathic patients, so that this group begins to approach the neurotic comparison group.

Any hypothesis which implies that the behavior of the psychopath is a consequence

TABLE 9-1 Percentage of Normal, Questionable, and Abnormal EEG Records

Group	Normal	EEG trace questionable	Abnormal
Normal control	90	4	6
Psychoneurotic patients	78	22	0
Psychopathic patients	48	32	20

SOURCE: *Knott and Gottlieb (1943).*

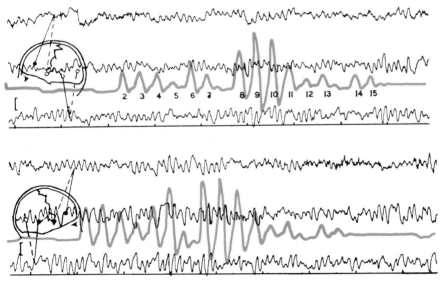

Figure 9-1. Psychopathic personality, predominantly aggressive and sadistic. Focus of slow wave activity in the posterior part of the right temporal lobe. (Hill, 1950.)

of immaturity has a certain appeal because of the social immaturity of the behavior itself. However, we must be cautious in jumping to this kind of conclusion, for the fact is that we do not have any good under-

Figure 9-2. Steeper decline of percentage of abnormal theta rhythm with age in psychoneurotic sample compared with psychopathic sample. (Hill, 1950.)

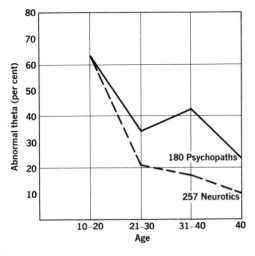

standing of the way in which particular EEG frequencies reflect specific activity in the central nervous system. Furthermore, many patients who are classified as psychopathic do not exhibit this sort of anomaly, nor do they show any other kind of EEG deviation.

While there have been some spasmodic attempts to identify other types of biological disorder in psychopaths, they have not met with any success. Partridge (1928) reported endocrine disorders in 13 out of 50 psychopaths, but there has been a paucity of similar evidence since.

Summary. The overwhelming majority of investigators report EEG anomalies in adult psychopaths. These anomalies tend to be in the direction of low-frequency waves in the theta band. Such frequencies are common in children and have led to the speculation that psychopathic behavior is a reflection of slow maturation of the central nervous system. In the present state of our knowledge of the relationship between the EEG and brain functioning, it is not possible to put this hypothesis into testable form.

CRIMINAL BEHAVIOR

The vast majority of convicted criminals do not present the syndrome of psychopathic behavior discussed above. Nevertheless, criminal activity is itself socially abnormal and an important problem for the psychopathologist. Law enforcement, the judicial system, and the penal system represent the tremendous effort that society makes to prevent and control crime. Crime costs the population, one way or another, nearly as much as the care and treatment of all other forms of psychopathology. Up to now, however, psychologists have spent little effort on research in this area, and much of what has been written suffers from the speculative nature of the observations upon which it is based. As the section below demonstrates, some of the major difficulties facing the research worker in this area are methodological.

Methodological Problems of Research in Criminal Behavior

Criminals are defined by the process of arrest and conviction. Of necessity, the criminologist is confined to studying the convicted person and has no ready way to study the offender who has managed to avoid detection or conviction. Also, some criminals are punished by fines or methods other than imprisonment and thus are not available as research populations. Likewise, the wealthy offender is more likely to have superior legal counsel and defense assistance and is less likely to go to prison than the poorer criminal. For all these reasons, the problem of the adequacy of the sample available for study is a major one for criminologists.

A second problem relates to the definition of the crime. Certain sequences of behavior can be defined as criminal under many different headings. Thus, when one man attacks another after having had a drink, he may be arrested under charges that range from "drunk and disorderly" to "assault with intent

to kill." This difficulty is akin to those we have already encountered in relation to psychiatric diagnosis: namely, that the same behaviors may elicit many different classifications, depending in large part upon who is doing the classifying. Thus, when we study a group of prisoners all convicted for the same crime, there may be considerable variation in the actual behaviors for which they were convicted. Certain categories are obviously narrower than others—as, for example, murder. But on the whole, the large majority of prison inmates are sentenced for crimes that might have been defined in some other criminal category.

Thirdly, researchers face the problem that the prisoner is studied after he has committed the crime and not while he is involved in it. Psychopathology may be studied in hospital patients as it reveals itself, with the pathological behavior occurring before the eyes of the hospital staff. Prisoners, on the other hand, are kept under conditions in which further criminal behavior is quite unlikely and where even minor infractions of rules may meet with severe punishment. What information we get about the criminal activity may depend upon casual witnesses, the prisoner's own memory and willingness to be frank, or the official accounts by the police. From a scientific point of view, none of these are good sources.

The remaining difficulties are the same as those found in any investigation of the determinants of human behavior where the investigator is not in a position to manipulate them directly. Thus, the problems of reliance on case history methods, indirect assessment of personality attributes, and so on all are relevant here.

Hypotheses Regarding the Determinants of Criminal Behavior

Granting the limitations outlined above, several hypotheses have been developed to account for the genesis of criminal behavior patterns. These are not mutually exclusive, but recognize the fact that identical behavior may be determined by many different combinations of factors.

The Subcultural Criminal. Many criminals acquire their behavior by processes that are indistinguishable from those by which physicians, lawyers, and bankers acquire their occupational responses. That is to say, they are raised in an environment in which criminal activity is approved and non-criminal "respectable" behavior is either unrewarded or directly punished. Just as the young man in middle-class society is praised and encouraged to study for a professional career, and just as he finds that the successful professional is admired and well paid, so the young man raised in a heavy-delinquency environment will find that successful criminal activity is admired and rewarded—and that ambitions to do otherwise are often unrewarded. In this sense, the young criminal is not psychologically deviant at all. He has responded to the reinforcements available to him in the same way that the budding medical student has responded to his reinforcements. Such a criminal may be termed *subcultural,* with the implication that his behavior is not psychologically deviant but has been acquired in the subculture of a criminal environment.

The writer once read a letter by a prisoner sentenced for automobile theft written to his younger brother, who was serving a sentence for the same crime but in another prison. As the younger prisoner was believed to be under the influence of his older brother, it had been decided to send him to a prison with a psychotherapeutic orientation, one in which inevitably many of the inmates were sexual offenders. This decision outraged the pride of the older man, who pointed out in his letter that "it is not right to send a decent thief like you to a prison with all those sex maniacs, people in our family have always been sent to a proper prison!" For the subcultural prisoner, being sent to prison represents one of the hazards of the occupation, to be avoided if possible,

but nevertheless part of the normal course of events when it happens. He learns how to adapt to life in prison, doing "easy time" rather than "hard time." Part of adapting to prison includes making gestures of rehabilitation by enrolling in vocational classes and being a "good" prisoner. These activities are likely to improve his chances of an early parole so that he can resume his criminal activities with minimal delay.

It is clear that there is no need to posit any unusual psychological theory to account for this behavior, and by the same token there is little likelihood of changing it without radical reform of the environments in which it is first acquired. These areas are usually well known to the larger community and have common characteristics. Typically, high-crime neighborhoods are conspicuous for poverty, poor housing, and low standards of living. Also, they are situated so that criminal activity is possible. Small towns or villages which are economically depressed may not have an unusually high crime rate, whereas in large cities the presence of prosperous individuals and neighborhoods provides the opportunity for crimes of theft, robbery, and so forth.

Differential Associations. A direct expression of the influence of subcultural learning in producing criminals was provided by Sutherland's concept of *differential association* (Sutherland & Cressey, 1960). Essentially this hypothesis accounts for development of the delinquent or criminal behavior as a direct consequence of the frequency, duration, priority, and intensity of contact with other criminals. People learn to be criminals by associating with existing criminals, and a criminal culture is thus transmitted by the same mechanisms that operate in the transmission of any other culture.

Sutherland's position has been criticized by some criminologists on the grounds that while it accounts for the manner in which criminal behavior is acquired, it does not account for the existence of the criminal culture in the first place. Cohen (1955), for example, points out that not all people exposed to a delinquent culture adopt it. He argues that there must be some additional factor to account for the differences in immunity or susceptibility to acculturation in a criminal environment. He also suggests that for the lower-income-group member, the discrepancy between the goals offered by conventional society and his lack of means to acquire them leads to frustration and so to aggression against the society. This serves to develop a subculture based upon malicious and destructive values.

Research evidence bearing on the differential association hypothesis is available. Glueck and Glueck (1950) studied 500 delinquents in Boston together with 500 nondelinquent controls. Of the controls, only 7 per cent had habitual associations with delinquent peers. On the other side, McCord, McCord, and Zola (1959) report that 75 per cent of children who associated with delinquents in childhood later had criminal histories, while of the children who did not associate with such gangs, the comparable figure was only 30 per cent. All these children were from high-delinquency areas.

The tenor of these data seems to be that associating with other delinquents or criminals is likely to result in the acquisition of criminal behavior. However, the act of associating with criminals is not inevitable in any given general environment, and there seems to be a good deal of selectivity on the part of the individual in establishing his associations. In fact, the high-delinquency area is likely to have a criminal subculture within it, but this subculture is still differentiated from the more conventional lower-class noncriminal culture in which it is embedded.

Frustration Hypothesis. Cohen's comments discussed above indicate that the selection of delinquent associates may be a reaction to frustrations engendered by the unavailability of conventional goals to the youth brought up in the conditions of a high-delinquency neighborhood, i.e., conditions of poverty, lowered educational standards, and so on.

Berkowitz (1962) has argued that frustrations generate hostility and aggression and thus "may predispose a person to associate with lawbreakers and accept their values." However, the frustrations that are important may be not only those produced by the unavailability of normal social goals. The more profound frustrations produced by parental rejection or harshness may be more central to this process.

Berkowitz suggests that the parents' neglect and indifference, their "refusing to recognize his worth and importance as a unique individual," may produce a child who will seek this acceptance from his peers. Where these peers are actively antisocial, they may be especially attractive to him because their behavior is consistent with his own hostility. Such a person becomes a socialized delinquent, likely to learn his behavior and practice it in company with other groups of delinquents. On the other hand, if the parental relationship to the child was one not of indifferent neglect but rather of active rejection, the child may learn to anticipate unfriendliness from others and thus develop his hostility alone. Such a person would be more likely to become a solitary delinquent than a gang member.

Parental Relationships. From the discussion in the preceding paragraph we should expect to find that the hostility or antisocial tendencies of the criminal are accompanied in a significant number of cases by hostility and negative attitudes toward parents. There are many studies (e.g., Merrill, 1947) indicating that delinquent children are found in homes where the parental relationship is marked by punitive and unloving behaviors. However, there have been surprisingly few studies concerning the nature of the correlation of attitudes toward the agencies of social control. One investigation (Watt & Maher, 1958) involved a study of the expressions of attitudes toward agencies of law and justice and attitudes toward home and parents as expressed by a group of 74 adult prisoners. The group was further divided into those convicted for murder, violent assault, forgery and fraud, sex offenses, and robbery without violence. Correlations were insignificant in all save the murder group; there were no differences in the intensity of hostility between the different kinds of criminal group. This study offers little support for any hypothesis that antagonism toward the law is mainly an offshoot of more profound antagonism to early parental authority. However, there is a distinct paucity of research evidence on this important issue, and much more is needed before any firm conclusion may be drawn.

The Gang Influence.   When the potentially delinquent youth has formed associations with other already delinquent peers, the major question of interest is the manner in which the delinquent behavior occurs. Most readers of the popular press in the United States have been exposed to reports of delinquent gangs run in an apparently highly organized manner, with a formal leader, a negotiator to handle interaction with other gangs, and a quasi-military discipline to provide control and cohesiveness within the group. Yablonsky (1959) has challenged this picture of the gang as an organized subculture. He questions Cohen's perception of the gang as a lower-class reaction to middle-class values and likewise the suggestion of Block and Nederhoffer (1958) that the gang represents an organization which satisfies the adolescent's striving for adult status.

The gang, he states, is more correctly described as a *near-group*, such groups being characterized by (1) diffuse role definition, (2) limited cohesion, (3) impermanence, (4) minimal consensus of norms, (5) shifting membership, (6) disturbed leadership, and (7) limited definition of membership expectations. Gang activities are relatively spontaneous and disorganized and differ sharply from the image of the gang that has been propagated both by the mass media and by professional workers in the field of delinquency. As an illustration of this discrepancy he cites the newspaper accounts of an alleged "gang war" to dispute "control

over the Riverside Park territory in New York City" on June 10, 1955, and compares them with interviews of 40 gang members who had been arrested at the scene of the trouble. Typical newspaper accounts were as follows:

Police Seize 38, Avert Gang Battle—Riverside Park Rule Was Goal

Police broke up what they said might have been a "very serious battle" between two juvenile factions last night as they intercepted thirty-eight youths. (*New York Herald Tribune,* June 11, 1955.)

Hoodlum War Averted as Cops Act Fast—38 to 200 Seized near Columbia

Fast police action averted what threatened to be one of the biggest street gang fights in the city's history as some 200 hoodlums massed last night on the upper West side to battle over "exclusive rights" to Riverside Park. (*World-Telegram & Sun,* June 11, 1955.)

However, the interviewees reported their presence as follows (Yablonsky, 1959, pp. 109–110):

"I didn't have anything to do that night and wanted to see what was going to happen."

"My father threw me out of the house; I wanted to get somebody and heard about the fight."

"Those guys called me a Spic and I was going to get even." (This comment was made although the "rival" gangs were mostly Puerto Ricans too.)

An additional insight is provided into the informal character of gang activity by the description one youth gave Yablonsky of how the gang's name, "the Balkans," was acquired.

"How did we get our name? Well, when we were in the police station, the cops kept askin' us who we were. Jay was studying history in school—so he said, how about the Balkans. Let's call ourselves the Balkans. So we told the cops—We're the Balkans—and that was it."

From close contact with these youths over a period of several years, Yablonsky emerged with a picture of the typical gang membership structure as consisting of three levels. The first of these, the core of the gang, is composed of the leaders, many of whom exhibit evidence of true psychological disturbance. These are the few individuals who perceive the gang as having some continuity and who spend time planning gang activities, "drafting" new members, and so forth.

A second level consists of youths who claim affiliation with the gang but who only participate in it according to their passing emotional needs, while a third peripheral membership consists of those who join in gang activity occasionally but do not claim any formal affiliation with it. Apart from the first-level central members—estimated by Yablonsky to be about 20 per cent of the total number associated with a gang—the gang does not appear to be a source of continuous and direct socialization into delinquent behavior. On the contrary, the gang seems to be a vehicle for the performance of certain kinds of delinquent activity by boys who have already developed hostilities for one reason or another.

Criminal Behavior as Immaturity. Although we have already distinguished between the psychopath and the other kinds of criminal in terms of their differences in anxiety and perception of the future consequences of their own behavior, there are many respects in which criminal behavior may be looked on as the persistence of childish techniques for solving personal difficulties. Roper (1950, 1951) has advanced this view. Crime is a disease of the young, he argues, which declines with advancing age. Some support for this observation is provided by the data available on the age of men convicted and imprisoned for various offenses. An example of such figures is given in Table 9-2. As the table shows, the percentage of men over forty years of age is quite low, even though these figures include men whose first offense may have occurred at a much earlier age. Not only is it fairly rare for an older man to enter a life of crime, but the general tendency is for existing criminals to abandon it as they get older. While these data are certainly open to the interpretation that increasing maturity leads to a cessation of crime, they should be regarded with caution. Much criminal activity is, in fact, rather strenuous and hazardous. The abandonment of it by men over forty may be as much a reflection of the demands made by a life of crime as it is of the man's personal development.

The Accidental Criminal. While it is clear that few older men commit a crime for the first time, nevertheless some do. The circumstances of their crimes suggest that an unfortunate concatenation of environmental pressures and the accidental opportunity to resolve a problem by criminal means produced the crime. One such example, drawn from the writer's experience, is of a man who had no criminal record at all but had been employed in a skilled occupation in an engineering plant. He was in the habit of gambling with his fellow workers for small sums during the lunch break. On one occasion he lost the money which had been

TABLE 9-2 Age Distribution of Male British Prisoners during 1946 and 1947 (Per Cent)

Age on conviction or examination	1946	1947
Under 21 years	18	45
21 years and under 30	37	23
30 years and under 40	23	16
40 years and over	22	16
Total prisoners	20,537	99,714

SOURCE: *Adapted from Roper (1951).*

given to him by his wife to buy groceries, and he was unable to face her to admit this. As the shift ended for the day and the employees were leaving, he approached one of them and struck him with a wrench, knocking him unconscious. He robbed the inert man of enough money to buy the groceries and proceeded on his way. Since the victim knew the offender personally, the latter was rapidly apprehended and convicted. During subsequent interviews the prisoner was confused and ashamed of his own behavior and attributed it to the extreme pressure he had felt regarding the loss of the money.

While the foregoing hypotheses have been offered to account for the genesis of generally criminal behavior, criminologists and psychologists have given special attention to certain classes of crime because of the extreme nature of the behavior involved. Murder and sexual offenses have been the focus of particular study.

MURDER

Murder is a crime that holds an abhorrent fascination for the human observer. It is the central dramatic theme of countless books and plays, and it makes headline news in the daily paper. In most societies it is the worst crime in the calendar and receives the most dire punishment. Probably, if one were to question most normal people, they would regard themselves as incapable of committing a murder. Legislation intended to reduce the severity of punishment for murder meets with the greatest opposition in many communities; it is the crime for which liberalized treatment is most suspect and hardest to develop. Under the circumstances, it is not surprising that much work has been done attempting to account for the genesis of the murderer and to understand the psychology of the act of killing. We may illustrate some of the findings that have been obtained by presenting two cases of murderers in Examples 9-2 and 9-3.

The man in Example 9-2 was sentenced to death, but this was later commuted to a life sentence. His case is not unusual: The murder was committed under considerable emotional stress in the face of a provoking situation. Part of the provocation lay in the fact that the intended victim was already a stimulus for anger because of his past relationship with the prisoner's wife. If the prisoner had not had the jackknife, he might simply have punched the man. The com-

EXAMPLE 9-2
Murder without Psychopathology

This man was fifty-two years old at the time of the offense. He was employed as a winchman in a coal mine, operating the machinery which controlled the high-speed elevators bringing miners to and from the coal face to the surface. This was a highly skilled and highly paid position. He had worked for many years and his financial situation was good. Apart from a period of military service, he had resided in the same mining town all his life and was well known as a sober and quiet citizen. He attended church regularly with his wife. His main recreations were watching the professional football games on Saturday and visiting a local men's club after the game to drink one or two beers and chat with his friends.

Shortly before the time of the murder, he discovered that his wife had established a sexual relationship with another man, a miner at the same coal mine as the prisoner. His reaction was to reproach her and then plead with her to give him up. She agreed to do so, and the trouble subsided. Some weeks later he met her in the street talking to the man and became very upset. "I just wanted to hurt him." He pulled out a large jackknife that he carried in his coat, opened it, and lunged at the man. The latter dodged the blow, but the knife struck the woman, who died some minutes later.

Character Disorders and Antisocial Behavior

bination of emotion and opportunity in an individual already set to aggress against the victim provided the essential ingredients in this affair.

Again in Example 9-3, the combination of anger and frustration mounted in an extended situation. It culminated in a provocation that proved too much for the murderer's self-control.

Empirical Studies

Many 'people have had experiences such as those described in the two examples, and yet did not commit murder. Is there any difference between the prior personality or histories of murderers and nonmurderers? One study (Palmer, 1960) suggests that the former have had more illnesses, accidents, and general frustrations than their non-murderous siblings. The same investigator found that the murder group had early histories of more aggressive acts (of a noncriminal kind) than their control brothers.

Some investigators have suggested that the murderer is of lower general intelligence than other types of prisoner, and that this is responsible for his greater history of frustration and for his recourse to lower levels of behavior when faced with frustration. This hypothesis, however, has not been universally supported by the data. Hulin and Maher (1959) reported that murderers in a population sampled at the Illinois State Penitentiary at Joliet were second only to forgers and embezzlers in their tested intelligence, with other crimes of violence and sex offenses coming somewhat lower on the scale.

It is significant, however, that the group of murderers cited in the Watt and Maher (1958) study was the only one in which hostility toward the law was correlated with hostility toward home and parents.

Socioeconomic factors are also significantly related to the incidence of murder. This crime is more common in lower-income groups than higher, and in white people it is more common in times of depression than in times of prosperity. If we assume that life on a low standard of living is fraught with frequent frustrations, and that this condition in turn produces increases in the tendency to aggression, the relationship between the two becomes clear.

However, from all present studies the emerging conclusion is that murder is a crime which, under extreme pressure, almost anyone might commit. There is no typical personality pattern for the murderer, and those who are released from prison appear to be quite unlikely to repeat the crime. The one notable exception to this is the hired killer. Such individuals who will murder a complete stranger for pay are more properly regarded as habitual criminals—indeed, the majority have records for other types of crimes. Since the murder is done without

---

EXAMPLE 9-3
Murder under Prolonged Provocation

The murderer was a merchant seaman aged forty. He had been continuously employed by the same shipping company for several years and had a good work record before that. He was single and had no previous record of criminal activity. On what was to be his last voyage, the ship acquired a new bo'sun who, according to the prisoner and other witnesses, harried and persecuted the prisoner for most of the voyage. When the ship docked for a few days in Hamburg, the prisoner went ashore and proceeded to get very drunk. He described this episode as being due to his wish to blot out the anger and anxiety that had now become chronic in his relationship with his tormenter. Later that night he returned to the ship and went to his quarters. When he entered the crew mess, the bo'sun appeared and began to abuse him sarcastically. The prisoner became explosively angry and siezed a brass hosepipe connection, bringing it down on the victim's head with great force and killing him almost instantly.

passion, the danger of recidivism if the person is released from prison is not less than that for any other habitual offender.

TREATMENT OF CRIME

Unlike psychopathology, the treatment of crime is beset with several different problems arising from contradictory goals. The historic purposes of punishment have been (a) revenge, (b) deterrence by example, (c) custodial prevention of further crime, and (d) reformation of the prisoner. Some of these goals rest upon quite specific assumptions about the *morality* of the criminal act, while others rest upon assumptions about the *empirical consequences* of punishment. Let us consider these goals in order.

Revenge

Those who support the punishment of crime on the grounds of revenge tend to invoke two arguments. One of these is not so much an argument as an assumption. This is that if one man injures another, then the other is entitled to even the account by injuring his assailant. An "eye for an eye, tooth for a tooth" principle is involved here. Revenge, in this sense, has not been a universal human reaction to injury. Early Anglo-Saxon law, for instance, placed upon the injurer the requirement of making good the damage done to the victim. If the damage done was murder, then the murderer could be required to make restitution to the widow of the victim, in the form of a money payment. Making restitution invariably cost the guilty party something, and thus one of the consequences of committing a crime was that the criminal was, in turn, hurt by the application of the law. But this was incidental, not the main purpose of the law.

The revenge motive is, in essence, based upon a moral premise which states that the guilty *ought* to suffer. There is no way for a behavioral scientist to argue the validity of a first premise such as this. The only

contribution that he can make is to study the consequences of actions based upon such beliefs.

A somewhat more complicated argument which is advanced in favor of revenge is that the need for revenge (moral or otherwise) is so strongly rooted "in human nature" that it is necessary for society to organize it to prevent the chaos that ensues what individuals take their revenge themselves. This shifts the argument from moral to practical grounds, so that the practice of punishing criminals is defended as necessary to maintain the social order. As there has never been any large-scale attempt to find out what happens when one does not punish criminals, it is not possible to evaluate this position.

Deterrence

Punishment of criminals is believed to have the effect of deterring others from committing crimes. This is an empirical question. In the absence of controlled experimentation, the only source of evidence lies in the study of changes in the crime rate following changes in the punishments assigned to a given class of crime, or in the comparison of societies where a crime is punished lightly with other societies where the same crime is punished heavily. Almost the only crime-punishment relationship that has been studied in this way is capital punishment. Some rather obvious and superficial comparisons spring to mind. The frequency of the murder of policemen in Britain, where the police officer is unarmed, is much lower than the corresponding figure in the United States. The murder rate generally in the United States is much higher than in Britain, although the probability of capital punishment actually being carried out in Britain is much lower than in the United States.

Historically, the progressive lessening of penalties for a crime has not been followed by an increase in the crime rate. Thus, in the nineteenth century, British criminals could be deported or hanged for comparatively minor crimes that would now be classed as petty larceny. Nevertheless, the incidence of petty larceny is no greater now than it was under the severer prohibitions of a century ago.

The argument in favor of deterrence would suggest that the more visible the deterrent is, the more effective it should be. Thus the practice of watching a public execution should have more effect upon people than simply reading a short announcement in the press the following day. The effect of the public deterrent is well described by Thackeray, who attended the public execution of F. B. Courvoisier in London in 1847. He commented:

I must confess . . . that the sight has left on my mind an extraordinary feeling of terror and shame. It seems to me that I have been abetting an act of frightful wickedness and violence, performed by a set of men against one of their fellows; and I pray God it may soon be out of the power of any man in England to witness such a hideous and degrading sight. Forty thousand persons (say the Sheriffs), of all ranks and degrees,—mechanics, gentlemen, pickpockets, members of both Houses of Parliament, street-walkers, newspaper writers, gather together before the Newgate at a very early hour; the most part of them give up their natural quiet night's rest, in order to partake of this hideous debauchery, which is more exciting than sleep, or than wine, or the last new ballet, or any other amusement they can have. Pickpocket and peer, each is tickled by the sight alike. (*Sketches and Travels in London.*)

Charles Dickens, witnessing a public execution in London two years later, was moved with disgust to comment that "a sight so inconceivably awful as the wickedness and levity of the immense crowd collected at the execution this morning could be imagined by no man" (letter to *The Times*, 1849, cited in Massingham & Massingham, 1958).

Clearly, observant witnesses at public punishment noted that the effects were more likely to encourage depravity in the audience than to lead to an improvement in their morals. Public deterrence has now been abandoned by most civilized countries, although a barbarous relic is to be found in the practice of permitting newspaper writers to attend executions in the United States, the better to stimulate the imagination of their readers the next day.

Custodial Prevention

That imprisonment serves to prevent the prisoner from committing any other crime while he is imprisoned is fairly obvious— although the murder of one prisoner by another is not uncommon, in spite of the security which is exercised in the observation of their activities. From the empirical point of view, custodial prevention is by definition effective. Its application to any given prisoner for any given crime may be argued on moral grounds if the term of deprivation of liberty seems to be excessive in relation to the crime. We may also wish to ponder the justice of any principle that permits society to inflict punishment upon a man for a crime that he has not yet committed. Preventive detention, if intended to keep the prisoner in a position where he cannot commit further crimes, and if prolonged beyond what appears to be appropriate to the crime for which he was imprisoned in the first place, rests upon rather dubious ethical foundations. The confusion between morality, justice, and social expediency is nowhere better exemplified than in this kind of treatment.

Reform

When prison or any other kind of punishment is administered so as to reform the prisoner, then it may be evaluated like any other kind of treatment. Most of the research in this area has been concerned with the effects of imprisonment rather than with other methods of punishment. These effects have been studied at two levels. One is the influence of the prison experience upon the man's attitudes toward crime and upon other broader areas of his behavior; the other is the probability that he will commit another crime on release—the rate of *recidivism*. The first of these two problems has been studied fairly intensively by criminologists interested in the processes by which the new inmate becomes acculturated to the prison culture. This process has been termed *prisonization* by Clemmer (1940).

Prisonization

As described by Clemmer, prisonization consists of the adoption by the inmate of a core set of behaviors and values that are maintained by the reinforcements controlled by other inmates, and that are in many respects at odds with the behaviors required of the inmate by the prison officials. In fact, one central theme of the inmate's code is the demand for loyalty to other inmates and opposition to the prison officials. Prisonization, when it occurred in complete form, tended to render the prisoner immune to the influences of conventional moral values. The extent to which an inmate became prisonized, Clemmer felt, was the major determinant of the probability that he would adjust to normal society after release.

How prisonized an inmate might become depended on the extent to which he was able to maintain contacts with people outside the prison, such as his family; the length of the sentence; and the chances that might place him in contact with other prisoners who were already prisonized. Prisonization is, of course, another instance of the acquisition of criminal behaviors in a criminal environment, and thus the concept employs the same basic assumptions that we noted in the discussion of differential association in the subculture as determinants of delinquency. Clemmer's own research led him to conclude that prisonization begins as the inmate enters the penitentiary and develops progressively with the passage of time. Two studies should be considered here, since they deal directly with the changes in moral code and attitude to conventional authority that occur with a prolonged stay in prison.

Hulin and Maher (1959) measured the expressed hostility of adult prisoners as a function of the length of time they had served in the prison. The measurement was further refined to distinguish between hostility directed at the specific agents of society concerned with the man's conviction, and agents of society and the law generally. On entering prison, for example, a man might well express pronounced hostility against the policeman who arrested him, the judge who tried his case, his own lawyer, and the prosecuting attorney. But at the same time, this man might adhere to the view that judges, policemen, and lawyers as a class are honorable and competent men.

The data in the study showed that (*a*) with increasing length of stay in the prison, the hostility expressed toward society's legal and moral codes and their agents became progressively more intense, and (*b*) the distinction formerly made between a personal experience and the law in general disappeared over time. Correlations ranged between 0.504 and 0.655. Prisonization was negatively correlated with intelligence, men who were more intelligent expressing fewer hostile responses. Whether this is a real effect, or whether it reflects the greater sophistication of the intelligent prisoner in concealing his attitudes, is not possible to assess.

Wheeler (1961) studied the complementary aspect of this process. Where the Hulin and Maher study recorded changes in the direction of rejection of conventional agents of law and justice, Wheeler studied the adoption of the prison code itself. Inmates were asked to select the appropriate behavior for a prisoner faced with a situation in which the inmate code and the official code were in conflict. One example is as follows:

Inmates Brown and Henry are planning an escape. They threaten Smith with a beating unless he steals a crowbar for them from the tool shop where he works. He thinks they mean business. While trying to smuggle the crowbar into the cell house, Smith is caught by an officer and charged with planning to escape. If he doesn't describe the whole situation, he may lose up to a year of good time. He can avoid it by blaming Brown and Henry.

The respondent is then asked what Smith should do—either keep quiet and take the punishment, or tell all and clear himself while getting Brown and Henry into trouble. Using this technique, Wheeler studied the responses of three groups of inmates. One was in the early phase of prisonization, having served less than six months; another was in the middle phase, having served more than six months and with more than six months to go for release; the third consisted of those who had less than six months imprisonment ahead of them. The relationship of phase to conformity to the staff expectations is shown in Table 9-3. As we can see from this table, there was a steady increase in the number of nonconforming responses, indicating an increase in adoption of the inmates' code. There was also a U-shaped curve in the appearance of high-conformity responses, these being highest among the early and late phases and least in the middle phase. Wheeler reports that this process is apparent not only in first-term prisoners, but also in those who have served previous sentences. The U curve of prisonization, with conformity high at the beginning and end, reflects the opposing effects of time producing prisonization being counteracted toward the end by the antic-

ipatory socialization back to the community as the inmate contemplates the approach of the problems of fitting in with normal society.

Dependency and Prison Experience

Quite apart from the process of prisonization, life in prison, as in any other total institution, deprives the inmate of the power of making any significant decisions for himself on a day-by-day basis. Times of rising, working, eating, sleeping, and recreation are all strictly prescribed, as well as the place and form they may take. While this may be necessary to the good order of the institution, it militates against the development of any personal maturity on the part of the prisoner. In this respect, the conditions of a large prison are almost exactly the converse of the conditions to which he will be exposed after release—when he will find himself very much on his own and more dependent on his own effort and initiative than people who have never lost the support of society by going to prison.

Some attempts have been made to counter this effect by giving prisoners more independence as they draw closer to the date of release. Maher (1957) describes one such project conducted at the British prison in Bristol. Here, selected prisoners were separated from the main body of inmates and housed in a small hostel. They were provided with civilian clothes and were found employment in the city of Bristol.

TABLE 9-3   Phase of Institutional Career and Conformity to Staff's Role Expectations

Institutional career phase	Per cent high	Per cent medium	Per cent low	Total	n
Early phase	47	44	09	100	77
Middle phase	21	65	14	100	94
Late phase	43	33	25	100	40
Total					211

$x^2(4df) = 20.48 p < .001$
$\gamma = -.21$
SOURCE: *Wheeler (1961).*

Their fellow workers did not know that at the end of the day they returned to the prison for the night—or indeed that they were prisoners at all. As an initiation into this project, the prisoner was given a small sum of money and sent out of the prison to buy some necessities—shaving soap, writing paper, stamps, etc., that were normally doled out by the officers. In spite of the many opportunities to escape (the prisoners were totally unguarded during their working day), the future careers of the men who passed through this system showed a pronounced drop in recidivism. This method of treatment seems to capitalize upon the loss of prisonization which is occurring as the sentence is drawing to a close, and provides needed experience in independence before the man is released to fend for himself in society.

Punishment, Morals, and Therapy

Behavioral science is based upon the view that human behavior is predictable—that if we were acquainted with all the factors operating at any time, we could accurately forecast the responses of the individual in the situation. While many people are perfectly willing to grant this assumption when it applies to the diagnosis and treatment of psychopathology, they are reluctant to accept it when the behavior concerned is criminal. Many, perhaps most, people feel that it is necessary to assume that man is the selector of his own behavior—that he has "free will"—before anyone else may honorably condemn him for bad behavior. On the face of it, it seems inappropriate to blame anyone for actions when he was not "free" to do otherwise at the time. This distinction is already written into the law: we absolve an individual for crimes he committed under threat of death or injury from another. The innocent driver who finds himself compelled at gunpoint to cooperate in the escape of a prisoner is not indicted for aiding the criminal.

Nettler (1959) has presented an illuminating account of the logical dilemma in which the advocate of free will and moral responsibility finds himself when pressing for punishment of the wrongdoer. If he believes that behavior is indeed not determined by past experience, then he must conclude that punishment will have no effect on the prisoner's future conduct. This, he must assume, is a product of the prisoner's free will and therefore not amenable to change by external factors. Granting this, the free-will doctrine compels us to conclude that the purpose of punishment is purely vengeful. The reform and deterrence approaches both assume that the behavior of people is modifiable by reinforcements and threat, and thus the free-will position must eschew either of these as possible goals of punishment.

Happily, this dilemma is entirely unnecessary. When evaluating criminal behavior, two decisions are necessary. One is the relatively factual issue of whether the supposed offender did do what he is alleged to have done. The other is the question of what treatment will change this behavior and lead him to behave differently under the same circumstances on a subsequent occasion. If this treatment is aversive, i.e., punishing to the individual receiving it, the rationale is precisely the same as that by which the physically ill are required to undergo medical treatments that may be both aversive and prolonged. An individual suffering from a contagious disease is not "blamed" for it; but this lack of blame does not prevent society from segregating him, depriving him of his liberty, and compelling him to take treatments that he may find unpleasant. The crucial problem for the determinist and indeterminist alike should be the fundamental one of what treatments are effective.

It is in this realm of inquiry that the psychopathologist has a major contribution to make. Let us hope that it will be made on a larger scale than has been evident in the past, and with clearer understanding of the role of the behavioral scientist.

SUGGESTED READINGS

1. Berkowitz, L. *Aggression.* New York: McGraw-Hill, 1962. A detailed examination of various psychological explanations of aggressive and violent behavior.
2. Cleckley, H. *The mask of sanity.* (3d ed.) St. Louis: Mosby, 1955. A classic work on the problem of psychopathy.
3. Clemmer, D. *The prison community.* New York: Holt, 1958. (A reissue of the first 1940 edition.) This is the first serious systematic study of prisonization and constitutes a landmark in the history of the study of this problem.
4. Karpman, B. *Case studies in the psychopathology of crime.* Washington: Medical Science Press, 1948. 4 vols. A fruitful source of clinical documentation in the area of criminal psychopathology.
5. Roche, P. *The criminal mind.* New York: Farrar, Straus & Cudahy, 1958. A forensic psychiatrist's view of the discrepancy between the legal-moral and the scientific-determinist approaches to criminal behavior, with special reference to the laws governing the plea of insanity.
6. Toch, H. H. (Ed.) *Legal and criminal psychology.* New York: Holt, 1961. A symposium on various aspects of the title topic.

REFERENCES

Bender, Lauretta. Psychopathic behavior disorders in children. In K. M. Lindner & R. V. Seliger (Eds.), *Handbook of correctional psychology.* New York: Philosophical Library, 1947.

Berkowitz, L., *Aggression.* New York: McGraw-Hill, 1962.

Block, H., & Nederhoffer, A. *The gang.* New York: Philosophical Library, 1958.

Brock, T. C., & Del Giudice, Carolyn. Stealing and temporal orientation. *J. abnorm. soc. Psychol.,* 1963, **66,** 91–94.

Clemmer, D. *The prison community.* New York: Holt, 1958. (Reissue of 1940 ed.)

Cohen, A. K. *Delinquent boys.* New York: Free Press, 1955.

Fairweather, G. The effect of selected incentive conditions on the performance of psychopathic, normal and neurotic criminals in a serial rote learning situation. Unpublished doctoral dissertation, Univer. of Illinois, 1954.

Franks, C. M. L'échelle de Taylor et l'analyse dimensionnelle de l'anxiété. *Revue de Psychologie appliqué,* 1956, **6,** 35–44.

Glueck, S., & Glueck, Eleanor. *Unraveling juvenile delinquency.* New York: Commonwealth Fund, 1950.

Hill, D., & Parr, G. *Electroencephalography.* New York: Macmillan, 1950.

Hill, D., & Watterson, D. Electroencephalographic studies of psychopathic personalities. *J. neurol. Psychiat.,* 1942, **5,** 47.

Hill, W. F. Learning theory and the acquisition of values. *Psychol. Rev.,* 1960, **67,** 317–331.

Hulin, C. L., and Maher, B. A. Changes in attitudes toward law concomitant with imprisonment. *J. crim. Law, Criminology police Sci.,* 1959, **50,** 245–248.

Kafka, F. *The Trial.* New York: Modern Library, 1937.

Knott, J. R., & Gottlieb, J. S. The electroencephalogram in psychopathic personality. *Psychosom. Med.,* 1943, **5.**

Kraepelin, E. *Psychiatrie.* Leipzig: Barth, 1915.

Lykken, D. A study of anxiety in the sociopathic personality. *J. abnorm. soc. Psychol.,* 1957, **55.**

McCord, W., McCord, J., & Zola, I. *Origins of crime.* New York: Columbia, 1959.

Maher, B. A. The pre-release treatment of persistent offenders. *J. crim. Law, Criminology police Sci.,* 1957, **48,** 315–316.

Massingham, H., & Massingham, P. *The London anthology.* London: Spring Books, 1958.

Merrill, Maud A. *Problems of child delinquency.* Boston: Houghton Mifflin, 1947.

Mosher, D. Interaction of fear and guilt

in inhibiting unacceptable behavior. *J. consult. Psychol.,* 1965, **29,** 161–167.

Nettler, G. Cruelty, dignity and determinism. *Amer. sociological Rev.,* 1959, **24,** 375–384.

Painting, O. H. The performance of psychopathic individuals under conditions of positive and negative partial reinforcement. *J. abnorm. soc. Psychol.,* 1961, **62,** 352–355.

Palmer, S. Frustration, aggression and murder. *J. abnorm. soc. Psychol.,* 1960, **60,** 430–432.

Partridge, G. E. Study of 50 cases of psychopathic personality. *Am. J. Psychiat.,* 1928, **7,** 953–973.

Prichard, J. C. *Treatise on insanity.* London: Gilbert & Piper, 1835.

Roper, W. F. A comparative survey of the Wakefield prison population in 1948, Part I. *Brit. J. Delinq.,* 1950, **1,** 15–28.

Roper, W. F. A comparative survey of the Wakefield prison population in 1948-1949, Part II. *Brit. J. Delinq.,* 1951, **1,** 243–270.

Sears, R. R., Maccoby, E., & Levin, H. *Patterns of child rearing.* New York: Harper & Row, 1957.

Sherman, L. J. Retention in psychopathic, neurotic, and normal subjects. *J. Pers.,* 1957, **25,** 721–729.

Siegman, A. W. The relationship between future time perspective, time estimation and impulse control in a group of young offenders and a control group. *J. consult. Psychol.,* 1961, **25,** 470–475.

Sutherland, E. H., & Cressey, D. R. *Principles of criminology.* (6th ed.) Philadelphia: Lippincott, 1960.

Thackeray, W. *Sketches and travels in London.* London: *Dent,* 1847.

Watt, N., & Maher, B. A. Prisoners' attitudes toward home and the judicial system. *J. crim. Law, Criminology police Sci.,* 1958, **49,** 327–330.

Wheeler, S. Socialization in correctional communities. *Amer. sociological Rev.,* 1961, **26,** 697–712.

Yablonsky, L. The delinquent gang as a near-group. *Soc. Problems,* 1959, **7,** 108–117.

PSYCHOSOMATIC
DISORDERS

Patients often seek treatment for bodily disorders in which the chief determinants are events in the environment that have psychological rather than physical malignance. One individual may develop an ulcer under the stresses occasioned by the conflict between his ambitions and his need for protection. Another may produce epileptic-like seizures whenever demands are made on him. A third patient may have contracted tuberculosis but finds that his condition fluctuates with his emotional states. There are endless instances of the interaction of psychological stressors and various kinds of bodily malfunction. For the sake of organization, psychopathologists have generally studied these disorders under three general headings:

1. Psychosomatic Disorders. There are disorders with clear evidence of true bodily disease, and medical treatment is necessary to alleviate or combat them. However, a significant proportion of the determinants of the disorder are psychological, and the disorder is likely to return and persist if the psychological problem is not resolved.

2. Hysterical Disorders. Here we are referring to a group of symptoms that may or may not involve bodily functions, but where minute examination of the malfunctioning organ reveals no physical defect at all. Medical therapies as such are completely ineffective—except insofar as any kind of treatment may produce improvement by psychological suggestion—and treatment is therefore predominantly psychological.

In general, *psychosomatic* disorders tend to involve the autonomic nervous system and related organ systems (circulatory, respiratory, digestive, etc.), while *hysterical* symptoms are more usually found in the special senses (hearing, vision, etc.) and in the skeletal musculature. Any such division does some violence to the realities of many cases, but it will serve as general guide in our discussion of these difficulties.

3. *Somatopsychological Disorders.* Most severe bodily diseases, occurring for purely physical, organic reasons, may begin to have effects upon the general behavior of the patient over and above the effects that are inherent in the disease itself. A man who loses a leg in an automobile accident finds that his life has changed in many ways and that he must make many psychological adjustments to these changes. Under some conditions the kinds of adjustment that he makes may be inappropriate. They may constitute a further handicap to the person and thus require treatment by psychological means. In some cases the kind of adjustment he makes may operate adversely upon the progress of the physical disease itself, and thus a circular relationship develops, to the detriment of the patient's welfare. Unlike the psychosomatic and hysterical disorders, the physical disease here is the original determining factor and is not itself amenable to cure by psychological means.

In some of our earlier chapters we discussed the rather complex relationships that exist between psychological stress, bodily reactions, and later bodily disorder. These relationships are subtle and sophisticated and are as yet poorly understood. Such findings as we have are rather general and crude. Let us consider the state of knowledge as it is at this time.

To begin with, it will be instructive to consider the case of a psychosomatic disorder, given in Example 10-1.

EXAMPLE 10-1
Psychogenic Urticaria

This patient was a single young woman in her twenties, who had a history of persistent, severe generalized urticaria (hives), especially about the face and eyes. However, thorough investigation by an allergist led to the conclusion that the patient was not reacting to any specific allergen. Many methods of direct treatment of the skin eruptions were used but with only temporary alleviation of the condition. Because of this, together with a history of emotional difficulties that the patient had suffered, the diagnosis of psychogenic allergy was made, and the patient was referred for psychological care. Quoting directly from the source of this case report, Saul and Bernstein (1941), we find that the patient ". . . gave the following history. Her mother divorced in order to marry the father when both were not yet 20. When the patient was one and a half her sister was born, and when she was two, her mother died, owing, it was rumored, to violence from the father. The father then married a divorcee and the children were placed in separate orphan homes when the patient was 4. A year later, in 1917, he took them back in order to avoid the draft. He was always engaged in shady or illicit enterprises and served several prison terms.

"The patient was well treated by the stepmother until the age of 6. Then the stepmother began to accuse her of things she had not done, for example, scratching the furniture, and would get the father to force a confession. This he did by cruel treatment with a sexual tinge. He stripped her and burned her with a poker, held her under water in the bathtub, forced her out into the cold scantily clad, and so on. This, she complained, was the only kind of attention she received from him. He never took her on his lap or was otherwise affectionate toward her. As soon as the children could help, they were put to doing charwork in the father's saloon and brothel. They knew abuse and drudgery, and the ostracism of the neighborhood and almost no pleasure. They longed for a good mother and a good father. Exposed to violence and promiscuous sexuality, they were forbidden all companionship with boys by the suspicious parents, who constantly accused them of sexual misbehavior and who threatened to shoot them and any boy they might be seen with.

"At the age of about 11, the patient made three suicidal attempts. At 12, she succeeded in getting a job in a near-by city. With her first salary she bought ice cream and consumed all she could possibly eat. Through hard work she brought the sister to live with her and helped her through school. The patient did well at secretarial work and helped the sister until the latter's marriage at the age of 22. The patient was then even more miserably lonesome. She was befriended by a girl her own age, Miss N, who took her to live in her own emotionally tense family. About this time the patient began going with a young man her own age upon whom she became dependent for male companionship, but who made no sexual advances, and who, despite his abilities and his intentions of marriage, was perpetually unable to find a position which would have made the marriage possible.

"Against this background the patient suffered a general attack of urticaria when she left the home of Miss N (subsequent to the latter's engagement). At the same time her father married a young woman the same age as the patient's sister and went to another city. Another friend of the patient, a young woman employed at the same office, was leaving for Christmas to spend the holiday with her father and invited the patient to come along. After a day of tension associated with preparation for an office party, and following a fight with the unsatisfactory boy friend, she broke out in a generalized urticaria of such severity that she remained in the hospital for three weeks and away from work for six months.

"The patient was referred for psychotherapy and there was a considerable improvement at this point. During the course of therapy, there were several recurrences of the disorder, each one coming closely after a disappointment of some kind in the patient's life. The failure of her fiancé to obtain a position for which he had applied provoked one such attack. A visit from her office girl friend also disappointed her because the friend did not pay enough attention, and this frustration was followed by an attack."

Several features of this case are important to note because they illustrate typical events in the development and recurrence of psychosomatic disorders. In the first place, we see that the patient had a history of continual psychological pressure and insecurity, and that the attacks began under circumstances in which she was subject to unusual stress, i.e., loss of her few emotional supports and fatigue from prolonged work and tension. Secondly, we note that the disorder is truly organic and may be alleviated on a temporary basis by purely medical forms of treatment. Thirdly, the onset of the disorder cannot be traced to some external physical agent.

We cannot emphasize too much the fact that the patient in cases such as this is suffering from an *organic* disorder, which if not treated may be fatal. Patients suffering from psychosomatic disorders sometimes die; there are reports of an asthmatic patient who died during an asthmatic attack following considerable emotional reactions in psychotherapy.

In disorders of this kind we have several

critical issues for psychopathological research, and we shall now consider them and the techniques available for their study.

GENERAL HYPOTHESES OF PSYCHOSOMATIC DISORDERS

There are two central questions in the area of psychosomatic disorder: (1) What determines the psychosomatic response in general, i.e., why does the patient develop a psychosomatic response rather than a neurotic symptom? (2) What are the determinants of the particular kind of disorder that afflicts a given patient? Many hypotheses have been advanced in answer to these questions, and we shall now consider them.

The Somatic Weakness Hypothesis

One hypothesis suggests that the kind of disorder which may arise in a patient is determined by the "weakest link" in his bodily functioning. Prior illness, genetic factors, and so forth may be adduced to account for the selective disruption of a given organic system in the first place, thereby making it more likely that it will develop a disorder when psychological stress occurs. From this point of view there need be no logical connection between the kind of psychological stress applied and the nature of the bodily disorder. This connection would, instead, be due to the accidental nature of whatever had weakened the organ in the first place.

A variant on this position has been advanced by Wolff (1950). He argues that each individual will respond to stress, any stress, with a typical preferred pattern of bodily response. The kind of response produced, he believes, is determined in large part by hereditary factors. However, the response is primarily an adaptive one, just as we have seen that many components of the general adaptation syndrome may be regarded as protective of further damage to the body.

Given patterns of somatic reaction will be accompanied by fixed patterns of emotion or feeling, so that when faced with stress the individual will always show a predictable pattern of psychosomatic response and will always experience a predictable pattern of emotional feeling. Much of this will not show until stress is brought to bear upon the person.

"A given protective pattern may remain inconspicuous during long periods of relative security, and then with stress, become evident as a disorder involving the gut, the heart and the vascular system" (Wolff, 1950, p. 312). From this position, certain deductions may be made: First, that an individual reacts to stresses of many kinds in the same way; second, that these reactions will tend to run in families; third, that the bodily reaction is accompanied by an appropriate and related set of emotional attitudes; and fourth, that people who all react with the same psychosomatic response will all experience a similar emotional reaction to the precipitating stress.

The Symptom-Symbol Hypothesis

Some workers have suggested that the symptom is determined by its symbolic relationship to the problems of the patient. This position is mostly associated with the earlier psychoanalytic speculations (e.g., Deutsch, 1922) and follows the same general lines as the psychoanalytic guesses about the symbolic origin of hysterical symptoms. Garma (1950), for example, has defended the hypothesis that peptic ulcer is a symbol of internalized aggression against the mother. Generally speaking, the symptom-symbol explanation has been abandoned, and there are few serious workers in the field of psychosomatics who operate within this framework.

The Personality-type Hypothesis

This hypothesis, mainly associated with the work of Flanders Dunbar (1943), suggests that persons who suffer from the same psychosomatic disorder have some personality traits in common. This core of traits would thus constitute a personality type for that disorder.

The Maternal Personality Hypothesis

A variant of the personality-type hypothesis is the view that psychosomatic disorders develop because of the interaction between the patient and his mother, the latter possessing particular traits that generate the subsequent psychosomatic reaction. Later in this chapter we see this hypothesis tested in the case of asthmatic children. Gerard (1953), for example, described asthmatic children as being mothered by "dependent, demanding, ungiving mothers who in all cases were charming and socially wooing, presenting an external appearance of good adjustment."

The Specific Emotion Hypothesis

Alexander (1950) argued that psychosomatic disorders are not due to the conversion of a symbol into a symptom, nor are they reliably correlated with particular personality types. Rather he argued that for each disorder there is a typical *conflict*. For example, in the case of peptic ulcers, he states that the patient's repressed need for love and protection are equated with the need for food (this being a primitive expression of a need for nurturance), and thus stomach activity is stimulated by what is essentially a need for affection. The excessive stomach activity produces the gastric secretions that generate the ulcer.

The Specific Attitude Hypothesis

A variant of the specificity hypothesis has been put forward by Grace and Graham (1952). They suggest that the central issue in the conflict is the attitude which the patient has toward it. If the person has been wronged by someone else, he might respond by trying to deny it, by brooding on it, by seeking revenge, by putting up with it, and

so forth. All these responses may be regarded as evidence of an attitude toward the problem. Particular attitudes, so the hypothesis states, determine the kind of psychosomatic symptom that develops, and as the attitude changes so will the symptom. This hypothesis has been provocative of rather more systematic research than most of the general hypotheses already described; this research is discussed in detail below. A brief summary of these various hypotheses is given in Table 10-1, p. 245.

EXPERIMENTAL APPROACHES TO PSYCHOSOMATIC DISORDER

In the study of psychosomatic phenomena, certain experimental techniques have been developed. Perhaps the two most important are (*a*) the establishment of a psychosomatic symptom as a conditioned response, and (*b*) the production by hypnotic suggestion of an autonomic pattern resembling that which characterizes a common psychosomatic disorder.

The Conditioning of Psychosomatic Responses

Experimental conditioning of psychosomatic response follows the same procedure as that outlined in our description of classical conditioning in Chapter 3. A stimulus is presented which will reliably evoke a psychosomatic response, e.g., an irritant is introduced that will produce a skin eruption or that will make breathing difficult when it is diffused in the air. Paired with this stimulus is some neutral stimulus that does not normally produce the psychosomatic response. After sufficient pairings, we observe the appearance of the response to the neutral stimulus when it is presented alone. A very good illustration is provided in an experiment by Ottenberg, Stein, Lewis, and Hamilton (1958).

A group of 30 guinea pigs were first sensitized to egg white by receiving three injections of it over a period of 1 week.

Allowing 2 more weeks for sensitization to occur, the animals were then placed in a small experimental box into which a fine solution of egg white was sprayed as the US, the various physical aspects of the box being the neutral stimulus. Spraying egg white into the atmosphere brought on the asthmatic attacks in all the presensitized animals on the first trial, but a decreasing number produced this unconditioned response on subsequent days. This observation is of some importance, as it underlines the factor of individual differences in susceptibility to this kind of disorder. Six of the animals were strongly reactive, producing attacks on at least 10 consecutive days. These animals were used to test the effects of extinction upon learned asthma. After 13 extinction trials (1 per day), all animals had extinguished the asthmatic response. Some indication of the process of extinction is given in Figure 10-1, which depicts the decreasing number of animals responding as extinction trials were extended.

In the same laboratory (Stein, Schiavi, Ottenberg, & Hamilton, 1961) a careful study was made of the mechanical properties of respiration during these attacks, because in the conditions of the experiment it was necessary to rely on the observer's judgments as to whether or not an attack was occurring. Using polygraphic methods of recording, the investigators measured the pressure in the lungs, tidal volume of air flow, and rate of air flow in and out of the lungs. A sample tracing is shown in Figure 10-2, where it can be clearly seen that the effect of the egg-white spray was to produce a marked asthmatic interference in respiration.

Experimental demonstrations of this kind do not compel us to conclude that all cases of asthma in the human patient are generated by a similar conditioning experience. Nevertheless, they serve to add plausibility to the position that psychosomatic responses represent learned reactions to stimuli that are themselves intrinsically innocuous.

Hypnotically Induced Responses

In a series of highly systematic studies, Graham and others (Grace & Graham, 1952; Graham, Stern, & Winokur, 1958; Graham, 1962) have studied the effect of hypnotically induced attitudes upon the de-

Figure 10-1. Extinction curve of learned asthma. The responses are expressed as the percentage of animals who had asthmatic attacks on consecutive daily trials. (Ottenberg et al., 1958.)

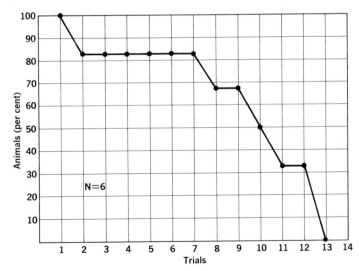

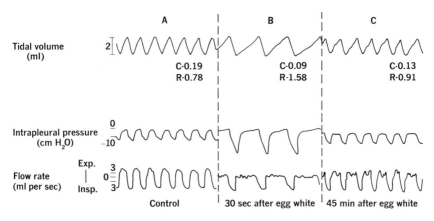

Figure 10-2. Sample tracings of guinea pig respiration. A. Tracing made during a control period. B. Tracing from the same sensitized animal 30 seconds after exposure to egg white. C. Tracing recorded 45 minutes after exposure. (Stein et al., 1961.)

velopment of autonomic patterns akin to psychosomatic disorder. Since their method has involved a sequence of logical steps, we shall trace it in that order.

A preliminary step was to elicit descriptions of their attitude from a large number of patients who were already suffering from various diseases. By *attitude* here is meant "a clear and unambiguous statement of what he (the patient) felt was happening to him, and what he wanted to do about it, at the time of the occurrence of the symptom" (Grace & Graham, 1952, p. 244). From questioning, the investigators were able to obtain data about 12 kinds of symptoms. They report that there was considerable consistency in the descriptions given by patients suffering from the same symptom. Their general findings are given in Table 10-1. These attitudes are more specific than any general description of an emotion would imply and represent the psychological situation in which the patient found himself rather than simply the emotional response to it.

Equipped with these data, the researchers' next step was to suggest to subjects under hypnosis that they were in the kind of situation and with the kind of attitude specific to one or the other of the symptoms. While the subject was responding to this suggestion, appropriate polygraphic measures were made to check whether or not the pattern of bodily response resembled that found in the disorder concerned. Employing this experimental tactic, Graham et al. (1958) hypnotized a group of normal young male subjects. After hypnosis had been achieved, the subjects were given suggestions designed to produce the attitudes specific either to (*a*) urticaria (hives) or (*b*) Raynaud's disease. These two disorders were selected for comparison in the same subjects because there is a clear difference in the skin temperature response associated with them. Urticaria patients produce high skin temperatures, while people suffering from Raynaud's disease have temperatures lower than normal. Thus the measure of skin temperature makes a logical provision for testing the effects of the attitudes. At no time during the experiment were the subjects told either (*a*) what disorder the attitude was supposed to be related to in disease entities, or (*b*) what physiological responses were diagnostic of any disorders. The actual instructions to the subjects were as follows:

For Hives Attitude. "Dr. X. is now going to burn your hand with a match. When he does so you will feel very much mistreated, but you will be unable to do anything about it. You can't even think of anything you

TABLE 10-1

Symptom	Number of patients	Attitude
Urticaria	31	Sees himself as being mistreated and is preoccupied with what is happening to him, not with retaliation. *Ex:* "The boss cracked a whip on me."
Eczema	27	Feels that he is being interfered with or prevented from doing something and cannot overcome frustration; is concerned with the obstacle rather than the goal. *Ex:* "I want to make my mother understand but I can't."
Cold, moist hands (Raynaud's disease)	10	Feels need to undertake some activity but may not know what to do. *Ex:* "Something had to be done."
	(4)	(Included in previous group.) The contemplated action was hostile. *Ex:* "I wanted to put a knife through him."
Vasomotor rhinitis	12	Facing a situation that he would rather avoid or escape. Essential feature was desire to have nothing to do with it. *Ex:* "I wanted to go to bed and pull the sheets over my head."
Asthma	7	Same as in vasomotor rhinitis.
Diarrhea	27	Desired to get a situation over with, to get rid of something or somebody. *Ex:* (Patient had bought a defective car.) "If only I could get rid of it."
Constipation	17	Individual grimly determined to carry on with a situation but with no expectation of improvement or success. *Ex:* "It's a lousy job, but it's the best I can do."
Nausea and vomiting	11	Preoccupied with a past mistake, something he wished he hadn't done or that hadn't happened. *Ex:* "I wish things were the way they were before."
Duodenal ulcer	9	Individual seeking revenge, wishing to injure a person or thing that had injured him. *Ex:* "He hurt me, so I wanted to hurt him."
Migraine Headache	14	When individual had been making an intense effort to carry out a planned program and was now relaxing. It made no difference whether or not the project had succeeded. *Ex:* "I had to meet a deadline."
Arterial Hypertension	7	Individual feels that he must be constantly prepared for threat. *Ex:* "Nobody is ever going to beat me. I'm ready for anything."
Low Back Pain	11	Individual thinking of walking or running away from something; physical movement involved. *Ex:* "I just wanted to walk out of the house."

SOURCE: *Grace and Graham (1952).*

want to do about it. You are thinking only of what happened *to* you."

For Raynaud's Disease Attitude.

The subject was given the same suggestion except that he was told, "You feel mistreated and you want to hit Dr. X. You want to hit him as hard as you can, you want to hit him and choke him and strangle him. That's all that you are thinking about, how much you want to hit him."

Both of these attitude suggestions represent examples of the basic attitude for each disease as given in Table 10-1. Each subject was used in the experiment under each of the two attitude conditions in order to ensure that the response could be attributed to the attitude independently of individual differences. From this investigation the results showed clearly and significantly that the "hives attitude" produced a rise in skin temperature, while the "Raynaud's disease attitude" produced a decline. Figure 10-3 provides an illustration of the effect.

We shall return to the other evidence of the validity of the specific attitude hypothe-

sis later. It is sufficient to note at this point the use that has been made of hypnosis and experimental manipulation of attitudes as a research technique in this field.

Studies of Personality Correlates

In the experimental research tactics described already, the subjects used are initially free from psychosomatic disorder. A symptom is then created, at least temporarily, by the experimenter, thereby providing a demonstration that psychosomatic disorders *may* be produced by the mechanism under scrutiny. Another and more widely used research technique depends upon the measurement of responses made by patients who are already suffering from psychosomatic disorders before the research starts. The response characteristics (or personality attributes) that are discovered are, of course, *correlates* of the disorder.

Three possible logical relationships might exist between the disorder and the personality correlate. After the physical disability has developed, there may be changes in the patient's behavior that represent ad-

Figure 10-3. Changes in hand temperature in the course of an experimental session. With the hives attitude, after a small initial drop there was a sustained rise; with Raynaud's, there was a steady drop. (Graham, Stern & Winokur, 1958.)

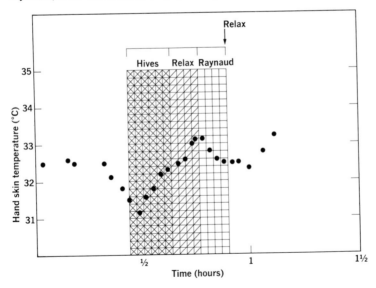

justments to the problems created by the disorder. For instance, we might find that all people who have peptic ulcers develop some common reactions to it; thus when we examine a group of ulcer patients (regardless of the factors responsible for the occurrence of the ulcer in the first place), they have some personality attributes that appear to be typical of them as a group. Putting this relationship in crude terms, we may say that the ulcer "caused" the personality.

A second possible relationship is where the personality features and the psychosomatic disorders are both the consequence of some more general set of determinants. For instance, if we find that people of a certain ethnic or social group tend to exhibit a particular kind of psychosomatic symptom, we might also find that they have certain personality resemblances. Both of these would be the result of influences in their cultural environment but would not be related to each other in any cause-and-effect sense. This is true of many kinds of behavior pathology. Alcoholism is a particularly serious problem in certain Irish groups. By the same token, these groups have some common beliefs and attitudes about religion, child rearing, discipline and obedience, and so on. These beliefs and attitudes have no necessary connection with alcoholism, however—as we can see when we study alcoholics from different social cultures.

A third possible connection is the one that is most emphasized in current studies of personality in psychosomatic patients. Here, the connection that is sought is one in which the personality of the patient reveals the presence of conflicts and ways of dealing with them which had predated the appearance of the psychosomatic symptom. Increases in the intensity of the conflict are accompanied by a worsening of the physical disorder. Resolution of the conflict is followed by disappearance of the symptom.

Methodological Considerations. Unfortunately, the bulk of research that has been reported on psychosomatic illness has been too poorly controlled to permit the reader to have confidence in the results. Commenting on this, Kissen (1960) cites an article that achieved publication in one of the leading journals, "based on data obtained from psychotherapeutic observation of three tuberculous women—private patients who had had tuberculosis many years previously. On the findings derived from these three female patients with long-standing tuberculosis, the author advances a 'hypothesis . . . regarding the mechanisms of connection between the state of ego integration and physical illness.'" Some time previously Kissen had himself conducted research into the psychology of tuberculosis patients over forty-five years of age. At his first session there were three males over forty-five, two of whom had glass eyes! What conclusions might have been drawn at that point from such a sample? Once again we must comment on the great paucity of scientific knowledge in the area of this kind of psychopathology. We shall consider what there is in the following sections.

GASTROINTESTINAL DISORDERS: PEPTIC ULCER

Disorders of digestion and elimination are among the more common psychosomatic diseases. Chief among this group are the ulcers, especially the peptic ulcer, and colitis, including ulcerative colitis as well as mucous and spastic colitis. Excessive appetite (bulimia) or pathological loss of appetite (anorexia) and vomiting and gastritis (local irritation of the stomach without actual tissue damage) are also reported frequently. Other disorders of elimination include chronic constipation and chronic diarrhea. Almost any function served by the gastrointestinal system may become the focus of a psychosomatic disorder.

Physiology of the Ulcer

A peptic ulcer is a lesion of the lining of the stomach or of the duodenum. It is an inflamed focal area and under some conditions may produce internal bleeding. In a normal person, acid secretion occurs when food enters the stomach and stops when digestion has been completed. In the ulcer patient, however, the acid activity occurs when there is no food in the stomach and consequently attacks the stomach tissues. Prolonged activity of this kind produces the damage which leads to the development of the ulcer.

Secretion of gastric juices is ordinarily activated by two sequences in the process of eating food. Chewing food in the mouth produces some secretion of gastric juice in the stomach, even in patients where the esophagus is blocked and it is not possible that some food could have already entered the stomach. This phase, the so-called *cephalic* phase, is responsible for about 20 per cent of the gastric juice produced by a given amount of eating. Activation of the cephalic phase seems to be dependent upon the activity of the vagus nerve, because destruction of vagal innervation leads to cessation of it. When food actually enters the stomach, the *gastric* phase occurs. Contact of food with the mucous membrane of the stomach produces the release of a hormone, *gastrin,* which mediates the production of gastric juices.

Ulcer patients are reported to secrete 4 to 20 times as much acid at night as normal subjects do, this oversecretion being at a time when the stomach is comparatively empty (Dragstedt, 1956). However, the overactivity can be cut nearly in half by severing the vagus nerve, and in an overwhelming number of patients this surgery led to disappearance of the ulcer.

Production of gastric juice by psychological stimulation may occur in several ways. Either we may find that simple conditioning of the cephalic phases is established by continued presence of food stimuli without any ever entering the stomach, or we may find that oversecretion of acid occurs in relation to emotional states and that these are sufficiently prolonged to create an ulcer, even though eating habits are normal.

Experimental Production of Ulcers: The "Executive" Monkey

Several striking demonstrations have been made of the way in which ulcers may be produced experimentally. One of the best known is the study of ulcers in "executive monkeys" conducted by Brady, Porter, Conrad, and Mason (1958). We mentioned related work briefly in Chapter 4.

Monkeys were placed in restraining chairs and subjected to a series of shocks that might be avoided by pressing a lever at least every 20 seconds. When a period of 20 seconds elapsed without depression of the lever, shock was delivered to the animal's feet. This technique produced ulcers in monkeys but left in doubt whether the psychological stress involved or the electric shock itself was the major factor. In order to solve this question experimentally, Brady devised a procedure whereby monkeys were paired in the apparatus. One of them (the executive) was trained as before, except that a failure to make a response in time to avoid shock resulted in the administration of shock to both animals. Thus the executive monkey was responsible for preventing shock to both itself and its control partner. In this way, the number of shocks was the same for both animals, but the executive was also subjected to whatever additional psychological stress is involved in an avoidance learning situation. The executives developed ulcers while the controls did not.

One suggestion offered was that the "social interaction" between the monkeys was in some way contributing to the stress. Accordingly the investigators later used soundproof isolation booths to house each of the yoked animals, and found that ulcers still developed in the executives. Clearly social variables were not important here.

During these experiments different cycles were used to program the "on" and "off" periods of the avoidance condition. The most destructive schedule was one that involved 6 hours of rest alternating with 6 hours of avoidance behavior. On the other hand, a schedule of 30 minutes rest—30 minutes avoidance behavior produced intense activity but no ulcers. Likewise a very demanding schedule of 18 hours on—6 hours off produced no ulcers.

Now that it seemed clear that a 6-hour cycle had particular importance in the formation of ulcers, the investigators turned to biological measurement of gastric secretion in animals living under this schedule. In order to assay gastric activity, the investigator (Brady, 1958) made a surgical opening (or *fistula*) in the abdomen and stomach, thereby permitting sampling of the stomach contents as required. When this was done, measurements were made of gastric activity under various periods of avoidance responding. The results are shown in Figure 10.4. A 1-hour session had no effect upon secretion, but there was considerable rise in acidity *after a 3-hour session had ended* and an even more intense rise after a 6-hour session had ended. The most important aspect of these results is that the gastric activity began *after* the session was over and did not occur during the actual avoidance responding at all.

Many questions are raised by these experiments, and the final explanations are not yet possible. Brady suggests the hypothesis that emotional stress brings on ulcers when (*a*) it is intermittent rather than continuous and (*b*) the period of its occurrence coincides with the natural periodicity of gastric secretions under normal circumstances.

Experimental Production of Ulcers: Conflict

In the experiments just described, the animals were not, in a technical sense, faced with a conflict. Sawrey and his colleagues (Sawrey & Weisz, 1956; Sawrey, Conger, & Turrell, 1956; Conger, Sawrey, & Turrell, 1958) have studied the effects of a chronic approach-avoidance conflict upon the production of gastric ulcers in the rat. This experimental technique was similar to that described in Chapter 3: the animals lived for approximately two weeks in an apparatus in which shock was received whenever they approached food or water. At the end of this period of time, many of the experimental animals had developed ulcers, and some of them died from gastrointestinal hemorrhages. Control animals deprived of food and water but not shocked were free from ulcers.

One interesting observation made during these experiments was that when the animals were placed in the conflict situation in groups of three at a time, the rate of ulceration was considerably less than when animals were used singly. This finding was explored experimentally in relation to the question of previous social experience of the animals. Subjects were raised in the laboratory either alone or in a group. At the end of this investigation, the evidence was quite clear that prior conditions of rearing had no significant effect upon ulceration but that the conditioning during conflict did. Conflict

Figure 10-4. Stomach acidity of executive monkeys, as shown in these highly simplified charts, did not Increase during avoidance sessions (dark) but rather during the subsequent rest periods. The greatest increase followed a 6-hour session; no rise followed a 1-hour session. (Brady, 1958.)

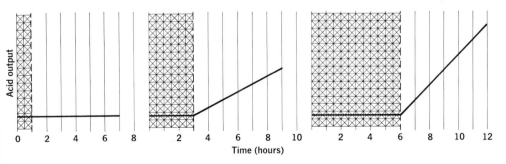

conditions were much less ulcerating when there were other animals present than when the conflict was experienced alone. Many explanations of this effect are possible. One interpretation is that the presence of other animals acts as an inhibitor of the stress response and thus reduces the intensity of the factors making for ulceration.

Predisposition to Ulcer Formation

Not all experimental animals develop ulcers when exposed to the kind of conditions we have described. Many people are exposed to the same life stresses that we find in ulcer patients, and yet they do not suffer from ulcers. Consequently, psychopathologists have been interested in the concept of susceptibility to ulcers as an explanation of the differences between individuals. Using rats, Ader, Beels, and Tatum (1960) studied the relationship between ulcer formation and the presence of *pepsinogen* in the subject. Pepsinogen levels are measures of gastric activity, and we might therefore expect that they would be higher in the ulcer patient. Mirsky (1958) has concluded that this difference is found reliably between patients suffering from duodenal ulcers and normal controls but not between patients with gastric ulcers and normal controls.

To generate ulcers, Ader et al. restrained rats for 20 hours while depriving them of food and water. Following this, a sample of blood was taken for analysis of plasma pepsinogen, and the animals were subject to autopsy examination of the stomach. Control animals were of the same sex and genetic strain but were not subject to any experimental procedure. Blood pepsinogen levels of the control and experimental animals did not differ significantly (in fact, the nonsignificant differences obtained were toward slightly higher levels for the controls). Those animals that developed gastric erosions in the experimental group showed considerably higher levels of blood pepsinogen than those that did not. Thus the combination of high blood pepsinogen level and experimental stress produced ulcers where

either of these factors alone did not. Among those animals that developed ulcers, the level of pepsinogen had no relation to the severity or number of gastric erosions produced. From these data we might conclude that high levels of pepsinogen are predictive of the susceptibility to gastric ulcers but not of the ulcers' severity. Although not in accord with Mirsky's findings with regard to type of ulcer, they confirm the importance of individual differences in ulcer susceptibility.

Turning from the animal data, we should note an interesting parallel set of findings by Weiner, Thaler, Reiser, and Mirsky (1957), who measured serum pepsinogen for 2,073 draftees. From these measures the investigators selected 63 who had values in the upper 15 per cent of the total distribution and 57 who fell in the lowest 9 per cent. Each of these was given a battery of psychological tests and a complete gastrointestinal-roentgenological examination before being sent to basic training in the usual way. Of these subjects, 107 were reexamined between the eighth and sixteenth week of training. A total of 9 peptic ulcer cases were reported, all of them from subjects in the high-pepsinogen group. Evaluation of the psychological test data led to the interpretation that the presence of a peptic ulcer was correlated with the presence of "persistent oral dependent wishes in conflict with environmental sources of oral gratification with resultant unexpressed reactive hostility toward such environmental sources."

Here we see that the determinants of the ulcer appear to be (a) the presence of stress, (b) predisposing biological factors, typified by the high pepsinogen level, and (c) the presence of certain kinds of personality predisposition. Careful analysis would suggest that the variable of "stress" cannot be readily dissociated from the matter of personality disposition; it may well be that basic military training is especially stressful for people with high needs for support and comfort from others, but not particularly stressful for other kinds of persons. To put it another way, the findings of "oral dependence" may be important only because of the kind of stress presented by military training. It is quite possible that individuals with other kinds of personality attributes will develop ulcers provided they are placed in situations that are stressful *for them,* if they possess the necessary biological predisposition.

Considering this study in conjunction with the preceding investigation of ulcers in rats, we can see rather nicely the role of the experimental analogue in filling out our knowledge about the nature of a phenomenon of interest in human psychopathology. We can also see, once again, the relatively complex interaction between environmental and biological variables in producing the final symptom pattern.

Summary of Experimental Data

Certain conclusions emerge from the data available to us. First, the individual must be placed in some stress situation for a relatively prolonged period of time. Secondly, the stress must occur when the subject is hyperactive gastrointestinally. The latter condition may be met by putting stress on individuals who are chronically hyperactive, as indicated by high pepsinogen levels, or by synchronizing the stress with periods of normal gastric hyperactivity—as is suggested by the study of the executive monkey. The personality pattern of the patient may be important chiefly as determining what a stress is. Within the data provided by experiment, it is quite possible to expect that a variety of personality patterns will occur in ulcer patients rather than one "central" or typical pattern.

Clinical Observation of Gastric Activity in Ulcer Patients

Several convincing demonstrations have been made of the relationship between gastric activity in the human and the presence of emotional stressful stimulation. An illustration is provided in Figure 10-5. It represents measures of gastric activity taken from an ulcer patient during an interview. At the beginning of the interview, the patient was discussing his resentment toward his wife, who had demonstrated her lack of love for him by being sexually promiscuous. His conversation is indicated by the following remarks.

"I'd come home at night and she'd be out—no supper was ready . . . she was running around with another man. . . . I found them accidentally in another house, she went to her mother. I felt downhearted and wanted to leave altogether. . . . I got a decent supper only on Saturday or Sunday. I did not want to believe the neighbor's gossip about her. . . . Pains started when I discovered she was running around. . . . She threatened to poison me." (Mittelmann & Wolff, 1942, pp. 34–35.)

We see that there is considerable gastric activity coincident with this conversation. Stomach contractions are frequent and intense. Level of hydrochloric acid in the stomach and total acid activity are high. All these measures reach a peak at the midpoint of the interview and then begin to decline. Paralleling this decline, the interviewer reported, the patient's attitude changed to one of acceptance of the experimental procedure and general security in his interaction with the interviewer.

The hyperactivity under stress, which falls to lower levels during relief, is quite evident in this record. It is also worth noting at this point that the patient refers with resentment to his wife's behavior in two ways. She had abandoned him, as evidenced by her sexual infidelity; she had also neglected to feed him. This connection between love and affection on one hand and giving of food on the other has been remarked upon many times by students of psychosomatic disorders.

Psychological Hypotheses

One of the leading hypotheses about the personality of ulcer patients has emphasized the importance of the need for comfort and affection and the conflict between this and social pressures on men to be strong, in-

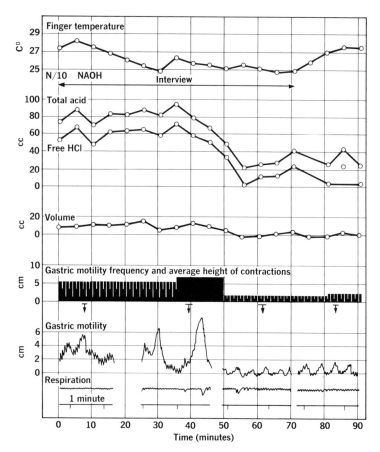

Figure 10-5. Gastroduodenitis and healed duodenal ulcer. Period of resentment with high acidity and peristaltic activity followed by decrease in both with induced feelings of security and relaxation. (Mittelmann & Wolff, 1942.)

dependent, and aggressive. This hypothesis has been chiefly associated with the work of Franz Alexander. He describes the *gastric type* of patient in this way.

In these patients the conscious attitude could be best verbalized as follows: "I am efficient, active, productive; or I give to everybody, help people, assume responsibilities, like to have people depend on me, like to be the effective leader and the self-sufficient, active or even aggressive personality." At the same time we find in the unconscious exactly the opposite attitude: an extreme and violent craving for love and the need for dependence and help. These tendencies we find in most of our cases repressed and denied by the patient and associated with violent conflicts. (Alexander, 1934.)

This conflict develops, Alexander hypothesizes, because of the early connections in infancy between being fed and being loved and cared for. We will dispense with the complex assumptions that gild the psychoanalytic explanation of this connection, and simply point out that the frequent pairing of loving and feeding during childhood is ideally suited to establishing each as a conditioned stimulus for the responses of the other. What is more important is the way in which a conflict may develop in this area. For example, affection-seeking behavior may have been punished in the patient. Thus the stimuli for an affection-seeking response provoke the response, but this in turn produces anxiety and suppression of the behavior. In due course the person exhibits only the behaviors appropriate to independence and aggressiveness, but the conditioned gastric component of the affection-eating pattern still occurs.

We might expect that ulcers would therefore be more common among people living in cultures or societies where (a) there is unusual emphasis upon the relationship between food and affection, and (b) there is unusual emphasis upon aggressive ambition in members of the group. In business society, great importance is attached to success in competition with others, especially in the Western world. The stereotype of the hardworking, ruthless, independent, successful business executive perhaps reaches its clearest development in the folklore of the American middle class. On the face of it, this should not necessarily produce conflict unless the ambitious individual is unable to find affection and fulfillment of his dependency needs at home. A particularly astute commentary on this has been made by Mittelman and Wolff (1942).

They surveyed the ratio of perforated ulcer cases in men and women at New York Hospital over the period 1901 to 1939. These ratios are given in Table 10-2. We can see that the ratio at the turn of the century was 2½ males to 1 female but that it increased many times in the subsequent 40 years. Over the same period there has been a change in the relationship between the sexes in marriage and at work. To this change the authors attribute the develop-ment of the kind of conflicts that produce ulcers. At the opening of the twentieth century

A man was expected to be "master" in his household, yet within this pattern of male dominance men were permitted emotional dependence upon their women . . . with the gradual change in domestic relationships, however, emotional dependence for a man has become more and more difficult, his freedom limited and his privileges curtailed. . . . Coupled with this change, women now compete with men at work . . . but they do not wish their financial contributions to be "counted upon," since there is social justification for the feeling that in giving themselves in marriage and in "running the household" they have already made an adequate contribution. A woman may become the important financial contributor in the home, in which case she often unwittingly creates in her partner a conviction of inadequacy. If she fails in an occupational venture she is justified by society in retiring and being provided for by her husband, brother or father, while such security for a man has no social approval. If a man fails to "provide" he may be denied the feeling of security which his wife's emotional support could give him. Her humiliation of him under these circumstances is endorsed by cultural sanctions. Thus, while society's requirements of the male are essentially as stringent as before, the emotional support accorded him in return is less. (Mittelman & Wolff, 1942, p. 18.)

Empirical Studies of Personality Variables

Very few studies have been reported in which the personality attributes of ulcer patients have been quantified. One of the most systematic was conducted by Scodel

T A B L E 1 0 - 2 Sex Incidence of Peptic Ulcer, New York Hospital

	Male	Female	Ratio
1901–1906	10	4	2.5/1
1907–1914	55	9	6/1
1915–1930	260	16	16/1
1932–1939	36	3	12/1

SOURCE: *Mittelmann and Wolff (1942).*

(1953). He applied the dependence-independence conflict hypothesis to deduce that there might be two personality types among a population of ulcer patients. The first of these is the person with strong needs for affection and dependence, but who is unable to accept this in himself and consequently denies it both verbally and by his behavior. Behaviorally, this is the active, striving, ambitious individual such as those described in general terms in the preceding paragraphs.

A second type of patient comes from lower socioeconomic status groups where ambition and drive for success are less fostered and satisfaction is more likely with lower-level, nonstriving pursuits. These ulcer patients, like those in the first group, also deny their dependence, but their overt behavior is inhibited and unassertive, in contrast to their perceptions of themselves as being active and energetic. Putting this distinction simply, the first type of patient is one who denies his dependence *behaviorally* and sees his own behavior—accurately—as independent. The second type of patient behaves dependently and denies his dependence *perceptually*—his self-perception being in this case inaccurate.

Scodel's investigation was focused on the latter group. He predicted that the behavioral passivity of these subjects would cause them to avoid failure in any task where such avoidance was possible; that where failure occurred, they would tend to deny or forget it sooner than nonulcer controls; and that they would passively persist in any response that seemed even minimally adequate when more effective responses could be found by active trial-and-error testing.

Experimental comparisons were made between 34 ulcer patients and 38 control subjects. All subjects were male veterans, and the control group included patients diagnosed as suffering from a wide range of psychological disorders, excluding psychosis. Anxiety states, obsessional neuroses, and conversion hysteria were included in this range, but no control patient was included who carried any diagnosis suggestive of psychosomatic disorder. Failure avoidance was tested by the use of a level-of-aspiration task, a task involving the recall of incompleted problems, and finally a task that required shifting from one method of solution to another as the first method became inadequate. Scodel's hypotheses were as follows:

Level-of-aspiration Task. Goals would be lower than those of the controls, low goals representing a method of preventing failure. *Recall of Incomplete Tasks.* While normal individuals typically recall tasks that are incomplete more easily than those that have been completed (the *Zeigarnik effect*), the ulcer patients will selectively recall successes rather than failures and thus reverse the normal response pattern. *Incomplete Problems.* Ulcer patients will tend to continue the use of a once-successful method of solution and will begin casting around for another method only after considerable failure with the first.

Both the first and second hypotheses were confirmed, but the third was not. Additional data of interest were provided by an analysis of the responses of these patients on the Minnesota Multiphasic Inventory—a questionnaire containing numerous items relevant to personality differences in the behavior disorders. On this questionnaire the patients described themselves as active, masculine, and efficient to a greater extent than did controls of neurotic nonulcer patients. Therefore the discrepancy between their behavior in the experimental tasks and their description of themselves is congruent with the original hypothesis.

Summary

From various kinds of investigation of human ulcer patients, it appears clear enough that gastric activity in these patients is readily stimulated by psychological stress. It also seems likely that whatever these stresses are, they are more common and critical in men than in women and that the dependence-independence conflict is a plausible source of it.

CIRCULATORY DISORDERS: ESSENTIAL HYPERTENSION

A second large group of psychosomatic disorders is found in relation to circulation and heart functioning generally. Of these, *hypertension* or chronic high blood pressure is by far the most important. Others include tachycardia, palpitations, fainting, and so forth. We shall consider hypertension in some detail because of its central importance in the cardiovascular group.

Physiology of Hypertension

When high blood pressure is found in a patient without accompanying signs of organic disease or disorder to account for it, it is referred to as *essential hypertension* or *functional hypertension*. In this kind of case, the sympathetic division of the autonomic nervous system is chronically hyperactive, keeping the activity of the heart in an accelerated condition. By the same process, the blood vessels are maintained in a constricted state. More blood is being pumped through narrower vessels than is normally the case; hence the blood pressure is unusually and consistently high. Protracted essential hypertension may bring about actual physical damage to the heart, blood vessels, and other tissues and may hasten death.

Essential hypertension often develops in two stages. In the preliminary stage there are frequent but temporary bursts of high blood pressure, presumably due to nonorganic stimuli, probably of a psychological kind. This gives way to a chronic, stable condition of hypertension. It seems quite probable that the second stage is a consequence of the organic changes produced by the first stage. These changes are presumably irreversible, except by direct physical intervention.

The maintenance of normal blood pressure in the human is of crucial importance for normal health. Deviations from the normal level produce reactions that tend to bring pressure back to the normal range. This process of adjustment is controlled by a set of receptor nerves known as *baroreceptors* that are located in the aortic arch and carotid sinuses. Baroreceptors are activated by arterial blood pressures of above 40 to 50 millimeters of mercury. Once above this level, the baroreceptors become active and serve to depress the blood pressure. The higher the blood pressure, the greater intensity the baroreceptor activity has. Permanent or temporary disruption of baroreceptor activity produces chronic high blood pressure. Many kinds of hormonal and drug effects may modify blood pressure, and the complete network of variables controlling it is remarkably complex. Our understanding of the manner in which psychological stresses interact in this system is rudimentary, but we shall consider the kinds of data that are available at this time.

Experimental Hypertension

Miminoshvili (1960), working in the Soviet Union, has studied the effects of an approach-avoidance conflict upon the development of hypertension in monkeys. A conditioned feeding response was placed in competition with a shock-avoidance response to produce the conflict. From this conflict the monkeys first developed a state of hypotension, which was followed by a transition to hypertension. One monkey developed an *infarct* of the heart—a degeneration of tissue that leaves the infarcted part "dead" insofar as its functioning is concerned.

Exposure to prolonged stress was also used by Schunk (1954). He placed cats in a situation of stress by exposing them to barking dogs for long periods over a duration of months. Some 50 per cent of the cats developed hypertension, and some of these also developed physical anomalies of the heart itself. The adrenal cortex also showed overdevelopment in part, testifying to the overactivity which we have seen is so characteristic of the stress syndrome.

Just as in the case of the experimental ulcer, we see that conflict and general stress produce hypertension in some animals but not in others. These differences in reaction may be determined by genetic factors and/or by various kinds of early experience. We do not yet know their source.

Hypertension and Anxiety

Malmo and Shagass (1952) turned their attention to the relationship between blood pressure and psychoneurotic symptomatology generally. Previous investigations of the differences in blood pressure between this kind of patient and normal controls had showed no reliable differences when the measurements were made in a condition of stable relaxation. However, because the main processes underlying the development of pathological behavior are those related to stress, Malmo and Shagass argued that it is under stress conditions that differences are most likely to show up. Accordingly they compared the blood pressure (arterial) changes in four groups of subjects. One group consisted of 37 patients diagnosed as neurotic, 27 of these having diagnoses which included anxiety. Another group included 10 acute psychotics, 8 with diagnoses of schizophrenia of one variety or another. The third group comprised 16 chronic schizophrenics, and the fourth group was made up of 20 normal controls. All subjects were exposed to three kinds of stress: stimulation with painful heat, a mirror-drawing test, and a rapid discrimination task.

Figure 4-11 (see Chapter 4) presents the blood pressure changes that were observed in three of the groups during the mirror-drawing test. Particular interest attaches to the fact that the neurotic group showed a continual rise in blood pressure beyond the point at which normals and chronic schizophrenic patients stabilized. Commenting on this, the authors remarked that "in psychoneurosis, there may be a basic deficiency in some regulatory mechanism which normally operates to check excessive rise in blood pressure." We have already seen how the baroreceptors serve this purpose. Their action in turn is regulated from the hypothalamus, and it is possible that some deficiency might exist at any level in this system.

Summary of Experimental Data

At this time, the general tenor of the conclusion to be drawn from empirical studies is (a) that an increase in blood pressure is a common response to conflict or stress, and that the pressure ordinarily returns to the normal level when the stressor has terminated; (b) that there appear to be differences between living organisms in their susceptibility to stress-produced hypertension; and (c) that extended tension of the kind which is found in individuals with neurotic behavior patterns is associated with a tendency for experimentally induced increases in blood pressure to be more prolonged than in normal subjects.

Clinical Observation of Blood Pressure in a Hypertensive Patient

Protracted observation of the fluctuations in blood pressure in a patient whose emotional state was varying during psychotherapy has been reported by Alexander (1939b). During each therapy session the therapist classified the emotional state of the patient as very disturbed, somewhat disturbed, or calm. Whenever the topic of conversation was emotionally disturbing, the patient's blood pressure rose, but when the therapist raised relaxing or nonthreatening issues, the patient's pressure level dropped. We can see that this technique of investigation of a psychosomatic illness has some general applicability. Our earlier case of gastric activity during a therapeutic interview, presented in Figure 10-5, is an instance of a similar technique.

Alexander interpreted this pattern of patient response to mean that his hypertension was functionally—although unconsciously—

determined by his inability to express hostility. As we shall see later, this is a very common psychoanalytic interpretation of hypertension, and one that draws some seeming support from such everyday observations that people who are angry commonly state that something "made their blood boil!" and so on. Unfortunately, in the study of the clinical case, we are faced with the problems that were raised in our earlier discussion of the clinical method. The chief problem, in a case such as this, is that, while we know that the patient is responding to stress with high blood pressure, we do not know whether this is because of repressed hostility or whether, perhaps, it has become his most likely somatic response to any stress.

Evidence in favor of the hostility hypothesis may be obtained more reliably by experimentation, and in the next section of this chapter, we shall examine the data that have been reported in that way. The value of the clinical case is, of course, its generation of the hypotheses that are tested experimentally.

Psychological Hypotheses

Psychological hypotheses advanced to account for the development of essential hypertension have tended to center around the conflict relating to hostile behavior on the patient's part. The kind of conflict that is envisaged is one in which stimuli occur that would normally arouse an aggressive retaliation by the patient. Aggressive behavior, it is assumed, has been punished in the patient's past history. Thus the stimuli arouse anger but also fear of performing the hostile acts for which the anger is normally a stimulus. Stemming from this hypothesis is the deduction that when the patient is enabled to perform some aggressive action, the condition of anger is reduced and the blood pressure subsides.

Experimental evidence bearing upon this deduction has been reported by Hokanson and his colleagues (Hokanson & Shetler, 1961; Hokanson & Burgess, 1962). In these experiments, normal subjects were deliberately angered by the experimenter while their blood pressures were being recorded. Another group was treated courteously by the experimenter. Later in the experiment, half of each group of subjects was given an opportunity to administer electric shock to the experimenter. The effect of this was to bring the blood pressure back to normal in the angry group. Blood pressure remained high in that half of the angry subjects who did not get the chance to aggress against the experimenter. One interesting aspect of these investigations is that when the provocation to the subjects was given by a person of presumably higher status and authority than they, their blood pressure quickly returned to normal whether or not they were provided with an opportunity to aggress against him.

Thus the essential conditions for hostility to produce hypertension seem to be that the subject should be set to aggress against a target and then be prevented from doing so. Maltreatment by another person may not produce the hostility-hypertension sequence if the maltreater is someone against whom it is not appropriate to aggress. What is important here is that the patient is well aware of his own anger and of the circumstances that are preventing his behaving aggressively. His anger may be said to be inhibited rather than repressed.

Much the same hypothesis was advanced by Alexander (1939a) and by Saul (1939). Alexander presents his description of the genesis of hypertension in the following words:

According to this assumption, the typical course of essential hypertension might be described as follows: The maturing individual in the course of his life gradually becomes more and more confronted with the complex problems of maintaining his and his family's existence, his social position and prestige. In our present civilization all these tasks unavoidably involve hostile competitive feelings, create fears, and require at the same time an extreme control of these hostile impulses. Those who through constitution or through early life experience have acquired a greater amount of inhibitions will handle their aggressions less efficiently than others and will tend to repress them. On account of their inhibitions they cannot find socially acceptable legitimate vents for their aggressive feelings, and thus these hostile impulses become accumulated and increase in intensity. It must also be borne in mind that the neurotic individuals who are more than normally blocked in relieving their hostilities and aggressions usually become inhibited also in many other respects, particularly sexual expression. All these inhibitions make them, in their struggle for life, less effective, create feelings of inferiority in them, stimulate their envy, and increase their hostile feelings toward their more successful, less inhibited competitors. These hostilities again require a greater amount of control and thus lead to greater inhibitions, greater inefficiency, and in turn again stimulate hostile, envious, and competitive tendencies. (Alexander, 1939a, p. 176.)

Summary

We have seen that hypertension may be induced when aggression is frustrated experimentally, and that many patients suffering from essential hypertension seem to be living lives where this is their lot. Prolonged elevation of blood pressure appears to bring about tissue changes that lead to permanent hypertension. Subsequent removal of the psychological stimuli that were producing hypertension in the first place may not necessarily return blood pressure to normal. Thus it is quite possible that we shall find many patients suffering from hypertension who show no present evidence that they are currently suffering from frustrated hostilities. They may have done so in the past, but demonstrating this presents obvious difficulties to the experimenter. We do not know whether or not hypertensive patients show changes in blood pressure when other kinds of stressors are applied, because this kind of experimental comparison does not seem to have been made.

BRONCHIAL ASTHMA

We have discussed peptic ulcers and hypertension in some detail, in part because they are among the most common of the psychosomatic disorders and in part because they have been studied more extensively than other problems in psychosomatic medicine. Perhaps the next greatest interest has been shown in the psychogenesis of bronchial asthma.

Physiology of Asthma

We have seen how an asthmatic attack may be produced by conditioning in an animal subject, and it thus qualifies as a learnable response. The physiological mechanisms underlying asthmatic symptoms involve contraction of the musculature of the bronchial tubes. This contraction hinders the passage of air through the respiratory tract in both inspiration and expiration. Parasympathetic efferent nerves produce this contraction, so that excessive parasympathetic activity is likely to be accompanied by asthmatic difficulties in breathing. Activation of these parasympathetic nerves is possible either by (a) a reflex response to local irritation of bronchial tissue or (b) direct innervation from central autonomic centers, especially the hypothalamus. As we can see, the machinery exists for emotional states to bring about asthmatic responses through the mediation of the hypothalamus.

Local irritation of the bronchi may produce asthmatic attacks without the mediation of any psychological factors at all. Many people are allergic to substances that they may inhale in the atmosphere. Animal danders, flower and weed pollens, certain food proteins, and so forth may irritate the mucous membrane of the respiratory tract in people who are unusually sensitive to them, thereby generating an asthmatic response by the reflex mechanism mentioned already. As many of these irritant substances, called *allergens,* are difficult to detect in the atmosphere, it is just as plausible to hy-

TABLE 10-3 Relationship of Asthmatic Attacks to Interaction of Patient with Psychological Stimulus (Mother)

Occurrence of asthma* —	Days with asthma 15	Days without asthma 70
Within 24 hours of being with mother	9 (60%)	14 (20%)
Not in contact with mother for preceding 24 hours	6 (40%)	56 (80%)

* χ^2 significant at 1% level of significance.
SOURCE: Metcalfe (1956).

pothesize some undetected allergen as to hypothesize some undemonstrated emotional stress when searching for an etiology in a particular patient's case.

Asthma and Stress

However, experimental work on animals has indicated that respiratory distress is an invariable manifestation of chronic experimental neurosis in animals, and that their breathing shows similarities to that found in bronchial asthma (Liddell, 1951). Cats that were exposed to an approach-avoidance conflict (food versus shock) developed, in some cases, a pronounced respiratory symptom resembling asthma (Seitz, 1959). Similar findings with a dog made experimentally neurotic (Gantt, 1947), and also with monkeys (Masserman & Pechtel, 1953) have been reported. Of particular interest in Seitz's data is the fact that the cats which developed the asthmalike symptoms were from a group that had been subjected to the stress of premature weaning. Other groups of cats, members of the same litters as the first, were not subjected to this kind of stress, and none of these developed asthmalike responses to conflict. The obvious implication is that susceptibility to this psychosomatic symptom is heightened by exposure to previous general stress.

Stimulus Control of Asthmatic Responses

Metcalfe (1956) has reported a careful analysis of a case of bronchial asthma that provides a neat demonstration of the manner in which the asthmatic seizure is controlled by a psychological stimulus. A patient, a young single female, was studied daily in an attempt to discover the stimuli precipitating the occurrence of an asthmatic attack. The patient kept a detailed daily diary over a period of 85 days, during which time she suffered attacks on 15 days. During all this period, the patient was in the hospital but free to visit outside, etc. Metcalfe plotted the frequency with which the attacks followed within 24 hours of a contact with the patient's mother versus those that occurred more than 24 hours after a contact with the mother. Her data are given in Table 10-3. The nine attacks following recent contact with the mother were, in turn, analyzed for setting, as shown in Table 10-4.

TABLE 10-4 Specificity of Asthma-producing Stimulus

	Followed by asthma	Not followed by asthma
Meeting mother at home	7	5
Meeting mother outside home	2	9

SOURCE: Metcalfe (1956).

Clearly we see that contact with the mother, in the home, represented the prime stimulus for the attacks.

After discharge from the hospital, the patient left home and subsequently married. In a postdischarge period of 20 months she suffered nine more attacks, eight of which occurred when she was in contact with her mother in her mother's home. This patient was of below-average intelligence (Wechsler-Bellevue IQ 82). Verbal and pictorial stimuli associated with the mother did not produce any attack, but as Metcalfe points out, this might well occur with a more intelligent patient, where ideas or symbolic representation may play more of a part in mediating behavior. This study is a good illustration of the possibility of demonstrating a valid relationship between an external stimulus and a symptom in a clinical case without resort to elaborate conceptions about the patient's motivations.

Asthma and Parent-Child Relationships

Systematic studies of the personalities of asthmatic patients have emphasized the importance of the mother-child relationship in the genesis of this disease. Since asthma, unlike ulcers or hypertension, is frequently found in children, it is possible to study the parents' attitudes and behavior directly, and many investigations have been conducted along these lines. Direct study of the personality and behavior of asthmatic patients has produced conclusions which, to cite Fitzelle (1959), "show that individuals suffering from bronchial asthma possess distinctive personality characteristics including a disproportionately large number of neurotic symptoms. Hypersensitiveness, sexual difficulties, over-protection, rejection, dependency, repressed hostility and anal and oral fixations are frequently ascribed to the asthmatic." It is difficult to imagine what has been left out!

Of particular importance in the study of the asthmatic patient is the fact that the asthmatic attack, especially in the child, places the patient in a very dependent position. During an attack it is necessary for the patient to be helped by someone else, in a manner that is much less true for the ulcer and hypertension patient. Under these circumstances we should expect to find that the patient develops dependent behavior patterns, the disease determining the personality and not vice versa. When studies are conducted comparing the already asthmatic patient with the nonasthmatic control, it is difficult to make valid measurements of the premorbid personalities of the asthmatic patients.

In the light of this, Fitzelle (1959) argued that the premorbid traits of the child could be measured directly by studying the personalities of the mothers. He hypothesized that this group of parents should possess some personality characteristics that would differ significantly from a control group. His control group consisted of a matched group of parents of children referred to the same pediatric clinic, but for disorders that excluded psychiatric referrals. No control child was included where a sibling suffered from asthma. Several standard measures of personality were taken of both the mothers and fathers of each group, but no differences could be found. What may be of some interest is that both groups of parents produced performances on one of the major measures, the MMPI (Minnesota Multiphasic Inventory), that deviated from norms for it. Parents of any child who is ill for prolonged periods may perhaps develop some responses that are not found in the parents of well children.

While Fitzelle's study represents a systematic rejection of the hypothesis that there are characteristic psychological features in the parents of asthmatic children, he reports that most of these parents were able to cite the significance of any kind of local emotional upset in triggering an attack in the child. He also noted statements, of which one is quoted below, which point to the fact that asthmatic attacks may be reinforced by parents and thus may become learned responses on the part of the child. For example, one mother reported:

He can work himself up into a spell. The first few days of school went fine. Then he heard that he could stay away from school by having asthma. He would work up an attack and come home. He would then be sick until noon and then be alright after it was too late to go back to school. I arranged to have him lie in the health room (in school) when an attack came on and he never got an attack at school again. (Fitzelle, 1959, p. 215.)

Here the asthmatic response was clearly not a simple reaction to the stresses of school, but was an avoidance response reinforced by its effect of removing the child from the school. We have already mentioned this process in our discussion of hysterical syndromes. For the moment it is worth noting that psychosomatic and hysterical mechanisms have some common aspects.

However, this conclusion is somewhat attenuated by the problems that surround the use of the personality measures involved and the rather vague nature of the original hypothesis. A more specific investigation was conducted by Little and Cohen (1951), bearing upon the hypothesis that the mothers of asthmatic children will be characterized by a tendency to set unrealistically high goals for their child's performance in any task situation. This hypothesis stemmed in turn from the more general observation that such mothers seem to be both over-ambitious and overprotective of their children, who themselves demonstrate dependency and obedience to these demands.

The investigators studied the goal-setting responses of 30 asthmatic children and their mothers compared with 30 nonasthmatic children and their mothers. Children in the two groups were matched for age, sex, intelligence, and school grade placement. The children were then required to perform a simple skilled task (shooting darts at a target) under conditions in which they predicted their score before each of 20 trials, thus providing a measure of the level of aspiration involved for the subject. Before the child's estimate was made and recorded, the mother of the child was asked to make her estimate of the child's performance.

Both groups of children set high positive goals, the asthmatic children setting significantly higher ones than the controls. The asthmatic children showed little tendency to modify their high goals in the face of low performance, while the control children tended to amend their estimates as the experiment progressed, bringing them into line with their actual performance. Aspiration behavior of the mothers of the two groups paralleled that of their children. Mothers of the asthmatic children maintained unrealistically high estimates and did not modify them with the child's failure to attain them. Mothers of the control children did modify their estimates in the direction of the child's real performance. In fact, the control mothers modified their estimates more accurately than did their children, the mothers apparently being more "realistic" than their children were.

There seems to be little doubt that this difference in goal setting is a reliable phenomenon, but it is open to several interpretations. Little and Cohen suggest that the mothers of asthmatics were more ego-involved in the child's performance and hence were displaying true "aspirations," while the mothers of controls, being less ego-involved, were giving impartial "judgments." Ego-involvement might be greater on the part of the former because the mother has developed protective attitudes due to the child's illness, or because she has high goals and it is important to her personally that her child do well, or because she is rejecting the child and is dealing with her guilt by overprotection.

None of these possibilities can be supported unequivocally within the bounds of this study, but they are amenable to separate test. Of great theoretical interest, granting the reliability of the empirical differences between mothers, is the relationship between high goal setting and *asthma*. Once again, we may invoke the probability that high goal setting is stressful to children and that given some predisposition to bronchial troubles, the stress interacts with it to produce the psychosomatic disorder. Some support from this comes from Little and Cohen's observation that while none of the mothers of the asthmatic children suffered from asthma themselves, many of their families had other members with a history of asthma.

From this possibility, we should expect that there are groups of children whose predispositions are toward other kinds of somatic difficulty and who have equally demanding mothers. In their case the stress should produce the relevant psychosomatic pattern, but not asthma. Put briefly, we might argue that there are many different ways in which a mother can stress a child; if the child has tendencies toward one or another kind of somatic reaction under stress, then the related psychosomatic pattern will emerge.

Some indication of the possible nonspecificity of the personality attributes of asthmatic children is given in a study by Neuhaus (1958). He investigated three groups of children—asthmatics, normal controls, and children with a long history of cardiac illness—in an attempt to discover to what extent the history of illness per se could account for signs of personality difficulty in the child. All children were tested psychologically with the Rorschach test, the Despert fables, and a personality inventory. From the results of these tests it emerged that the asthmatic group produced more evidences of general maladjustment than did normal controls—particularly of anxiety, insecurity, and dependency. The same pattern was true for the cardiac children. Both of these groups differed in the same way from normal healthy controls, lending Neuhaus to suggest that "children who suffer from a chronic physical illness display an emotional pattern that deviates from the normal." Clearly, some aspects of the personality of the asthmatic child (or any child with a long history of psychosomatic illness) are due to the illness itself.

Summary

We may summarize the current state of knowledge about asthma by concluding that (a) there is no compelling evidence for the presence of any characteristic pattern of personality in the asthmatic patient, separate from the effects of the asthmatic handicap itself; (b) asthmatic attacks may be produced by a variety of stresses, including conflict, by simple conditioning where a neutral stimulus is paired with an allergen, or by the reinforcing consequences that an attack may have.

GENERAL CONSIDERATIONS IN PSYCHOSOMATIC ILLNESS

We have considered ulcers, hypertension, and bronchial asthma in some detail. Many other symptom syndromes have been studied with regard to their possible psychological etiology, but space will not permit discussion of them here. Now that we have had some opportunity to see what kind of hypotheses have been advanced and what kind of data have been collected, it is possible to give thought to the problems that exist in this field.

Psychoanalytic Speculations

For many decades the major influence in the study of psychosomatic disorder has been the clinical experience of psychoanalysts. There have been several consequences of this. One has been the usual preference for clinical intuition over controlled observation and measurement of the behavior of patients. Another has been the elaboration of complicated psychological mechanisms to account for the development of the symptom. The following quotation from Wittkower and White (1959) will illustrate the situation clearly. Discussing the etiology of asthma, they comment:

Fenichel has suggested that asthma may represent an unconscious attempt by the patient on a regressive basis, to protect himself permanently and omnipotently from loss of maternal love by respiratory introjection of the ambivalently regarded mother. Fenichel's theory is complementary to Saul's. According to both theories, the aim of the asthmatic patient is to be united with the mother— projectively (Saul), or introjectively (Fenichel). But the patient rejects his wish (which is alien to his adult self), and he rejects the negative aspects of the mother, that is, the mother who has deprived him of love. The mother is then both a loved and hated object, and the asthmatic seeks to retain the "good" mother and rid himself of the "bad" mother. (Wittkower & White, 1959, p. 697.)

It is difficult to know what this could mean in terms of testable research hypotheses, or of possible functioning of the respiratory response, but it is fairly typical of much that has been written in the field. Besides illustrating the kind of speculation that has been offered, it provides an example of the third and perhaps most sterile consequence of the application of psychoanalytic theory to the etiology of bodily ailments. This is the compulsion to find psychological "meaning" in the kind of physical ailment that the patient develops. To return for the moment to asthma, we find that asthma may represent "fear of drowning"—hence the suffocation aspects of the asthmatic attack (Wittkower & White, 1959); that it represents "repressed weeping," even in cats (Seitz, 1959); or that it is to be explained as the physiological concomitant of introjection. Thus Fenichel (1945) suggests that respiratory introjection is achieved by "smelling" in which a "particle" of the external world may be regarded "as taken into the body."

Rival hypotheses about any scientific problem are very useful when they can be tested against each other in some experimental situation. How testing could be carried out with the three hypotheses just mentioned is not clear, and they must be regarded as contributions to literature rather than science at this point. Paradoxically, the confusion engendered by psychoanalytic speculations is also compounded by the tendency for the same hypothesis to appear for widely different bodily syndromes.

For example, with respect to ulcerative colitis, we find some writers persuaded that "the essential psychological condition operating with somatic factors towards the onset of ulcerative colitis is an affective state characterized by helplessness and despair arising from a deep disturbance in a key object relation which is lost or threatened, or whose loss is imagined" (Titchener, Riskin, & Emerson, 1960, p. 127). Wittkower and White (1959) tell us there is general agreement among psychoanalytic writers that one of the problems of severe asthmatic patients is that "they are afraid of losing their mothers or destroying them" (p. 696). Flarsheim (1958) places the occurrence of physical symptoms in tuberculosis "after the loss of an important relationship." Cancer, as we shall see shortly, has been described as triggered by depression and grief following the loss, or fear of loss, of an important personal relationship, and so forth.

It is quite possible that all these observations are true, and useless. Loss of a significant relationship produces grief and general stress. The important ingredient of all these precipitating circumstances may well be simply that they are stressors, not that they specifically involve loss of relationships. The emphasis upon the local characteristics of the stressors may be quite misleading; it certainly has not led to any substantial addition to our knowledge of the mechanisms of psychosomatic illnesses. When the same stressor produces a different symptomatic breakdown in different patients, then we may look at the bodily processes involved in order to find some explanation of this. A systematic attempt to discover such differences has been made by workers studying the problem of autonomic dominance.

We do know that stress situations trigger and exacerbate many psychosomatic responses. We know that some of these responses represent relative dominance of either the sympathetic or parasympathetic divisions of the autonomic nervous system.

We know that individuals differ in this relative dominance, and we may suspect that this disposes them to some kinds of autonomic dysfunction rather than to others. We also know that prolonged exposure to the handicaps of an illness, psychosomatic or not, produces certain kinds of life adjustment, and thus we may expect to find some commonality in the behaviors of patients who have suffered from a similar illness for some time.

When we find that conflicts which produce ulcers in some patients produce hypertension in others, we may turn to the study of the autonomic components of the disorders for clues about the nature of these individual differences. A comprehensive series of hypotheses about the control of autonomic functions has been presented by the concept of autonomic tuning.

Autonomic Tuning

One of the grosser ways in which individuals differ from each other in bodily functions is in the matter of autonomic tuning. This concept has been developed by Gellhorn (1957) as a broad basis for the analysis of a range of autonomic responses. It has special implications for psychosomatics. Basic to its definition is the fact that the same stimulus may produce a predominantly sympathetic response in the autonomic nervous system in one subject, while producing a parasympathetic response in another. Likewise, the same individual may react sympathetically at one time and parasympathetically at another. We can speak of the autonomic nervous system being "set" or "tuned" to respond in one way or another so that a stimulus which has the power to provoke responses in either division of the system produces responses only in the division that is currently dominant.

Tuning of the autonomic system may be altered by many variables. As it is currently conceived (e.g., Gellhorn & Loofbourrow, 1963), the main center for the regulation of the balance between sympathetic and parasympathetic activity is the hypothalamus.

Consequently, direct stimulation of the hypothalamus—with drugs, direct electrical stimulation, etc.—will bring about changes in tuning. However, the most probable daily source of changes in tuning is simple external stimulation. The main principle behind the tuning concept is, in fact, that prior stimulation alters the kind of response that may be produced by a standard stimulus. If the prior stimulation is of a kind that ordinarily provokes parasympathetic activity, then a subsequent stimulus will find the organism tuned parasympathetically. The minor frustration that may produce rage in an already angry man may produce amusement in him should it occur after a good meal.

Developing this thesis further, Gellhorn and Loofbourrow argue that existing data seem "to indicate that the hypothalamic balance in different persons follows the normal distribution curve, showing that those with a marked preponderance of the parasympathetic division represent a minority." Experimental and clinical studies support the assumption that vagotonia (parasympathetic dominance) is related to peptic ulcer and that sympathotonia (sympathetic dominance) is related to hypertension. Thus, from this point of view, the basic dimension along which psychosomatic patients might be considered is the nature of their autonomic dominance.

It is not necessary to accept the hypothesis of autonomic tuning in order to accept the somewhat simpler notion that there are reliable differences between individuals in the manner in which their autonomic nervous systems respond to stress. These differences may be determined in part by hereditary factors and in part by interaction of the hereditary factors with subsequent experience. The work of Seitz (1959) cited above and of Levine cited in Chapter 4 suggests the importance of certain kinds of early experience upon later responses to stress, in the case of animal subjects. Measures of autonomic reactivity in the human infant, taken before the postnatal environment has had much effect, have also been reported and give us some insight into the possibilities of genetically determined individual differences.

Autonomic Functions in the Neonate

In an outstanding series of systematic studies (Lipton, Steinschneider, & Richmond, 1960, 1961a, 1961b; Richmond, Lipton, & Steinschneider, 1962), differences in autonomic responses in newborn infants were measured. The goal of these investigations was to discover stable individual differences at an age when environmental effects had had little opportunity to occur. One of the early studies indicated that certain kinds of stimulation produced motor activity and also changes in heart rate. Such a correlation leaves unanswered the question of whether the changes in heart rate were autonomous responses to the stimuli (which were mainly tactile), or whether the increased motor activity produced the heart-rate changes. This problem was tackled by studying cardiac responses in infants both when they were swaddled to prevent movement and when they were loose. Using an experimental layout depicted in Figure 10-6, the responses of 10 infants aged 2 to 5 days were recorded.

From this investigation it transpired that swaddling per se had the effect of reducing heart rate, motor activity, and respiratory rate. In this respect, at least, the swaddled infant seems to be more at rest than the unswaddled. Responsiveness to an air tactile stimulus was no different under the two conditions, some infants being more reactive when swaddled than when free. The amount of change in heart rate under conditions of stimulation did not seem to be explainable solely in terms of the effect of motor activity, and thus we must assume that some other innate differences are influencing this. Detailed examination of the form of the cardiac responses supported the view that stable individual differences in response are to be found in newborn infants, not only in the magnitude and speed of the cardiac response but also in the rapidity with which it returns to prestimulus levels. Employing the concept of homeostasis, we might consider the data as suggesting that ability to restore a homeostatic level is different

Figure 10-6. Infant subject with attached electrodes and plastic cone above umbilicus for delivery of oxygen stimulus. Diaper holds legs in extension, and light receiving blanket restricts movement of all body parts except head. (Lipton et al., 1960.)

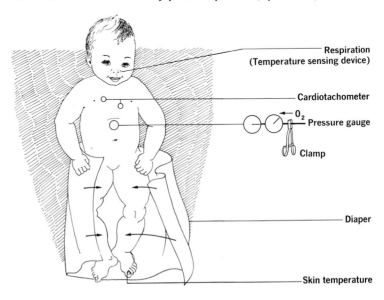

among individuals from the beginning of life.

An interesting measurement of the same capacity at a later age is reported by Sternbach (1960), who observed the magnitude and speed of the *startle response* in college students. A blank cartridge was fired from a pistol close to the subjects, who were required to make a key-pressing response on hearing it. Autonomic measures were taken of several parameters, but the major finding was in the measurements of cardiovascular responses (systolic blood pressure, pulse pressure, heart rate, etc.): these were higher in the subjects who were slowest to press the key. Magnitude of the autonomic response pattern was correlated with slow recovery time, this return to homeostasis seeming to be an important individual difference.

The Significance of Psychological Etiologies

From the clinical point of view, the importance of etiology is its significance in determining therapy. Assuming for a moment that we have valid reason to believe that a patient's hypertension was in some way determined by emotional experiences, then the crucial question is whether or not psychotherapy will reduce the hypertension. If it will not, and if the patient will require medical treatment just as any other patient might with an illness of purely organic origin, then knowledge of the psychological etiology may be interesting but irrelevant in practice. A more common state of affairs is that the medical treatment may be ineffective without some attention to the psychological determinants, presuming that these latter are still operative in the patient's life. Where this is the case, it is necessary to show that psychotherapy can be effectively adjusted to specific conflicts, and thus that there are specific psychotherapies for particular psychosomatic disorders. Success in adjusting psychotherapy to purely psychological disorders has been conspicuously lacking so far. It seems to be unusually optimistic to hope for better outcomes where biological variables complicate the picture

even more. In brief, not only has the hunt for specific psychogeneses been so far chimerical; it is not clear what we would do with such information if we had it.

Summary

The problems of psychosomatic illness are the problems of individual differences in response to stress. In its brief history, the study of psychosomatics has been largely dominated by theories that have tried to relate the form of the bodily ailment to particular determinants in the psychological life history of the patient. Such efforts have met with no measurable success. What is clear is that these disorders can be modified and intensified by psychological variables, largely stressors. In most cases it is necessary for the stress to be prolonged before the disorder develops. Some disorders may be acquired by processes similar to those operating in simple learning; by the same token, they may be extinguished.

For the psychopathologist the central problem is that of predisposition. Before we can hope for a satisfactory solution, this problem will involve genetics, the biology of stress, the influence of early experience upon stress resistance, and the mediation of autonomic responses by learning.

PSYCHOSOMATIC FACTORS IN OTHER DISEASES

In the preceding section we have considered the processes governing diseases that have become regarded as peculiarly liable to psychological influences. However, attention has been turned also to the possibility of psychological influences in many other diseases where the pathological process is known or believed to be predominantly organic. Because of the great interest in them as major health problems, cancer and tuberculosis have come in for considerable attention. We shall consider here some of the work that has been done and the problems that exist in doing it.

Cancer

Incidence in Psychosis. The term "cancer" covers a wide variety of pathologies, the central feature of which is the overproduction of certain kinds of cell by the body to the detriment of the integrity of healthy tissue. Inasmuch as the biological processes that control this overproduction are poorly understood at the present time, there is no obvious point at which we might expect psychological variables to play a part in them. Consequently the research into possible relations between psychological and biological aspects of cancer has been of the crudest empirical kind. One of the grosser approaches has involved the assumption that cancer may be accelerated or triggered by emotional distress, and thus we may expect to find a higher incidence of deaths from cancer in a mental hospital population than we do in a normal population at large. Many statistical studies have been reported along these lines, with conflicting results. A major problem in such studies is that the death of a state hospital patient is more likely to be followed by an autopsy than is the case with the normal population. In earlier studies, done in the first two decades of the century, the death rate for hospitalized psychotics was higher than that for normals; that is to say, the hospitalized patients were likely to die sooner than normals born at the same time. A probable source of this difference was the much greater incidence of syphilis and tuberculosis in the mental hospital group. Being more likely to die early from the diseases of poverty, the patient was less likely to live long enough to die of cancer—a disease of the middle and later years of life.

When such methodological difficulties have been controlled, the most recent data give no strong evidence of a significantly higher death rate from cancer in psychotic patients than in normals. An excellent summary of these data, from Perrin and Pierce (1959), is provided in Table 10-5.

Personality Factors in Cancer. Beliefs about the existence of personality types in whom susceptibility to cancer is unusually high have been reported in the literature for many years. In general these beliefs appear to have been based upon informal observation of cancer patients by the attending physician. Such beliefs have included the notion that grief or disappointment could act as catalysts for a cancerous process in the body. This view, apparently shared by many writers in the eighteenth and nineteenth centuries, has persisted in the form of a hypothesis that depression is carcinogenic. Freud (1905) claimed to have seen this relationship in several of his patients, but reports no quantitative data beyond citing seven particular cases. A somewhat more systematic study was described by Greene (1954), and further work has been done by Greene, Young, and Swisher (1956). In these investigations, patients suffering from lymphomas and leukemias were interviewed to obtain data regarding the psychological events that had immediately preceded onset or recognition of the disease. In a group of 20 males, it was re-

TABLE 10-5 Ratios of Cancer Incidence in Psychotic Patients to Cancer Incidence in Control Population

Commissioners in Lunacy	$2.98/1.39 = 2.14$
Copeman & Greenwood	$1.58/1.34 = 1.18$
Ehrentheil	$46/33.6 = 1.37$
Lord & McGrath	$3.1/1.8 = 1.72$
Opsahl (Age 60–70)	$6.39/5.20 = 1.23$
Peller (White patients)	$125/150.2 = .83$
Rudolph & Ashby (males 1907–13)	$.588/.428 = 1.37$
Scheflen ("Endogenous" psychoses)	$4.4/3.8 = 1.16$

SOURCE: *Perrin and Pierce (1959).*

ported that most cases of the disease developed while the patient was trying to adjust to a loss of emotional support. Loss of emotional support was rather loosely defined and included not only such obvious events as loss of a near relative, but also a change of school, and so forth. In other cases a different kind of stress was detected in the immediate past of the patient. However, the most recent conclusions derived by the authors were that "one of the multiple conditions determining the development of lymphoma and leukemia in adults may be a separation from a key object or goal with ensuing depression."

Combining the notion that psychological stress may precipitate cancer in a predisposed patient with the notion that such predisposition is correlated with a certain kind of personality, Evans (1926) examined 100 cancerous patients drawn from a larger population of neurotic patients. She concluded that these patients were extraverts and had lost hope following the loss of some important relationship. Loss of hope was presumed to have precipitated the cancer.

Quantification of personality variables has been comparatively rare in research into the psychological antecedents of cancer. In the few studies that have used statistical comparison of such measures, no striking significances have emerged. Thus a study by Stephenson and Grace (1954) produced only 5 significant differences between women suffering from cancer of the cervix and women suffering from cancer at some other site. As they tested at least 25 comparisons, the few significances that were obtained must be regarded with caution. Not surprisingly however, these few related to difficulties regarding sexual intercourse. Shrifte (1962) failed to find a predicted difference in general emotional tension between patients who had been able to recover from cancer following treatment and those who did not recover. In spite of this, she remarks upon the possibility that poor host resistance to cancer is related to general vitality and energy in daily life. Passivity,

she claims, is a good prognostic factor. Unfortunately, these conclusions are obtained from post hoc inspection of the data, and the data themselves are derived from projective measurement of unknown validity.

Lung Cancer, Smoking, and Personality. Few impartial observers doubt that smoking causes lung cancer. The evidence is too convincing to deny or distort. Insofar as there may be psychological determinants of smoking, then these may also be coincidental determinants of lung cancer. A very thorough study conducted by Kissen (1962) reports that in a population of 212 males found to have lung cancer, there was a significantly higher incidence of peptic ulcer than in a control group of noncancerous males or in a comparison group of 47 males suffering from other psychosomatic disorders. In brief, there is a consistent correlation in his data between smoking, peptic ulcer, and lung cancer. An additional feature of the results was that lung cancer patients also have a more frequent history of psychosomatic complaints in general than did the normal controls. These normal controls were not selected for histories of good health; they were a group of men who had been referred for possible diagnosis of lung cancer but had been found free of it.

These data raise the possibility that heavy smoking is found in people who are under continual psychological stress. Thus we might expect to find a higher incidence of stress disorders among smokers than among nonsmokers. However, since smoking is directly carcinogenic, the high incidence of lung cancer in smokers does not lead us to regard lung cancer as psychosomatic. It is not produced by a bodily reaction to stress, and it may occur in a heavy smoker where the latter is not smoking in response to stress. McArthur, Waldron, and Dickinson (1958) have studied the personality correlates of smoking and report that heavy smoking is determined by a variety of influences, with anxiety reduction being only one of many factors. In fact, the general tenor of the data suggests that the heavy smoker is likely to be overtly unemotional and self-controlled rather than visibly tense and stressed. Nonsmoking was found to be associated with an emphasis upon middle-class morality and conventional career striving.

All in all, we may conclude there is no reason to suppose that heavy smokers are under more stress than nonsmokers, and thus the relation between smoking and cancer does not rest upon the assumption that cancer is in any way a consequence of the smoker's other psychological stresses.

Methodological Problems. At the present time research in this area has been much less thorough than could be desired. Unfortunately the methodological weaknesses are of the more obvious varieties. Cancer sites are rarely identified; few studies have used any kind of control group at all; undefined interviews and casual observation have been used in lieu of quantifiable measures; statistical treatment of data has been often lacking; and finally, there has been little attempt to distinguish between the reaction of the patient to the trauma of having discovered that he has cancer and any presumed premorbid personality characteristics. Nobody could be surprised, for example, to find that cancer patients are depressed, unmotivated, and tending to withdraw from the world. We should be very cautious indeed before concluding, from the data currently available, that depression catalyzes cancer.

Summary. The organic processes which lead cells to multiply malignantly are not yet understood by pathologists. Methods for arresting or preventing this are few and largely empirical. It is obviously possible that emotional stress may deplete the power of the body to resist any disease activity. At this time there is absolutely no convincing evidence that cancer patients have suffered more premorbid stress than non-cancer patients, or that psychological therapies are of any value in the treatment of cancer.

Tuberculosis

Tuberculosis, especially pulmonary tuberculosis, seems to have possessed an unusual fascination for writers[1] as well as psychologists for many years. As a disease, tuberculosis has certain psychological aspects that may be of special importance. The course of the disease is often protracted, treatment has generally depended upon long periods of relative inactivity in a hospital, and many of the patients have been comparatively young. As Christian (1953) points out, despite the recent developments in chemotherapy, antibiotic treatment, and surgery, the treatment of tuberculosis is still based upon a regimen of rest, diet, and climate. For most patients, he comments, "Tuberculosis remains essentially a disease of long duration needing careful management for years" (p. 126).

Fatigue is sufficiently important in the aggravation of the disease that any situation which is likely to lead to stress or overactivity will represent a threat to the cure of the patient. By the same token, easy fatigability is a feature of the disease. We should not be surprised to find that patients who are finally diagnosed as tuberculous have been living for some time under conditions likely to impair their self-sufficiency. We should also expect to find that life stresses worsen the disease to the point where it becomes diagnosable and thus that hospitalization frequently occurs shortly after a period of psychological distress.

Long periods of hospitalization are likely to produce certain kinds of change in life adjustment. Planning for posttreatment goals, such as a career, marriage, and so on, may have to be suspended because of the

[1] Examples are found in Thomas Mann's novel *The Magic Mountain*, W. Somerset Maugham's short story *The Sanatorium*, Puccini's opera *La Bohème*, etc.

total uncertainty as to when action about them may be possible. Under these circumstances, the patient may focus his interests entirely upon his life and activities in the sanatorium. To a spectator this may seem like a pathological narrowing of interest, but in fact it may be simply the same phenomenon that is found in hospitalized psychiatric patients, prisoners of war, and any other group who are confined for indefinite periods and permitted only rather limited activities. To attribute this behavior to the disease process itself would be unwise.

Many patients find themselves unable to tolerate a lengthy sojourn in hospital and leave against medical advice. Lewis, Lorenz, and Calden (1955) estimated that the rate of irregular discharge from tuberculosis hospitals runs around 50 per cent. Irregular discharges here refer to those "against medical advice" (AMA), absence without official leave (AWOL), and disciplinary discharges. Subsequent reports show a death rate among the irregular dischargees of over twice that for the patients who remain in hospital for a full course of treatment. Personality factors appear to play a large part in determining whether or not a patient leaves a sanatorium irregularly. Psychologists have been interested in discovering these factors in the hope of devising ways in which such discharges can be anticipated and prevented.

Predisposing Personality Characteristics. Once again we find that many writers have speculated that dependency and conflicts relating to it are precipitants of tuberculosis. Among many other studies we may consider that reported by Muldoon (1957). He administered psychological tests to four groups of patients, tuberculous and nontuberculous, subdivided into those who had been hospitalized for less than 3 months versus those who had been in hospital for 11 months or more. The main measures used were the MMPI and the California F Scale (a test believed to measure rigidity of personality). From the MMPI, a dependency score was computed which differed significantly between the tuberculous and the nontuber-

culous. Mean dependency scores for tubercular patients who had been hospitalized for a long time were higher (although not significantly so) than for those who had been in hospital less than 3 months.

At first sight this seems to suggest that dependency is a trait which predates the onset of tuberculosis. However, we must consider the fact that the tubercular patient in this study was much freer to leave the hospital AMA than the controls—who were severely crippled—were. Consequently we might expect that dependent patients would be likely to remain in hospital while independent ones among the tuberculous group would leave. Since the handicaps of the controls were severe, such patients would be likely to remain in hospital a long time, whether they were dependent or not.

Considerations such as these make it extremely difficult to conclude anything about the effect of hospitalization upon dependency, because the latter may determine the former in tuberculous patients. As in the case of cancer, we have no solid data to substantiate that there is any specific emotional problem determining susceptibility to tuberculosis. The matter must be regarded as unresolved.

Personality and Hospital Course. A thorough investigation of the problem of irregular discharge has been provided by Lewis et al. (1955). Exhaustive study of the personality factors, environmental pressures, and demographic characteristics of patients who seek irregular discharge versus those who remain in hospital for the full course of treatment led them to conclude that the following factors were important. Patients seeking irregular discharge were:

1. Emotionally isolated patients or patients whose personal attachments were firmly fixed on figures outside the hospital
2. Patients who have specific developmental adjustment problems which are reactivated in relation to hospital personnel (see below)
3. Impulsive patients

These workers felt that particular psychological importance is attached to the sequence of events through which a patient goes in the routine course of hospital treatment. Their conceptualization of this is as follows:

Early in hospitalization, patients are forced to accept complete bed rest. This, in effect, enforces a regression to an "infantile" stage. As their condition improves, they are allowed to get up and circulate at greater and greater distances from their bed and from their "ward family." Still later in hospitalization their freedom of activity is such that they behave like adolescents. The role played by the ward personnel and the hospital staff changes with the "growing up" of the patient. For a time the patient is dependent upon doctor and nurse as upon father and mother. Later he is allowed to function more and more independently. Still later he makes his own judgments (sometimes rebelliously), and finally, on recovery (with "parental" medical approval) he leaves the support and guidance of the Hospital family. (Lewis et al., 1955, p. 279.)

SUMMARY

Most of the caveats that we mentioned in our discussion of cancer apply with equal force to the work on tuberculosis. No clear interpretation has yet been offered of the way in which psychological variables may play a part in this disease, if indeed they play any significant part at all. We are once again compelled to conclude, at this juncture, that the most parsimonious construction of the evidence is that stressors may increase the probability of any disease occurring in the human body. We do not have any reason to suppose that the type of psychological stress involved is related to the type of disease that develops.

Where there is evidence, as in the case of the traditional group of psychosomatic disorders, that the disease can be established as a learned response, there is great reason for enthusiasm in going forward with psychological research. A thorough understanding of the processes by which autonomic responses come under stimulus control seems to be our most desirable goal in this work.

SUGGESTED READINGS

1. Alexander, F., & French, T. M. *Studies in psychosomatic medicine.* New York: Ronald, 1948. An interesting illustration of the application of psychoanalytic speculation to the problems of psychosomatics.
2. Gellhorn, E., & Loofbourrow, G. N. *Emotions and emotional disorders.* New York: Hoeber-Harper, 1963. Part V of this text covers the biological aspects of hypertension, peptic ulcer, and other psychosomatic disturbances.

REFERENCES

Ader, R., Beels, C. C., & Tatum, R. Blood pepsinogen and gastric erosions in the rat. *Psychosom. Med.,* 1960, **22,** 1–12.

Alexander, F. The influence of psychologic factors upon gastrointestinal disturbances: general principles, objectives and preliminary results. *Psychoanal. Quart.,* 1934, **3,** 501–539.

Alexander, F. Emotional factors in essential hypertension. *Psychosom. Med.,* 1939, **1,** 153–216. (a)

Alexander, F. Psychoanalytic study of a case of essential hypertension. *Psychosom. Med.,* 1939, **1,** 139–152. (b)

Alexander, F. *Psychosomatic medicine.* New York: Norton, 1950.

Brady, J. V. Ulcers in executive monkeys. *Scientific Amer.,* October, 1958, **199,** 95–100.

Brady, J. V., Porter, R. W., Conrad, D. G., & Mason, J. W. Avoidance behavior and the development of gastroduodenal ulcers. *J. exp. Anal. Behav.,* 1958, **1,** 69–72.

Christian, H. A. (Ed.) *The Oxford medicine.* Vol. VIII. *Medical treatment of disease.* Fair Lawn, N.J.: Oxford, 1953.

Conger, J. J., Sawrey, W. L., & Turrell, E. S.

The role of social experience in the production of gastric ulcers in hooded rats placed in a conflict situation. *J. abnorm. soc. Psychol.*, 1958, **57**, 214–220.

Deutsch, F. Psychanalyse und organkrankhester. *Internat. Ztschr. f. Psychoanal.*, 1922, **8**, 290.

Dragstedt, L. R. A concept of the etiology of gastric and duodenal ulcer. *Amer. J. Roentgenol.*, 1956, **75**, 219–229.

Dunbar, F. *Psychosomatic diagnoses.* New York: Hoeber-Harper, 1943.

Evans, E. *A psychological study of cancer.* New York: Dodd, Mead, 1926.

Fenichel, O. *The psychoanalytic theory of neurosis.* New York: Norton, 1945.

Fitzelle, G. T. Personality factors and certain attitudes toward child-rearing among parents of asthmatic children. *Psychosom. Med.*, 1959, **21**, 208–217.

Flarsheim, A. Ego mechanisms in three pulmonary tuberculosis patients. *Psychosom. Med.*, 1958, **20**, 475–483.

Freund, W. A. Naturgeschichte der krebskiankheit nach klinisches ehrfaheunger. *Ztschs. Kreboforsch.*, 1905, **3**.

Gantt, W. H. *The origin and development of behavior disorders in dogs.* Psychosomatic Medicine Monographs. New York: Hoeber-Harper, 1947.

Garma, A. On the pathogenesis of peptic ulcer. *Int. J. Psycho-Anal.*, 1950, **31**, 53–72.

Gellhorn, E. *Autonomic imbalance and the hypothalamus.* Minneapolis: Univer. of Minneapolis Press, 1957.

Gellhorn, E., & Loofbourrow, G. N. *Emotions and emotional disorders.* New York: Hoeber-Harper, 1963.

Gerard, R. W. What is memory. *Scientific Amer.*, September, 1953, **189**, 118–126.

Grace, W. J., & Graham, D. T. Relationship of specific attitudes and emotions to certain bodily diseases. *Psychosom. Med.*, 1952, **14**, 243–251.

Graham, D. T. Some research on psychophysiologic specificity and its relation to psychosomatic disease. In R. Roessler & N. S. Greenfield (Eds.), *Physiological correlates of psychological disorder.* Madison: Univer. of Wisconsin Press, 1962.

Graham, D. T., Stern, J. A., & Winokur, G. Experimental investigation of the specificity of attitude hypothesis in psychosomatic disease. *Psychosom. Med.*, 1958, **20**, 446–457.

Greene, W. A. Psychological factors and reticuloendothelial disease: I. Preliminary observations on a group of males with lymphomas and leukemias. *Psychosom. Med.*, 1954, **16**, 220–230.

Greene, W. A., Young, L. E., & Swisher, S. N. Psychological factors and reticuloendothelial disease: II. Observations on a group of women with lymphomas and leukemias. *Psychosom. Med.*, 1956, **18**, 284–303.

Hokanson, J. E., & Burgess, M. The effects of three types of aggression on vascular processes. *J. abnorm. soc. Psychol.*, 1962, **65**, 232–237.

Hokanson, J. E., & Shetler, S. The effect of overt aggression on physiological tension level. *J. abnorm. soc. Psychol.*, 1961, **63**, 446–448.

Kissen, D. M. A scientific approach to clinical research in psychosomatic medicine. *Psychosom. Med.*, 1960, **22**, 118–126.

Kissen, D. M. Relationships between primary lung cancer and peptic ulcer in males. *Psychosom. Med.*, 1962, **24**, 133–147.

Lewis, W. C., Lorenz, T. H., & Calden, G. Irregular discharge from tuberculosis hospitals: a major unsolved problem. *Psychosom. Med.*, 1955, **17**, 276–290.

Liddell, H. S. The influence of experimental neuroses on the respiratory function. In H. A. Abramson (Ed.), *Somatic and psychiatric treatment of asthma.* Baltimore: Williams & Wilkins, 1951.

Lipton, E. L., Steinschneider, A., & Richmond, J. B. Autonomic function in the neonate: II. Physiologic effects of motor restraint. *Psychosom. Med.*, 1960, **22**, 57–65.

Lipton, E. L., Steinschneider, A., & Richmond, J. B. Autonomic function in the neonate: III. Methodological considerations. *Psychosom. Med.*, 1961, **23**, 461–471. (a)

Lipton, E. L., Steinschneider, A., & Richmond, J. B. Autonomic function in the neonate: IV. Individual differences in cardiac reactivity. *Psychosom. Med.*, 1961, **23**, 472–484. (b)

Little, Sue W., & Cohen, L. D. Goal setting behavior of asthmatic children and of their mothers for them. *J. Pers.*, 1951, **19**, 376–389.

McArthur, C., Waldron, Ellen, & Dickinson, J. The psychology of smoking. *J. abnorm. soc. Psychol.*, 1958, **56**, 267–275.

Malmo, R. B., & Shagass, C. Studies of blood pressure in psychiatric patients under stress. *Psychosom. Med.*, 1952, **14**, 82–93.

Masserman, J. H., & Pechtel, C. Conflict engendered neurotic and psychotic behavior in monkeys. *J. nerv. ment. Dis.*, 1953, **118**, 408–411.

Metcalfe, M. Demonstration of a psychosomatic relationship. *Brit. J. med. Psychol.*, 1956, **29**, 63–66.

Miminoshvili, D. I. Experimental neurosis in monkeys. In I. Rurkin (Ed.), *Theoretical and practical problems of medicine and biology in experiments on monkeys.* New York: Pergamon Press, 1960.

Mirsky, I. A. Physiologic, psychologic and social determinants in the etiology of duodenal ulcer. *Amer. J. digest. Dis.*, 1958, **3**, 285–314.

Mittelmann, B., & Wolff, H. G. Emotions and gastroduodenal function. *Psychosom. Med.*, 1942, **4**, 5–61.

Muldoon, J. F. Some psychological concomitants of tuberculosis and hospitalization. *Psychosom. Med.*, 1957, **19**, 307–314.

Neuhaus, E. C. A personality study of asthmatic and cardiac children. *Psychosom. Med.*, 1958, **20**, 181–186.

Ottenberg, P., Stein, M., Lewis, J., & Hamilton, C. Learned asthma in the guinea pig. *Psychosom. Med.*, 1958, **20**, 395–400.

Perrin, G. M., & Pierce, I. R. Psychosomatic aspects of cancer: a review. *Psychosom. Med.*, 1959, **21**, 397–404.

Richmond, J. B., Lipton, E. L., & Steinschneider, A. Autonomic function in the neonate: V. Individual homeostatic capacity in cardiac response. *Psychosom. Med.*, 1962, **24**, 66–74.

Saul, L. J. Hostility in cases of essential hypertension. *Psychosom. Med.*, 1939, **1**, 153–216.

Saul, L. J., & Bernstein, C. The emotional setting of some attacks of urticaria. *Psychosom. Med.*, 1941, **3**, 351–369.

Sawrey, W. L., Conger, J. J., & Turrell, E. S. An experimental investigation of the role of psychological factors in the production of gastric ulcers in the rat. *J. comp. physiol. Psychol.*, 1956, **49**, 457–461.

Sawrey, W. L., & Weisz, J. D. An experimental method of producing gastric ulcers. *J. comp. physiol. Psychol.*, 1956, **49**, 269–270.

Schunk, J. Emotionale faktoren in der pathogenese der essentiellen hypertonie. *Z. klin. Med.*, 1954, **152**, 251–280.

Scodel, A. Passivity in a class of peptic ulcer patients. *Psychol. Monogr.*, 1953, **10** (Whole No. 360).

Seitz, P. F. D. Infantile experience and adult behavior in animal subjects: II. Age of separation from the mother and adult behavior in the cat. *Psychosom. Med.*, 1959, **21**, 353–378.

Shrifte, M. L. Toward identification of a psychological variable in host resistance to cancer. *Psychosom. Med.*, 1962, **24**, 390–397.

Stein, M., Schiavi, R. C., Ottenberg, P., & Hamilton, C. The mechanical properties of the lungs in experimental asthma in the guinea pig. *J. Allergy*, 1961, **32**, 8–16.

Stephenson, J. H., & Grace, W. J. Life stress and cancer of the cervix. *Psychosom. Med.*, 1954, **16**, 287–294.

Sternbach, R. A. Correlates of differences in

time to recover from startle. *Psychosom. Med.,* 1960, **22**, 143–148.

Titchener, J. L., Riskin, J., & Emerson, R. The family in psychosomatic process. *Psychosom. Med.,* 1960, **22**, 127–142.

Weiner, H., Thaler, Margaret, Reiser, M. F., & Mirsky, I. A. Etiology of duodenal ulcer: I. Relation of specific psychological characteristics to rate of gastric secretion. *Psychosom. Med.,* 1957, **19**, 1–10.

Wittkower, E. D., & White, K. L. Psycho-physiologic aspects of respiratory disorders. In S. Arieti (Ed.), *American handbook of psychiatry.* New York: Basic Books, 1959.

Wolff, H. G. Life situations, emotions and bodily disease. In M. L. Reymert (Ed.), *Feelings and emotions.* New York: McGraw-Hill, 1950.

11 PSYCHOPATHOLOGY WITH BRAIN PATHOLOGY

When damage occurs to the brain, or to the nervous system generally, it is sometimes accompanied by behavioral changes. These changes may resemble those found in other kinds of psychopathology, or they may be relatively specific to the brain-injured condition. Damage may arise from several sources.

GENERAL EFFECTS OF BRAIN DAMAGE

Degenerative and Age-related Changes

With the onset of the aging process many changes occur that affect the functioning of the central nervous system. Some of these involve the thickening of arterial walls and the consequent reduction in blood supply to the nervous tissue. Other changes probably occur, but much remains to be understood about them. Before the onset of aging some patients develop degenerative diseases. Amongst the best known of these are *Alzheimer's disease* and *Pick's Disease*.

In Alzheimer's disease (first described by Alzheimer in 1906), the patient progresses from a state of intellectual deterioration that includes disturbances of perception and reasoning, loss of memory for recent events, and some aphasic difficulties. From this initial stage his behavior becomes less goal-directed, and speech difficulties increase. Finally the patient deteriorates to a relatively primitive condition of existence with very limited speech and little responsiveness to the environment.

Alzheimer's disease has been regarded as a *presenile* disorder, because the age of onset is usually in the period before senescence. While it is still categorized in this way, there have been some recent suggestions that the fundamental neuropathology may be found in younger people. This neuropathology includes the development of atypical cell structures, especially in the ganglion cells of the cortex. The changes caused by the disease are quite similar to many changes observed in the aged. Alzheimer's disease is statistically infrequent and of relatively little interest to students of psychopathology. It is described here chiefly as an illustration of a degenerative process.

Senile brain disease is a term used to classify the elderly patient who develops a psychotic pattern of behavior in later life. It is intended as a distinctly different descriptive category from that of normal senility; the distinction implies the development of senile deterioration to an extent exceeding that found normally and requiring institutional care. While the assumption is that these psychotic changes are the consequence of a brain syndrome, their general content is not unlike that found in normal senility. The distinction is thus a matter of degree.

Specifically, the category of senile brain disease includes roughly one-tenth of all new admissions to mental institutions. These admissions typically occur from the age of sixty onward. Women are more often admitted with this diagnosis than are men. There is no precise picture of the behaviors of the senile psychotic. Usually the psychopathology represents an extreme development of the person's ordinary behavior tendencies, coupled with gross deterioration of personal habits (toilet and grooming), suspiciousness, disorientation, lapses of memory, and poor judgment.

These changes are often quite gradual and may not be noticed for some time, even by the patient's family and close friends. Memory defects of an apparently minor kind are common early signs, together with some unpredictability and impulsiveness of behavior. As shown in Example 11-1, some male patients develop impulsive pathological sexual interests involving children, and such behavior may be the first event that attracts attention to their condition.

Very similar patterns of psychopathology are found in patients suffering from *cerebroarteriosclerosis,* a disorder associated with the hardening of cerebral blood vessels. Differential diagnosis between this condition and senile psychosis may be difficult or impossible in many cases.

Degenerative Changes and Compensatory Patterns

The degenerative and slowly developing cerebral disorders are of some interest to the psychopathologist because they offer an opportunity to study the processes of compensation that may develop in the patient's behavioral repertoire. Where a difficulty—such as memory loss—comes on gradually, the patient may begin to develop ways of coping with its consequences. Thus he may begin to "invent" memories of events rather than admit that he cannot remember. Where the invention is a more or less total fabrication, the process is known as *confabulation.* Alternatively, he may develop ways in which he can get someone else to supply the missing description or provide him with a cue that will aid his own recall. Or the patient may say, "I don't want to talk about that," as if the memory were distasteful to him—a more acceptable response than admission of memory loss.

Complex tasks and experiences are often threatening to the patient who is undergoing deterioration, and he may avoid them entirely. Or he may be willing to accept lower levels of his own performance than he would previously have been satisfied with.

EXAMPLE 11-1
Behavior Deterioration with Degenerative Changes due to Aging

The patient was a male, sixty-seven years of age, serving a sentence in prison for a sexual assault on a minor girl. His prior history was uneventful. He was a widower his wife having died some nine years previously, and he had been living with his married daughter and her family. Two years previously he had retired from his occupation as engineman in a coal mine and had had no occupation since. Inquiry showed that during the last two years of his employment his performance on the job—a skilled one—had begun to deteriorate to the point that the safety of others was involved. Consequently his supervisor had arranged to assign him to the care of the machinery rather than the operation of it, and in this way had been able to keep him employed until his retirement came due.

The patient had been arrested for molesting a neighborhood child, doing so more or less in public view. At the time of his conviction his behavior did not seem to have been sufficiently bizarre to attract the attention of the court, and hence he was sentenced to a term of imprisonment. His deterioration in the prison was marked. On interview he repeated "Stop that shouting!" at spasmodic intervals, paying no attention to the examiner but responding as if to hallucinatory stimuli. His personal grooming was very poor, and it was necessary to "point" the patient physically toward the door of a room before he could find his way out of it. He had only a scattered recollection of the circumstances of his arrest—or of any of the events of his life during the latter four or five years.

The patient deteriorated further in the prison and was subsequently transferred to a psychiatric hospital.

In a study of the performance of patients suffering from cerebro-arteriosclerosis, Maher and Martin (1954) asked them to assemble small colored plastic pieces into designs (the Lowenfeld Mosaic Test). This kind of task may elicit many levels of response. Individuals of superior intelligence commonly make complicated multicolored abstract designs, while lower levels of performance may include assembling pieces of the same shape into one group, or putting a piece next to another to form a simple shape such as a straight line or circle. Maher and Martin reported that the cerebro-arteriosclerotic group produced a significantly larger number of the latter kind of performance than did controls matched with them for age and resident with them in a home for the aged.

Focused Injuries

The kinds of neuropathology described in the preceding paragraphs have been diffuse, involving widely spread areas of the brain.

A second general group of brain-damaged patients includes those who have suffered a specific and localized disturbance of brain tissue. Sources of such disturbances include external traumata—such as blows to the head and gunshot wounds—or internal foci —such as those produced by local tumors, local vascular accidents (the rupture of a cerebral blood vessel with concomitant damage to surrounding areas), or "strokes." In these disorders the site of the damage may affect the kinds of psychopathology exhibited by the patient, and indeed the behavioral consequences are frequently used in the attempt to diagnose the probable site of the lesion.

Knowledge of the functions of various brain areas has come from many sources: from animal studies, from studies of brain damage in humans, and from brain stimulation. Any attempt to summarize the major areas and their functions will suffer from oversimplification, but with this caution we shall present some of the most reliable generalizations.

Figure 11-1 provides a general view of the human brain with the major topographical areas marked.

The Frontal Lobes. The functions of the frontal lobes are far from clear at the present time, and a wide variety of hypotheses has been advanced to account for their functions. As will be seen in the discussion of psychosurgery in the final chapter of this book, two widely held beliefs are that the frontal cortex exercises some inhibitory function upon impulsive activity and that the experience of acute emotion is dependent upon its being intact. Neither of these hypotheses can be accepted unequivocally; the frontal areas of the cortex remain to a large extent a mystery.

The Temporal Lobes. The mediation of verbal behavior appears to be significantly dependent upon the integrity of the temporal lobe; more specifically, it is dependent upon the intactness of the temporal area of the dominant hemisphere. In the ordinary right-handed person, the dominant hemisphere is, of course, the left. Verbal and speech behavior generally seem to be impaired in patients where there is evidence of damage to, or of focal epilepsy in, the left temporal lobe (Meyer & Jones, 1957).

Penfield and Rasmussen (1950) report that where there is evidence of malfunctioning of the temporal lobe, there is likely to be loss of stored memory traces. However, as Meyer (1961) points out, subsequent evidence indicates that the recall of past events is not adversely affected by damage to this area, but that the recording of present events is impaired—and hence they are difficult to recall on later testing. This deficit in the "recording" of contemporary input is seemingly only true when the damage includes both hemispheres. Where the damage is confined to one hemisphere, the effects appear to be mainly an impairment in the registration of verbal material presented audibly, but with no impairment in material presented visually (Quadfasel & Pruyser, 1955).

The Parietal Lobes. In the parietal areas of the cortex are found both motor and sensory-somatic functions. Stimulation of the motor areas is accompanied by motor responses by the muscle groups of the body, while stimulation of the somatic areas produces reports of bodily sensations. From

Figure 11-1. The lobes of the cerebral cortex. (Morgan, 1961.)

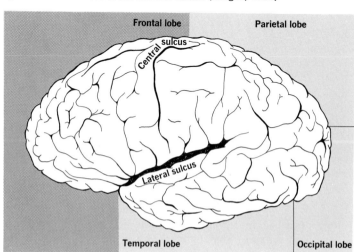

this we would expect that brain damage to the parietal areas would produce deficits in sensory input from the skin surface—such as the ability to detect fine-point or two-point stimulation. The results of investigations of this hypothesis have been somewhat equivocal also. Several investigators have found impairment in judgments of weight, tactile thresholds, etc., as predicted; but others find similar impairments in patients where the brain damage does not involve the parietal lobe.

Where damage to the parietal cortex involves motor areas, the behavioral consequences are more readily seen. For example, the removal of large parts of the motor area may lead to flaccid paralysis, or general lack of motor responsiveness. Because the continuous feedback of input from the body and its position is important to the maintenance of orientation in space, we shall not be surprised to find that damage to the parietal areas is often accompanied by confusion in spatial orientation. Likewise, the ability to initiate a motor performance—especially a skilled performance—is impaired in some cases of parietal injury.

The Occipital Lobes. The occipital lobe in the posterior cortex is primarily concerned with the mediation of vision and with some aspects of visual memory. Widespread damage to the occipital cortex may produce blindness, while damage to some of the occipital association areas is accompanied by difficulties with the recollection of visually recorded events. Spatial judgment is also impaired where vision is the main cue.

The Parietal-Occipital-Temporal Association Areas. The classic divisions between the four lobes of the cortex are not entirely congruent with the distribution of function that is found across brain areas. Some neuropsychologists identify the parietal-occipital-temporal association area as a functional unit. This area is concerned with the storage and recognition of sensory input from all the major sense modalities. When points on this area are stimulated electrically, the patient frequently reports the experience of a familiar "memory" in image form. Damage to this area may produce any of a very wide range of defects of recognition of familiar objects or words, including the disruptions of language known as the *aphasias*. Patients suffering from epilepsy where the focus is in this area may report temporary lapses of consciousness, or may find that their seizure is heralded by an advanced sensation similar to those produced by the electrical stimulation experiments.

Bearing these general comments in mind, we can see that the consequences of a focused injury to the brain may include a wide variety of specific behavioral patterns. There is, therefore, no standard picture of the psychopathology following on localized injuries. Each one may differ considerably from the next.

The Localization of Focused Injuries

With the exception of surgical injury and injuries produced by penetrating external objects, the accurate localization of a focused internal lesion is quite difficult. It is not uncommon, for example, for an injury that is localized in one hemisphere to produce EEG abnormalcies in both hemispheres —or even, on occasion, in the contralateral hemisphere only. Damage resulting from concussive blows to the head may produce temporary disturbances of the EEG pattern at other parts of the cortex.

The consequences of a localized injury may fade in time, or by the same token, some of the consequences may be quite delayed. There is some reason to believe that under appropriate circumstances the functions of a damaged area in the dominant hemisphere may be assumed by the non-dominant area. The data supporting this inference suggest that such a take-over is more likely to occur in younger patients than in older. All in all, the development of

confident conclusions about the effects of localized brain injury in the human subject is still a long way ahead.

Brain Injury and Learning

Bearing in mind that the consequences of brain injury will depend in large part upon the site and nature of the injury, we may now turn to the study of the effects of injury upon learning. There has been a vast number of investigations of the effects of particular kinds of brain lesion upon animal learning. A thorough review of their findings is beyond the scope of the present chapter. However, certain general principles may be discerned from these studies, and we shall present them here.

Where the tissue destroyed is localized in a sensory association area, there is evidence that the retention of learned material mediated by that area is impaired. Thus, for example, Stewart and Ades (1951) and Meyer, Isaac, and Maher (1958) have reported that when a response is conditioned to a particular kind of sensory cue, auditory or visual, then destruction of the auditory or visual association areas of the cortex will be followed by loss of the response.

Parallel findings with human subjects have been reported. Morrell (1956) found that patients with symptoms indicating a sharply localized temporal lobe pathology (i.e., localized in the auditory areas) were impaired in the ability to form a conditioned alpha response to a sound stimulus. Responses to a tactile stimulus were unimpaired. Meyer (1956, 1959) reports similar findings but notes that the extent of impairment depends upon whether or not the damage is located in the dominant hemisphere. Thus, patients who had a temporal lobectomy on the dominant side revealed disruption of auditory learning ability, whereas those in whom the operation had been performed on the nondominant side showed no learning loss.

Evidence exists to suggest that many injuries produce only temporary effects upon learning and that after a sufficient interval, subcortical areas may take over the function of a cortical area which has been destroyed. Whether or not this will happen is also a function of the complexity of the performance that is involved. This was the case in the Stewart and Ades (1951) and Meyer et al. (1958) studies mentioned above.

Brain Damage and Intelligence

Perhaps the most voluminous research on brain damage effects in humans has been concerned with possible deficits in intelligence. For a variety of reasons it is difficult to conduct this research except in a *post facto* situation—measuring the intelligence of patients known to have suffered brain damage. The methodological problems involved in this kind of work are enormous. They have been discussed elsewhere in some detail (Maher, 1963), but we may profitably summarize them here.

The diagnosis of brain damage and the localization of the damage often depend upon inference from indirect measures. Thus the use of EEG localization, the examination of reflexes, and inference from the patient's general pattern of complaint all are common. An ideal diagnosis would be based upon direct observation of the injury, which is rarely possible except in the case of penetrating wounds to the head. Lacking this kind of data, the investigator might confirm the diagnosis of brain damage by autopsy—a difficult condition to achieve and one involving long delays between the measurement of intelligence and the subsequent confirmation of the diagnosis. Where the injury has been induced by surgery, localization is possible—as in the case of surgical extirpation of tumors, etc. Where the surgery was performed for psychological reasons (see Chapter 17), then we are faced with the problem that the subject was behaving in a deviant manner before the operation, and it is difficult to apply results from such research to the normal population.

There are few studies that have successfully coped with these difficulties. However, the work of Weinstein and Teuber (1957) is a good example of such an effort. They used a population of military patients who had taken a general measure of intelligence before suffering penetrating head wounds. Ten years after the injury, the test was administered again, and differences between this performance and the preinjury performance were noted. A control group who had suffered peripheral nerve injuries was also studied. Both groups had the same preinjury test scores; comparison of the postinjury scores showed some striking deficits in intelligence concomitant with the development of aphasia. However, even when aphasics were excluded from the comparison, patients with left-hemisphere injuries in the parietal or temporal areas showed deficit.

Another study conducted under well-controlled conditions has been reported by Williams, Lubin, and Gieseking (1959). Their procedure was much the same as Weinstein and Teuber's. Military subjects were used who had undergone intelligence testing upon entering the service and had subsequently suffered damage to the brain. These subjects had diffuse rather than focal damage, and the extent of brain tissue involved varied considerably in each subject. Controls were a group of hospitalized non-brain-damaged soldier patients and a second group of non-hospitalized soldiers. In the comparison of preinjury and postinjury test performance, the data indicated that verbal tests were much more affected by brain injury than tests of spatial ability. While these differences were statistically significant, they were too small to constitute a reliable basis for the diagnosis of brain damage in a single case.

Brain Damage and the Abstract Attitude

Among the many consequences that are ascribed to diffuse brain damage, one of the most persistent is the loss of the "abstract attitude." This hypothesis, most elaborately

developed by Goldstein, is presented in more detail in Chapter 14. Its main features are that the patient finds it difficult to maintain a mental set—that is, to continue to concentrate upon a given problem or stimulus while excluding attention to surrounding distraction; to plan ahead; or to make relative judgments which require forming superficially contradictory assessments of the same object (such as that a stick which is longer than one stick can also be shorter than another).

Most of the evidence that brain damage brings this kind of deficiency is clinical—that is to say, it stems from observations of patients under relatively uncontrolled conditions. Nevertheless, these observations have been made so often that the hypothesis must be regarded as a reasonable one. The difficulty in ascribing a general deficit of this kind to a patient suffering from diffuse brain damage is that many of his failures on tasks may be due to the various specific effects of the damage at various points in the brain.

However, there is strong evidence that brain damage of a diffuse kind may be accompanied by deficiencies in the maintenance of attention. Inability to maintain a mental set, or inability to concentrate on some aspects of a total stimulus while ignoring others, may readily be understood if we assume that focused attention is achieved by the active suppression of irrelevant stimulus input. The destruction of the tissue which is involved in the suppression or *inhibition* of input should be expected to have consequences for performance on many different kinds of tasks.

Brain Damage and Inhibition

As we have repeatedly pointed out in various parts of this book, the maintenance of attention can be thought of as the process of inhibiting from consciousness those aspects of a total stimulus environment that are not relevant to the performance of some task at hand. In a general sense, the process

of inhibition can be regarded as damping down the intensity of irrelevant stimuli rather than completely excluding them from awareness. Any task that requires the subject to give careful and selective attention to some parts of a stimulus while ignoring others is especially likely to be impaired when the inhibitory mechanisms are deficient. Tasks of this kind are frequently used to study brain injury. Among them, particular attention has been given to the figure-ground perception task.

In this task the subject is required to detect a picture of a common object that is displayed in a context of distracting surrounding patterns of stimuli. To see the central or *figure* stimulus, it is necessary to ignore the background or *ground* stimuli. A typical figure-ground stimulus is shown in Figure 11-2.

Strauss and Lehtinen (1947) have studied the responses of brain-damaged and normal children to this kind of stimulus. Three groups of subjects were used: brain-injured and retarded children, retarded children not believed to be suffering from brain injury, and normal controls. Stimuli such as those in Figure 11-2 were shown briefly through a tachistoscope and the child was asked to report what he saw. The investigators recorded all responses in which the subject included some reference to the "background" in his report, and they found that

75 per cent of the responses of the brain-injured group were in this category. Of the responses by normals and nondamaged retardates, only 9 and 14 per cent, respectively, included background references.

Extending this kind of investigation to the sense of touch, an analogous study was performed using figures embedded among patterns of dots, all carved in relief on a wooden board. The child explored the contours of the board by touch alone; he was not permitted to inspect it visually. He was then asked to draw what he had perceived, and the responses were scored in terms of the extent to which the background dots were included in the drawing. Here again, the brain-injured group produced many more responses which included the background, often with no tactile perception of the figure at all.

Spivack (1963) has reviewed the work of Strauss and Lehtinen, together with several studies performed since on the same topic. Although some results have been contradictory (notably Coleman, 1960), he concludes:

Research in this area suggests that brain injury rather than retardation produces responses to background or intrusion of background in perception. The question remains open about whether such performance reflects a basic defect in brain injured subjects in the capacity to disregard background or the ten-

Figure 11-2. Tactual-motor test used in figure-ground perception studies. (Strauss & Lehtinen, 1947.)

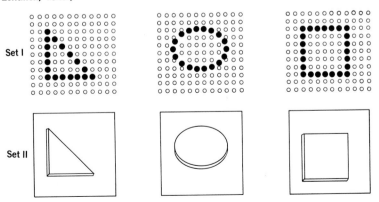

dency for dominant aspects of complex stimuli to intrude upon or dampen out less dominant features, or whether the research techniques have allowed non-perceptual response characteristics to guide performance. (Spivack, 1963, p. 485.)

For obvious reasons, it is difficult to determine how general this kind of inhibitory deficit is in brain damage in humans. To study its effects in terms of localization of injury in particular parts of the brain, we must turn to animal studies. Much of this work on localization has been focused on the functions of the frontal lobes. A particularly scrupulous analysis of the problem of loss of inhibition following frontal lobe ablation has been given by Rosvold and Mishkin (1961). The fundamental technique used in their animal studies has involved the establishment of a response to one of two conditioned stimuli and the inhibition of this response to the other CS. These two responses and their related CSs may be termed excitatory and inhibitory respectively. Following frontal ablation, the excitatory response is often magnified in amplitude, while the inhibitory response disappears, i.e., the animal begins to make the excitatory response to both stimuli. Behaviorally, this may also be described as a failure of a previously learned discrimination. Similar ablations to the parietal areas of dogs do not produce these effects. A summary of the results obtained by several investigators is given in Table 11-1. It will be apparent that disinhibition is almost uniformly reported with frontal ablation, while in two comparisons with parietal ablations, no such effect was observed.

Generalization from animal to human behavior is especially problematic when we are dealing with nervous system phenomena. Thus for the time being, the question of the nonspecific nature of disinhibition following brain injury must remain a matter for continued study.

Brain Damage and Language

Among the many behavioral consequences of injury to the brain are the *aphasias*. The aphasias are disturbances of language and of symbolic functioning generally. In order to understand the many points in communication at which a disruption might occur, let us consider a patient who is given a common object, an apple, and asked to speak its

TABLE 11-1 The Effects of Prefrontal and Parietal Lesions on CR

Reinforcement	Type of CR	Conditioned response observed	Prefrontal ablation		Parietal ablation	Authors
			Excitatory CR	Inhibitory CR		
Food	Instrumental	Lifting of the foreleg	Normal (15)*	Disinhibited (15)	Normal (4)	Brutkowski et al. (1956) Brutkowski (1959) Ławicka (1957) Ławicka (unpublished) Chorzyna (unpublished)
Food	Instrumental	Barking	Normal or enhanced (4)	Disinhibited (4)		Ławicka (1957)
Food	Classical	Salivation	Normal or enhanced (6)	Disinhibited (6)	Normal (4)	Brutkowski (1957)
Water	Instrumental	Lifting of the foreleg	Normal (2)	Disinhibited (2)		Zernicki (in preparation)
Electric shock	Classical	Lifting of the hindleg and breathing	Enhanced (3) Normal (1)	Disinhibited (3) Normal (1)		Brutkowski & Auleytner (in preparation) Ławicka (unpublished)
Acid into the mouth	Classical	Salivation and breathing	Enhanced (3)	Disinhibited (3)		Brutkowski & Auleytner (in preparation)
Electric shock	Instrumental (avoidance)	Lifting of the foreleg	Normal (2)	Normal (1) Disinhibited (1)		Zbrozyna (unpublished)

* The numerals indicate the number of dogs used in a given experiment.
SOURCE: *Rosvold and Mishkin (1961).*

name. In the first place, he might not recognize the object at all—it might appear strange to him. This would be the case if the processes involved in the storage of his recollections of apples were in some way disrupted. Secondly, he might recognize the apple, but be unable to recall the word that goes with it. This would be somewhat analogous to the experience that we sometimes have of seeing a once familiar face but being unable to recall the person's name. Thirdly, he may recognize the object, recall the name, but be unable to recall the movements required to say the name.

All these possible difficulties arise when the task is to speak the name aloud. Parallel difficulties are possible when the task is to recognize the name spoken by someone else, to write the word, or to recognize the word in written form. Where the brain injury causes an inability to produce the required word, it is referred to as an *expressive* aphasia or a motor aphasia. Difficulty in recognizing the word when it is spoken or written by someone else is frequently referred to as a *sensory* aphasia. A variety of subtypes of language and symbolic disturbances includes the following:

Alexia. Inability to understand the written language. The patient may be able to read the word, i.e., say it correctly on sight, but cannot understand its meaning. In many cases he is unable to understand the meaning of words that he writes himself.

Agraphia. Here the patient is unable to write words that he hears, although he is well able to conduct a spoken conversation.

While these are the major varieties of disturbance recognized by psychopathologists, it is clear that a given patient may exhibit more than one, or he may exhibit only a limited version of one.

An excellent account of an aphasic conversation is provided by Laffal (1965) in the following extract. The patient was suffering from aphasia following a stroke that had occurred some six months before this con-

versation took place. It is worth noting that the patient's difficulty is less evident when he is conversing freely, choosing his own words, than when he is required to find the correct specific word in answer to a question.

Pt. Good. All right. And . . . the boys went . . . out there Saturday morning and over there, and over there in the corner there. Saturday morning I gave someone cigarettes, I suppose, over there, corner.

Dr. Could you speak a little louder, Mr. Wilson?

Pt. All right.

Dr. So I can hear you?

Pt. And I gave him something over there.

Dr. Who, who are you talking about?

Pt. Over there, there, over there . . . too, I guess, I gave him something too. God Almighty, and then I gave him something over there. I gave him cheese and everything else, I guess. I gave him something over there. I gave him something over there.

Dr. What did you give him?

Pt. Yes, I know. And I gave him something.

Dr. What did you give him?

Pt. Cookies, chocolate, something else, over there. God Almighty, I gave him something over there in the corner, over there, I gave him something, I . . . over there in the corner over there, once. Once I gave him something that, I gave him something, God damn it, I gave him something, something. I gave him something. And I gave him something, God Almighty. I gave him something too. I gave him something, also. Also I gave him something.

Dr. To whom did you give something? To whom, to whom did you give something?

Pt. There in the corner over there.

Dr. Who was it?

Pt. I. . . .

Dr. Who was it?

Pt. God Almighty, I gave him something. God damn it, I gave him something (*Patient cries.*)

Dr. Take it easy, Mr. Wilson. Relax. You don't have to cry if you can't think of the word.

Pt. All right?

Dr. Take it easy.

Pt. I gave him something, God damn it, I gave him something too. I gave him something . . . I gave him something and ah, and ah,

and ah, and I gave him something. I gave him something, gave him something, over there, corner. God Almighty, I gave him something over there.

(Laffal, 1965, pp. 169–179.)

The patient above was suffering from expressive aphasia. An example of sensory or receptive aphasia is provided by Van Riper (1954), who gives a patient's description of her reactions upon hearing the word "your" spoken:

I mentally heard it but it had no meaning. I felt that it was related to the word "you" but I could not figure out the relationship between the two. I continued to puzzle over this until the speaker had finished his lecture and sat down. . . . More generally when I do not recognize the meaning I do not recognize the sound. The word is a jumble of letters. (Van Riper, 1954, pp. 32–33.)

Receptive aphasia has been described by Diamond, Balvin, and Diamond (1963) as a "perceptual palsy." They argue that the problem may be seen as one of auditory figure-ground perception, with loss of the inhibition necessary to keep the voice of a speaker relatively dominant over the background of surrounding noises in the room. Children with receptive aphasia frequently show other signs of loss of inhibition, being easily distractible and behaviorally impulsive.

Brain Damage and Emotional Responses

We have already seen that attention deficiencies in vision and audition are common accompaniments of diffuse brain injury and that they may reveal themselves in the form of deficits in a wide variety of performances. These deficiencies may be regarded as instances of inhibitory failure—specifically, failure to inhibit external sensory input in appropriate ways. However, sensory input also arises from internal organs, and it is quite reasonable to expect that inhibitory deficiencies might include excessive awareness of visceral input and impairment of the inhibitory mechanisms responsible for damping down the state of visceral arousal generated by emotional stimuli.

Gastaut and Fischer-Williams (1959), for example, describe a partial epilepsy that includes such symptoms as abnormal abdominal sensations, chewing, salivation, deglutition, and strong impulses to urinate or defecate, all accompanied by disorders of attention and concomitant symptoms of anxiety or rage. In the light of this symptom picture, they suggest that the rhinencephalon and diencephalon are involved—structures that are also regarded as crucial in the production of *psychomotor epilepsy*, to be discussed later in this chapter.

Hyperreactivity of the visceral-emotional system may be expected to take the form of excessive outbursts of emotional behavior without any strong emotional stimulus necessarily being present. Diamond, Balvin, and Diamond (1963) cite an instance of this pattern:

Robin, a 15-year-old Negro boy who reads on a fourth grade level, is another difficult behavior problem. His parents are devoted to each other, and were hopeful that their son would be a credit to their race. Yet periodically the boy does outrageous things. His teacher says that Robin is sometimes very good and polite, then all of a sudden he breaks loose. When he was eight his mother sought advice. Robin was reported to have rushed into the school auditorium while a class play was in rehearsal, flipped down all the aisle seats, making a great clatter while he hallooed at the top of his lungs. He became "ugly in mood," fighting and kicking at the teacher. He was diagnosed by the school psychologist as severely emotionally disturbed due to the "over ambition" of his mother. Robin had an undiagnosed illness when he was nine years old. He was rushed to the hospital, had convulsions, ran a high fever and was lethargic for several days. At this time it was learned that he had had repeated seizures up to the age of 4½. The pediatrician had assured his mother that he would outgrow them. He has had no more seizures since then, but periodically becomes involved in some antisocial behavior. He is always most contrite: "I don't

know why I do it, I don't want to. Something just happens." (P. 330–331.)

Emotionally spasmodic behavior of this kind may well be triggered by relatively minor stimuli. Thus situations that we might think of as being merely irritating may produce intense frustration in the patient suffering from this kind of defect. Observations of the intense overreaction of brain-damaged patients to frustrations have been noted for many years. Goldstein (1942) has described what he termed the *catastrophic reaction* on the part of brain-damaged patients who were unable to complete a simple arithmetic problem.

Here is a man with a lesion of the frontal lobe, to whom we present a problem in simple arithmetic. He is unable to solve it. But simply noting and recording the fact that he is unable to perform a simple multiplication would be an exceedingly inadequate account of the patient's reaction. Just looking at him, we can see a great deal more than this arithmetical failure. He looks dazed, changes color, becomes agitated, anxious, starts to fumble, his pulse becomes irregular; a moment before amiable, he is now sullen, evasive, exhibits temper, or even becomes aggressive. It takes some time before it is possible to continue the examination. Because the patient is so disturbed in his whole behavior, we call situations of this kind catastrophic situations. (P. 71.)

Goldstein himself interprets this reaction in terms of the psychological threat that is involved in such incompetence, but regards the reaction as being more immediate and primitive than would be the case with a normal patient. However, he assumes that the magnitude of the reaction is the cumulative consequence of many such experiences of failure, rather than being attributable directly to biological factors. While this frustration experience may be a significant source of the overreaction, we must give due consideration to the possibilities that the brain damage itself has resulted in disinhibition of emotional patterns.

Summary

We have seen that the effects of brain injury may be studied at several levels. Firstly, there are the effects of specific lesions or injuries that reveal themselves by specific sensory or motor handicaps. Secondly, there are general disinhibitory effects, the consequences of which may be shown by disorganization in perception and in the monitoring of sensory input from all sources, together with related difficulties in understanding or communicating in symbolic terms.

Finally, we noted that the general behavior of the brain-damaged patient may reflect his attempts to adjust to his own deficiencies by seeking out simpler environments, by adopting lower-level responses to complex problems, or by avoiding responding to difficult tasks.

EPILEPSY

One large and heterogeneous group of brain-damaged patterns of behavior is classified under the general heading of the *epilepsies*. As we shall see, this term covers many dissimilar pathological phenomena but is applied to classes of behavior in which the overt pathological condition is seen spasmodically rather than continuously. It is the transient character of the defects that is the general diagnostic feature rather than their behavioral attributes. Let us first consider the descriptive classification of the major patterns.

Major Classes

Grand Mal Epilepsy. The most striking aspect of the grand mal episode is the onset of severe motor convulsions involving much of the gross skeletal musculature and leading into rapid coma. During the convulsions it is usual to distinguish a *tonic* phase of brief rigid muscular tension, followed by a *clonic* phase of rapid tremor and movement of the

arms and legs, etc. In many patients, the onset of the grand mal seizure is preceded by a phenomenon known as the *aura*. The aura is a brief motor, sensory, or conscious event, tending to recur in the same form on each occasion. Visual hallucinations, sensations of odor or sound, muscular twitches, recurring obsessive thoughts, and so forth are included in this category.

Petit Mal Epilepsy. In petit mal epilepsy the diagnostic feature is the occurrence of momentary interruptions of consciousness in which the patient may suspend his ongoing activity, appear unresponsive to external stimulation, and lack awareness of the discontinuity. Gross motor activity is not present, and the typical "seizure" may last only a few seconds.

Jacksonian Epilepsy. A third variety of epilepsy is the so-called "Jacksonian epilepsy" (named after J. Hughlings Jackson, the British neurologist). In this pattern there is a preliminary motor spasm in a very circumscribed muscle group—e.g., in one finger—that spreads temporarily to include larger and larger groups of muscles.

Psychomotor Epilepsy. The final classification is that of *psychomotor* epilepsy, a condition in which the patient suffers interruptions of consciousness during which he performs some relatively organized sequence of behavior. This behavior is then terminated by the end of the seizure and the return of consciousness. Thus a patient may suddenly break off in the middle of a conversation, commence an activity such as scrubbing the floor, and resume the conversation some time afterwards. Typically he has no recollection of the interruption. From time to time there are cases reported of this kind of epilepsy in which the patient assaults someone violently with criminal consequences. Because of the difficulty of establishing clearly that such an action is occurring under epileptic control, it is not uncommon for a psychomotor seizure to be offered as legal defense by people accused of homicide or violent assault.

These categories are neither exhaustive nor exclusive. Patients sometimes show more than one pattern, and atypical patterns—for example, episodes in which the seizure is experienced purely as an alien experience in consciousness—are not rare in the literature.

Processes in Epileptic Seizures

The common feature of epileptic seizures is that they are generated by spontaneous and massive discharge of groups of neurons. At first the discharge may be localized in a small region of cerebral gray matter, but it then spreads to adjacent tissue areas. Spreading of this kind is subject to many influences. The discharge may die down, apparently spontaneously. Or it may spread with sufficient speed and scope to produce a general seizure of the grand-mal variety. If the original focus of the discharge is subcortical, the route of spread may include both cerebral hemispheres.

Whatever the mechanism or route, the spread of discharge activity is accompanied by the normal activity of the cortical tissue involved. Thus if the discharge spreads across visual areas, visual sensations will be experienced. Where motor regions are involved, muscular activity will result. Should the discharge spread across memory or association areas, then the individual will have "dreamlike" experiences of familiar past events. Because of this, the nature of the first component of the seizure often provides a useful clue to the probable site of the original focus of discharge.

After a neuron has discharged in this way, it is temporarily inactive and unresponsive to further stimulation. General seizures are thus followed by general unconsciousness or coma, while partial seizures may be accompanied by lack of consciousness of the events of the seizure itself.

Discharges of this kind may have several

origins. Any local pathology of the brain tissue may serve to generate the focal discharge. Thus, tumorous growths, scarring caused by old injuries or undetected hemorrhages, and the like may be the basic sources of the difficulty. However, many patients with epileptic conditions do not reveal clear evidence of such foci, and there is considerable support for the notion of a general hereditary tendency to epileptic seizures.

Although the origin of the seizure may be biological in the sense that there is an identifiable and localized lesion involved, psychological stimulation plays a major role in the onset of many specific episodes. Thus if normal sensory input has the effect of stimulating the area of the cortex that is the site of the focus, these cells will be activated normally but hence will be much more likely to pass over into spontaneous discharge of a seizure type. Where, for example, the focus is in the visual cortex, intense visual stimulation may well be sufficient to trigger the seizure sequence.

Major work on this problem has been reported by Penfield and Rasmussen (1950). They have studied the effect of direct electrical stimulation of the brain surfaces of epileptic patients upon whom neurosurgery was being performed. In many cases they found it possible to localize areas in brain tissue that produced, on stimulation, the same experiences that occurred in the epi-

leptic aura. They describe such a case as follows:

Case M. G. Auditory Hallucinations

The patient complained of seizures which were ushered in by the hallucination of music. Her right hemisphere was exposed at operation . . . [Figure 11-3]. Stimulation at A, up above, produced extension of the fingers of the left hand, and the patient observed that the fingers had moved of themselves. Stimulation at K produced sensation in the fingers, and at L puckering of the lips.

Stimulation in the temporal region produced auditory hallucinations as follows: Stimulation at O—"I hear funny things; I've heard that before; I think it is like an attack." When point Y was stimulated, she made no response. Finally she said: "I had a dream, I wasn't here." It was not like her habitual seizure. When the point was restimulated she said, "Dream." She explained, "I seem to be here but things sound different," and she then said she heard "funny things." The third time the same point was stimulated she remarked, "I hear music" and at the fourth stimulation, "dream, people coming in."

In this case the hallucinations were nearly all auditory. But hallucinations of different content were produced by restimulation at the same point. Except for the music, which was a familiar air and which had come to her at the beginning of her attacks, she did not remember anything like it in her "dreamy state" seizures. She was conscious of her surroundings and of her hallucination simultaneously.

Years later she recalled the hallucinations

Figure 11-3. Craniotomy, as shown by broken line. (Penfield & Rasmussen, 1950.)

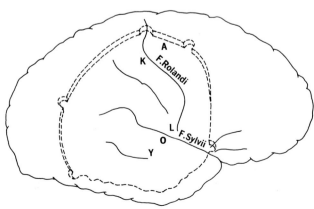

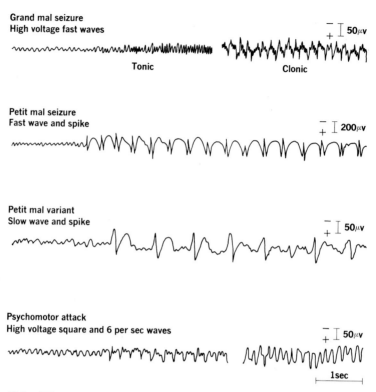

Figure 11-4. EEG patterns of various types of epileptic seizure. (From F. A. Gibbs, E. C. Gibbs, and W. G. Lennox, *Archives of Neurology and Psychiatry*, 38, 1939, p. 1112.)

which we had induced during operation and she said she remembered people coming into the operating room with snow on their clothing and she remembered wondering that they should be allowed in. As she was a French-Canadian young woman and we were operating in the month of February, this illustrates the fact that the hallucinations were made up from remembered experiences, like the music she had heard.

In summary, the music which this patient heard was what she described as a "funny little piece," a lullaby her mother had been in the habit of singing to her. Often that bit of music was the prelude to a major convulsion. But other hallucinations produced by stimulation bore no relation to the experience of any previous seizures so far as she could recollect. It was obvious that the hallucinations produced by the stimulating electrode were made up from memories, some of them quite recent. (Penfield & Rasmussen, 1950, pp. 171–173.)

Epilepsy and the Electroencephalogram

In the diagnosis of epilepsy, the use of electroencephalography (EEG) has assumed a prime role. Epileptics often (although not always) present abnormal tracings in the EEG. These abnormalcies may be of several kinds. The most common is illustrated in Figure 11-4.

For clinical purposes, the use of EEG is mainly helpful in cases where individuals have not demonstrated gross unmistakable seizures, or where some behavior suggestive of a seizure has been reported and confirmation of its epileptic origin is required. As mentioned already, the psychomotor seizure is a particularly troublesome diagnostic issue, and the EEG is the basic method used in making a decision about it. Earlier in this book (see Chapter 4) we men-

tioned the major methodological difficulties attached to the use of EEG measurements—namely, the relatively large number of deviant traces for which no accompanying seizure activity can be found, plus the rather large borderline area of trace analysis in which the decision that a pattern is abnormal is a matter of clinical judgment.

Epilepsy and Personality

Some workers in the field of psychopathology have advanced the view that epilepsy is associated with a typical personality pattern and that the seizure activity may be regarded as significantly related to basic conflicts which trouble the patient. Maslow and Mittelmann (1951) describe the epileptic "character" as hostile, withdrawn, self-centered, and suspicious. Characteristics such as these may well develop as a consequence of the socially aversive consequences that the epileptic patient might meet because of his susceptibility to seizures. Thus the personality of the patient may be interpreted as a pattern of secondary adjustment to the difficulties caused by the underlying organic disorder.

Tizard (1962) has identified four basic theoretical positions relating to the question.

1. The majority of epileptics share a common personality structure. The presumed central trait of this personality is emotional impulsiveness or "explosiveness."

2. Epileptic patients have a larger share of other neurotic disturbances than are found in a sample of nonepileptic subjects.

3. There is a personality structure seen in epileptic patients which is also found in other patients suffering from organic disabilities. The structure is not peculiar to epilepsy as such.

4. There is a personality pattern characteristic of patients with temporal lobe epilepsy, but it is not found in patients with other kind of epilepsies.

A fifth position—not appropriately called a theory—is that there is no typical epileptic pattern of personality. A random sample of epileptic patients would be expected to reveal the same distribution of personality attributes that would be found in any similar sample of nonepileptics.

At the present time it is difficult to evaluate any of these views because of the enormous methodological problems that beset the investigator. As Tizard comments, "What has to be studied, in fact, is the behavior of individuals with malfunctioning nervous systems, damaged in different areas at different stages of development, controlled to a greater or lesser extent by different drugs, acting on and responding to different kinds of environment" (Tizard, 1962, p. 207).

Nevertheless, certain gross observations seem to be possible. These are presented in the following paragraphs.

Temporal Lobe Epilepsies. The majority of investigators agree that temporal lobe epilepsies are accompanied by a high incidence of personality disorders of all kinds. Thus Hill (1957) reports that of a group with temporal lobe focus, 50 per cent suffered from measurable personality disorder. Of these, 25 per cent were psychotic. Similar figures have been given by Gibbs (1958), who reported 40 per cent disturbed and 33 per cent of these psychotic. A similar trend is noted when the kinds of epilepsy found in psychiatrically hospitalized epileptics are compared with the kinds found in nonhospitalized samples. Thus Roger and Dongier (1950) and Liddell (1953) report that while 30 per cent of outpatient epileptics reveal temporal lobe foci, 64 per cent and 50 per cent of mental hospital epileptics in the two studies, respectively, were of the temporal lobe type. In both studies, the most common feature in the personality disturbances of the temporal lobe patients was explosive and chronic aggressiveness.

In the case of temporal lobe epilepsies, the hypothesis relating the brain focus to personality is on somewhat more solid ground than the theories dealing with other epilepsy-personality relationships. Klüver and

Bucy (1939) studied the effects in the monkey of ablation of the temporal lobes (including the hippocampus, the amygdala, and the uncus). Among a variety of behavioral changes, the animals became placid. In operations performed on cats (Bard & Mountcastle, 1948) in which the underlying structures were removed but not the temporal lobes themselves, the effect was to produce rage behavior. An oversimplified interpretation of these results would suggest that the temporal cortex and hippocampus are in an excitatory-inhibitory relationship governing emotional behavior and that disorders of emotional control may be expected whenever there is a temporal lobe pathology in epilepsy.

Meyer, Falconer, and Beck (1954) have found that in all cases of temporal lobe epilepsy (diagnosed by EEG) which have come to autopsy, temporal lobe lesions were observable. This gives support for the use of anatomically based theory to account for the relationships between temporal lobe EEG foci and the emotionality of the patients' behavior.

Other Epilepsies. In the case of other types of epilepsy, the available data are insufficiently reliable to do other than indicate that patients with histories of seizures develop a variety of maladjustments. There is no scientific support for the hypotheses which suggest that the seizure is *generally* determined by motivational antecedents, although individual cases of convulsive response patterns may be found where there are no signs of biological pathology and where the "epileptic" behavior is apparently being maintained because its consequences are reinforcing to the patient.

Summary

The term "epilepsy" refers to a range of biologically based pathologies in which the common features are (*a*) transient interruptions in consciousness and/or in overt behavior, and (*b*) the presence of intermittent neuronal discharges that may be focused or diffuse and that appear to determine the psychological symptomatology.

In any case, the nature and sequence of the psychological phenomena will be a consequence of the areas of brain tissue involved in the discharge and the sequence of spread that occurs. Localized preliminary accompaniments of the discharge may produce sensory, conscious, or motor phenomena known as the aura. At the present time, the major method of diagnosis—other than observation of the seizures themselves —is the electroencephalogram.

Many investigators have sought to find relationships between epilepsy and the personality of the patients. Some support exists for the hypothesis that temporal lobe patients suffer from irregular emotional control, and anatomical relationships exist that would make this plausible. No satisfactory evidence has yet been found for other kinds of personality factors in these disorders.

MENTAL DEFICIENCY

One of the largest groups of people institutionalized because of their behavior is the group of the mentally *retarded* or mentally *deficient*. As in the case of brain damage or the epilepsies, the term "mental deficiency" is a broad one. Included in it are a wide variety of children and adults who share a common deficiency in acquiring adaptive behaviors, but whose etiologies may range from mechanical brain injury during birth to genetic anomalies or severely unfavorable early environments.

For practical purposes, the term mental deficiency refers to inadequacy in acquiring adaptive behavior, inadequacy that (*a*) is sufficiently severe to require some protection for the patient and (*b*) occurs sufficiently early in life that there is no long history of normalcy prior to institutionalization. Within these rather broad limits, however, there has been considerable controversy about the appropriate criteria for classifying the presence and degree of deficiency necessary for institutionalization.

Criteria for a Diagnosis of Mental Deficiency

British practice has tended to emphasize the *social adequacy* of the patient as the basis for classification. The Mental Deficiency Act of 1913 (as amended by various acts in 1927, 1933, 1944, and 1946) recognizes four categories of mental deficiency, which are defined as follows:

1. Idiots. Persons in whose case there exists mental defectiveness of such a degree that they are unable to guard themselves against common physical dangers.

2. Imbeciles. Persons in whose case there exists mental defectiveness which, though not amounting to idiocy, is yet so pronounced that they are incapable of managing themselves or their affairs, or—in the case of children—of being taught to do so.

3. Feebleminded. Persons in whose case there exists mental defectiveness which, though not amounting to imbecility, is yet so pronounced that they require care, supervision and control for their own protection or for the protection of others and, in the case of children, that they appear to be permanently incapable by reason of such defectiveness of receiving proper benefit from the instruction in an ordinary school.

4. Moral Defectives. Persons in whose cases there exists mental defectiveness coupled with strongly vicious and criminal propensities and who require care, supervision and control for the protection of others.

(Lyons & Heaton-Ward, 1953, p. 9.)

These definitions make it clear that the major concern is with the social survival and effectiveness of the patient rather than with any specific quantitative measurement of his abilities.

A predominantly quantified approach has been taken by many clinicians in the United States, where an intelligence quotient of 69 or below has been regarded as the prima-facie definition of mental deficiency. Indeed, the categories of *idiot* and *imbecile* mentioned in the previous paragraphs are defined in terms of IQ ranges of 0 to 19 and 20 to 49, respectively. Patients with an IQ range of 50 to 69 are classified as *moron*, and those with IQs of 70 to 79 as *borderline*.

Several important problems exist with this kind of approach, the more important because the use of intelligence test scores as legal criteria of mental deficiency has been adopted by some states. First, this system assumes that the test score is reliable enough to be used in making a decision to institutionalize a child with little risk of serious error. Secondly, it assumes that the validity of the intelligence test used is appropriate to the kind of decision that is being made. This point may be considered in the following way: Is it the case that a child who receives a test score producing an IQ of 55 during preadolescent years will continue to be ineffective in later life—i.e., will fail to become self-supporting, etc.?

There are now several sources of response to such a question. This writer has concluded elsewhere that:

Formal tests of intelligence are not universally good predictors of the future social efficiency of subjects whose test scores indicate retardation. The studies of Anderson and Fearing (1923), Fairbank (1933), Baller (1936), Muench (1944), Kennedy (1948), and Charles (1953) suggest the extent of this unreliability. Indeed, as Masland, Sarason, and Gladwin (1958) have pointed out, when children thus identified as retarded leave school, the majority cease to be defined as retarded, having presumably made a satisfactory adjustment. Anyone who has worked professionally within an institution for the mentally retarded will be aware that one of the significant factors which are taken into account when deciding to discharge a patient is the nature of the social environment to which he will return—not evidence of improved intellectual functioning. (Maher, 1963, p. 238.)

Acute difficulties of this kind with the IQ criteria have led to greater sophistication in the combining of intellectual and social competence variables into more comprehensive definitions. Doll (1941) suggested that a total definition would include "(1) social incompetence, (2) due to mental sub-

normality, (3) which has been developmentally arrested, (4) which obtains at maturity, (5) is of constitutional origin, and (6) is essentially incurable."

Purposes of Criteria

Criteria are, necessarily, arbitrary. They cease to be arbitrary when it is shown that they successfully identify a class of individuals whose condition has a sufficiently common etiology that treatment or prevention may be selected sensibly by the criteria. If the etiologies are heterogeneous and the treatments likewise, then the decision to define the class on the basis of irrelevant superficial similarities is essentially capricious. There is, therefore, no obvious way to decide between the various criteria that have been discussed except in terms of the inherent unreliability of applying any particular one of them (as, for example, the IQ criterion). In day-to-day practice, it is failure to follow the expectations of minimal normal progress through school that tends to secure the critical diagnosis of mental retardation. Except in the severe early congenital arrest of development, the age of school attendance and performance in the early grades may be the most significant reasons for seeking referral for diagnosis. As we have already mentioned, the large body of patients in institutions for the retarded includes such a miscellaneous group of etiologies that it would be difficult to select a criterion that would apply adequately to the majority of patients and yet be correlated with etiology. About the closest correlation that we may find is between diagnosis of mental retardation and the presence of some organic pathology—and this correlation is far from perfect, or even from being uniformly accepted by psychopathologists.

Brain Damage, Genetics, and the Environment

The first of the possible statements about the etiology of mental retardation is that failure to proceed through school learning tasks at the normal rate may be due to some general structural damage to those parts of the body necessary for learning—especially the sensory systems and the central nervous system. This damage may be externally induced—by mechanical trauma or toxic interference—or it may represent a failure of complete development of some part of the system. To the extent that the damage is irreversible, the precise nature of its origin may be largely an academic issue.

Secondly, we can say that if the rate and level of learning of which any individual is capable is itself a function of subtle characteristics of the central nervous system, then it is possible for two people to be different in learning ability without the less adequate of the two presenting anything that would be described as a "lesion" or "pathology." Their differences may be of genetic origin, or may stem from some combination of genetic factors and early stimulation experiences. People in whom genetic endowment at the lower end of the normal curve of intelligence has coincided with especially unfavorable early experiences might thus develop into unusually inadequate learners.

Thirdly, we might expect to find a group of people who had early developed an active aversion or disinterest in academic performance, but who had no intrinsic deficiency in intelligence. In this group, the emphasis placed upon school performance in making a diagnosis of mental retardation would be an unfortunate accident, producing inferences about their intelligence that would be invalid. However, if academic motivation, etc., can be improved in these individuals, their behavior may be expected to show a change toward greater normalcy.

With these three points in mind, we can recognize three general groupings of patients in the mental retardation category. First are those with clear evidence of brain damage (externally caused or inferred from gross signs of developmental arrest). Second are those who do not present evidence of biological pathology but who seem unable to learn at a normal rate in spite of special teaching methods, whose family history has records of similar difficulties, and who seem to have had no specific learning experiences that would lend support for an emotional interference explanation. Third, where the learning difficulty is relatable to emotional factors and there is no sign of any of the other correlates, the patient is unlikely to be regarded as a mental retardate, even though various other considerations may lead to his being placed in an institution for the retarded. Thus, the majority of the retarded fall into one of the first two groups.

These groups have been given various gross labels. Lewis (1933) used the terms *pathological* (meaning that the retardation was associated with and in most cases due to some definite organic lesion or abnormality) and *subcultural* (designating those individuals who are at the lower end of the normal genetic curve of endowment of intelligence). Strauss and Lehtinen (1947) preferred the terms *exogenous* and *endogenous* for the same distinction. On the whole, however, the term *garden variety* has passed into most general use for the large percentage of patients who show no overt signs of brain damage and who tend to be at the upper end of the ability range of the mentally retarded population.

Mental Deficiency with Genetic Factors: Down's Syndrome

One hundred years ago a British physician, Dr. J. Langdon Down, suggested that the features and facial structures of various types of mental retardate would permit them to be classified on the basis of normal ethnic groupings. Among these groupings was that of *mongolism,* and although the rest of Down's classification was soon abandoned, the term mongolism survived as a label for a particular kind of exogenous defective. In some respects, the superficial facial characteristics of this kind of patient resemble normal features of members of the Mongol ethnic groups—hence the term. Recently, the word has been dropped from technical usage and been replaced by the label *Down's Syndrome.*

Physical characteristics of this syndrome include a small flattish skull, a downward and inward slope to the eyes, a protruded and fissured tongue, large flabby hands, and fissuring between the great toe and the other toes on the foot. There are many instances of heart and respiratory disorders and a host of other minor physical deviations. For many years the origin of Down's Syndrome was a matter for theoretical controversy. Among the correlations reported were paternal alcoholism, family histories of tuberculosis, ill health of the mother during pregnancy, syphilis in the family, and late age of the mother at the time the patient was born.

Hypotheses advanced to account for the condition have included "infusion of Mongol blood" somewhere among the ancestors, pressure on the foetus during the sixth and seventh week of pregnancy, and unhealthy condition of the uterine mucus at the time of conception. However, in 1959, Lejeune, Turpin, and Gautier discovered the presence of a third (extra) chromosome (trisomy) in position 21 in the karyotype of Down's Syndrome patients. This was followed by the discovery by Shaw and Chu (1961) of partial trisomy in the mothers of affected children. Later Lejeune and Turpin (1961) reported a deficiency in tryptophan metabolism in these patients and the possibility that there is a concomitant deficiency in brain serotonin. Thus the mechanism most likely to account for the disorder involves genetically controlled enzyme dysfunction and a consequent widespread pattern of physical and behavioral abnormalities. The possibility of chemical treatment for Down's Syndrome is also raised, although at the time of writing no concrete progress has been reported.

Mental Deficiency with Brain Damage

Where the patient is brain-damaged from birth in a manner that produces permanent decrement in learning ability, the diagnostic picture of retardation is likely to be complicated by the usual accompaniments of brain damage. These have been discussed at length earlier in this chapter and do not need elaboration here. However, there is the question of the generality of brain-damage symptoms in mental retardates where no overt evidence of actual organic pathology has been found. Here again, the psychological processes of attention and inhibition have been the focus of much work.

Baumeister, Spain, and Ellis (1963) studied attention via the measurement of EEG alpha blocking in normal and mentally retarded groups. Subjects were allowed to relax until alpha was obtained, and they were then stimulated with a brief, intense light that blocked alpha. The duration of the alpha blocking was measured, and a subsequent trial was not begun until alpha had reappeared on the trace. Under these conditions, the results (Figure 11-5) showed clearly that alpha blocking (attention) was

much briefer in the retarded group than in the normals under conditions of identical stimulation. As will be seen from the figure, adaptation begins to appear in the normals by the eighth trial, making the two groups comparable at this point.

Further studies on inhibition in massed practice learning, paired-associate learning, delayed discriminations, and so forth support the general conclusion that random samples of high-grade mental retardates show the defects of inhibition and attention that are so commonly found in the brain-damaged.

Therapy for Mental Deficiency

At the present time there are no therapies for mental retardation that produce changes of sufficient magnitude to be called "cures." Many workers have found it helpful to use

Figure 11-5. Attention in normals and retardates as measured by alpha blocking. (Baumeister, Spain, and Ellis, 1963.)

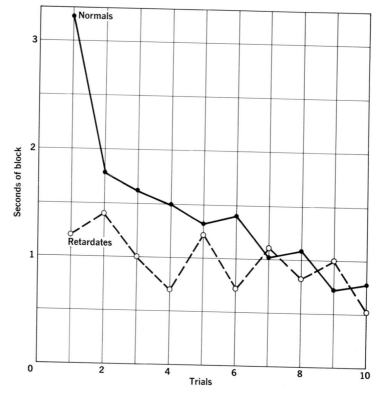

simple forms of psychotherapy in dealing with the associated personality difficulties often found with retarded patients. In recent years it has begun to seem more fruitful to use straightforward principles of reinforcement and concentrate on methods of training the patient to acquire socially adequate behaviors, and it is in this sphere that psychology has the greatest contribution to make.

The group of conditions known as mental retardation includes a range of symptoms characterized by inadequate learning abilities from an early stage in life. It has a variety of possible biopsychological origins and necessitates special care, often in an institution. Even where there is no overt evidence of brain damage, much of the behavior of the retardate shows those deficiencies of attention and inhibition that are found in the brain-damaged. This, plus the relative incurability of the vast bulk of institutionalized retardates, suggests that all these disorders have a fundamental biological nature. The main contributions of behavioral science appear to lie in the application of the principles of learning to the training of patients in socially adequate behaviors.

SUMMARY

In this chapter we have seen that injuries to the human brain may arise from a number of sources. Degenerative changes with aging, externally caused traumatic damage, tumors, infections, and many other agents may be involved. In each case, the specific effects upon the patient will depend in part upon the functions that are normally served by the damaged area. However, many psychopathologists have been interested in the problem of whether or not there are general effects of brain damage—effects that may be seen in many patients with different kinds of injury.

There is some evidence to suggest that there are some general effects that represent the reaction of the patient to the injury and incapacity itself. Much as a man may develop psychological reactions to the handicaps caused by the loss of an arm, so we may find similar "compensatory" or defensive reactions to the difficulties that arise in brain damage.

Apart from reports of these general reactions, there have been studies that suggest that the loss of the abstract attitude is a common feature of many kinds of brain damage. We have suggested that much of these data may be subsumed under the more general notion that loss of inhibition is involved whenever there is serious injury to higher centers.

Mental deficiency has also been considered. Here we have noted the general and rather vague definition of mental deficiency as an entity and have indicated some of the recent discoveries in genetics and their implications for the study of retardation.

SUGGESTED READINGS

1. Delafresnaye, J. (Ed.) *Brain mechanisms and learning.* Oxford: Blackwell Scientific Publications, 1961. A symposium volume dealing with advanced work in the correlations between brain function and learning. While not directed specifically to questions of brain damage, it is of great value in understanding the rationale for relating brain injury to various kinds of behavior deficit.

2. Ellis, N. (Ed.) *Handbook of mental deficiency.* New York: McGraw-Hill, 1963. A comprehensive handbook of empirical research on the performance characteristics of the retarded, with chapters on genetics, concepts of intelligence, and the social psychology of the retarded, together with numerous contributions on learning, motivation, psychophysiology, etc. A major source book for this topic.

3. Hill, D. (Ed.) *Electroencephalography.* London: Macmillan, 1950. A handbook source for work on EEG. Chapters on

the epilepsies and EEG methodology are especially valuable.

4. Meyer, V. Psychological effects of brain damage. In H. J. Eysenck (Ed.), *Handbook of abnormal psychology*. New York: Basic Books, 1961. A comprehensive account of the major trends in research work on the problems of brain damage and behavior. It is especially useful in discussing problems of methodology in this area.

5. Sarason, S. *Psychological problems in mental deficiency*. New York: Harper, 1949. A brief but now classic consideration of the problems of mental deficiency with special emphasis upon the "garden variety" concept.

REFERENCES

Alzheimer, A. Uber eine eigenartige Erkrankung der Hirnrinde. *Centralbl. Nervenheit. Psychiat.*, 1907, **18**, 177.

Anderson, W. W., & Fearing, F. M. *A study of the careers of 322 feeble-minded persons*. New York: National Committee of Mental Hygiene, 1923.

Baller, W. R. A study of the present social status of adults who, when they were in elementary schools, were classed as mentally deficient. *Genet. Psychol. Monogr.*, 1936, **18**, 165–244.

Bard, P., & Mountcastle, V. B. Some forebrain mechanisms in expression of rage with special reference to suppression of angry behavior. *Res. Publ. Ass. Res. nerv. ment. Dis.*, 1948, **27**, 362–404.

Baumeister, A. A., Spain, C. J., & Ellis N. R. A note on alpha block duration in normals and retardates. *Amer. J. ment. Defic.*, 1963, **67**, 723–725.

Charles, D. C. Ability and accomplishment of persons earlier judged mentally deficient. *Genet. Psychol. Monogr.*, 1953, **47**, 3–71.

Coleman, T. W. A comparison of young brain-injured and mongolian mentally defective children on perception, thinking and behavior. Unpublished doctoral dissertation, Univer. of Michigan, 1960.

Diamond, S., Balvin, R. S., & Diamond, F. R. *Inhibition and choice*. New York: Harper & Row, 1963.

Doll, E. A. The essentials of an inclusive concept of mental deficiency. *Amer. J. ment. Defic.*, 1941, **46**, 214–219.

Fairbank, R. The subnormal child seventeen years after. *Ment. Hyg., N. Y.*, 1933, **17**, 177–208.

Gastaut, H., & Fischer-Williams, M. The physiopathology of epileptic seizures. In H. W. Magoun (Ed.), *Handbook of physiology*. Vol. 1. Washington, D.C.: American Physiological Society, 1959.

Gibbs, F. A. Abnormal electrical activity in the temporal regions and its relationship to abnormalities of behavior. *Res. Publ. Ass. Res. nerv. ment. Dis.*, 1958, **36**, 278–294.

Goldstein, K. *Aftereffects of brain injuries in war*. New York: Grune & Stratton, 1942.

Goldstein, K. Mental changes due to frontal brain damage. *J. Psychol.*, 1944, **17**, 187–208.

Hill, D. N. Epilepsy. In Lord Cohen (Ed.), *The British encyclopaedia of medical practice: medical progress*. London: Butterworth, 1957.

Kennedy, R. J. A. *The social adjustment of morons in a Connecticut city*. Hartford: Southbury Training Schools, 1948.

Klüver, H., & Bucy, P. C. Preliminary analysis of functions of the temporal lobes in monkeys. *Arch. Neurol. Psychiat.*, 1939, **42**, 979–1000.

Laffal, J. *Pathological and normal language*. New York: Atherton, 1965.

Lejeune, J., & Turpin, R. Chromosomal aberrations in man. *Amer. J. hum. Genet.*, 1961, **13**, 175–184.

Lejeune, J., Turpin, R., & Gautier, M. Le mongolism, premier example d'aberration autosomique humaine. *Ann. Genetique*, 1959, **2**, 41–49.

Lewis, E. D. Types of mental deficiency and their social significance. *J. ment. Sci.*, 1933, **79**, 298–304.

Liddell, D. W. Observations on epileptic

automatism in a mental hospital population. *J. ment. Sci.*, 1953, **99**, 732–748.

Lyons, J. F., & Heaton-Ward, W. A. *Notes on mental deficiency.* Bristol: John Wright & Sons, 1953.

Maher, B. A. Intelligence and brain-damage. In N. Ellis (Ed.), *Handbook of mental deficiency.* New York: McGraw-Hill, 1963.

Maher, B. A., & Martin, A. W. Mosaic productions in cerebro-arteriosclerosis. *J. consult. Psychol.*, 1954, **18**, 40–42.

Masland, R. L., Sarason, S. B., & Gladwin, T. *Mental subnormality.* New York: Basic Books, 1958.

Maslow, A. H., & Mittelman, B. *Principles of abnormal psychology: the dynamics of psychic illness.* New York: Harper & Row, 1951.

Meyer, A., Falconer, M. A., & Beck, E. Pathological findings in temporal lobe epilepsy. *J. Neurol. Neurosurg. Psychiat.*, 1954, **17**, 276–285.

Meyer, D. R., Isaac, W., & Maher, B. A. The role of stimulation in spontaneous reorganization of visual habits. *J. comp. physiol. Psychol.*, 1958, **51**, 546–548.

Meyer, V. Learning changes following temporal lobectomy. *Bull. Brit. Psychol. Soc.*, 1956, **29**, 21.

Meyer, V. Cognitive changes following temporal lobectomy for the relief of temporal lobe epilepsy. *Arch. Neurol. Psychiat.*, 1959, **81**, 299–309.

Meyer, V. Psychological effects of brain damage. In H. J. Eysenck (Ed.), *Handbook of abnormal psychology.* New York: Basic Books, 1961.

Meyer, V., & Jones, H. G. Patterns of cognitive test performance as functions of the lateral localization of cerebral abnormalities in the temporal lobe. *J. ment. Sci.*, 1957, **103**, 758–772.

Morgan, C. T. *Introduction to psychology.* New York: McGraw-Hill, 1961.

Morrell, F. Interseizure disturbances in focal epilepsy. *Neurology*, 1956, **6**, 327–334.

Muench, G. A. A follow-up of mental defectives after eighteen years. *J. abnorm. soc.*

Psychol., 1944, **39**, 407–418.

Penfield, W., & Rasmussen, T. *The cerebral cortex of man: a study of the localization of function.* New York: Macmillan, 1950.

Quadfasel, A. F., & Pruyser, P. Cognitive deficit in patients with psychomotor epilepsy. *Epilepsia*, 1955, **4**, 80–90.

Roger, A., & Dongier, M. Correlations electrocliniques chez 50 epileptiques internes. *Rev. Neurol.*, 1950, **83**, 593–596.

Rosvold, H. E., & Mishkin, M. Non-sensory effects of frontal lesions on discrimination learning and performance. In J. Delafresnaye (Ed.), *Brain mechanisms and learning.* Oxford: Blackwell Scientific Publications, 1961.

Shaw, M. W., & Chu, E. H. Y. Chromosome analysis of a mother of two mongols. *Program Amer. Soc. hum. Genet.*, 1961. (Abstract)

Spivack, G. Perceptual processes. In N. Ellis (Ed.), *Handbook of mental deficiency.* New York: McGraw-Hill, 1963.

Stewart, J. W., & Ades, H. W. The time factor in reintegration of a learned habit lost after temporal lobe lesions in the monkey *Macaca Mulatta. J. comp. physiol. Psychol.*, 1951, **44**, 479–486.

Strauss, A. A., & Lehtinen, L. E. *Psychopathology and education of the brain-injured child.* New York: Grune & Stratton, 1947.

Tizard, B. The personality of epileptics: a discussion of the evidence. *Psychol. Bull.*, 1962, **59**, 196–210.

Weinstein, S., & Teuber, H. L. Effects of penetrating brain injury on intelligence test scores. *Science*, 1957, **105**, 1036–1037.

Williams, H. L., Lubin, A., & Gieseking, C. F. Direct measurements of cognitive deficit in brain-injured patients. *J. consult. Psychol.*, 1959, **23**, 300–305.

Van Riper, C. *Speech correction: principles and methods.* (3d ed.) Englewood Cliffs, N.J.: Prentice-Hall, 1954.

12 SCHIZOPHRENIA: CLINICAL AND THEORETICAL ASPECTS

Of all the problems in the field of psychopathology, that of schizophrenia is at once the most important and the most baffling. As a general descriptive category, it includes the largest single proportion of patients in most mental hospitals. Human effort in research and treatment of the schizophrenic patient probably exceeds that devoted to any other behavior deviation. As a condition or group of conditions, as a process or several processes, the puzzles presented by the behavior of schizophrenic patients remain to a significant extent unsolved. Because of its great importance, we shall devote a considerable amount of our discussion to this pattern of behaviors, beginning with the clinical aspects.

One of the first systematic descriptive terms applied to a certain kind of behavior disorder was *dementia praecox*. The term was first used by Morel (1860), but its application to a systematically conceived category of behavior was first proposed by Kraepelin (1896). Kraepelin's major concern was to differentiate a pattern of disorder from that of manic-depressive psychosis. The syndrome as defined by Kraepelin consisted of hallucinations, delusions, inappropriate emotional responses, negativism, stereotyped behavior, and deficient attention, but no disorder of sensory process. Four types of dementia praecox were recognized by Kraepelin: *hebephrenic, catatonic, paranoid*, and *simple*.[1] Implicit in Kraepelin's handling of the problem of descriptive

[1] Kraepelin added the simple type (following the distinction made by Bleuler) to the other three which were his own classification.

diagnosis was the belief that he was dealing with an organic disease process, probably of metabolism. His contribution was largely a descriptive one, and there was very little in the way of an articulated theory attached to it.

Following Kraepelin, although overlapping him chronologically, was Bleuler (1911). In his classic work *Dementia Praecox, or the Group of Schizophrenias*, Bleuler modified the account given by Kraepelin in many ways. Abandoning the notion that the basic process of the disorder was a progressive deterioration, he emphasized rather the "splitting" of the personality whereby many functions and responses became disengaged from the environment. The behavior of these patients did not necessarily begin to show signs of pathology early in life, as the term "praecox" implied, nor did it always terminate in deterioration or dementia. Central to these patterns of behavior, Bleuler felt, were *autism* (the predominance of internal fantasy over external determinants of behavior) and the divorce of affective states from reality factors. For this new concept of the behavior he developed the term *schizophrenia* and presented a detailed account of a group of behavior patterns referred to as the schizophrenias. This concept of several varieties is important and has become standard in most subsequent thinking on the topic. *Schizo-phrenia* means literally "split personality." Semantically this usage is a little unfortunate, because the term split personality has passed into popular use with reference to cases of hysterical multiple personality. The splitting to which Bleuler referred was the presumed splitting off of some components of the personality from others.

Bleuler offered some dynamic theoretical hypotheses to account for the main features of schizophrenic behavior. The major processes were loosening of associations—shown by many features of disordered language and behavior sequences—and autistic thinking, in which wishes and fears, expressed in symbolic form, dominate the thinking proc-esses of the patient to the detriment of logical or rational thought and behavior.

A third figure in the development of the groundwork of modern thinking about schizophrenia was Meyer (1906, 1910). Of particular importance was his extension of scientific interest to the premorbid history of the schizophrenic patient and his conception of the disordered behavior as lying on a continuum with the earlier prepsychotic responses of the patient. His general conception was of the slow building up of faulty habits of living which gradually spread and degenerate to the point that institutionalization is necessary. He is of interest, therefore, as one (*a*) who pointed up the need for study of the conditions under which the premorbid personality of the patient developed, and (*b*) who suggested by implication the importance of learning poor adjustment techniques as a precursor of the final psychotic adjustment.

A new emphasis upon the interpersonal relationships of the patient, especially his childhood interactions with his parents, was introduced by Harry Stack Sullivan. He presented his theory in a now classic monograph, (Sullivan, 1953) in, which he advanced the so-called "interpersonal theory" of psychiatry. Although much of his thinking was presented in rather obscure terminology, he drew attention to the importance of the communications between parent and child, as well as to the role of rejection and the ensuing anxiety and defense, in the development of severe psychopathology. Largely owing to his influence, many recent studies of patterns of family interaction in schizophrenia have been conducted.

CLINICAL FEATURES

We shall study the clinical features of the varieties of schizophrenic pattern under the presently accepted headings. First let us consider the most common features of the disorder, regardless of the specific variations peculiar to the subtypes.

General Features

At the time of admission to a hospital the patient is typically young, not likely to be older than the late thirties. While there is usually some precipitating incident that has led to the decision to admit him to the hospital, this incident is the latest in a series of behavioral anomalies that have become increasingly apparent over the preceding years. A decline in interest in life generally, especially in other people, may have been slowly developing, accompanied by a preoccupation with some event or idea that is assuming unusual significance for him.

As these private preoccupations develop, they are likely to determine the person's perception of reality. Commonly the patient will begin to interpret the behavior of others as significantly related to his own ideas, concluding that he is being followed, that trivial conversations or phrases have special significance as messages to him, that he is being observed and victimized by some threatening outside agency, and that "they" are exercising power over his bodily and mental functions. (See the case described in Example 12-1.)

The patient's beliefs that events have a special significance for him are called *ideas of reference*. They are components of the more systematized erroneous belief patterns called *delusions*. Delusions may be of *persecution* or of *grandiosity*. In the former the patient sees himself as the target of hostile forces, whereas in the latter he sees himself as possessed of great power and importance. These two aspects of a delusional belief are sometimes integrated, so that the persecutors are inimical to the patient precisely because of his importance and power.

Complaints that the world appears distorted to perception are also common. Other people and objects are described as looking flat, hollow, or two-dimensional. Extreme perceptual anomalies occur—as when the patient "hears" voices, which usually appear to be upbraiding him for his behavior; accusing him of being incestuous, criminal, or inadequate; and threatening reprisals. These anomalies are termed *hallucinations*. Auditory hallucinations are probably the most common, but visual hallucinations are frequently reported. Hallucinations of touch, taste, and smell are less common.

Emotional behavior is also markedly pathological. Patients typically exhibit patterns of emotionality that range all the way from apathy and withdrawal to intense but inappropriate emotional responses. Anger, fear, laughter, and suspicion may be elicited by trivial or unidentifiable stimuli and may

---

EXAMPLE 12-1

Delusions in a Schizophrenic Patient

A seventeen-year-old girl was admitted to a psychiatric hospital with a clinical diagnosis of schizophrenia, paranoid type. For some months previously she had begun to exhibit delusional fears of observation. The first evidence of this, according to the patient's parent, was her statement one day that she was being watched out of the television set by a well-known entertainer who had sexual designs on her. At first she would take care to seat herself in the room in such a way that she was not directly in the line of vision of the television screen. Some days later she complained that this was not effective and insisted on switching off the television set entirely whenever she was in the room. Following this she began to express belief that the same entertainer was now "listening to her thoughts" via the household appliances plugged into the power outlets, such as the electric iron, the vacuum cleaner, and so on. She now demanded that these be unplugged from the wall whenever she was in the room, and she refused to talk aloud in case she could be overheard by her tormentor. It was at this juncture that her parents sought psychiatric advice.

Schizophrenia: Clinical and Theoretical Aspects

change in unpredictable fashion. However, the most characteristic aspect of the patient's mood is likely to be detected by the effect he has on the observer. In conversation with the schizophrenic patient, the observer may feel an unusual lack of real contact; a feeling often described in terms such as "There seems to be a glass wall between us," or the like.[2]

Verbal behavior is sometimes bizarre. The patient may utter strings of words with no

[2] The behavior of a patient during a conversation under the conditions in which it usually takes place, i.e., after involuntary incarceration in an institution under circumstances damaging to his self-esteem, is likely to be cynical and aloof. When considering this description of the schizophrenic's mood, it is important to distinguish between the primary behavioral pathology and the secondary consequence of the immediate environment.

apparent coherence, termed *word salad*. Negativism and mutism in speech are seen, and *opposite speech* is sometimes reported, as in Example 12-2.

Capacity for sustained or directed attention appears to be impaired also, a phenomenon that will be discussed in detail in later chapters. Because of this, many other behaviors are inadequate, such as behavior involved in learning, retention, conceptualization, and related performances.

It must be appreciated that the foregoing characteristics are common and to a large extent "typical" but are by no means universally found in all patients diagnosed as schizophrenic. There are additional clinical patterns, usually regarded as subtypes of the general category. Four widely accepted patterns have been incorporated into the language and thinking of psychopathologists: the *simple, hebephrenic, catatonic,* and

EXAMPLE 12-2
Opposite Speech in a Schizophrenic Patient

Peter is a twenty-four-year-old single man who first exhibited psychotic behavior while serving as a gunner with a mortar company in combat in Korea. At the time of admission to the field hospital he was mute, and he neither ate nor talked for three days. Information accompanying him to the field hospital revealed that he had been hearing voices telling him that he was dirty, that he spread disease, that he was an SOB and a pervert.

He was transferred to the United States one month later. At that time he ate very little because he felt that his food contained chopped-up people and worms. He equated worms with penises. After a total of 45 electric shock treatments without sustained improvement, he was transferred to a Veterans' Administration hospital. There he was better oriented and in fair contact, and during the next few months, he was given several passes and leaves of absence. Finally he was placed on trial visit approximately fourteen months after his initial breakdown on the battlefield. Three months after the beginning of the trial visit, he became quite agitated, telling his mother that one of the girls in the neighborhood was calling his name and would not leave him alone. He began to pound on the wall and shout that he wanted the name calling to stop. It was at this point that the patient was brought to his present Veterans' Administration hospital. There was no mention in the fairly detailed Army and previous Veterans' Administration hospitalization records of the opposite speech.

The patient is an only child. His parents are frugal, lower-middle-class people, who apparently were always able to provide their son with the things other boys had. They describe him as having been shy and introverted but always a good boy. He was an average student and was graduated from high school at the age of eighteen. Concerned about his slender physique, he sometimes worked enthusiastically with weights to build himself up. He was too bashful to go out with girls, and as far as can be ascertained, had no heterosexual relations. Following graduation from high school, he worked in an upholstery shop until drafted into the Army. The family matrix includes an exceedingly protective, indulgent, and yet controlling mother and a relatively ineffectual father.

In asking the patient routine questions at admission, the resident was struck by the confusing answers that he received. The patient appeared to substitute "yes" for "no" and "always" for "never." The patient's parents first noted this type of reversal on the day prior to his admission when the patient said at lunchtime, "I'm hungry." His mother prepared a sandwich, and when she offered it to him he rejected it. In his behavior on the ward, the patient was withdrawn, uncommunicative, compliant, and well behaved, despite some agitated periods when he hallucinated a marriage and the presence of his "wife" in the hospital, and when he hallucinated the presence of his mother on the ward. The hallucinatory and delusional content was mainly sexual and religious in nature. Neurological studies were noncontributory.

When interviewed by two clinicians, the patient engaged in the following conversation.

Dr. X Peter, I want to ask you something. I'm holding a pipe here in my hand. Do you see this pipe?
Pt. No.
Dr. X Dr. Y, do you see this pipe?
Dr. Y Yes, I see the pipe.
Dr. X Peter, how is it when I show you the pipe, you say, no you don't see it, and Dr. Y says yes, he does see it. How is it he says yes and you say no?
Pt. Well . . . the doctor says he don't see it?
Dr. Y I do see it.
Pt. You do see it?
Dr. X What do you say, Peter?
Pt. I do see the pipe.
Dr. X You do see the pipe?
Pt. Unnnhhh.
Dr. X Now, wait, you tell me. I've got the pipe here in my hand. Do you see the pipe?
Pt. Nope, I don't see it.

(Laffal, Lenkoski, & Ameen, 1956.)

paranoid varieties. Additional distinctions have been made between *process* and *reactive* schizophrenia, a classification which cuts across the four subtypes; between *good premorbid* and *poor premorbid*, a distinction which is quite similar to the *process-reactive* dichotomy; and between the *acute* and *chronic* stages of any of the subtypes.

Schizophrenic Reaction: Simple Type

Beginning at an early age, often before or during early adolescence, the patient shows a slow development of apathy and withdrawal. A declining interest in other people and events around him is coupled with a comparable deterioration in intelligent behavior. Responsiveness to interrogation is limited: questions elicit inferior and barren answers. Generally there is an absence of the dramatic delusions and hallucinations described in the previous section, the patient's thinking being *impoverished* rather than bizarre.

Diagnostic problems are often encountered with these patients, the difficulty being that of distinguishing between this condition and mental retardation. Generally speaking, the differential diagnosis is resolved in favor of simple schizophrenia when there is evidence in the case history of a decline from some earlier more adequate level of functioning. Simple environments sometimes make it possible for the patient to make a minimal adjustment and avoid detection or hospitalization. The population of tramps, hoboes, and the like found in many cities undoubtedly includes many people who have made this kind of adjustment.[3]

In the case in Example 12-3, we note that the patient appears to be unresponsive to the external environment, but we have no inkling as to the possible internal stimuli to which she may be attending. If we were to conclude that she is preoccupied with some inner events, we would be speculating without evidence. The most parsimonious inference we can make is that she is not responding to anything very much—internal or external. However, we shall postpone problems of interpretation to a later part of this chapter, turning now to examine

[3] An excellent study of such a population is to be found in Vexliard's (1957) investigation of the clochards of Paris.

another common type of schizophrenic reaction.

Schizophrenic Reaction: Catatonic Type

Although the catatonic type of reaction is regarded as one of the major varieties of schizophrenic pattern, there is some reason to believe that examples of it are becoming rarer in psychopathological experience (Arieti, 1959). The characteristics of this reaction are the so-called *catatonic excitement* and *catatonic stupor*. In the state of excitement the patient is active and agitated in a disorganized way, although dangerous and destructive behavior may also be present. In the stuporous stage, the patient may be completely apathetic and immobile. Other people may have to spoon-feed him, dress him, and tend to all his physical needs. Questions may not elicit any response; in some cases he may not speak at all. Sometimes he may adopt a particular posture and hold it for hours. Should the clinician place him in some such posture, even an uncomfortable one, he may maintain it in the same way. This phenomenon is referred to as "waxy flexibility" (*flexibilitas cerea*).

EXAMPLE 12-3
Simple Schizophrenia

Lotte is a forty-year-old woman who was examined and admitted to the hospital at the request of her mother. Shortly before this, her father had died and had left her mother and Lotte with no financial support. Lotte had "sat around the house" for the previous twelve years, having lost her temporary employment in the office of a government agency because of inefficiency. She had no friends, interests, or hobbies. According to her own account, she did not read or watch television but did occasionally perform a few simple household tasks when pressured by her mother. Her one job had been secured during the manpower shortage of World War II and had consisted of simple filing and sorting of documents. She found this work "too fast" and was ultimately discharged for incompetence. From her high school days on, Lotte seemed to have had no relationship of even a casual kind with men. She did not finish high school; her parents took her out of it "because it made her nervous."

On admission, she was quiet and almost completely passive about the prospect of hospitalization. She was neat and clean and obedient to the instructions of her mother regarding such matters as where to sit, when to remove her hat and coat, etc. This pattern of behavior was repeated on the admission ward during the subsequent weeks.

Many patients classified in this way also exhibit *negativism* in the form of resistance to instructions given by clinicians or attendants. A more extreme version of the same behavior is seen where the patient actively does the opposite of that which he has been asked. If asked to sit, he may stand. If forbidden to perform some action, he will do it.

While the most dominant pattern of the catatonic stupor is the motor pathology, there is reason to suppose that during these periods of apparent inactivity hallucinatory or delusional experiences are occurring.

These are not immediately evident to the observer, but descriptions given by patients after emerging from the inactive phase refer to them. Thought processes seem to center on death and destruction; the patient feels that he is already dead or undergoing torture and that universal catastrophe has struck the world.

All these behaviors are accompanied by a deterioration in personal habits, and in some instances the patient may regress to a relatively vegetative state of behavior. Example 12-4 (Meehl, 1947) illustrates some of these features.

EXAMPLE 12-4

Catatonic Schizophrenia

L. W., a forty-five-year-old unmarried schoolteacher, was hospitalized following complaints by her family that she was overactive and assaultive, talked irrationally, acted peculiarly, and was generally "out of her head." Her psychotic behavior had developed only four days before admission to hospital. Having come to her parents' home from the town in which she was employed, she seemed to them to be unwell. Her complaints were largely somatic and seemed to involve a headache. A local physician prescribed sulfa drugs for her condition, but the next day grossly psychotic symptoms appeared.

"She first began to mumble somewhat unclearly about having stolen or lost $100 from the school milk fund. The family went to the trouble of checking this with the school superintendent, who reported that there was no money missing. She would stand motionless for long periods merely staring vacantly into space; then would suddenly shift to a marked degree of activity. She talked vaguely about someone coming to take her away. At times she would creep around the floor on her knees with her hands outstretched, exclaiming repeatedly, 'A child is born! A child is born!' (possibly a connection with the Christmas play she was directing). With considerable difficulty her parents managed to get her back into bed.

"On Saturday she continued to behave peculiarly. She wandered aimlessly around the house, whined and cried a good deal, and said puzzling things. On one occasion she knelt before her mother and cried, 'Mother, mother—come!' She still seemed to be under the impression that someone was coming to take her away. Various members of the immediate family remained at her bedside all that night, which on the whole was reasonably peaceful. She was able to carry on a more or less lucid conversation with her sister, although she was not very voluble and still stared for extended intervals into space.

"When she awoke Sunday morning, she had a very difficult time putting on her stockings. She ate a hearty breakfast, and then at her parents' suggestion lay down for a nap. Upon awakening from this nap, she called her parents into the library, saying that she had something important to talk to them about. However, when they had come to listen, she seemed to have some sort of blocking which kept the words from coming. After manifesting this difficulty in speech, she grasped her father's hand without saying anything and squeezed it so hard that he cried out in pain. When her mother asked her what was the matter with her, she said that her stomach hurt and that she wanted a hot-water bottle for it. Upon being given the hot-water bottle, the patient began to 'tear it apart.' Then she suddenly became 'stiff and rigid.' This phenomenon alarmed the mother, who ran to the telephone saying that she was going to call the physician, whereupon the patient again became active and fought to keep her mother from the telephone. When the physician arrived and decided to administer an intravenous sedative, it required the combined efforts of four people to hold the patient down. During the half hour or so before this injection took effect, the patient ran and rolled 'all over the floor,' bumping into furniture and grabbing at people so that it was necessary to keep objects clear of her to prevent her from injuring herself. Late that afternoon she was brought to the university hospital and admitted to the psychiatric ward."

Once in the hospital, this patient's behavior was marked by active and passive negativism. She would perform actions the opposite of those requested by the nurse. When her temperature was to be taken, she would close her mouth tightly. She would sometimes spit out the food that she had allowed to be put into her mouth, and it was necessary to catheterize her because of urinary retention. At times she would be fairly quiet and able to speak easily, but within a short time would become tense, hold her arms rigid, and two hours later have to be put into restraints because of violent activity and assaultiveness. (Meehl, 1947, pp. 72–77.)

Differentiation between catatonic schizophrenia and manic-depressive psychosis is sometimes problematic because of the overactivity common to both patterns of pathology. However, Example 12-4 includes the characteristic negativism, mutism, and blocking that define the catatonic pattern, and these are central to the diagnostic decision.

use of the term *hebephrenic silliness* to describe it. Continued deterioration of behavior to the point where the patient may become incontinent in excretion, utterly heedless of grooming, liable to eat dirt or rubbish found around the ward, and so forth, is a frequent outcome. A case of this kind is given in Example 12-5.

Schizophrenic Reaction: Hebephrenic Type

The characteristics of the hebephrenic type of schizophrenic reaction are vaguer and less well defined than the others. Delusions and hallucinations are common, but they are of a disorganized kind and have little in the way of systematic content. Bizarre ideas about his body are not unusual in a patient —delusions that his body is hollow, that his brain has frozen and has been removed, and so forth. Delusions and hallucinations are likely to have a pleasant emotional tone and to be accompanied by expressions of self-satisfaction, grandiosity, and pleasure. Irrelevant joviality and outbursts of laughter without apparent stimulus are common. The whole pattern of behavior is marked by a bizarreness and absurdity that has led to the

Schizophrenic Reaction: Paranoid Type

Far and away the most common variety of schizophrenic reaction is the paranoid type. The distinguishing aspect of this diagnostic definition is the presence of more or less *systematized* delusions. Such delusions are organized with regard to the rest of the patient's beliefs and in some cases are comparatively logical provided that one accepts the patient's (incorrect) first premise. More often than not these delusions are based upon the belief that the patient is being persecuted or attacked by some outside agency or people. He attributes a variety of bodily and psychological problems to these outside forces; for example, his thoughts are "being stolen" or are being wiped out by malevolent "radiations" directed by his

EXAMPLE 12-5

Hebephrenic Schizophrenia

The patient is a twenty-two-year-old single white woman. She graduated from college with an M.A. in mathematics at the age of twenty. After graduation she worked in accounting and clerical positions. She was very seclusive and had few friends, but she had one male friend whom she had known for about two years. The possibility of marriage to him had been discussed.

The onset of her psychotic condition was marked by depression. She ". . . cried a great deal, expressed unfavorable opinions about members of her family and great dissatisfaction with home conditions; grew increasingly absent-minded, could not keep her mind on her work, and was sent to a hospital for observation where she remained for about seven months. Here she was overproductive and irrelevant in conversation. She had a habit of defining words used and describing her feelings in meticulous detail. The physicians thought that she probably had been mentally ill for a long time. In about seven months she was transferred to a state hospital in an unimproved condition.

A report 21 days after admission described her as pleasant, compliant, and well oriented. A month later no change was noted. A few weeks later she was reported as irritable and cross, as sullen and evasive during an interview, and as quoting the Bible on occasions. A month later she was still irritable.

Her mental status was described as: "At least average intelligence; memory, retention, and immediate recognition—good; no impairment in her thinking capacity; continually quotes the Bible hoping that it can help her since medical science has failed to do so. Prognosis guarded."

Three months after this description, the patient was reported to be worse. Awareness of her surroundings had diminished, she appeared to be immune to any external stimulation, and the general slowness of her mental processes had increased appreciably. (From Babcock, 1947, pp. 40–43.)

---

enemies. Auditory hallucinations are often reported, again usually of a threatening nature.

Some of these delusional systems are elaborated into complicated *world schemes.*[4] These schemes, or even more modest delusional systems, are sometimes written up by the patient and distributed widely to public figures. Preoccupation with problems of geopolitics, the law, and other abstractions is common. Religious and philosophical issues are often developed in delusional form.

Part of the delusional aspect of the patient's thinking is the tendency to interpret trivial events within the delusional framework. *Ideas of reference*, as they are termed,

refer to the manner in which the patient reads personal significance into the actions of others, overheard phrases, and the like.

Although the patient may act according to his delusions, he is also likely to remain in gross contact with his environment in other respects most of the time: he is able to engage in conversation, and he remains oriented as to time and place with reasonable accuracy. The onset of paranoid schizophrenia is possible at almost any age past puberty. Frequently it occurs in the fourth or fifth decade of life. An illustration of this kind of reaction is provided in Example 12-6.

Schizophrenic Reaction: Undifferentiated Type

The four types described so far may be thought of as models or hypothetical types rather than as four clearly distinct categories.

[4] For example, the author has in his possession a document of many pages which provides a "computer program for world peace" written in computer terminology!

EXAMPLE 12-6

Paranoid Schizophrenia

Mr. S was first admitted to the hospital at the age of forty-eight. He was admitted at the insistence of his two sons, who had become alarmed at his increasing suspiciousness and irascibility. Some weeks prior to admission, he had taken to sealing the cracks under doors and in window sashes with the metal from empty toothpaste tubes to "keep out radio waves" that were being directed at him by agents of "the Tsar Nicholas." He lost his job as a skilled glass stainer around this time because of similar behavior at work, but he attributed his dismissal to similar machinations of enemies and unnamed fellow workers.

On admission, he was well groomed to the point of being dapper, and he expressed considerable interest in the professional status of the resident who interviewed him, the national reputation of the hospital, and so forth, pointing out the international fame that would accrue to the institution from his presence. On the ward he was condescending to the other patients, demanding many privileges for himself and giving lengthy accounts of the importance attached to him by both the Russians and the White House. He spent many hours perusing newspapers to see if his movements were reported there. He also devoted much time to brushing his hair and grooming himself, and he made sexual overtures to the student nurses.

Within a short time of admission, his delusional system became more elaborate. He accused his two sons of being in league with his enemies and plotting to keep him in hospital. He finally reached a point where he attempted to obtain legal counsel to arrange to nullify their kinship relationship with him. After a period of seven months on the ward, his symptoms subsided and he was released to the care of his oldest son. When he was leaving the hospital he was full of praise for the kindness and acumen of this son for getting him out of the hospital.

Many patients exhibit patterns of pathological behavior that show features of some or all of these types, and it has been found convenient to add the category of an *undifferentiated type* to describe them. Inasmuch as there is no typical pattern in this category, we may dispense with any case description.

THE PATIENT'S EXPERIENCE

Clinical descriptions, such as those given in the preceding section, are descriptions from the viewpoint of the professional observer. Many aspects of the description are readily amenable to operational measurement. It is comparatively simple to develop measures of motor activity, frequency of use of neologisms, and the like. Feelings of unreality, however, are extremely difficult to describe in observational terms. To get some notion of the quality of these features of the patient's pathology, we should consider the statements made by patients who have been able to record their experiences. Let us turn first to a description given by a twenty-two-year-old woman, as reported by Meyer and Covi (1960).

Feelings of Depersonalization

The patient had been an inpatient for 16 months. During the first year of this period, she had been chronically frightened, withdrawn, inarticulate, and actively suicidal. She had begun to improve at the time the following document was written, and she was discharged 4 months later. Here is the document.

"In order to explain the feeling of not being real, it is necessary to go into a long unreal definition of the feeling, for it is so far from reality, that in order to be made into a concrete real definition, it has to be described in an abstract, unreal way, if it is to be fully understood. Probably it is not worth fully understanding, for the feeling itself is one of unworthiness, in the way that a counterfeit bill might feel when being examined by a banker, with a good understanding and appreciation of real currency.

"It makes each day assume a magnitude and importance that would not ordinarily be expected of it. Little things that could be thought of as small, when one has the will to decide big and small and to put things in their relative positions as much as is possible, become huge and assume frightening proportions. It is as if everything that is done during the day is done automatically and, then, examined by the feeling that would have been put into the act, had it been committed in a reasonably normal way. Just as the Church was rent apart by schisms, the most sacred monument that is erected by the human spirit, i.e., its ability to think and decide and will to do, is torn apart by itself. Finally, it is thrown out where it mingles with every other part of the day and judges what it has left behind. Instead of wishing to do things, they are done by something that seems mechanical and frightening, because it is able to do things and yet unable to want to or not to want to. All the constructive healing parts, that could be used healthily and slowly to mend an aching torment, have left, and the feeling that should dwell within a person is outside, longing to come back and yet having taken with it the power to return. Out and in, are probably not good terms though, for they are too black and white and it is more like gray. It is like a constant sliding and shifting that slips away in a jelly-like fashion, leaving nothing substantial and yet enough to be tasted, or like watching a movie based on a play, and having once seen the play, realizing that the movie is a description of it and one that brings back memories and yet isn't real and just different enough to make all the difference.

"Even a description of it is unreal and tormenting, for it is horrifying and yet seems mild and vague, although it is acute. It is felt in an unreal way in that it isn't constant torture and yet never seems to leave and everything seems to slip away into impressions. What seems to be is more important that what is and nags, rather than throws

temper tantrums. For what is, is, and yet what seems to be is always changing and drifting away into thought and ideas, rather than actualities. The important things have left and the unimportant stay behind, making the loss only more apparent by their presence." (Meyer & Covi, 1960, pp. 215–216.)

Perceptual Changes

We have seen that patients complain that objects in the external environment appear to be flat, unreal, or remote. In the following extracts we see some of the changes in this kind of experience as described by patients.

"I awoke again, reverberating to the intermittently deafening noise of a radio blaring into my ears. My eyesight had undergone another transformation and seemed linked in some way to my hearing. As great waves of blaring music poured into me, my vision became steadily clearer only to fade almost to blindness as the music descended into near silence. As far as I was able to judge in moments of visual clarity, the sound came from behind a screen which surrounded part of the bed next to me, concealing all but the lower half of a body. The sound was so loud, or suddenly so soft, that it was impossible to identify exactly what it was but it seemed to me the playing and singing of various popular songs simultaneously, accompanied by continuous static. After some moments of listening, I contributed to the din in the room by beginning to scream at regular intervals: 'Quiet! Quiet! Can't we please have some quiet?' " (Peters, 1949, pp. 53–54.)

The disturbance in perception of the intensity of stimulation is paralleled by disturbances in the perception of depth and of time. The following two quotations will illustrate these effects.

"Around us the fields spread away, cut up by hedges or clumps of trees; the white road ran ahead of us; the sun shone in the blue sky and warmed our backs. But I saw a boundless plain, unlimited, the horizon infinite. The trees and hedges were of cardboard, placed here and there, like stage accessories, and the road, oh, the endless road, white glittering under the sun's rays, glittering like a needle; above us the remorseless sun weighing down trees and houses under its electric rays." (Sechehaye, 1951, pp. 15; 17.)

"I do not remember that first day in five as a day. This is not surprising, because for a long time no day seemed to me like a day, and no night seemed like a night.

"But this day, in particular, has no shape in my memory. I used to tell the time by meals, but as I believed that we were served with several sets of meals in each real day—about half a dozen sets of breakfast, lunch, tea, and dinner in each twelve hours—this was not much help." (Harrison, 1941, p. 32.)

Delusional Thinking

In the following extract, a former patient is describing the development of her delusional thinking and some accompanying perceptual anomalies.

"There has been so much written about acute schizophrenic illnesses, and there is so much material available on delusions and hallucinations, that I won't go further into those. What I do want to explain, if I can, is the exaggerated state of awareness in which I lived before, during and after my acute illness. At first it was as if parts of my brain 'awoke' which had been dormant, and I became interested in a wide assortment of people, events, places and ideas which normally would make no impression on me. Not knowing that I was ill, I made no attempt to understand what was happening, but felt that there was some overwhelming significance in all this, produced either by God or Satan, and I felt that I was duty-bound to ponder on each of these new interests, and the more I pondered the worse it became. The walk of a stranger on the street could be a 'sign' to me which I must interpret. Every face in the windows of a passing streetcar would be engraved on my mind, all of them concentrating on me and trying to pass me some sort of message. Now, many years later, I can appreciate what had happened. Each of us is capable of coping with a large number of stimuli, invading our being through anyone of the senses. We could hear every sound within earshot and see every object, line, and colour within the field of vision, and so on. It's obvious that we would be incapable of carrying on any of our daily activities if even one-hundredth of all these available stimuli invaded us at once. So the mind must have a filter which functions without our conscious thought, sorting stimuli and allowing only those which are relevant to the situation in hand to disturb consciousness. And this filter must be working at maximum efficiency at all times, particularly when we require a high degree of concentration. What had happened to me in Toronto was a breakdown in the filter, and a hodge-podge of unrelated stimuli were distracting me from things which should have had my undivided attention.

"New significance in people and places was not particularly unpleasant, though it got badly in the way of my work, but the significance of the real or imagined *feelings* of people was very painful. To feel that the stranger passing on the street knows your innermost soul is disconcerting. I was sure that the girl in the office on my right was jealous of me. I felt that the girl in the office on my left wanted to be my friend but I made her feel depressed. It's quite likely that these impressions were valid, but the intensity with which I felt them made the air fairly crackle when the stenographers in question came into my office. Work in a situation like that is too difficult to be endured at all. I withdrew farther and farther, but I became more and more aware of the city around me. The real or imagined poverty and real or imagined unhappiness of hundreds of people I would never meet burdened my soul, and I felt martyred. In this state, delusions can very easily take root and begin to grow. I reached a stage where almost my entire world consisted of tortured contemplation of things which brought pain and unutterable depression. My brain, after a short time, became sore with a real physical soreness, as if it had been rubbed with sandpaper until it was raw. It felt like a bleeding sponge. Meaningful distractions from the real world, such as the need to carry on a conversation with a friend, sometimes brought welcome relief from the pain and depression, but not always. By the time I was admitted to hospital I had reached a stage of 'wakefulness' when the brilliance of light on a window sill or the colour of blue in the sky would be so important it could make me cry.

I had very little ability to sort the relevant from the irrelevant. The filter had broken down. Completely unrelated events became intricately connected in my mind." (MacDonald, 1960, pp. 175–176.)

Later in this book we shall examine the importance of perceptual changes in schizophrenia. From some theoretical points of view, they are of central importance to understanding the pathology. When reading the extracts given above, we should remember that the writers were intelligent and well-educated. In this respect they are somewhat atypical of the hospital population as a whole, but the insights that they offer may be of great general value in understanding the mechanisms determining schizophrenic behavior.

DIMENSIONAL DESCRIPTIONS

Although the fourfold typology given in the previous section is the most common, some investigators have been interested in developing ways of describing schizophrenic pathology along some unitary dimension. On this basis patients may be compared with each other as they exhibit different degrees of some single process, or as they occupy different points along some continuum of pathology. Let us now consider some of the more important of these.

The Process-Reactive Distinction

The process-reactive distinction, in its general form, states that within the category of schizophrenia two subgroups may be distinguished. One of these is *process* schizophrenia and the other is *reactive* schizophrenia. A major difference between the process and reactive groups is that the reactives are marked by sudden onset of schizophrenic behavior with little or no history of prepsychotic pathology and have a favorable prognosis for recovery. Process schizophrenia, on the other hand, is marked by a long history of psychological diffi-

culties, gradual onset of the symptoms of schizophrenia, and poor prognosis for recovery. This distinction was noted by Bleuler (1911), although never followed up by him. A more detailed account of the distinction between the two groups is provided in Table 12-1.

While it is possible to conceive of this distinction as being between two types of schizophrenia, the clinical data suggest instead, as Becker (1956, 1959) has remarked, that we might more suitably think of the two categories as the two end points of a continuum along which various gradations are possible in any single case. This continuum, Becker suggests, is one based upon *levels of personality organization*. Such a concept is exceedingly complex, and the problem of measuring levels of organization is quite difficult. In principle, however, the lowest level of personality organization is marked by poor perceptual constancy, inadequate differentiation of needs and interests, and poor emotional or adaptive functioning under stress.

King (1958) extended this notion of a process-reactive continuum to include physiological measures. He has specifically considered the reaction of the patients' blood pressure to injections of the drug mecholyl and has reported that autonomic reactivity of this kind was correlated with the patient's prepsychotic history. Process schizophrenics showed little autonomic reaction, while the reactive group did produce significant blood pressure changes.

As Chapter 14 discusses, the process-reactive distinction has been used in studies of various psychological functions and represents one of the more recent trends in the study of schizophrenia. The fundamental distinction that it makes is between patients who have a more or less normal life history up to the time they are admitted to hospital and those who have a history of inadequacy and pathology for many years before admission. Other attempts have been made to measure premorbid (i.e., preillness) status, and we shall consider these now.

TABLE 12-1 Items Defining Frame of Reference for Case History Judgments

Process schizophrenia	Reactive schizophrenia
Birth to the fifth year	
a. Early psychological trauma	a. Good psychological history
b. Physical illness—severe or long	b. Good physical health
c. Odd member of family	c. Normal member of family
Fifth year to adolescence	
a. Difficulties at school	a. Well adjusted at school
b. Family troubles paralleled by sudden changes in patient's behavior	b. Domestic troubles unaccompanied by behavior disruptions; patient "had what it took"
c. Introverted behavior trends and interests	c. Extroverted behavior trends and interests
d. History of breakdown of social, physical, mental functioning	d. History of adequate social, physical, mental functioning
e. Pathological siblings	e. Normal siblings
f. Overprotective or rejecting mother, "momism"	f. Normally protective, accepting mother
g. Rejecting father	g. Accepting father
Adolescence to adulthood	
a. Lack of heterosexuality	a. Heterosexual behavior
b. Insidious, gradual onset of psychosis without pertinent stress	b. Sudden onset of psychosis; stress present and pertinent; later onset
c. Physical aggression	c. Verbal aggression
d. Poor response to treatment	d. Good response to treatment
e. Lengthy stay in hospital	e. Short course in hospital
Adulthood	
a. Massive paranoia	a. Minor paranoid trends
b. Little capacity for alcohol	b. Much capacity for alcohol
c. No manic-depressive component	c. Presence of manic-depressive component
d. Failure under adversity	d. Success despite adversity
e. Discrepancy between ability and achievement	e. Harmony between ability and achievement
f. Awareness of change in self	f. No sensation of change
g. Somatic delusions	g. Absence of somatic delusions
h. Clash between culture and environment	h. Harmony between culture and environment
i. Loss of decency (nudity, public masturbation, etc.)	i. Retention of decency

SOURCE: *Kantor, Wallner, and Winder (1953).*

Premorbid Status and Social Competence

Adequacy of premorbid adjustment has been scaled by Phillips (1953). The Phillips Premorbid Scale is a method of estimating adjustment by differential weighting of various items in the patient's case history. An illustration of the manner of scaling for male patients is provided in Table 12-2.

Premorbid adjustment has been shown to be related to prognosis in the case of schizophrenia (Phillips, 1953); to success in the rehabilitation of schizophrenic patients (Farina & Webb, 1956); to the level of perceptual cognitive development shown by normal subjects (Lane, 1955); and to reactivity to stimulation (e.g., Crider, Maher, & Grinspoon, 1965). Underlying the notion of premorbid adjustment is the concept of *social competence* or social maturity. Phillips and his associates have conceived of this within the general framework of personality development. They see the person as passing through stages of development in which differing kinds of social demand are placed upon his behavior. For every maturity level there is a normal and adequate pattern of adaptive behavior; there is also an inadequate or pathological pattern of deviation. In this way psychopathology may be regarded as encompassing various forms of ineffective solutions to the social demands made at given levels. The various syndromes of pathological behavior may be ordered or ranked as being representative of inadequacies at particular stages of maturity.

Normal behavior, seen from this standpoint, is not just the absence of pathology. What is normal and what is pathological depend upon the level of development of the individual and its relation to the social demands placed upon him. Improvement— i.e., remission—of a pathological syndrome is represented by the achievement of a successful solution to the patient's difficulties at his own level of maturity rather than at some ideal state. In pathological individuals, the patient with the higher degree of maturity should have a greater possibility of producing adequate solutions. Thus his level of maturity should be related to the prognosis for him. It should also be related to the kind of pathological behavior he displays when an adequate resolution has not yet been reached.

Measurement of Social Competence

A scale for rating the relative social maturity of an individual patient has been worked out by Zigler and Phillips (1960) in the following way. Six areas of development and

three levels of adequacy in each area are defined. These are presented in Table 12-3.

The investigators classified common symptoms of pathological behavior into those that entail (1) *self-deprivation and turning against the self,* (2) *self-indulgence and turning against others,* and (3) *avoidance of others.* The classification is based upon the assumption that different levels of problem resolution are involved in each of the three classes. If such is the case, we should expect that scores on the scale of social competence should be related to the kind of symptom exhibited by a patient. Data reported by Zigler and Phillips indicate that this is so. Table 12-4 illustrates the way in which different symptoms are found in patients of different levels of social competence. As the table shows, category 1 of self-deprivation and turning against the self is related to the highest levels of social competence, whereas the other two categories are ranked lower in this respect.

Examination of this table makes it clear that the symptoms most strongly associated with social incompetence are those included under the avoidance-of-others category. By the same token, these symptoms are most definitive of the diagnosis of schizophrenia. Direct evidence of this relationship has been provided by Zigler and Phillips (1960) in their study of the frequency of appearance of each category of symptom in four major psychiatric diagnostic classifications—manic-depressive psychosis, psychoneurosis, character disorder, and schizophrenia (including the four major types described earlier in this chapter). Their findings indicate the tendency for symptoms of the lowest social competence category to be definitive of schizophrenia.

The Action-Thought Parameter

Quite apart from the social competence dimension, it is possible to consider the process of normal development as involving a shift from action to thought in response to states of need. Early stages of development, this argument holds, are characterized

TABLE 12-2 Phillips Scale of Premorbid Status in Schizophrenia: Partial Extract

	Numerical Weight
A. Recent sexual adjustment	
1. Stable heterosexual relation and marriage	0
2. Continued heterosexual relation and marriage, but unable to establish home	1
3. Continued heterosexual relation and marriage broken by permanent separation	2
4. a. Continued heterosexual relation and marriage but with low sex drive	3
b. Continued heterosexual relation with deep emotional meaning but emotionally unable to develop it into marriage	3
5. a. Casual but continued heterosexual relations—"affairs"	4
b. Homosexual contacts with lack of or chronic failure in heterosexual experiences	4
6. a. Occasional casual heterosexual relations or homosexual experience with no deep emotional bond	5
b. Solitary masturbation; no attempt at heterosexual or homosexual experiences	5
7. No sexual interest in men or women	6
B. Social aspects of sexual life during adolescence & immediately beyond	
1. Always showed healthy interest in girls, with steady girl friend during adolescence	0
2. Started taking girls out regularly in adolescence	1
3. Always mixed closely with boys and girls	2
4. Consistent deep interest in male attachment, with restricted or no interest in girls	3
5. a. Casual male attachments with inadequate attempts at adjustment to going out with girls	4
b. Casual contact with boys and girls	4
6. a. Casual contacts with boys with lack of interest in girls	5
b. Occasional contact with girls	5
7. No desire to be with boys and girls; never went out with girls	6
C. Social aspects of recent sexual life: 30 years +	
1. Married and has children, living as a family unit	0
2. Married and has child but unable to establish or maintain a family home	1
3. Has been married and had child, but permanently separated	2
4. a. Married, but considerable marital discord	3
b. Single, but has had engagement or deep heterosexual relation—emotionally unable to develop into marriage	3
5. Single, short engagements/relationships with females which do	

	Numerical Weight
not appear to have emotional depth for both partners, i.e., "affairs"	4
6. a. Single, has gone out with a few girls, but no indications of a continuous interest in women	5
b. Single, consistent deep interest in male attachments, no interest in women	5
7. a. Single, occasional male contacts, no interest in women	6
b. Single, no interest in men or women	6

D. Social aspects of recent sexual life: below 30

1. Married, living as family unit with or without children	0
2. a. Married, with or without children, but unable to establish or maintain a family home	1
b. Single but engaged in a deep heterosexual relationship (presumably leading to marriage)	1
3. Single, has had engagement or deep heterosexual relation; emotionally unable to carry to marriage	2
4. Single, consistent, deep interest in male attachments, with restricted or no interest in women	3
5. Single, casual male relationships with restricted or no interest in women	4
6. Single, has gone out with a few girls casually but without indications of continued interest in women	5
7. a. Single, never interested in or associated with men or women	6
b. Antisocial	6

E. Personal relations: history

1. Always had a number of close friends but did not habitually play leading role	1
2. From adolescence on had a few close friends	2
3. From adolescence on had a few casual friends	3
4. From adolescence on stopped having friends	4
5. a. No intimate friends after childhood	5
b. Casual but never any deep intimate mutual friendships	5
6. Never worried about boys or girls; no desire to be with boys or girls	6

F. Recent premorbid adjustment in personal relations

1. Habitually mixed with others, but not a leader	1
2. Mixed only with a close friend or group of friends	3
3. No close friends; only very few friends; had friends but never quite accepted by them	4
4. Quiet; aloof; seclusive; preferred to be by self	5
5. Antisocial	6

SOURCE: *Phillips (1953)*.

TABLE 12-3 Categories of Social Competence

1. Age: 24 and below; 25–44; 45 years and above.
2. Intelligence: IQs obtained on a standard intelligence test of 84 or less; 85–115; 116 and above.
3. Education: none or some grades including ungraded or special classes; finished grade school, some high school, or high school; some college or more.
4. Occupation: *The Dictionary of Occupational Titles* (United States Government Printing Office, 1949) was employed to place each occupation into the categories of unskilled or semiskilled, skilled and service, or clerical and sales or professional and managerial.
5. Employment history: usually unemployed; seasonal, fluctuating, frequent shifts, or part-time employment; regularly employed.
6. Marital status: single; separated, divorced, remarried, or widowed; single continuous marriage.

SOURCE: *Zigler and Phillips (1960).*

by immediate, direct, and unmodulated responses to external stimuli or internal needs. Higher levels of maturation, on the other hand, are marked by the emergence of indirect, ideational, conceptual, symbolic, or verbal behavior patterns. This dimension of development has been termed the *action-thought parameter* (Phillips & Zigler, 1961).

Using this parameter in much the same manner as the social competence dimension, it is possible to predict that patients who are relatively mature (socially competent) should develop symptoms that are largely ideational, verbal, or symbolic. Directly active motor symptoms should be rare in the behavior patterns of this kind of individual. A reversal of this situation would be expected for individuals with a low level of premorbid social competence.

Case records of patients were examined by Zigler and Phillips with the following division of symptoms in mind.

Action Symptoms: Accused of murder, assault, perversions (except homosexuality), compulsions, rape, robbery, suicidal attempt, irresponsible behavior, etc.
Thought Symptoms: Suspiciousness, phobias, fear of own hostile impulses, bizarre ideas, obsessions, suicidal ideas, depersonalization, etc.

They found that patients with high social competence scores showed thought symptoms significantly more often than those with low social competence scores. Since they also obtained the reverse finding for the frequency of action symptoms, this investigation supports the general suppositions of developmental differences in symptomatology and their relation to premorbid social competence.

TABLE 12-4 Summary of Relationships between Symptom Categories and Social Effectiveness in Both Men and Women

	Men			Women		
	No. & %	No. & %	No. & %	No. & %	No. & %	No. & %
Symptom category	+	0	−	+	0	−
Category 1 Self-deprivation and turning against the self	32 (91%)	3 (9%)	0 (0%)	21 (72%)	6 (21%)	2 (7%)
Category 2 Self-indulgence and turning against others	5 (14%)	9 (26%)	21 (60%)	1 (5%)	2 (10%)	18 (85%)
Category 3 Avoidance of others	5 (28%)	2 (11%)	11 (61%)	6 (32%)	5 (26%)	8 (42%)

SOURCE: *Zigler and Phillips (1960).*

Summary

Dimensional descriptions of the kind we have just discussed offer a possibility of discovering systematic regularities underlying the bewildering array of symptoms that we observe. As such, they are in accord with the position that the shift from normal to pathological behavior is continuous, the dividing line between one and the other being open to many definitions. A position such as this is not consistent with the Kraepelinian hope that separate syndromes would be defined, each with its own etiology. It is consistent, however, with what we know about the way in which behavior is acquired. It is also consistent with the view that the principles of psychological science apply to the understanding of all behavior and that no special concepts or laws are necessary for the description of pathological behavior.

SOCIAL DETERMINANTS OF SCHIZOPHRENIA

Deficiency in normal social responses is an essential characteristic of schizophrenic pathology. Consequently one of the obvious lines of investigation is the nature of the immediate and broader social environments in which the patient is raised.

Family Patterns

Parents are the chief reinforcers of a child's behavior in early life. If the subsequent pathology of the schizophrenic patient is to be understood in terms of his early learning of inadequate methods for resolving problems of living, then we should expect to find some distinctive kinds of experiences in his early relationship with his parents. Many workers have studied the possibility of discovering *schizophrenogenic* influences in the family of the patient, and we shall look at some of these now. Our later discussion of the "double-bind" hypothesis will have obvious implications for the kind of relationship that might exist between the communicating parent and the child victim. However, that hypothesis lays major stress upon the manner of communication, whereas in this section we shall be more concerned with general patterns of family interaction.

Parent Dominance. Considerable attention has been given to the extent to which one parent dominates the other in the family of the schizophrenic patient. Marriages can be described in terms of the relative equality of the partners, varying from complete equality to complete dominance of one partner by the other. Both of these extremes are, of course, hypothetical, and it is unlikely that they would be found in actual marriages.

Many investigators report that the families of schizophrenic patients show the dominance of one parent by the other more often than is true of normal samples. There is some suggestion (Rodnick & Garmezy, 1957) that patients who come from father-dominated families tend to be married, to have numerous friends of both sexes, and to present a better premorbid history than patients from mother-dominated families. The latter tend to remain single, to be social isolates, and to make a poor social and sexual adjustment before hospitalization.

Parental Conflicts. A series of studies by Lidz and his colleagues (Lidz & Lidz, 1949; Lidz, Cornelison, Fleck, & Terry, 1957) emphasizes the existence of what they call *marital schism* and *marital skew* in the schizophrenic family. Marital schism refers, simply, to direct conflict between the two parents. Each partner is hostile and disappointed in the other, in both cases because of feelings that the partner has not fulfilled expectations in the relationship. Conflicts of this kind, so it appears, are generally accompanied by attempts on the part of both parents to recruit the child to their side of the dispute. Marital skew refers to the tendency for the pathological attributes of one of the parents—the dominant parent—to be accepted and adopted by the other. From a situation of this kind, the child might well be expected to learn pathological responses much as the child of normal parents learns normal behavior.

Direct investigation of these questions has been carried out, usually within a clinical observational framework. Farina (1960) observed the actual verbal interactions of the parents of male schizophrenic patients and recorded several measures of dominance and conflict between them, comparing their behavior with that of a group of controls (parents of male patients hospitalized for tuberculosis). His psychiatric subjects were further divided into good premorbid and poor premorbid on the basis of the Phillips scale. The results of this investigation revealed a marked relationship between sex of the dominant parent and level of premorbid adjustment achieved by a schizophrenic son. The interactions of parents of good-premorbid patients were marked by father dominance, whereas in the poor-premorbid group, the parental relationship was dominated by the mother. General conflict measures were also higher in the parents of the schizophrenic groups. Of great importance in this study is the fact that the high-conflict scores were largely contributed by the poor-premorbid group, there being no significant differences between the control and the good-premorbid parents on these measures. These observations may not, of course, be applicable to female schizophrenics.

Interpretation of correlational data such as these is always open to doubt. If we assume that the male child acquires adequate maturity as a male by having a dominant father to provide a model, then we may claim that Farina's results support this. Good-premorbid patients display more normal adult male behavior prior to the psychosis than is found in poor-premorbid patients. Although the good-premorbid patient may be living in a family which is psychologically unhealthy, with poor marital relationships between parents, nevertheless the father is dominant and therefore in a position to reinforce the behaviors of his son when the latter copies him. As a model the father may be an unfortunate one, but he may still make it possible for the son to acquire some integrated male behavior. In the mother-dominated family, this would not be possible.

Parental Personality. Over and above the question of parental interactions, many students of schizophrenia have sought for a pattern of personality that might characterize each parent individually. A rationale for such a search is obvious, since the personality of the parent presumably has a profound effect by its behavioral impact upon the child. The *schizophrenogenic mother* has been described by Arieti (1959) as "overprotective, hostile, overtly or subtly rejecting, overanxious, cold, distant, etc." Lidz, Parker, and Cornelison (1956) describe the father of the schizophrenic patient as insecure in his masculinity, in need of great admiration to bolster his shaky self-esteem, and not infrequently paranoid or given to irrational behavior.

The problem with these interpretations, based largely upon clinical observations, is that they are made without clear reference to measures of the behavior of normal people's parents. Fortunately we have data from Schofield and Balian (1959) that fill this gap. They studied intensively a large number of hospitalized schizophrenics and medical patient controls, recording important variables in their relationships with parents and with siblings. There was a considerable overlap between both groups on all variables (i.e., many of the schizophrenic patients had family relationships indistinguishable from those of the normal controls). While it was found that there were significant differences between normals and schizophrenics, the latter more often having poor relationships with father or mother, this was true for only about one-third of the cases.

As we shall see immediately below, many investigators have been concerned with the relationship between social class and schizophrenia. Empirical details of these relationships will be discussed later, but we should note here that family patterns of interaction are themselves heavily influenced by social class. Hence, the finding that a particular kind of parent-child relationship predominates in the families of schizophrenics is likely to be confounded by the fact that the patients most often come from lower social-class levels. Thus the "schizophrenogenic" family may be a largely normal low-social-class pattern.

Lane and Singer (1959) have developed this argument in some detail. They conducted a detailed study comparing the family attitudes of male patients who were diagnosed as paranoid schizophrenic with those of patients who were hospitalized for nonpsychiatric medical illnesses. Both groups, in turn, were subdivided into lower socioeconomic and middle socioeconomic levels, based upon evaluation of the patient's father's occupation, type of neighborhood the patient lived in as a boy, family ownership of real estate, and family history of requiring public assistance or relief.

On the basis of a wide range of previous investigations of the "schizophrenogenic family," they deduced the following hypotheses about family relationships in schizophrenia.

Normal-Schizophrenic Differences. (*a*) The schizophrenics reveal stronger feelings of rejection by their parents. (*b*) The schizophrenics indicate greater control by parents. (*c*) The schizophrenics reveal greater dependence upon parents. (*d*) The schizophrenics manifest evidence of a greater problem regarding the expression of hostility (as shown either by more repression or denial of hostility or by more direct hostility). (*e*) The schizophrenics place a greater value on being a "good boy," a more conventional submissive type of personality. (*f*) The schizophrenics describe a greater

degree of maternal overprotection. (*g*) The schizophrenics reveal more evidence of Oedipal conflict. (*h*) The schizophrenics describe their parents as more unhappy with each other or ill-suited to each other.

From previous work on differences in family patterns in different social classes, a second set of hypotheses was derived, unrelated to the problem of schizophrenia. These hypotheses were as follows.

Socioeconomic Class Differences. (*a*) The middle-class subjects describe parental figures as more ambitious and concerned with their achievement than do lower-class subjects. (*b*) The middle-class subjects are less able to express hostility. (*c*) The middle-class subjects describe their mothers as more overprotective. (*d*) The lower-class subjects describe their parents as using more direct forms of control. (*e*) The middle-class subjects reveal a different relationship with father figures. (*f*) The lower-class group manifests less evidence of Oedipal conflict. (*g*) The lower-class subjects reveal a greater degree of interparental friction. (*h*) The lower-class subjects indicate greater independence.

Family attitudes were measured by a battery of questionnaire scales and semi-projective instruments. From the data, the authors concluded that many of the significant differences between schizophrenic and normal subjects could be accounted for by social class differences. That is to say, the "schizophrenogenic" family pattern appeared to differentiate middle-class schizophrenics from middle-class normals. In the lower-class comparisons there were fewer differences of any kind between patients and controls.

All in all, we must regard the data from studies of family interaction as suggesting that some kinds of family pattern are contributory to the pathology, but only as one of several etiological factors, and mainly in some social classes.

The Extended Family

Some attention has been turned to the wider family and kinship relations of the schizophrenic patient. One of the more systematic approaches to this part of the patient's environment has been made by Bell (1962). Bell's thesis is that a marriage produces a temporary disruption of existing arrangements in the families of the marriage partners. The principal focus of friction is the relationship between one partner and the parents of the other (the "in-law" problem). In America and many areas of Western Europe, the marriage creates a new and separate family, requiring the dissolution or weakening of ties to the old families. As both sets of in-law relatives are equally important—the wife's family has the same claims to make on the new marriage as the husband's—the success of the marriage in the long run is influenced by the ability of the people involved to establish some minimum of harmonious equilibrium between the new demands.

Bell argues that this equilibrium has not been established in the families of disturbed patients, but is usually evident in the families of well people. "Disturbed families," he claims, "have a deficiency of family boundaries, which leads them to involve extended kin in their conflicts and makes them sensitive to influence from extended kin. Directly or indirectly a considerable segment of kindred systems becomes part of a pathological drama until pathology is a characteristic of the system, not of individual persons or families."

Social and Cultural Influences

Moving further into the study of broad social influences upon the patient, we may turn to the investigations of *epidemiology* as it is related to the social class of the patient. Epidemiology is the study of the distribution of illness throughout a community or society. One of the better-known investigations of the epidemiology of mental illness is that reported by Hollingshead and Redlich (1958). They investigated the incidence of mental illness in New Haven, Connecticut, and found that there were considerably more schizophrenic patients in the lower socioeconomic groups than in the higher. This observation is in line with those made much earlier by Faris and Dunham (1939). They reported that high rates of first hospital admission for schizophrenia are found in areas of the city where residents are generally of low social class and where residential stability is poor. Members of particular ethnic groups living in non-ethnic areas of the community were likewise more prone to exhibit schizophrenic behavior, as were foreign-born residents of slum areas.

From this finding, Faris and Dunham developed their *social isolation* hypothesis, namely that any way of life which tends to cut a person off from intimate social contacts with others for an extended period of time is likely to lead to schizophrenic pathology. They felt that the early childhood experiences are less important than the circumstances that produce social isolation. "In a majority of cases the early childhood was reported to be normal and without any indications of schizophrenic symptoms. These symptoms developed after the isolating factors had been at work" (Faris, 1944).

Some twenty years after Faris and Dunham's original report, an extended investigation of this hypothesis was made by Kohn and Clausen (1955). Intensive study of the histories of 45 schizophrenic patients led them to conclude that significant elements of schizophrenic behavior were evident in childhood and before any environmentally produced social isolation could occur. Social isolation, they concluded, was a symptom, "to be viewed as a sign that the individual's interpersonal difficulties have become so great that he is no longer capable of functioning in interpersonal relationships. The question of how he got that way is not a question of social isolation *per se*."

There is little doubt that social class is correlated with the frequency of diagnosed mental illness within that class and with the kind of diagnosis that is made. Diagnoses of schizophrenia are more common in lower socioeconomic groups. In order to understand this kind of correlation, we need to know something about the specific influences in a social class that impinge upon the individual. Certain kinds of physical diseases are also prevalent in lower socioeconomic groups, but the class correlation does not tell us anything about the pathological organisms responsible for the spread of the disease. An additional observation that we might make is that the majority of the members of the lower socioeconomic groups do not exhibit schizophrenic pathology, or any other pathology for that matter. Clearly we need to identify the specific psychological influences operating on the person who develops schizophrenic behavior before we can arrive at a systematic account of the way in which the social class correlation occurs.

Now that we have had an opportunity to consider the general character of the social environment of the schizophrenic, we may begin to examine the work that has dealt with specific etiological agents. One of the first areas to consider is that of interpersonal communication—the channels through which social reinforcements have their effect upon the acquisition of behavior by the patient.

COMMUNICATION AND SCHIZOPHRENIA

The Double-bind Hypothesis

Gregory Bateson and his colleagues (Bateson, Jackson, Haley, & Weakland, 1956; Weakland, 1960) have proposed a hypothesis to account for the origin of schizophrenic behavior that focuses on the communications made to the patient by others, especially by his parents. This hypothesis describes the individual as being in a *double-bind* situation, which is characterized as follows.

1. The person is faced with a significant communication involving two separate messages, each belonging to a different level or logical type. The two messages are related to each other (i.e., they refer to the same problem or event) but are incongruent.
2. A response of some kind to this communication is mandatory, so that ignoring it or leaving the situation is not possible.
3. The basic contradictions in the messages are concealed, denied, or inhibited in some way so that it is not possible to recognize them overtly when responding.

An excellent example of a parent placing a child in a double bind of this kind was provided by Samuel Butler in the novel *The Way of All Flesh*. Mrs. Pontifex is speaking to her son, Ernest.

"Papa does not feel," she continued, "that you love him with that fulness and unreserve which would prompt you to have no concealment from him, and to tell him everything freely and fearlessly as your most loving earthly friend next only to your Heavenly Father. Perfect love, as we know, casteth out fear: your father loves you perfectly, my darling, but he does not feel as though you loved him perfectly in return. If you fear him it is because you do not love him as he deserves, and I know it sometimes cuts him to the very heart to think that he has earned from you a deeper and more willing sympathy than you display towards him. Oh, Ernest, Ernest, do not grieve one who is so good and noble-hearted by conduct which I can call by no other name than ingratitude."

Ernest could never stand being spoken to in this way by his mother: for he still believed that she loved him, and that he was fond of her and had a friend in her—up to a certain point. But his mother was beginning to come to the end of her tether; she had played the domestic confidence trick upon him times without number already. Over and over again had she wheedled from him all she wanted to know, and afterwards got him into the most horrible scrape by telling the whole to Theobald. Ernest had remonstrated more than once upon these occasions, and had pointed out to his mother how disastrous to him his confidences had been, but Christina had always joined issue with him and showed him in the clearest possible manner that in each case she had been right, and that he could not reasonably complain. Generally it was her conscience that forbade her to be silent, and against this there was no appeal, for we are all bound to follow the dictates of our conscience. (Butler, 1903.)

Butler's fictional example illustrates an important feature of the double bind. The attempt to point out the incongruity of the message leads to a denial of this incongruity on the part of the message sender (Ernest's mother), who points out that her betrayal of the victim's confidence was "necessary" for the sake of a higher principle. Denial of the incongruity is one of the critical ingredients of the double bind. Not only does it prevent any escape from the dilemma facing the victim, but it involves an additional contradiction; the victim is being told something contradictory and then being told that no contradiction exists. In this way, any particular instance of a contradictory communication may be seen as contributing to a larger overall relationship between the communicator and the victim, a relationship that itself possesses the central characteristics of the double bind.

As the only adequate responses possible to incongruent communications would be those that recognize the incongruity, the effect of the double bind is to generate inadequate behaviors of various kinds. Complete withdrawal is one possibility. Reactions to messages of even a normal kind by seeking for hidden meaning is another, a habit perhaps developed by a long history of trying to make unitary sense from the incongruities that the victim has experienced throughout his life. In any event, the process of communication should acquire many aversive factors.

The Double-bind and Conflict

Messages are psychologically important insofar as they are stimuli for some response on the part of the listener. Messages that require no response from the listener would not constitute a double bind of any significance. Thus, should we hear a political speaker claiming that the national economy is becoming healthier each week, while also remarking on the growing rate of unemployment, we might not even notice the incongruity because no response is required.

Where a response is called for, however, it is clear that the double-bind situation is directly analogous to the approach-avoidance conflict model presented in Chapter 6. A communication is made that evokes incompatible responses in the same way that a stimulus possessing characteristics of separate stimuli associated with both punishment and reward evokes incompatible responses. In Chapter 6 we have seen how the existence of conflict states, coupled with an inability to get away from the situation (i.e., coupled with restraint in the situation), leads to a variety of disorganized responses. We have also seen how, in the laboratory, the experimental neurosis makes the entire experimental setting aversive to the subject. If this analogy holds up, we should expect that the schizophrenic patient will eschew social interactions with others. When these are unavoidable, he may adopt protective devices that will nullify the interaction and maintain his protective posture. A very similar analysis is to be found in Bannister's *serial invalidation hypothesis* of schizophrenic thinking discussed at length in Chapter 15.

ROLE TAKING IN SCHIZOPHRENIA

Role Taking and Discrimination Learning

Different social situations require differing social responses. Patterns of behavior appropriate to a particular social environment are termed *roles*,[5] and the learning of roles may be regarded as one of the most important processes in the acquisition of behavior by an individual. Every person learns many roles in his life. That is, he learns to respond discriminatively to different people.

[5] For an extended discussion of the application of principles of learning to the concept of social role, the reader is referred to Lewis (1959).

A failure to do this will produce unpleasant results, and if sufficiently striking will be regarded as pathological.

Role behavior is generally acquired initially in the home. Hartley and Hartley (1952) describe the process as one whereby the child "finds that one kind of behavior brings comfort and another brings discomfort, or that one kind obtains for him what he wants and another fails to do this. . . . In accordance with what his parents notice or disregard, reward or punish, the child develops a pattern of behaviors that correspond to the social role in his family group." Naturally we should expect that where the behavior of the parent does not permit the child to acquire consistent role behavior, the whole process of learning discriminative responses for different social settings would be impaired. For role learning to take place, it is necessary for the child to be living in an environment where there are systematic punishments and rewards for adequate role taking. If we assume that this was not the case for the schizophrenic patient, then we should expect that his role-taking ability in later life will be poor.

Cameron's Hypothesis

Norman Cameron has concluded that deficiency in role taking is a central feature of schizophrenic pathology. A socially immature, solitary, and anxious person enters adulthood lacking "the degree of role-taking skill necessary for ease in shifting perspective under stress. He has learned to rely heavily upon fantasy; but he has not mastered the techniques of social validation, of sharing his interpretations and conclusions, and of modifying them in accordance with the attitudes of others. When, through attempted social interaction he encounters severe conflict, thwarting or delay, and develops marked anxiety, he is almost sure to show disorganization" (Cameron & Magaret, 1951).

This general hypothesis has been tested by reference to the concept of *empathy*. Empathy may be thought of as the ability to perform the behavior of another person in a specified situation. Playing a role is an instance of empathic behavior and is assumed to involve some understanding of the ways in which people other than oneself might behave in some particular circumstances. The experimental method employed in studies of empathy typically demands that the subject give his own responses to some test or task. Following this performance, he is asked to repeat the same task as it would be done by someone else—the "someone else" being defined for him beforehand.

Empirical Data

Helfland (1956) asked four groups of subjects to sort a selection of statements in a way that would reflect their own feelings and attitudes. These statements had already been sorted by a criterion patient, who also prepared an autobiography. After the subjects had performed the initial task, they were asked to read the autobiography and reperform the sorting as they thought the author of the autobiography would do. Their performance was then compared for accuracy with that of the criterion patient. Among the groups of patients tested, chronic schizophrenics showed inferior performance, whereas a group of improved schizophrenics were superior to controls and to tubercular patients who were also tested. However, the deficiency of the chronic patients was markedly greater than any of the differences between the other groups.

Similar tactics were used by Bloom and Arkoff (1961), who asked schizophrenic patients to respond to the MMPI and the Rorschach test as a "typical, average, ordinary person" would. Their general results suggest that chronic schizophrenic patients were less able to simulate normalcy than were the acute patients.

Role taking, as we have seen already, represents a particular form of discrimination learning. An inability to shift from one role to another as required suggests that the subject is responding with a very limited repertoire of responses to a wide range of different stimulus situations. This failure to make effective social discriminations, or to make effective discriminations in responding to impersonal objects, has been noted by many observers of schizophrenic behavior. We shall meet it many times again in our discussion of schizophrenic language and learning. At this point, we should note that role-taking ability certainly seems to be impaired in schizophrenic patients; the more impaired it is, the profounder the pathology and the poorer the prognosis for the individual. Whether this deficiency is central to schizophrenic behavior, or is simply an instance of impaired discrimination in one more area of performance, is a question that requires consideration of much more evidence. This evidence will be presented in the following chapters.

ANXIETY AND SCHIZOPHRENIA

Withdrawal is a prime aspect of schizophrenic behavior, and withdrawal is a very predictable consequence of fear or anxiety. It is inevitable, therefore, that we should try to understand schizophrenic pathology as a derivative of anxiety. Many attempts have been made along these lines.

Anxiety and Perceptual Incongruence

The interpretations that an individual makes of events around him may be disconfirmed by some later happenings. A person may have developed the belief that a friend is very intelligent and be surprised to find him behaving stupidly in some respect. Such disconfirmations may generate anxiety and lead to attempts to reinterpret the events so as to make consistent sense. In this way, *incongruity*, or *cognitive dissonance* (Festinger, 1957), *perceptual disparity* (Peak, 1955), or the *invalidation of constructs* (Kelly, 1955) may be regarded as a source of aversive stimulation that will lead to the development of anxiety and the occurrence of responses that reduce it.

McReynolds (1960) has developed a systematic attempt to apply this notion to the understanding of schizophrenia. He says that the process of assimilating new events into an existing system of interpretation and belief is accompanied by pleasure, provided that the rate at which new events happen is optimal (neither too slow nor too fast). It is also necessary that perceived events be sufficiently novel. Marked deviations from these two requirements will create discomfort for the perceiver. He identifies four main deviations which might produce difficulties in assimilation and thus cause anxiety.

1. An excessively high rate of influx of percepts, so that things are happening faster than they can be handled or understood.
2. Extreme novelty. Events that are very different from past experience are relatively more difficult to interpret.
3. Considerable uncertainty about future events. Assimilation of percepts related to them would then be difficult.
4. Incongruency of percepts and the system into which they are to be assimilated. This is the major source of anxiety, as we have already suggested.

Anxiety is presumed to be a function of how much perceptual material is yet unassimilated. From this assumption it would follow that certain behaviors should be expected of the anxious person. In the first place, he should tend to assimilate new percepts so as to avoid the addition of more unassimilated material, i.e., he should attempt to keep his anxiety level from rising. In the second place, by the same reasoning he should be slow to abandon or alter any existing interpretations that he has, as this would add to the burden of unassimilated percepts. Thirdly, and most obviously, the person should avoid or deny incongruent stimuli.

Following from these deductions, McReynolds has suggested that schizophrenic withdrawal should be interpreted as an attempt to reduce the level of stimulation impinging upon the patient—a kind of functional sensory deprivation. We would expect also that the tendencies seen in the paranoid schizophrenic to assimilate everything, no matter how trivial, into his delusional system, represent an attempt to obtain maximum congruence between his beliefs and events in the external world.

Much the same idea was presented earlier by Cameron in his concept of *reaction sensitivity* and *reaction insensitivity* (Cameron, 1947). This concept refers to the tendency of patients with various pathologies to become especially insensitive to certain kinds of stimuli or especially reactive to some kinds of events. This is worthy of mention largely to indicate that the notion of insensitivity to external stimulation has often been suggested as a mechanism in psychopathology.

McReynolds argues that hallucinations may be understood as the inevitable result of decreased sensory input. We have already seen that experimental sensory deprivation produces hallucinations in normal subjects. We have also seen that this may be understood as the normal and natural outcome when there are no external stimuli to enable the perceiver to judge between the reality of external events and the fantasy of internal images and thoughts. If the patient has developed avoidance of perceptual recognition of external stimuli, the effect should be the same as if there were in fact no stimuli there.

This kind of argument is not inconsistent with the possibility that there is some biological deficiency in the ability of the person to deal with perceptual input of a kind which would not bother the normal person. The former schizophrenic patient cited earlier in this chapter who described the experience of delusional thinking (MacDonald, 1960) commented on her inability to sort the relevant from the irrelevant—"The filter had broken down." Malfunctioning of the process by which stimulus material is assimilated or ignored may occur either because of excessively incongruent input, or because of sheer deficiency in the handling of normal input. In either case, we might expect anxiety to result.

SUMMARY

There are many theories regarding the etiology and the pathology of schizophrenic behavior. To do even scant justice to them all would require a separate book, and many such books have been written. In this chapter we have considered some of the kinds of explanation that have been offered, selecting for examination only those that are capable of experimental test. In the next three chapters many other explanations and hypotheses will be considered. Meantime, more detailed accounts of some of the many approaches to schizophrenia can be found in the list of suggested readings which follows.

SUGGESTED READINGS

1. Arieti, S. *Interpretation of schizophrenia.* New York: Brunner, 1955. A significant development in the theory of schizophrenia.

2. Bateson, G., Jackson, D. D., Haley, J., & Weakland, J. H. Toward a theory of schizophrenia. *Behav. Sci.,* 1956, **1,** 251–264. A concise account of the double-bind hypothesis of parent-child interaction in schizophrenia.

3. Bleuler, E. *Dementia praecox, or the group of schizophrenias.* New York: International Univer. Press, 1950. The English translation of Bleuler's classic text on schizophrenia. An essential foundation for all serious students of this disorder.

4. Cameron, N. *The psychology of the behavior disorders.* Boston: Houghton Mifflin, 1947. One of the major landmarks in the development of a systematic understanding of environmental influences in the development of pathological behavior. A stimulus for much of the important research that has been done on schizophrenia.

5. Hollingshead, A. B., & Redlich, F. C. *Social class and mental illness: a community study.* New York: Wiley, 1958. A major example of the study of dis-

tribution of mental illness within a community.

6. Jackson, D. D. (Ed.). *The etiology of schizophrenia.* New York: Basic Books, 1960. An organized presentation of several writers on topics dealing with the psychology, physiology, and genetics of schizophrenia.

7. Jaco, E. G. *The social epidemology of mental disorders.* New York: Russell Sage, 1960. A useful account of the distribution of psychopathology in social classes and groups.

8. Kaplan, B. (Ed.). *The inner world of mental illness.* New York: Harper, 1964. A series of autobiographical accounts by patients of the experience of mental illness.

REFERENCES

Arieti, S. *Interpretation of schizophrenia.* New York: Brunner, 1955.

Arieti, S. Schizophrenia: the manifest symptomatology, the psychodynamic and formal mechanisms. In S. Arieti (Ed.), *American handbook of psychiatry.* New York: Basic Books, 1959.

Babcock, H. Schizophrenia, hebephrenic form. In A. Burton & R. L. Harris (Eds.), *Case histories in clinical and abnormal psychology.* New York: Harper & Row, 1947.

Bateson, G., Jackson, D. D., Haley, J., & Weakland, J. H. Toward a theory of schizophrenia. *Behav. Sci.,* 1956, **1,** 251–264.

Becker, W. C. A genetic approach to the interpretation and evaluation of the process-reactive distinction. *J. abnorm. soc. Psychol.,* 1956, **47,** 489–496.

Becker, W. C. The process-reactive distinction: a key to the problem of schizophrenia? *J. nerv. ment. Dis.,* 1959, **129,** 442–449.

Bell, N. W. Extended relations of disturbed and well families. *Family Process,* 1962, **1,** 175–193.

Bleuler, E. *Dementia praecox, or the group of schizophrenias.* Leipzig: Deutsche, 1911. English translation, New York: International Univer. Press, 1950.

Bloom, B. L., & Arkoff, A. Role playing in acute and chronic schizophrenia. *J. consult. Psychol.,* 1961, **25,** 24–28.

Butler, S. *The way of all flesh.* New York: Dodd, Mead, 1957. First published, London, 1903.

Cameron, N. *The psychology of the behavior disorders.* Boston: Houghton Mifflin, 1947.

Cameron, N., & Magaret, A. *Behavior pathology.* Boston: Houghton Mifflin, 1951.

Crider, A., Maher, B. A., & Grinspoon, L. The effect of sensory input on the reaction time of schizophrenic patients of good and poor premorbid history. *Psychonomic Sci.,* 1965, **2,** 47–48.

Farina, A. Patterns of role dominance and conflict in parents of schizophrenic patients. *J. abnorm. soc. Psychol.,* 1960, **61,** 31–38.

Farina, A., & Webb, W. W. Premorbid adjustment and subsequent discharge. *J. nerv. ment. Dis.,* 1956, **124,** 612–613.

Faris, R. E. L. Reflections of social disorganization in the behavior of the schizophrenic patients. *Amer. J. Sociol.,* 1944, **50,** 134–141.

Faris, R. E. L., & Dunham, H. *Mental disorders in urban areas.* Chicago: Univer. of Chicago Press, 1939.

Festinger, L. *A theory of cognitive dissonance.* New York: Harper & Row, 1957.

Harrison, M. *Spinners lake.* London: Lane, 1941.

Hartley, E. L., & Hartley, R. E. *Fundamentals of social psychology.* New York: Knopf, 1952.

Helfland, I. Role taking in schizophrenia. *J. consult. Psychol.,* 1956, **20,** 37–41.

Hollingshead, A. B., & Redlich, F. C. *Social class and mental illness: a community study.* New York: Wiley, 1958.

Kantor, R. E., Wallner, J. M., & Winder, C. L. Process and reactive schizophrenia. *J. consult. Psychol.,* 1953, **17,** 157–162.

Kelly, G. A. *The psychology of personal constructs.* New York: Norton, 1955.

King, G. F. Differential autonomic responsiveness in the process-reactive classification of schizophrenia. *J. abnorm. soc. Psychol.,* 1958, **56,** 160–164.

Kohn, M. L., & Clausen, J. A. Social isolation and schizophrenia. *Amer. sociol. Rev.,* 1955, **20,** 265–273.

Kraepelin, E. *Lehrbuch der Psychiatrie.* (5th ed.) Leipzig: Barth, 1896.

Laffal, J., Lenkoski, D., & Ameen, L. Case report: "opposite speech" in a schizophrenic patient. *J. abnorm. soc. Psychol.,* 1956, **52,** 409–413.

Lane, J. E. Social effectiveness and developmental level. *J. Pers.,* 1955, **23,** 274–284.

Lane, R. C., & Singer, J. L. Familial attitudes in paranoid schizophrenics and normals from two socio-economic classes. *J. abnorm. soc. psychol.,* 1959, **59,** 328–339.

Lewis, D. J. Stimulus, response and social role. *J. soc. Psychol.,* 1959, **50,** 119–127.

Lidz, T., Cornelison, A. R., Fleck, S., & Terry, D. The intrafamilial environment of schizophrenic patients: II. Marital schism and marital skew. *Amer. J. Psychiat.,* 1957, **114,** 241–248.

Lidz, R. W., & Lidz, T. The family environment of schizophrenic patients. *Amer. J. Psychiat.,* 1949, **106,** 332–345.

Lidz, T., Parker, B., & Cornelison, A. R. The role of the father in the family environment of the schizophrenic patient. *Amer. J. Psychiat.,* 1956, **113,** 126–132.

MacDonald, N. Living with schizophrenia. *Canad. med. J.,* 1960, **82,** 218–221.

McReynolds, P. Anxiety, perception, and schizophrenia. In D. D. Jackson (Ed.), *The etiology of schizophrenia.* New York: Basic Books, 1960.

Meehl, P. Schizophrenia, catatonic form. In A. Burton & R. L. Harris (Eds.), *Case histories in clinical and abnormal psychology.* New York: Harper & Row, 1947.

Meyer, A. Fundamental conceptions of dementia praecox. *Brit. med. J.,* 1906, **2,** 757–764.

Meyer, A. The dynamic interpretation of dementia praecox. *Amer. J. Psychol.,* 1910, **21,** 385.

Meyer, E., & Covi, L. The experience of depersonalization: a written report by a patient. *Psychiatry,* 1960, **23,** 215–217.

Morel, B. *Traités des maladies mentales.* Paris: Masson, 1860.

Peak, H. Attitude and motivation. In M. R. Jones (Ed.), *Nebraska symposium on motivation: 1955.* Lincoln: Univer. of Nebraska Press, 1955.

Peters, F. *The world next door.* New York: Farrar, Straus, 1949.

Phillips, L. Case history data and prognosis in schizophrenia. *J. nerv. ment. Dis.,* 1953, **117,** 515–525.

Phillips, L., & Zigler, E. The action-thought parameter and vicariousness in normal and pathological behaviors. *J. abnorm. soc. Psychol.,* 1961, **63,** 137–146.

Rodnick, E. H., & Garmezy, N. An experimental approach to the study of motivation in schizophrenia. In M. R. Jones (Ed.), *Nebraska symposium on motivation: 1957.* Lincoln: Univer. of Nebraska Press, 1957.

Schofield, W., & Balian, L. A comparative study of the personal histories of schizophrenic and non-psychiatric patients. *J. abnorm. soc. Psychol.,* 1959, **59,** 215–225.

Sechehaye, M. *Autobiography of a schizophrenic girl.* New York: Grune & Stratton, 1951.

Sullivan, H. S. *The interpersonal theory of psychiatry.* New York: Norton, 1953.

Vexliard, A. *Le clochard: étude de psychologie sociale.* Bruges: Desclée de Brouwer, 1957.

Weakland, J. H. The double-bind hypothesis of schizophrenia and three-party interaction. In D. D. Jackson (Ed.), *The etiology of schizophrenia.* New York: Basic Books, 1960.

Zigler, E., & Phillips, L. Social effectiveness and symptomatic behaviors. *J. abnorm. soc. Psychol.,* 1960, **61,** 231–238.

SCHIZOPHRENIA: BIOLOGICAL AND GENETIC ASPECTS

In this chapter we shall examine some of the attempts that have been made to discover biological and/or genetic determinants for the behaviors which are seen in patients classed as schizophrenic. There have been many such endeavors, and in the space of one chapter we can hope to do no more than describe and discuss some of them in order to show the problems and methods that are generally involved.

BIOLOGICAL ASPECTS

Biochemical Hypotheses

Some investigators have developed theories which postulate that the patterns of deviant behavior described in Chapter 12 originate in a physical pathology, which in turn is caused by the presence of some organism or substance in the body of the patient. This kind of theory then relates the clinical behavior of the patient to a fundamental biological disorder, with the implication that a cure is dependent upon the discovery of some technique for removing or destroying the pathogen.

Possibilities such as this have been envisaged for many years. Kraepelin had suggested that glandular poisons affected the brain, while Jung suggested in 1906 that a specific toxin, which he referred to as *toxin X,* would be found to be responsible for schizophrenic psychosis. Many attempts to discover such a substance met with failure, so much so that in 1958 Benjamin commented, "We are at present in the midst of an upsurge of activity in this field, as well as a gradual lessening of its almost complete isolation from the mainstream of psychiatry. I feel strongly that such a direction is to be welcomed. . . . At the same time there is reason to fear that the field will again, as in the past, become somewhat discredited through poorly conceived and designed investigations and particularly through over-enthusiastic and premature publication of unsubstantiated findings." (Benjamin, 1958, p. 428.)

In spite of the depressing lack of results from biochemical approaches, a major impetus to this kind of research was provided by work done on the chemical nature of certain hallucination-producing drugs (hallucinogens). Mescalin and lysergic acid diethylamide (LSD 25) in particular were known to produce vivid experiences when taken by normal subjects, and these experiences showed some resemblances to the symptoms of schizophrenia. Knowledge of the structure of these drugs provided a basis for hypothesizing about the type of substance in the body which might be responsible for schizophrenia. This served to focus biochemical research upon the discovery of mescalin-like substances in the human, with results which we shall now examine.

The Adrenochrome Hypothesis. One major hypothesis about the pathogenesis of schizophrenia points to the central importance of the substance *adrenochrome*. The hypothesis was first advanced by Osmond and Smithies (1952) and has since been elaborated by Hoffer and Osmond (1955, 1959). A preliminary observation had been made that mescalin and adrenalin are chemically similar. Mescalin, a substance obtained from the Mexican peyote, produces psychological effects upon human subjects that resemble the symptoms of schizophrenia in many ways. In view of the fact that adrenalin is present in the human body, it seems not impossible that in some individuals it might be metabolized into a substance with the same properties as mescalin. Those persons who metabolize adrenalin in this way would be schizophrenic.

Adrenochrome was first suggested as the pathogenic metabolite of adrenalin, although this possibility ran into certain difficulties. Specifically, it turned out to be difficult to prepare adrenochrome for research uses, because there were questions about its chemical stability. However, following a series of studies with available supplies of adrenochrome, the investigators developed the further hypothesis that adrenochrome itself became converted in the body into one of two substances—*adrenolutin* and *5.6-dihydroxy-N-methylindole*. This sequence of events may be diagrammed as shown at the bottom of this page.

In schizophrenic persons, the major product will be adrenolutin; in the nonschizophrenic the major reaction will be that which produces the dihydroxy indole. An additional aspect of this hypothesis is that the dihydroxy indole is regarded as a possible antitension substance which might oppose the effects of adrenalin in the body. Adrenolutin, however, is hypothesized to be both an antitension substance and also pathogenic for the occurrence of schizophrenic symptoms.

Those who have been working with the adrenochrome hypothesis have suggested that one of the primary processes in psychosis is disturbance in perception. Perceptual disturbances, accompanied by disturbances of mood or emotion, provide the basis for the other symptoms. Thus, from this point of view, the disorders of thought and language which are so often described

Adrenalin ————————→ adrenochrome ⟶ 5.6-dihydroxy-N-methylindole / adrenolutin as characteristic of schizophrenia are to be interpreted as reactions that develop on the basis of a fundamental distortion of perception. This position is derived from the observation that the most marked reactions of volunteers to the experience of taking mescalin are those of changed and distorted perception—the environment appears strange to sight, hearing, taste, and smell. Perception of the passage of time seems to undergo erratic distortions.

These investigators have reported that the effects of adrenolutin could persist for a week or more and that evidence has been reported by Braines (1959) in Moscow which suggests that complex and recently acquired skills were impaired by adrenochrome whereas simpler, earlier responses were not. The observations in Moscow were made on monkeys. Further evidence for the adrenochrome hypothesis comes from studies by Schwarz, Hakim, Bickford, and Lichtenheld (1956), who reported that intraventricular injections of adrenochrome in monkeys produced a drowsy state with higher thresholds for the sensation of pain.

A deductive test of the adrenochrome hypothesis was made by Lea (1955) when he argued that since adrenochrome is antihistaminic in action, schizophrenic patients should be unusually resistant to the development of allergies. Comparing military schizophrenic patients with other military patients, he found that his prediction was confirmed.

Negative evidence has been forthcoming also. Szara, Axelrod, and Perlin (1958) were unable to detect the presence of adrenochrome in either schizophrenic or healthy subjects; Holland, Cohen, Goldenberg, Sha, and Leifer (1958) were unable to find differences in the manner in which circulating adrenalin was utilized by schizophrenic and normal controls.

Criticisms based upon the inability of the investigator to find a substance in the body create some special problems. Biochemical assay techniques are often highly complicated and delicate procedures with many possibilities for error. Contradictory results obtained by different investigators may be due to differences in technique or in the skill with which the same technique is applied. Logically it is not possible to conclude that because an investigator failed to find a particular substance, it cannot have been there to be found. When several investigators working independently fail to find a substance, using the technique described by the original discoverer, then doubts may become more plausible.

The Taraxein Hypothesis. Another well-known and systematically developed biological hypothesis is that offered by Heath (cf. Heath, 1960). His basic hypothesis is that there is a genetically determined disorder which is characterized by the presence of a substance in the body of the patient. He has named this substance *taraxein*. Taraxein is a protein which forms a compound with other bodily substances, these compounds being toxic and producing disturbances of function in the central nervous system. This toxic process is believed by Heath to be due to the faulty metabolism of amines. He assumes that amines are released into the bloodstream during stress, so that the consequences of this metabolic defect are more pronounced when the subject is undergoing a stressful situation.

The major result of this chemical aberration is, according to Heath, the development of a defect in the *pleasure-pain* mechanism. For him, therefore, the fundamental symptom of this disorder is the inability of the patient to experience pain and pleasure as other people do. Such an explanation of the fundamental *psychological* deficit in schizophrenia has already been advanced by Rado, Buchenholz, Dunton, Karlin, and Senescu (1956), and Heath's description of the psychological characteristics of schizophrenia follows their account closely.

An inevitable consequence of this deficit is that the patient becomes aware that he does not "feel" as other people do, and thus begins to feel alienated and unsure of his own identity. Coupled with the deficit in pleasure-pain feeling, anxiety about his own identity and about his contact with reality therefore constitute a second fundamental symptom for the patient. For Heath the presence of these two symptoms defines the basic personality of the schizophrenic individual. Such persons are classified as *schizotypes;* the classic clinical symptoms of schizophrenia are secondary symptoms and arise when a schizotype is placed under stress. Heath, therefore, considers "that the schizophrenic symptoms are a complication of a fundamental disease and are precipitated by psychological pressures in predisposed individuals only" (Heath, 1960, p. 147).

Stress which affects the schizotype so as to produce the symptoms of schizophrenia appears to be a reaction to features of the basic deficiencies rather than to be due to prior learning. For Heath, the neurotic disorders represent the consequences of faulty learning, but the behavior of the schizophrenic is a qualitatively different matter. Regarding this, Heath has stated, "Most psychiatrists and psychoanalysts, in describing the disease process, present their data as if schizophrenia were a more extensive form of neurosis. In our experience this is not true. In the neurotic and the normal individual, the psychiatric data suggest that inferior adaptive patterns in current behavior are related to past faulty learning experiences. . . . In contrast, it is our experience that only a very small amount of stress is derived from the area of faulty learning in the schizophrenic" (Heath, 1960, p. 151).

The crucial stresses, for the schizophrenic, are those situations in which the uncertainty of his own identity is aroused. Because the basic disorder is presumed by Heath to vary in intensity in different schizotypal individuals, mild schizotypes may be able to cope with their identity problems by copying other people, play-acting behaviors which they have learned intellectually are socially appropriate, and so forth. In patients with

more serious deficit, these measures would be inadequate, and the secondary clinical symptoms of schizophrenia would develop. As an aid to understanding the structure of Heath's hypothesis, the general outlines are presented in Figure 13-1.

Evidence for the taraxein hypothesis is of several kinds. At the level of brain physiology, Heath and his colleagues report that after administration of taraxein, alterations of electrical activity have been recorded from the limbic system of normal volunteers. Similar activity in the limbic system had been recorded from psychotic patients, the intensity of the activity being related to the degree of psychotic behavior. In one case reported, the abnormal recordings were most pronounced when the patient was withdrawn and angry, the focus of the abnormality being the right posterior hippocampus—a part of the limbic system. Animals to which psychotomimetic drugs have been administered show somewhat similar recordings from the same areas of the brain (Heath, 1954, 1955, 1958, 1959; Heath, Martens, Leach, Cohen, & Angel, 1957, and Heath, Martens, Leach, Cohen, & Feigley, 1958). All in all, the tenor of this evidence suggests that psychotic behavior may arise from aberrant activity in the limbic system and that this aberrant activity may be produced when taraxein is present in the body.

At the psychological level, the same writers present evidence that the administration of taraxein to normal volunteers produces behavioral changes similar to psychotic behavior, and that deviant behavior is also observed in animals under like conditions. For example, Heath et al. (1957) gave varying doses of taraxein to volunteers from a prison population. They report their general reactions as follows:

The characteristic general change is evidence of impairment of the central integrative process resulting in a variety of symptoms. There is marked blocking with disorganization and fragmentation of thought. There is impairment of concentration. Each subject has described this in his own words—some saying

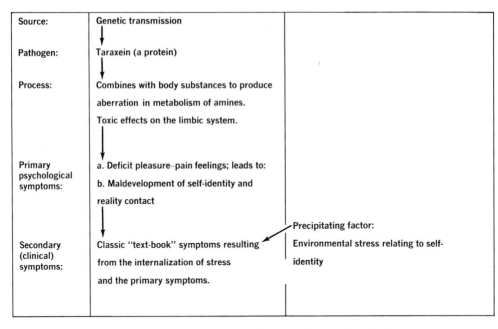

Source:	Genetic transmission
Pathogen:	Taraxein (a protein)
Process:	Combines with body substances to produce aberration in metabolism of amines. Toxic effects on the limbic system.
Primary psychological symptoms:	a. Deficit pleasure–pain feelings; leads to: b. Maldevelopment of self-identity and reality contact
Secondary (clinical) symptoms:	Classic "text-book" symptoms resulting from the internalization of stress and the primary symptoms.

Precipitating factor: Environmental stress relating to self-identity

Figure 13-1. Hypothesized relationship between taraxein and schizophrenic behavior.

merely "I can't think"; "my thoughts break off"; others, "I have a thought but I lose it before I can tell you anything about it," etc. "My mind is a blank" is another common expression. It becomes impossible to express a complete thought. Often they will state only a part of a sentence. They appear generally dazed and out of contact with a rather blank look in their eyes. They become autistic, displaying a lessening of animation in facial expression. Subjective complaints of depersonalization are frequent. Attention span is markedly shortened with increase in reaction time. The symptoms often produce apprehension in the patients. The commonest verbalization of their concern is "I never felt like this in my life before." Virtually all have made this statement. Memory was impaired only during states of profound stupor. Recall was excellent in all cases except for what transpired during periods of deep stupor. Sensorium has always been clear when subjects are capable of reporting. (P. 21.)

There has been some criticism of the taraxein hypothesis. Siegel, Niswander, Sachs, and Stavros (1959) report themselves to be unable to isolate taraxein in schizo-

phrenic patients. However, since other investigators working at other laboratories have reported doing so, their failure cannot be considered theoretically crucial at this point.

The hypothesis itself is a little unclear on some important points. If we are to assume that the pleasure-pain deficit produces a developmental deficit in the sense of identity, which in turn leads to the secondary symptoms of schizophrenia under stress, it seems unlikely that this mechanism could lead to the rapid development of such symptoms in normal volunteers shortly after administration of taraxein. Secondly, it rests rather heavily upon the assumption that there is a pleasure-pain system of a physiological nature and that this is a function of the limbic system. Finally, the evidence for the genetic transmission of taraxein (assuming the substance itself to be stable) has not yet been provided.

All in all, we may conclude our discussion of the taraxein hypothesis with the comment that it appears to have some distinct possibilities for explanation at the biochemical level, although the major body of evidence necessary to develop it has not yet been collected.

The Serotonin Hypothesis. A different kind of biochemical approach to the understanding of schizophrenia has developed around the discovery of a substance, *serotonin,* in the human brain. Serotonin (also known as 5-hydroxytryptamine) is found in many parts of the body, but is particularly evident in the limbic system of the brain (see Figure 13-2), an area which is believed to have importance in the regulation of emotional states. Certain properties of serotonin are of interest to students of the biochemistry of behavior.

Structurally, serotonin is characterized by the *indole nucleus,* also seen in substances which produce psychotic-like behavior, such as LSD and adrenochrome as well as some tranquilizing compounds like reserpine. This similarity suggests that these substances are all capable of occupying the same sites in the body and thereby of preventing any other substance of like structure from exerting its action at those sites at the same time. Substances which may compete for occupancy of the same site in this way are referred to as *pharmacological antagonists;* one is often said to "block" the action of the other. Thus serotonin and LSD block each other's actions.

Physiologically, serotonin performs a specific function in the transmission of nerve impulses along the cholinergic division of the nervous system. This transmission is achieved when the substance acetylcholine is released at the nerve ending and is taken up at the receptor site at the postsynaptic membrane in the manner described in detail in Chapter 4. Serotonin combines with some of the acetylcholine which is released during the transmission of a nerve impulse, thereby preventing it from reaching the receptor site. It will be apparent that the amount of serotonin available to act in this way will determine how much acetylcholine is blocked and therefore will determine the extent to which cholinergic nerve impulses are transmitted across the synapse. An excess of serotonin could produce a marked reduction in cholinergic activity, whereas an absence of serotonin would lead to an increase in it.

Insofar as the maintenance of normal behavior is dependent upon the existence of a stable balance between the activity of the cholinergic division and the antagonistic adrenergic division of the nervous system, any disruption of this balance might be expected to lead to behavioral deviations of

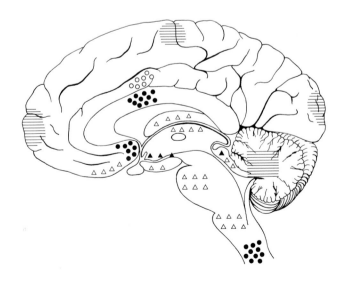

Figure 13-2. Serotonin content of the human brain. The areas with the highest concentration of serotonin, an indole amine, include the hypothalamus. A lower level is observed in the mammillary bodies, fornix, thalamus, and medulla oblongata. Serotonin is found in the cingulate gyrus, hippocampus, and amygdaloid nucleus in greater concentrations than in the neocortex or cerebellum, which contain the least amounts. Lines indicate 0.01 to 0.05 γ/g; ○, 0.05 to 0.1 γ/g; ●, 0.1 to 0.3 γ/g; △, 0.3 to 0.6 γ/g; ▲, more than 0.6 γ/g. (Costa and Aprison, 1958.)

some kind. An excess or a deficiency of serotonin would disturb this balance and thus might bring about aberrations in behavior. By the same token, any substance which acts as an antagonist to serotonin in the normal person should bring about temporary changes in behavior if it is introduced artificially into the body.

Support for this deduction comes from the observations made about the effects of LSD upon serotonin levels in the body. Acting as an antagonist to serotonin, LSD has been shown to inhibit the activities of cholinergic nerves in some cases, but to produce effects which are similar rather than contradictory to those of serotonin in others (e.g., Shaw & Woolley, 1956). Clearly the effects of LSD can either diminish or increase the effects of serotonin depending upon the concentration of LSD administered (Costa, 1956), large concentrations acting to antagonize the effects of serotonin and weak concentrations facilitating them.

Turning more directly to research on schizophrenic patients, we find that there is some evidence drawn from studies in which a substance tryptophan is administered to the patient. Tryptophan in the body produces serotonin, and one of the consequences of the production of serotonin is an increase in the urinary excretion of *5-hydroxyindoleacetic acid*. Thus by administering tryptophan and measuring the subsequent excretion of 5-hydroxyindoleacetic acid, we can infer the extent to which serotonin had been produced and was active in the patient's body. Lauer, Inskip, Bernsohn, and Zeller (1958) reported that schizophrenic subjects excreted significantly less in this respect than did normals, but this finding has not been consistently repeated (e.g., Bannerjee & Agarwal, 1958; Kopin, 1959).

Direct estimation of the levels of serotonin in schizophrenic patient groups has also been reported (Toderick, Tait, & Marshall, 1960; Feldstein, Hoagland, & Freeman, 1959), with the general conclusion that the serotonin level of acute schizo-phrenic subjects was significantly lower than that of chronic schizophrenic groups. However, abnormally deviant levels were also found in patients with organic psychoses and patients who were disturbed but not psychotic. Thus the general tenor of this kind of evidence is to suggest that serotonin levels in psychiatric patient groups do deviate from the norm, but not in any way which allows us to assume with confidence that serotonin deviation is especially related to schizophrenia.

In the main, the serotonin hypothesis has depended heavily upon the assumption that the behavioral deviations produced by LSD are essentially the same as those which are commonly called schizophrenic. This is a questionable assumption. Many observers who have reported their own experiences under the influence of LSD describe them in terms which cast doubt upon the identity of the LSD experience and schizophrenic states.

Methodological Problems in Biochemical Research. The kind of research that has been reported in connection with the three previous hypotheses has been severely criticized by Kety (1959). Most of his strictures refer to matters that might well have been controlled by the investigators, but were not. Chief among them is the fact of the generally heterogeneous patient populations that are described as schizophrenic for the purposes of the research. This is a severe problem, and one that in the context of biochemical research might best be resolved by selecting patients for the presence of certain rather specific kinds of behavior pathology, rather than by trying to refine existing Kraepelinian categories. Additional methodological problems relate to the generally atypical diets provided by mental hospitals—a factor that needs control and/or better knowledge of the effects of such diets upon normal metabolism. The influence of previous therapies, especially shock therapies, chemotherapies, etc., represents a profound contamination with any biological measure, and yet few studies indicate that the investigators have taken steps to control for them.

Perhaps the most difficult problem of all is the question of experimenter bias. While a fuller discussion of this in behavioral science is available elsewhere (e.g., Rosenthal, 1964), it is necessary to note here that much of the literature of psychological biochemistry is marred by a polemic tone and thinly veiled hostility toward rival biochemical hypotheses (and their adherents) and more especially toward those who reject biochemical explanations in principle.

While this situation may serve to amuse the reader, it does not give much grounds for confidence regarding the impartiality with which the investigator in question is collecting and viewing his own data. The chief demand placed upon us by science is that we search with enthusiasm for data that may run counter to beliefs in which we have a great deal of ourselves invested. To do this is not easy, and yet if we fail to do so then we become mere propagandists lobbying in the journals for our personal convictions. Unfortunately, a significant segment of biochemical research is reported in a manner that raises some doubt about the care with which negative evidence is sought.

Summary. The three hypotheses which have been discussed have all been concerned with the functioning of particular biochemical compounds—adrenochrome, taraxein, or serotonin. Each hypothesis envisages that faulty metabolism on the part of the patient produces either the formation of toxic compounds or the blocking of normal bodily processes. Evidence in favor of these hypotheses is dependent to a very large extent upon the discovery of the products which these substances are presumed to form. As we have seen, none of the hypotheses enjoys clear support from experimental evidence; nevertheless, they have produced sufficient data to justify the further investigations which continue to be reported.

Physiological Stress Hypotheses

Time and again we have noted that the schizophrenic patient seems to be unable to cope with the pressures of the environment. His response to stress appears to be extremely maladaptive, at least at the behavioral level. The possibility that the schizophrenic is characterized by an inadequate response to stress at the physiological level has been explored also. We shall examine some of these explorations now.

The Adrenal Cortical Functions in Schizophrenia. Clinical observation of schizophrenic subjects has frequently revealed disorders in bodily processes which are consistent with the possibility that these patients are suffering from some inadequacy of the adrenal functions.

Included among these findings are the frequent occurrence of lassitude and tiredness, low blood pressure, various deviations from normal sugar metabolism, and especially the failure to produce certain adrenal cortical steroids when the patient is placed under stress. We are already familiar with the outlines of the general adaptation syndrome described by Selyé and discussed in detail in Chapter 4. We have seen that when a normal subject is exposed to stresses of various kinds, the stress response which occurs involves a complicated series of bodily reactions, among the most important of which is the secretion of a number of substances by the *adrenal cortex*. For research purposes, it has been found comparatively simple to measure this activity by using two indices. One of these is the output of *17-ketosteroids* in the urine; the other is the lymphocyte count in circulating blood. These measures are inversely related to each other. Stress produces an increase in the output of 17-ketosteroids, whereas the lymphocyte count declines.

In normal subjects there is a characteristic daily rhythm in the output of 17-ketosteroids. The schematic diagram in Figure 13-3 shows the daily rise and fall in output both for normals and for schizophrenic patients, the latter being derived from the reports of Hoskins (1946). The daily curve of the patients deviates from that of the normal group in two major respects: The overall curve is flatter than that of the normal population, and the variability is much greater.

Particularly interesting differences are observed when we turn to the effects of various stresses upon the adrenal responses of the patients. In one investigation of these differences, experimenters (Hoskins, 1946) compared chronic schizophrenic patients with normal males in their responses to the stresses produced by a psychomotor task (using a pursuitmeter), a frustration task (the target-ball task), exposure to heat, and the breathing of air with reduced oxygen content. Particularly striking is the fact that the schizophrenic patient is disabled by an inadequate adrenal cortical response to stress. An additional approach to verification of this hypothesis involves, once again, the study of the effects of psychotomimetic drugs such as LSD. Here the argument is simply that if LSD produces schizophrenic-like behavior, then we might expect to find that it also produces changes in adrenal responses similar to those found in the schizophrenic. Investigations along

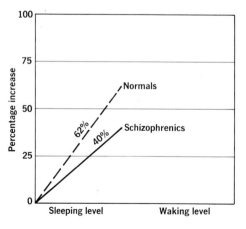

Figure 13-3. Schematic curve of the rise in output of 17-ketosteroids after awakening in normal and chronic schizophrenic subjects. (After Hoskins, 1946.)

these lines have been reported by Rinkel and his colleagues (Rinkel, Hyde, Solomon, & Hoagland, 1955), where the physiological responses to the stress of ACTH administration was observed in normals under conditions of LSD administration and no drug. The results suggested that the effect of the LSD was to diminish the responsiveness of the adrenal cortex to ACTH, a finding which parallels the apparent diminished responsiveness of the schizophrenic.

Criticisms of this hypothesis have come from many quarters, and we should note some of the problems which exist. The methods used to determine adrenal activity are open to objection because of unreliability. The assumption that such tasks as the pursuitmeter are emotionally stressful to schizophrenic patients and normals in the same way is also arguable.

A deduction which we may make from the hypothesis is that chronic malfunctioning of the adrenal response should bring about psychotic symptoms after a sufficient time has elapsed, or should aggravate such behavior in patients who are already psychotic. Apter (1958) studied four patients who had been operated upon to remove both adrenals, thereby cutting adrenal activity to nil. These patients had already exhibited psychotic behavior for some time before the operation, but the removal of the adrenals did not produce any worsening of the symptoms. Apter finds it difficult to reconcile this observation, which was made for a period of six years postoperatively, with the prediction that lowered adrenal activity produces a deterioration in behavior.

At this time, it seems possible that the aberrations of adrenal activity which have been reported in schizophrenics may be secondary consequences of some other biological activity in the patient not directly centered in the adrenal glands.

General Autonomic Responses to Stress. While a general picture of sluggish and diminished responsiveness to stress is given by the material discussed in the preceding paragraphs, a somewhat different picture is provided when we look at the responses of *acute* schizophrenic patients to threat. Malmo and Shagass (1949) conducted an intensive investigation of various responses to painful stimulation on the part of several groups of patients. Many measures were taken from the patients during stimulation, including heart rate, muscular tension, the galvanic skin response, and motor movements of the finger. (See Figure 13-4.)

The group of early acute schizophrenic patients produced responses quite similar to those of the patients whose chief clinical picture was anxiety. Thus the conclusion which emerges is that responsiveness to painful stress is very marked in the early stages of schizophrenia. In a much earlier study, Pfister (1938) noted that in the early stages of schizophrenic disorder there was a heightened responsiveness of the cardiovascular system, but that this diminished as the patient progressed toward chronicity. Finally, in the chronic state, such reactivity

was less than normal. This difference between the reactivity of the acute and the chronic schizophrenic patient to stress has been reported in further studies by Malmo, Shagass, and Davis (1951). The difference is most marked, however, when the painful stimulus is of low intensity. Very painful stimulation does produce an increase in reactivity on the part of the chronic schizophrenic, bringing his response level up to that of the acute patient. This effect, where muscle tension is the response, is shown in Figure 13-5.

Contradictory evidence has been provided by Ray (1963). He compared groups of chronic schizophrenics, differentiated on the basis of "adequate" versus "inadequate" overt verbal behavior, and found no difference between them and normal controls in level of autonomic activation or in autonomic reactivity to threat-pain thresholds. It is difficult to know whether or not the groups in question correspond to the acute-

Figure 13-4. Subject with head in frame ready for stimulation. Note left hand strapped down for GSR recording, and right forefinger resting on button. In the actual experiments, electrodes were attached to the neck, right arm, and left leg, and a pneumograph was employed. (From Malmo & Shagass, 1949.)

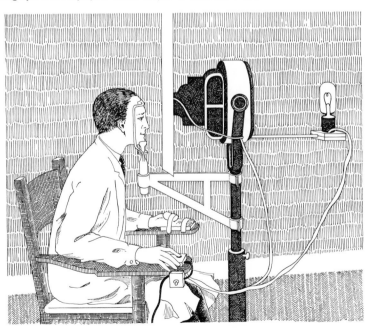

Schizophrenia: Biological and Genetic Aspects

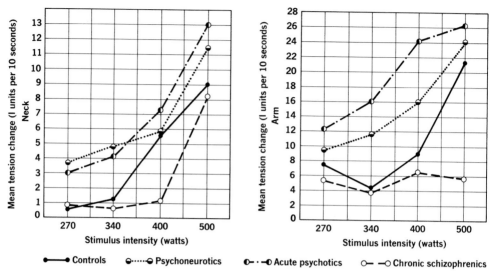

Figure 13.5 Mean changes in arm and neck tension of control and psychopathological groups under pain stimulation (see text). (Malmo, Shagass, & Davis, 1951.)

chronic distinction that we have in mind, since all patients were drawn from a chronic population. On balance, the evidence seems to favor the conclusion that autonomic reactivity is lower in chronic than in acute schizophrenics.

Here again, therefore, the hypothesis suggests that the chronic schizophrenic patient is slow to respond to stimuli which are sufficient to arouse normal subjects, and that this condition in the chronic patient is preceded by hyperresponsiveness in the initial acute stage. This transition from high levels of anxiety, easily aroused, to chronically low anxiety in the later stages has been utilized at the behavioral level by Mednick (1958) in developing his hypothesized explanation of thought disorders in schizophrenia (see Chapter 15).

Arousal and Schizophrenia

The observations described in the previous section also permit an interpretation almost entirely contradictory to the one offered there. Large reactions to stress stimuli are possible only in individuals who are not already in a highly aroused state. Patients who are in a chronically high state of arousal may be close to the ceiling of their potential for further arousal. Thus, experimental observation of their responsiveness may reveal little or no change in autonomic functions to the experimental stimulus. On the other hand, patients who are in a state of low arousal may produce very marked responses to comparatively minor stimulation. Considering the data on the responses of the chronic schizophrenic, therefore, we are uncertain as to whether the lack of reaction is evidence that the patient is pathologically "sluggish" or that he is already so aroused that nothing higher can reasonably be expected. This view is, essentially, that put forward by Venables (1964).

Inasmuch as the measurement of reactivity itself does not permit us to discriminate between the two hypotheses, it is necessary to turn to other approaches. One of these involves the manipulation of the patient's level of arousal by drugs or other techniques. If it is true that chronic patients are in a high state of arousal, we should expect that the use of depressant drugs would lead to an improvement of their behavior concomitant with a more appropriate level of attention under lowered arousal. Fulcher, Gallagher, and Pfeiffer

(1957) report that when the depressant amobarbital was given to chronic patients, an increase was noted in the frequency of lucid intervals. More impressive evidence was provided by Stevens and Derbyshire (1958), who obtained remission of catatonic stupor under amobarbitol and found that there was a corresponding reduction in level of arousal as measured by EEG and polygraph recording.

We have already noted the use of the sedation threshold to measure resting levels of arousal, and the implications of the research in the previous paragraph have been supported by the appearance of predictably higher thresholds for chronic schizophrenics than for simple schizophrenics or normals. Acute schizophrenic patients, on the other hand, have lower sedation thresholds than any of the groups.

Fulcher et al., in the study just cited, also investigated the use of the drug *arecoline*, which has a parasympathetic action and may be regarded as more obviously opposed to arousal than amobarbitol. The latter has a much more involved sequence of processes in reducing arousal. This drug also produced an increase in lucid intervals in chronic schizophrenic patients, providing additional support for the high-arousal hypothesis.

Confirmation of this hypothesis by measurement of resting rates of autonomic activity is, as we have said, difficult to obtain in view of the great individual differences in resting rates and the problems related to assigning meanings to the actual values. Nevertheless, Williams (1953) and Malmo et al. (1951) show that resting rates in chronic schizophrenic patients tend to be higher than those of acutes, especially in skin conductance and heart rate—both of which tend to be the most reliable correlates of arousal stimulation in normal subjects. Venables and Wing (1962) have shown that the extent of social withdrawal in hospitalized chronic patients is closely related to their skin potential: the more withdrawn the patient, the higher the skin potential, and presumably, the higher the level of arousal. The general form of the data is shown in Figure 13-6.

Within the framework of this hypothesis, one might speculate that the withdrawal on the part of highly aroused chronic schizo-

Figure 13-6. Skin potential and withdrawal measures of clinical subgroups of schizophrenics. (Venables & Wing, 1962.)

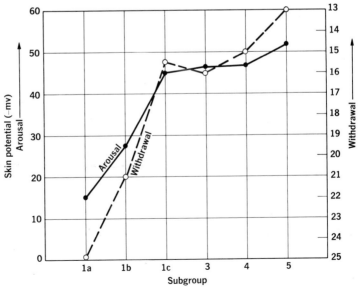

phrenics represents an attempt to cut down external stimulation and to keep arousal within bearable limits. Thus, the avoidance behavior would be seen as "avoidant" in the technical sense of the term, i.e., a response that is reinforced by the reduction of a noxious state. In this respect there is a certain congruence between Mednick's and Venables's formulations. That is to say, the shift from acute to chronic schizophrenia is characterized by responses that are increasingly avoidant. The difference in the two formulations lies largely in the inferences that are made about anxiety—if anxiety is defined as autonomic arousal. Whereas the Mednick position supposes that the avoidance is successful and that the chronic patient is not anxious and hence not aroused, Venables adduces evidence to indicate that the avoidance is only minimally effective and that the chronic patient is highly aroused even though he is in a withdrawn state.

Paranoid Schizophrenia. Nearly all the comments upon autonomic reactivity in schizophrenia must be withdrawn in discussing paranoid schizophrenic patients. For example, where the patient suffered from *coherent* delusions, the relationship between skin potential and withdrawal did not hold up in the Venables and Wing study. Shakow (1962) has summarized many years of research into schizophrenia with the observation that on a majority of measures the paranoid patient resembles the normal control more often than he resembles the other classes of schizophrenic. Stevenson, Derrick, Hobbs, and Metcalfe (1957) report that paranoid patients are unlike others in the adrenocortical response. As we shall see in the next chapter, there are many other ways in which paranoid patients differ from nonparanoid schizophrenics, a fact which suggests that different processes may be involved in the development of delusional behavior.

The chief problem with the Venables formulation seems to arise when we consider the fact that admission to a hospital with a diagnosis of acute schizophrenia is frequently preceded by some specific stress. Under these circumstances, the hypothesis must argue that stress has produced a lowered arousal state—an inference that is a little paradoxical. Two possible solutions to this might be suggested. One is that under stress, the patient may be responding with parasympathetic dominance, in line with Gellhorn's notion of autonomic tuning. Another solution might be that the patient is in a pathologically low state of arousal and that this, with its concomitant excessive broadening of attention, produces difficulties in the maintenance of organized behavior. These difficulties do not become evident until the patient is in a situation that demands complicated sequences of responses, and it is then that his behavioral difficulties become manifest. Since complicated situations are by definition stress situations, the behavioral disorganization is incorrectly attributed to stress. In fact, the stress situation was crucial only in revealing the consequences of a deficit that was there, but not evident, in less demanding environments.

Arousal, Avoidance, and Etiology. Consideration of the preceding paragraphs raises the general question of etiology. Should we regard the patient as suffering from some excessive sensitivity to external threat, a sensitivity acquired by experience? Or should we assume that there is a basic dysfunction in the maintenance of autonomic balance, so that high arousal states occur and are maintained more or less regardless of the nature of the environment? Because all the evidence is correlational in its logic, there is no sure way to answer this. We do know that stress produces sympathetic arousal in the normal individual anyway, and thus we might expect an interaction between stress and biological imbalance to produce an excessive sympathetic dominance in individuals with some predisposition to this dominance anyway. It is also possible that prolonged stress will produce this kind of imbalance in a relatively irreversible fashion. Thus we cannot regard the evidence from autonomic functioning as demonstrating a biological origin for the disorder, but simply as suggesting a biological vehicle by which many of the psychological phenomena might be understood.

Russian (Pavlovian) Formulations

Many investigators in the Soviet Union have also been concerned with autonomic functions in schizophrenia. Their work stems more or less directly from a theory of schizophrenia derived from the neuropsychology of Pavlov (cf. Pavlov, 1941). Two major Pavlovian concepts are necessary for the understanding of Russian work: protective inhibition and internal inhibition.

According to Pavlovian principles, when a nerve cell is exposed to prolonged or excessive stimulation it ceases to react or to transmit impulses. This functional inertness is assumed to have a protective purpose, preventing the cell from harm that might accrue from excessive excitation. Such a state of inactivity is termed *protective inhibition*. In this state, any nervous system function is dulled or missing, whether it is sympathetic or parasympathetic in nature, or whether it is mediated by the internal processes of excitation or inhibition.

Internal inhibition, however, is best illustrated by the process of extinction of the conditioned response when it is not reinforced. It is an internal process that leads to the suppression of conditioned responses when they are not paired with the unconditioned response. This kind of inhibition is presumed to be produced by the *activity* of specific neural tissue. Thus, any inertness in this system would lead to a failure to suppress an unreinforced response.

Protective inhibition would, therefore, lead both to poorer conditioning and to poorer extinction of a conditioned response that had been established already. If it involves the entire cortex, protective inhibition would lead to lack of cortical control or integration of behavior at the subcortical level. Thus, some kinds of pathological behavior might be thought of as functionally

"decorticate" in their character. On the other hand, if massive protective inhibition has spread to involve subcortical centers, then we should expect extreme lack of responsiveness to any stimulation.

Various combinations of protective inhibition have been invoked by Russian theorists to account for schizophrenic behavior. In catatonic stupor, for example, it is hypothesized that protective inhibition has included subcortical and sympathetic centers generally, as well as cortical.

One of the prime methods for the testing of these hypotheses has been the use of the *orienting response.* This consists of three components: (1) motor responses, such as muscular tension and physical turning toward the origin of the stimulus; (2) autonomic changes, such as dilation of the pupils, increases in palmar skin conductance, vasodilation in the head with vasoconstriction in the limbs, and various changes in heart rate and respiration rate; (3) EEG changes, chiefly of the alpha blocking type. It will be clear that the operations defining the orienting response are the same as those that are commonly used here to define arousal or activation. Other investigators have sometimes used the term "vigilance reaction" for the same group of changes.

Orienting Responses in Schizophrenia. One group of investigators (Traugott, Balonov, Kauffman, & Luchko, 1958) reports the responses of chronic schizophrenics to a range of orienting stimuli. These included sounds of a whistle, a bell, and a tone; visual stimuli of lights; and tactile stimuli. In many of their chronic patients there were no orienting responses at all, and where some responses were obtained, these were much more depressed in the autonomic sphere than in the motor component. Similar results were described by Gamburg (1958), who found little or no response from simple schizophrenics and anxiety reactions from paranoid patients. In the nonresponding patients, the response was elicited under dosage of caffein.

Other investigators have reported low

sympathetic measures in the resting state and low reactivity to stimulation in schizophrenic patients. For example, Ekolovia-Bagalei (1955) studied 85 catatonic patients and reported low resting measures for pulse and respiration rates, blood pressure, sweating, and pupillary diameter. Reactions in these channels to external stimulation were likewise missing or minimal.

Pupillography. Streltsova (1955) conducted systematic investigations into the response of pupil dilation under stimulation. She used hot and cold tactile stimuli, an odor, and a bell. The vast majority of her schizophrenic patients showed either no response to stimulation or else greatly reduced reactivity. A few subjects showed excessively high reactions, i.e., abnormally large dilation; while a small percentage produced pupil constriction—a response that the investigator states is never found in normal subjects. Following this finding, she studied the effect of caffein upon the elicitation of the response, arguing that caffein counteracts inhibition. With small doses, she obtained responses from 13 of 15 patients who had previously given no response at all. However, by increasing the dosage strength beyond that value, she then obtained a reduction in the number of patients responding. This effect follows the curvilinear form that is typical in arousal-behavioral efficiency functions, as we have seen before. In Pavlovian terminology, the explanation is that high doses of the excitatory drug provoke protective inhibition, thus producing the paradoxical effect described.

Pavlov argued that protective inhibition builds up in the normal individual as the day progresses, being dissipated during sleep. Thus, protective inhibitory effects ought to be seen at their least values early in the morning, just after waking. Accordingly, it might be expected that failure to give orienting responses should be most evident in the latter part of the day and least evident upon waking. This prediction was confirmed by Streltsova (1955). Upon waking, 21 of

22 patients gave normal orienting responses, but failed to respond when retested from 2 to 5 hours later.

Electroencephalography. Many investigators have reported in the English-language literature that no reliable differences may be found between schizophrenics and others in the form of the EEG trace. This problem is reviewed later in this chapter. However, Soviet psychopathologists have emphasized the appearance of *constellations* and *overflows* in such traces, and regard them as additional evidence of pathology of the inhibitory process. A constellation is a burst of high-amplitude activity lasting from ½ to 2 seconds in one area of the cortex coincident with low-amplitude responses from other areas. Overflows are spreading excitations in the cortex, starting at one location and enveloping larger segments—much like the phenomena seen in some epileptic traces and in normal sleeping traces.

Constellations have been reported by Belenkaya (1960), who states that they are to be found in acute and agitated patients. To explain this, he argues that the pathological protective inhibition affects both excitatory and inhibitory processes in the cortex, but that the first weakening occurs in inhibitory processes—thereby creating an imbalance in favor of excitation. Any strong stimulus will add to this and provoke protective inhibition sufficient to exclude reaction to the stimulus. Paradoxically, a weak stimulus will produce a response because it has not added a sufficient increment to the excitatory state to provoke further protective inhibition. Once the weak stimulus has activated the cortex, it will produce a very strong reaction because of the excitatory tone of the patient's nervous system at that juncture.

On the other hand, overflows induced by external stimulation have been reported by Gavrilova (1960) in paranoid schizophrenic patients. From this she argues that the overflow represents an initiation of excitation at subcortical levels which spreads to the cortex, and that in these patients the proper balance of subcortical-cortical relationship is impaired.

Belenkaya (1960, 1961) has approached the problem of overflows with a four-stage model of the development of paranoid schizophrenia. The first stage is paranoid delirium without hallucinations; the second stage is paranoid delirium with hallucinations; the third stage is paraphrenic delirium; and the fourth stage is catatonic state with hallucinations. Reactions to light decline progressively when measured in patients who are grouped in these stages, and EEG activity is generally lessened also. All these groups showed overflows. Overflows are assumed to be signs of increasing inhibition, as in sleep—presumably protective inhibition. Treatment of these patients with the drug chlorpromazine produced an increase in overflows for a brief period of weeks, after which the EEG trace began to return to normal—a process that Belenkaya attributes to the restoration of normal internal inhibition following the "damping out" of excitation via the action of chlorpromazine on the reticular formation.

Summary. The general tenor of the work of Russian investigators has been well summarized by Lynn (1963). His conclusions were as follows:

1. The Russians have described two types of schizophrenic patient. One of these includes mainly catatonic and simple schizophrenics and is characterized by low sympathetic tone and low reactivity. This group is numerically in the majority. A second and less numerous group has abnormally high tone and reactivity and chiefly includes acute and agitated patients. These differentiations are quite similar to the views of Venables and Mednick, discussed elsewhere in this book.

2. Russian workers in the field of EEG do not confirm the negative findings of Western investigators, who have by and large found little or no differences between the traces of schizophrenics and other classes of patient. However, the methods of analysis of the trace differ, and it may be that the failure of American and European scientists to discover differences is due to this fact.

3. Conditioning speed is impaired in all schizophrenic patients, but especially in catatonic patients. Once established, conditioned responses are very unstable, requiring very large numbers of reinforced trials to achieve stability. These responses are easily inhibited by distracting stimuli or by quite minor variations in the conditioning situation. Conditioned discrimination is particularly difficult for the patient to make. With clinical improvement in the patient's status, there is usually a parallel improvement in his conditionability and in related response phenomena.

4. These deficiencies of conditioning and of autonomic responsiveness may be improved with the aid of stimulant (disinhibiting) drugs in moderate doses. However, increased doses tend to reverse the effect.

It is apparent that much of this work is in agreement with the studies discussed in the previous account of autonomic reactivity and arousal. At the operational level it is difficult to distinguish between the various hypotheses advanced by Russian and Western psychopathologists. However, there are some differences between, for example, Venables's notion that the chronic schizophrenic patient is in a state of high arousal, and the Russian hypothesis that he is suffering from excessive inhibition. Venables's position has the merit of being simple, while the Pavlovian theorists resort more frequently to complex hypothetical events in the brain to explain some seeming paradoxes in the data.

Brain Pathology and Schizophrenia

In the next chapter we shall see that many psychological investigations have been conducted into what we might describe as the general *brain pathology* hypothesis of schizophrenia. These studies all utilize behavioral similarities between patients known to suffer from brain pathology of some kind and patients whose behavior is overtly schizophrenic. Direct investigation of brain pathology in schizophrenic patients is also a common topic of research. We shall consider it at this point.

Electroencephalography. Many studies have been performed with the intention of discovering differences between the cortical rhythms of schizophrenic and nonschizophrenic subjects. In our earlier discussion of the taraxein hypothesis, we have seen that Heath and his associates have attempted to use deep recordings from patients and volunteer subjects in order to demonstrate

the effects of taraxein in producing "psychotic" brain waves.

To summarize some of the information on EEG presented earlier in this book, normal subjects in the resting state produce EEG rhythms which are generally composed of two frequencies. Alpha rhythm is in the range of 20 to 30 cps. These frequencies are usually observed to be distributed with a predominance of alpha from the occipital area of the brain and beta over the remainder. A typical EEG pattern is presented in Figure 13-7. The nature of the processes occurring in the brain which determine these frequencies is not clearly understood. However, where there is brain pathology, as in such conditions as brain tumor, mechanical damage to the brain, toxic and infectious

Figure 13-7. EEG pattern: normal adult male.

Alpha

Beta

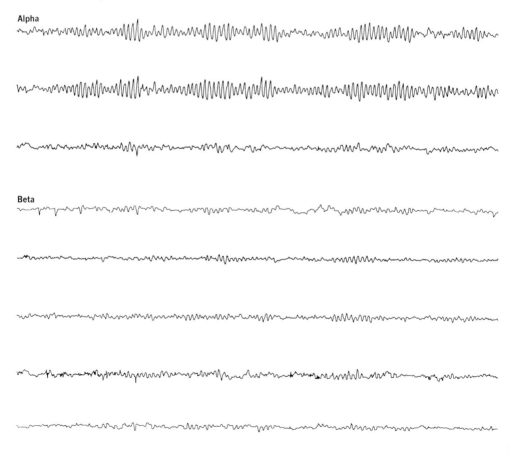

conditions, etc., the wave form of the EEG is likely to deviate from the normal. Certain kinds of deviant frequency are found to be consistently related to certain kinds of brain pathology. Epileptic conditions in particular tend to produce characteristic wave patterns, and this has resulted in the use of the EEG as a major diagnostic tool where epilepsy is suspected. Apart from epilepsy, the kind of abnormal EEG pattern which is found may be of many kinds, and it is difficult for even a skilled diagnostician to identify clearly what kind of brain pathology is present simply by examining the EEG tracing.

In the light of this we can see that a primary approach to the study of schizophrenia with the EEG involves establishing that patients whose behavior is schizophrenic have a significantly high proportion of abnormal EEG tracings. The discovery of any specific "schizophrenic EEG" would be a much more remote possibility. Many problems, some of which have already been discussed, exist in interpreting the outcomes of research of this kind. Unreliable diagnoses due to ill-defined categories represent a familiar source of error. In addition, we must recognize that brain pathologies may well be present in any sample of the population; thus any large number of subjects—including schizophrenics—may be expected to include cases of brain pathology. A final problem which we face is that the EEG procedure itself is liable to error. Although the figure varies, most EEG investigators report the routine occurrence of "abnormal" EEG patterns in about 10 per cent of normal subjects.

Using a simple distinction between abnormal and normal tracings, Kennard and Levy (1952) found that 40 per cent of their schizophrenic sample had normal traces, but also discovered that the earlier the onset of schizophrenic symptoms and the more prolonged had been the illness, the more likely it was that the subject would exhibit EEG abnormality. A similar distribution of abnormal EEGs in a sample of 500 schizophrenics was reported by Finley and Campbell (1941), 60 per cent of this group producing abnormal traces and 40 per cent normal ones. Data obtained by Turner, Lowinger, and Huddleston (1945) suggest that the presence of abnormal rhythms may be related to prognosis for response to treatment. They found that of those patients with abnormal EEG patterns, none recovered after shock therapy sufficiently to be discharged, whereas 25 per cent of those without abnormal EEGs were discharged.

A slightly more specific finding was reported by Davis (1940), who described an erratic pattern of low voltage ranging from 26 to 50 cps in approximately 60 per cent of a sample of schizophrenics. Slow waves in the 2 to 6 cps range were reported by Walter (1942) in catatonic schizophrenic patients, but these findings were not constant.

We may summarize the present state of EEG findings in schizophrenia by noting that as a group, schizophrenic patients present a higher frequency of abnormal EEG records, but that no data have yet been forthcoming to support any systematic relationship between the psychological aspects of the disorder and the EEG deviations. There is some reason to suppose that the presence of an abnormal brain rhythm in a schizophrenic patient augurs poorly for his recovery or responsiveness to treatment.

Histopathology. While the EEG is an indirect measure of brain functioning in the living patient, more visible evidence of brain pathology may be obtained by direct postmortem inspection of the brain and tissue samples. Where psychosurgical procedures are performed on living patients, it is possible to obtain samples of brain tissue for biopsy. Once again, before proceeding to consider the evidence from histopathological studies, we must note the problems which are encountered in this kind of research. In the first place, autopsy studies are performed when the patient has died from some disease process which may itself have brought about changes in brain tissue. Tissue changes which accompany aging may also confound the investigation. Biopsy analyses are hampered by the difficulty of obtaining control samples from normal subjects, a procedure which is necessary in order to ascertain what tissue damage is caused by the surgical procedure itself.

Many studies of both autopsy and biopsy material have been reported. Perhaps the most systematic use of histopathological findings was made by Papez and Bateman in a series of investigations reported between 1948 and 1952 (Papez, 1948, 1952; Papez & Bateman, 1949, 1950, 1951).

Papez Hypothesis: Inclusion Bodies. In Papez's laboratory, studies were made of nerve cell changes in biopsy material from the brains of schizophrenic patients. The investigators identified microorganisms within the biopsy material which when stained, produced evidence of dark staining particles in the cytoplasm of the nerve cells. Papez termed these particles *inclusion bodies* and identified them as living organisms of a parasitic nature. The investigators studied these microorganisms in living preparations of cortical tissue, reporting that they were able to preserve them alive over periods of hours.

Invasion of the nerve cell by these organisms was the central process in a disease which Papez described as consisting of three phases. In the first phase, the inclusion bodies were found in the cytoplasm of intact nerve cells. Cell nuclei showed some deformity in this phase. Following this a second phase was identified which was marked by a pronounced increase of inclusion bodies in the cytoplasm and by further changes in the structure of the cell nucleus. A final phase included the appearance of nuclei denuded of cytoplasm as well as the occurrence of other degenerative changes. As drawn from microscope observation, these changes are pictured in Figure 13-8.

Papez and Bateman hypothesize that this parasitic invasion of nerve cells is the central disease process in schizophrenia, and that the many other histopathological findings of previous investigators are evidences of the effects of the various phases of this process

upon the nerve cells. In support of the Papez and Bateman position, another investigator, Schadewald (1953), confirmed many of their observations from his own study of 34 biopsy samples. The problem, however, is that there was no accompanying observation of the presence of inclusion bodies in a normal sample; no control samples were obtained by Papez and Bateman or by Schadewald. Thus the crucial linkage between histopathology and psychopathology cannot be made on the basis of the evidence so far available.

General Structural Changes. Space does not permit us to consider in detail all the particular changes in nerve tissue which have been reported by various investigators. They may be summarized as follows:

1. Loss in number of nerve cells, especially in anterior brain areas.
2. Disappearance of myelin substance.
3. Degenerative changes in nerve cells and in glial cells, including cell shrinkage, and increase in fat content of cells.

While these changes are reported with sufficient frequency to suggest that they are reliable, it is difficult at this time to integrate the information into a systematic understanding of the biology of schizophrenia. A lack of equally thorough examination of brain tissue of nonschizophrenic subjects means that we do not yet possess a knowledge of the limits within which the tissue of normal subjects varies—a knowledge which is essential to the interpretation of this kind of research.

GENETIC ASPECTS

The first part of this chapter examined some current hypotheses about the biology of schizophrenia which have one common feature: that schizophrenic behavior is significantly determined by some deviant organic process in the body of the patient. Granted this assumption, the task which the patholo-

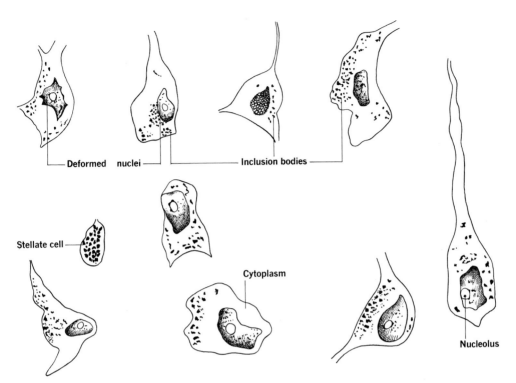

Deformed nuclei

Inclusion bodies

Stellate cell

Cytoplasm

Nucleolus

Figure 13-8. Nerve cells from cortex of dementia praecox in the first stage, showing intact cytoplasm with inclusion bodies and the local deformities in the nuclei due to irregular growths of chromatin material. (Mag. 1200 X.) (Papez & Bateman, 1949.)

gist has set himself is to discover the nature of this deviant process by examination of the bodily processes and tissues of the patient. When such a process is identified, or at least suspected, it is then regarded as the immediate biological determinant of the symptomatic behavior.

However, a complete understanding of the entire disorder would entail knowledge about the conditions which led to the development of the biological deviation itself. Generally speaking, there are a limited number of possibilities for the origin of a bodily disorder. One of these is that a pathogenic organism has entered the body after conception or after birth. The introduction of malarial organisms into the body of a human by a mosquito would be an example of this. A second possibility is that the biological environment in which the person develops

is inadequate in some way—as, for example, in the case of disorders due to oxygen deprivation at birth, vitamin deficiency in the diet, etc.

Neither of these possibilities has received much attention as explanations of the origin of schizophrenic disorders. Major interest has been focused upon hereditary or genetic factors wherever the primary etiology of schizophrenia has been studied. The methods available for the study of genetic factors in human behavior have been presented in detail in Chapter 5, and the reader is advised to refer to it where necessary in the discussions which follow. Before proceeding to examine the data that have been reported, let us first consider the implications of the heredity-environment argument that is so often raised whenever genetic explanations of behavior pathology are offered.

Heredity versus Environment

Human behavior is the end product of many influences acting together at any given time. The influence of past experiences (learning), the factors operating in the environment at the time the behavior is elicited (situational variables), and the biological endowment of the subject all affect the outcome. Consequently any dispute about whether or not a particular response is due to environmental versus biological factors is inherently nonsensical. The most meaningful question which can be asked is what relative effects one kind of variable has on the other. If we were to find that a particular kind of behavior is extremely resistant to environmental modification, we would tend to conclude that the most important determinants of its occurrence are biological. Consequently the question which we may wish to ask about any behavior is the extent to which changes in it correlate with environmental changes. If we find that such correlations are low, then we may deduce either (a) that we have not yet discovered the significant environmental influences—i.e., we are correlating the behavior with irrelevant changes in the environment or with only some of the relevant ones—or (b) that environmental influences are truly unimportant in determining changes in the behavior.

Behavior geneticists have attempted to quantify the contribution of heredity to the incidence of behavior by comparing the concordance of behavior in identical twins with the concordance in fraternal twins. If a particular pattern of behavior were exclusively determined by genetic factors, we should expect to find that whenever it is observed in one member of a pair of identical (MZ-monozygotic) twins, it invariably occurs in the other member. On the other hand, if it were exclusively determined by environmental factors, the incidence of the behavior pattern in the members of a pair of MZ twins would be no greater than that which would be found in any two children living in the same environment but unrelated to each other.

Needless to say, these instances are much too simple, and the actual comparisons are not easy to make. For practical purposes, it is common to compare the concordance rates for a behavior disorder in MZ twins with the rates for the same disorder in fraternal or dizygotic (DZ) twins. Because the latter are assumed to have had environments as similar to each other as would be the case for MZ twins, the difference between the two kinds of twin represents the similarity of their genetic endowment. Expressing this comparison in proportions, Neel and Schull (1954) have developed the following equation:

$$H = \frac{\text{CMZ} - \text{CDZ}}{100 - \text{CDZ}}$$

where H = an approximate index of the proportion of phenotypical variance to be attributed to genetic factors

CMZ = concordance rate for MZ twins, %

CDZ = concordance rate for DZ twins, %

This formula assumes that the similarity observed between DZ twins is to be assigned entirely to their common environment. However, we know that they have some similarities in their genetic endowment, being born of the same parents. Thus the effect of the formula is to provide a somewhat reduced value for H than that which we might get if we were comparing MZ twins with concordance rates for unrelated pairs.

Chromosomal Anomalies in Schizophrenia

In Chapter 5 we noted the use of the karyotype in detecting abnormal structure or translocations of chromosomes. While this method has not yet been applied widely to the study of psychotic patients, some work has been reported by Cowie (1963).

TABLE 13-1 Concordance Rates for Schizophrenia in Twins

Source	Number of pairs		Concordance, %*	
	MZ	DZ	MZ	DZ
Kallman (1946)	174	517	69	10
Kallman (1953)	268	685	86	15

* Concordance rates corrected to nearest whole number.

She studied those cases where the patient's physical measurements were more characteristic of the opposite sex, assuming this to be a preliminary indication of some possible genetic aberration. In this sample no chromosomal anomalies were detected. Nevertheless, she points out that "The visible sign of a genetical mechanism originally seen in mongolism seemed to hold out promise of similar discoveries in other conditions. However, the demonstration of the genetical origin of a condition as clearcut as that evidenced in an abnormal chromosome pattern evidently requires an exceptional piece of good fortune. It cannot be too strongly emphasized that a genetical aetiology cannot be dismissed just because the chromosome pattern appears to be normal" (Cowie, 1963, p. 32).

While this argument is certainly defensible, it recognizes the fact that with techniques currently available there is as yet no knowledge about the manner in which genetic factors might mediate the development of schizophrenic behavior. On the whole, those psychopathologists who have focused on the problems of autonomic balance and arousal in schizophrenia might not be surprised at the lack of evidence of gross genetic anomaly. So far, the support for a genetic explanation of schizophrenia still rests upon statistical inference from twin and family resemblances.

Guidance from Twin Studies

Perhaps the best-known study of concordance rates for schizophrenia in twins is that reported by Kallman in 1946 and later in 1953. He studied the frequency with which, given one member of a pair of twins who was hospitalized with a diagnosis of schizophrenia, the other member of the pair was also diagnosed in this way. His data are presented in Table 13-1. The application of the formula for H, given above, to the accumulated 1953 figures provided in the table produces a value of $H = 0.839$, which would suggest that a large amount of the variance in phenotypic schizophrenic development might be attributed to hereditary influences.

The figures reported by Kallman should be considered in the light of the reports of previous investigations of twin pairs. The comparable figures from these studies are given in Table 13-2, together with the calculated values of H (after Gregory, 1960). Although the values derived from the other investigators are somewhat smaller than that calculated from Kallman's data, they are of considerable magnitude.

TABLE 13-2 Concordance Rates for Schizophrenia in Twins

Source	Number of pairs		Concordance, %		
	MZ	DZ	MZ	DZ	H
Luxenburger (1928)	21	60	67	3	0.655
Rosanoff et al. (1934)	41	101	67	10	0.633
Essen-Möller (1941)	7	24	71	17	0.657
Slater (1953)	41	115	76	14	0.723

Twin Concordance and Severity of Psychopathology

In the studies so far cited, the criterion of concordance has been the rather simple one of "schizophrenic or well." Yet our previous discussion of the biological data relevant to schizophrenia has suggested that there appear to be degrees of disturbance among patients and probably differences in the degree to which biological mechanisms may be operating in a schizophrenic population. Gottesman and Shields (1965) studied 57 pairs of twins who had attended the Maudsley Hospital, London. Their sample was extremely carefully selected and included all patients admitted to the hospital between 1948 and 1964 who (a) were diagnosed schizophrenic and (b) were members of a twin pair where the other member was of the same sex. Because in some cases the other member of the twin pair entered the sample independently, there were actually 61 index cases—patients drawn into the study by virtue of their admission to the hospital—coming from a total of 57 different pairs of twins. Only 6 index cases were lost (and not included in the figures given above) due to death or departure from the country. The vast majority of the cases were identified as monozygotic or dizygotic by blood typing and fingerprint comparisons, providing much more reliability than many of the methods used in previous studies.

The index patient and his twin were contacted personally by the investigators in 106 cases, leaving only 8 cases in which second hand reports were used to provide data. With these data, the psychopathologi-cal status of each co-twin was graded according to the following scale.

Grade I   Close Concordance. The co-twin had been hospitalized psychiatrically and diagnosed schizophrenic.

Grade II   Moderate Concordance. The co-twin had been psychiatrically diagnosed, but with a diagnosis other than schizo-phrenia.

Grade III   Least Concordance. The co-twin: was in treatment as an outpatient for psychiatric disorder; was receiving some psychotropic drug while under treatment by a general practitioner; or demonstrated paranoid/schizoid tendencies either in behavior to the interviewer or on psychometric evaluation with the MMPI.

Grade IV   No Concordance. The co-twin was free from psychiatric disturbance.

Concordance percentages for grade I represent the strictest test of the prediction that schizophrenia in one twin will be accompanied by closely similar psychopathology in the other member of the pair. By including the figures for grade II and grade III, the test is made progressively less severe. These comparisons are shown in Table 13-3. It is quite clear that the impressive magnitudes of Kallman's figures must be viewed in the light of the fact that more careful definitions of concordance produce significantly lower estimates. A more appropriate inference might be that high concordance seems to exist between schizophrenic twins on the general level of susceptibility to the

TABLE 13-3 Schizophrenia Continuum and Twin Similarity (Cumulative Percentages)*

	I	II	III	N
MZ	42	54	79	24
DZ	9	18	46	33

* Not age corrected. Kallman's method of age correction would produce concordances in grade I of approximately 65 and 18 per cent for MZ and DZ respectively.
SOURCE: *Gottesman and Shields (1965).*

development of some kind of psychopathology in the course of the life span.

Having gathered these empirical estimates of "true" close concordance, Gottesman and Shields then analyzed their findings with respect to a criterion of the severity of the illness in the index cases—all of whom, it will be remembered, were diagnosed schizophrenic. Each index case was classified as "well" if he had managed to stay out of the hospital and remain gainfully employed for more than 6 months at the time of the study; he was classified as "sick" if he had not been able to achieve this level of social competence. The co-twin was then recorded as schizophrenic or not, on the basis of the data already described. The concordance rates for sick and well index twins are shown in Table 13-4. Here is striking evidence that high concordance rates—indicative of a strong genetic component—are more relevant to the understanding of severe schizophrenic pathology than of less disturbed patients. While no direct measure of the process-reactive classification was involved in this study, there are strong resemblances between that and the criteria for sick and well used here, suggesting that the reactive (good-premorbid) pattern involves a minor genetic factor, the contrary being true for the process or poor-premorbid patient.

The Gottesman and Shields study is of considerable importance as an instance both of careful control in methodology and of sophistication in the analysis of results. Its relevance to other work involving distinctions between types and severity of schizophrenia makes it much more informative than simple presence-absence studies have been in the past. Similar evidence, contrary to the implications of Kallman's reports, has been provided by Tienari (1963) and Kringlen (1964). The first of these found complete discordance in a sample of 16 MZ twins, while the latter found 6 discordant cases among 8 twins.

Conclusions to be drawn from twin studies, as indeed from any genetic studies, are often a matter of heated debate. Gregory (1960) cites the remark of Muller (1956) that "the heredity-environment controversy is an excellent example of wishful thinking by two sets of fanatical opponents, both of whom ought to know better." While avoiding debates of this kind, we should nevertheless consider the problems which arise in interpreting twin data.

Commonality of Environment. The assumption behind the comparison of MZ and DZ twin pairs is that the similarity of the environment for a pair of identical twins is equal to that for a pair of fraternal twins. It is quite possible to question this assumption. In many respects a pair of identical twins may be treated exactly alike, especially when young, while fraternal twins may be treated differently in important ways.

Diagnosis of Zygosity. Decisions regarding the zygosity of a pair of twins are not always easily made. Modern procedures use refined techniques of blood serum analysis, whereas many of the studies described did not. They depended instead upon such measures as eye color, hair color, fingerprints, height, skull dimensions, and so forth. Any significant bias toward a diagnosis of monozygosity would tend to exaggerate the contribution of heredity to the psychopathology.

TABLE 13-4 Effects of Severity on Concordance

Co-twin status	MZ proband			DZ proband		
	"Well"*	"Sick"	Total	"Well"*	"Sick"	Total
SC	2	12	14	0	4	4
Non-SC	10	4	14	16	14	30
Concordance, %	17	75	50	0	22	12

* Gainfully employed and out of hospital, more than 6 months.
SOURCE: Gottesman and Shields (1965).

Diagnosis of Schizophrenia. The diagnosis of schizophrenia is a rather unreliable matter, as we have already seen. Unfortunately, the use of twin pairs demands that once a member of a pair has been found to be schizophrenic, some attempt must be made to diagnose the other member. Since this diagnosis is carried out with the knowledge of the status of the first twin, it is difficult to rule out the effects, albeit unconscious, of bias toward finding schizophrenia. In other words, the extent to which the investigator believes that heredity is a significant determinant of schizophrenia may influence his diagnostic findings.

Biological Biases in Twins. A member of a pair of twins is not a random member of the population at large, because his uterine environment was different from that of the majority of babies. Twins of both kinds have lower birth weight than babies born singly (Allen, 1955), and the incidence of certain forms of epilepsy and mental retardation is somewhat higher in twins. It is difficult to estimate the importance of features of this kind in affecting the normalcy of any sample of twins. Some negative evidence is provided by the study of Gottesman and Shields cited above. They report that the incidence of twins in 48,000 consecutive admissions to the Maudsley Hospital was 2.4 per cent —the same as that for the population at large.

Family Studies

If a disorder is inherited, then by the same logic as that which is involved in twin studies, it should be most likely to appear in a close blood relative of a patient (the MZ twin being the ideal example of this) and increasingly less likely to be found in relatives of increasingly distant blood kinship. The base line against which these frequencies can be evaluated is the rate of schizophrenia in the total general population. Most estimates of this rate place it at about 0.8 to 0.9 per cent. Using his twin cases as the starting point, Kallman (1946, 1950) also observed the frequency of appearance of schizophrenia in various blood relatives of the patients, as well as in non-blood relatives (spouses and step-siblings). As Table 13-5 shows, his data indicate a falling off in the probability of finding schizophrenia in relatives of the patient as the relationship becomes more distant.

Examination of Table 13-5 shows that while the probability falls away as expected, it does so more sharply than would be expected by any simple Mendelian model of genetic transmission. The Mendelian expectancies for assumptions of either completely dominant or completely recessive genes are also shown (from Gregory, 1960). Gregory concludes from an examination of various possible models that whatever the genetic determinants of this disorder may be, it seems most likely that polygenic assumptions would be necessary to make sense out of the available information.

Calculations of the expected frequencies of schizophrenia are rendered rather complex because of certain facts about the mortality rates and marriage rates of patients.

Selective Mating. Some investigators have suggested that a person who is already schizophrenic or who comes from a family with a history of schizophrenia is more likely to marry another such person than would be the case if he were normal. Thus, the mating of people who are theoretically liable to be "carriers" of schizophrenic genes is not strictly random.

Mortality Rates. Various investigators have reported estimates of the mortality rates for schizophrenic patients as being from two to three times as high as that of the general population. Thus the potential transmission of schizophrenic susceptibility is substantially reduced compared with that for any normal genetic characteristic (e.g., Malzberg, 1934).

TABLE 13-5 Risk of Schizophrenia for Relatives of Schizophrenics: Empirical and Mendelian Theoretical Expectancy

Class	Percentage risk of schizophrenia	Theoretical expectancy	
		Completely dominant gene	Completely recessive gene
Children of two nonschizophrenic parents (general population)	0.9		
Relatives of adult schizophrenic index cases—			
Not consanguineous {Step-sibs	1.8		
{Spouse	2.1		
First cousins	2.6	.13	.03
Nephews and nieces	3.9	.25	.05
Grandchildren	4.3		
Half-sibs	7.1	.25	.15
Parents	9.2	.50	.09
Full-sibs	14.2	.50	.30
Dizygotic co-twins	14.5	.50	.30
Dizygotic co-twins of same sex	17.6	.50	.30
Children with one schizophrenic parent	16.4	.50	
Children with two schizophrenic parents	68.1	.75	1.00
Monozygotic co-twins	86.2	1.00	1.00
Monozygotic co-twins living apart for at least five years	77.6	1.00	1.00
Monozygotic co-twins not so separated	91.5	1.00	1.00

SOURCE: *After Kallmann (1946, 1950), Shields and Slater (1961), and Gregory (1960).*

Fertility Rates. The marriage rate of male schizophrenic subjects is lower than that for normal men, for obvious reasons. One effect of this is that the reproduction or fertility rate is lower than that for the general population, an effect which should militate against the maintenance of a consistent pool of schizophrenic subjects in the population. There is also some indication that in married schizophrenic females, the direct fertility rate is somewhat lower than that for normal women.

The total effect of these factors would be to reduce the number of offspring produced by schizophrenic adults, and we would therefore expect to find that the percentage of schizophrenics in the population is diminishing from one generation to another. As far as we can tell, however, this is not the case, a fact which argues for an environmental explanation of the disorder.

While genetically oriented studies have generally been confined to the gross characteristics of schizophrenia, Mednick and Schulsinger (1964) have reported an ingenious investigation of family resemblances between parents and their children in the shape of the curve of stimulus generalization and in general GSR responsivity to stress. Children from schizophrenic mothers comprised the experimental group, while normal control children were matched with them for age, sex, father's occupation and educational level, and area of residence. Preliminary results indicated that the experimental children had lower basal levels of GSR and produced higher, broader curves of generalization for a conditioned GSR. Insofar as these data reflect differences in autonomic responsiveness, they tend both to support the autonomic explanation of schizophrenia and to be congruent with a genetic explanation of the disorder.

Interpretation of Genetic Studies

None of the data which we have described are contradictory to the genetic hypothesis. However, concordance percentages are sufficiently deviant from simple Mendelian ratios that a complex, polygenic model would be necessary to account for them. Critics of the genetic position have sometimes gone even further and denied that the evidence necessarily supports any genetic hypothesis at all.

If we suppose that the major determinants of schizophrenic disorders are the pattern of family relationships and accompanying pressures on the child, then we might expect that as we examine the more distant relationships, the probability of finding a similar environment would be reduced. Thus the figures which we have presented in Table 13-5 might also be regarded as showing the effects of increasingly dissimilar environments upon the probability of finding a schizophrenic relative to an already identified patient.

However, at the present time the nature of the environment which generates schizophrenic behavior is no more clear than the nature of the genetic influences which have been postulated. It is not possible to argue that the data favor the environmental explanation any more than the genetic one. The environmental argument is especially difficult to apply to the discrepancy in concordances between MZ and DZ twin pairs. Allowing for the probability that the environment of MZ twins is more similar than that for DZ twins, the sheer magnitude of the difference in concordance rates is such as to cast doubt upon the environmental explanation.

Overshadowing any attempt to clarify this problem is the fact that the definition of schizophrenic behavior is itself vague. Without clearly defined phenotypical criteria for a diagnosis, the whole question of genetic versus environmental etiology becomes difficult to resolve. The possibility that there are many behavioral phenomena of differing etiologies which are all classed together as schizophrenic is considerable and must be borne in mind whenever we are attempting to discover some order in the material which we have discussed.

The present state of opinion on the issue is illustrated by the following quotations. Kallman (1959) after reviewing his own studies, concludes:

The deeply rooted reluctance to recognize genetically determined elements in the etiology of mental illness will inevitably have harmful consequences. The common denominator for damaging trends of this kind may be seen in the toleration or promotion of general attitudes that are liable to divert attention from important public health issues.

Apparently the tendency to de-emphasize genetic factors as potential causes of behavior disorders is an occupational hazard of all mental health professions and is older than psychiatry itself as a social phenomenon. (P. 191.)

Indicative of the opposition to genetic interpretations is the following statement from White (1949):

From a biological standpoint, the differences among men appear to be insignificant indeed when compared with their similarities. From the standpoint of human behavior too, all evidence points to an utter insignificance of biological factors as compared with culture in any consideration of behavior variation. As a matter of fact, it cannot be shown that any variation of human nature is due to variation of a biological nature. (P. 124.)

Unfortunately the question of biological and genetic influences in the development of human behavior has been clouded by the emotions of the participants on both the biological and the environmental sides. As long as the question is posed as being whether schizophrenic behavior is genetically determined *or* environmentally determined, there seems to be little prospect that we shall advance much further in our understanding of any of its determinants. We do have ample evidence that manipulation of biological variables produces changes in behavior; we also have ample evidence that manipulating the environment changes behavior. The important problem is the discovery of the processes by which these influences operate and the nature of the interaction between them.

SUGGESTED READINGS

The most useful reading sources on the topics covered in this chapter are rather scattered, and the reader will require access to several kinds of technical and scientific journals.

1. Benjamin, J. D. Some considerations of biological research in schizophrenia. *Psychosom. Med.,* 1958, **20,** 427–445. A brief review of the recent history of biological research in schizophrenia, from the point of view of dynamic psychiatry.
2. Hoskins, R. G. *The biology of schizophrenia.* New York: Norton, 1946. An account of the early research on adrenal function, now mainly of historic and systematic interest.
3. Lang, P. J., & Buss, A. H. Psychological deficit in schizophrenia. II. Interference and activation. *J. abnorm. Psychol.,* in press. A review summary of recent literature on the general topic of deficit. The arousal-inhibition variable is reviewed in detail.
4. Sankar, D. V. S. Some biological aspects of schizophrenic behavior. *Ann. N.Y. Acad. Sci.,* 1962, **96,** 1–490. A symposium of collected research papers on the title topic. Includes papers dealing with experimental psychoses, indole metabolism, serotonin hypothesis, human serum fractionations, etc.
5. Venables, P. Input dysfunction in schizophrenia. In B. A. Maher (Ed.), *Progress in experimental personality research.* Vol. I. New York: Academic Press, 1964. An excellent brief summary of the arousal-schizophrenia relation.

REFERENCES

Allen, G. Comments on the analysis of twin samples. *Acta genet. med. Gemelli,* 1955, **4,** 143–160.

Apter, N. S. Bilateral adrenalectomy in chronic schizophrenic patients. *Amer. J. Psychiat.,* 1958, **115,** 55–59.

Bannerjee, S., & Agarwal, P. S. Tryptophan—nicotinic acid metabolism in schizophrenia. *Proc. Soc. exp. Biol. Med.,* 1958, **97,** 657–659.

Belenkaya, N. Y. Electroencephaloscopic investigations of paranoid schizophrenics using meratran. *Zh. Nevropat. Psikhiat.,* 1960, **60,** 224–230.

Belenkaya, N. Y. The result of an electro-encephalographic investigation of paranoid schizophrenics under amizin therapy. *Zh. Nevropat. Psikhiat.,* 1961, **61,** 218–227.

Benjamin, J. D. Some considerations of biological research in schizophrenia. *Psychosom. Med.,* 1958, **20,** 427–445.

Braines, C. H. (Ed.). *Collected papers in experimental pathology.* Moscow: Academy of Medical Sciences, 1959.

Costa, E. Effects of hallucinogenic and tranquilizing drugs on serotonin evoked uterine contractions. *Proc. Soc. exp. Biol. Med.,* 1956, **91,** 39–41.

Costa, E., Aprison, M. H. Distribution of intracarotid by injected serotonin in the brain. *Amer. J. Physiol.,* 1958, **192,** 95–100.

Cowie, V. The psychiatric significance of chromosome anomalies. *Ciba Sympos.,* 1963, **11,** 28–33.

Davis, P. A. Evaluation of the electro-encephalograms of schizophrenic patients. *Amer. J. Psychiat.,* 1940, **96,** 851–860.

Ekolovia-Bagalei, E. M. The effect of cocaine on catatonics. In *Proceedings of the All Union theoretical-practical conference dedicated to the centenary of S. S. Korsakov.* Moscow: Medgiz, 1955.

Essen-Möller, E. Psychiatrische Untersuchungen an einer Serie von Zwillingen. *Acta psychiat., Kbh.,* Suppl. 23, 1941.

Feldstein, A., Hoagland, H., & Freeman, H. Blood and urinary serotonin and 5-hydroxyindoleacetic acid levels in schizophrenic patients and normal subjects. *J. nerv. ment. Dis.,* 1959, **129,** 62–68.

Finley, K. H., & Campbell, C. M. Electroencephalography in schizophrenia. *Amer. J. Psychiat.,* 1941, **98,** 374–381.

Fulcher, J. H., Gallagher, W. J., & Pfeiffer, C. C. Comparative lucid intervals after amobarbitol, CO_2 and arecoline in chronic schizophrenics. *Arch. neurol. Psychiat.,* 1957, **78,** 392–395.

Gamburg, A. L. The orienting and defensive reaction in simple and paranoid forms of schizophrenia. In N. N. Traugott et al. (Eds.), *The orienting reflex and orienting investigating activity.* Moscow: Academy of Pedagogical Sciences of R.S.F.S.R., 1958.

Gavrilova, N. A. Investigations of the cortical mosaic in different forms of schizophrenia. *Zh. Nevropat. Psikhiat.,* 1960, **60,** 453–460.

Gottesman, I. I., & Shields, J. Personal communication, 1965.

Gregory, I. Genetic factors in schizophrenia. *Amer. J. Psychiat.,* 1960, **116,** 961–972.

Heath, R. G. *Studies in schizophrenia.* Cambridge, Mass.: Harvard Univer. Press, 1954.

Heath, R. G. Correlations between levels of psychological awareness and physiological activity in the central nervous system. *Psychosom. Med.,* 1955, **17,** 383–395.

Heath, R. G. Correlation of electrical recordings from cortical and subcortical regions of the brain with abnormal behavior in human subjects. *Confinia Neurol.,* 1958, **18,** 305–315.

Heath, R. G. Physiological and biochemical studies in schizophrenia with particular emphasis on mind-brain relationships. In C. C. Pfeiffer and J. R. Smythies (Eds.), *International review of neurobiology.* Vol. 1. New York: Academic Press, 1959.

Heath, R. G. A biochemical hypothesis on the etiology of schizophrenia. In D. D. Jackson (Ed.), *The etiology of schizophrenia.* New York: Basic Books, 1960.

Heath, R. G., Martens, S., Leach, B. E., Cohen, M., & Angel, C. Effect on behavior in humans with the administration of taraxein. *Amer. J. Psychiat.,* 1957, **114,** 14–24.

Heath, R. G., Martens, S., Leach, B. E., Cohen, M., & Feigley, C. A. Behavioral changes in nonpsychotic volunteers following the administration of taraxein, the substance obtained from serum of schizophrenic patients. *Amer. J. Psychiat.,* 1958, **114,** 917–919.

Hoffer, A., & Osmond, H. Schizophrenia: an autonomic disease? *J. nerv. ment. Dis.,* 1955, **122,** 448–452.

Hoffer, A., & Osmond, H. The adrenochrome model and schizophrenia. *J. nerv. ment. Dis.,* 1959, **128,** 18–35.

Holland, R., Cohen, G., Goldenberg, M., Sha, J., & Leifer, A. I. Adrenaline and noradrenaline in the urine and plasma of schizophrenics. *Fed. Proc.,* 1958, **17,** 378.

Hoskins, R. G. *The biology of schizophrenia.* New York: Norton, 1946.

Kallman, F. J. The genetic theory of schizophrenia—an analysis of 691 twin index families. *Amer. J. Psychiat.,* 1946, **103,** 309–322.

Kallman, F. J. *Genetics of psychoses.* Paris: Hermann, 1950.

Kallman, F. J. *Heredity in mental health and disorder.* New York: Norton, 1953.

Kallman, F. J. The genetics of mental illness. In S. Arieti (Ed.), *American handbook of psychiatry.* New York: Basic Books, 1959.

Kennard, M. A., & Levy, S. Meaning of abnormal electroencephalogram in schizophrenia. *J. nerv. ment. Dis.,* 1952, **116,** 413–423.

Kety, S. Biochemical theories of schizophrenia. *Science,* 1959, **129,** 1520, 1590, 3362.

Kopin, I. J. Tryptophan loading and excretion of 5-hydroxyindoleacetic acid in normal and schizophrenic subjects. *Science,* 1959, **129,** 835.

Kringlen, E. Discordance with respect to schizophrenia in monozygotic male twins:

some genetic aspects. *J. nerv. ment. Dis.,* 1964, **138,** 26–31.

Lauer, J. W., Inskip, W. M., Bernsohn, J., & Zeller, E. A. Observations of schizophrenic patients after iproniazid and tryptophan. *Arch. neurol. Psychiat.,* 1958, **80,** 122–130.

Lea, A. J. Adrenochrome as the cause of schizophrenia: investigation of some deductions from this hypothesis. *J. ment. Sci.,* 1955, **101,** 538–547.

Luxenburger, H. Vorläufiger bericht über psychiatrische serien untersuchungen an Zwillingen. *Z. ges. Neurol. Psychiat.,* 1928, **116,** 297–326.

Lynn, R. Russian theory and research on schizophrenia. *Psychol. Bull.,* 1963, **60,** 486–498.

Malmo, R. B., & Shagass, C. Physiologic studies of reaction to stress in anxiety and early schizophrenia. *Psychosom. Med.,* 1949, **11,** 9–24.

Malmo, R. B., Shagass, C., & David, F. H. Electromyographic studies of muscular tension in psychiatric patients under stress. *J. clin. exp. Psychopathol.,* 1951, **12,** 45–66.

Malzberg, B. *Mortality among patients with mental disease.* Utica, N.Y.: State Hospital Press, 1934.

Mednick, S., & Schulsinger, J. Unpublished data. Kommunhospitalet, Copenhagen, 1964.

Muller, H. J. Genetic principles in human populations. *Amer. J. Psychiat.,* 1956, **113,** 481–491.

Neel, J. V., & Schull, J. W. *Human heredity.* Chicago: Univer. of Chicago Press, 1954.

Osmond, H., & Smithies, J. Schizophrenia: a new approach. *J. ment. Sci.,* 1952, **98,** 309–315.

Papez, J. W. Inclusion bodies associated with destruction of nerve cells in scrub typhus, psychoses, and multiple sclerosis. *J. nerv. ment. Dis.,* 1948, **108,** 431–434.

Papez, J. W. Form of living organisms in psychotic patients. *J. nerv. ment. Dis.,* 1952, **116,** 375–391.

Papez, J. W., & Bateman, J. F. Cytological changes in nerve cells in dementia praecox. *J. nerv. ment. Dis.,* 1949, **110,** 425–437.

Papez, J. W., & Bateman, J. F. Cytologic changes in cells of thalamic nuclei in senile, paranoid and manic psychoses: the significance of the dorsal thalamus in psychoses. *J. nerv. ment. Dis.,* 1950, **112,** 401–403.

Papez, J. W., & Bateman, J. F. Changes in nervous tissues and the study of living organisms in mental diseases. *J. nerv. ment. Dis.,* 1951, **114,** 400–412.

Pavlov, I. P. *Lectures on conditioned reflexes.* New York: International Univer. Press, 1941.

Pfister, H. O. Disturbances of autonomic function in schizophrenia and their relations to insulin, cardiazol and sleep treatments. *Amer. J. Psychiat.,* 1938, **94,** 109–118.

Rado, S., Buchenholz, B., Dunton, H., Karlin, S. H., & Senescu, R. A. Schizotypal organization: a preliminary report on a clinical study of schizophrenia. In S. Rado & G. Daniels (Eds.), *Changing concepts in psychoanalytic medicine.* New York: Grune & Stratton, 1956.

Ray, T. S. Electrodermal indications of levels of psychological disturbance in chronic schizophrenia. *American Psychologist,* 1963, **18,** 393.

Rinkel, M., Hyde, R. W., Solomon, H. C., & Hoagland, H. Experimental psychiatry. II. Clinical and physio-chemical observations in experimental psychosis. *Amer. J. Psychiat.,* 1955, **111,** 881–895.

Rosanoff, A. J., Handy, L. M., Plesset, I. R., & Brush, S. The etiology of the so-called schizophrenic psychoses with special reference to their occurrence in twins. *Amer. J. Psychiat.,* 1934, **91,** 247–286.

Rosenthal, R. The effect of the experimenter on the results of psychological research. In B. A. Maher (Ed.), *Progress in experimental personality research.* Vol. I. New York: Academic Press, 1964.

Schadewald, M. Cerebral cortical inclusions in psychoses. *J. comp. Neurol.,* 1953, **99,** 23–41.

Schwarz, B. E., Hakim, K. B., Bickford, R. G., & Lichtenheld, F. R. Behavioral and electroencephalographic effects of hallucinogenic drugs. *Arch. neurol. Psychiat.*, 1956, **7**, 83–90.

Shakow, D. Segmental set. *Arch. gen. Psychiat.*, 1962, **6**, 1–17.

Shaw, E., & Woolley, D. W. Some serotonin like activities in lysergic acid diethylamide. *Science*, 1956, **124**, 121–122.

Shields, J., & Slater, E. Heredity and psychological abnormality. In H. J. Eysenck (Ed.), *Handbook of abnormal psychology*. New York: Basic Books, 1961.

Siegel, M., Niswander, G. D., Sachs, E., & Stavros, D. Taraxein: fact or artifact. *Amer. J. Psychiat.*, 1959, **115**, 819–820.

Slater, E. *Psychotic and neurotic illnesses in twins*. London: H. M. Stationery Office, 1953.

Stevens, J. M., & Derbyshire, J. A. Shifts along the alert response continuum during remission of catatonic stupor with amobarbitol. *Psychosom. Med.*, 1958, **20**, 99–107.

Stevenson, J. A. F., Derrick, J. B., Hobbs, G. E., & Metcalfe, E. V. Adrenocortical response and phosphate excretion in schizophrenia. *Arch. neurol. Psychiat.*, 1957, **78**, 312–320.

Streltsova, N. L. The characteristics of some unconditioned reflexes. In *Proceedings of the All Union theoretical-practical conference dedicated to the centenary of S. S. Korsakov*. Moscow: Medgiz, 1955.

Szara, S., Axelrod, J., & Perlin, S. Is adrenochrome present in the blood? *Amer. J. Psychiat.*, 1958, **115**, 162–163.

Tienari, P. Psychiatric illnesses in identical twins. *Acta Psychiat. Scand.*, 1963, **39**, Suppl. 71, 1–195.

Toderick, A., Tait, A. C., Marshall, E. F. Blood platelet 5-hydroxytryptamine levels in psychiatric patients. *J. ment. Sci.*, 1960, **106**, 884–890.

Traugott, N. N., Balonov, L Ya., Kauffman, D. A., & Luchko, A. E. O. On the dynamics of the destruction of orienting reflexes in certain psychotic syndromes. In *The orienting reflex and orienting investigating activity*. Moscow: Academy of Pedagogical Sciences of R.S.F.S.R., 1958.

Turner, W. J., Lowinger, L., & Huddleston, J. H. Correlation of pre-electric shock electroencephalogram and therapeutic result in schizophrenia. *Amer. J. Psychiat.*, 1945, **102**, 299–300.

Venables, P. Input dysfunction in schizophrenia. In B. A. Maher (Ed.), *Progress in experimental personality research*. Vol. I. New York: Academic Press, 1964.

Venables, P. H., & Wing, J. K. Level of arousal and the subclassification of schizophrenia. *Arch. gen. Psychiat.*, 1962, **7**, 114–119.

Walter, W. G. Electroencephalography in cases of mental disorder. *J. ment. Sci.*, 1942, **88**, 110–121.

White, L. A. *The science of culture, a study of man and civilization*. New York: Farrar, Straus, 1949.

Williams, M. Psychophysiological responsiveness to psychological stress in early chronic schizophrenic reactions. *Psychosom. Med.*, 1953, **15**, 456–461.

14 SCHIZOPHRENIA: SENSATION, PERCEPTION, AND LEARNING

The previous chapter described the attempts that have been made to discover a primary biological dysfunction which might account for the psychological deficits and the various secondary symptoms that have been classified under the general heading of schizophrenia. On the other hand, a major contribution to research has been made by investigators who have turned their attention to the definition of the primary psychological deficit itself. A large body of literature has been built up, and it is beyond the scope of this work to cover even a major portion of it. However, we shall examine some of the most popular hypotheses and consider the experimental findings that they have generated.

GUIDING HYPOTHESES

For the sake of simplicity we have divided the experimental psychopathology of schizophrenia into two general areas: (a) the basic processes of sensation, perception, and learning and (b) research into language, thinking, and concept formation. This division is, of course, arbitrary, and the reader will probably hit upon other ways of integrating the data that will be presented. Inasmuch as the hypotheses that have guided research in one area frequently have pertinence to the other, we shall see that certain general notions reappear from time to time in the work of different experimenters tackling problems that differ at the level of the specific response concerned.

The General Organic Hypothesis

For want of a better title, we may use the term "general organic hypothesis" to refer to the implicit assumption that schizophrenia arises from a biological deficit of an undetermined type. However, the tactical procedure of the investigator tends to be directed to showing that the behavioral symptoms of the disorder possess some crucial resemblances to the behavioral symptoms of patients known to have brain damage—or other biological deficit.

It is difficult to give this assumption the full status of a hypothesis because of its vaguely articulated character. Furthermore, it involves two rather troublesome questions. First, when the experimenter seeks to make a comparison of the responses of his schizophrenic subjects with brain-injured subjects, he must assume that there is a general consequence of brain injury that is common to all such patients, regardless of the site and extent of the injury. The empirical status of this belief has been examined in an earlier chapter, and we have seen that it is most tenuous. Alternatively, he must select a group of brain-injured patients who all suffer from a similar and well localized injury. If the investigation is to be of any information value, comparison of such subjects with schizophrenic patients implies that the experimenter is hypothesizing the existence of a similar localized lesion in the schizophrenic group.

Secondly, this type of experimental work places the investigator in the position of accepting the argument that like effects must arise from like causes. This, we have also seen, is not logically compelling, and a favorable outcome for such an investigation leaves the experimenter with the problem of demonstrating by biological measurement that the supposed brain injury is actually present.

In fact, this general organic hypothesis is not usually stated explicitly, and we shall

see that investigators tend to make the comparison without going deeply into the rationale for it. An instance of this kind of research is to be found in the work of Saucer upon the problem of the perception of apparent motion (Saucer & Deabler, 1956; Saucer, 1958, 1959), which is discussed later in this chapter.

Defective Inhibition

In the previous chapter we saw that Pavlovian psychologists have argued that schizophrenia is the outcome of disordered inhibitory processes and have cited biological evidence in support of their view. Many of the experimental operations that have been used to demonstrate this hypothesis behaviorally lie directly in the field of learning rather than neuropsychology. Specifically, the acquisition and extinction of conditioned responses, and especially of discriminations, are presumed to depend upon the adequate operation of inhibition.

For example, when a subject acquires a conditioned response to a light of a given color, it will generalize to other colored lights until the training procedure has extinguished this generalized response by the absence of reinforcement. Extinction of these responses is regarded as due to the buildup of inhibition to the stimuli. Failure to build up such inhibition would be indicated by the continued appearance of the responses after prolonged extinction trials. Where the subject is required to acquire one response to one stimulus but another response to the similar generalized stimulus, then failure of inhibition should produce continual interference of one response with another to either stimulus.

By the same token, the gradient of stimulus generalization may be regarded as dependent upon the correct operation of inhibitory processes—responses becoming weaker to stimuli that are progressively less similar to the original CS. Failure of inhibition here should lead to less marked weakening, i.e., a less steep gradient. Thus the stimulus generalization gradient of schizophrenic patients should tend to be flatter than that of normal controls or other kinds of patient.

Inhibition, in the foregoing sense, refers to the suppression of responses. However, it is also used to refer to the suppression of responses to ongoing stimulation necessary to permit the appearance of the orienting response to new stimuli, and to permit the maintenance of attention to a given stimulus when circumstances demand it. Thus, deficient inhibition would lead us to expect (a) difficulty in getting the subject to attend to those aspects of a situation in which the experimenter is interested, *i.e.*, the experimental task, and (b) difficulty in keeping his attention on the same aspects when the environment contains random stimulation that might distract him.

While these expectations may be tested in experiments that demand close attention to task elements, they are likely to be seen clinically in a variety of ways. The inability of the schizophrenic to follow a systematic train of thought or sequence of responses can be understood as a part of his difficulty in ignoring (inhibiting) local irrelevant stimuli. Where stimuli have more than one meaning, i.e., as in the case of many symbols, then the inability to ignore the inappropriate meaning may lead to considerable confusion in communication and organization of behavior generally. Thus the inhibitory deficiency may appear as a general deficiency in "attention" or "concentration" or the ability to maintain a "mental set."

The deficient-inhibition explanation is, at the behavioral level, largely a matter of demonstrating that schizophrenic behavior is consistently deducible from certain propositions about the role of inhibition in the normal learning process. However, the "inhibitory process" is here a hypothetical one, inferred from behavior and not demonstrated by any direct biological measure. It has merit only to the extent that it permits a wide range of schizophrenic symptomatology to be encompassed in a parsimonious explanatory system.

Activation Deficit

While the previous hypothesis emphasizes the importance of deficient inhibition, other workers have regarded schizophrenia as a disorder of arousal or activation. One of the most sophisticated versions of this hypothesis has been advanced by Venables (1964). He draws a distinction between the acute and the chronic states of the disorder, as well as between subtypes of diagnostic classification, believing that there is a transition from acute to chronic in at least some cases which is accompanied by a change in the character of the primary deficit.

The acute patient (and perhaps both the reactive and the paranoid) is believed to suffer from an inability to restrict the range of attention and is thus at the mercy of a variety of sense impressions from all parts of the environment. Any function that requires the selective ignoring of some input will be disrupted, especially the perception of figure and ground relationships—the distinguishing of stimuli as separate from the background of stimulation in which they occur. The broad span of attention is presumed to reflect a low level of activation, or parasympathetic dominance in the autonomic balance. Any drug or procedure that would raise the level of activation should raise the behavioral efficiency of the patient by narrowing his attention span.

Chronic patients—and possibly process patients—are believed, on the other hand, to be suffering from unusually high levels of activation, with a consequent narrowing of attention. Thus, many external sensory items do not enter consciousness at all. Drugs or other techniques that reduce arousal would serve to improve the subject's perception of the environment and his behavioral efficiency.

Particular interest attaches in this hypothesis to the phenomena of the perceptual constancies. The basic mechanisms have already been discussed in an earlier chapter, but it may help to review them here. When a subject correctly perceives a distant man to be taller than a nearby child, he does so even though the size of the retinal image is smaller for the man than for the child. His correct estimate is based in large part upon the availability of many other local cues to the true relationship of their sizes, such as the apparent size of nearby buildings, the distance perspective indicators, and so on. Where these are either eliminated or not perceived, the subject is more likely to perceive the man in terms of the retinal image —and thus will make errors of size judgment. High states of activation, with accompanying narrowed attention, should therefore lead to underestimates of the size of distant objects. We shall see the importance of this hypothesis later in the chapter.

Social Disarticulation

In contrast to the foregoing approaches, Cameron has suggested that the origin of schizophrenia lies in the social history of the individual. Pathological thought processes and the other cognitive anomalies found in schizophrenia are secondary consequences of this. The schizophrenic is presumed to have undergone a progressive withdrawal from the controlling influences exerted by reality upon his thinking. Consequently, the patient's cognitive processes become increasingly autistic and idiosyncratic, dominated by fantasy and his private associations. Because this withdrawal is most marked in his relations with other people and the social environment generally, the impairment in thinking would be most evident when the solution to a problem is defined in terms of social reality. However, as thinking or conceptualizing of any kind requires constant and regular validation through contact and discussion with other people, lack of this contact would be followed by deficiencies in thinking with any kind of material. Turning directly to Cameron, we find him remarking that

Thinking must be made to correspond with operations in the shared social field of interbehavior, if it is to remain socially valid. For all but the exceptionally well-integrated social person, this means that one must continually engage in cooperative and competitive activities with other social persons, or at least return repeatedly to participative behavior, where conclusions privately arrived at can be publicly verified or contradicted. (Cameron & Magaret, 1951, p. 507.)

From an experimental point of view, certain general deductions might be made from Cameron's hypothesis. Preoccupation with inner, autistic stimuli should lead to a relative insensitivity to external stimulation, or to difficulty in distinguishing consistently between inner and outer stimuli. Social disarticulation might be expected to create particular difficulties for the patient in dealing with stimuli which have social significance, but relatively less difficulty in dealing with tasks which employ impersonal stimuli. By the same token, where the motivation for performing the task at all is social (e.g., receiving experimenter approval or disapproval), the behavior of the patient might be different from his behavior under biological motivations (e.g., hunger, thirst, physical pain, etc.).

While Cameron has thus presented what is essentially an etiological hypothesis, he has also described varieties of thinking pathology which he feels are characteristic of schizophrenic cognitions. Specifically, he has referred to *overinclusion* and *underinclusion* in concept formation. Overinclusion is the process of including in a concept items which would ordinarily be regarded as inappropriate and therefore omitted by normal subjects. Underinclusion refers to the process of leaving out items which the normal subject would regard as logically within the definition of a concept. Two further cognitive disturbances cited by Cameron are those of *fragmentation* and *interpenetration*. The occurrence of a miscellany of discontinuous or abortive responses, or sudden reaction which is not followed by resumption of the original theme, represents Cameron's definition of fragmentation. Interpenetration is used by him to mean the appearance in an ongoing sequence of an intrusive word, movement, or thought which belongs to some other coordinated activity sequence. This hypothesis is discussed in detail in the next chapter.

Insensitivity to Reinforcement

Several investigators have considered that schizophrenia might be characterized by insensitivity to particular classes of reinforcer (e.g., reward, punishment, social versus physical reinforcers, etc.) without regard to the possible origin of such insensitivity. While all these possibilities are plausible in Cameron's hypothesis, they may be studied without reference to it, simply as hypotheses about the nature of the primary deficit rather than its origin.

Of the foregoing general hypotheses, Cameron's is the only one that makes specific estimates about the kind of etiology involved in the genesis of the primary deficits. The others are essentially attempts at theoretical parsimony—at incorporating a wide range of symptoms into a smaller number of categories or at relating the symptoms to a small number of psychological systems. Not all empirical research into schizophrenic responses in sensation, perception, or learning has adopted these hypotheses. Many investigators have conducted research into such functions with nothing more than a desire to see if there is a difference in some normal response class.

All the hypotheses suffer because of the inherent simplicity of the concept of schizophrenia that they imply. Experimental groups suffer from lack of homogeneity on many counts. Before we can reasonably study the data, we should first consider some of the methodological problems that have been encountered.

METHODOLOGICAL PROBLEMS

Correlated Variables

People who are hospitalized with a diagnosis of schizophrenia are sociologically atypical in other ways. Specifically, we find that they tend to be less well educated than the normal population, to have lower economic status, and to be more likely to come from an immigrant group (in the United States) and from an urban rather than a rural area. Many of these factors could well influence behavior in a variety of experimental situations, as well as mislead clinical observers, who themselves generally come from middle-class or higher strata of society. For deductions to be made about schizophrenia, it is necessary, therefore, to either control for these factors by careful matching of patients and normals before the experiment begins, or to have some other way of estimating their influence separately from the influence of schizophrenia.

A second source of confusion in studies is the effect of hospital-produced factors. Chronic schizophrenic patients are, by definition, patients who have spent considerable time in hospitals. Some of the behavior which they exhibit might be attributable to the effect of institutionalization itself. Chronic patients are also typically older than acute patients, a difference which may be important in comparing the two groups.

Third, in order to participate as a subject in an experiment, the patient must be able to attend to the experimenter, understand instructions, and manipulate whatever apparatus or materials might be involved. This requirement serves to eliminate many patients from studies; indeed, it is common for the experimenter to conduct some preliminary screening of his subjects to select the ones who are capable of participating. Provided this screening is reported, the procedure is perfectly reasonable. It is difficult to see how many studies could be done otherwise. But it also means that research findings are necessarily restricted to a class of patients who are sufficiently in contact with the experimental situation to permit them to make measurable responses.

Diagnostic Entities

The previous chapter describing the clinical aspects of schizophrenia indicated that we might more appropriately speak of the *group* of schizophrenias. We shall not repeat the discussion of the validity of disease entity concepts here, but it will be obvious that inadequacies in diagnostic groupings of this kind can have the effect of obscuring differences between patients, where these differences might be important for psychopathological theory. More useful distinctions might be made between patients by using criteria other than gross clinical features of the patients' behaviors. Experimental psychopathologists have found that certain classifications are more predictive than the formal psychiatric diagnoses; the more prominent of these are given in the following section.

Quite apart from the questionable validity of orthodox diagnostic groupings within schizophrenia, there is the question of the reliability of such diagnoses anyway. Two or more diagnosticians may, and frequently do, observe the same patient behaving in the same way and yet arrive at contradictory conclusions as to the correct diagnostic label to be applied to the case. Some diagnosticians seem to have a favorite diagnosis which is applied to a remarkably heterogeneous group of patients. A major source of this confusion is the inherent vagueness of the traditional diagnostic definitions; some of it stems from different emphases in the institutions in which diagnosticians are trained. Whatever the reasons, the unreliability of diagnostic classification is such that its use as a criterion for selecting groups of experimental subjects is surrounded by pitfalls for the investigator.

PREMORBID FACTORS

Because of the many problems involved in the use of traditional classifications in schizophrenia, attention has been turned to certain other aspects of the history and behavior of schizophrenics. One of the more striking differences between patients diagnosed as schizophrenic is the manner of onset of the disorder. Another is the prognosis for a favorable recovery. The process-reactive

distinction has already been described. Another categorization is the good-premorbid–poor-premorbid distinction developed by Phillips (1953). The Phillips Rating Scale of Premorbid Level of Adjustment in Schizophrenia provides a quantitative value for the premorbid status of the patient. The scale has been used by experimental psychopathologists to distinguish good-premorbid from poor-premorbid subjects in various studies. Typical items from the Phillips scale are given in Table 12-2 (see Chapter 12). A fuller review of work done in relation to this scale has been provided by Higgins (1964).

Bearing these classifications in mind, we may now turn to examine the findings which have been made by experimental psychopathologists on various aspects of schizophrenic behavior.

EXPERIMENTAL FINDINGS

Sensation and Perception

Perceptions of reality which are at variance with those of a normal population are common symptoms of the schizophrenic psychoses. Hallucinations represent an extreme example of misperception, but other anomalies of perceptual accuracy are also frequent in the descriptive clinical literature. Consequently, it is not surprising that experimental psychopathologists have turned their attention to perception in an attempt to discover the variables which determine the kind and extent of misperceptions by patients under various circumstances. One of the first problems of interest was the investigation of differences in threshold perceptions by using controlled stimuli and different sense modalities.

Sensory Thresholds.   Early work on *tactual* thresholds was reported by Franz (1910). He found no differences between psychotics and normals. Huston (1934) found no differences between the thresholds for faradic stimulation of schizophrenics and normals.

At the present time, there is no substantial evidence to suggest that schizophrenic patients differ from normals in their thresholds for tactile perception.

Related to tactual thresholds are the thresholds for the perception of *pain*. Hall and Stride (1954) used a device for producing heat stimulation of the skin of the forehead on various classes of patient, recording the patient's verbal report of warmth perception and pain perception, and finally reaching the point in stimulus intensity at which a reaction of wincing or withdrawal from the stimulus was recorded (pain reaction point). Only 14 schizophrenic patients were observed in this way, but they produced high mean verbal report of pain and pain reaction point values. Caution was used by the investigators in interpreting this observation because of the unreliability of the mental set of these subjects—a problem which has already been mentioned in the Goldstein hypothesis.

Particular interest has been focused on the study of *visual* perception, but no reliable differences in absolute thresholds or in visual acuity have been reported. A series of investigations has dealt with the problem of the threshold value for *critical flicker frequency* (CFF). This measure, which is based on the alternation between light and dark of a fixed light source, may be defined as the slowest rate of alternation at which the subject will see a steady (unflickering) light. The periods of light and dark are equal, the rate of alternation in on-off cycles per second being the critical measure. Psychopathologists have been interested in this measure because variations in CFF are presumed to be related to brain damage. Neuropathological conceptions of schizophrenia would lead to the presumption that deviant CFF values might be found for the schizophrenic population.

However, studies by Ricciuti (1948), Irvine (1954), and McDonough (1960) provide evidence to indicate that no reliable differences exist between schizophrenic and normal subjects in the CFF threshold. In McDonough's study, the schizophrenic sample was divided in terms of the process-reactive distinction, and the mean CFF threshold of the reactive group was higher than that of the normals. However, the obtained significance of the difference was just at the .05 level (the mean for the normals was 16.38 cps; for the process, 16.43 cps; and for the reactive, 16.67 cps.), and it seems difficult to attach any theoretical importance to differences of such small absolute magnitude. Here, as in the case of tactual thresholds, there appears to be little justification for hypothesizing that schizophrenic patients are characterized by perceptual differences at this level.

When two lights close to each other are illuminated momentarily, with a suitably brief interval of time between the two flashes, the result is that an observer perceives them as a single light in motion. This effect is sometimes referred to as the phenomenon of *apparent movement*. Many investigations have suggested that brain pathologies of some kinds may result in changes in the frequency threshold for perception of apparent motion under normal conditions. We have already seen that many investigators approach the problems of schizophrenia with a general hypothesis that it is basically an organic disorder. With this in mind Saucer has conducted a systematic series of studies of apparent movement perception in schizophrenia (Saucer & Deabler, 1956; Saucer, 1958, 1959). His conclusions are as follows: Undifferentiated schizophrenic patients see apparent movement at a much lower rate of oscillation than do normals; but when patients are subdivided into paranoid and nonparanoid groups, the paranoid patients are equal in performance to normals. Nonparanoid patients under chlorpromazine see the apparent motion effect at the same frequency as normals. Saucer interprets his results as supportive of a general hypothesis that schizophrenia is a disorder of "functional decortication." We may wish to suspend judgment upon this interpretation but to note that nonparanoid schizophrenics appear to be consistently different from normals and paranoids in this kind of perception.

Auditory thresholds have been investigated by L. E. Travis (1924), R. C. Travis (1926), and Morel (1936). Again they found no evidence to support the notion that there are differences in schizophrenic thresholds, although the data of Morel indicate that thresholds may vary when the patient is actively hallucinating during the experiment. This observation may perhaps be regarded as evidence of responsiveness to autistic stimulation rather than as any temporary deficit in auditory sensory processes.

From these data we may summarize in Box 14-1 some general conclusions about threshold perception in schizophrenia.

Estimates and Judgments

It is a common hypothesis in psychology that the estimation of the physical characteristics of a rewarding (or threatening) object will be partly determined by the intensity of the needs of the perceiver in relation to the object. Thus the estimate made by a subject will be a resultant of the "true" value of the physical variable combined with the motivational influences operating at the time of perception. The investigations of Bruner and Goodman (1947) and Dukes and Bevan (1952) exemplify this hypothesis. Many other factors will, of course, modify judgments, including the context in which the object is perceived and the past experience of the subject in making such estimates.

From this general hypothesis, it seems possible that greater distortion of estimates might be expected from individuals whose perceptual processes are unusually impervious to reality factors. Thus, the definition of the schizophrenic condition as being marked by poor reality contact would lead to the prediction that patients will be less accurate than normals in judging measurable attributes of a physical stimulus. This possibility has been explored in several studies.

Visual Estimates. Judgments of the *size* of a stimulus object have been obtained from schizophrenic subjects by Harris (1957). He presented adult male schizophrenics with a series of pictures projected upon a screen. The pictures were selected to represent certain mother-child relationships designated as dominance, acceptance, ignoring, and overprotection. Two neutral pictures were also provided in the series, one being a square and the other a picture of two trees. Figure 14-1 illustrates the stimulus material. The subject was asked a series of questions designed to arouse preoccupations with his emotional ties to his own mother before he was shown the pictures portraying abstract mother-son relationships. The size estimates

BOX 14-1 Sensory Thresholds in Schizophrenia

Sense modality	Sensory variable	Differences
Tactual	Pressure	No differences between patients and normals
	Pain perception	Schizophrenics had higher thresholds than normals
Auditory		No differences
Visual	Acuity	No differences
	Brightness	No differences
	CFF	No major differences; reactive schizophrenics slightly higher than process and normals
	Apparent movement	Nonparanoid patients lower than paranoids and normals

Figure 14-1. The stimulus figures. 1. Neutral 2. Dominance 3. Acceptance 4. Ignoring 5. Overprotection 6. Square. (Courtesy of J. G. Harris.)

produced by the normal subjects and by the schizophrenic patients, subdivided into the good-premorbid and poor-premorbid dichotomy provided by the Phillips rating scale, are given in Table 14-1. Not all the differences between groups are statistically significant. However, it can be seen that, in general, the schizophrenic group divides clearly on the task in terms of premorbid adjustment, thereby strengthening the view that this factor should be taken into account

in any investigation of schizophrenic groups.

A similar investigation is reported by Zahn (1959), who proceeded from the findings of Harris. Punishment and reward were used to establish punishing and rewarding values for certain otherwise neutral pictures. The flashing on of a sign reading either "right" or "wrong" constituted the reinforcement and was administered by a prearranged schedule during preliminary training in what purported to be a size discrimination task.

TABLE 14-1 Comparison of Mean Size Estimates with the Standard Size for Good- and Poor-premorbid Groups

Picture theme	Good-premorbid group df = 8		Poor-premorbid group df = 7	
	t	Level of significance	t	Level of significance
Neutral (trees)	.054	NS	2.350	.10
Dominance	2.306	.05	2.124	.10
Acceptance	1.865	.10	2.063	.10
Ignoring	1.029	NS	3.898	.01
Overprotection	.679	NS	3.167	.02
Neutral (square)	.370	NS	1.049	NS

SOURCE: *Harris (1957).*

Social reward affected the good-premorbid group differently from the other two groups, the rewarded picture being judged as significantly smaller than the punished one. The poor-premorbids and normals produced comparable results on all variables. Zahn suggests that in his good-premorbid group, there existed a high degree of anxiety and sensitivity to stress, whereas the poor-premorbid group might have developed withdrawal adjustments resulting in less involvement in the experimental task. Another difference in the two studies, unmentioned by Zahn, is the deliberate arousal of preoccupations with familial relationships by Harris, which was not a feature of Zahn's procedure. It is likely that this may have had a determining influence upon behavior of such a specific type as estimating the size of a stimulus object.

Systematically pursuing the hypothesis derived from his first investigation, Zahn (1960) looked at the relationship between anxiety, as measured by the Taylor Manifest Anxiety Scale (MAS), and sensitivity of size judgments to the effects of social punishment and reward. The subjects were college students. Students who were classified as high anxious on the MAS overestimated the size of the punished picture compared with the low-anxious group. Zahn's general conclusion is that experimental punishment of this kind makes the picture stimulus "personally relevant" to the anxious subject, and that personal relevance leads to an overestimation of stimulus size.

On this basis, therefore, the crucial variable is not positive versus negative reinforcement, but the relevance versus nonrelevance of the stimulus in the emotional life of the subject.

Size estimation as it is affected by contextual variables has also been studied, using the phenomenon of *size constancy* as the response measure. In studies of this kind the perceptual task usually involves judging the size of an object placed at some distance from the eye subtending a known angle to the retina. Thus the size of the object as it is seen under the experimental condition varies in measurable manner from its true maximum size as measured metrically along its major dimensions. Judgments of size made under these conditions by normal subjects are typically modified by their previous experience with the "true" dimensions.

In the case of schizophrenics, Raush (1952) advanced the general hypothesis that size constancy ought to be impaired and that judgments of size would be closer to the value of the proximal stimulus—in this case the retinal image. His rationale for this prediction was based upon the assumption that size constancy is a phenomenon associated with good reality contact and is in fact necessary for effective dealings with the world of real objects. However, Raush drew a distinction between the probable constancy mechanisms of the paranoid and nonparanoid schizophrenic. Delusions may be regarded as marked by considerable imperviousness to change, even in a changing environment. Thus, the paranoid interprets reality with great constancy, even though with considerable inaccuracy. On this basis he deduced that paranoid schizophrenic patients would exhibit overconstancy (would judge the size of a stimulus object more closely to its actual dimensions than normal controls would), whereas the nonparanoid schizophrenic would judge the stimulus more closely to its proximal dimensions than normals would. In the outcome, his data indicated significant overconstancy for the paranoid group, compared with both normals and nonparanoid patients. However, the last two groups did not differ significantly from each other. All differences were reduced when size judgments were made with increased availability of cues.

Pursuing this problem, Raush (1956) further investigated the effect of the value, or symbolic significance, of the stimulus objects upon size constancy. This problem arises directly from the earlier finding with normal subjects that the value of a coin, for instance, influences estimates of its size. Raush called for estimates of the sizes of objects which were presumed by him to have special psychological significance on the basis of psychoanalytic theory. His neutral object was a button; his significant objects were a scoop of ice cream and the cross section of a cigar. Actually, his subjects were presented with circles of varying diameters and required to select those which would be about the same size as a typical button, etc.

As predicted, the schizophrenics selected relatively larger circles to represent the two symbolic objects than that selected to represent the button, and this discrepancy was significantly smaller in a normal control group. It should be noted here that, strictly speaking, this is not a study of perceptual constancy, since the subject was not required to estimate the characteristics of an object present at the time of judging. However, the data may be regarded as supportive of the more general hypothesis that object distortion in schizophrenia may be influenced by the symbolic value of the object.

This conclusion is congruent with the belief in the importance of personal relevance noted by Zahn above. Paranoid schizophrenics did not differ from nonparanoids in this part of Raush's study, but were significantly more restricted in the range of circle sizes which they selected to represent the smallest button and largest button, etc. This observation leads Raush to conclude that rigidity in perceiving reality is characteristic of the paranoid schizophrenic state.

The influence of contextual distance cues upon size constancy in schizophrenics was investigated by Lovinger (1956). The observation that availability of cues reduced the differences between patients and normals in a size constancy task has already been noted in Raush's first study. Lovinger systematically varied the availability of cues, using groups of schizophrenics who were in turn divided on the basis of contact with reality into good-contact and poor-contact groups. He discovered that the poor-contact group was significantly different from both the good-contact group and normal controls under conditions of minimal cue availability, but that there were no differences between groups under maximal-cue and no-cue conditions. Among other things, Lovinger points out the necessity of taking the contact-with-reality variable into account when making predictions about perceptual phenomena. Before leaving this study, it is well to point out that the conclusions to be drawn are (a) that patients defined as being in poor contact with reality demonstrate perceptual anomalies in size constancy tasks, thereby extending our interpretation of the notion of reality contact, and (b) that the diagnosis of schizophrenia per se does not justify the assumption that perceptual anomalies of this kind will be found in the patient.

Finally we may turn to the work of Weckowicz and his colleagues (Weckowicz, 1957; Weckowicz, Sommer, & Hall, 1958; Weckowicz & Hall, 1960). They investigated both size and distance constancies in schizophrenic patients and found that constancy was inferior; i.e., estimates of size were closer to the size of the proximal stimulus than was the case in normals. This confirms a similar study by Crookes (1957).

These data about visual estimates in schizophrenia are summarized in Box 14-2.

An interesting finding by Weckowicz (1958) is that when the drug mecholyl is administered to schizophrenics, those who respond by a rise in blood pressure also show better size constancy than those who show little or no rise. This finding has been interpreted by Weckowicz to suggest that the central problem in schizophrenia is pathological reactivity of the autonomic nervous system.

While this conclusion is stated in somewhat general terms, it does imply that the reactivity or arousability of the autonomic system is correlated with the constancy effect—an important relationship for those investigators who argue that deficiency in arousal is the primary deficit in schizophrenia. This position has been espoused most explicitly by Callaway and Thompson (1953). When an organism is faced with a threat, they argued, there is an increase in sympathetic activity of the autonomic nervous system. Increased arousal of this sort should narrow attention and thus produce constancy perceptions closer to the true size of the retinal image. Any other stimulus that produces increased arousal and narrowed attention should have the same effect. Callaway and his colleagues tested this hypothesis with a variety of stimulant conditions designed to increase arousal. Included in these were cold pressor stimulation (placing the subject's foot in cold water), amyl nitrate, adrenalin, and metamphetamine (Callaway & Dembo, 1958; Callaway, 1959). In each case the effect of the arousal condition was to produce a reduction in the size estimate of a test object, thereby confirming the hypothesis.

It is quite clear that the measurement of size constancy is not simply a matter of identifying yet another response in which the patient is deviant. The manner in which it deviates seems to implicate the biological mechanisms underlying the maintenance of attention—thus supporting the view that it is this deficit that may be the most fundamental in the patient's disorder.

Time Perception. The problem of time perception is one which has fascinated psychologists and others for many decades. What is it that leads us to feel that one period of time has been longer than another, when we do not have a clock to measure it?

BOX 14-2 Visual Judgments in Schizophrenia: Size and Constancy

Variable	Effect
Schizophrenic vs. normal	Size and distance constancy generally inferior in schizophrenics
Premorbid adjustment	Good-premorbid schizophrenics are more deviant in estimating size of personally relevant objects
Paranoid vs. nonparanoid	a. Paranoid schizophrenics overestimate in a size constancy judgment b. Paranoid schizophrenics do not differ from normals and nonparanoid schizophrenics in estimating size of symbolically significant objects
Reality contact	a. When *few* cues are available, patients in poor contact are inferior to normals and good-contact patients in size constancy b. When *many* cues or *no* cues are available, normals and both groups of schizophrenics are the same in size constancy responses

A thorough review of this problem would be out of place here, but may be found elsewhere (Woodrow, 1951). Theories of time perception tend to emphasize (a) the importance of the rate of change of events during a given time interval or (b) the importance of bodily rhythms, such as breathing, pulse rate, and so forth. In either case, we might expect that insensitivity to outer stimulus changes and/or preoccupation with one's own bodily functions would lead to differences in time perception. Clinical descriptions of schizophrenia mention both of these processes, and it is therefore plausible to seek for experimental evidence of a typical time perception in schizophrenic patients.

Early descriptions of disruption of "time sense" were given by Schilder (1936) but direct investigation of disturbances of time perception did not develop for some time. Rabin (1957) asked schizophrenics to estimate the time taken in interviews and found a significant tendency to overestimate time periods passed in this way. Lhamon and Goldstone (1956) and Weinstein, Goldstone, and Boardman (1958) found that schizophrenic patients overestimate clock times of one second and are much more influenced in their judgments of short time intervals by the immediate "anchor" or time sample presented to them in the experimental situation. Speculating about these results, the authors suggest that (a) schizophrenics are judging time by the rate of change of their inner fantasy events, rather than by the changing outer stimuli, and (b) schizophrenics appear to deal with experimental tasks of this variety as though they were unable to use their past experience with time sequences, being at the "mercy" of the conditions of a particular experiment. On the principle that fantasy events change more rapidly than actual environmental events, we would expect preoccupation with inner fantasies to lead to an overestimation of time, and on the whole the data appear to confirm this phenomenon, although they do not necessarily corroborate the explanation of it.

Weight Judgment. Two possible anomalies of weight judgment have been suggested in schizophrenia. Rado (1953) has suggested that proprioceptive disorder is an inherent aspect of schizophrenia and that judgments based upon proprioception would be poor in schizophrenic patients. A second possibility has been adduced by Salzinger (1957). He points out that, in view of Goldstein's notion of deficiency of the abstract attitude in schizophrenia, schizophrenics ought to be more influenced by stimuli within the experiment, and therefore more easily shifted by the kind of anchor stimulus provided in a judgment task. The *anchor stimulus* is the standard stimulus used to define the end of the series which the subject is to judge, and *shifting* is the phenomenon whereby judgments change in magnitude because of the influence of the anchor stimulus used in any experiment. Salzinger's own investigations confirm that schizophrenics do shift more in a weight-judging task but do not differ from normals in their ability to discriminate between weight stimuli. Thus the Rado hypothesis draws no support from this result, but the data are congruent with Goldstein's views.

Attention

Reaction Time. Goldstein's hypothesis included, among other things, the statement that deficiency in capacity to hold the abstract attitude would be marked by inability to assume or hold a *mental set*. Mental set may be defined as the process of being prepared to respond to an expected stimulus or of being selectively attentive to certain classes of stimulus or aspects of stimuli. The maintenance of a mental set requires adequate attention mechanisms. One possible measure of readiness to respond is the reaction time (RT) of the subject's response to a signaling stimulus when he has been warned to expect it. Slow or erratic reaction times might be regarded as indicative of difficulty in maintaining a mental set.

With this possibility in mind, a series of

investigations was begun on the question of RTs in schizophrenia. Much of the original work was done at the Worcester State Hospital by Shakow and his colleagues, one of the earliest being the study reported by Huston, Shakow, and Riggs (1937). They recorded the RTs of schizophrenics to signaling stimuli of both light and sound. The presentation of the stimulus was preceded by a preparatory interval, and the intervals were varied in length and presented regularly (the same interval being repeated several times) or irregularly (the interval being varied randomly). Reaction times of the schizophrenics were generally longer and more variable than those of the normals under the same conditions.

This inquiry was extended by Rodnick and Shakow (1940), whose data indicated that the RTs of schizophrenics were shorter for brief regular intervals than for brief intervals in an irregular series. The reverse relationship was found for longer intervals. On the other hand, normal subjects were consistently faster on the regular series, except in the case of long intervals, where the regular condition did not lead to greater speed. With these findings in mind, the investigators established a measure which they called the *set index*, using a system of differential weightings for the interval length and condition of presentation. Application of this index to samples of normals and schizophrenics discriminated between the samples without overlap. Computation of the set index is conducted using the following formula.

$$\text{Set index} = \frac{1}{2}\left(\frac{M\,7.5r}{M\,7.5i} + \frac{M\,15r}{M\,15i}\right)$$
$$\times Mh + \frac{M\,2r}{M\,4r} \cdot M2r$$

Where M = mean for that series of trials

Mh = longest mean RT for any series of 10 trials

r = regular procedure

i = irregular procedure

Numbers stand for preparatory interval in seconds.

On the basis of these data, the investigators favored the hypothesis that the behavior of schizophrenic patients was determined by an inability to maintain set, or the state of "readiness to respond." Shakow (1950) regarded this as an essential feature of the schizophrenic condition; whether it might be referred to some more fundamental process or deficiency then became a further question for research. Additional investigations of the significance of the regular versus irregular series have been conducted by Zahn et al. (Zahn, Rosenthal, & Shakow, 1963). Their data lead them to conclude that the difficulties experienced by schizophrenics in maintaining set during the long preparatory intervals are due to the interference of "minor sets" which intrude upon the major set to respond to the stimulus. These minor sets are presumed to arise because of the demands made upon the patient by the experimental situation. Other aspects of their data seem to militate against any interpretation in terms of fatigue or reactive inhibition.

Hunt and Cofer (1944) suggested that the reaction times of schizophrenics might be symptomatic of a general reduction of responsiveness to social stimuli. In this case, the social stimulus is provided by the experimenter, and the schizophrenics would be more difficult to motivate when the prime motivation is the social one of cooperating with him. Some support for this notion comes from the fact that the schizophrenic subjects who were reported as "cooperative" by Huston, Shakow, and Riggs (1937) performed more nearly like the normals. However, the hypothesis that differential sensitivity to social stimuli is characteristic of schizophrenics has been investigated in other situations and will be discussed later.

Some important aspects of this issue are illuminated by an investigation conducted by Cromwell, Rosenthal, Shakow, and Zahn (1961). He explored the relationships between RT efficiency and an *autonomy-control* variable in the presentation of the stimulus. In the autonomous condition, the subject selected his own preparatory interval before the stimulus tone was presented, while under the control condition, the experimenter selected the onset of the stimulus in the usual way, but informed the subject of what the interval would be. Under a third (controlled-blind) condition, the experimenter selected the setting but did not inform the subject of what this would be.

The relative efficiency of a group of 15 male schizophrenics under these various conditions is shown in Figure 14-2. A control group of normal males provides the comparison. The experimenter computed an autonomy-control index (A-C index), which was essentially the sum of an individual's performance under the autonomous conditions minus his performance under controlled plus controlled-blind conditions. A high index means that reaction times were relatively higher (i.e., slower) under the autonomy condition than under the controlled conditions. The A-C index was significantly lower for normals than for patients (79.5 versus 124.8).

In this investigation, questionnaire measures were also taken of the tendency to perceive events in general as being under one's own (internal) control or under external control. Among normal controls, this measure had a +.74 correlation with the A-C index: those individuals who tend to perceive events as being under internal control were most effective in the autonomy condition. However, among the schizophrenics this correlation was not found. But since the schizophrenics were significantly more "external" anyway, their general performance supports the notion that the higher the tendency to external control, the higher the A-C index. In simpler terms, people who see events as being controlled by others are less effective in situations where control is in their own hands than in situations where it is in the hands of another. Schizophrenics, generally, are at this end of the continuum.

An alternative explanation of the reaction time phenomena was put forward by Knehr (1954). He maintained that speed of response is related to general intellectual functioning and that any deficiency in this will be accompanied by changes in reaction time. Using acute schizophrenics, and providing them with a narrower range of preparatory intervals, he obtained data which cast doubt upon the discriminative validity of the set index. Knehr's interpretation of the reaction time phenomena leads to the prediction that similar responses would be obtained with subjects who were not schizophrenic but who were comparable to a schizophrenic population in their intellectual functioning. A test of this prediction was made by Tizard and Venables (1956). Replicating the Rodnick and

Figure 14-2. Reaction time (RT) as a function of experimental conditions I (autonomy), II (control), III (controlled-blind), and IV (autonomy) for normals and schizophrenics. (Cromwell et al., 1961.)

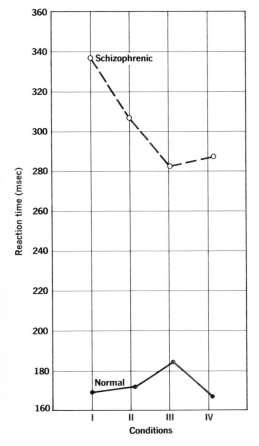

Shakow experiment in essential details, they added a group of high-grade mentally retarded adults in an attempt to control for the variable of intellectual level. The set index discriminated reliably between the normal and schizophrenic samples, only two of the latter falling within the response distribution of the former. Responses from the mentally retarded sample were similar to those of the normals.

While the work of Tizard and Venables is implicitly supportive of the use of the set index, it is questionable whether or not the inclusion of the control group of mentally retarded subjects is adequate to resolve the issue raised by Knehr. Overall IQs obtained from schizophrenic patients may equal those of mentally retarded subjects, and yet there may be differences between the two samples in the patterns of errors they make on formal tests of intelligence. Considering this possibility, Rosenthal, Lawlor, Zahn, and Shakow (1960) examined the relationship between the set index, the severity of schizophrenic disorganization, and a nonverbal measure of intelligence. The set index correlated significantly (rho $= 0.89$) with a rating of severity of schizophrenic disorganization, while the intelligence measure produced a nonsignificant correlation with both of these. Besides supporting the value of the set index, these investigators report that their data permit the extension of the Rodnick-Shakow conclusions. Specifically, they found that schizophrenics who rated higher in mental health (showed least disorganization) were better able than disorganized schizophrenics to take advantage of shorter preparatory intervals relative to longer ones, especially in the regular condition as compared with the irregular one.

Returning to the defective attention hypothesis, we find that some investigators have sought to determine whether or not drugs which improve clinical symptoms in schizophrenics produce parallel improvements in measures of attention. Huston and Senf (1952) obtained measures of the set index in samples of patients which included both early and chronic schizophrenics. All subjects were tested under normal conditions and after intravenous injection of sodium amytal with amphetamine sulfate. Under the normal condition, the set index discriminated the chronic schizophrenic group almost perfectly from a neurotic comparison sample. It did not successfully distinguish between the early and chronic schizophrenic groups. In the drugged condition, the set index of the chronic schizophrenic group improved to a degree which approached but did not reach statistical significance. However, the *level of attention,* based upon the relationship between regular and irregular conditions of stimulus presentation, did improve significantly in the chronic group. A general conclusion drawn from this study is that the set index measures the resultant of several different attention variables, each of which may vary independently of the others.

While the general tenor of the data, therefore, seems to support the validity of the set index, we must bear in mind that these results do not, in themselves, confirm the inference that defective attention is the crucial variable involved. Slowness and variability in reaction times of patients suffering from the so-called "functional psychoses" have been reported for many years, but this phenomenon permits many possible explanations.

Speed of response is used systematically in general psychology as a measure of the strength of a habit, as well as of its reaction potential at any given time. In the case of any simple learned response which would be elicited by a conditioned stimulus, we might expect to find longer latencies when the response had been learned only minimally, when the response was being elicited under conditions of low motivation, when the response was being elicited after an extinction process had begun, or when the CS aroused competing responses. Variability of response latency during a series of trials given in a limited period of time suggests that the motivational level of the subject is fluctuating from trial to trial, or that the CS evokes competing responses in some inconsistent fashion.

Low habit strength, without competing responses either because of incomplete acquisition or partial extinction, would not lead to variability of response. Thus the most likely source of explanation is in either the motivational state of the patient or in the presence of competing responses.

Experiments which use the set index involve two kinds of stimuli; one is the visual or auditory stimulus to which the formal response is to be made, while the other is the experimenter and his instructions to respond to the presented stimulus. In these studies the possible reinforcements are those provided by the approval (implicit or explicit) of the experimenter or his disapproval, and the intrinsic reinforcements to be obtained from performing the required movements. While it is quite possible in many studies that there is intrinsic reinforcement in the task which the subject performs, it is most probable when the task involves complex and novel material. Repetitious tasks of a very simple type seem to have little likelihood of arousing interest.

Granting that the motivation in reaction time studies is largely a matter of seeking experimenter approval, we might expect to find that the schizophrenic is deviant in his social motivations and that his slow, erratic reaction times are diagnostic of motivational difficulties rather than of some cognitive process required in maintaining set. Alternatively, we might consider that the schizophrenic is, by definition, characterized by a tendency to respond to private inner stimuli. In an experiment he may be responding in unpredictable fashion to these inner stimuli in a manner which competes with his responses to the controlled stimulus of the study.

Thus we can summarize three major hypotheses which may be advanced to account for the reaction time data:

1. The patient is suffering from a primary deficit in a cognitive function required to maintain attention to a stimulus.
2. The patient is relatively unresponsive to the social reinforcements provided by the approval or disapproval of the experimenter, i.e., the patient is deviant in terms of the strength and character of his social motivation.[1]
3. The patient is responding from time to time during the experiment to inner autistic stimuli, and these responses compete with those which would normally be elicited by the experimental stimulus.

Before closing this discussion of reaction time data, we should note that the possibility that the deviant RTs of schizophrenics may be due to neurological pathology has been explored by Huston (1935) in a carefully controlled study of matched groups of schizophrenic and normal subjects. Using the latency of the patellar reflex as the RT measure, he found no differences between his groups. Similar results were obtained by Strecker and Hughes (1936). At the present time there is little enthusiasm for a neurological explanation of RT data in schizophrenia. We may conclude by noting that RT measures in schizophrenic patients seem to be consistently deviant compared with those of normal subjects, but that the reaction time measure—or latency of response measure—is sensitive to differences in variables of motivation, learning, and cognition. Consequently it is not permissible at this juncture to assume that the RT data necessarily confirm the defective attention hypothesis. A summary presentation of the general findings of RT studies is given in Box 14-3.

Controlled Shifting of Attention. Deficiency in controlling attention to a situation or stimulus may be evidenced not only by irregularity in response to a predictable

[1] Reaction time measures may be affected by deviant motivation in more ways than one. Rosenbaum, Grisell, and Mackavey (1957) identify three sources of motivational deficiency in a patient population studied by them: reduced responsiveness to biological incentives; reduced responsiveness to social incentives, and descriptive anxiety motivation. These three factors were, they claim, relatively independent of each other.

BOX 14-3 Reaction Times in Schizophrenia

Variable	Findings
Stimulus mode; light vs. sound	As a group schizophrenics give faster RTs to light than to sound. In normal controls this is reversed. However, slow normals also respond faster to light than sound, while fast schizophrenics show the same pattern as controls.
Preparatory interval (PI)	Schizophrenics show longer RTs to long and irregular PIs, their slowness differentiating them from normals under these conditions, but not when PIs are short and regular.
Control of PI by subject or experimenter	Schizophrenics perform better when PI is under experimenter control than when it is under their own control. This pattern is reversed in normals.
Intelligence and clinical status of subject	RT as measured by set index differentiates between schizophrenics and normals or mental retardates. The latter two cannot be differentiated from each other by the set index. Set index correlates with rated severity of schizophrenic disorganization, but not with measures of verbal intelligence in a schizophrenic sample.
Distracting stimuli	Schizophrenic performance is more disrupted by the presence of irrelevant stimuli than is the performance of normal controls.
Collateral "arousal" input (noise, light)	Collateral arousal input facilitates performance of all subjects (schizophrenics and normals), but the improvement is more marked in the patients, who start from a slower rate of responding. Poor-premorbid schizophrenics show most improvement, with good-premorbid patients being very similar to normals.
Escape RTs	When the response serves to terminate noxious physical stimulation (electric shock, unpleasant noise), subjects improve. Schizophrenics produce responses similar to those of normals. Under noxious social stimulation (blame or reproof) the same effects are seen, with schizophrenic RTs becoming faster, although not equaling those of normals.

stimulus; it may also result in an inability to shift attention from one stimulus to another. Goldstein, as we have seen already, commented upon the seeming inability of schizophrenics to "shift voluntarily from one aspect of the same situation to another." Even as early as 1909, Gatewood conducted a psychometric study which led him to consider the possibility that "loss of thought control" might be a fundamental characteristic of the schizophrenic process. Similar conclusions were drawn by Malamud

and Palmer (1938) and Kendig and Richmond (1940). While the empirical data generally support the notion that shifting of set presents difficulties for the schizophrenic, the suggestion has also been made that the primary deficit in tasks of this variety is in the patient's motivation.

Using arithmetic problems, Huston, Cohen, and Senf (1955) investigated the ability of chronic schizophrenics to change from one type of simple arithmetic problem to another under varying degrees of distraction and with different numbers of shifts involved between groups. Their data led them to conclude that the deficit observed in schizophrenics may be limited to tasks in which the stimulus material permits personal and social interpretations to intrude into the objective aspects of the task. Arithmetic items, being less susceptible to idiosyncratic responses, would therefore tend to be more easily handled by the patient. Support for this inference, at least so far as arithmetic items are concerned, comes from studies by Hunt (1935) and Magaret (1942). Once again we seem to be justified in remarking that motivational difficulties may account for these apparent difficulties in shifting attention.

Learning

The behavior of psychotic individuals may be interpreted as the outcome of a long history of the learning of maladaptive responses. In its most naïve form, a purely environmental account of psychosis would rest upon this assumption. However, a recurring objection to such an assumption is the observation that many people present histories of unfavorable learning conditions without developing psychotic behavior patterns; by the same token, many psychotic patients do not have notably deviant histories in this regard. Consequently, the simple learning position is modified to include the assumption that there may be fundamental individual differences in learning, which will lead to differing effects of the same experiences for different individuals.

If these individual differences are not, in themselves, the result of some primary learning experience, then we are faced with the necessity of thinking of some kind of theory of learning types based upon congenital differences. It is not at all impossible that such a typology could be explained on the basis of primary learning experiences. The work of Harlow and his associates (Harlow, 1958) points up the usefulness of the notion of "learning how to learn," while Schroder

and Rotter (1952) have reported the effectiveness of training in rigidity in problem-solving behavior in an experimental situation. Nevertheless, there has been little elaboration of this possibility in dealing with the learning characteristics of psychotics.

In fact, the major interest in schizophrenia has been in discovering empirical differences in learning rather than in formulating theories that might predict them. Naturally, the occurrence of such differences does not, in itself, indicate the reasons for them.

Conditioning. Schizophrenics were reported by Shipley (1934) to be slower to establish conditioned responses (CRs) than either manic-depressive patients, neurotics, or normals. Likewise Paintal (1951) reported that psychotic subjects produced significantly smaller galvanic skin responses (GSRs) than normals to the threat of shock. Howe (1958) studied the establishment and extinction of conditioned GSRs in chronic schizophrenic patients, in patients diagnosed as suffering from anxiety state, and in normals. His chronic schizophrenic patients were not significantly different in this respect from his normals, while his anxious subjects were more resistant to extinction than either of the other two groups. However, examination of some schizophrenic patients who were not at all conditionable suggested that they were more severely disturbed than his experimental chronic group. From this, Howe speculates that there is a relationship between chronicity and autonomic conditionability.

In a study of both GSR and verbal conditioning, O'Connor and Rawnsley (1959) report that there were no differences between normals, chronic paranoid schizophrenics, and chronic nonparanoid schizophrenics, but that the paranoid group took significantly longer to condition on the verbal procedure. In this part of the study the subject was required to press a key when the experimenter said "Good." As we shall see later on, the significance of social reinforcements for schizophrenics is such that this part of the study may be as much a measure of social motivation as it is of conditionability.

Peters and Murphree (1954) report that normals and chronic schizophrenics who had been through a period of treatment in problem solving were noticeably more responsive in producing a GSR to an unconditioned stimulus and were quicker to establish a conditioned GSR than a group of untreated chronic schizophrenics. The investigators conclude that their data lend support to the belief that schizophrenia may be thought of as a kind of functional decortication of the patient, with the conditioned response being a measure of cortical functioning. We have already noted this hypothesis in our discussion of Saucer's work.

Similar investigations begun at the State University of Iowa (Spence & Taylor, 1953; Taylor & Spence, 1954) revealed that schizophrenics showed *superior* conditionability to either normals or neurotics. These studies incidentally found no difference between anxiety neuroses and other categories of neurosis on this measure. The obvious contradiction between the results of Howe and those of the Iowa investigations invites comment. Howe has suggested that the schizophrenic patients in the Iowa studies were less chronic than his, and that conditionability increases as chronicity decreases. A further difference which appears worthy of note is that whereas the work of Paintal and of Howe involved an autonomic response, the studies of Spence and Taylor involved a conditioned eyeblink, which is not autonomic. The possibility that schizophrenic patients are more deviant in autonomic functioning than in sensory or motor behavior makes it necessary to distinguish between anomalies of autonomic conditioning and anomalies of other kinds of conditioning. A further limitation upon our conclusions about conditioning in schizophrenia is the fact that in all these investigations the unconditioned stimulus (US) has been noxious, and the procedure has been that of classical conditioning.

Some light may be shed on this problem by considering the role of the orienting response in the establishment of a conditioned response. When the CS is presented for the first time, it produces the orienting response —itself an aspect of the general arousal of the individual by the stimulus input. Attention is narrowed and focused and the subject attends to the conditioned stimulus, inhibiting awareness of other irrelevant aspects of the environment. Stanishevskaya (1955) has used changes in blood pressure as measures of the orienting response and has described two stages in its occurrence in normal control subjects. With the appearance, there is a general vasopressor response recordable at several points, but this rapidly gives way to a localized response, which he ascribes to the development of inhibition in all but the local area. This sequence might be thought of as analogous to the initial stage of general arousal followed by the selective attention to a limited part of the environment. Using this technique, Stanishevskaya reports that in simple schizophrenics, only the general arousal stage appears—a fact which presumably reflects defective inhibition—while in catatonic patients, neither stage appears—which argues for the existence of massive inhibition preventing any arousal response.

The details of this Russian investigation are difficult to ascertain, but it serves to illustrate that deficiency in establishing a conditioned response may be attributed to preliminary difficulties in producing attention to the stimuli rather than to any central defect in establishing neural connections.

Operant conditioning has been utilized in the study of schizophrenics and psychotics generally by Lindsley and his colleagues (e.g., Lindsley, 1960). Using a room constructed on the principle of the Skinner box, they have studied rates of bar pressing in psychotics as these are influenced by different kinds of reinforcement under varying schedules of reward. Rewards used have included money, food, candy, cigarettes, bursts of music, display of color slides, etc.

Typical illustrations of operant-conditioning apparatus are shown in Figures 14-3 and 14-4.

However, Lindsley has not been mainly interested in deficiencies in learning ability as such. Instead he has been concerned with using the changes in learned responses as measures of the current state of the patient. After the patient has acquired the conditioned response of pressing the bar to receive the reward, his rate of responding (the number of times he presses the bar per minute or per hour) will tend to stabilize at a constant rate. This rate may be changed by varying the conditions of the reward, but it is also sensitive to other influences not introduced by the experimenter. Among the other influences which may lower the rate or interrupt responding altogether is the presence of competing stimuli. As the experimental room is free from any stimulus which would elicit competing responses in the nonpsychotic individual, competition would have to occur through autistic stimulation in the psychotic. Lindsley (1960) suggests that many forms of psychosis act as a competing response system on the free operant behavior of these patients. As an example of this possibility, we may consider a patient described by Lindsley. The patient is

. . . a male, 58 years old and he has been continuously hospitalized for 29 years. His experimental behavior has been under study for five years. Admitted in 1930 at the age of 29, he was diagnosed dementia praecox, paranoid type. The recent "blind" diagnoses were simple schizophrenia (by the clinical psychologist), and schizophrenia, mixed (by the psychiatrist). His recent Wechsler-Bellevue I.Q. was 60 and he scored in the 3rd percentile on the Hospital Adjustment Scale and lives on a locked ward. His personality picture is "that of a withdrawn, colorless patient who shows

Figure 14-3. Data recording room for operant conditioning of psychotic patients. (Courtesy of Dr. Ogden Lindsley, Metropolitan State Hospital, Waltham, Mass.)

Schizophrenia: Sensation, Perception, and Learning

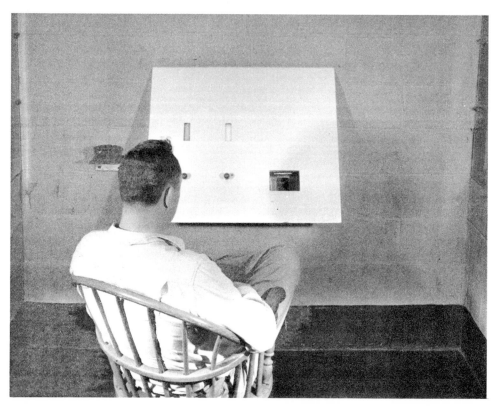

Figure 14-4. Interior of operant-conditioning room for human subjects. Subject is facing the panel containing plungers which he presses to receive reinforcements. (Courtesy of Dr. Ogden Lindsley, Metropolitan State Hospital, Waltham, Mass.)

little evidence of acting-out and whose general defense is that of compulsivity in terms of wanting a fixed routine, his own things, and to be left alone." He is very untidy, but not incontinent. He collects worthless objects and eats cigarette butts. He cleans the hospital basement floors but needs almost constant supervision. He is a good worker unless provoked, when he has tantrums and runs about, yelling, biting his fists, and pounding the walls.

The patient behaved in this fashion during the psychotic episode shown in Figure 14-5, and it is this behavior which keeps him on the locked ward. In Figure 14-5, we see two response records, one a record of the level of the bar-pressing rate of response and the other a record of vocalizations registered by a voice key. We can clearly see the decline in rate of bar pressing as the patient

begins to make vocal responses, presumably to some private auditory stimulus.

Used in this way, the operant-conditioning technique becomes a measure of the presence or absence of distractibility by any stimulus, including autistic ones. As there is some evidence that the bar-pressing rate may fluctuate when no gross overt indications of autistic behavior exist, this technique may possess advantages as a measuring device compared with simple clinical observation.

This use of the operant-conditioning procedure must be clearly distinguished from its use as a measure of learning. Lindsley reports that the vast majority of his chronic schizophrenic subjects (90 per cent) fail to develop stable normal levels of responses under standard conditions. He attributes this phenomenon to psychotic "debility"—a concept which is primarily descriptive rather than explanatory.

Stimulated by Lindsley's research, King et al. (King, Merrell, Lovinger, & Denny, 1957) investigated the general hypothesis that rate of responding in an operant-conditioning apparatus is related to "depth of psychosis." Their data do not support the specific hypothesis that response rate declines with severity of psychosis; rather, their results suggest that a curvilinear relationship exists. This curve is presented in Figure 14-6. The investigators speculate about the possibility that motivation and task attitude are the major variables producing this curve, but suggest even more strongly that since psychopathology is usually defined in terms of impaired personal-social relationships, it is unlikely that severity of psychosis would have a clear functional relationship with a response (bar pressing for candy or cigarettes) which is largely nonsocial in its motivational aspects.

All in all there has, as yet, been no large-scale systematic study of operant conditioning in schizophrenia, or in the psychoses generally. However, the increasing develop-ment of devices such as teaching machines which incorporate the principles of operant conditioning will undoubtedly have an impact upon the scientific study of psychopathology.

Reactive Inhibition. We have already noted the development of the hypothesis that schizophrenics are characterized by deficiencies in inhibition, which results in a deterioration of performance in a learning task, or indeed in level of performance on any task. The investigation of this problem is fraught with difficulties. Chief among them is the fact that decrements of performance or decline in learning rate may occur as a result of many influences, perhaps especially as a result of fluctuating motivation. The difficulties of ensuring adequate motivation in psychiatric patients have been discussed already. In the case of withdrawn schizophrenics, they are particularly important.

In 1917 Clark Hull studied the learning of paired associates in paretics, schizophrenics, and controls. The task involved learning to associate a nonsense syllable with

Figure 14-5. Effect of psychotic incident upon an operant response. (Lindsley, 1960.)

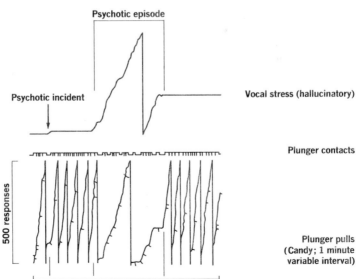

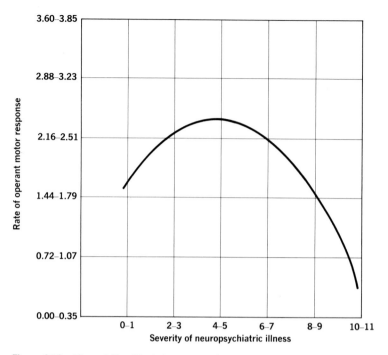

Figure 14-6. The relationship between severity of neuropsychiatric illness and rate of operant motor response. (Rate of operant motor response is based on a logarithmic transformation.) (King et al., 1957.)

a Chinese character, there being 12 such pairs in the list. Paretics were slower to learn this list than the schizophrenics, and both were inferior to the controls. Several measures of retention were then used, and from his results Hull concluded that the major deficit was in acquisition rather than in retention.

Reactive inhibition would have the effect of producing a falling off in learning after an initially normal learning process had been demonstrated, and this effect would supposedly be especially evident when learning had been carried out with massed practice (repeated trials with little rest between them). By the same token, since the effect of rest is to dissipate reactive inhibition, we would expect that the schizophrenics would show more gain from rest (such gain or improvement being described as *reminiscence*). As shown in Figure 14-7, Venables and Tizard (1956) did in fact obtain results of this kind when comparing nonparanoid chronic schizophrenics with depressive patients. It will be evident that the schizophrenics demonstrated a slower rate of improvement before the rest period, greater reminiscence as a function of the rest period, and greater inhibition buildup after the rest period. These results are in line with some earlier studies (Hoch, 1901; Kraepelin, 1913) which suggest that performance shows a falling off after an initial rise in schizophrenics, but a reversal of this in the case of manic-depressive patients.

In passing, we should note that a subsequent investigation (Venables, 1959) failed to find these differences when a task which permitted a more rapid rate of response was used. The effect of this was, of course, to accentuate the massed-practice phenomenon, and this built up reactive inhibition to a greater extent in normals and depressive patients—making their performance indistinguishable from that of schizophrenics.

Testing a deduction from the reactive inhibition hypothesis, Tizard and Venables

(1957) argued that the performance of schizophrenics should be improved by disinhibition. Disinhibition should be produced by presenting external distracting stimuli during the experiment, and thus we should expect the rather paradoxical effect that schizophrenics would perform better under distraction than without it. This effect was in fact found in the case of groups of nonparanoid and withdrawn subjects. Patients who were paranoid or were rated "sociable" did not benefit from distraction. While the reactive inhibition hypothesis is thus partially supported, Tizard and Venables speculate upon the possibility that the distracting stimulus acts simply as a form of increased sensory input, which would facilitate the nonspecific arousal system in the patient.

Stimulus Generalization. Schilder commented that it is characteristic of the schizophrenic syndrome that "generally everybody who approaches the patient is reacted to in the same way" (1939). This statement was refined by Garmezy (1952) to bring out the implication that schizophrenic patients mani-

Figure 14-7. Mean scores per minute of schizophrenics and endogenous depressives on a repetitive task. N = 5 in each schizophrenic group and 10 for the depressive group. Reminiscence effect is most marked in the schizophrenic group. (Venables & Tizard, 1956.)

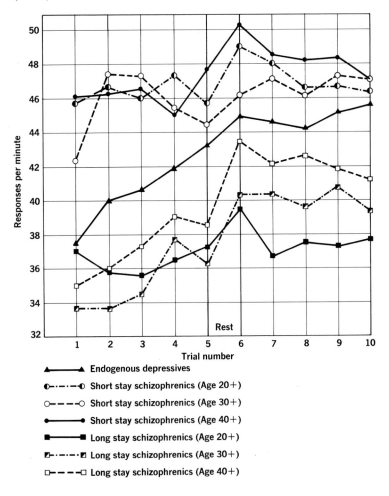

Endogenous depressives

○‐‐‐‐○ Short stay schizophrenics (Age 20+)

○‐ ‐ ‐○ Short stay schizophrenics (Age 30+)

●————● Short stay schizophrenics (Age 40+)

■————■ Long stay schizophrenics (Age 20+)

◪‐‐‐‐◪ Long stay schizophrenics (Age 30+)

□‐ ‐ ‐□ Long stay schizophrenics (Age 40+)

fest a relative inability to make differential responses to different stimuli within a given class. In a word, these patients exhibit wide gradients of stimulus generalization.

Garmezy turned then to investigate the shape of stimulus generalization gradients in schizophrenics. He used acute patients, including paranoids and others, in a task requiring that the patient respond to a predetermined auditory tone by moving a lever. A sufficient number of correct responses accumulated on a scoreboard marker and entitled the patient to a reward of candy or cigarettes. Under a reward-punishment condition, a response to a tone of the wrong pitch would lead to a reduction of the accumulating score. Gradients of generalization were then obtained for the various groups of subjects under the different conditions. They are presented in Figure 14-8. Clearly the data indicate that under the reward-punishment condition, the schizophrenic group produced a broader gradient of stimulus generalization. However, under a reward-only condition, the schizophrenic patients did not differ from normals in their generalization. Garmezy points to the probable importance of avoidance of punishment by withdrawal on the part of the schizophrenic group, suggesting that this provides the chief difference between them and the normals.

Mednick (1955) found some inconclusive differences between schizophrenic and normal subjects' generalization gradients where the spatial separation of lamps was the dimension along which generalization might take place. Here the motivation was simply that involved in cooperating with the experimenter. Thornton (1958) failed to find differences between similar groups using generalization to words in a paired-associate learning task. Here again the motivation was that of general cooperation with the experimenter. Carson (1958) likewise failed to elicit differences between normals and schizophrenics. He did, in fact, find a slightly contrary tendency in his data, getting somewhat less SG (stimulus generalization) from his psychotics than from his normals.

The data on this question seem to point fairly clearly to the conclusion that under conditions of nonpunishing motivation, there are no reliable differences between schizophrenic patients and normals in the gradient of stimulus generalization. Under threat of punishment, the gradient of SG for the schizophrenic group is both flatter and lower than that obtained from normals.

Motivation

Time and time again in our discussion of research on schizophrenia, we have come across the observation that motivational factors appear to be particularly important in creating differences between schizophrenic patients and other groups in various kinds of behavior. Two distinctions seem to

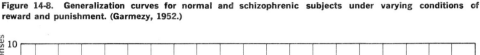

Figure 14-8. Generalization curves for normal and schizophrenic subjects under varying conditions of reward and punishment. (Garmezy, 1952.)

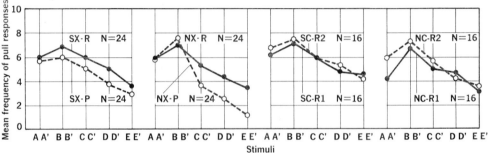

occur with particular frequency. One is the difference between positive reinforcements (rewards) and negative reinforcements (punishment, or threat of it). The other is the difference between social reinforcements (verbal rewards or punishments given by an individual) versus nonsocial reinforcements (physical stimuli such as candy, cigarettes, or shock).

It is, of course, not possible to make a distinction between the efficiency of certain kinds of reinforcements and the influence of certain kinds of motivational states. If we find, as Garmezy did, that schizophrenics become poorer at discriminating between stimuli when they are punished for errors, then we are also finding out something about the influence of fear motivation in these patients. For our purposes, we shall consider the relevant research under the general rubric of reinforcement, pointing out the implications for motivation as necessary.

Punishment and Threat. The influence of punishment or threat of punishment might be due to its creating response sets which are incompatible with the effective performance of a task. In a simpler sense, threat might serve as an inhibitor of effective performance, much the same as reactive inhibition does. If schizophrenics are more sensitive to the interference effects of threat, then we might expect them to show greater decrement in performance when threatened —but also more reminiscence following rest. If this argument is correct, we would expect that schizophrenics would benefit more from rest following performance under threat than from rest following performance under reward.

This hypothesis was investigated by Bleke (1955) and was substantiated for poor-premorbid schizophrenic patients, who showed reminiscence under punishment but not under reward. Correct responses were "rewarded" by the flashing of a sign reading "Right;" errors were followed by the flashing of the word "Wrong." The fact that no reminiscence occurred under the reward condition suggests that reactive inhibition was not operative in this kind of task. Inasmuch as those patients who had a poor premorbid history were believed to have had generally earlier and more intense exposure to punishment experiences, they were presumed to be most susceptible to the interference of threat.

Bleke's findings are of interest especially because of the earlier reports of Dunn (1954), Garmezy (1952), and Webb (1955) which indicate that performance is affected adversely in schizophrenics under threat. However, the discrepancy between these two sets of results is neatly resolved when we note that interference will impair performance while the subject is responding, but that it will dissipate rapidly with rest, producing the reminiscence effect after a rest period.

Turning from verbal reward and punishment to physical reinforcers, we find that the typical schizophrenic deficit in reaction time is eliminated in male patients but not in female when the response terminates a mild faradic current delivered to the finger at the same time as the signal (Rosenbaum, Grisell, & Mackavey, 1957) and that substantially similar results were obtained by Pascal and Swenson (1952) using "white" noise as the punishing stimulus. White noise has been found equally effective in improving the performance of schizophrenics on a concept formation task (Cavanaugh, 1958). Cohen (1956) and Cohen and Cohen (1960) report that mild shock had facilitating effects upon the performance of schizophrenics in a learning task, but that social rapport and verbal reinforcements were ineffective as reinforcers. This distinction is subject, however, to the limitation that the experiments were set up to study physical punishment versus social reward, thus confounding the reward-punishment and social-nonsocial influences. Some light is cast on this question by the work of Leventhal (1959), who demonstrated clearly that schizophrenic patients will selectively acquire those responses which serve to avoid verbal punishment.

In line with the hypothesis developed by Cameron, it has seemed likely that schizophrenic patients would be (*a*) especially sensitive to social censure, and (*b*) especially unresponsive to social rewards. Two major lines of experimentation have developed to explore this possibility. The first involves the general hypothesis that schizophrenic patients will find any social stimuli unpleasant or threatening and will, therefore, perform tasks which involve social stimuli less adequately than they perform nonsocial tasks. In general, we might regard this as the notion that schizophrenic patients will display poor competence in dealing with social stimuli. A second line of experimentation emphasizes the social reinforcements given by the experimenter, such as approval or expressions of displeasure, but the task does not itself require responses to social stimuli.

Competence with Social Stimuli. Investigating the differences between the Goldstein and Cameron hypotheses, Whiteman (1954) conducted a study of the performance of nondeteriorated male schizophrenics compared with that of normals on tests of *formal concepts* and of *social concepts*. The latter consisted of a series of sets of four cards depicting people in social situations. Three of the cards had a common theme (e.g., one person rescuing another) while the fourth was irrelevant.

Solution of the problem presented by each set required the subject to eliminate the irrelevant card and give a verbal explanation of the theme common to the other three. The performance of the normal group was significantly superior to that of the patient group, but this superiority was significantly greater in the task involving the formation of social concepts. Whiteman concluded that the position taken by Cameron seems to be borne out by these results, which thus support the inference that social withdrawal is a determinant in the etiology of schizophrenic cognitive deficit.

Qualitative analysis of his data (Whiteman, 1956) revealed that the schizophrenics'

responses included a high percentage of certain types of conceptualization. Unique responses (responses made by only one subject) were characteristic of the patient group, as were responses which were determined by physical features of the stimulus and responses in which the sorting of cards to define the concept was correct but the patient's verbal explanation of the common concept was inappropriate. An unexpected result was the failure to find any difference between patients and normals in the frequency with which they gave negatively or nonnegatively toned responses to the cards. Whiteman attributes this to the lack of ambiguity of his pictures, which might militate against conceptualization upon a projective emotional basis. White (1949) came to a like conclusion from the responses of schizophrenics and normals to a word preference measure.

Further evidence that the performance of schizophrenics is disrupted by the presence of social (human) aspects in the stimulus is provided by the data of Davis and Harrington (1957). They found no difference between patients and normals on problem-solving tasks involving nonhuman stimuli, but significant inferiority of the patients when human stimuli were involved.

Using cartoons, Senf, Huston, and Cohen (1956) investigated the social comprehension of several groups of psychiatric patients. The patients were required to identify the environment shown in the cartoon, the speaker and listeners, their social roles, the action going on in the scene, the motivation of the figures, and finally the cartoon's humorous aspect. The chronic schizophrenic group was significantly inferior to all other groups in its responses to every category except that of environmental description. The other groups did not differ significantly from each other at any point. Some importance may be attached to the fact that the decrement in performance was not observed in the group of early schizophrenics, a finding which has been reported in other studies of schizophrenia. Dunn (1954) measured the performance of schizophrenics on a task which involved discriminating variations in silhouette pictures of social interactions between mother and child. The pictures, which include one with a nonsocial theme, are presented in Figure 14-9. On the "scolding" picture series, discrimination by the schizophrenics was significantly less accurate compared with that of a normal group. Differences on the other items showed no consistent inferiority for the schizophrenics. Dunn suggested that the scolding represents an attack upon social status, whereas whipping or feeding deal with the bodily status of the recipient, and hence responses to the latter might not be affected by the presumed sensitivity of the schizophrenic to social situations.

From these studies it becomes clear that schizophrenics appear consistently inferior to normals on tasks in which the stimuli are representative of human social interactions. Where the stimulus material is of a nonpersonal kind, this inferiority is less consistent.

Social Reinforcements.   The effect of social threat has been investigated by Reisman (1960), who used pictures which were presumed to be threatening as negative reinforcers to control the rate at which patients performed a sorting task. Reactive schizophrenic patients were motivated to avoid the pictures, whereas a process schizophrenic group was not. Reisman concluded that the need to avoid social censure is characteristic of reactive patients, rather than of schizophrenics considered as a group. Olson (1958) reported that praise produced greater facilitation of performance than did verbal censure in a group of schizophrenics, but that verbal censure did produce some improvement in performance compared to the effects of giving no reinforcement (positive or negative) at all. Atkinson (1958) reports the greater facilitation of social punishment over social reward in the performance of schizophrenic women, whereas the reverse was the case for normal women. Stotsky (1957) found that praise

Figure 14-9. Pictures used in study of discrimination in schizophrenia. The 4 scenes which were used in the experiment: a. Whipping, b. Scolding, c. Feeding, d. Object. (Dunn, 1954.)

served to improve the performance of schizophrenic patients, but that it proved to be less effective on complex tasks than on simple ones.

From what appears a welter of confusing research data, certain general conclusions seem to emerge:

1. Schizophrenic patients will learn to avoid physically noxious stimulation. They will also learn if rewarded by physical rewards such as candy, cigarettes, etc.

2. Noxious stimulation seems to inhibit the *performance* of schizophrenics more than it does that of normals; but it appears to facilitate *learning* by schizophrenics more than reward does.

The responses of these patients to punishing stimuli lend themselves to several interpretations. Silverman (1963), for example, has argued that "the schizophrenic's perceptual, conceptual and motor behaviors are geared to maximizing the probability of detecting and then avoiding or reducing aversive stimulation. When it is not possible to avoid censure by task-inappropriate responses such as inattentiveness, but only by increased attentiveness . . . then task performance will improve."

Such an interpretation of attention deficit is in line with Mednick's hypothesis to the effect that the distractibility or remoteness of associations found in schizophrenics is learned because it serves to reduce anxiety. However, we may equally well note that noxious stimuli are generally "arousers" and should thus serve to direct attention when it is most important that this be done—during the acquisition of the learned connection between stimulus and response. However, when the performance must be maintained in a condition of threat—and involves the possibility of disruption by competing responses—then the gain in attention ceases to be of importance and is offset by the disruption at the response level.

3. Both praise and censure serve to improve the learning of responses by schizophrenics, when compared with learning without social reinforcement. Praise seems to be, on the whole, more effective than censure in this respect.

4. Tasks in which the stimuli are social are done less well by the schizophrenic than those in which stimuli are impersonal, presumably because of the disruptive effect of social situations.

5. There appear to be some sex differences in responsiveness of patients to various reinforcements.

SUMMARY

We began this chapter with the intention of outlining the major hypotheses and findings from research into basic psychological processes in schizophrenia. It is obvious that we are far from being able to describe laws which govern schizophrenic behavior. Nevertheless, some general conclusions seem to stand out. In the first place, the weight of the data does not appear to give much support to gross organic explanations of schizophrenic defect.

Secondly, the probability that deficiencies in attention are central to the problem of schizophrenia is well supported by a wide range of data. Reaction time measures, the perceptual constancies, and the effects of arousal stimuli, all combine to suggest that there may be some fundamental pathology in those biological systems that mediate the focusing of attention and the inhibition of response to irrelevant stimuli.

Thirdly, it seems clear that motivational factors enter into almost all measures of schizophrenic behavior, with particular importance being attached to social motives.

Finally, the general diagnostic category "schizophrenia" is less useful than certain other ways of categorizing schizophrenic patients. Distinctions between process and reactive, between chronic and acute, and between paranoid and nonparanoid patients have been fruitful in helping psychopathologists to make some discoveries. There appears to be little justification for continuing to use the grosser category of schizophrenic versus nonschizophrenic subjects, at least insofar as research is concerned.

SUGGESTED READINGS

1. Buss, A. H., & Lang, P. J. Psychological deficit in schizophrenia. I: Affect, reinforcement and concept attainment. *J. abnorm. Psychol.,* 1965, **70,** 2–24. A detailed survey of recent experimental work on the title topic. Considers punishment, regression, interference, inadequate motivation, and affective sensitivity hypotheses.

2. Eysenck, H. J. (Ed.). *Handbook of abnormal psychology.* New York: Basic Books, 1961. A major reference book for research reports in experimental psychopathology, with an emphasis on the work of the psychological laboratories of the Maudsley Hospital, University of London.

3. Hunt, J. McV., & Cofer, C. N. Psychological deficit. In J. McV. Hunt (Ed.), *Personality and the behavior disorders.* Vol. II. New York: Ronald, 1944. A thorough survey of the early experimental literature.

4. Silverman, J. Psychological deficit reduction in schizophrenia through response-contingent noxious reinforcement. *Psychol. Rep.,* 1963, **13** (Suppl. No. 2V13), 187–210. A survey of the effect of punishment upon schizophrenic performance.

5. Silverman, J. The problem of attention in research and theory in schizophrenia. *Psychol. Rev.,* 1964, **71,** 352–379. A careful review of the research relating to attentional deficit in schizophrenia, together with a summary of the major relationships that have been discovered.

6. Winder, C. L. Some psychological studies of schizophrenics. In D. D. Jackson (Ed.), *The etiology of schizophrenia.* New York: Basic Books, 1960.

A survey of the major topics of research, with discussion of some recent studies.

REFERENCES

Atkinson, R. Paired associate learning by schizophrenic and normal subjects under conditions of verbal reward and verbal punishment. Unpublished doctoral dissertation, Indiana Univer., 1958.

Bleke, R. Reward and punishment as determiners of reminiscence effects in schizophrenic and normal subjects. *J. Pers.,* 1955, **23,** 479–498.

Bruner, J. S., & Goodman, C. C. Value and need as organizing factors in perception. *J. abnorm. soc. Psychol.,* 1947, **42,** 33–44.

Callaway, E. The influence of amobarbitol (amylobarbitone) and metamphetamine on the focus of attention. *J. ment. Sci.,* 1959, **105,** 382–392.

Callaway, E., & Dembo, D. Narrowed attention. *Arch. Neurol. Psychiat.,* 1958, **79,** 74–90.

Callaway, E., & Thompson, S. Sympathetic activity and perception: an approach to the relationship between autonomic activity and personality. *Psychosom. Med.,* 1953, **15,** 443–455.

Cameron, N., & Magaret, A. *Behavior pathology.* Boston: Houghton Mifflin, 1951.

Carson, R. C. Intralist similarity and verbal rote learning performance of schizophrenic and cortically damaged patients. *J. abnorm. soc. Psychol.,* 1958, **57,** 99–106.

Cavanaugh, D. K. Improvement in the performance of schizophrenics on concept formation tasks as a function of motivational change. *J. abnorm. soc. Psychol.,* 1958, **57,** 8–12.

Cohen, B. D. Motivation and performance in schizophrenia. *J. abnorm. soc. Psychol.,* 1956, **52,** 186–190.

Cohen, E., & Cohen, B. D. Verbal reinforcement in schizophrenia. *J. abnorm. soc. Psychol.,* 1960, **60,** 443–446.

Cromwell, R., Rosenthal, D., Shakow, D., & Zahn, T. Reaction time, locus of control, choice behavior and descriptions of parental behavior in schizophrenic and normal subjects. *J. Pers.*, 1961, **29**, 363–379.

Crookes, T. G. Size constancy and literalness in the Rorschach test. *Brit. J. med. Psychol.*, 1957, **30**, 99–106.

Davis, R. H., & Harrington, R. W. The effect of stimulus class on the problem solving behavior of schizophrenics and normals. *J. abnorm. soc. Psychol.*, 1957, **54**, 126–128.

Dukes, W. F., & Bevan, W. Size estimation and monetary value: a correlation. *J. Psychol.*, 1952, **34**, 43–53.

Dunn, W. L. Visual discrimination of schizophrenic subjects as a function of stimulus meaning. *J. Pers.*, 1954, **23**, 48–64.

Franz, S. I. Touch sensations in different bodily segments. *Bull. Govt. Hosp. Insane*, 1910, **2**, 60–72.

Garmezy, N. Stimulus differentiation by schizophrenic and normal subjects under conditions of reward and punishment. *J. Pers.*, 1952, **20**, 253–276.

Gatewood, L. C. An experimental study of dementia praecox. *Psychol. Monogr.*, 1909, **11** (45).

Hall, K. R. L., & Stride, E. The varying response to pain in psychiatric disorders: a study in abnormal psychology. *Brit. J. med. Psychol.*, 1954, **27**, 48–60.

Harlow, H. F. Learning set and error factor theory. In S. Koch (Ed.), *Psychology: a study of a science*. Vol. II. New York: McGraw-Hill, 1958.

Harris, J. G. Size estimation of pictures as a function of thematic content for schizophrenic and normal subjects. *J. Pers.*, 1957, **25**, 651–671.

Higgins, J. The concept of process-reactive schizophrenia: criteria and related research. *J. nerv. ment. Dis.*, 1964, **138**, 9–25.

Hoch, A. On certain studies with the ergograph. *J. nerv. ment. Dis.*, 1901, **28**, 620–628.

Howe, E. S. GSR conditioning in anxiety states, normals, and chronic functional schizophrenic subjects. *J. abnorm. soc. Psychol.*, 1958, **56**, 183–189.

Hull, C. The formation and retention of associations among the insane. *Amer. J. Psychol.*, 1917, **28**, 419–435.

Hunt, J. McV. Psychological loss in paretics and schizophrenics. *Amer. J. Psychol.*, 1935, **47**, 458–463.

Hunt, J. McV., & Cofer, C. N. Psychological deficit. In J. McV. Hunt (Ed.), *Personality and the behavior disorders*. Vol. II. New York: Ronald, 1944.

Huston, P. E. Sensory threshold to direct current stimulation in schizophrenic and normal subjects. *Arch. Neurol. Psychiat.*, 1934, **31**, 590–596.

Huston, P. E. The reflex time of the patellar tendon reflex in normal and schizophrenic subjects. *J. gen. Psychol.*, 1935, **13**, 3–41.

Huston, P. E., Cohen, B. D., & Senf, R. Shifting of set and goal orientation in schizophrenia. *J. ment. Sci.*, 1955, **101**, 423.

Huston, P. E., & Senf, Rita. Psychopathology of schizophrenia and depression. I. Effect of amytal and amphetamine sulphate on level and maintenance of attention. *Amer. J. Psychiat.*, 1952, **109**, 131–138.

Huston, P. E., Shakow, D., & Riggs, L. A. Studies of motor function in schizophrenia. II. Reaction time. *J. gen. Psychol.* 1937, **16**, 39–82.

Irvine, R. Critical flicker frequency for paretics and schizophrenics. *J. abnorm. soc. Psychol.*, 1954, **49**, 87–88.

Kendig, I., & Richmond, W. V. *Psychological studies in dementia praecox*. Ann Arbor, Mich.: Edwards, 1940.

King, G. F., Merrell, D. W., Lovinger, E., & Denny, M. R. Operant motor behavior in acute schizophrenics. *J. Pers.*, 1957, **25**, 317–326.

Knehr, C. A. Schizophrenic reaction-time responses to variable preparatory intervals. *Amer. J. Psychiat.*, 1954, **110**, 585–588.

Kraepelin, E. *Psychiatrie.* Leipzig: Barth, 1913.

Leventhal, A. M. The effects of diagnostic category and reinforcer on learning without awareness. *J. abnorm. soc. Psychol.,* 1959, **59,** 162–166.

Lhamon, W. T., & Goldstone, S. The time sense: estimation of one second durations by schizophrenic patients. *Arch. Neurol. Psychiat.,* 1956, **76,** 625–629.

Lindsley, O. R. Characteristics of the behavior of chronic psychotics as revealed by free-operant conditioning methods. *Dis. nerv. Syst., Monogr. Suppl.,* 1960, **21,** 66–78.

Lovinger, E. Perceptual contact with reality in schizophrenia. *J. abnorm. soc. Psychol.,* 1956, **52,** 87–91.

McDonough, J. M. Critical flicker frequency and the spiral aftereffect with process and reactive schizophrenics. *J. consult. Psychol.,* 1960, **24,** 150–155.

Magaret, A. Parallels in the behavior of schizophrenics, paretics, and pre-senile non-psychotics. *J. abnorm. soc. Psychol.,* 1942, **37,** 511–528.

Malamud, W., & Palmer, E. M. Intellectual deterioration in the psychoses. *Arch. Neurol. Psychiat.,* 1938, **39,** 68–81.

Mednick, S. A. Distortions in the gradient of stimulus generalization related to cortical brain damage and schizophrenia. *J. abnorm. soc. Psychol.,* 1955, **51,** 536–542.

Morel, F. Examen audiométrique de malades présentant des hallucinations auditive verbales. *Ann. méd-psychol,* 1936, **94,** 520–533.

O'Connor, N., & Rawnsley, K. Incentives with paranoid and non-paranoid schizophrenics in a workshop. *Brit. J. med. Psychol.,* 1959, **32,** 133–143.

Olson, G. W. Failure and the subsequent performance of schizophrenics. *J. abnorm. soc. Psychol.,* 1958, **57,** 310–314.

Paintal, A. S. A comparison of the galvanic skin responses of normals and psychotics. *J. exp. Psychol.,* 1951, **41,** 425–428.

Pascal, G. R., & Swenson, C. Learning in mentally ill patients under conditions of unusual motivation. *J. Pers.,* 1952, **21,** 240–249.

Peters, H. N., & Murphree, O. D. The conditioned reflex in the chronic schizophrenic. *J. clin. Psychol.,* 1954, **10,** 126–130.

Phillips, L. Case history data and prognosis in schizophrenia. *J. nerv. ment. Dis.,* 1953, **117,** 515–525.

Rabin, A. I. Time estimation of schizophrenics and non-psychotics. *J. clin. Psychol.,* 1957, **13,** 88–90.

Rado, S. Dynamics and classification of disordered behavior. *Amer. J. Psychiat.,* 1953, **110,** 406–416.

Raush, H. L. Perceptual constancy in schizophrenia. *J. Pers.,* 1952, **21,** 176–187.

Raush, H. L. Object constancy in schizophrenia: the enhancement of symbolic objects and conceptual stability. *J. abn. soc. Psychol.,* 1956, **52,** 231–234.

Reisman, J. M. Motivational differences between process and reactive schizophrenics. *J. Pers.,* 1960, **28,** 12–25.

Ricciuti, H. A. A comparison of critical flicker frequency in psychotics, psychoneurotics and normals. *Amer. Psychologist,* 1948, **3,** 276.

Rodnick, E., & Shakow, D. Set in the schizophrenic as measured by a composite reaction-time index. *Amer. J. Psychiat.,* 1940, **97,** 214–225.

Rosenbaum, G., Grisell, J. L., & Mackavey, W. R. The relationship of age and privilege status to reaction time indices of schizophrenic motivation. *J. abnorm. soc. Psychol.,* 1957, **55,** 202–207.

Rosenthal, D., Lawlor, W. G., Zahn, T. P., & Shakow, D. The relationships of some aspects of mental set to degree of schizophrenic disorganization. *J. Pers.,* 1960, **28,** 26–38.

Salzinger, K. Shift in judgment of weights as a function of anchoring stimuli and instructions in early schizophrenics and normals. *J. abnorm. soc. Psychol.,* 1957, **55,** 43–49.

Saucer, R. T. A further study of the perception of apparent motion by schizophrenics. *J. consult. Psychol.,* 1958, **22,** 256–258.

Saucer, R. T. Chlorpromazine and apparent motion perception by schizophrenics. *J. consult. Psychol.*, 1959, **23**, 134–136.

Saucer, R. T. & Deabler, H. L. Perception of apparent motion in organics and schizophrenics. *J. consult. Psychol.*, 1956, **20**, 385–389.

Schilder, P. Psychopathology of time. *J. nerv. ment. Dis.*, 1936, **88**, 530–546.

Schilder, P. The psychology of schizophrenia. *Psychoanal. Rev.*, 1939, **26**, 380–398.

Schroder, H. M., & Rotter, J. B. Rigidity as learned behavior. *J. exp. Psychol.*, 1952, **44**, 141–150.

Senf, Rita, Huston, P. E., & Cohen, B. D. The use of comic cartoons for the study of social comprehension in schizophrenics. *Amer. J. Psychiat.*, 1956, **113**, 45–51.

Shakow, D. Some psychological features of schizophrenia. In M. L. Reymert (Ed.), *Feelings and emotions: the Moosehart symposium.* New York: McGraw-Hill, 1950.

Shipley, W. C. Studies of catatonia. VI. Further investigation of the perseverational tendency. *Psychiat. Quart.*, 1934, **8**, 736–744.

Silverman, J. Psychological deficit reduction in schizophrenia through response-contingent noxious reinforcement. *Psychol. Rep.*, 1963, **13**, 187–210.

Spence, K. W., & Taylor, Janet A. The relation of conditioned response strength to anxiety in normal, neurotic and psychotic subjects. *J. exp. Psychol.*, 1953, **45**, 265–272.

Stanishevskaya, N. N. A plethismographic investigation of catatonic schizophrenics. In *Proc. all union theoretical-practical conference dedicated to centenary of S. S. Korsakov and to current psychological problems.* Moscow: Medgiz, 1955.

Stotsky, B. Motivation and task complexity as factors in the psychomotor responses of schizophrenia. *J. Pers.*, 1957, **25**, 327–343.

Strecker, E. A., & Hughes, J. Functional changes in the patellar reflex as seen in the psychoses. *Amer. J. Psychiat.*, 1936, **93**, 547–557.

Taylor, Janet A., & Spence, K. W. Conditioning level in the behavior disorders. *J. abnorm. soc. Psychol.*, 1954, **49**, 497–502.

Thornton, T. E. Stimulus generalization in schizophrenic, brain-injured, and normal subjects. Unpublished doctoral dissertation, Northwestern Univer., 1958.

Tizard, J., & Venables, P. H. Reaction time responses by schizophrenics, mental defectives and normal adults. *Amer. J. Psychiat.*, 1956, **112**, 803–807.

Tizard, J., & Venables, P. H. The influence of extraneous stimulation on the reaction time of schizophrenics. *Brit. J. Psychol.*, 1957, **48**, 299–305.

Travis, L. E. Suggestibility and negativism as measured by auditory threshold during reverie. *J. abnorm. soc. Psychol.*, 1924, **18**, 350–368.

Travis, R. C. The diagnosis of character types by visual and auditory thresholds. *Psychol. Monogr.*, 1926, **36**, 18–37 (Whole No. 168).

Venables, P. H. Factors in the motor behavior of functional psychotics. *J. abnorm. soc. Psychol.*, 1959, **58**, 153–156.

Venables, P. H. Input dysfunction in schizophrenia. In B. A. Maher (Ed.), *Progress in experimental personality research.* Vol. I. New York: Academic Press, 1964.

Venables, P. H., & Tizard, J. The performance of functional psychotics on a repetitive task. *J. abnorm. soc. Psychol.*, 1956, **53**, 23–26.

Webb, W. W. Conceptual ability of schizophrenics as a function of threat of failure. *J. abnorm. soc. Psychol.*, 1955, **50**, 221–224.

Weckowicz, T. E. Size constancy in schizophrenic patients. *J. ment. Sci.*, 1957, **103**, 475–486.

Weckowicz, T. E. Autonomic activity as measured by mecholyl test and size constancy in schizophrenic patients. *Psychosom. Med.*, 1958, **20**, 66–71.

Weckowicz, T. E. Perception of hidden

pictures by schizophrenic patients. *A. M. A. Arch. Gen. Psychiat.*, 1960, **2**, 521–527.

Weckowicz, T. E., & Hall, R. Distance constancy in schizophrenic and non-schizophrenic mental patients. *J. clin. Psychol.*, 1960, **16**, 272–276.

Weckowicz, T. E., Sommer, R., & Hall, R. Distance constancy in schizophrenic patients. *J. ment. Sci.*, 1958, **104**, 1174–1182.

Weinstein, A. D., Goldstone, S., & Boardman, W. K. The effect of recent and remote frames of reference on temporal judgments of schizophrenic patients. *J. abnorm. soc. Psychol.*, 1958, **57**, 241–244.

White, M. A. A study of schizophrenic language. *J. abnorm. soc. Psychol.*, 1949, **44**, 61–74.

Whiteman, M. A. The performance of schizophrenics on social concepts. *J. abnorm. soc. Psychol.*, 1954, **49**, 266–271.

Whiteman, M. A. Qualitative features of schizophrenic thought in the formation of social concepts. *J. nerv. ment. Dis.*, 1956, **124**, 199–204.

Woodrow, H. Time perception. In S. S. Stevens (Ed.), *Handbook of experimental psychology*. New York: Wiley, 1951.

Zahn, T. P. Acquired and symbolic affective value as determinants of size estimation in schizophrenic and normal subjects. *J. abnorm. soc. Psychol.*, 1959, **58**, 39–47.

Zahn, T. P. Size estimation of pictures associated with success and failure as a function of manifest anxiety. *J. abnorm. soc. Psychol.*, 1960, **61**, 457–462.

Zahn, T. P., Rosenthal, D., & Shakow, D. Reaction time in schizophrenic and normal subjects in relation to the sequence of series of regular preparatory intervals. *J. abnorm. soc. Psychol.*, 1963, **67**, 44–52.

SCHIZOPHRENIA: 15
LANGUAGE AND THOUGHT

In the entire spectrum of schizophrenic behavior, the pathologies of language and thought occupy the most colorful positions. Bizarre and distorted thought processes are seen readily in simple clinical observation. They can often be recognized as deviant with little reference to the context in which they are observed. Their presence in the behavior of a patient tends to provoke a diagnosis of schizophrenia more readily than almost any other response in the schizophrenic syndromes. It is perhaps ironic that the behaviors that are regarded as most definitive of the schizophrenic categories have been less investigated than the behaviors that are deduced from hypotheses generated by the clinical phenomena. Speaking of the study of language, for example, psycholinguists point out:

> The research in the area of language disturbance has been quite unsatisfactory from a psycholinguistic point of view. This is not to make light of the difficulties of working with abnormals. . . . Still the fact remains that we have little by way of systematic knowledge of disturbed language and that very little more has accrued during the past five years. (Rubenstein & Aborn, 1960, p. 308.)

Distinguishing between language and thought is very difficult. Investigations of thought processes have leaned heavily on the analysis of verbal statements made by patients, and it is frequently a matter of the researcher's choice whether or not he regards his work as bearing upon thought rather than language. For our purposes here, we shall distinguish between those hypotheses and studies that have used verbal responses and those that have used categorizing, sorting, or conceptualizing as the main data. Even this distinction is likely to be a little blurred from time to time. However, it is based upon a discrimination between the classes of response observed rather than the processes presumed to mediate these responses, and thus may be applied with less overall confusion.

GROSS CHARACTERISTICS OF SCHIZOPHRENIC LANGUAGE

Clinical Examples

Here are some extracts from documents written by schizophrenic patients. They will serve to convey the nature of the phenomenon which we are attempting to understand in the pages that follow.

1. "I am St. Michael the Archangel and the Red Horse of the Apocalypse. Some may say I have delusions of grandeur, but like Jesus Christ, I glorify myself for my Father's sake. For additional proof, I refer you to metaphysicians and Jehovah's Witnesses. I am in disguise and one might say a blessing in disguise. . . . I am for Goals for Americans, Strategy of Peace, Medical Care for the Aged, the Common Market, Peaceful Co-existence, and Self-Preservation not survival of the fittest, and also for freedom of religion."

2. "If things turn by rotation of agriculture or levels in regards and 'timed' to everything; I am re-fering to a previous document when I made some remarks that were facts also tested and there is another that concerns my daughter she has a *lobed*[1] bottom right ear, her name being Mary Lou. . . . Much of abstraction has been left unsaid and undone in this product/milk syrup, and others, due to economics, differentials, subsidies, bankruptcy,

---

[1] The words in italics have been so printed in order to identify them as *neologisms,* which were described briefly in Chapter 11.

tools, buildings, bonds, national stocks, foundation craps, weather, trades, government in levels of breakages and fuses in electronics too all formerly 'stated' not necessarily *factuated.*"

3. "The players and boundaries have been of different colors in terms of black and white and I do not intend that the futuramas of supersonic fixtures will ever be in my life again because I believe that all known factors that would have its effect on me even the chemical reaction of ameno [sic] acids as they are in the process of *combustronability* are known to me."

All these documents were written spontaneously by the patients. They were not produced in response to an experimenter's request, and in this respect are examples of written language occurring in the natural habitat. We do not know what stimuli provoked them, nor do we know the significance that they have for the writers.

Nevertheless, probably none of us would fail to judge these documents to be seriously deviant or pathological, even though we may find it difficult to identify exactly what it is about them which leads us to that judgment. The extent to which agreement can be reached regarding the deviance of language behavior has been studied systematically by Hunt and his students at Northwestern University. We shall consider his results before proceeding to a discussion of hypotheses.

Cues for Judging Schizophrenicity

The investigations of Hunt have been concerned with several questions.

1. Do experienced clinicians agree with each other as to the extent to which a given sample of language is pathological?
2. Do individual clinicians produce reliable judgments; that is, do they make the same judgments about language material when asked to repeat their estimates after some time has passed?
3. Do naïve laymen agree with each other

and do they make reliably repeatable judgments?

4. What validities do these judgments, made by either experienced clinicians or laymen, have in terms of the severity of the pathology shown by the patient in his total behavior?

These studies were carried out on samples of language contained in answers to the Comprehensive Vocabulary Scale of the Wechsler-Bellevue Intelligence Scale (1944). In the vocabulary test the subject is required simply to state the meanings of various words. Some typical answers obtained by Hunt are:

Word	Patient's response
Fable	"The right thing when someone else is equally right."
Fur	"The method of warmth of an animal."
Hero	"We got the hero like some people in service in the front lines."
Bicycle	"A riding transportation for people." (Hunt & Jones, 1958.)

Degree of Schizophrenicity. When experienced clinicians were asked to judge responses such as those given above for degree of "schizophrenicity" (i.e., "How schizophrenic is each of these responses?"), the agreement between each individual judge and the group judgment ranged from .73 to .92 on a first judgment task, .69 to .95 when they were asked to repeat the judgment 3 months later, and .81 to .92 on a third judgment 18 months later. On the first and second judgings, the test-retest correlations (those that indicate how well the judge agrees with his previous estimates when asked to judge the same material again) ranged from .65 to .91 for vocabulary and .68 to .90 for comprehension (Hunt & Arnhoff, 1956). From these results it seems clear that there is a high degree of agreement between clinicians in their identification of a language sample as being schizophrenic. However, nothing in these data

indicates what stimulus aspects a language sample must have to be rated high or low with regard to schizophrenicity.

Dimensions of Schizophrenicity. Hunt and Jones (1958) proceeded further with this method of judging to see if agreement could be reached in like manner on the degree of communicability, intelligence, and concreteness-abstractness present in verbal responses. Experienced clinicians and naïve college undergraduates were used as judges. Two kinds of data emerged from this study. The first refers to the extent to which either group of judges could agree upon the presence of the three attributes. The second was the extent to which judgments of schizophrenicity were essentially similar to judgments of the three separate attributes. In other words, perhaps the judgment of schizophrenicity is largely determined by the same cues that produce a judgment of concrete-abstract.

The relevant figures are given in Table 15-1. From it we see that there was good agreement on the part of clinicians and undergraduates upon the judgment of schizophrenicity and of communicability. Furthermore, the correlation between the judgments of these two attributes suggests that judgments of schizophrenicity are largely influenced by the amount of communicability present in the response. The relationship between schizophrenicity and concreteness-abstractness was statistically significant but rather small ($-.28$), and it was also more difficult for clinicians to agree upon their ratings of this dimension (median agreement was .55).

Validity of Judgments. Our last question is whether or not these judgments are related accurately to the observed severity of the patient's pathology. Jones (1959) compared estimates of pathology made in the hospital with the ratings made by experienced clinical judges of patients' answers to the vocabulary and comprehension subtests of the Wechsler Adult Intelligence Scale (1958). The hospi-

TABLE 15-1 Reliability and Validity Coefficients for Judgment of Schizophrenicity of Language

Factors	Clinicians			Naïve		
	High	Median	Low	High	Median	Low
Schizophrenia	.94	.88	.63	.89	.72	−.50
Intelligence	.83	.70	.22*	.83	.61	.14*
Communicability	.91	.80	.70	.85	.75	.39
Concrete-abstract	.71	.55	.38	.73	.60	−.54

	Clinicians	Under-graduates
Schizophrenia & intelligence	−.11	−.52‡
Schizophrenia & communicability	−.90‡	−.84‡
Schizophrenia & concrete-abstract	−.28†	.66‡
Intelligence & communicability	.23	.57‡
Intelligence & concrete-abstract	.79‡	−.58‡
Concrete-abstract & communicability	.34†	−.71‡

* *With these two exceptions all r's were significant at the .01 level.*
† = *significant at .05 level*
‡ = *significant at .01 level*
SOURCE: *Hunt & Jones (1958).*

tal estimates of pathology were based upon a consideration of various diagnostic test data, case history material, and observation of an interview with the patient. The Wechsler verbal responses were judged for schizophrenicity by experienced clinicians and by undergraduates in the same manner as in the previous studies. The validity correlations obtained for clinicians ranged from .61 to .71; for undergraduates from .43 to .48. From this we can see that (*a*) the experienced clinicians were more accurate in their estimates of the severity of the patient's pathology than were the naïve judges, and (*b*) the absolute sizes of the correlations obtained were quite impressive.

Significance of Language. Some additional light is shed upon the use of language judgments in estimating the severity of schizophrenic pathology by a study conducted by Cohen (1961). Using the same patients that Jones had studied, he presented samples from the recorded interviews to a group of undergraduate judges. One group was given a typescript only, another the recording only, a third group both typescript and recording, a fourth group the recording with consonants filtered out (thus making the content of the interview unintelligible, but leaving volume and other noncontent cues intact), and the fifth group both the filtered record and the typescript. Of all these comparisons, the only significant correlation with actual degree of pathology was obtained by the typescript group alone (.65). The worst result was provided by the group with the filtered record (−.038). Cohen correctly concluded from these data that verbal cues are adequate bases for making valid judgments of pathology, and that the addition of vocal cues does not improve these predictions.

Summary. From the foregoing we can conclude that the language of schizophrenics is characterized by some unidentified attributes which can be recognized by clinicians with a high degree of agreement. The fact that these attributes can be placed along a dimension from low to high suggests that there is some regularity which also produces judge's agreement. What the Northwestern studies demonstrate is that there is a phenomenon which can generate observer agreement as to both its presence and certain of its gross characteristics. These studies do not, in themselves, indicate what were the cue or stimulus features to which the judges reacted. Data on this kind of investigation require more detailed analysis.

Detailed Analyses of Formal Characteristics

Several investigations have been conducted in recent years that attempt to identify reliable formal characteristics of schizophrenic language. The typical procedure has involved eliciting either written or spoken language from patients in various categories and then conducting a fine-grain tabulation of the uses of various kinds of language units (e.g., verbs, adjectives, nouns, or ratios between them) and of various kinds of content theme. Content themes include references to the self, sex, anxiety, or indeed any category of meaning that may be of psychological interest.

Many investigations have been directed toward the discovery of formal differences between schizophrenic language and other kinds of language without regard to the testing of hypotheses. Other studies have attempted to find similarities between schizophrenic language and that of other specific groups in the hope of adding to the probability that schizophrenia may be subsumed under some more general category or process.

Generally speaking, we may regard these studies of formal characteristics as having two possible values. First, they attempt to discover simple differences per se, and as such they might provide empirical bases for the development of hypotheses about the processes involved in schizophrenic language. However, their second value lies in their relevance for existing hypotheses. We shall consider these now.

As we shall see later, there is a widely held belief that the schizophrenic patient's thinking is characterized by *overinclusion,* or the tendency to lump into one category events or items that ordinarily would be distinguished from each other and placed in separate categories. Put another way, the patient is believed to lack the ability to make accurate and adequate discriminations in his environment. Now the fundamental mechanism for many daily discriminations is the use of different words for subclasses of larger groups of events. Thus, we may distinguish between certain people by calling one of them *intelligent,* another *cunning,* another *shrewd,* and another *ingenious.* Reflection upon these words will show that while they all describe people who have something in common, each different adjective has a slightly different meaning. A person who could not make this kind of distinction might well class all the people the same way, e.g., as *intelligent.*

Thus in a running sequence of writing or conversation, we might argue that the more limited the use of different words, the fewer are the discriminations that the patient is making. We should expect this to be most marked in the use of words that are especially designed to aid discrimination, i.e., adjectives and adverbs. In order to show that a particular individual is notably deficient in the use of adjectival discrimination, we should compute the ratio of these to some word whose frequency is likely to be unrelated to the use of adjectives. Thus, the more nouns a sample of language includes, the more adjectives we should expect to find also, since adjectives qualify nouns. On the other hand, the use of verbs should not influence the frequency of adjectives, and thus the adjective-verb quotient provides a crude index of the extent to which the patient is using discriminators in his language.

By the same token, word frequency measures imply that the fewer of any kind of words that a person uses, the fewer discriminations he has available to him. Thus we should expect to find lower indices here, as well as in the ratio of adjectives to verbs for schizophrenic populations than for normals.

Frequencies of Word Usage. Several investigators have been interested in whether patients use a wide range of different words to convey their meaning, or show on the other hand a tendency to repeat words in a given length of verbal sample. Some investigators have adopted the term *type token ratio* (TTR) or refer to numbers of *different words* (DW) per sample length. In the TTR, the investigator computes the ratio of the number of different *types* (i.e., words) to the total number of *tokens* (words) in the sample. Thus the sentence "To be or not to be, that is the question" has a total of ten tokens but eight types, giving a TTR of .80. Exactly the same effect is achieved by simply counting different words—in this case eight—and giving a DW count for samples of comparable length. As the fundamental operations are the same, we shall discuss them together. Baker (1951) analyzed the letters of a female paranoid schizophrenic using the DW index and found that (*a*) the woman's vocabulary expanded at a steady rate and (*b*) she used approximately the same number of different words (about 67) in each hundred-word sample. Baker also noted a tendency for a word to occur about the same number of times in each hundred-word sample. Smith (1957) applied the DW to the letters of a woman written at each decade of her life. She concluded that the DW declined with age and served as a good measure of the deterioration in written-language behavior with age.

The TTR was employed by Fairbanks (1944) and Mann (1944) in their studies of language samples from groups of schizophrenics and university freshmen. Fairbanks analyzed spoken samples and found that the difference between the two groups in mean TTR was significant, with the schizophrenic group being generally lower, although both groups showed inner consistency in terms of means and variability. Mann analyzed written samples and found that the schizophrenics' TTRs were significantly more variable in the number of types used per hundred-word segments than the freshmen's. The mean segmental TTR and the mean overall TTR were both found to be significantly lower for the schizophrenics than the freshmen, indicating that schizophrenics have less variability in their vocabulary than do freshmen. The schizophrenics showed greater variability within their own group than did the freshmen. Comparison of these data with the results obtained by Fairbanks showed that the mean TTR for both types of subjects ran considerably higher for the written than for the spoken language samples, probably owing to the fact that written language is a more finished and worked-over product.

Comparable measures of flexibility have been used by other investigators. Whitehorn and Zipf (1943) analyzed the language of normals, children, and paranoid schizophrenics for repetition (reduced number of different words in the vocabulary) and diversification (increased number of different words). They theorized that these two opposing tendencies—to have a word for each meaning versus having one word for all meanings—lead to a compromise in actual speech. They computed the rank frequencies of words for normal adult speech and found that the rank multiplied by the frequency equaled a constant, or in other words, that the two tendencies were inversely proportional to each other. When the letters of a paranoid schizophrenic were analyzed in the same way, a curve with a steeper slope was observed, indicating that the tendency to repetition was greater for the schizophrenic than for the normal adults. This finding corroborates Fairbank's and Mann's data.

In analogous word-count data for a variety of populations, Lorenz and Cobb (1954) report finding greater constriction in the vocabulary of neurotic patients than of either schizophrenics or psychotics. However, in the studies no tests of statistical significance were applied and it is difficult to regard them as more than indicative of trends. A general summary of these findings appears in Box 15-1.

Word Class Ratios.   Another characteristic of interest to psychopathologists is the ratio of one kind of word to another, or the various distributions of words within pa-

BOX 15·1 Findings from Studies of Formal Characteristics of Normal and Pathological Language

DW and TTR findings		
Investigator	Subjects used	DW or TTR (in %)
Baker (1951)	Female schizophrenics	67*
Fairbanks (1944)	Schizophrenics, spoken	57†
	Freshmen, spoken	64
Mann (1944)	Schizophrenics, written	66†
	Freshmen, written	71
Lorenz & Cobb (1954)	Schizophrenics	32‡
	Manics	31
	Obsessive-compulsives	28
	Hysterics	29
	Normals	34
AVQ findings		
Boder (1940)	Conversational (drama)	11
	Normative (legal statutes)	20
	Narrative (fiction)	35
	Journals (Emerson's)	47
	Descriptive (science)	76
Fairbanks (1944)	Schizophrenics, spoken	20
	Freshmen, spoken	29
Mann (1944)	Schizophrenics, written	43
	Freshmen, written	51
Lorenz & Cobb§ (1954)	Manics	60
	Obsessive-compulsives	60
	Hysterics	69
	Schizophrenics	75
	Normals	94
Maher, McKean, &	Reactive schizophrenics	39
McLaughlin (1966)	Process schizophrenics	31
	nonschizophrenics (all written)	35

* DW/100 words
† TTR (Fairbanks and Mann data)
‡ DW/1,000 words (explains lower values)
§ The difference in absolute values is probably due to counting differences between the Lorenz and Cobb study and the other two. Mann and Fairbanks adopted the Boder method, while Lorenz and Cobb counted traditional grammatical categories and thus had a much higher adjective frequency. Both groups separated main verbs from auxiliaries, but Mann and Fairbanks counted only adjectives before nouns, as did Boder.

tients' language samples. Fairbanks (1944), in her grammatical analyses of spoken language, found that schizophrenics used significantly fewer nouns, conjunctions, prepositions, adjectives, and articles than did the freshmen controls, and significantly more pronouns, verbs, and interjections. Mann's (1944) companion grammatical analysis of written samples produced no significant differences between groups except in the relative frequency of usage of nouns. Mayers and Mayers (1946) noted that schizophrenic responses in a story-telling task showed omission of articles and pronouns; confusion of sexes through pronoun switch; and a lack of prepositions which, coupled with the lack of articles, indicated a tendency to spatial disorientation.

Ellsworth (1951) used sentence completion responses to test the hypothesis that schizophrenic language is like that exhibited by children. He found that both children and schizophrenics used more nouns and pronouns and fewer verbs and adjectives than a control group of comparable age to the schizophrenics. Ellsworth attributed the lack of adjectives to the fact that the schizophrenics "see no need to clarify or redefine their language: and assume that others know what they mean." The lack of verbs, he hypothesized, indicated a trend toward emotional instability. Ellsworth also noted that schizophrenics used third-person pronouns with high frequency. When he divided his schizophrenic subjects into organized (written language in socially meaningful form) and disorganized (regressed language) groups:

The organized schizophrenic group used approximately the same parts-of-speech percentage in their sentence completions as the normal control group. The disorganized schizophrenic groups "regressed" even further in their language than did the fifth grade children by using more nouns and pronouns and fewer verbs and adjectives than the fifth grade group. (1951, p. 389.)

Mabry (1955) also used a sentence completion task and found that schizophrenics did not differ from normals in their use of the various parts of speech, thus partially corroborating Ellsworth's results.

Lorenz and Cobb (1954) compared the use of different parts of speech in four patient groups and a normal control group. For use of nouns, the hysterics and obsessive-compulsives were the lowest, with manics and schizophrenics next and normals highest. Normals and schizophrenics used about the same percentage of adjectives, with manics lowest and the neurotic patient groups in between. The neurotic groups used more adverbs, with schizophrenics and normals in the middle and manics lowest. All four patient groups used more verbs than normals,

with the neurotic groups slightly above the manics and schizophrenics. The patient groups were also considerably higher than normals on the use of pronouns, with the neurotic groups highest. The use of conjunctions and prepositions (connectives) tended to be lower for the patient groups than for normals. Articles also appeared to be less frequently used by the patient groups.

The Adjective-Verb Quotient (AVQ). The adjective-verb quotient was originally developed by Busemann as the ratio of the number of verbs (action words) to the number of qualitative descriptions (adjectives, nouns, and participles of verbs). Boder (1940) inverted this ratio and counted only adjectives before nouns and main verbs. Thus a low Boder AVQ is indicative of a lack of qualification or description and a high amount of action, and a high AVQ indicates a relative lack of action and a high degree of qualification and description.

Boder applied this measure to various styles of writing to determine AVQs for them (see Box 15-1). Balken and Masserman (1940) found that anxiety patients (including obsessive-compulsives) had active fantasies (a low AVQ) and that conversion hysterics had more descriptive fantasies with little forceful action expressed (a high AVQ). Mann (1944) found that the AVQ was almost significant in favor of the freshmen controls in her study of normal and schizophrenic written language. Fairbanks (1944) also found that the freshmen had a slightly higher AVQ than the schizophrenics in her companion study of spoken language. Lorenz and Cobb (1954) found that all their patient groups (schizophrenics, manics, obsessive-compulsives, and hysterics) differed significantly from the normal group in their AVQs. These data are also reported in Box 15-1.

Stone, Bales, Namenwirth, and Ogilvie (1962) have devised a technique for the analysis of language by a computer, thus permitting the study of large quantities of material and the conduct of many different kinds of tabulation. Maher, McKean, and McLaughlin (1966) used this technique to analyze several samples of written documents produced by schizophrenic patients under conditions of spontaneity.

The computer program, termed the General Inquirer, "reads" the document and tabulates the words used with reference to a dictionary of categories already established by the investigators. Each sample is then tabulated in terms of the number of times each category was used, and also in terms of the use of certain grammatical categories. The content categories are referred to as *tags*, and the distribution of content categories in a particular sample is called the *tag tally*. Analysis of syntax is achieved in essentially the same manner. A typical passage from a document is given below, in its original form:

The subterfuge and the mistaken planned substitutions for that demanded American action can produce nothing but the general results of negative contention and the impractical results of careless applications, the natural results of misplacement, of mistaken purpose and of unrighteous position, the impracticable serviceabilities of unnecessary contradiction. For answers to this dilemma consult Webster.

When coded and prepared for computer reading, the same passage appears as in Figure 15-1.

In the first of a series of studies that used this technique, a large collection of documents (letters, diaries, manifestos, etc.) was obtained from a group of hospitals throughout the United States. Each of these had been written spontaneously and thus, presumably, was a sample of verbal behavior in the natural habitat. From this source two groups of documents were selected, of which clinicians judged one to exhibit language pathology and the other to be free from any overt signs of it. Given this division, it seemed possible to identify the characteristics of language that lead to such judgments in more detail than had been possible in the investigations of Hunt and his associates cited earlier.

From this comparison, certain differences emerged between the two groups. The group judged to exhibit language pathology showed a tendency to use more objects per subject, fewer qualifiers per verb, fewer different words, and more varieties of negative words. Since these findings are in line with those already cited, there appears to be good agreement in this kind of investigation. An interesting aspect of the study was that the investigation was of documents rather than people. When the study was completed, data were obtained on the authors of the various writings. Some differences appeared in the composition of the two groups. Both groups had the same age of onset of their psychopathological condition, but the age at the time of writing the letter was later for the pathological samples. Thus there is a relation between chronicity and the appearance of disordered language patterns.

Following this investigation, letters written by patients who were classified into *process* and *reactive* schizophrenics by the Phillips scale (Phillips, 1953) were studied in conjunction with documents produced by nonschizophrenic psychiatric patients. In this analysis, the process group showed a tendency to use fewer different words than the reactive. Process subjects had a lower AVQ and also used shorter thought units (units of writing that could stand by themselves as sentences).

Figure 15-1. Language sample prepared for computer analysis. (Maher et al., 1966.)

```
093Y01  THE SUBTERFUGE/1 AND THE MISTAKEN/1 PLANNED/1 SUBSTITUTIONS/1 FOR THAT
093Y01  DEMANDED/2 AMERICAN/2 ACTION/2 CAN PRODUCE/3 NOTHING/5 BUT THE GENERAL/5
093Y01  RESULTS/5 OF NEGATIVE/6 CONTENTION/6 AND THE IMPRACTICAL/5 RESULTS/5
093Y01  OF CARELESS/6 APPLICATIONS/6, THE NATURAL/5 RESULTS/5 OF MISPLACEMENT/6,
093Y01  OF MISTAKEN/6 PURPOSE/6 AND OF UNRIGHTEOUS/6 POSITION/6, THE
093Y01  IMPRACTICAL/5 SERVICEABILITIES/5 OF UNNECESSARY/5 CONTRADICTION/5.  FOR
093Y01  ANSWERS/4 TO THIS DILEMMA/4 (YOU/1) CONSULT/3 WEBSTER/5.
```

Summary. From the analyses which have been made of formal language characteristics, certain conclusions appear. Schizophrenic language is generally characterized by the following formal attributes:

1. Schizophrenic subjects generally have *lower DW or TTR* counts than do normals. Process schizophrenics have relatively lower counts than reactive schizophrenics.
2. The *adjective-verb quotient* (AVQ) is lower for schizophrenics than for normals. Once again, this effect is more marked in process than in reactive subjects.

Thematic Characteristics

A second aspect of schizophrenic language is the appearance of particular kinds of content or theme. There are, of course, many kinds of themes for which language may be analyzed, and we shall consider only those having theoretical relevance.

The Discomfort Relief Quotient (DRQ). Dollard and Mowrer (1947) have developed the *discomfort relief quotient* or DRQ as a method for measuring tension in written documents. The DRQ is a ratio of the number of discomfort words to the number of discomfort words plus the number of relief words. The authors did not give a list of "discomfort" or "relief" words, but specified that "only words which would stand alone, out of context, as indicating drive-tension were included" and that the words included in each category were "identified by the common sense of intelligent people." Smith (1957) used the DRQ in her analysis of letters written by a woman at each decade in her life and concluded that the DRQ showed closer relationship to the content of the letters and the emotional state of the writer than to her age.

In the General Inquirer study cited earlier (Maher et al., 1966), the DRQ was computed for both pathological and non-pathological samples. The DRQ for the pathological sample of documents was considerably lower than that for the nondis-turbed samples. Repeating this analysis in the process-reactive comparison, the investigators found the process group to have lower DRQs than the reactive group. Both of these findings would tend to support the notion that with process or long-hospitalized patients, there is a shift toward the reduction of anxiety. However, the nature of the process is perhaps more complicated than might appear from this statement, and we shall have more to say on the issue later in the chapter.

Self-reference. One of the principal areas of interest in content analyses has been the subjects' use of the personal pronoun "I." Balken and Masserman (1940) noted that while conversion hysterics show a minimum use of the first person, anxiety-state patients and obsessive-compulsives use the first person quite often.

Whitehorn and Zipf (1943) equated repetitiousness with a self-oriented approach and diversity with an other-oriented approach and found that paranoid schizophrenics show a shift toward the repetition-self end of the curve indicative of an autistic personality. Shneidman (1948) also noted an extreme interest of schizophrenics in themselves. But White (1949), in her study of schizophrenics' responses to word stimuli, observed that her subjects tended to avoid personal themes or references and preferred moral and impersonal themes of religion and life and death.

Fairbanks (1944) analyzed spoken samples and found that schizophrenics used more first-person singular pronouns and fewer of all other personal pronouns than her freshmen controls. In her companion study, however, Mann (1944) analyzed written samples and did not find any differences in the frequencies with which certain pronouns occurred. In fact, Mann's freshmen controls used relatively more first-person singular pronouns in writing, while the schizophrenics used fewer as compared with their frequencies in spoken language. In interpreting these conflicting results, Mann cited both the task of writing a life history and the formality of the writing situation as sources of bias.

Ellsworth (1951) noted that both schizophrenics and children use more pronouns (particularly "I") than adult controls. Lorenz and Cobb (1954), comparing five groups on the use of "I" per thousand words, found that hysterics and obsessive-compulsives used "I" significantly more frequently than did manics, paranoid schizophrenics, or normals. These three groups were almost identical in their frequency of use of "I." However, in all groups, "I" was the word used most frequently. This measure has been of some interest largely because of its relevance to the hypothesis that schizophrenia is marked by high levels of egocentricity and self-concern. Additional tests of this distribution were made in the General Inquirer investigations. No support for the hypothesis was provided by the data. All in all, it does not appear that there is any reliable ground for asserting that self-references are pathognomic for schizophrenic language.

Content Topics. One of the earliest systematic studies of thematic aspects of schizophrenic language was reported by White (1949). She found that in a sentence completion task, schizophrenics tended to use more "universal" themes. These are themes that deal with humanity in general, religion, science, and the like. In the computer study by Maher et al., the thought-disordered sample used many more instances of legal, military, political, religious, and scientific tags than did the comparison group. By the same token, the comparison group used more experiences closer to the patient's own life, i.e., family and recreational tags were higher.

A very similar kind of analysis has been reported by Gottschalk and his colleagues (Gottschalk, Gleser, Daniels, & Block, 1958; Gottschalk, Gleser, Magliocco, & D'Emura, 1961). Their method involved eliciting five minutes of speech, which was then tape-recorded. Each subject was invited to speak on a matter of personal interest to him. Analysis of the recorded sample was made with reference to a number of variables. The majority of these were content categories, and the investigations led to the development of a scoring system for language entries in these categories that distinguished between a variety of psychopathological groups. Two kinds of data were obtained for this purpose: one was the frequency of given content themes for each group, and the other was a derived total score on a schizophrenia scale that was based upon the occurrence of typical schizophrenic themes.

Table 15-2 presents the rating system used in these studies. The investigators reported on the typical scaled scores of seven groups of subjects, including chronic and acute schizophrenics. Chronic schizophrenic patients and those suffering from chronic brain syndrome produced very similar distributions. Acute schizophrenic patients did not, as a group, make very high schizophrenic scores on this scale, although they were higher than any other nonschizophrenic groups. However, a more informative discrimination is possible when we compare the kinds of content produced by these groups. Table 15-3 presents the data. We see, for example, that the chronic schizophrenic group differs from the brain syndrome sample by its more frequent references to "Self unfriendly to others" and "Others unfriendly to self." Repetition of words is also characteristic of both acute and chronic schizophrenic patients and distinguishes them from all other groups.

Analysis of Contextual Associates

Another investigation of interest has been conducted by Laffal (1963). He has approached the analysis of free speech by schizophrenics from the standpoint of three assumptions. These have been derived from the study of word association, many investigations of which have been performed in the history of psychological research.

Scores (weights)	Categories and scoring symbols
	I. Interpersonal references (including fauna and flora)
	A. To thoughts, feelings or reported actions of avoidance, leaving, deserting, spurning, not understanding of others
0	1. Self avoiding others
+1	2. Others avoiding self
	B. To unfriendly, hostile, destructive thoughts, feelings, or actions
+1	1. Self unfriendly to others
+⅓	2. Others unfriendly to self
	C. To congenial and constructive thoughts, feelings, or actions
−2	1. Others helping, being friendly toward others
−2	2. Self helping, being friendly toward others
−2	3. Others helping, being friendly toward self
	D. To others (including fauna, flora, things, and places)
0	1. Bad, dangerous, low value or worth, strange, ill, malfunctioning
−1	2. Intact, satisfied, healthy, well
	II. Intrapersonal references
	A. To disorientation—orientation, past, present, or future. (Do not include all references to time, place, or person, but only those in which it is reasonably clear the subject is trying to orient himself or is expressing disorientation with respect to these. Also, do not score more than one item per clause under this category.)
+2	1. Indicating disorientation for time, place, person, or other distortion of reality
0	2. Indicating orientation in time, place, person
0	3. Indicating attempts to identify time, place, or person without clearly revealing orientation or disorientation
	B. To self
0	1. a. Physical illness, malfunctioning (references to illness or symptoms due primarily to cellular or tissue damage)
+1	b. Psychological malfunctioning (references to illness or symptoms due primarily to emotions or psychological reactions *not secondary* to cellular or tissue damage)
0	c. Malfunctioning of indeterminate origin (references to illness or symptoms not definitely attributable either to emotions or cellular damage)
−2	2. Getting better
−1	3. Intact, satisfied, healthy, well
+½	4. Not being prepared or able to produce, perform, act, not knowing, not sure
+½	5. To being controlled, feeling controlled, wanting control, asking for control or permission, being obliged or having to do, think, or experience something
+3	C. Denial of feelings, attitudes, or mental state of the self
	D. To food
0	1. Bad, dangerous, unpleasant, or otherwise negative; interferences or delays in eating; too much and wish to have less; too little and wish to have more
0	2. Good or neutral

TABLE 15-2 (Continued)

Scores (weights)	Categories and scoring symbols
	E. To weather
−1	1. Bad, dangerous, unpleasant, or otherwise negative (not sunny, not clear, uncomfortable, etc.)
−1	2. Good, pleasant, or neutral
	F. To sleep
0	1. Bad, dangerous, unpleasant, or otherwise negative; too much; too little
0	2. Good, pleasant, or neutral
	III. Miscellaneous
	A. Signs of disorganization
+1	1. Remarks or words that are not understandable or audible
0	2. Incomplete sentences, clauses, phrases; blocking
+2	3. Obviously erroneous or fallacious remarks or conclusions; illogical or bizarre statements
	B. Repetition of ideas in sequence
0	1. Words separated only by a word (excluding instances due to grammatical and syntactical convention, where words are repeated, e.g., "as far as," "by and by," and so forth. Also, excluding instances where such words as "I" and "the" are separated by a word)
+1	2. Phrases, clauses (separated only by a phrase or clause)
+1	IV. A. Questions directed to the interviewer
+½	B. Other references to the interviewer
+1	V. Religious and Biblical references

SOURCE: *Gottschalk & Gleser (1964).*

1. When a particular stimulus word is presented to a subject, there are very high probabilities that some, and not other, words will occur to the subject as associates of the stimulus.

2. In the absence of pathology, unusual motivation, or unusual sets, the response most likely to be produced is the one given by a large random population to the same stimulus word.

3. Where there are unique sets or motivations, an unusual response will occur, the character of this response being determined by the set or motivation.

While written or spoken conversation is not a resultant of discrete verbal stimuli, as is the word association test, nevertheless the two contain many common elements. Laffal points out that many verbal errors in normal speech appear to reflect the intrusion of a strong associate into a sentence that is ordinarily governed by the speaker's attempt to convey meaning. An example of this, originally quoted by Simonini (1956), is cited by Laffal:

"His battalion was swallowed up in the Bulgium belch" [Belgium Bulge].

In his analysis of this slip of the tongue, Laffal points out:

The speaker, intending to tell of the destruction of a unit at the Battle of the Bulge, and at the same time preoccupied with alimentary needs, utters words (swallow) both appropriate to his rational intention and to his alimentary needs, but at one point produces words more appropriate to the preoccupation than to the rational intention. A possibility which should not be overlooked in this particular case is the presence of the word *bulge* in the intention, led to the choice of the word *swallow*, and with this accumulation of alimentary stimuli, the tongue slip into an alimentary response (belch) was made more likely. (1963, p. 54.)

In order to analyze contextual associations in free speech, Laffal has constructed a dictionary of roughly 5,000 words divided into about 100 categories—the decisions regarding category membership being partly on logical grounds of synonymity and partly on psychological-theoretical grounds. Given this method of categorizing speech, it is possible to select a topic word—such as "female"—and tabulate all other associates that occur in conjunction with it. Laffal has applied this method to the autobiography of Daniel Schreber (Schreber, 1955), using it to identify the contextual significance of certain key concepts in the account (Laffal, 1960, 1965).

So far, this technique has been used to study internal significance of individual speech or writing and has not been applied to the characteristics of schizophrenic language pathology in general. However, the rationale behind it gives promise for application to that problem.

We may now conclude our discussion of the formal aspects of schizophrenic language. The findings derived from studies of content aspects of schizophrenic language are given in Box 15-2.

Interpretation.   While the conclusions stated in the box are borne out by research, it is quite possible that a document might contain all the schizophrenic signs and yet pass the test of judgment for normalcy. At best, these findings give us some general hints about the nature of schizophrenic language and the underlying thought processes. They represent data about which it is possible to draw more testable hypotheses. We shall

now examine some of the attempts that have been made to derive and test such hypotheses. The investigators who have tested them have studied language or conceptualization by a variety of methods, and we shall therefore evaluate their work with reference to all data, whether from language or other kinds of response systems.

HYPOTHESES FOR SCHIZOPHRENIC THOUGHT

The Regression Hypothesis

One of the commonest hypotheses to be advanced regarding schizophrenic thinking is that it represents a regression to a previous less mature level. Schizophrenic thinking, so this view holds, is essentially "childish" thinking.

An early explicit formulation of this kind was advanced by Gardner (1931). He pointed out that the concept of regression has two implications. One of these is that the schizophrenic thinks and acts as a "primitive" man, and that we may regard him as having regressed to a precivilized mode of thought. The second implication of regression is that the patient's thinking has regressed to a mode which he used earlier in his own life, namely, during his childhood. There is an accompanying assumption that the thinking of a child recapitulates the mental growth of the human race. Thus there would be a resemblance between the thinking of a regressed psychotic and that of a primitive man.

Proceeding from these premises, Gardner attempted to develop a scale of regression which would provide a "psychotic age" for a patient—determined by the similarity of his thinking and behavior to that of a normal child of a given age. While reviewing the purely psychological explanations for regression, Gardner suggested that we can best account for this reactivation of age levels in infancy in the psychoses by assuming some innate defect in the patient's sym-

TABLE 15-3 Comparison of Diagnostic Groups on Categories of Verbal Expression Used in the Schizophrenic Scale

Categories scored with positive weights (schiz. responses)	Chronic schiz. (113)		Acute schiz. (29)	
	% giving response	Sample avg.*	% giving response	Sample avg.*
I A$_2$ Others avoiding self	22.1	.15	27.6	.11
I B$_1$ Self unfriendly to others	21.3	.16	20.7	.07
I B$_2$ Others unfriendly to self	37.2	.27	34.5	.18
II A$_1$ Disorientation	8.0	.07	0.0	.00
II B$_{1a}$ Physical illness, malfunctioning	15.3	.17	24.2	.10
II B$_{1b}$ Psychological malfunctioning	76.6	1.03	75.9	.78
II B$_{1c}$ Malfunctioning of indeterminate origin	28.8	.26	51.8	.40
II B$_4$ Unsure, unable to perform	85.0	1.53	75.9	.73
II B Needing or wanting control	54.0	.44	51.8	.23
II C Denial of feelings, affect	30.1	.10	24.2	.05
III A$_1$ Words inaudible	51.3	1.08	6.9	.06
III A$_3$ Erroneous or bizarre statements	54.9	.56	55.2	.37
III B$_2$ Repetition of phrases, clauses	85.8	1.74	86.2	1.19
IV A Questions to interviewer	45.1	.64	51.8	.47
V Religious and Biblical references	15.9	.24	34.5	.55
Categories scored with negative weights (nonschiz. responses)				
I C Self, others, friendly, helpful, loving	81.4	1.14	75.9	1.32
II B$_2$ Self improving, better	27.4	.12	20.7	.04
II B$_3$ Self well, adequate	62.8	.78	75.9	.85
Categories weighted zero for predicting differences in degree of illness among schizophrenics				
I A$_1$ Self avoiding others	25.7	.14	20.7	.11
I D$_1$ Others bad, ill, strange	61.1	.75	58.6	.40
I D$_2$ Others well, achieving, adequate	45.1	.34	58.6	.41
II D$_1$ Food bad, interference with eating	8.8	.05	3.4	.01
II D$_2$ Food good, adequate	16.8	.13	17.2	.08
II E$_1$ Weather bad	5.3	.02	3.4	.01
II E$_2$ Weather good	2.7	.01	0.0	.00
II F$_1$ Sleep bad, dangerous	2.7	.01	10.3	.02
II F$_2$ Sleep good, sufficient	8.0	.04	6.9	.02
III A$_2$ Blocking	61.1	.40	75.9	.49
III B$_1$ Repetition of words	69.0	1.04	93.2	1.11
IV B References to interviewer	52.2	.60	44.8	.21

* *Average frequency (per 100 words) of verbal references scored in each category.*
SOURCE: *Gottschalk & Gleser (1964).*

pathetic nervous system which prevents a normal and orderly emotional development.

While the parallels that Gardner observed between psychotic and childish behavior are provocative, they represent a hypothesis rather than a conclusion. We might therefore turn to consider the research findings on this kind of problem.

The Cameron Studies. An impressive series of systematic studies was conducted by Cameron bearing on the hypothesis of

Brain syndrome (18)		Psychiat. nonschiz. (26)		General medical (48)		"Normal" employee (60)	
% giving response	Sample avg.*	% giving response	Sample avg.*	% giving response	Sample avg.*	% giving response	Sample avg.*
22.2	.10	23.1	.08	12.5	.06	10.0	.02
11.1	.02	15.4	.08	4.2	.02	13.3	.03
22.2	.10	30.8	.18	6.2	.03	8.3	.02
22.2	.07	7.7	.04	0.0	.00	0.0	.00
22.2	.20	15.4	.07	50.0	.57	13.3	.04
72.2	1.11	92.3	1.01	56.2	.59	58.3	.29
44.4	.26	50.0	.30	64.6	1.31	13.3	.03
72.2	.74	61.5	.60	62.5	.96	71.7	.40
33.3	.19	57.7	.21	39.6	.27	36.7	.11
22.2	.17	19.2	.04	14.6	.05	10.0	.02
44.4	.84	23.1	.16	22.9	.15	8.3	.05
44.4	.34	26.9	.12	16.7	.08	11.7	.02
88.9	1.85	96.2	.93	87.5	1.06	88.3	.66
44.4	.76	46.2	.27	35.4	.21	31.7	.16
11.1	.18	23.1	.13	27.1	.20	5.0	.01

Categories scored with negative weights (nonschiz. responses)

72.2	1.05	96.2	1.47	79.2	1.28	90.0	1.22
5.6	.06	26.9	.14	39.6	.31	6.7	.01
66.7	1.14	84.6	.86	70.8	.95	91.7	1.36

Categories weighted zero for predicting differences in degree of illness among schizophrenics

16.7	.10	30.8	.11	8.3	.03	10.0	.02
66.7	.52	84.6	.75	54.2	.38	75.0	.60
55.6	.51	80.8	.80	54.2	.48	85.0	.88
5.6	.03	11.5	.04	18.8	.08	10.0	.02
11.1	.02	23.1	.15	27.1	.18	33.3	.14
5.6	.02	3.8	.05	8.3	.08	21.7	.07
5.6	.02	7.7	.03	8.3	.06	10.0	.03
5.6	.01	11.5	.04	10.4	.04	3.3	.01
5.6	.01	11.5	.04	10.4	.04	3.3	.01
77.8	.74	76.9	.43	33.3	.19	53.3	.17
23.3	.65	73.1	.57	64.6	.59	78.3	.49
87.7	.07	11.5	.17	10.4	.04	13.3	.06

regression in schizophrenic thinking (1938a, 1938b, 1939, 1944). Comparing the verbal responses of children, normal adults, disorganized schizophrenics, and psychotic senile patients to a test which required them to complete sentences, he failed to find the predicted resemblances between childish and schizophrenic logical processes. From these and other data collected by him, he concluded that there were only superficial resemblances between the language, logic, and conceptualization of children and schiz-

BOX 15-2 Findings from Studies of Content Characteristics of Schizophrenic Language

Self-reference themes

Investigator	Findings
Balken & Masserman (1940)	Hysterics use fewer personal pronouns than do anxiety-state or obsessive-compulsive patients
White (1949)	Schizophrenics avoid reference to personal themes
Fairbanks (1944)	Schizophrenics use more first-person singular pronouns than do freshman controls in spoken language
Mann (1944)	No differences in self-reference frequency between schizophrenics and freshmen controls in written language
Ellsworth (1951)	Schizophrenics and children use more pronouns (especially "I") than normal adults do
Lorenz & Cobb (1954)	Hysterics and obsessive-compulsives used "I" more often than do manic, paranoid schizophrenic and normal adult groups; no differences between these latter three groups
Maher, McKean, & McLaughlin (1966)	No reliable differences between good-premorbid and poor-premorbid schizophrenics.

Theme topics

White (1949)	Schizophrenics use more "universal" themes, i.e., science, religion, politics, etc.
Maher, McKean, & McLaughlin (1966)	Thought-disordered schizophrenics use more universal themes while non-thought-disordered schizophrenics use more personal, domestic, and family themes

ophrenics. The differences between them were much more striking.

The Pascal-Suttell Studies. A similar research tactic has been employed by Pascal and Suttell (1951) and Suttell and Pascal (1952). They studied the similarities between the drawings of the Bender-Gestalt figures produced by children, adult schizophrenics, adult psychoneurotics, and adult normals. Their findings did not support the contention that regression is peculiar to schizophrenia. They concluded:

Where schizophrenic perceptual-motor behavior is similar to that of a young child this similarity is based on disruption of a learned motor response, apparently regulatory in nature, and not on a return to an earlier behavioral capacity; and . . . regression as defined in this study is not peculiar to the schizophrenic. The findings of this study, in regard to psychomotor performance, corroborate those [of] Cameron in the area of language and thought, both indicating only a superficial similarity between the performance of adult schizophrenics and of young normal children. (Suttell & Pascal, 1952, p. 656.)

While these studies are not concerned with language, they are cited here because of their general relevance for the problem of regression.

Ellsworth's Study. In a direct analysis of the formal aspect of schizophrenic language, Ellsworth (1951) compared the usage of nouns, pronouns, verbs, and adjectives by adult schizophrenics, adult normals, and schoolchildren of various grade levels. He found resemblances between the frequency with which various parts of speech were used by the schizophrenics and fifth-grade children. The resemblance diminished as the patients were compared with older children and normal adults. In this study, "regression" was characterized by the greater use of nouns and pronouns and the lesser use of verbs and adjectives. Ellsworth concludes by stating that "on the basis of parts of speech, . . . the language of the schizophrenic is 'regressed' as compared with the language of a comparable normal group" (P. 390.)

Critique of the Concept of Regression. The studies so far discussed have all tested the regression hypothesis by seeking similarities between the performance of children and of adult schizophrenics in certain language or thinking tasks. Only in the matter of parts of speech do we find any indication of such a similarity.

A major problem here is that there are several difficulties in dealing with the measurement of regression. A child may fail to give the correct "adult" answer to a test item because he has not yet had the opportunity to learn it. On the other hand, the adult schizophrenic patient may fail to give the correct answer because he is not paying attention to the task, because something about the item has aroused an irrelevant association that then interferes with his responding, or for any of a large variety of reasons. In this respect the overall characteristics of performances produced by the two groups may well be the same, i.e., they may both be equally incompetent at the task. To assume that this similarity reflects the presence of some process which has led the schizophrenic "backwards" to an earlier stage of mental development is quite unjustified.

A good example of this problem is provided in Ellsworth's study just cited. Both patients and fifth-grade children used equally high percentages of pronouns. However, the children used more first-person pronouns, while the patients used more third-person pronouns. This lack of similarity in language patterns may be of much greater importance than the gross resemblance in totals, and might justify the conclusion that the schizophrenics are *not* using parts of speech in the same way that fifth graders do!

In an earlier chapter, the phenomenon of regression was defined as involving the reappearance of earlier response patterns. An investigator using this definition must demonstrate that the patient has regressed to a form of behavior which he had exhibited before but had since abandoned. This definition also involves the assumption that the regressive behavior is inadequate to the situation in which it is now being demonstrated. Unless one uses the patient as his own "control" when defining his response patterns as regression, then we are faced with the problem of inferring regression by argument from analogy. Given an explanation of the conditions under which a person will revert to an earlier but inadequate form of behavior, we are in a position to hypothesize about this whenever we see it happening clinically. Merely to demonstrate a resemblance between some facet of schizophrenic behavior and that of another group (in this case, children) does not move us forward in the attempt to deal with the disordered behavior. All in all, we may conclude that the concept that schizophrenia is a "psychosis of regression" has not been demonstrated insofar as language is concerned. Additionally, it seems unlikely that such demonstrations will be of particular value in the study of psychopathology.

Cameron's Hypothesis

One of the most complete descriptions of schizophrenic language has been provided by Cameron from the studies already mentioned. Summarizing these findings, Cameron has characterized the language of schizophrenics as marked by the following:

Asyndesis. The speech is lacking in essential connectives. Thus, important conjunctions such as "because" or "but" may be omitted. The basis for putting two phrases or concepts into the same sentence may be unclear without further explanation. The author was once working with a female schizophrenic patient and observed her during a Christmas party which had been organized by the occupational therapy service. At one point the patients were required to cut out pictures from magazines and assemble them to represent the title of a popular song. This patient announced her intention of presenting the title "There's no place like home." She promptly placed a clipping of a necktie next to one of a telephone. On inquiry by the writer, the patient explained that the necktie represented "my ties with home" and the telephone because "you call home whenever you're away for a long time."

Metonymy. The language is lacking in precise definitive terms, many concepts being dealt with instead by loose figures of speech or other private idioms. The tendency to write figuratively or literally when these are inappropriate is thus regarded as characteristic of schizophrenic language usage.

Fragmentation. By fragmentation is meant the "occurrence of a miscellany of discontinuous and abortive responses, or of sudden inaction that is not followed by resumption of the original theme" (Cameron & Magaret, 1951, p. 454). While the phenomenon may be discerned in many kinds of ongoing behavior, in language and thought it is usually characterized by so-called "thought blocking." The patient seems to be unable to remember what he had intended to say; he may complain of this, stating that his thoughts "are being stolen," or that competing and conflicting thoughts are "being put into his mind."

Interpenetration. Language dealing with events in the external world is continually intertwined with material from the ongoing fantasy of the patient. As the fantasy material is highly personal, the effect is to interrupt and destroy the continuity of communication.

Interpenetration has been defined by Cameron as an intrusive movement, word, or thought that appears in an ongoing sequence of activity but that belongs to some other sequence. Simple examples are to be found in humorous descriptions of professorial absentmindedness, slips of the tongue, and so on. The very term "absentminded" is descriptive of the lack of coordination between the overt behavior and the thinking of the person at a given moment in time.

It will be apparent that both fragmentation and interpenetration are related to the same underlying process—namely, that of the interruption of a sequence of thought or behavior by another response or other responses. Whether this interruption takes the form of blocking or the appearance of unrelated behaviors may be relatively unimportant theoretically.

Overinclusion. Perhaps the most important of the observations made by Cameron was his description of overinclusive uses of language. The phenomenon of overinclusion is most clearly seen in experimental studies of thinking, especially when an object-sorting task is used to define thinking. Overinclusion may be regarded as related to interpenetration, because the central feature of overinclusion is the inability to exclude from a thought sequence material that is irrelevant to the major theme of the thought. Thus in language samples we would expect to find the continual juxtaposition of material that appears to be related only by some private association which is veiled from the observer.

All the features identified by Cameron may be regarded as instances of a general phenomenon: In language and thought, the schizophrenic is not able to keep his responses to the external world separate from the fantasy processes that are going on at the same time. His behavior, especially his language, thus presents a picture of frequent interruptions. As these interruptions are also in the form of words, the total effect is of long sequences of disorganized and bizarre communications, some elements of which are responses to his environment and some of which are determined by fantasy.

Interruptions of these kinds may be caused by the fact that a particular word in a sentence has many common associations. Take, for example, the word "blue." It is the first word of many common phrases, e.g., blue ribbon, blue book, blue baby, blue blood, and so forth. Besides its meaning as a color, it also has the common figurative meaning of "moody" or "depressed." For an adult raised in a Western English-speaking culture, these associations may be assumed to have some strength. However, they do not interfere with the use of the word "blue" in other contexts, because their strength in such situations is low. Thus, when we are asking for a blue shirt in a haberdashery, we do not find these associations to "blue" reaching sufficient strength to disrupt our communication.

The schizophrenic in his use of language may therefore be seen as suffering from a process whereby irrelevant associations reach a strength equal to those of relevant associations, leading to a breakdown in the discriminations necessary to the precise use of words. The following sentence, written by a patient, may illustrate this process. Intrusion of associations to the word "blue" are very much in evidence here:

"I may be a 'Blue Baby' but 'Social' Baby not, but yet a blue heart baby could be in the Blue Book published before the war."

Once an irrelevant association has interrupted a train of thought, it may initiate a new train of thought. This, in turn, may be interrupted in the same way. We could hypothesize that the original thought was related to the fact that this patient had suffered from heart trouble. Thus the first communication might have been intended as "I was a blue baby." This, in turn, may have prompted the association with "blue blood" in the sense of social status, hence the interruption of "Social Baby not." This interplay between the two meanings of blue then appears as the next thought: "yet a blue heart baby could have been in the [Society] Blue Book."

The illustration above includes examples of interpenetration and overinclusion. However, a crucial problem for the psychopathologist is whether there is some consistent schizophrenic tendency toward overinclusion and interpenetration, or whether these char-

acteristics are simple consequences of a more fundamental process by which all or many of the possible associations to a word are at equal strength. Let us examine the evidence from the research available.

Empirical Evidence for Overinclusion. An early study by Zaslow (1950) investigating overinclusive thinking required schizophrenics to sort a series of figures ranging along a continuum from triangularity to circularity (see Figure 15-2). In the experimental procedure, the patients were required to arrange the cards along the appropriate dimension, to classify them into triangular and circular cards, and to indicate the group of cards which did not fall into either of these two categories. Zaslow's patients produced two kinds of performance: very narrow (where only one or two cards were accepted as triangles), or very broad (where the boundary for triangularity was at a card much beyond that selected by normal controls). These two kinds of performance are characterized as either rigid or fluid by Zaslow. Fluidity and rigidity, Zaslow remarks, may be differential aspects of a single underlying process, differing in quantitative rather than qualitative terms.

Another way to approach the investigation of overinclusion is to study the extent to which irrelevant behavior is likely to enter

Figure 15-2. Designs used in the test of conceptual thinking. The designs, when placed in one row, form a continuum extending from perfect triangularity to perfect circularity. In testing, each design is drawn on a card 2 inches square. The side of the equilateral triangle is 1½ inches, and the diameter of the circle is 1¾ inches. (Zaslow, 1950.)

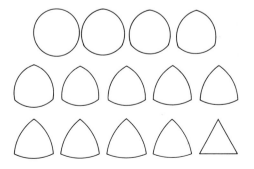

into the performance of a language task. An early investigation of this kind was conducted by Epstein (1953). He used a verbal task, called the inclusion test, in which the patient was required to underline all words which designated things or concepts required for the complete thing described by the key word. An example was as follows:

Key word: man
Response words: arms, shoes, hat, toes, head, none

In this example the words *arms, toes,* and *head* should be underlined. When a subject omitted one of the correct words, he received a score of one point for underinclusion. When a word was underlined that should have been omitted, one point for overinclusion was scored.

Epstein compared the performance of 38 schizophrenic patients and 45 normal adult controls. He reported that normal controls made as many errors of underinclusion as of overinclusion, 12.10 and 12.49 being the mean scores, respectively. The schizophrenic group, on the other hand, made roughly the same numbers of errors of underinclusion as did the normals (12.20), but reached a mean score of 20.92 for overinclusion. Analysis of the test items which produced the highest overinclusion scores revealed that they involved key words which were neologisms or response words which were clang (rhyming) associations to the key word.

Another type of experimental approach to this problem has been employed by Chapman (1956a, 1956b). Here the use of language was avoided and the patients were faced with a task requiring them to sort cards with figures on them. The design of these figures was such that several different methods of sorting were possible, but only one was "correct"—this one being explained by the experimenter to the patient before the task began. Many aspects of the designs were irrelevant to the correct method but could act to distract the patient and thus impair his performance. Under these conditions, patients tended to be inferior to controls in limiting themselves to the correct method, and they tended to be distracted when there was some basis of resemblance between the correct figure and an attribute of the distracting figure.

Following up this observation, Chapman and Taylor (1957) directly investigated the hypothesis that overinclusion in a sorting task is positively related to the degree to which incorrect items share common qualities with the correct items in a given conceptual category. They constructed a task requiring the subject to sort objects (named on cards) into three groups. The three groups were distinct from each other, but two of them were subclasses of a more abstract category. Thus a particular set of cards included names of (*a*) trees, (*b*) flowers, and (*c*) musical instruments. The first two categories are obviously part of a larger category—botanical objects. Given a deck of cards which included these three classes, the subject was asked to sort out all cards which listed, for example, names of fruit, and to put all nonfruit cards into a second category.

Clearly this method establishes the possibility that the patients will be overinclusive by placing irrelevant cards under the fruit category. If the general botanical similarity is a factor making for overinclusion, then more of the "tree" cards should be missorted than the musical instrument cards. This expectation was confirmed.

In a second stage of the experiment, the subjects were asked to sort all the abstract category, e.g., fruit and trees, into one group and the dissimilar category into another. This procedure thus permitted errors of underinclusion whereby the patient might fail to include all items appropriate to the abstract category. No difference in underinclusion scores was obtained between the patient and control groups.

Considering these data, Chapman (1961a) suggested:

Schizophrenics often appear to deal with test materials in ways which they prefer rather than the ways in which they are instructed. It may be that the more basic phenomenon in errors of conceptual sorting is, at least in part, not a tendency towards overexclusion or overinclusion but rather a tendency to use concepts of a specific preferred breadth regardless of appropriateness.

Should this be the case, then whether we get overinclusion or underinclusion would be determined by the relative breadth of the experimentally "correct" concept and that of the patient's preferred concept. This suggestion was investigated by a modification of the card-sorting task used in the earlier studies. In the modified task the breadth of the concept that the patient was required to use was varied systematically. As the instructed concepts became broader, the errors made by patients shifted from overinclusion to underinclusion, thus confirming the original hypothesis. Among the most comprehensive studies conducted on the topic of overinclusion are those of Payne and his associates (cf. Payne, 1964). In an early study (Payne, Matussek, & George, 1959), they attempted to reformulate the concept of overinclusion in the following terms:

Concept formation can be regarded as largely the result of discrimination learning. When a child first hears a word in a certain context, the word is associated with the entire situation (stimulus compound). As the word is heard again and again, only certain aspects of the stimulus compound are reinforced. Gradually the extraneous elements cease to evoke the response (the word), having become "inhibited" through lack of "reinforcement." This "inhibition" is in some sense an active process, as it suppresses a response which was formerly evoked by the stimulus. "Over-inclusive thinking" may be the result of a disorder of the process whereby "inhibition" is built up to "circumscribe" and "define" the learned response (the word or "concept"). In short, it could be an extreme degree of "stimulus generalization."

The same theory can be expressed in different terms. All purposeful behavior depends for its success on the fact that some stimuli are "attended to" and some other stimuli are ignored. It is a well-known fact that when concentrating on one task, normal people are quite unaware of most stimuli irrelevant to the task. It is as if some "filter mechanism" cuts out or inhibits the stimuli, both internal and external, which are irrelevant to the task in hand, to allow the most efficient "processing" of incoming information. Over-inclusive thinking might be only one aspect of a general breakdown of this "filter mechanism."[2] (P. 631.)

Their empirical data are quite extensive. In an object-sorting task, the prediction was made that acute schizophrenic patients should include many more details in the bases for sorting than normal controls would. Thus such factors as shadows cast by the objects, personal associations to the objects, etc., might be used to form categories. This hypothesis was confirmed (Payne, 1962; Payne & Friedlander, 1962).

Payne and Hewlett (1960) demonstrated that schizophrenic patients gave longer, more complex, and overinclusive explanations to proverbs. In this same study, the patients did not differ from normal controls on tests of concreteness of thinking. A more complicated aspect of the study involved an investigation of the relationship between overinclusive scores and scores on tests of psychomotor retardation. There was a significant tendency for patients who showed overinclusive thinking to be free from retardation, while those who evidenced psychomotor retardation were significantly freer from overinclusiveness.

From this observation, the investigators suggested that there might be a basis for distinguishing between two subvarieties of schizophrenia, defined by the presence or absence of overinclusiveness or retardation. Proceeding from this, Payne, Ancevich, and Laverty (1963) studied the frequency of retardation and overinclusiveness in treated schizophrenic patients judged to be symptom-free and similar groups who were acutely

[2] The reader will probably notice the striking similarity between the wording of this hypothesis and the description of perceptual breakdown given by MacDonald (1960) and quoted in Chapter 12.

psychotic just after admission. No significant evidence of overinclusiveness or retardation was found in the treated group, while the newly admitted group gave the expected signs of both types of symptom. The investigators concluded that overinclusive thinking and retardation are not fundamental personality characteristics of patients who later become schizophrenic, but rather are true symptoms of the psychotic condition, rising and falling with the acuteness of the patient's psychotic state.

Payne, Caird, and Laverty (1963) tested a further implication of the concept of overinclusiveness. They argued that overinclusive thinking might produce delusions (although not all delusions need be explained in this way). For example, a patient may have developed avoidance tendencies toward a certain individual and may extend the concept of that individual to include all other people who look like him, are the same sex, age, etc. Thus the development of an extensive delusional system might arise on the basis of overinclusion. By the same token, the common clinical observation that the paranoid patient appears to notice very wide ranges of stimuli may be induced to account for the fact that the patient feels compelled to attach significance to what he notices. The normal person, since he does not notice many irrelevant details in his environment, does not assign any significance to them. Here again, we see the concept of the loss of a "filter" as a fundamental problem in the patient's perceptual processes.

These investigators gave the proverbs test, as before, to deluded schizophrenics, to nondeluded schizophrenics, and to nonschizophrenics. The deluded group was significantly more overinclusive than either of the other samples, and the investigators conclude that overinclusiveness is associated with greater proneness to the development of delusions.

In all these studies, the schizophrenic samples were drawn from *acute* patient populations. If overinclusion is in some way a central process in schizophrenic behavior, it would be reasonable to suppose that it would become more marked in patients who deteriorate to the chronic state. As an early pilot study indicated that this was not the case, Payne, Friedlander, Laverty, and Haden (1963) conducted a comprehensive investigation of 40 long-stay chronic schizophrenics. They were found to be no more overinclusive on the proverbs test than normals are. However, at the time of the study the patients were on a regimen of drug treatment, and there was some possibility that this might have influenced the outcome. A further study with patients who were taken off drug therapy produced essentially similar results.

The full implications of this finding are ambiguous. Not all acute patients show overinclusive thinking in the type of study described already; Payne estimates that 50 per cent do. It may be that the presence of overinclusion is, in some way, a good prognostic sign—those who do not show it being more likely to remain hospitalized and become classed as chronic. An alternative possibility is that overinclusion is somehow eliminated by the apathy that develops with institutionalization, and thus its disappearance may be, in effect, hospital-induced. Much of this confusion is probably a reflection of the rather arbitrary nature of the acute-chronic distinction; it is quite possible that a process-reactive classification might produce less ambiguous results.

Finally, we should note an interesting study by Payne (1964) in which he argued that if overinclusion is related to the breakdown of the hypothetical "filter" that ordinarily operates to maintain narrowed perception, then overinclusive patients should have wider spans of attention than controls do. As a test of the range of stimuli perceived by the patient, he presented pictures in a tachistoscope beginning at exposure intervals too short to permit identification of the picture. When the interval in this kind of test is lengthened, there is usually a period where the subject is uncertain of the exact nature of the picture but will make a guess when he has noticed enough to form some percept. The point at which a subject begins to make incorrect guesses may be used as a rough index of the point at which he is receiving enough input to warrant a guess. On this basis the over-inclusive patient ought to make such guesses sooner (i.e., at shorter exposure times) than controls would, for the patient would notice more in the picture for any given exposure time. Payne found a correlation of +.90 between the tendency to make early incorrect guesses and a score of overinclusiveness derived from their performance upon an object classification test. Subjects were 43 mixed psychotic patients newly admitted to hospital and tested before any treatment had begun.

Summary. It is clear that overinclusiveness, as measured by the tendency to include more items in a concept than normal controls do, is readily obtained in newly admitted or acute schizophrenic patients. By suitable manipulation of the demands of the experimental situation, the same kind of patient can be made to appear "underinclusive." It is perhaps most parsimonious to assume that the patient generally tends to include into concepts more items than are ordinarily relevant to the concepts, but when he is required to extend them to meet an experimental demand, he is unable to do so constructively.

The second important observation is that overinclusiveness seems to be most typical of some kinds of patient, notably those with good prognoses. It is therefore likely to be associated with the reactive rather than process schizophrenic. By the same token, it appears to be symptomatic of the patient's thinking during the florid state of the disorder only and not reliably characteristic of his thinking during periods when there is no other evidence of psychosis.

Many of the concomitants of overinclusion seem to be derivatives of excessively broad attention. We may note once again that some process which limits input into consciousness in the normal individual seems to be defective in these patients. In the light of our earlier discussions of the possibilities of low arousal and broader attention in acute patients, these findings make some sense.

Chapman's Hypothesis

Stemming from their many previous studies, some of which were designed to test the validity of Cameron's hypothesis, Chapman and his associates (Chapman, Chapman, & Miller, 1964) have developed a hypothesis to account for schizophrenic thinking that draws heavily from some learning theory principles. Their argument stems from the empirical observation that the kinds of error which are thought to be typical of schizophrenic thinking are also found, although less readily, in the thinking of normal controls. Specifically, these are:

1. The intrusion of associations into conceptual performance (Chapman, 1958)
2. Overinclusive interpretation of common concepts so as to incorporate incorrect items that are in some respect similar to the correct ones (Chapman & Taylor, 1957; Chapman, 1961a)
3. Confusions between literal and figurative usages of language (Chapman, 1960)
4. The solution of formal syllogisms by inferring an identity of objects that share a common quality (Chapman & Chapman, 1959; Gottesman & Chapman, 1960)

Because all these are errors, they may be regarded as instances of response biases. By a response bias is meant the tendency to give a particular kind of wrong answer when the cues for the production of the correct answer are minimal. A typical example is the response that involves a simple strong association. Bleuler (1950, p. 26) cites a patient who began describing a walk with her family and when enumerating the people accompanying her, commented, "Father, son . . . and Holy Ghost." This is a strong associative chain, even though in context it is inappropriate.

Response biases are mediated, the argument proceeds, by *meaning responses*. This is a "hypothetical internal event which mediates a person's overt behavioral response to a word" (Chapman, Chapman, & Miller, 1964). They are especially concerned with the denotative meaning of words, i.e., the objective referent to which the word applies. Thus the meaning response to the word "pen" might be an object used in writing, etc., or a fenced enclosure to keep cattle. Many simple words have several denotative meanings derived from both conventional and colloquial use. In normal speech or writing, the selection of the appropriate denotation will depend upon the context. Which is the "correct" meaning of pen may depend upon the general topic under discussion at the time.

Some denotative meaning responses are less common than others. For example, if we were to ask a large number of people to define "table," we would probably get back the meaning that refers to an item of furniture. A second meaning, a layout of data in a book or journal, would probably be much rarer unless we happened to pick a sample of printers as our respondents. The other meanings, such as parliamentary procedure (tabling a motion) or geology (tablelands) would be even weaker. However, normal communication requires that the stronger meaning response not be emitted when the context calls for the use of a weaker one. A failure to inhibit the strong meaning response might occur either because the subject is particularly insensitive to the cues that call for the weaker meaning, or because some hypothetical inhibitory process is not functioning correctly. Whichever of these two processes is inferred is somewhat irrelevant to the empirical prediction to be made. This is that the schizophrenic will produce strong meaning responses whether or not the context calls for them. Where the context does call for them, the schizophrenic communication will be correct and meaningful to the listener; where the context calls for the weaker meaning response, then the schizophrenic communication will be incorrect and confusing.

Naturally, this hypothesis requires that there be an independent method of measuring the relative strength of meaning responses. To achieve this, the investigators presented words to a group of judges and asked them to identify the first meaning that came to mind and then the second, etc. For example, the word "pit" produced the meaning "hole in the ground" for 92 per cent of judges, while only 8 per cent gave "hard stone of a fruit" as the strong meaning.

Armed with these quantifications of meaning strength, the experimenters studied the production of errors by chronic schizophrenics. The typical experimental procedure involved presenting subjects with multiple-choice items in which the sentence to be defined contained some minimal cues as to the correct meaning response to be given. For each item in which a strong meaning response was correct, there was a parallel item in which the strong meaning response was incorrect. The hypothesis predicted that the schizophrenic patients would be relatively adequate in responding when the item called for the strong response, but would make errors when the item called for inhibiting the strong response in favor of the weaker. A typical item used the word "pen." The strong meaning of pen referred to its definition as a writing instrument, while the weak meaning referred to its definition as an enclosure for cattle. Both meanings appeared in two items as follows:

When the farmer bought a herd of cattle he needed a new pen. This means:
A. He needed a new writing implement   (Strong meaning but incorrect here)
B. He needed a new fenced enclosure   (Weak meaning, correct here)
C. He needed a new pick-up truck   (Irrelevant error)

The professor loaned his pen to Barbara. This means:
A. He loaned her a pick-up truck   (Irrelevant error)
B. He loaned her a writing implement   (Strong meaning and correct here)
C. He loaned her a fenced enclosure   (Weak meaning, incorrect here)

Chapman's hypothesis predicts that the schizophrenic would be likely to pick the alternative A in the first item and thus be in error, but would pick the same meaning (alternative B) in the second item and be correct. Impressive support was obtained for this prediction from three experiments conducted with a population of chronic schizophrenic patients. A typical finding, presented in Table 15-4, shows the marked tendency of the patient group to make misinterpretations based upon the strongest meaning response, and somewhat fewer based upon the weakest meaning response.

Proceeding from these data, Chapman et al. have pointed out that the dimension of "abstract-concrete" discussed previously lends itself to interpretation in the same terms. Where the strongest meaning similarity between two objects is "abstract," then this should be used by schizophrenics for categorization, while similarities mediated by strong "concrete" meanings should be used also under appropriate circumstances. In other words, the patient will use the strongest meaning whether or not it be concrete or abstract. Shifting from the stronger to the weaker of two possible meanings should be particularly difficult for the schizophrenic, and thus the ability to recategorize or reconceptualize objects already categorized in terms of their strongest similarity should be impaired.

The Concrete-Abstract Dimension

The concrete-abstract hypothesis of the schizophrenic process is discussed in Chapter 12. In dealing with schizophrenic conceptualization the same hypothesis has been applied extensively. A failure to use abstract concepts has been defined by an inability on the part of the subject to group objects, shapes, etc., together on the basis of some common property. This is the same operation that was used in the studies of over-inclusion, except that in those cases the patient was dealing with verbal symbols rather than objects.

The most important studies carried out

TABLE 15-4 Mean Number of Misinterpretations Mediated by Stronger and Weaker Meaning Responses

	Total groups	
	Schizophrenic	Normal
Stronger	3.80	.89
Weaker	1.24	.44
Strong minus weak	2.56	.45

SOURCE: *Chapman, Chapman, & Miller (1964).*

with the specific intention of testing the abstracting ability of schizophrenics have been based on a series of tasks devised by Goldstein and his associates. These include the Goldstein-Weigl test, in which the subject is required to sort shaped tiles on the basis of either color or form and then to re-sort them again on whichever basis was not used the first time. A second test in the series is the Goldstein-Scheerer Object Sorting Test, which consists of a large number of small common objects that the subject is required to sort into categories as he sees fit.

Historical. A complete review of the history of the hypothesis that schizophrenic thinking is concrete would be impossible here. Beginning with Vigotsky (1934) and continuing to the present time, there have been a welter of conflicting reports on this issue. The central problem has been whether or not patients diagnosed as schizophrenic are capable of arriving at conceptual bases for grouping objects together. In spite of the many experimental evidences that this group of patients is defective at conceptualizing, strikingly contradictory evidence has been provided by Cameron. Summarizing his work, Cameron states:

If one accepts Goldstein and Scheerer's criteria for the "abstract capacity level" [1941], it is obvious to the writer on the basis not only of test situations but of several years devoted to daily close communication with intelligent schizophrenics of every degree of severity, that the "abstract capacity level" can be found in most schizophrenics provided the painfully patient technique necessary for effectual rapport with this group is developed. (Cameron, 1944.)

The McGaughran-Moran Studies. Cameron, as we have seen in Chapter 9, has preferred to think of schizophrenia as a disorder that is primarily one of defective social communication. The issue, then, is whether or not the patient's thinking is marked by a loss of ability to use abstract concepts or whether it can be more adequately described as an impairment of skills in social communication without impairment of abstracting ability. To test these two divergent views directly, an important study was carried out by McGaughran and Moran (1956).

They developed a systematic classification of concepts along two dimensions. One of these was called the *public-private* dimension and the other the *open-closed* dimension. A highly *public* concept is one that is defined by an attribute which is easily communicated to another person. Thus objects grouped together because they are "circular" would define a highly public concept, whereas objects grouped "because I like them" would be considerably less public. A maximally *open* concept is one that uses only a single attribute to define the concept —such as a grouping based upon all "red" objects irrespective of their shape, weight, use, etc. A maximally *closed* concept would represent the other end of the continuum, where objects are grouped together only when they have all their attributes in common, i.e., they are identical.

Examples of the four broad combinations possible are seen in Table 15-5.

This type of classification was developed as a method of categorizing the *conceptual area* in which the patient might prefer to use concepts. Some reflection upon the position taken by Cameron suggests that the schizophrenic should be expected to use more private-open concepts, while the normal individual with a stable orientation toward reality should use more public-closed concepts.

This study also used a method of scoring sorting responses based upon the abstract-concrete dimension. The dimension was termed the *conceptual-level* score. In simplified form this score assigned a concrete notation to any responses that were based upon "inessential detail," while those that were based upon "essential detail" received an abstract score.[3]

With this method the experimenters studied the responses of a group of chronic male paranoid schizophrenics and a control group of nonpsychiatric hospital patients matched for intelligence, age, and educational level. They used the Goldstein-Scheerer Object Sorting Test, scoring responses both for level and for area of concepts used. Their results were quite clear and showed that the schizophrenic group produced as many abstract responses as the control group (in fact, some of their abstraction scores were significantly higher than those of the controls!) but that they produced significantly fewer closed-public and more open-private concepts than the controls. Thus the conclusion is clearly favorable to the deductions from Cameron's position and does not support the Goldstein hypothesis.

[3] It is clear that the terms *abstract* and *concrete* have limited definition here.

TABLE 15-5 Dimensions of Concepts in Object Sorting

Area	Grouped objects	Concept basis
Closed-Public	Two sugar cubes	"They are exactly alike."
Open-Public	Red circle, red ball, red eraser	"They're red."
Open-Private	Several mixed objects	"They please me."
Closed-Private	Green square, matches, cigarette	"Have on my desk at home."

SOURCE: *McGaughran & Moran, (1956).*

Summary. The concrete-abstract dimension, with the concomitant hypothesis that schizophrenia is a disorder of deficiency in abstracting, has proved to be a singularly sterile approach to the understanding of the very complex problems presented by the thinking of these patients. The terms "abstract" and "concrete" are themselves poorly defined. At best they are descriptive of certain kinds of limited response obtained sometimes by experimenters and sometimes not. While the hypothesis has had some value in stimulating research into schizophrenic conceptualizing, the time has clearly come to place it in proper historical perspective and turn to more promising lines of attack on these most baffling problems.

Mednick's Hypothesis

Mednick (1959) has applied the notion of the gradient of stimulus generalization to develop a model for the explanation of thought disorder in schizophrenia. His analysis assumes that the patient's method of dealing with anxiety passes through three stages in the following way.

Incipient Stage. Initially the patient is suffering from intense anxiety, and anxiety motivation will therefore lead to a raising of the generalization gradient to the threatening stimuli in the patient's environment. Thus the aversive or avoidant behaviors which he has learned will be readily invoked by stimuli which are more or less irrelevant, i.e., dissimilar to the originally threatening stimulus. The effect of this is to render the formerly nonthreatening stimuli threatening, thereby increasing anxiety even further. This, in turn, will raise the gradient of generalization and the process will be repeated. As a consequence of this spiraling situation, there will be a gradual shift into the second or transitional stage.

Transitional Stage. As the stimuli to which the patient's responses generalize become more and more irrelevant, there will be an increasing probability that stimuli will be included which had been previously associated with anxiety reduction. They will serve to reduce the patient's anxiety and thus will be additionally reinforcing to him. In this way, seemingly irrelevant responses and preoccupations will become habitual on the part of the patient and thus will become more and more evident in his behavior pattern. They should become particularly evident whenever he is in unusually anxiety-provoking situations. Gradually, this type of preoccupation will dominate the patient's life, and he will pass into the third stage.

Chronic Stage. With irrelevant responses and thoughts predominating, the anxiety level of the patient is reduced to a stable low level, and in the absence of therapeutic or circumstantial intervention, will remain so. Overt anxiety will be minimal, but autistic and bizarre ideation will be relatively permanent.

Some technical criticisms have been leveled at this hypothesis by de Mille (1959) and have produced clarifications by Mednick (1959). For our purposes it may be regarded as a descriptive hypothesis, inasmuch as Mednick does not offer any specific suggestions as to the conditions which produce abnormally high anxiety in the first place. Deductively, his hypothesis leads to the expectation that schizophrenics should show flat generalization gradients, especially in conditions of threat or avoidance motivation, and that these gradients might be different in the acute versus the chronic stages of schizophrenia.

Justifying the assumptions contained in this analysis, Mednick has pointed out that "(a) schizophrenics more easily acquire a conditioned response; (b) schizophrenics show greater stimulus generalization responsiveness; (c) schizophrenics have great difficulty performing well in complex situations, being plagued by irrelevant, tangential associative responses competing with the adequate mode of response. However, they do at least as well as normals on low complexity tasks" (Mednick, 1958, p. 319). All these characteristics are found in individuals suffering from high anxiety, and thus he infers that schizophrenic patients are also high in anxiety. The progress through the three stages described above is therefore predicated upon this similarity.

Experimental Evidence. An ingenious investigation of Mednick's hypothesis has been reported by Woods (1961). Two lists of category words were selected, one being rated as high-anxious and the other low-anxious. Presented with a given category word, the subjects were asked to give instances of the category. Thus if the category word was "insect," responses might include "ant," "bee," etc. Thirty-two female schizophrenics were presented with these lists, and their responses to the two lists were compared for remoteness of the association produced. Remoteness was more marked in responses to the high-anxiety categories

These data are thus generally congruent with the model developed by Mednick.

Bannister's Analysis

Considering some of the data that have been reviewed here, Bannister (1960) has concluded that many of the current approaches to schizophrenic conceptualizing, including the "overinclusion" hypothesis, "are limited in that they describe the schizophrenic *condition* rather than define the schizophrenic *process*." He goes on to argue for the utilization of a theoretical framework dealing with thinking and conceptualizing generally, specifically the *personal construct* theory developed by G. A. Kelly.

Personal Constructs. A detailed account of personal construct theory is not possible here; the reader is referred to Kelly (1955). However, in simplified form, Kelly may be said to have adopted the object-sorting situation as a model for the understanding of social perception by individuals. He has used the term "construct" to refer to the basis upon which a person sorts the events, ob-

jects, or people in his environment. We may look at this situation as being the obverse of the concept formation task typically employed in research into overinclusion. The person, in Kelly's view, develops his own constructs for sorting the environment in which he lives. The task of the clinician is to discover the basis upon which these sortings are made, rather than to see if the patient can sort according to some predetermined construct developed by the experimenter. In order to do this, Kelly has developed a measuring procedure known as the Repertory Test. The patient is presented with words naming three figures known to him, usually typed on cards, e.g., "your father," "your mother," and "your best friend." He is then asked to sort this trio into a pair versus one on any basis that he deems appropriate; he is only required to see some similarity between the two which is not shared by the odd member of the trio. Many different trios are sorted, and after each sorting the patient is asked to describe the basis for it.

Within the framework of Kelly's theory, the supposition is made that the constructs used by any given person are relatively stable. If we elicit them by having him sort many figures in his environment, we will get much the same kind of picture if we have him repeat the process using another list of figures from his environment. The extent to which this is the case may be measured statistically, and the resulting measure is described as the consistency score for this individual. Other measures of various kinds may be derived from this procedure, such as the extent to which any patient tends to sort figures along the same dimensions that normal controls do, etc.

Construct Validation and Conceptual Loosening. A construct is said to be invalidated when the property which has defined it turns out to be unstable. For example, a child might construe his mother as being "reassuring" only to find that under some conditions she is punitive. As neither "reassuring" nor "punitive" are stable characteristics of his mother's behavior, this construct will be abandoned in favor of one which is stable. Both of these kinds of maternal behavior might be regarded as "just" if they are consistently related to the child's behavior. Thus the child might abandon the reassuring-versus-punitive construct for a just-versus-unjust one, in which case the mother can now be permanently placed and predicted from the child's point of view. This kind of modification of an invalid construct is effective and adaptive, because the child does now have a better basis for predicting his mother's behavior and for interacting with her.

However, another way of dealing with the invalidation of the reassuring-punitive construct would be to *loosen* the definition of the terms "reassuring" and "punitive" so that many behaviors could be classed under this dichotomy. The effect would be to make the construct unpredictive of any behavior in particular. Now if we consider that constructs are interrelated by a complex network of meanings, we can see that a highly private and unique construct will be difficult to integrate into the subject's systematic thinking in general. When we ask a person what he "means" by a certain remark, we usually expect to get an answer that uses words other than those contained in the original remark. If the speaker has a very unique and situational definition for each word in the remark, there is no way in which he can say the same thing in other words. From one very important aspect, his remark has no meaning to anyone else. In an extreme case the patient might develop a construct sufficiently private that no existing word is entirely satisfactory as a verbal label for it. Under these circumstances it would be "necessary" to create a word, which would be a neologism.

Bannister's Serial Invalidation Hypothesis. From the foregoing considerations, Bannister (1960, 1962, 1964) developed a systematic approach to the problem of schizophrenic conceptualization. His first concern was to examine the possibility that the Repertory Test would reveal differences between patient populations and normal controls, with schizophrenics showing "looser" constructions. He considered several clinical features of schizophrenic thought to be instances of loosened construing. Specifically, he believed that the *inconsequential following of side issues* and *clinging to unimportant detail*[4] common to schizophrenic language may be regarded as evidence of what has become important and definitive in the patient's construct system. "Unimportant detail" is judged by the clinician from the context of normal, common constructs. We should consider the possibility that the patient is clinging to details not because they are unimportant or because he does not discriminate between the important and the trivial. Rather, he may be emphasizing seemingly trivial details because they are important *to him.* Likewise the *vagueness and poverty of ideas*[4] seen in the schizophrenic may be interpreted as consistent with a loosening of construing. Where particular thoughts have little meaning in terms of their relation to other ideas or constructs, we may expect them to become vague and devoid of significant content.

On theoretical grounds, Bannister deduced that the schizophrenic loosening of conceptualization probably arises from the experience of *serial invalidation* of his constructs. If the individual's categorizing of other people—especially important people such as parents—turns out to be invalid, then the categories are likely to be changed until one is found that is valid. However, repeated invalidation may lead the subject to abandon the attempt to develop stable concepts for the people in his environment. Each concept is likely to become idiosyncratic and unrelated to general ways of perceiving.

Empirical Findings. The first task was to demonstrate that schizophrenic concep-

[4] This particular terminology of clinical description is taken from Mayer-Gross, Slater, and Roth (1954).

tualizing is, in fact, looser than that of normal controls when both are measured by the Repertory Test. In the first investigation (Bannister, 1960) a version of the Repertory Test was administered to several groups of patients and normal controls. Among the patient groups were two defined by diagnosis as thought-disordered and non-thought-disordered. Bannister was particularly interested in Kelly's suggestion that schizophrenic patients might be regarded as suffering from a process that involves "loosening" of their construct system. Hence, the prediction made here was that the consistency score of the thought-disordered patients would be much lower than that of normals or of non-thought-disordered patients tested in the same way.

While the first experiment required the patient to sort real people known to him, a second asked him to sort photographs of strangers in the same way. The results of these two studies in terms of consistency scores are shown in Table 15-6.

These data clearly support the hypothesis. However, they require some interpretation, for as they stand they are still descriptive. In essence they imply that the thought-disordered schizophrenic patient tends to develop constructs for each particular sorting task, but to find these constructs inapplicable to any other group of figures. Bannister has speculated on the process that might produce this effect.

If we accept for the sake of the argument that weak construct relationships in the sense in which they have been here experimentally demonstrated are central to schizophrenic thought-disorder, then we can refer to construct theory as a whole for a possible hypothesis concerning process. The line of thought which immediately suggests itself hinges on the idea that changes in construct systems are related to their *validational history*. (Bannister, 1960, p. 1246. Italics added.)

As it now appeared that the looseness of schizophrenic constructs could be demonstrated through the use of the Repertory Test, Bannister (1964) proceeded to attempt the production of "schizophrenic looseness" in a normal population by the use of an experimental analogue. Ten normal adults were used. On the first day of the experiment they were given an array of 10 photographs of people unknown to them. Each was asked to rank-order the array of photographs along a dimension of *"likable."* This ranking task was repeated for 9 more adjectives (*"mean," "good," "unusual," "narrow-minded," "sincere," "selfish," "intelligent," "unreliable,"* and *"kind"*). On the second day, the subjects were required to repeat this task, using a new array of photographs; and so on for a total of 10 days and 100 photographs. On each day after the first, each subject was told that he had been very incorrect in his ranking for 5 of the adjectives, but had been very successful for the other 5. The successful and failed adjectives were the same each day.

In the outcome, the data revealed that while there were day-by-day differences in the coherence with which subjects used one construct in relation to another, there were no significant differences attributable to the "validated-invalidated" treatment. However,

TABLE 15-6 Comparison of Schizophrenic and Other Populations for Looseness of Conceptualization as Measured by the Repertory Test

Low consistency (loose)		High consistency (coherent)		
Thought-disordered schizophrenics	**Non-thought-disordered schizophrenics**	**Depressive**	**Normal**	**Neurotic**
10.25[1]	29.42	31.70	36.00	46.50
14.5[2]	47.9	33.1	50.1	4-.4

[1] *People as stimuli* (Bannister, 1960).
[2] *Photographic stimuli* (Bannister, 1962).

the possibilities for significant change in an individual's method of conceptualizing his world are very slim when the experience supposed to produce the change is limited to a brief period in a laboratory. From Bannister's data it did appear that some of his subjects developed the predicted loosening, and it is possible that some kinds of constructs are more open to the effects of serial invalidation than others. At the present time we must conclude that the basic hypothesis is, as yet, without empirical support.

Summary. There appears to be little doubt that thought-disordered schizophrenics exhibit looser and less consistent constructs, as these are defined by Kelly. So far, however, this remains a descriptive hypothesis. The processes that may underlie it are still a matter of speculation. Bannister's suggestion that inconsistent validation of constructs may lead to loosening is congruent with some views that we have already met, as, for example, the double-bind hypothesis of Bateson. Thus the mother mentioned above who issues messages which imply that she is loving and hostile toward the child cannot readily be construed as either one or the other. However, when faced with prolonged experience of this kind, it is possible that the child might develop a construct of "inconsistent" that would handle the mother's behavior while leaving constructs of loving and hostile still useful for the conceptualizing of the behavior of other people. As we have seen, one crucial characteristic of the double bind is that the recipient of the messages is not permitted to regard them as inconsistent, the message sender explicitly denying that there is any inconsistency. Thus, in Kelly's terms, the construct of "inconsistent" would itself be continually invalidated by continued rejection of it by the mother.

Von Domarus's Principle

One of the most discussed hypotheses of schizophrenic thought has been the principle enunciated by Von Domarus (1944), which is essentially a definition of schizophrenic thought disorder in terms of the presence of certain kinds of logical error. The "prelogical" thinking of the schizophrenic is judged against the canons of formal logic in the way indicated by the now classic dictum.

Whereas the logician accepts only the Mode of Barbara, or one of its modifications, as basis for valid conclusions, the paralogician concludes identity from the similar nature of the adjectives. (Von Domarus, 1944, p. 111.)

This kind of error he called *paralogical* because it constitutes a deviation from reasoning by the formal laws of logic. He also suggested a rephrasing of his own principle, omitting some of the technical terminology of formal logic:

This idea might have been expressed by Vigotsky as follows: whereas the logician accepts identity only upon the basis of identical subjects, the paralogician accepts identity based upon identical predicates.

Two further modifications of Von Domarus's original formulation have been developed. Perhaps the best known is Arieti's, which reads:

Whereas the *normal person* accepts identity only upon the basis of identical subjects, the *paleologician* accepts identity only upon identical predicates. (Arieti, 1955, p. 194. Italics added.)

Arieti's changes are quite serious in the light of the subsequent research that has been done on this problem. Firstly, Arieti is here assuming that the formal laws of logic are representative of how normal persons think in everyday situations. Secondly, the substitution of "paleologician" for "paralogician" is based upon his belief that the Von Domarus principle is describing a regression to a primitive or prelogical form of thought, normal among primitive individuals or children. Von Domarus had, himself, raised the possibility that this kind of nonlogical thinking might be "in the nature of an atavism" but did not elaborate the suggestion to any great degree.

Yet another variation has been proposed by Nims (1959), who suggested that the typical error in schizophrenic thinking is the willingness to adopt the fallacy of the *undistributed middle.*

The normal draws a conclusion only when the middle (linking) term is distributed and provides a valid basis for concluding a relationship between the subject and the predicate of a conclusion. The paleologician will conclude that a relationship exists even though the middle term is not distributed. (Nims, 1959, p. 14.)

In fact, Nims was technically incorrect in interpreting Von Domarus in this way, as there are other manners of comitting the fallacy of the undistributed middle than by assuming identity from similar predicates.

Before we can turn to the empirical investigations of this problem, we should review briefly some of the fundamental terms of formal logic[5] as they appear in the study of syllogistic reasoning.

Syllogistic Reasoning. A syllogism consists of three statements or *propositions*. The first two propositions are premises. That is, they are known or assumed to be true. The third proposition is the *conclusion* which is inferred or deduced from the preceding premises. Correct application of the rules of syllogistic reasoning permits us to decide whether or not a given conclusion follows validly from the premises.

A conclusion consists of asserting something (the *predicate*) about a person or object, etc. (the *subject*). Many different subjects may have the same predicate. For example, we may correctly state, "All men

[5] For a thorough discussion of the rules of syllogistic reasoning, the reader is referred to any standard text in logic. Here we present only an outline sufficient to make the nature of Van Domarus's principle clear.

are mortal," and "All horses are mortal." However, from two premises such as these, no valid conclusion is possible. A possible kind of invalid inference would be made if we were to conclude "Therefore all horses are men." An error of this kind clearly develops should we assume that identity of the predicate (being "mortal") justifies accepting identity of the subject ("horses are men"). It is this kind of invalidity which is involved in Van Domarus's principle, and which is assumed to be typical of the reasoning of the schizophrenic.

Von Domarus's Principle and Overinclusion. Before turning to the experimental evidence bearing on it, we should consider in more detail what is involved in paleologic. When we say that a patient accepts two dissimilar things as being identical, we mean that he behaves toward both of them in the same way—that he does not discriminate between them either in his verbal responses or in his other behavior in relation to them. Insofar as he is responding to the attribute that the predicate describes, his behavior is appropriate. It is when he is responding to attributes not covered by the predicate that his lack of discrimination becomes pathological. Even here, the behavior is only pathological when it is applied to one of the subjects; it may be quite appropriate when applied to the other. Let us consider a hypothetical example.

A patient reasons as follows: "General Eisenhower is a veteran. My therapist is a veteran. Therefore my therapist is General Eisenhower." He then addresses his therapist as "General," salutes him whenever they meet, stands to attention in his office, and so forth. All of this is inappropriate behavior in relation to the therapist. Should he happen to meet General Eisenhower, the same behavior would be appropriate. Thus the behavioral consequences of paleological reasoning are exactly the same as the behavioral consequences of extended stimulus generalization. Behavior which is appropriate to one set of stimulus conditions is elicited by a stimulus of minimal (but some) similarity. What makes this generalization pathological is that it is being elicited by a degree of similarity that would be too small to elicit it in the normal subject.

Looked at in this way, the problem of paleological reasoning is not that it is assuming identity on the basis of similar predicates. The problem is that the patient assumes identity on the basis of the similarity of very *limited* predicates. Where the range of attributes covered by a predicate is comparatively broad, the absence of discrimination between the subjects of those predicates is not at all unusual.

Consider now a normal example. A person who has been ill-treated by someone with a foreign accent avoids the next person he meets who has a foreign accent. We should say that this is an example of simple avoidance learning generalizing to the stimulus of the foreign accent. Regarding the same events as the outcome of "reasoning," we might argue that the person was thinking paleologically in the following way: "The man who injured me had a foreign accent. This man has a foreign accent. Therefore this is the man who injured me." The avoidance behavior would then be seen as the outcome of a serious error in logic!

At this point the reader will probably have noticed that the error of *overinclusion,* discussed at some length earlier in the chapter, seems to have behavior consequences that are much the same as those described in this section. Both overinclusion and the Von Domarus type of error can be regarded as instances of a failure to respond to differences between objects of people and hence to regard them as members of a single category (overinclusion) or as being identical (Von Domarus principle).

Empirical Evidence. Nims (1959), using the expanded definition of the Von Domarus principle quoted above, found no differences between hospitalized male schizophrenics and normal controls on overall performance on logical reasoning tasks. The verbal intelligence of both groups was controlled, and items in the syllogisms included both neutral and emotionally toned terms. Gottesman and Chapman (1960) compared 30 normal and 30 schizophrenic males on an experimental task which involved the selection of the correct (i.e., valid) conclusion to be derived from a set of premises. A typical example is as follows:

All of Tom's ties are red.
Some of the things Ada is holding are red.
Therefore:
1. At least some of the things Ada is holding are Tom's ties.
2. At least some of the things Ada is holding are not Tom's ties.
3. None of these conclusions is proved.
4. None of the things Ada is holding are Tom's ties.
5. All of the things Ada is holding are Tom's ties.

Alternative 3, is, of course, the correct conclusion. Von Domarus's principle would lead us to predict that the patient will choose either number 5 or number 1, both of which involve assuming identity of subject on the basis of the identity of predicates. In the outcome, the performance of the schizophrenic group did not differ significantly from that of the controls. Further, the data indicated that both groups had a slight tendency to commit the paleological error in preference to other errors.

However, this study has two possible weaknesses. The schizophrenic group had a mean verbal intelligence score of 89.3, while that of the normal controls was 107.2. Another problem is the impersonal non-affective nature of the items that were incorporated into the syllogisms. If the Von Domarus principle is envisaged as a statement of a fundamental deficit in thinking, then this criticism is irrelevant. If, on the other hand, the schizophrenic is regarded as reverting to paleologic mainly when he is required to think about emotionally toned matters, then the technique used by Gottesman and Chapman is not an adequate test of it.

Perhaps the most comprehensive study of this whole problem has been made by

Williams (1964). He used 50 normal and 50 hospitalized male schizophrenic subjects. No differences existed between the two groups on educational level or verbal intelligence. The normal controls were slightly older than the schizophrenics (significant at the .05 level), the mean ages being 40.7 and 36.60 respectively.

Three classes of syllogism were used, 96 items in all, labeled according to the traditional classification of formal syllogisms as *figures*. These are shown in Figure 15-3. Variations of these figures were included with *positive and negative* premises, with *personal and impersonal* material and with *concrete and abstract* terms. The main errors possible were asserting valid conclusions when none could be drawn from the premises, and failing to draw a valid conclusion when one was possible.

Williams's results were quite clear. On positive items, the schizophrenics were not inferior to the normals in their total error score. Schizophrenics were not inferior to normals in the solution of abstract syllogisms. Both groups were generally inferior in their performance upon abstract items compared with concrete items. Both groups were inferior in their performance on personal compared with nonpersonal items. Of particular interest was the finding that both groups did better on positive problems cast in the form of figure II (the figure closest to the usual formulation of the Von Domarus principle!) than on either of the other two figures. This

finding was reversed in the case of negative items, but again there was no difference between patients and controls in this respect.

All in all, the tenor of the empirical evidence is quite clear. There is absolutely no basis for accepting the Von Domarus principle as being a valid description of an error tendency pathognomic to schizophrenia. The error that this principle describes is quite likely to occur in the everyday thinking of the normal individual, and it is therefore unwise to assume that the formal laws of logic depict the typical thinking of the normal person. Cohen and Nagel (1934) have argued that the formal laws of logic are simply the laws that govern the relationships between propositions or statements. They do not assume that normal people, in fact, follow these principles in their daily thinking. One might, for example, specify the principles for the correct maintainance of dental health, but they would probably be very different from an account of how most people actually do take care of their teeth.

Williams's study confirms what other investigators (Sells, 1936; Morgan and Morton, 1944; Thistlethwaite, 1950) had reported some time before: Personal, affective material produces different thinking sets from impersonal material, and affirmatively stated conclusions are regarded differently from negatively stated ones. In both of these respects the schizophrenic is the same as the normal person. Thus we can conclude that

Figure 15-3. Schematic summary of simple logical premises and conclusions in syllogistic reasoning. (Williams, 1964.)

	Figure I	Figure II	Figure III
First Premise (example)	M—P Some frogs are poets.	P—M Some poets are frogs.	M—P Some frogs are poets.
Second Premise	S—M Some bullies are frogs.	S—M Some bullies are frogs.	M—S Some frogs are bullies.
Conclusion	S—P Some bullies are poets.	S—P Some bullies are poets.	S—P Some bullies are poets.

the Von Domarus principle is unsupported by observation of the actual reasoning processes of schizophrenics. Much of the *behavior* of patients may be hypothesized to arise from this kind of reasoning, but the simpler model of stimulus generalization will account for the same behavior more parsimoniously. At the present time the latter explanation is to be preferred.

The Organic Hypothesis

Elsewhere we have seen that a common and persistent hypothesis about schizophrenic pathology is that it represents an example of a cerebral pathology. At the behavioral level, this hypothesis generates research which is designed to discover if there are similarities between the psychopathological features of schizophrenia and the behavioral consequences of known brain pathology. In Chapter 3 we discussed the research that had been performed on simple learning and perception. Much the same kind of investigation has been made into the language and thought of schizophrenics.

Schizophrenia and Brain Injury: Metaphorical Thinking. Several clinicians have noted what they believe to be a confusion of literal and metaphorical meanings in the thinking of schizophrenics, while the same observation has been made by others about the brain-injured. Examples of metaphorical usage in normal speech include the extension of the meaning of a word from one sense mode to another, e.g., "The man is wearing a *loud* tie"; the extension of the meaning of a word from one object to another, e.g., the reference to a "space*ship*," and the extension of a word from a physical to a psychological mode, e.g., "I was feeling very *low*."

Consideration of metaphoric usage suggests to us that confusion of the literal and figurative meanings of a word may go either way. For example, when we refer to someone who is politically powerful by saying, "He has the Governor's ear," we incur the possibility that this may be taken literally. On the other hand, when we say of someone who was injured at work, "He fell down on the job," there is the possibility that this will be misinterpreted as meaning that he was incompetent. Now the most likely kind of error in schizophrenic and brain-injured patients is that of using metaphorical utterances in a literal and concrete way. Thus we should expect the patient to make the mistake of concluding that the politician had taken the Governor's ear, but not the mistake of assuming that the injured workman was incompetent.

With this rationale in mind, Chapman (1960) conducted a careful study of the kinds of errors made by schizophrenics, by brain-injured patients, and by a group of normal subjects. Each subject was given a paper and pencil test consisting of a number of multiple-choice items such as the following:

David turned yellow when he faced the enemy.

This means:
A. David became cowardly.
B. David became hungry.
C. David's skin became discolored.

Miss Bailey's illness turned her yellow.

This means:
A. Miss Bailey became cowardly.
B. Miss Bailey became hungry.
C. Miss Bailey's skin became discolored.
(Chapman, 1960, p. 413)

Three kinds of errors are possible in this test. One is the incorrect use of a figurative answer (e.g., answer A in the second item), the incorrect use of a literal answer (e.g., answer C in the first item), or an unidentified error (answer B in both items). The data obtained in this investigation are given in Table 15-7. Analysis of these results shows that schizophrenic patients made significantly more literal misinterpretations than figurative, while the brain-damaged group produced the opposite effect. Eliseo (1963) has reported data on a comparable group of patients where vocabulary level was controlled, and suggests that much of the variance found by Chapman stems from differences in this ability.

Schizophrenia and Brain Injury: Object Sorting. More pressing claims to the similarity of schizophrenic and brain-damaged patients have been made with respect to their performance in dealing with concepts. Many of the original proponents of the significance of the abstract-concrete dimension for understanding schizophrenia have also pointed to an alleged similarity of patients in both of these pathological groups, both being described as "concrete" in their conceptualization (e.g., Vigotsky, 1934; Bolles, 1937; Bolles & Goldstein, 1938; Hanfman & Kasanin, 1942).

Using the same technique as that described earlier in this chapter, McGaughran and Moran (1957) compared the performance of the same group of schizophrenics with that of a group of male patients suffering from cerebral disorder. Their results indicated that the brain-injured patient was much more likely to use a *closed* concept than an *open* one. On the *public* versus *private* dimension, no difference between the two groups was found. Both of these findings are in line with the experimenters' original hypothesis, namely, that while the public-private dimension (or dimension of *communality*) distinguishes schizophrenics from normals, the open-closed dimension (or dimension of *degree of conceptual classification*) would differentiate between the schizo-

phrenic and the brain-damaged patient. Their general conclusion reflects the inutility of the heterogeneous definition of abstract-concrete as used by its proponents.

Social Content and Thinking

Supposing the schizophrenic to be differentially sensitive to social stimuli, which are presumed to arouse anxiety and disruptive responses, some investigators have predicted that the sorting of objects with social content will be less adequate than the sorting of objects without it. The same is held to be true of any tasks in which the social content of the items may be varied. Experimental investigation of this problem is comparatively straightforward, requiring mainly the substitution of social for nonsocial items in a task and a comparison between schizophrenic and normal subjects in terms of the discrepancy in their scores on the two types of material.

Chapman (1961b), for example, has studied the adequacy of performance on *arithmetic* items where the content is social or not. A "social" problem reads: "If Al kisses 5 aunts and 3 cousins, how many of these relatives does he kiss altogether?" whereas a nonsocial item reads: "If a highway passes 6 houses and 3 barns, how many of these buildings does it pass altogether?" The data indicate that closed-ward schizophrenic subjects were significantly poorer on the social items, whereas an open-ward

T A B L E 1 5 - 7 Median Scores of Predicted and Unidentified Errors

	Schizophrenic	Brain-damaged	Normal
Figurative error items			
Figurative errors	2.6	1.9	1.0
Unidentified errors	.3	.2	.0
Corrected figurative error score (figurative minus unidentified)	1.4	1.4	.9
Literal error items			
Literal errors	5.3	.6	.4
Unidentified errors	.7	.1	.0
Corrected literal error score (Literal minus unidentified)	3.1	.4	.4

SOURCE: *Chapman (1960).*

group was equally efficient at both. Davis and Harrington (1957) studied a similar effect, comparing schizophrenics with normals, and found that human content in a problem-solving task disrupted the performance of the patients but not that of the controls.

Summary. In general, experimenters have found that human content in a problem task selectively disrupts the performance of schizophrenic patients, presumably by raising anxiety and thereby generating competing and irrelevant responses. Possibly these responses lead to inadequate perception of the stimulus material.

Once again, the data fail to substantiate the usefulness of the gross assumption of cerebral pathology. It is clear that such a concept is much too crude and vague to be of value in developing a model of the nature of schizophrenic deficit. A biological model of this disorder will require more specification of the probable locus of organic pathology before comparisons with patients known to have suffered injury in these loci could be of any value to us.

PERCEPTUAL PROCESSES

Turning now from the immediate problems of language, logic, and concept formation, we shall consider some complex perceptual phenomena. In the previous chapter we noted that disturbance in simple sensory functions has been widely investigated, stemming from the observation that the schizophrenic patient's reactions to the external world might be determined by disorders in the sensory-perceptual systems. The same possibility has been studied with reference to more elaborate perceptual processes. Let us consider some of these.

Closure

The tendency to perceive incomplete figures as complete, and the tendency to perceptually "improve" the symmetry of complete but irregular figures, is a main tenet of the Gestalt school of psychology. Koffka (1935) has stated it in the following way. "If the unit is 'open' or 'incomplete,' then that part of the field which corresponds to a gap will be a seat of very particular forces, forces which will make the arousal of processes of closure easier than the arousal of any others." A fundamental aspect of this principle is that the normal operation of tendencies to perceptual closure is dependent upon certain activities in the brain and may therefore be disrupted in cases of brain pathology.

Some early workers in this problem reported that psychiatric patients were less likely to produce closure in Gestalt tasks than were normals, and that patients suffering from brain damage were least likely of all (Street, 1931, 1934). However, the diagnoses of the psychiatric patients were unclear. Systematic investigation of this phenomenon in schizophrenic patients was first reported by Snyder, Rosenthal, and Taylor (1961).

Using a series of simple Gestalt copying tasks, these investigators measured the extent of closure produced by schizophrenic patients, some of whom were on drug regimen at the time (chlorpromazine) and some of whom were not. Both of these groups were compared with normal controls, and the extent of closure was measured in millimeters from the gaps in the subject's attempts to copy an incomplete figure. In Figure 15-4 the zero line represents complete accuracy of copying, while the deviations on either side indicate the tendency to close or to open. Inspection of this diagram indicates that the patients showed considerably less closure than the controls, especially in the drugged condition. This finding fits in with the earlier studies, but raises some rather interesting issues.

Lack of closure is, in fact, also a measure of accuracy. The patient group reproduced the figures more precisely than did the controls, and thus their perception cannot be regarded as intrinsically erroneous. When we turn back to the data on size constancy

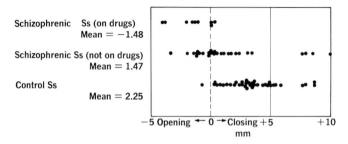

Schizophrenic Ss (on drugs)
         Mean = −1.48

Schizophrenic Ss (not on drugs)
         Mean = 1.47

Control Ss
         Mean = 2.25

−5 Opening ← 0 → Closing +5   +10
mm

Figure 15-4.   Closure scores of schizophrenic and control subjects. (Snyder, Rosenthal, & Taylor, 1961.)

reported in the previous chapter, we find that once again the schizophrenic patient is more likely to perceive a simple stimulus as it really strikes his eye at the moment rather than in terms of its more stable attributes. Further evidence for this comes from the studies on time perception and weight judgment discussed in the same chapter. Here, it will be recalled, the investigators generally found that the behavior of the patient in such tasks suggested that he was more "at the mercy" of the specific values of a stimulus used in the experiment. By the same token, the patient is less likely to make judgments that utilize his general past experience with the class of stimulus involved.

Snyder et al. have concluded that the data on closure are congruent with two possible hypotheses of schizophrenia—one of these being psychological and the other physiological. On the one hand, it is possible that the subjects paid less attention to the figure as a whole and copied it part by part —a procedure which would militate against the closure effect occurring. On the other hand, the data could be explained in terms of the deficit-of-arousal hypothesis described in Chapter 13. Gestalt theory argues that the phenomenon of closure is mediated by processes in the brain of the perceiver. Those theories which hold that the disorder of schizophrenia is chiefly one of deficiency in the mobilizing or energizing of the brain functions would predict that closure would be lacking in patients in the conditions of this experiment.

Perceptual Selectivity and Thought Disorder

Stemming from the studies of the perceptual constancies conducted by himself and his associates, Weckowicz has advanced a hypothesis of *personal selectivity* to account for the perceptual anomalies found in schizophrenia. From this point of view, the patient is deficient in the ability to perceive selectively objects and events in their environment. The hypothesis is stated in the following way:

There is a redundancy of information in the sensory input from the environment to the organism. The "cognitive process" is to a great extent concerned with reduction of this redundancy and with "selection" or "abstraction" of some information according to certain principles and suppression of all other information. In the perceptual process it will manifest itself in the ability to perceive stable "things" or objects, in spite of a constant change in the sensory input—the ability which is usually described as "constancy of perception." It will also manifest itself in more artificial perceptual tasks such as the ability to "break down gestalts" (e.g. tasks using embedded figures.) The rationale for this is as follows: constancy of perceptions depends on selecting certain cues and rejecting other cues. Therefore it could be related to the ability to break down gestalts, if, by gestalts, are understood primary and total configurations of visual cues, which are perceived "literally," as a pattern of light and not as denoting certain objects. Crookes' finding mentioned before is relevant here that in schizophrenics, poor size constancy correlates highly with "literalness" of the Rorschach responses. In the thought process this selectivity will manifest itself in the ability to form stable "classes" of "things" or objects, which is the essence of the concept formation.

Thus there is a common factor involved in the constancy of perception—ability to "break down" gestalts and capacity for abstract thinking. If this factor is affected by schizophrenic illness there should be a positive correlation between constancy of perception, ability to break down "gestalts" and capacity for abstract thinking. In the special case of the experiments reported in this paper there should be a positive correlation between poor size constancy, impaired ability to see embedded figures and impaired ability to form concepts. (Weckowicz & Blewett, 1959.)

With this hypothesis at hand, these investigators examined the relationship between size constancy and several other measures, including the open-closed and public-private scores developed by McGaughran, two tests of the ability to break down gestalts, and several other measures of abstraction in thinking.

Their results need not be presented in detail here, but it is of interest to note that size constancy correlated with several measures of abstraction, but not with the measures of ability to break down gestalt figures. This aspect of the results is given in Table 15-8. Considering abstraction as the process of selectively attending to some aspects of an event or object while ignoring others, these correlations make a good deal of sense. They also fit in with the picture of the patient as someone who is unable to maintain a set, in the way suggested by Shakow and his colleagues, where maintaining a set necessarily involves selectively attending to some events and not to others.

SUMMARY

The vast array of data accumulated so far on the behavior of the person described as schizophrenic fill the reader with puzzled dismay. Hypothesis struggles with hypothesis in a conflict in which new contenders enter the field but the defeated never retire. Are there any generalizations to be made at this point? If there are, where do they lead us? Fully aware of the fragility of the evidence, we shall present some conclusions which seem justified by the general tenor of data so far reported. These conclusions emerge from a consideration of the material discussed at length in the three preceding chapters.

Sensory Functions

There is no solid evidence to suggest impairment in simple sensory functions, such as thresholds for stimulation and so forth.

TABLE 15-8   Correlations between Size Constancy Measures and Measures of Conceptualization in Schizophrenia

	Abstraction level combined ("abstract-concrete" dimension)	McGaughran score of "openness"	McGaughran score of "closedness"	Letter-finding test	Gottschaldt's figures	Stroop test	Goldstein Scheerer colour/ form test
Size constancy, distance 7.5 m	.33*	.43†	.38*	.25	.01	−.11	.07
Size constancy, distance 15 m	.46†	.31*	.33*	.20	.19	−.06	.02

* Sig. < .05.
† Sig. < .01.
SOURCE: *Weckowicz & Blewett (1959).*

Attention

The mechanisms responsible for the direction and maintenance of attention in the normal individual seem clearly to be disrupted in many schizophrenic patients. Our understanding of these mechanisms is far from being complete. However, we may point to several possibilities.

1. The physiological mechanisms responsible for directing attention to external stimulation, i.e., the mechanisms comprising the arousal response, are defective. This defect may consist primarily of a lowered capacity for arousal with a consequent unresponsiveness to external stimulation in general, and/or a deficit in the capacity to damp down or "tune out" irrelevant stimuli after arousal has been achieved.
2. Another possibility, the obverse of the previous one, is that the processes by which attention is directed by external stimulation are dominated by those responsible for attention to internal autistic events. Both of these possibilities presume some biological aberration likely to involve the reticular system and related structures.
3. Disregarding biological possibilities for the moment, we may assume that attention in both its arousal and its selective aspects is readily modifiable by learning, and likewise may be extinguished when no reinforcements are forthcoming. From this point of view the schizophrenic is a predictable product of an environment which has provided little reinforcement when the individual has interacted with it. Equally possible is that the reinforcements and punishments have been provided on a schedule that is essentially random, and thus the individual ultimately learns to ignore an environment where stimuli do not represent consistent signals for reinforcement.
4. A fourth possibility is that the patient is unusually susceptible to stimulus change in an environment which has been predominantly punitive and has therefore learned a repertoire of habits the majority of which are avoidant. Thus he is literally responding to the environment, but most of his responses are of the same kind, i.e., aversion. Thus there is no defect in attention in the strictly biological denotation of the term.

Learning

Generalizations about learning by schizophrenic subjects require some precision in indicating the relevant variables. However, the following conclusions appear to be plausible.

1. Aversive physical stimuli appear to be more effective in producing adequate learning in schizophrenic subjects than reward is.
2. Intense sensory stimulation raises schizophrenic performance closer to the normal level.
3. Impersonal verbal reward and impersonal verbal punishment act differentially upon patients, the general division being that performance is more improved by punishment in process schizophrenics and by reward in reactive schizophrenics.
4. Social reward and punishment administered by a human experimenter appear to have discriminable effects upon patient learning and performance. Broadly speaking, patients appear less responsive to social reinforcements than are normal subjects, and this unresponsiveness is more pronounced in social punishment conditions.
5. Where biological, impersonal-verbal, and social reinforcement have been compared directly, the evidence favors the inference that biological motivation is more likely to be effective than social motivation, especially for patients who have a history of prolonged hospitalization.

These conclusions, as they stand, are compatible with more than one of the alternative hypotheses developed here. We may reasonably predict that increasing stimulus input either by adding intense stimulation or by punishment will serve to produce arousal. In a subject where level of arousal is pathologically low, such a procedure should produce an increase in the adequacy of performance in response to external stimuli. These effects would be less evident in a situation where the social reinforcement variable was, in physical terms, the sound of a voice. Thus the distinction between biological and social reinforcement could well be a distinction between intense and mild physical stimulation.

However, a theory of social learning would predict the same differences. If we assume that the patient, although normal biologically, has learned to ignore the social reinforcements of a basically unreliable social world, the same outcome would result. Electric shock, loud white noise, and the like are difficult to ignore in the *normal* individual trying to attend to something else. So the problem is unresolvable at this level.

Conceptualization

There seems to be no valid reason for concluding that the ability to perform *logical* operations is impaired in the patient compared with the normal person. Concept formation tasks are performed in ways which deviate from the modes preferred by nonpatients, the patient not making the same distinctions between relevant and irrelevant aspects of objects when grouping them together. The kinds of attributes used to make distinctions are unstable, being likely to change from one administration to another. Fluctuation and idiosyncrasy of this kind are equally evident with social stimuli or with simple common objects, shapes, figures, etc. Performances of this type are quite predictable if we assume fluctuating attention, but are less obviously deducible from a social learning position. Data currently available are not congruent with the notion that there is some basic deficiency in the capacity to think abstractly, and there is reason to conclude that the classical *concrete-abstract* dimension has been largely confounded with the dimension of communicability, privateness, and commonness.

FINAL ANALYSIS

Bearing these generalizations in mind, we may now suggest a model for the understanding of the behavior of schizophrenic patients. A model of this kind is obviously tentative and depends upon weighting some kinds of evidence more heavily than others. The reader may, and probably should, consider the evidence from other points of view.

Dimensionality

Gross schizophrenic behavior—consisting essentially of reduced responsiveness to the environment, depersonalization, and perceptual distortions—is variable rather than dichotomous. Under certain extreme conditions of fatigue, anxiety, sensory deprivation, and pharmaceutical intervention, these behaviors can be elicited in normal individuals. These behaviors disappear when the eliciting condition has been eliminated; but within the broad continuum of normalcy there are individual differences in the ease with which schizophrenic behavior can be produced and the readiness with which it will dissipate. Within the broad continuum of schizophrenic patient status, there are similar differences, measurable in a crude way by study of the patient's premorbid efficiency.

Biological Basis

Like all complex behavior, schizophrenic behavior is limited and determinable by biological factors. We know that attention depends upon an intact complex of neurological systems, chiefly involving the reticular formation. Given that such tissue systems exist, it is reasonable to suppose that they are susceptible to developing organic pathologies like any other tissue. Pathologies of this kind should produce syndromes in which defective attention is present and other symptoms of the kind commonly termed schizophrenic will develop. Thus a gross distinction may be made between primary and secondary symptoms, the latter being the consequences of the kind of experiences that such a patient will experience in his life span.

Tissue conditions of this kind may exist in all degrees from pathology to minor individual differences in normal individuals. Such differences will be expected to have their counterpart in the differences between normal individual susceptibility to schizophrenic reactions to external conditions.

Social Learning

Given a fundamental deficit of greater or lesser degree in attention-perception systems, the learning experiences of the individual will be more or less different from those of a normal individual. Organic pathologies do not always confine themselves to tissue systems as categorized by the neuroanatomist, and we may expect that systems other than those concerned with arousal may be involved. Deficit in emotional reactivity is probable, and we might expect some differences between subjects in terms of the possibility of manipulating their behavior by interpersonal reinforcements. In the adult patient, much if not most of the overt clinical picture might require an interpretation in terms of his past learning experience. However, a learning explanation based upon the assumption that the patient learned to become schizophrenic by the operations of systems of attention-perception and acquisition identical to those which produce a nonschizophrenic personality may be too naïve.

Chronicity

Prolonged sojourn in a mental hospital is itself a learning experience of massive proportions. Apathy, obedience, and lack of spontaneity are reinforced, together with the concomitant lowering of self-esteem which occurs as a consequence of the stigma attached to the patient by sheer virtue of having been diagnosed as deviant in the first place. Disentangling the effects of insti-

tutionalization from those pathological processes which would have developed anyway is an enormous task. Current research methods and knowledge do not permit us to make this distinction yet. However, insensitivity to social reinforcements in the usual experimental arrangement is hardly surprising, and we might conclude that the testing of the social learning explanation of schizophrenic behavior becomes less and less convincing the longer the subject has been hospitalized before the test is carried out.

The Process-Reactive Distinction

Granted the assumption that there is a continuum of primary schizophrenicity, we should find that there is a body of people who will develop the behavioral features of the central syndrome simply under the gradual erosion of everyday living. Others who do not develop these behaviors except under unusual pressure will, in the ordinary way, not break down and stabilize at the schizophrenic level. They will break down and then return to their premorbid adjustment as soon as the transient pressures may have passed. The distinction made between process and reactive schizophrenia should not be thought of as a dichotomy. Rather it should be thought of as a reflection of the interaction of relative degrees of stress upon individuals of varying degrees of development of the primary pathology.

Inhibition

While the data reported from different quarters support various hypotheses that have been mentioned, the writer believes that the evidence gives the most weight to the notion that the schizophrenic patient suffers from defective inhibition. Many of the specific defects that are noted in the behavior of schizophrenic patients seem to consist of the failure to prevent the intrusion of responses other than those demanded by the stimulus situation. Excessive stimulus generalization is easily seen as a failure to inhibit responses to the generalization stimuli. The many phenomena of language and conceptualization are readily interpretable as instances of the intrusion of associative responses that should have been inhibited. Failure to maintain a "set" or general deficiency of attention is, almost by definition, a failure of inhibitory mechanisms to prevent the continued arousal effects of a multitude of irrelevant stimuli. The impressive body of evidence from Russian investigators to the effect that inhibitory effects are difficult or impossible to obtain in schizophrenic patients also supports this general view.

Throughout this book so far, we have repeatedly pointed out that the practice of investigating clinical entities in terms of Kraepelinian terminology necessarily generates large quantities of error variance in group results. The foregoing argument regarding the role of inhibition of schizophrenia might better be put another way. This is that there are probably psychotic syndromes for which the primary deficiency is failure of inhibition. Behavioral consequences of this deficiency are likely to be quite complex and to ramify into many areas of functioning. Many of the patients suffering from this basic deficiency will be diagnosed as schizophrenic, especially if the sequelae of deficient inhibition have become evident in the areas of language and thinking. On the other hand, some of these patients, at least, may well receive other diagnoses, depending upon which aspect of the secondary symptomatology has most impressed the admitting clinician.

By the same token, the classification of schizophrenia will be applied to some patients who do not suffer from inhibitory deficit, as for example the patient who develops delusional ideas because he has been living, in fact, in a threatening social environment. In other words, it is not possible to state that "schizophrenia" is a deficiency of inhibition, but simply that deficiency of inhibition will produce psychotic patterns, many features of which will look like schizophrenia as the classic texts describe it.

Prolonged hospitalization is likely to blur the central features of this syndrome, as it blurs the features of any acute clinical picture. Thus the investigation of chronic patients is particularly unlikely to reveal the basic nature of this or any other disorder. It is clear that the hypothesis of inhibitory deficiency has biological implications; the writer intends this, and much recent research adds plausibility to the proposition that the deficiency is one that involves the reticular system and/or the balance of adrenergic and cholinergic activity.

The task of the psychopathologist is indeed exemplified beautifully in the problem of schizophrenia; namely, the search to discover the determinants of disordered behavior wherever these may lie, without preconceptions about the precedence of one discipline over another.

SUGGESTED READINGS

1. Arieti, S. *Interpretation of schizophrenia*. New York: Robert Brunner, 1955. A major contribution to recent theoretical discussion about the disorder.
2. Kasanin, J. S. (Ed.) *Language and thought disorder in schizophrenia*. Berkeley, Calif.: Univer. of California Press. A valuable collection of articles by different authors dealing with the title topic. Includes the hypotheses of Von Domarus, Goldstein, Cameron, etc.
3. Laffal, J. *Pathological and normal language*. New York: Atherton, 1965. This book presents the detailed procedures for the application of the method of analysis of contextual associates. It also includes excellent brief chapters on the associational structure of language and reviews pertinent studies.
4. Payne, R. W. *Cognitive abnormalities*. In H. J. Eysenck (Ed.), *Handbook of abnormal psychology*. New York: Basic Books, 1961. A very thorough review of the experimental literature covering the areas of concept formation, intelligence, attention mechanisms, etc., in a variety of psychopathologies. Considerable attention is given to schizophrenia.

REFERENCES

Arieti, S. *Interpretation of schizophrenia.* New York: Robert Brunner, 1955.

Baker, S. J. A linguistic law of constancy. II. *J. gen. Psychol.,* 1951, **44**, 113–120.

Balken, E. R., & Masserman, J. Language of phantasy. *J. Psychol.,* 1940, **10**, 75–86.

Bannister, D. Conceptual structure in thought disordered schizophrenics. *J. ment. Sci.,* 1960, **106**, 1230–1249.

Bannister, D. The nature and measurement of schizophrenic thought disorder. *J. ment. Sci.,* 1962, **108**, 825–842.

Bannister, D. The genesis of schizophrenic thought disorder. (Mimeo.) Univer. of London, 1964.

Bleuler, E. *Dementia praecox or the group of schizophrenias.* New York: International Univer. Press, 1950.

Boder, D. P. The adjective-verb quotient. *Psychol. Rec.,* 1940, **3**, 309–343.

Bolles, M. M. The basis of pertinence. *Arch. Psychol.,* 1937, **30** (212).

Bolles, M., & Goldstein, K. A study in the impairment of "abstract" behavior in schizophrenic patients. *Psychiat. Quart.,* 1938, **12**, 42–66.

Cameron, N. Reasoning, regression and communication in schizophrenics. *Psychol. Monogr.,* 1938, **50**, 1–34. (a)

Cameron, N. A study of thinking in senile deterioration and schizophrenic disorganization. *Amer. J. Psychol.,* 1938, **51**, 650–664. (b)

Cameron, N. Deterioration and regression in schizophrenic thinking. *J. abnorm. soc. Psychol.,* 1939, **34**, 265–270.

Cameron, N. Experimental analysis of schizophrenic thinking. In J. Kasanin (Ed.), *Language and thought in schizophrenia.* Berkeley, Calif.: Univer. of California Press, 1944.

Cameron, N., & Margaret, A. *Behavior pathology.* Boston: Houghton Mifflin, 1951.

Chapman, L. J. Distractibility in the conceptual performance of schizophrenics. *J. abnorm. soc. Psychol.,* 1956, **53**, 286–291. (a)

Chapman, L. J. The role of type of distracter in the "concrete" conceptual performance of schizophrenics. *J. Pers.,* 1956, **25**, 286–291. (b)

Chapman, L. J. Intrusion of associative responses into schizophrenic conceptual performance. *J. abnorm. soc. Psychol.,* 1958, **56**, 374–379.

Chapman, L. J. Confusion of figurative and literal usages of words by schizophrenics and brain-damaged patients. *J. abnorm. soc. Psychol.,* 1960, **60** (3), 412–416.

Chapman, L. J. A reinterpretation of some pathological distrubances in conceptual breadth. *J. abnorm. soc. Psychol.,* 1961, **62**, 514–519. (a)

Chapman, L. J. Emotional factors in schizophrenic deficit. *Psychol. Rep.,* 1961, **9**, 564. (b)

Chapman, L. J., & Chapman, Jean P. Atmosphere effect re-examined. *J. exp. Psychol.,* 1959, **58**, 220–226.

Chapman, L. J., Chapman, Jean P., & Miller, G. A. A theory of verbal behavior in schizophrenia. In B. A. Maher (Ed.), *Progress in experimental personality research.* Vol. I. New York: Academic, 1964.

Chapman, L. J., & Taylor, Janet A. Breadth of deviate concepts used by schizophrenics. *J. abnorm. soc. Psychol.,* 1957, **54**, 118–123.

Cohen, A. J. Estimating the degree of schizophrenic pathology from recorded interview samples. *J. clin. Psychol.,* 1961, **17**, 403–406.

Cohen, M. R., & Nagel, E. *An introduction to logic and scientific method.* New York: Harcourt, Brace, 1934.

Davis, R. H., & Harrington, R. W. The effect of stimulus class on the problem-solving behavior of schizophrenics and normals. *J. abnorm. soc. Psychol.,* 1957, **54**, 126–128.

de Mille, R. Learning theory and schizophrenia: a comment. *Psychol. Bull.,* 1959, **56**, 313–314.

Dollard, J., & Mowrer, O. H. A method of measuring tension in written documents. *J. abnorm. soc. Psychol.,* 1947, **42**, 3–32.

Eliseo, T. S. Figurative and literal misinterpretation of words by process and reactive schizophrenics. *Psychol. Rep.*, 1963, **13**, 871–877.

Ellsworth, R. B. The regression of schizophrenic language. *J. consult. Psychol.*, 1951, **15**, 387–391.

Epstein, S. Overinclusive thinking in a schizophrenic and a control group. *J. consult. Psychol.*, 1953, **17**, 384–388.

Fairbanks, Helen. The quantitative differentiation of samples of spoken language. *Psychol. Monogr.*, 1944, **56** (255), 19–38.

Gardner, G. E. The measurement of psychotic age: preliminary report. *Amer. J. Psychiat.*, 1931, **10**, 963–975.

Goldstein, K., & Scheerer, M. Abstract and concrete behavior: an experimental study with special tests. *Psychol. Monogr.*, 1941, **53** (2).

Gottesman, L., & Chapman, L. J. Syllogistic reasoning errors in schizophrenia. *J. consult. Psychol.*, 1960, **24**, 250–255.

Gottschalk, L. A., & Gleser, G. C. Distinguishing characteristics of the verbal communications of schizophrenic patients. *Disord. Commun.*, 1964, **42**, 400–413.

Gottschalk, L. A., Gleser, G. C., Daniels, R., & Block, S. The speech patterns of schizophrenic patients: a method of assessing relative degree of personal disorganization and social "alienation." *J. nerv. ment. Dis.*, 1958, **127**, 152–166.

Gottschalk, L. A., Gleser, G. C., Magliocco, E. B., & D'Emura, T. L. Further studies on the speech patterns of schizophrenic patients. *J. nerv. ment. Dis.*, 1961, **132**, 101–113.

Hanfman, E., & Kasanin, J. *Conceptual thinking in schizophrenia.* New York: Nerv. Ment. Dis. Publ. Co., 1942.

Hunt, W. A., & Arnhoff, F. The repeat reliability of clinical judgment of test responses. *J. clin. Psychol.*, 1956, **12**, 289–290.

Hunt, W. A., & Jones, N. F. Clinical judgment of some aspects of schizophrenic thinking. *J. clin. Psychol.*, 1958, **14**, 235–239.

Jones, N. F. The validity of clinical judgment of schizophrenic pathology based upon verbal responses to intelligence test items. *J. clin. Psychol.*, 1959, **15**, 396–400.

Kelly, G. A. *The psychology of personal constructs,* Vol. I–II. New York: Norton, 1955.

Koffka, K. *Principles of gestalt psychology.* New York: Harcourt, Brace, 1935.

Laffal, J. The contextual associates of sun and God in Schreber's autobiography. *J. abnorm. soc. Psychol.*, 1960, **61**, 474–479.

Laffal, J. The use of contextual associates in the analysis of free speech. *J. gen. Psychol.*, 1963, **69**, 51–64.

Laffal, J. *Pathological and normal language.* New York: Atherton, 1965.

Lorenz, Maria, & Cobb, S. Language patterns in psychotic and psychoneurotic patients. *Arch. Neurol. Psychiat.*, 1954, **72**, 665–673.

Mabry, M. Language characteristics of scattered and non-scattered schizophrenics compared with normals. *Dissert. Abst.*, 1955, **75**, 457–458.

MacDonald, N. Living with schizophrenia. *Canad. med. J.*, 1960, **82**, 218–221, 678–681.

McGaughran, L. S., & Moran, L. J. "Conceptual levels" versus "conceptual area," analysis of object sorting behavior of schizophrenic and neuropsychiatric groups. *J. abnorm. soc. Psychol.*, 1956, **52**, 43–50.

McGaughran, L. S., & Moran, L. J. Differences between schizophrenic and brain-damaged groups in conceptual aspects of object sorting. *J. abnorm. soc. Psychol.*, 1957, **54**, 44–49.

Maher, B. A., McKean, K. O., & McLaughlin, B. Studies in psychotic language. In P. Stone (Ed.), *The general inquirer: a computer approach to content analysis.* Cambridge, Mass.: M.I.T. Press, 1966.

Mann, Mary B. The quantitative differentiation of samples of spoken language. *Psychol. Monogr.*, 1944, **56** (255), 41–74.

Mayer-Gross, W., Slater, E., & Roth, M.

Clinical psychiatry. London: Cassel, 1954.

Mayers, A. N., & Mayers, E. B. Grammarrhetoric indicator. *J. nerv. ment. Dis.,* 1946, **104,** 604–610.

Mednick, S. A. A learning theory approach to research in schizophrenia. *Psychol. Bull.,* 1958, **55,** 316–327.

Mednick, S. A. Learning theory and schizophrenia: a reply to a comment. *Psychol. Bull.,* 1959, **56,** 315–316.

Morgan, J. J. B., & Morton, J. T. The distortion of syllogistic reasoning produced by personal convictions. *J. soc. Psychol.,* 1944, **20,** 39–59.

Nims, J. P. Logical reasoning in schizophrenia: the Von Domarus principle. Unpublished doctoral dissertation. Univer. of Southern California, 1959.

Pascal, G. R., & Suttell, B. J. *The Bender Gestalt Test.* New York: Grune & Stratton, 1951.

Payne, R. W. An object classification test as a measure of overinclusive thinking in schizophrenic patients. *Brit. J. soc. clin. Psychol.,* 1962, **1,** 213–221.

Payne, R. W. The measurement and significance of overinclusive thinking and retardation in schizophrenic patients. Paper presented to Amer. Psychopathological Ass., 1964.

Payne, R. W., Ancevich, S. S., & Laverty, S. G. Overinclusive thinking in symptomfree schizophrenics. *Canad. psychiat. Assoc. J.,* 1963, **8,** 225–234.

Payne, R. W., Caird, W. K., & Laverty, S. G. Overinclusive thinking and delusions in schizophrenic patients. *J. abnorm. soc. Psychol.,* 1963, **68,** 562–566.

Payne, R. W., & Friedlander, D. A short battery of simple tests for measuring overinclusive thinking. *J. ment. Sci.,* 1962, **108,** 362–367.

Payne, R. W., Friedlander, D., Laverty, S. G., & Haden, P. Overinclusive thought disorder in chronic schizophrenics and its response to "proketazine." *Brit. J. Psychiat.,* 1963, **109,** 523–530.

Payne, R. W., & Hewlett, J. H. Thought disorder in psychotic patients. In H. J. Eysenck (Ed.), *Experiments in personality.* Vol. II. London: Routledge, 1960.

Payne, R. W., Matussek, P., & George, E. An experimental study of schizophrenic thought disorder. *J. ment. Sci.,* 1959, **105,** 627–652.

Phillips, L. Case history data and prognosis in schizophrenia. *J. nerv. ment. Dis.,* 1953, **117,** 515–525.

Rubenstein, H., & Aborn, M. Psycholinguistics. In R. P. Farnsworth (Ed.), *Annual review of psychology.* Vol. II. Palo Alto, Calif.: Annual Reviews, 1960.

Schreber, D. P. *Memoirs of my nervous illness.* Cambridge, Mass.: Robert Bentley, 1955.

Sells, S. B. The atmosphere effect: an experimental study of reasoning. *Arch. Psychol. N.Y.,* 1936, **200.**

Shneidman, E. Schizophrenia and the MAPS test. *Genet. Psychol. Monogr.,* 1948, **38,** 145–223.

Simonini, R. C. Phonemic and analogic lapses in radio and television speech. *Amer. Speech,* 1956, **31,** 252–263.

Smith, M. H. The application of some measures of language behavior and tension to the letters written by a woman at each decade of her life from 49 to 89 years of age. *J. gen. Psychol.,* 1957, **57,** 289–295.

Snyder, S., Rosenthal, D., & Taylor, I. A. Perceptual closure in schizophrenia. *J. abnorm. soc. Psychol.,* 1961, **63,** 131–136.

Stone, P. J., Bales, R. F., Namenwirth, J. Z., & Ogilvie, D. M. The General Inquirer: a computer system for content analysis and retrieval based upon the sentence as a unit of information. *Behavioral Sci.,* 1962, **7,** 1–15.

Street, R. F. A gestalt completion test. *Teach. Coll. Contrib. Educ.,* 1931, 481.

Street, R. F. The gestalt completion test and mental disorder. *J. abnorm. soc. Psychol.,* 1934, **29,** 141–142.

Suttell, B. J., & Pascal, G. R. "Regression" in schizophrenia as determined by performance on the Bender-Gestalt test. *J. abnorm. soc. Psychol.*, 1952, **47**, 653–657.

Thistlethwaite, D. L. Attitude and structure as factors in the distortion of reasoning. *J. educ. Psychol.*, 1950, **45**, 442–458.

Vigotsky, I. S. Thought in schizophrenia. *Arch. Neurol. Psychiat.*, 1934, **31**, 1063–1077.

Von Domarus, E. The specific laws of logic in schizophrenia. In J. Kasanin (Ed.), *Language and thought in schizophrenia.* Berkeley, Calif.: Univer. of California Press, 1944.

Weckowicz, T. E., & Blewett, D. B. Size constancy and abstract thinking in schizophrenia. *J. ment. Sci.*, 1959, **105**, 909–934.

White, M. A. A study of schizophrenic language. *J. abnorm. soc. Psychol.*, 1949, **44**, 61–74.

Whitehorn, J., & Zipf, G. Schizophrenic language. *Arch. Neurol. Psychiat.*, 1943, **49**, 831–851.

Williams, E. B. Deductive reasoning in schizophrenia. *J. abnorm. soc. Psychol.*, 1964, **69**, 47–61.

Woods, P. J. A test of Mednick's analysis of the thinking disorder in schizophrenia. *Psychol. Rep.*, 1961, **9**, 441–446.

Zaslow, R. W. A new approach to the problem of conceptual thinking in schizophrenia. *J. consult. Psychol.*, 1950, **14**, 335–339.

PSYCHOLOGICAL 16
METHODS OF TREATMENT
IN PSYCHOPATHOLOGY

Treatment of psychopathological disorders has two possible aims. One of these is to change the behavior of the patient so that it is acceptable in the environment to which he will return. Another goal is to find an environment in which such changes as have been made will be most likely to gain acceptance. These two aims are not independent, and an effective program of therapy will usually combine both of them as far as possible.

During the course of treatment, a hospitalized patient is likely to be subject to some combination of three kinds of influence, all of which will operate to change his behavior in some way. The first of these is the hospital environment per se. Secondly, he may be exposed to some professional techniques believed to bring about changes by psychological processes, especially psychotherapy. Thirdly, and in many cases more commonly, he may be subjected to the somatic or bodily therapies. Psychotherapy and somatic therapy are directed, as we shall see, to eradicating the pathological behaviors that brought the patient into hospital in the first place. In recent years there has been increasing interest in the provision of certain kinds of social skills and occupational qualifications that are likely to make it possible for the patient to maintain himself once he has returned to society. Such procedures are usually termed *rehabilitation* and are employed with concern for the kind of environment to which the patient will return.

Estimates of the efficacy of given kinds of treatment are plentifully available in the professional literature. The problems of arriving at reliable estimates are extremely complex. We shall consider the problems and data now in some detail.

THE MENTAL HOSPITAL

Patients who are hospitalized for the treatment of behavior disorders are to be found in three kinds of hospital. By far the largest percentage are maintained in hospitals financed and administered by the state, so much so that in the majority of states in the United States, the term "state hospital" is synonymous with "mental hospital." A second major group of hospitals is that administered by agencies of the Federal government, especially the Veterans' Administration. Finally, there are many private mental hospitals, unavailable to the majority of patients because of the tremendous expense involved. An exception to this problem may be found in the inpatient service of teaching hospitals, where low-income patients may be admitted in order to provide teaching experience for students.

The caliber of state mental hospitals varies enormously with regard to the physical plant, the number and qualifications of the professional staff, and the extent to which the hospital administration views its function as the provision of treatment rather than custody. Differences between state hospitals are to be found not only from one state to another, but also within the same state. There are, of course, differences in the internal organization of hospitals. However, most mental hospitals are organized around the assumption that there is a natural progression in the hospitalization of the patient.

Hospital Routine and the Patient

Typically the newly arrived patient is received and housed in an admissions unit. Apart from the routine clerical procedures of admission, this unit may be used for preliminary observation or diagnosis and/or for some kind of initial intensive treatment

designed to produce a rapid discharge before the patient stabilizes at some chronic prolonged level of pathological behavior. Where this fails, or is not even tried, the patient may be assigned to a general ward in the hospital. In the simplest kind of administration, these ward assignments are made on the basis of sex and degree of overt disturbance of the patient. The least manageable patient whose behavior is regarded as most "regressed" is likely to be assigned to a ward along with other similar patients. Significant changes in the manageability of the patient's behavior are likely to be accompanied by shifts from one ward to another in the appropriate direction.

Improvements in the patient's behavior are, in effect, rewarded by changes in his standard of living in the hospital. Living conditions in the regressed wards are conditioned by the fact that the patients in them may destroy furniture, soil themselves, throw food, and so forth. Consequently, the kind of furniture available is of necessity minimal, heavy, and uncomfortable. The writer has seen patients in such a ward sitting for long periods on a heavy bench, which was bolted to the floor, gazing at a television set from which the picture tube had been removed to prevent breakage. As the loudspeaker was left in, the patients could hear the sound portion of the program but could see nothing accompanying it.

Whatever the rationale, conditions in the better wards are generally more attractive. Thus the typical hospital system includes a graded series of reinforcements for improved behavior—and a graded series of punishments for undesirable behavior. It should be noted that this system of behavior control is largely concerned with the manageability of the patient and not with his mental health. An important feature of the system is that the reward for an improvement in behavior may be considerably delayed, while the punishment for unacceptable behavior may be instant. When a patient shows some signs of improving, the tendency of the staff is to wait for at least some days to see if the improvement promises to be stable. If sufficient time elapses without incident, the patient may be transferred to a "better" ward. On the other hand, once he is in a better ward, a sudden burst of violence on his part is apt to lead to his expulsion to a regressed ward with minimum delay. As we have seen, delayed reinforcement is relatively ineffective, and the system is thus poorly equipped to reinforce positive improvement in the patient's behavior. Per contra, the system is efficiently equipped to punish regressive behavior, a combination of circumstances that is most likely to produce fear in patients rather than more positive motives.

This feature of hospital treatment, seen at its worst in older, autocratically run hospitals, is of major importance in the development of certain kinds of behavior in the patient—behavior that is often quite independent of the factors that produced the psychopathology for which he was admitted in the first place. Immediate control of the patient's fate in the hospital from day to day rests, in common practice, in the hands of the staff member most likely to be present and affected by the patient's actions, namely, the nurse or attendant. The relationship between patients and the various ranks of staff represents a major source of influence upon the development of the patient's behavior after admission.

Staff and Patients

In institutions such as mental hospitals it is possible to recognize three categories of staff member whose behavior and attitudes have an effect, direct or otherwise, upon the fate of the patient. One group comprises the professional administrators, especially those concerned with the budget, who see their job as that of running the housekeeping side of the hospital in accordance with some mandate given by the state government, or other agency that provides the money. If the budgetary administrator is relatively free from control by the professional medical administrator, then many therapeutic decisions or policies may be negated by a decision that they are financially improper.

However, the main staff categories of interest are the professionals (the psychiatrists, psychologists, social workers, and other therapeutic or diagnostic specialists) and the ward staff who are in continuous and daily contact with the patient. Many hospitals are grossly understaffed, especially at the professional level. Of necessity, much of the working day of the professional staff is spent writing reports, attending case conferences, and performing other activities that do not bring them into direct contact with individual patients. Consequently, the implementation of the hospital's therapeutic policy is largely in the hands of the ward staff.

For a therapeutic policy to operate effectively when carried out by ward staff it is necessary both that the staff understand and agree with it and that carrying it out does not conflict with other responsibilities assigned to them. For example, where an attendant is held responsible for the cleanliness of the ward and is dependent upon patient labor for this, it is not possible for him to act in accordance with a policy that requires him to be accepting of spontaneous urination on the ward. In such a case it is much easier for a supervisor to tell whether or not the ward is clean than it is to know whether or not the attendant is suitably therapeutic in his attitude to patients. Thus the system is likely to reinforce the attendant for fulfilling housekeeping needs more than for carrying out the subtle duties of a therapeutic policy.

In effect, the ward attendant is the main manipulator of the patient's environment. He has at hand the threat of demotion to a back ward and the promise of promotion to a better ward with which to control the patient. As understaffing at the attendant level is also common, he may require more than good behavior from his patients if he is to get through the day. At least some of the patients may act as his assistants, such cooperation being rewarded by the attendant with small favors in the form of cigarettes, extra food, and the extension of unofficial privileges in general.

For the attendant to secure the demotion or promotion of a patient, it is necessary for him to induce the relevant member of the professional staff to make the decision. In much the same way, the military NCO finally resorts to reporting to an officer the behavior of a private who has proved recalcitrant to the unofficial punishments that have been applied to him. Essentially, the problem for the attendant is to get the professional clinician to see the patient's behavior the same way that the attendant sees it. Under these circumstances the pressure to omit or distort events may be great; the information reaching the clinician is likely to have undergone a good deal of filtering by the attendant beforehand, thus increasing the gulf between the patient and the professional even more than shortage of time has already made it.

The Hospital and the Medical Model

Once a patient has been diagnosed and placed in hospital, the ostensible goal is the elimination of psychopathology. If the diagnosis tends to imply a pessimistic prognosis, as in the disorders of senility, then the goal may be the more simple one of custody and maintenance. Should the treatment policy of the hospital be mainly built upon the notion that individual psychotherapy is necessary and sufficient for improvement, then the function of hospitalization is to hold the patient and protect him during the long hours between psychotherapy sessions. The model is analogous to the treatment of cancer by radiation therapy, where the patient may be receiving no specific treatment between radiation exposures other than general care and feeding. What happens to the patient between exposures is assumed to be more or less irrelevant to the course of treatment.

When this assumption is made about psychotherapy with hospitalized patients, it implies the belief that the interaction between therapist and patient for one-hour sessions is vastly more important than his daily routine on the ward, and is discon-tinuous with it. Clinicians who hold this view might be willing to go along with the attendant's views about ward management because they believe them to be relatively unimportant in the cure of the patient.

On the other hand, if the clinician faces the fact that everything that happens to the patient influences his behavior in proportion to the power of the motivations and reinforcements involved, then psychotherapy assumes a role of lesser significance in the course of treatment. Facing this fact makes it necessary to accept the further conclusion that the professional disciplines most valuable in hospital treatment would be those concerned with the effects of continuous social environments upon behavior, i.e., social psychology and especially the psychology of learning. As the majority of psychiatrically trained clinicians have no claim to competence in these disciplines, it is not surprising that the medical model is still predominant in the formulation of hospital policies.

Notwithstanding this predominance, there are factors operating in recent years that herald significant changes in the concept of hospital care. We shall discuss them in detail later, but can mention here that as drugs make management easier, the distinction between manageable and unmanageable patients is reduced, with concomitant reduction in the difference between "good" and "bad" wards. Some psychiatrists have begun to see the importance of social psychology and sociology in determining optimal environments for patients and have made significant advances in changing hospital attitudes and routines. Appreciation of the disadvantages of even the best hospital environment has brought interest to bear upon the possibilities of emphasizing outpatient therapy and preventive measures generally. Finally, the enormous cost and discouraging results of the reliance upon individual psychotherapy have perforce led to the movement to concentrate upon the learning of social and occupational skills (rehabilitation) rather than upon the reconstruction of personality. The use of large-scale restraining techniques for these purposes is also appearing.

All these are, however, straws in the wind of change, and at this time the vast majority of patients are being treated in hospitals under the conditions described in the opening pages of this chapter. In these pages we attempted to point out some of the important influences operating on the patient in a large hospital, factors that have an antitherapeutic effect upon the patient's behavior. These effects are sufficiently common that they are often characterized by terms such as *institutionalism* (e.g., Wing, 1962) or *secondary adjustments* (e.g., Goffman, 1961).

Institutionalism

Long stay in a total institution produces certain kinds of change in the behavior of the inmate. A *total institution* has been defined by Goffman (1961) as "a place of residence and work where a large number of like-situated individuals, cut off from the wider society for an appreciable period of time, together lead an enclosed, formally administered round of life" (p. xiii). Typical total institutions are prisons, leprosariums, cloistered religious orders, naval vessels at sea, and mental hospitals. Central characteristics of these institutions include the facts that work, sleep, and play are not separated in location as they are in normal society; that there are two (at least) classes of persons associated with the institution, the inmate proper and the staff, officers, or guards; and that contact with the wider society by the inmate is prohibited or regulated by the staff.

The purposes, activities, and living conditions of institutions may vary a good deal from one to another. Likewise the degree of coercion that is exercised to prevent the inmate from leaving the institution may vary from the complete restriction placed upon the prisoner to the moral pressures brought to bear upon the nun. Coercive institutions demand that the inmate adjust to them, the form of acceptable adjustments depending upon the goals of the institution. In order to make these adjustments, the inmate must change some of the behavior patterns with which he entered the institution. Where the demands of the institution are markedly different from the demands of society at large, the process of adjustment to the former may involve growing maladjustment to the latter.

Total institutions tend to have certain demands in common. Obedience and dependency upon the part of the inmate toward the staff, adjustment to an unvarying routine with regard to meals, activities, dress, etc., and the inhibition of personal tastes and preferences in such matters are practically standard requirements of most total institutions. While this uniformity is enforced by the staff, they are usually unwilling to be regarded as the authors of it. Military commanders and religious superiors are themselves subject to higher authority, which is usually located elsewhere and is invisible to the inmate. Physicians may appear to be bound by the dictates of good medical practice; prison wardens are bound by the letter of the law. Thus not only is the inmate faced with a demand that he forgo his individuality; he is faced with this demand in a form that gives him little reason to suppose that it could be modified by the staff.

Total institutions dealing with inmates who enter as adults, disturbed or otherwise, expect to find tension and resistance upon the part of the new entrant when the demands of the institution are made clear to him. Many total institutions present a different public version of institutional life from that which actually exists within its confines. The eager military recruit may be violently disillusioned to find that his experiences in the army are not in line with the descriptions given him by the recruiting sergeant; the mental patient may find that his expectations of a "hospital," based upon knowledge of medical hospitals, are not fulfilled when he enters a mental hospital. Disillusionment coupled with restriction of departure from the hospital is likely to produce a certain sequence of events.

Initially the patient may deny his patient status violently now that he can see clearly what it entails, rejecting any of the facilities of the hospital and especially any of the procedures that serve to make his patient status clearer—such as wearing hospital dress, surrendering his valuables for safe-keeping, being bathed, and so on. Coupled with this will be strenuous demands to be released and the possible belief that he was deceived by someone into coming to the hospital in the first place. His family physician, his spouse, and his relatives are the logical candidates for suspicion, since they may have resorted to deception in order to get the patient into the hospital. In this way a patient may conclude that he is the victim of a plot and in one sense be quite correct in his suspicions.

All these responses are more than likely to confirm the diagnosis that the patient is disturbed and should not be released. If they have any effect upon his status, it is to lead to his greater restriction and control by the hospital staff. Obedience and acceptance (at least overtly) of the status of patient are the only bases upon which the patient can gain whatever privileges and freedoms are available to the inmates of the hospital. When he has learned these behaviors adequately, he is likely to have extinguished some of the important ties that he had with society outside the walls. It is this final adjustment that is termed "institutionalism." As a syndrome it has been noted by many observers, both scientific and literary. Wing (1962) designates the central elements as apathy,

resignation, dependence, depersonalization, and reliance on fantasy. Other elements are doubtless involved, and there are several varieties of adjustment possible within this syndrome.

Empirical Studies of Institutionalism

In view of the widespread recognition of institutionalism as a serious concomitant of a prolonged stay in hospital, it is somewhat surprising that there have been few well-controlled quantitative studies of its effects. One such study is reported by Wing (1962). He investigated the stated wish to leave the hospital in 256 male schizophrenic patients, inmates of two London hospitals. The patients were classified into groups on the basis of the length of time that they had been in hospital. Data obtained on this point are presented in Table 16-1. From this table we see a striking shift, as time of hospitalization increases, in the proportion with a definite wish to leave the hospital versus those who wish to stay. This severing of interest in return to society is paralleled by a decline in the extent to which society is interested in the patient.

The percentage of patients who were either visited by someone from outside or made a visit home themselves showed the same trends. Table 16-2 presents the percentage of social contacts with the non-hospital world as it was related to length of stay in hospital. During this investigation, data were collected regarding the clinical deterioration of the patients in other respects

TABLE 16-1 Effects of Length of Stay in Hospital on Wish to Return to Society

	Length of stay in hospital, years											Total over 2 years	
	<1:11		2-4:11		5-9:11		10-19:11		20+				
Attitude to discharge	N	%	N	%	N	%	N	%	N	%		N	%
Definite wish to leave	36	50.7	12	29.3	13	23.6	6	11.3	1	2.8		32	17.3
Vague wish to leave	17	23.9	15	36.6	14	25.5	6	11.3	5	13.9		40	21.6
Indifferent or wish to stay	18	25.4	14	34.2	28	50.9	41	77.4	30	83.3		113	61.1
Total	71	100.0	41	100.1	55	100.0	53	100.0	36	100.0		185	100.0

SOURCE: *Wing (1962).*

as a function of the length of stay in the hospital. From these data it was concluded that there was no demonstrable relationship between length of stay and severity of pathology. Wing suggests that clinical deterioration may be complete, where it is going to occur at all, within two years of first onset of the illness (this onset not necessarily being coincident with admission to hospital). Institutionalism as a syndrome may take much longer to reach a maximum.

NEW POLICIES IN HOSPITAL CARE

Hospital authorities have been aware of the need to adopt new methods of patient care and control in order to avoid the problems that have been described in the foregoing paragraphs. Several goals are obvious. One is to eliminate the barrier between society and the patient by bringing voluntary visitors into the hospital, by increasing visits from the hospital to the home, by providing day-care or night-care arrangements, and especially by retraining the patient so that he may maintain a satisfactory adjustment in society, no matter how minimal this adjustment may be.

Besides working to get patients out of the hospital as rapidly as possible, some hospitals have taken significant steps to decrease the dependent role of the inpatient. Patient government and the institution of the *therapeutic milieu* are being utilized to give the patient more autonomy in deciding his own fate and being a party to the decisions that may be made about him. At a much more drastic level, there is a thoroughgoing reappraisal of the wisdom of using large mental hospitals at all. An alternative is to locate inpatient wards in general medical hospitals, providing the less disturbed patients with the opportunity to interact with normal medical patients. We shall consider some of these techniques now.

Liberalization of the Hospital Environment

The belief that patients should be treated humanely rather than custodially is not new. Pinel's transformation of the Bicêtre and Salpetrière hospitals in France during the early years of the French Revolution is a turning point in the history of hospital treatment of pathological behavior. However, it was not until after World War II that there developed a recognition of the need to use all the influences of the hospital environment for positive changes in the patient, a step beyond that of removing the detrimental consequences of custodial care. While it may be hard to date precisely the beginning of an active attempt to turn the hospital into a totally therapeutic environment, one starting

T A B L E   1 6 - 2   Decline in Interest by Society in Patients with Long Hospital Stay

	Length of stay in hospital, years							
	2-9:11		10-19:11		20+		Total	
Nonhospital social contacts	N	%	N	%	N	%	N	%
Goes home, or is visited regularly	43	74.1	16	35.6	3	10.3	62	47.0
Visited less than once a month. Does not go home	6	10.3	11	24.4	10	34.5	27	20.5
Never visited and never goes home	9	15.5	18	40.0	16	55.2	43	32.6
Total	58	99.9	45	100.0	29	100.0	132	100.0

SOURCE: *Wing (1962).*

point was the *Northfield Experiments* in Britain in 1943 and subsequently.

Two psychiatrists, W. R. Bion and J. Rickman, were assigned to the Northfield Military Hospital to handle some problems of discipline that had arisen in one section of the hospital. Bion undertook the radical steps of abandoning the authoritarian organization of the hospital in this unit and relinquishing his own disciplinary control of the group of patients concerned. The patients were given the choice of developing self-government of their own community or living in the confusion that prevailed when every man was left to his own devices. The temporary experiment was successful and later was applied to a complete hospital, being coupled with a program of group psychotherapy. Kräupl-Taylor (1958) has suggested that the second Northfield experiment marks the first systematic attempt to organize a hospital along the lines of a therapeutic community.

British hospital administration has, on the whole, been perceptibly ahead of that in other countries in developing new ideas of patient care in hospitals. Even before the first Northfield experiment J. Bierer had established a patient-governed social club for inpatients at Runwell Hospital in 1938. This was followed soon after by other clubs for outpatients, many in the London area. Removing restraints and easing disciplinary controls also increased apace in British hospitals during the late 1940s and since. A striking instance of this change is reported by May (1956), who noted that at Netherne Hospital only 5 per cent of patients had had ground privileges in 1932 and that no open wards or units existed in the hospital. In 1956 nearly two-thirds of the wards were open and 60 per cent of the patients were on ground parole.

In the United States, one of the early large-scale liberalizations of hospital care was conducted at the former Boston Psychopathic Hospital (now renamed the Massachusetts Mental Health Center). In a complete description of this liberalization,

Greenblatt, York, and Brown (1955) present a vivid picture of the kinds of changes that were made over a period beginning around 1946 and continuing since. In 1948, steps were taken to institute patient government by establishing an elected council of patients which negotiated with the administration with regard to matters of ward management and daily care. Parallel with this was the reduction in physical restraint, hydrotherapy, and other restrictive methods of dealing with agitated patients. A graphic illustration of the decline in the use of seclusion is shown in Figure 16-1. Similar humanizing influences have been at work in mental hospitals throughout the country during the past two decades. Perhaps the best known model of the therapeutic community concept is that developed and described by Maxwell Jones.

Maxwell Jones and the Therapeutic Community

In 1947, a *social rehabilitation unit* was opened at Belmont Hospital in England. Behind this unit was a concept of the *therapeutic community* where "each individual, whether patient or staff, has definite roles to play, and everything is done to help the individual bring his emotional problems to the group" (Baker, Jones, Merry, & Pomryn, 1953). The patients not only are treated themselves but are also involved in the treatment of other patients. Certain specific therapeutic activities were established, mainly in group form.

Individual Interviews.   Individual therapeutic interviews with a psychiatrist are held at least once weekly. They are aimed largely at giving supportive guidance in relationship to the patient's activities in the hospital, not at discovering underlying dynamics of his behavioral problems.

Group Psychotherapy.   Each patient is also a member of a therapy group meeting more than once a week. The techniques used in

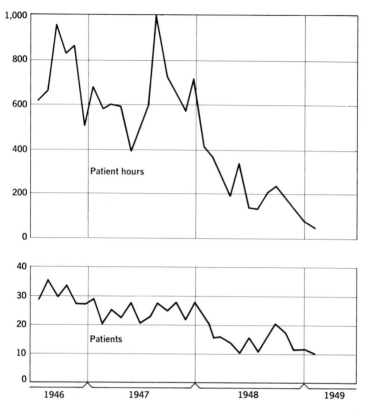

Figure 16-1. Patient hours and patients in seclusion, Boston Psychopathic Hospital, July, 1946, to January, 1949, showing shifts in hospital practices. (Greenblatt, York, & Brown, 1955.)

group therapy resemble those in general use elsewhere and require no special comment.

The Morning Meeting. Disciplinary infractions by patients posed some difficulties for a hospital system that was moving toward giving patients greater freedom in determining their own fate. Some of these infractions could be serious to the extent of involving hazard to the patient. Thus on one occasion, three patients were observed crossing an electrified railroad track late at night under the influence of alcohol, running imminent risk of being electrocuted. To handle such problems, a morning meeting was established to which defaulting patients were asked to come. The patient was free

to come or not, and if he came was at liberty not to enter into discussion of his behavior. In this meeting the therapist was at pains to avoid punitive or blaming comments. Permissive discussions of this kind appeared to facilitate expressions of guilt by individual patients and to work some change in the direction of an ability to see the unit rules as being developed for the patient's welfare rather than for the hospital autocracy.

The Ward Meeting. Once each week the patients of each ward meet with the charge nurse, two social worker therapists, and the ward physician. The purposes of this meeting are largely related to the solution of problems in the management of the ward, the development of social activities, and so forth. As far as is feasible, the goal is to encourage self-government in these matters by the patients.

Community Discussion. Each morning at 9 A.M., the entire patient and staff populations meet to present problems, with frequent use of psychodrama and other methods for the description and analysis of community issues. Much of the burden of therapeutic interaction in this community lies with the social therapists, mainly women trained or in training as social workers. These therapists maintain active affiliation with the wards and also receive tutorial supervision. An additional feature of the arrangement is the provision of group therapy for the social therapists themselves, partly with the hope that this might improve their effectiveness and partly as a device for teaching the principles of group dynamics.

The majority of the patients in the unit appeared to have had trouble in accepting ordinary authority relationships outside the hospital. Thus the "democratization" of the community and the diffusion of authority among the patients themselves may have had particular significance in reducing their typical rebellious behavior. However, the democratic control of the patients had clear limits, and in the final analysis the hospital staff could and sometimes did step in to exert the control that they deemed necessary.

Evaluation of the Therapeutic Community

There have been no controlled studies of the efficiency of the therapeutic community as a method of changing patient behavior. Consequently it is simply impossible to offer any evaluation of it in those terms. However, upon the ground of common humanity any step is desirable that increases the self-respect of the patient and decreases dependency. From this point of view the techniques of Maxwell Jones seem to be laudable.

THERAPEUTIC USE OF OPERANT-CONDITIONING TECHNIQUES IN WARD MANAGEMENT

Moving from the relatively integrated and reality-oriented patients of the therapeutic community, we shall now consider some recent developments in the hospital management of chronic patients. Of particular interest is the use of operant techniques for the production of behavior changes in chronic patients. Successful application of simple reinforcement procedures has been reported by several workers in this field, and we shall consider one of these in detail.

Reduction of Feeding Problems by Reinforcement Techniques

While planning an experiment involving the use of food as a reinforcer, Allyon and Haughton (1962) became interested in the possibilities of using food reinforcement methods to control feeding problems in chronic schizophrenic patients. As the investigators commented, many such patients exhibit bizarre symptomatology associated with refusal to eat. Some patients might complain that the food was poisoned, or that God commanded them not to eat. Symptoms of this kind commonly elicit complex interpretations on the part of the clinician, such as explanations based upon the symbolic nature of eating, regression to "oral level," and so forth. Explanations of this kind imply that until the more fundamental dynamic problems have been cleared up, there is little prospect that the symptomatic behaviors can be changed in any enduring way. It was from this general background that these investigators decided to study the management of feeding problems by using simple food reinforcement for normal eating behavior, and by withholding it when pathological feeding responses occurred.

Typical orthodox methods of dealing with the patient who refuses to eat include coaxing, escorting him to the dining room, expressing concern and sympathy, spoon feeding, tube feeding, and so on. In this experiment, all nursing personnel were excluded from contact with the patients at mealtime. When a meal was due, the meal was called and a period of 30 minutes was allowed to elapse during which the patients were free to enter the dining room. After this time had passed, the door was locked and no further access was possible. In order to eat a meal, each patient had to walk, unescorted and without personal attention, to the dining room within the half-hour period. As the study progressed, the access period was reduced by stages to 20, 15, and finally 5 minutes. The study involved 32 patients, including 7 chronic feeding problems. In this group, 30 had been diagnosed as chronic schizophrenics, 1 as mentally retarded, and 1 as depressed.

The outcome of the arrangement is shown in Figure 16-2. Over all conditions of access, the feeding-problem group maintained stable eating rates, although these rates were lower than those for patients with acceptable eating behavior. However, they were now eating without any of the coaxing or persuasion that had been necessary before the

experimental regimen was instituted. During the early stages of the experiment, the patients were noted to engage in a wide range of behaviors directed at seeking encouragement and physical assistance from the nurses. For example, some patients would go to the dining room door and just wait, as if waiting to be urged to go in. One patient was recorded approaching a nurse and commenting, "I haven't eaten yet today, should I go eat now?" All these approaches were ignored by the nurse, as instructed. When these help-seeking behaviors were not reinforced, they began to extinguish.

The experimenters then introduced a penny-in-the-slot arrangement whereby the patients were given a penny and required to place it in a slotted collection can before being granted access to the dining room. All patients learned the responses involved. Once this point had been established, the experimenters were able to use the pennies as reinforcers for other kinds of behavior, especially behavior of more importance in the patient's recovery than improvement in eating was. They established a situation in which social cooperation was essential in order for the patients to get the pennies.

Figure 16-2. The unassisted eating by mental patients. All assistance, persuasion, and spoonfeeding at mealtimes were removed. Following meal call, access to the dining room was gradually reduced from 30 minutes to 20, to 15, and finally to 5 minutes. (Allyon & Haughton, 1962.)

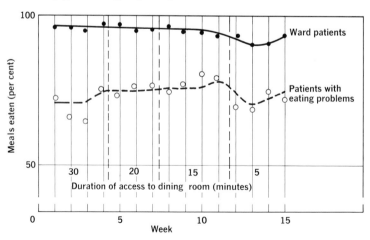

The task hinged on a device consisting of a table with doorbell buttons at each end and a red-light buzzer in the middle. To acquire pennies, the patients had to turn on the light and bell, which could only be done when both buttons were pressed simultaneously. As the buttons were 7½ feet apart, two people had to cooperate to push them at the same time. In order to get such co-operation, verbal interaction between patients was necessary, and thus they began to communicate with each other in a realistic manner. One year after this series of experiments was begun, all the patients, including the group who had had feeding problems, were continuing to take a diet as good as or better than they had before the experimental techniques were introduced.

Significance for Ward Management

Two general issues arise from this kind of demonstration. One is the simple fact that it is possible to change behavior without knowing the "underlying dynamics." From one point of view, we may argue that these patients' eating difficulties were generated by the hospital and thus were evidence of the excessive dependence that mental hospitals tend to foster. Thus the removal of reinforcement for help-seeking behavior is perhaps undoing a difficulty that was not central to the patient's psychopathology but was acquired as a concomitant of being institutionalized. What is hard to avoid is the observation that such behavior is most usually "explained" by recourse to complicated motivational speculations, and that these speculations are of little practical value in bringing about improvement in the patient. On the other hand, knowledge of what reinforcements are maintaining the behavior is of immense practical value in determining how to change it.

Secondly, these experiments indicate the possibilities for therapeutic changes by manipulating the ward environment, without prolonged, costly, and ineffective recourse to individual psychotherapy. Where the problem facing society is the large-scale rehabilitation of the hospitalized patient, methods such as this have encouraging possibilities.

PSYCHOTHERAPY

Definition

There are many definitions of psychotherapy current in the field of psychopathology. By the American Psychological Association it has been defined as "a process involving interpersonal relationships between a therapist and one or more patients or clients by which the former employs psychological methods based on systematic knowledge of the human personality in attempting to improve the mental health of the latter" (Raimy, 1950). Eysenck has suggested a definition involving six criteria, mainly taken from Winder (1957):

1. There is an interpersonal relationship of a prolonged kind between two or more people.
2. One of the participants has had special experience and/or has received special training in the handling of human relationships.
3. One or more of the participants have entered into the relationship because of a felt dissatisfaction with their emotional and/or interpersonal adjustment.
4. The methods used are of psychological nature, i.e. involve such mechanisms as explanation, suggestion, persuasion etc.
5. The procedure of the therapist is based upon some formal theory regarding mental disorder in general, and the specific disorder of the patient in particular.
6. The aim of the process is the amelioration of the difficulties which cause the patient to seek the help of the therapist.

(Eysenck, 1961, p. 698)

Both of these definitions have much in common, although the APA definition omits the criterion of "felt dissatisfaction" on the part of the patient. Some patients enter psychotherapy rather unwillingly, as the lesser of two evils—the other alternative being criminal prosecution for their behavior. Such patients may have little feeling of dissatisfaction with themselves, and so this criterion is probably less generally valid than are the others in Eysenck's definition. However, we shall base the discussion that follows upon his six points. Let us examine this definition from the point of view of the principles of general psychology.

Psychotherapy and General Psychology

A careful study of the details of the above definition reveals some terms that can stand further psychological analysis. One of these is the term *interpersonal relationship*. Consider two people who are responding to each other; their behavior is visible and audible to each other, and the responses of either member are contingent upon the prior responses of the other. When each member brings into the situation some response habits learned in previous situations, we shall find certain regularities in his behavior, regularities that may be discerned apart from the immediate factors in the present interaction. Thus the individual who is habitually witty, or querulous, or taciturn, etc., may behave in this way in many different interactions with many different people. When two people, such as a therapist and a patient, meet and interact over a number of separate occasions, their relationship might be defined by the kind of dominant pattern of responses that emerges from both of them. If one member is continually attacking the other, and the other is retaliating in kind, the relationship might be described as hostile or unfriendly.

But such statements are abstractions; the "relationship" is nothing more nor less than the behavior of the two people toward each other. There is no mystical communication, no immeasurable phenomenon involved. With long experience the two persons may begin to respond to nonverbal stimuli provided by each other, such as facial expressions, posture, manner of lighting a cigarette, etc. When this stage is reached, it is easy to assume that some unusual kind of communication has been established, and that this kind of communication occurs only or mainly in something defined as psychotherapy. From such assumptions it is natural to conclude that a psychotherapeutic relationship is different *in kind* from the interaction that takes place between two travelers conversing during a chance meeting on a train. There is no scientific basis for this assumption. We suggest strongly at this point that the variables operating in a psychotherapeutic relationship are those that operate in any social interaction, and that a special set of concepts is not necessary to describe or understand them.

Next let us consider the role of theory in the practice of psychotherapy. It is quite possible for an effective therapy to develop without benefit of theory at all. The history of medicine, indeed of science generally, is replete with examples of accidental discoveries of a purely empirical kind. Nearly two thousand years ago Celsus (cited by Francis Bacon) notes the usual sequence of events with his comment, "Medicine and cures are first found out and then afterwards reasons and causes were discussed; and not the causes first found out, and by light from them the medicines and cures discovered" (Bacon, 1605). The discovery of the antibacterial action of penicillin by Sir Alexander Fleming and its therapeutic development by Sir Howard Florey is now a classic example of just such chance empirical observation.[1]

When a therapy is derived from some prior body of knowledge about the disorder to which it is to be applied, it is termed a *rational* therapy. If the therapy is known to be effective, but the mechanisms by which it operates are unknown, then it is termed *nonrational*.[2] Effective therapies may be developed from theoretical bases as well as

[1] An excellent discussion of the role of chance discoveries in science and medicine is to be found in Beveridge (1950).
[2] Techniques that have neither rational basis nor evidence for their effectiveness are typical of the charlatan.

from fortuitous observation; because we cannot sit around waiting for accidental solutions to the problems of psychopathology, the gathering of knowledge about behavior seems to be the most sensible course to follow in our search for effective treatment methods.

Some thought should be given here to the extent to which the effectiveness of a therapy serves to *validate* the theory from which it was derived. Two sequences of events are likely in the development of therapy-theory relationships. In the first sequence, an effective therapy is discovered accidentally. The discoverer speculates about the processes by which the therapeutic variable brings about the observed improvement, and elaborates these speculations into a theory, or at least a series of articulated hypotheses. At this point, the theorist may test deductions from the theory (deductions having to do with events *other* than those that were originally observed in the therapy); as these deductions are confirmed, the theory gains validity. Alternatively, he may repeat his therapeutic procedures with another patient and find that they are still as effective as before. This procedure serves to establish the reliability of the therapy, but *it tells us nothing about the validity of the theory.*

A second sequence of events commences with the observation of behavior outside the therapy situation, let us say in the laboratory. From a large number of controlled studies a theory of behavior is built up. At an appropriate stage, this theory may be used to deduce that pathological behavior should be amenable to change by the application of certain techniques. These techniques are applied, the behavior changes, and a therapeutic outcome has been achieved. From the patient's point of view this was therapy; from the scientist's point of view it was a test of a theory using observations other than those that had given rise to the theory in the first place. As such, the success of the therapy serves to add to the validity of the theory.

The distinction that we have made between these two sequences is vitally important when we seek to evaluate claims that the success of a therapy supports the validity of the therapist's theory. It does so only in the second sequence, not in the first. Claims of this kind are not uncommon, and we should regard them conservatively until it is clear that they are not simply instances of the reliability of the therapy itself.

We may now consider the possible processes of psychotherapy, bearing in mind the definition and our reflections upon it. Let us do so at the outset from the point of view of the general psychology of learning.

PSYCHOTHERAPY AND THE PSYCHOLOGY OF LEARNING

Regardless of who referred the patient, the purpose of psychotherapy is to change some aspect of his behavior. Our discussion of pathology in Chapter 1 noted that there are certain gross categories of behavior which may be altered. We may seek to reduce the expression of distress—the verbal complaints made by the patient—without substantially altering other aspects of his behavior. Or we may be concerned to change some pattern of responses that may or may not be accompanied by verbal complaints. Eliminating delusional behavior, accentuating goal-seeking and socially effective behavior, and so on, would be examples of the latter. In brief, the purposes of psychotherapy are the *acquisition* and *extinction* of particular kinds of behavior. Some therapists may be satisfied with changes that are rather minimal, as in getting the patient to accept his own symptoms without altering the symptom. Whatever the goal of therapy, and however elaborate the therapist's account of what is going on "in" the patient, the evidence that any kind of change has occurred is necessarily behavioral—verbal or otherwise.

We have already seen that behavior may be changed in certain ways. Reinforcement, removal of reinforcement, and punishment will bring about significant alterations in ongoing response patterns. Modification of the biological mechanisms that mediate behavior will also produce changes. A learning approach to psychotherapy is concerned largely with the manipulation of reinforcements. It seeks also to discover the nature of the reinforcements that produce change in any kind of psychotherapy.

Principles in Reinforcement Manipulation

Much of our explanation of neurotic behavior rests upon the assumption that the symptoms develop from a conflict between approach and avoidance response tendencies. What makes us consider the response pathological is, in part at least, the facts that the avoidance component is inappropriate in terms of the reality in which the patient is living and that the symptom does not resolve the conflict. Thus one process that we may wish to instigate in therapy is the elimination of an avoidance response. Now as we saw several chapters ago, the extinction of an avoidance response is extremely difficult, requiring that the subject remain in the presence of the conditioned stimulus long enough to be influenced by the lack of an associated noxious stimulus. Because the defensive nature of the avoidance response prevents precisely this state of affairs from occurring naturally, it is necessary to restrain the subject from removing himself from the conditioned stimulus. Laboratory apparatus permits this to be done to animals with comparative simplicity. For the human patient in the natural habitat, such arrangements are not readily made.

Consequently, the extinction of the avoidance response must be accompanied by the reinforcement of the approach response, with the goal of reducing the conflict in favor of the dominance of the approach behavior. For example, let us consider a young woman patient who would like to marry and enjoy normal heterosexual relationships, but is unable to make even a preliminary approach to meeting a man because she has been punished by her mother for any interest in sexuality during her childhood. Consequently, she avoids men and becomes extremely anxious should circumstances compel her to be in male company for any length of time.

The task of the therapist here would be to reinforce any preliminary approach responses that the patient might exhibit and to ensure that they are not inadvertently punished. Ultimately, his task is to produce this behavior in the general environment of the patient, not just in the weekly hour of psychotherapy. On the face of it, there are two possibilities open to him. One of these is to attempt to manipulate the patient's environment directly by working with relatives, friends, employers, etc., instructing them in techniques for reinforcing the patient's actions. With outpatients this may not be a practical possibility, although there is very little evidence that it has been tried systematically as yet. Hospitalized patients, however, are living in an environment in which great control over the actions of others in relation to him is possible. Nurses, attendants, and staff generally can be "programmed" to reinforce behavior that the therapist regards as desirable.

A second possibility, and one that is implicit in the vast bulk of individual psychotherapy, is that the therapist will be able to act as a reinforcer personally during therapy, and that the changed behavior of the patient in his office will generalize to the rest of the patient's environment. For this to happen, the therapist must become a potent reinforcer for the patient, so as to establish the desired responses with sufficient strength to ensure generalization to the patient's natural habitat. Additionally the therapist must be somewhat similar to the important figures in the patient's conflict, so that generalization and not discrimination will occur. This latter requirement poses some rather interesting problems, since the therapist must also be sufficiently different from the key figures in the patient's life that he will not produce strong avoidance responses in the patient.

Many therapies of an avowedly nonlearning-theory type are based upon the principle that the patient must undergo a learning experience in relation to the therapist, and not merely spend the time in describing experiences that he has had or is having elsewhere. Learning experiences of this kind are sometimes labeled a "transference neurosis" (e.g., by psychoanalysts) and involve the generalization into the therapy session of the behaviors that are related to the problems existing outside the session. Once the transference neurosis has been resolved, i.e., when the therapist has manipulated the reinforcements in therapy so that the patient is now responding in a desirable fashion, it is assumed that the new behaviors will carry over to the key situations in the environment. Improvement of the patient's behavior during therapy may not generalize to other circumstances. Hence the judgment of the therapist that the patient has improved in therapy is irrelevant to the question of cure unless it is supported by evidence that the patient is behaving more appropriately outside.

Returning to our hypothetical woman patient, we can see that a therapist might be in a position to extinguish her fear of verbalizing sexual interests by initiating lines of discussion likely to elicit such expressions, by threatening therapeutic failure should she keep anything hidden, and by expressing interest and maintaining a nonpunitive attitude when she responds with sexual material. As the patient makes this kind of response and is not punished for it, her anxiety is reduced slightly by extinction, and it will be a little more probable that she can make another response of the same kind. What we should expect to find is that the patient experiences episodes of anxiety following each new emergence of the developing approach response, and thus that there will be attempts to escape from therapy, to avoid discussing dangerous topics, and so on. The therapist must not permit these to be effective, and thus his task will be to bring the patient back to face the avoided topic. This may be accompanied by admonishment for "resistance."

Somewhere in this process, if the therapist is a male, the reduction in the fear of sexual response may lead to the occurrence of sexual approaches in some form to the therapist. If the therapist is not to undo all that he has achieved, he is faced with a rather subtle task. He must avoid punishing the behavior while managing to avoid reinforcing it. One possible method is to ignore preliminary indications of this kind, anticipating that some of these responses will now be occurring outside therapy in relation to some suitable male who will reinforce them directly, thus solving the problem. If this does not happen, the therapist may decide to "interpret" the patient's behavior in such a way that he is excused from having to take it personally. Thus if the patient is permitted to get to the point of telling the therapist that she loves him, the therapist does not punish her by saying, "Well, I don't love you." What he may do is to point out that while her behavior is appropriate as such, her choice of goal object is not, and is instead an indication that she loves someone else (e.g., her father).

An excellent illustration of this kind of sequence is given by Goldstein and Palmer (1963), discussing the course in treatment of a young married woman who was experiencing difficulties in her sexual relationship with her husband. During 2½ years the patient was seen in outpatient therapy three times weekly.

At first she was quite loquacious, reciting much of the above history with many brief intellectual insights. She attributed much of her problem to the fact that she was "Daddy's little girl," saying that she had never really grown up. She began to dress in a more adult fashion, using more cosmetics and wearing revealing blouses or knit dresses that emphasized her shapely figure. Her walk and mannerisms became markedly seductive. She made many slips of speech, particularly referring to her father as her husband or vice versa. Once she slipped and said "Daddy" instead of doctor in addressing her therapist. When these slips were called to her attention, and it was suggested that she confused her husband, father and therapist, she would either smile sweetly and remain silent or attempt to make a joke of it, "Oh you and your psychology!" After several months she reported that her sexual relations with her husband had improved markedly. "I'm so sexy every night that poor Bobby just can't keep up with me." She interpreted this change in her feelings to mean that her main problems had been resolved. She had about decided to stop treatment, but changed her mind, saying, "I guess you've just become a habit with me." Shortly thereafter she became increasingly silent and obviously depressed. Whereas previously she had always been prompt for her appointments now she was frequently late and several times cancelled the appointment. It was suggested to her that her resistance might be the result of some feelings she might have regarding the therapist. She hotly denied this interpretation and became increasingly angry at the therapist, saying that she felt that he was pressuring her into something, to the extent that she felt as if she were being raped. Attempts to get her to explore these feelings further met with stormy silence. Finally, in tears, she admitted that she had recently had several dreams wherein she imagined the therapist making love to her. Following this revelation she had another brief amnesic period which lasted one day. She wandered the streets not remembering who she was, and finally found herself standing in front of the clinic. (P. 77.)

Generalization and Psychotherapy

We may summarize the main burden of the previous paragraphs by itemizing the major steps in psychotherapy in the following way.

1. The patient brings into the psychotherapy session a set of responses to the therapist that are largely generalized from important conflicts existing in the patient's life.

2. The therapist deals with these responses by appropriate handling of the social reinforcements that he is providing, seeking to produce resolutions of the neurotic behaviors of the patient in relation to himself.

3. When, and if, this is achieved the expectation is that the new behaviors learned in therapy will now generalize back to the patient's daily life.

We can see, therefore, that the meaning of the patient's behavior in therapy demands that we assume the operation of generalization. The expectation that improvement in therapy will be accompanied by improvement in the rest of the patient's life is also based upon the assumption that generalization will take place.

Clearly, the successful manipulation of reinforcements is a highly skilled task, and one that requires the therapist to be aware of the nature of the reinforcements that are maintaining the neurotic behavior generally. Also, he must be aware of the many behaviors that he may be reinforcing inadvertently during therapy, behaviors that may militate against improvement. We have already seen how the solicitude of a nurse can help to maintain a feeding problem in psychotic patients. Let us consider some of the possible reinforcements available in psychotherapy that may be detrimental to improvement.

Inadvertent Reinforcement in Psychotherapy

Certain kinds of psychotherapy are extremely expensive. Thus the fact that a patient is undergoing psychoanalysis may have implications of affluence much like those related to driving an ostentatious automobile. In addition, the status of a patient in psychotherapy may imply that he is sufficiently complicated to have problems and is likewise undergoing an experience of some special value not shared by more humdrum acquaintances. In brief, in some social groups there is a certain kind of superficial prestige to be obtained by making it known that one is undergoing psychotherapy. Reinforcements of this kind tend to keep the patient in therapy and to operate against the kind of behavior changes that the therapist is seeking to achieve.

If the therapist is convinced that the process of psychotherapy inevitably requires some self-revelations along specified lines, e.g., the description of previously forgotten material, the discussion of aggression, sexuality, guilt, and so forth, he is likely to be uninterested in material that seems to be covering up the crucial discussions. When the patient talks about material that the therapist has been trained to believe has special significance, the therapist is apt to be interested and attentive. When the patient talks about material that the therapist believes to be "superficial," the therapist is likely to be bored and unresponsive or negative. Under such circumstances the therapist is very likely to reinforce certain kinds of verbal behavior and to punish or extinguish others. These reinforcements and punishment are quite subtle, and consist of expressions and gestures of attention, or signs of disinterest and complaints of the patient's "resistance."

Should the therapist be unaware of his own effect upon the patient's conversation in this way, then all he may notice is that the content of the therapy session is getting more and more "significant." This may appear to confirm his theory that when you have time "to get down deep" you invariably discover that the problem is one of the few that the theory predicts. In fact, all it confirms is that the therapist is interested in some kinds of topics and not in others. Unfortunately this process of reinforcing the patient for discovering problems that the therapist would like to see him admit may be utterly irrelevant to the problem of changing the patient's behavior. At one extreme it may simply conclude with the patient accepting the therapist's definition of his problem and the therapist's theory about its connection with the behavior. Meanwhile the behavior may remain much as it was before therapy started.

Summary. Our contention here is that the verbal interactions that go on in any kind of face-to-face communication constitute reinforcing, punishing, and extinguishing experiences for some kinds of verbal response. The changes of behavior that are thus induced may generalize to the non-therapy environment of the patient. If they do not, then the relearning that has taken place in therapy has been of little avail. The relearning processes that are central to psychotherapy may not be recognized by the therapist, who may have very elaborate conceptual schemes to account for the changes that he sees. We should expect that, inasmuch as a marked improvement in a patient constitutes a reinforcement for the therapist, experienced therapists learn techniques that are increasingly similar and effective and that are largely unrelated to the theoretical language in which they choose to describe their cases.

However, some psychotherapists have systematically sought to apply the principles of learning in therapy, and we should examine the methods and results of some of these.

PSYCHOTHERAPY BASED UPON BEHAVIORAL SCIENCE

Psychotherapy Based upon Learning Theory

Two significant applications of learning theory to psychotherapy have been reported in recent years. One of these is the *social learning* theory of J. B. Rotter (1954), and the other is the *interference* theory of E. Lakin Phillips (1956). Earlier attempts were made to translate the terms and concepts of psychoanalytic theory into a learning framework, notably by Dollard and Miller (1950), but since this attempt did not lead to any modification in the recommended practices of psychotherapy, it had little practical import. We shall discuss the other two theories here at this point.

Rotter's Social Learning Theory. Rotter (1954) has emphasized the necessity for the therapist to deliberately reinforce certain kinds of behavior in therapy. Of central importance, he feels, is the reinforcement of the response of looking for alternate solutions to problems of life. We may perhaps regard the neurotic person as suffering from a rigidity of behavior whereby his anxieties lead him to overlook the solutions to his difficulties. On this point, Rotter comments:

It is the purpose of therapy not to solve all of the patient's problems, but rather to increase the patient's ability to solve his own problems. . . . From a social learning point of view, one of the most important aspects of treatment, particularly face-to-face treatment, is to reinforce in the patient the expectancy that problems are solvable by looking for alternative solutions. (Rotter, 1954, p. 342.)

One experimental investigation in the effectiveness of this technique is reported by Morton (1949), who gave a group of maladjusted students training in methods of seeking alternative solutions to human problems. A matched group of similar students did not receive this training. Measures of adjustment both before and after taken in both groups showed a significant improvement in adjustment indices for the experimental group over the control group. Maher and Katkovsky (1961) studied the long-term outcomes of therapy in a clinical setting where the technique emphasized the manipulation of reinforcements by parents of children with psychological problems. The role of the therapist was to counsel the parent in appropriate techniques for the acquisition and extinction of relevant behavior. Compared with the parents of this group was a group of parents who sought such help but did not receive it for lack of facilities. These data are given in Table 16-3. As the table indicates, there were several areas of significant improvement for the treated versus the nontreated group. In this study, the criterion of improvement was provided by the parents' estimate of the posttreatment status of the child's difficulties, thereby eliminating the ambiguities that arise when the therapist is judge of his own effectiveness.

Principles of scientific psychology, derived from controlled experimentation, have now begun to be used as a basis for the treatment of the deviant behavior of individual patients. Two general approaches are used by learning-theory therapists. One employs the therapist as a verbal reinforcer in face-to-face verbal therapy. Thus the therapist is using learning-theory principles to guide his own responses to the patient, but is dealing mainly with the behaviors that he can elicit in the therapy session. Since much of the time he will not be observing the major

TABLE 16-3 Parents' Estimates of Severity of the Problem, and of Their Worry about It, Following Brief Therapy

	Treatment group			Control group		
1. In general would you say the problem about which you consulted us:						
a. no longer exists	20	20*	40%	8	8	19%
b. has improved	23	23	46%	15	15	37%
c. is about the same	6⎫			15⎫		
d. is worse than before	1⎭	7	14%	3⎭	18	44%
		N = 50			N = 41	
2. If the problem has not completely cleared up, how would you describe your present feelings about it compared to time of consultation?						
a. more worried	2⎫			10⎫		
b. worries us about as much	3⎭	5*	17%	15⎭	25	76%
c. less worried	16⎫			6⎫		
d. not worried at all	9⎭	25	83%	2⎭	8	24%
		N = 30			N = 33	

* *Difference of the distributions between the two groups significant beyond the .05 level.*
SOURCE: *Maher & Katkovsky (1961).*

pathology of the patient, but only some generalized version of it, the effectiveness of this procedure hinges largely upon the extent to which new behaviors learned in therapy generalize outside. However, a second group of workers emphasize direct application of conditioning to the patient's behavior and use procedures that are taken, *mutatis mutandis,* from the laboratory. Let us examine both of these approaches.

Lakin Phillips's Assertion Therapy. The theoretical position taken by Lakin Phillips (1956) notes that the behavior of people is determined by their beliefs about the outcomes (reinforcements) that a given course of action will produce. When these beliefs conflict with other beliefs that imply a contradictory outcome, then a state of tension arises. Tension may also arise when the environment fails to provide the expected outcomes but where the belief is held with high strength because of a long history of reinforcement. Tension, acting as a motivator, produces stronger responses and also engenders symptomatic responses. Phillips has preferred the term "assertion" to denote a belief about the reinforcement that will attend a given response.

For Phillips the specific form or "content" of a symptom is largely irrelevant to the nature of the conflict between assertions. Thus detailed examination of the symptom will tell us little about the events that gave rise to it. Because the symptom does not dispel the assertion, the tension continues and the assertion meets with even greater frustration when the patient attempts to get the environment to confirm it, i.e., to provide the hoped-for reinforcement.

Therapeutic techniques devised by Phillips consist in large part in drawing the attention of the patient to what he is doing and to the inadequacy of his current solutions. In the sense that the patient is being helped to become aware of his current behavior patterns, the therapist might be said to be providing "insight." Insofar as "insight" means that the patient is being led to accept a certain theory about the childhood origins

of his disorder, assertion therapy is not an insight therapy.

Empirical research on the effectiveness of this kind of therapy has been reported by Phillips (1956), who deals incidentally with the crucial factor of the *efficiency* as well as the effectiveness of assertion therapy versus "depth" therapy of the psychoanalytic kind. Efficiency, an extremely important criterion to consider in evaluating any therapy, may be computed by taking the number of cases who actually improved (by some objective measure) as a percentage of those who *applied* for therapy, whether or not the therapist accepted them. Many patients, as we shall see shortly, improve whether they are treated or not. The control group data in the Maher and Katkovsky (1961) study, for example, show that some kinds of problems improve anyway. An experienced clinician soon learns that some behavioral problems have a good prognosis and others a poor prognosis; by selecting those with a good prognosis and rejecting those with a poor one, the clinician's effectiveness may seem to be quite impressive. If we include the number of cases rejected by the clinician for reasons other than lack of time (e.g., because they are "poor risks" for therapy), then we can compute a general index of efficiency, which might be much lower than the index of effectiveness. Phillips's comparison is shown in Table 16-4. We see that the efficiency and effectiveness of the assertion therapy method is the same, no applicants having been refused by the therapist. It is also higher than either index for the psychoanalytically oriented therapy.

So far the results of verbal therapy based upon established principles of learning seem to be promising. We may now turn to consider the recent developments in the application of direct conditioning procedures to pathological behavior. As a matter of fact, we have already encountered the basic technique as it was applied by Allyon and Haughton (1962) in their modification of feeding problems in schizophrenic patients. The use of direct conditioning, counter-

TABLE 16-4 Comparing the Efficiency and Effectiveness of Hypothetical (Ideal) Therapy, Assertion-structured Therapy, and Depth-oriented Therapy

	No. applying for therapy	No. treated from among applicants	No. refused treatment by clinicians	No. who themselves refuse treatment	No. completing 3 or more interviews	No. benefited by 3 or more interviews	Percentage of original applicants benefited
Hypothetical group	100	90	5	5	90	90	81%
Assertion-structured therapy	59	53		6	53	51	86.4%
Psychoanalytic depth-oriented therapy	190	45	103	42	45	21* (patients' rating) 33* (therapists' rating)	11.05%* (patients' rating) 17.3%* (therapists' rating)

* Therapists' ratings were available for all 45 patients who completed 3 or more interviews. Only 27 of these 45 patients returned questionnaires rating their therapy experience; the 21 who rated themselves as having improved somewhat supplied the figure used here.
SOURCE: *Phillips (1956).*

conditioning, extinction, and other procedures in the treatment of pathology has been generally described under the heading of *behavior therapy.* Eysenck, his colleagues, and students in London have been particularly active in developing these techniques, and we shall be drawing largely from their work in the following account of behavior therapy.

Behavior Therapy

In an excellent, though brief, account of behavior therapy, Rachman (1963) has tentatively identified the major relearning and unlearning techniques that have been used by behavior therapists.

1. Desensitization based upon relaxation.
2. Operant conditioning of the adaptive response.
3. Aversive conditioning.
4. Training in assertive behavior.
5. Use of sexual responses.
6. Use of feeding responses.
7. Extinction based upon negative practice.
8. Anxiety-relief responses.

One of the earliest illustrations of behavior therapy in practice was provided by Jones (1924). She treated a three-year-old boy (Peter) who showed fears of white rats, rabbits, fur objects, cotton, and so forth. Jones decided to eliminate the fear of rabbits by inducing a competing response in the presence of the rabbit. Peter was placed in a playroom with three fearless playmates, and a rabbit in a cage was introduced into the room at some distance away. Peter continued to play, and the rabbit was progressively brought closer to him as his toleration of it improved. Finally Peter was able to tolerate the rabbit moving freely in the room, and ultimately was able to fondle it. Another technique employed by Jones was the provision of food (a positive reinforcement) in the presence of the rabbit, so that the latter became a conditioned stimulus for the positive responses associated with the food.

Such methods are not startling. The technique of providing pleasant rewards when a child overcomes some fear is not at all unusual in the practices of many parents. The fact that this technique is not uncommon suggests that it is relatively effective in the natural habitat and that we might hesitate to abandon it for less rational procedures until they have proved more effective.

Aversive Conditioning. The principle employed in aversive conditioning is that of punishing some preliminary aspects of the pathological behavioral sequence. When this is done, the preliminary aspects become conditioned stimuli for the onset of anxiety. Termination of the pathological behavior produces removal of the punishing stimulus —the US—and thus the response involved in termination becomes reinforced by its power to reduce the anxiety generated by the preliminary pathological responses. Repeated trials should have the effect of conditioning anxiety to preliminary responses that occur at progressively earlier points in the chain, including the stimuli that ordinarily invoke the pathological response. Behaviorally this means that during the first treatment trials, the patient should become anxious as he begins to make the pathological response and should terminate it "in midstream." This termination point will occur sooner and sooner on subsequent trials until the point is reached at which the patient does not even begin the pathological sequence at all.

Blakemore, Thorpe, Barker, Conway, and Lavin (1963) report the techniques of aversive conditioning as they were used to treat a patient who had a behavioral symptom of transvestism (wearing the clothes of the opposite sex). This case, described in Example 16-1, illustrates the procedure of aversive conditioning.

EXAMPLE 16-1
Aversive-conditioning Therapy

The patient was a male, aged thirty-three, married, who had engaged in transvestite behavior from approximately the age of twelve years. He had dressed in his mother's and sister's clothes before that age, but the frequency of the compulsion to do so did not become clear until this point. His transvestism was interrupted by military service, but was replaced during that time by transvestite fantasies. During this period he developed a duodenal ulcer.

He subsequently married, but found that it was necessary for him to cross-dress in order to engage in normal sexual relations. He frequently went about in public at night dressed in female attire and wearing a female wig. His motivations for treatment appeared to be strong: they included a fear of legal difficulties were he discovered cross-dressed in public, consideration for his wife, and concern about his young son should the latter discover his problem. The patient had had six years of psychotherapy and had been using sodium amytal to reduce tension. He had become addicted to the drug, and the symptoms remained unchanged.

The treatment consisted essentially of repeated trials wherein the patient received painful shock at a point where he had partially completed the sequence of getting dressed in female clothes. During treatment the patient was standing on a grid through which shock could be delivered, and the details of the method are given by the authors as follows:

"At the beginning of each session the patient, dressed only in a dressing gown, was brought into a specially prepared room and was told to stand on the grid behind the screen. On the chair beside him was his "favorite outfit" of female clothing, which he had been told to bring with him at his first attendance. These clothes had not been tampered with for the most part, with the exception that slits had been cut in the feet of nylon stockings and a metal plate fitted into the soles of the black court shoes to act as a conductor. Each trial commenced with the instruction to start dressing, at which he removed the dressing gown and began to put on female clothing. At some point during the course of dressing, he received a signal to start undressing irrespective of the number of garments he was wearing at that time. This signal was either a shock from the electric grid or the sound of a buzzer, and these were randomly ordered on a fifty per cent basis over the 400 trials. The shock or buzzer recurred at intervals until he had completed his undressing. He was allowed a one minute rest period between each of the five trials which made up a treatment session.

"In order that the number of garments put on should not be constant from trial to trial, the time allowed from the start of dressing to the onset of the recurrent shock or buzzer was randomly varied between one and three minutes among the trials. It was possible, also, that the patient's undressing behavior would become stereotyped if the interval between the successive shocks or soundings of the buzzer remained constant from trial to trial, therefore, while these intervals were kept constant within a trial, they were randomly varied between 5, 10 and 15 seconds among trials. The explanation of the procedure given to the patient before treatment commenced did not contain any reference to the randomization of these variables, and did not include any instructions pertaining to the speed of undressing. At the start of each new trial the patient did not know, therefore, how long it would be before he received the signal to undress, whether this would be a shock or the buzzer, or the frequency with which these would recur during his undressing." (Blakemore et al., 1963, pp. 31–32.)

Following this treatment, the patient was discharged. A follow-up report showed no recurrence of transvestism over a six-month period. Of perhaps equal if not greater importance is the patient's observation that he was generally less anxious than he had been for some time and was taking less sodium amytal than he had for several years. If we insist on regarding symptoms as merely the "surface" evidence of a more fundamental anxiety, then elimination of the symptom should leave the anxiety untouched, and a new symptom should appear rapidly to take the place of the old one. Such a sequence seems not to have occurred here, indicating the fact that symptoms may persist in life largely as learned responses, and that their existence may *generate* anxiety, rather than be a consequence of it.

Operant Conditioning. We have already seen how the principles of operant conditioning may be utilized to reinforce desired behaviors and extinguish undesirable behaviors (Allyon & Haughton, 1962). A more detailed account of the rationale for the procedures used is presented in Example 16-2, a case demonstration by Allyon (1963).

Desensitization Techniques. Wolpe (1954, 1958, 1962) has used the principles of conditioning to develop a technique that he calls *systematic desensitization*. The technique is in turn based upon the principle of reciprocal inhibition. Because neurotic behavior is acquired in anxiety-provoking conditions, successful treatment of neurosis requires the reinforcement of some response that is antagonistic to anxiety. This response should be reinforced in the presence of a stimulus that ordinarily generates the neurotic anxiety. Wolpe has emphasized the importance of muscular relaxation as a counteragent to anxiety, and this is one of the more important responses that he attempts to establish.

An additional technical aspect of this kind of therapy is the use of the principle of stimulus generalization. The antagonistic response is first conditioned to a stimulus that has only minor power to evoke anxiety, but whose power to do so is based upon its relationship to the most anxiety-provoking stimulus. Stimuli that produce neurotic anxiety are therefore ranked into *hierarchies* by the patient from the most to the least anxiety-arousing. Such hierarchies clearly represent a gradient of stimulus generalization, with the least disturbing elements being further out on the gradient. Once these hierarchies have been categorized, the therapist introduces one of the least disturbing items in the presence of the patient while the latter is relaxing; the patient is instructed to signal to the therapist any onset of tension, whereupon the stimulus is removed.

Once a patient has established relaxation as a response in the presence of a low item on the hierarchy, items of higher rank are introduced over a number of sessions. Each therapeutic session is terminated with an item that is lower on the hierarchy, to ensure that the patient does not leave the

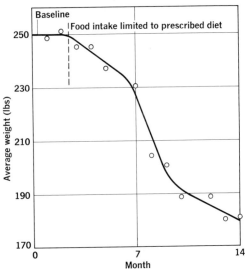

Figure 16-3. The effective control of food stealing results in a notable reduction of body weight. As the patient's food intake is limited to the prescribed diet, her weight decreases gradually. (Allyon, 1963.)

EXAMPLE 16-2

Operant-conditioning Therapy

The patient was a female, aged forty-seven years, who had been hospitalized for nine years. She presented three behavioral symptoms that had incapacitated her socially and caused considerable nursing problems on the ward. These consisted of food stealing, hoarding hospital towels in her room, and wearing excessive clothing. She typically wore half a dozen dresses, many pairs of stockings, towels draped over her head, and so forth. Her overeating had constituted a serious hazard to her health, as she had weighed over 250 pounds for some years. Although placed on a special diet, she refused to cooperate with this arrangement and continued to steal food from other patients and from the dining room counter. The current nursing technique with this patient included coaxing, explanations, and so forth.

To eliminate this behavior, it was necessary to ensure that it did not receive reinforcement. Consequently all coaxing and cajoling was discontinued, and the nurses were instructed to remove the patient from the dining room whenever she approached a table other than her own or picked up unauthorized food from the dining counter. This technique was continued until the patient's weight fell to 180 pounds. The effect of the treatment upon the patient's weight is given in Figure 16-3.

In dealing with the patient's towel hoarding, the therapist utilized the principle of *stimulus satiation*. Ordinarily, a count of towels in this woman's room revealed anywhere from 19 to 29 on hand, not including those that the nurses recovered between counts. Treatment consisted of discontinuing the practice of removing surplus towels from the patient's room. Instead, intermittently during the day a nurse would take a towel to the patient and hand

Psychological Methods of Treatment in Psychopathology

it to her without comment. During the first week she was given an average of 7 towels a day, and in the third week this figure was raised to 60 towels a day. When the towels in her room totaled 625, she began to take some of them out. At this point the technique was discontinued. During the following year the mean number of towels found in her room was between 1 and 2 per week. The manner in which satiation succeeded in making the towels aversive to the patient is well illustrated by the following comments made to the nurse as the latter brought a towel to her room.

First week: "Oh, you found it for me, thank you."
Second week: "Don't give me no more towels, I've got enough."
Third week: "Take them towels away . . . I can't sit here all night and fold towels."
Fourth week: "Get these dirty towels out of here."
Sixth week: (After beginning to take the towels out of her room): "I can't drag any more of these towels, I just can't do it."

The third problem, that of overdressing, was handled by requiring the patient to be below a certain weight (measured on the scales) before being allowed to enter the dining room. Specified weights were established that represented the patient's known body weight plus some extra pounds for clothing. Thus she could reduce her weight to the desired maximum by removing some of her clothing. Initially the limit set was 2 pounds less than her usual weight when overdressed. As the patient met each requirement, the limit was set successively lower until she reached a point where the clothing worn weighed only 3 pounds.

Figure 16-4 indicates the progress of this patient from the beginning to the end of the experiment. The patient removed excess clothing to this extent over a ten-week period. One accompaniment of this improvement was that the patient's social activities improved: her parents took her home for a visit for the first time in the nine years that she had been hospitalized. Previously they had been unwilling to do this because they felt that her overweight plus the excessive dressing made her look like a "circus freak."

therapy situation while experiencing anxiety. If this precaution were not observed, there would be some measurable risk that leaving the therapist's office would be associated with anxiety reduction, making it unlikely that the patient would return for further treatment.

Where the stimuli in the hierarchy are not directly available for the therapist's use, their introduction may be managed by instructing the subject to visualize one of the stimulus situations. This use of visualization is itself assisted by the state of deep and almost hypnotic relaxation that is achieved with the patient. Visualization of items higher up the hierarchy then proceeds as it

would with the actual stimuli. Example 16-3 illustrates the process.

General Considerations of Behavior Therapy. From the standpoint of science, behavior therapies have two outstanding merits. In the first place, the methods used are derived systematically from principles established many times in the laboratory; the behavior therapist has not been driven to develop a vast mental apparatus to account for his results. Secondly, the methods of treatment and the measurements of improvement are readily communicable to another person. Thus the treatment procedures may be replicated elsewhere, the results quantified, and

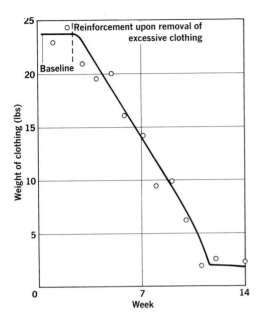

Figure 16-4. A response, excessive dressing, is eliminated when food reinforcement is made dependent upon removal of superfluous clothing. Once the weight of the clothing worn by the patient drops to 3 pounds, it remains stable. (Allyon, 1963.)

conclusions drawn about the efficacy of the technique. As such the behavior therapies resemble the rational therapies used in medical treatment of organic disease, or in the educational treatment of ignorance.

On the doubtful side, there are few accounts yet of long-term follow-up measures, i.e., for five years or more. Such data are desirable not because of any problems of "repressed symptoms," but because of what we know about the spontaneous recovery of previously extinguished responses.

Behavior therapy is not predicated upon any rejection of the notion that maladaptive responses may have developed as a consequence of childhood experience. It is predicated upon the belief that the circumstances of acquisition are often irrelevant to the problem of extinction. Length processes of "digging" to "uncover" the details of the acquisition do not produce removal of the behavioral problem, whereas systematic application of the principles of learning to bring about behavior change will. It seems difficult to doubt that the behavior

EXAMPLE 16-3

Desensitization Therapy

The patient was a woman, married, aged thirty-one. As reported by Clark (1963), she suffered from a phobia of birds and feathers. Amongst the consequences of this she was unable to go for walks out of doors, to go to parks, or to take her two-year-old son to zoos for fear the birds might come near her or swoop over her. She had been compelled to use foam rubber pillows in her house and had had an anxiety attack when a store clerk offered a hat with a feather in it for her to try on.

"Systematic desensitization was then instituted by the following technique. It was arranged for the patient to be available as an out-patient for about 30 to 45 minutes once a week. The patient was asked to sit in a comfortable armchair in the psychologist's darkened office, and told to relax. Mild hypnosis was then induced after the dorsal-palmer electrodes of a G.S.R. apparatus had been fixed to her left hand and the apparatus balanced. In this drowsy and suggestible state the patient was then told that she would feel utterly relaxed and free from anxiety, that she would be unworried throughout the course of the entire session. At this point it was usually noted that skin resistance tended to go up and the G.S.R. was rebalanced. The patient was then told that she would gradually return to full wakefulness, but would continue in a limp and relaxed posture and mood, as the psychologist counted from 10 to 1. After some words of reassurance the patient was then shown, on the first occasion, a single feather at some 12 ft. distance. If any subjective feelings of apprehension were felt she was to say so immediately and the stimulus, i.e. feather, would be withdrawn. The galvanometer needle was also watched carefully for drops in resistance reflecting sympathetic nervous system changes below the threshold of subjective appreciation. This was of some importance, since autonomic reactions were to be deconditioned as much as subjective feelings. If no adverse signs were noticed the feather was brought closer to the patient until it was no more than a foot away. The stimulus was then removed and further efforts at relaxation and calmness were suggested to the patient hypnotically. One session consisted of 3 or 4 such trials. At the slightest sign of apprehension the stimulus was immediately removed, and reiterations of instructions were soothingly made until G.S.R. readings returned to normal. If the patient, after these trials showed, either objectively or subjectively, no apprehension or anxiety, then the next item in the stimulus hierarchy was proceeded with at the next session. Each session lasted about 30 to 40 minutes." (Clark, 1963, p. 64–65.)

therapies represent the most rational and promising avenues to the treatment of neurotic behavior that we have seen.

OTHER FORMS OF VERBAL TREATMENT

We have already discussed the probable kinds of learning experience that occur in verbal interactions between a therapist and his patient, no matter what the doctrinal persuasion of the former. However, there are many different doctrines current among professional psychotherapists, and it is customary to describe them in the same terms as their protagonists might use. We shall not do so here. Detailed discussion of these doctrines would fill (and has filled) many books. Some appropriate sources are listed at the end of the chapter as an aid to the curious reader.

The Evaluation of Psychological Therapeutic Methods

Evaluation of the effects of a treatment must be conducted in the same way as any other experimental comparison between two conditions of an independent variable. Because psychological therapies are conducted with people in distress, and carried on with an appropriate sense of compassion and urgency, the processes of random assignment

to treatment, withholding of treatment for research purposes, and so forth are very unlikely to occur. Published figures issued by hospitals and clinics therefore provide a very poor basis for scientific conclusions about therapeutic effectiveness. Nevertheless, this kind of report constitutes the most common source of data available for such assessments. Most of the methodological requirements for reliable comparison have been outlined already in Chapter 5 to which the reader is referred at this point. However, some other issues deserve especial study because of their significance in evaluating the reports presently available to us in the literature.

Selection of Patients for Psychotherapy

Considerable point to Phillips's comparison in efficiency is given by an excellent example of the variables that enter into the application of a particular kind of therapy to a patient. Discussing the phenomena of drop-out rate (i.e., premature termination of therapy) at the Hutchinson Memorial Clinic of Tulane University, Lief, Lief, Warren, and Heath (1961) describe the application procedure as follows:

All applicants fill out an application. On the basis of the information on the application, a few patients are rejected without being seen. This group includes patients with repeated hospitalizations for psychosis, severe psychopaths and a miscellaneous group of patients who seem like poor risks for intensive psychotherapy. This screening eliminates less than 5 per cent of the applicants. . . .

Those applicants who pass this screening are then interviewed for admission, and a decision is made on the basis of two or sometimes three interviews by the clinic psychiatric staff. From these interviews and an admissions conference, a decision is made whether or not to accept the patient in psychotherapy. Over a ten-year period, this clinic received 1,261 applications, of which 627 were accepted, the rejection rate being therefore almost exactly 50 per cent. Comparisons of demographic data on the rejected and accepted groups from a consecutive sample of 350 in these two categories show that the accepted patient is likely to be younger and better-educated than the rejected patient. Commenting on the fate of the rejected applicants, the authors noted:

> Since we feel an obligation to place in treatment as many of the applicants to the Tulane Clinic as possible, we refer those who are rejected to other clinics and agencies. Many of the better treatment cases are referred to the "medical students clinic," a clinic in which the therapists are third and fourth year medical students supervised by members of the department of psychiatry. . . . Other patients are referred to the Tulane University outpatient psychiatry clinic at Charity Hospital and to other treatment centers or agencies in New Orleans. (P. 110.)

Here we see in operation a selective filtering whereby the "best" patients are admitted to the clinic, the next-best are sent to a preferred alternative clinic, and the others end up elsewhere. In this clinic the preferred method of treatment is therapy involving "insight," but the authors comment upon the potentialities of "new methods of psychotherapy being evolved based on greater activity of the therapist as well as on methods of desensitization. These may involve hypnosis, relaxation and suggestion or com-

binations of these. Certainly drug therapy would have its greatest application with this group of patients," and later, "It is a wasteful procedure to include the lower classes of patients in clinics where the main emphasis is on teaching insight therapy. At the same time we cannot effectively perform our jobs as psychiatrists in terms of the mental health of the community unless we can discover methods of treatment appropriate to those people in the lower class positions, or utilize more effectively those now in existence." As the kind of patient being described here—the lower-class patient—is more numerous in fact and more likely in terms of probabilities to develop pathological problems, it seems to this writer a striking waste of time to continue to train clinicians to perform a service even the practitioners of which report is of no value to the bulk of the population of the mentally ill!

Clearly, when we wish to evaluate the relative effects of a treatment upon a given class of disorders, we must ensure that both methods of treatment are applied to comparable samples of patients, preferably being assigned randomly to one method or the other. Likewise, if we wish to compare treatment versus no treatment, we must make sure that the patients are not preselected into the treatment group. Otherwise we may be demonstrating nothing more than the ability of the admissions officer to detect the kind of patient who will get better anyway.

Spontaneous Recovery

When patients are not given specialized psychotherapeutic treatment, many of them show improvement in their psychological condition anyway. One of the most exhaustive studies of this spontaneous recovery effect is provided by Denker (1946). He reported on the course of recovery of individuals diagnosed as neurotic who had disabilities severe enough to warrant insurance payments for nonemployment. These patients were treated by their own physicians with sedatives, suggestion, tonics, and reassurance, but in no case was any treatment given that would constitute other than very superficial "psychotherapy." Denker's patients were all insured with a private life insurance company for health insurance. They had some financial incentive to remain sick, as they were receiving payment while they were disabled. All of them appear to have been drawn from income classes comparable to those accepted at Tulane as described in the previous section.

Denker reports the rate of improvement over a five-year period as shown in Figure 16-5. We note, for instance, that after two years 72 per cent of these patients recovered. Denker used a very severe criterion of improvement, including the requirement that the patient have had no recurrence of work disability for at least five years after the termination of the current disability. It is difficult to do other than conclude that effective psychotherapy must be judged by its ability to produce improvements significantly faster than this base rate reported by Denker.

It would be astonishing if spontaneous recovery rates were low. The environment of patients, like other people, is constantly changing. As these changes occur, the inadequacy of the patient's behavior rises and falls in relation to the new demands placed on him, or to the elimination of the circumstances and events that generated his previous problems. The longer a patient lives, the more likely it is that some beneficial change will occur. By the same token, the longer a patient persists in inadequate behavior, the more likely it is that he will begin to accumulate a series of extinction experiences and punishments and will learn more adaptive behavior.

Therapeutic Error

When a physician is faced with a case of organic disease, he usually attempts to make a diagnosis. If the physician is incompetent, tired, or inefficient for one reason or another, he may make a mistake and misdiagnose the disease. Should he then proceed

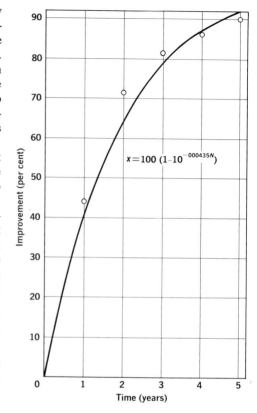

Figure 16-5. Improvement shown by 500 severe neurotics, not receiving psychotherapy, over 1 to 5 years. In the formula, X denotes the proportional improvement while N denotes the number of weeks elapsing from the beginning of the experiment. (Eysenck, 1961.)

to treat the disorder on the basis of his mistake, he might do serious damage to the patient, causing organic destruction that would not have occurred by the disease process alone. Possibly he might kill the patient. If the patient, or his next of kin, discover that there was a faulty diagnosis, they may take legal action against the physician. Physicians may also make genuine judgments that would be supported as reasonable by any other physician, but may make these judgments in the face of less than 100 per cent certainty of the outcome. Sometimes the result will be unfavorable. This kind of outcome reflects the lack of current knowledge about the disease, and it would be unreasonable to blame the physician for it.

An incompetent therapist is in a position to create problems that his patient did not have before entering therapy. This is equally true for the physical therapy of organic disease and for psychotherapy of behavioral disorders. In the many published statistics of the improvement of patients during the time they were receiving psychotherapy, there is a paucity of data on the percentage of patients whose condition worsened. In any evaluation of the effects of a physical therapy, we would expect to compare the number of patients who were cured by a procedure with the number who were injured by it. Surgery, for example, sometimes carries with it a risk of fatalities brought about by the surgery itself. Surgeons take this into consideration when assessing the values of the technique.

In exactly the same way, the effectiveness of any psychotherapeutic technique should involve a comparison not only of the percentage improved compared with the spontaneous remission rate, but also the percentage deteriorated compared with deterioration in an untreated population. Such a comparison need not be unfavorable to psychotherapy, which may serve to prevent behavior from becoming more pathological without actually improving it. However, in the absence of this kind of statistic, it is difficult to arrive at sophisticated conclusions about psychotherapeutic effectiveness.

Problems in Criteria of Improvement

An additional problem in evaluating the outcome of two different kinds of therapy is the criterion used to define "improvement." Generally speaking, we may look for evidence of some behavioral change in the direction of effectiveness, some change in expressions of distress in the direction of greater comfort, or some change in the patient's account of his problems in the direction of greater awareness or "insight." Many

workers use these three criteria in a global or total fashion, assuming implicitly that they are all representative of some single general process of improvement. In a careful study of changes in patients following group therapy, Kelman & Parloff (1957) found that measurements of all these criteria, taken on all patients, showed insignificant intercorrelations in 20 of 21 correlations. The other achieved minimal significance. It seems clear that the conclusions drawn about the effects of therapy may vary tremendously, depending upon the measures used to define improvement.

General Empirical Outcomes of Various Psychotherapies

Many published reports exist of the improvement rates claimed by nonlearning psychotherapists of various allegiances. There is not space here to discuss them all in detail; the reader will find excellent reviews in Levitt (1957) and Eysenck (1961). Suffice it to say that in reviewing the percentage of patients for whom some degree of improvement was claimed, Levitt reports that 67 per cent of all children (studied in investigations of over 4,000 children) improved. This rate increased to 78 per cent when improvement was measured some time after the termination of therapy, a fact implying that the period after treatment produced continuing improvement, presumably to be attributed to spontaneous recovery. Untreated controls showed an improvement rate of 72 per cent.

Similar data are reported by Eysenck from a survey of studies of therapeutic improvement in neurotic adults. Using Denker's figures as a base rate for spontaneous recovery, he presents the recovery rate for patients treated psychoanalytically as 44 per cent, while those treated by other "eclectic" methods have a rate of 64 per cent. Denker's two-year recovery rate is 72 per cent, and in this comparison Eysenck is compelled to draw the conclusion that psychotherapy is associated with a lower rate of recovery than no psychotherapy at all! One may well question the wisdom of drawing conclusions of this kind from populations of patients who were not matched with each other for pathology, age, etc. However, what is indisputable is that the published data present no positive evidence *in favor* of psychotherapy at all.

TREATMENT AND MORAL VALUES

Up to this point we have considered psychological treatments as technical procedures applied to bring about behavior change. We have evaluated them in terms of their scientific rationality and their practical effectiveness. While doing this, we have suspended discussion of some philosophical issues that are implicit in any process whereby one human being is changing the behavior of another. These issues have plagued applied psychology for many years, and there is no ready answer to the questions that have been raised. There are, however, some things to be said about them.

When a patient seeks out a therapist and asks him to help eliminate a phobia, a tic, or some other specific symptom, it may be presumed that the patient has decided that he would be better off without the symptom than with it. In accepting the patient for treatment, the therapist is implying that he has the skills to eliminate the problem. This is a straightforward arrangement, much as may be the case where a patient approaches a physician to set a broken bone. Should the therapist have a private goal in therapy which differs from that of the patient, then it seems clear that it is his duty to tell him as soon as possible. Should the therapist feel that the only feasible goal is "acceptance of the symptom" by the patient, then this must be explained.

Changes of therapeutic goal are not rare, and many therapists who have begun therapy with more optimistic aims will conclude that acceptance is the only plausible goal. Provided that the patient is apprised of this, then the relationship is free from deception and may be continued in a straightforward, though changed, fashion. On the other hand, a therapist who is convinced that changing symptomatic behavior is irrelevant and that the desirable course is to change the patient's "philosophy of life" is deceiving the patient if he accepts him for treatment on any other grounds. Put in its simplest possible terms, the patient is most in control of his own fate to the extent that he knows what the purposes of the therapist are.

Lawyers are often approached by clients seeking legal aid in securing a divorce. Many lawyers, on the basis of their observation, conclude that divorce creates as many problems as it solves and therefore feel morally obliged to try to persuade the client to seek some other solution. But the decision is in the client's hands; the lawyer does not deceive him by going through the motions of preparing a divorce suit while privately planning to prevent it coming before the judge. If he considers that the client has a weak case, he tells him that success is unlikely and why. If the client wishes to assume that risk, then the proceedings go forward.

Where a patient has a definable psychological difficulty, there seems to be no reason why a therapist cannot operate in the same way. The more crucial problem arises where the patient's difficulties are diffuse and ill-defined. Thus the patient who is generally unhappy, has vague, unstable symptoms, and complains of the "meaningless" nature of his life may not be able to decide what it is he wants the therapist to do except make him "happy."

It cannot be emphasized too strongly that the science of psychology possesses no knowledge of how to make people happy or how to give meaning to their lives. Psychologists, as persons, sometimes develop convictions on these topics. Physicists, physiologists, scientists, and artists frequently do the same. In this matter the training of the psychologist in no way equips him to provide answers to questions of happiness, the meaning of life, beauty, or reality. These matters are decided by every man, and if there are professions into whose domain they properly fall, they are the professions of religion and philosophy.

For a man to dedicate his life to helping others find personal answers to these problems is a noble course. The fact that he has no science to draw on diminishes the merit of his activities not one whit. Men who do this are to be found in the ranks of professional psychology and psychiatry and are hence likely to be mistaken for scientists. It is necessary to emphasize that the moral value of these endeavors is unrelated to the scientific nature of their bases. It is also necessary to emphasize that questions of a scientific nature are not amenable to answer from nonscientific activities, and that the latter are irrelevant to the science of psychopathology.

We are presently at a stage in the history of psychopathology where this confusion is becoming apparent. The irrelevance of metaphysical notions of mental apparatus for the problems of etiology and treatment has been demonstrated by the barrenness of these views for the practical relief of disordered behavior. With the entry of the techniques of experimental psychology and the biological sciences into the field of the behavior disorders, our prospects of progress seem considerably brighter.

SUGGESTED READINGS

1. Ford, D. H., & Urban, H. B. *Systems of psychotherapy.* New York: Wiley, 1963. A detailed comparative survey of the major modes of psychotherapy. Provides a basic coverage for the intermediate student.
2. Goffman, E. *Asylums.* Garden City, N.Y.: Anchor Books, 1961. A collection of four essays on the social life of the mental patient. An essential source in the study of this problem.
3. Greenblatt, M., York, R. H., & Brown, Esther L. *From custodial to therapeutic*

patient care in mental hospitals. New York: Russell Sage, 1955. An account of the transition from a closed to open environment in a mental hospital and a description of the changes in behavior that accompanied it.
4. Rotter, J. B. *Social learning and clinical psychology.* Englewood Cliffs, N.J.: Prentice-Hall, 1954. A systematic theory of personality, based upon concepts of learning and expectancy, together with a discussion of its application to psychotherapy.
5. Stanton, A. H., & Schwartz, M. S. *The mental hospital: a study of institutional participation in psychiatric illness and treatment.* New York: Basic Books, 1954. A classic study of the manner in which the milieu and administrative policies of a mental hospital contribute to the factors of mental illness.
6. Wolpe, J., Salter, A., & Reyna, L. J. *The conditioning therapies.* New York: Holt, 1964. A collection of essays, research reports, and case data on various topics in behavior therapy. A useful introduction to the scope and nature of those therapies.

REFERENCES

Allyon, T. Intensive treatment of psychotic behavior by stimulus satiation and food reinforcement. *Behav. res. Ther.,* 1963, **1,** 53–61.

Allyon, T., & Haughton, E. Control of the behavior of schizophrenic patients by food. *J. exp. Anal. Behav.,* 1962, **5,** 343–352.

Bacon, F. *The advancement of learning.* 1605.

Baker, A. A., Jones, M., Merry, J., & Pomryn, B. A. A community method of psychotherapy. *Brit. J. med. Psychol.,* 1953, **26,** 222–244.

Beveridge, W. I. B. *The art of scientific investigation.* New York: Norton, 1950.

Blakemore, C. B., Thorpe, J. G., Barker, J. C., Conway, C. G., & Lavin, N. T.

The application of faradic aversion conditioning in a case of transvestism. *Behav. res. Ther.*, 1963, **1**, 29–34.

Clark, D. F. The treatment of a monosymptomatic phobia by systematic desensitization. *Behav. res. Ther.*, 1963, **1**, 63–68.

Denker, W. Cited in H. J. Eysenck (Ed.), *Handbook of abnormal psychology.* New York: Basic Books, 1961.

Dollard, J., & Miller, N. E. *Personality and psychotherapy.* New York: McGraw-Hill, 1950.

Eysenck, H. J. Classification and the problem of diagnosis. In H. J. Eysenck (Ed.), *Handbook of abnormal psychology.* New York: Basic Books, 1961.

Goffman, E. *Asylums.* New York: Doubleday, 1961.

Goldstein, M. J., & Palmer, J. O. *The experience of anxiety.* Fair Lawn, N.J.: Oxford Univer. Press, 1963.

Greenblatt, M., York, R. H., & Brown, L. *From custodial to therapeutic patient care in mental hospitals.* New York: Russell Sage, 1955.

Jones, Mary. A laboratory study of fear: the case of Peter. *Ped. Sem.*, 1924, **31**, 308–315.

Kelman, H. C., & Parloff, M. B. Interrelations among three criteria of improvement in group therapy: comfort, effectiveness, and self-awareness. *J. abnorm. soc. Psychol.*, 1957, **54**, 281–288.

Kräupl-Taylor, F. A history of group and administrative therapy in Great Britain. *Brit. J. med. Psychol.*, 1958, **31**, 153–173.

Levitt, E. E. The results of psychotherapy with children: an evaluation. *J. consult. Psychol.*, 1957, **21**, 189–196.

Lief, H. I., Lief, V. F., Warren, C. O., & Heath, R. G. Low dropout rate in a psychiatric clinic. *Arch. gen. Psychiat.*, 1961, **5**, 200–211.

Maher, B. A., & Katkovsky, W. The efficacy of brief clinical procedures in alleviating children's behavior problems. *J. indiv. Psychol.*, 1961, **17**, 205–211.

May, A. R. The changing pattern of psychiatric care in a mental hospital. *Proc. Royal Soc. Med.*, 1956, **49**, 1027–1030.

Morton, R. B. A controlled experiment in psychotherapy based on Rotter's social learning theory of personality. Unpublished doctoral dissertation, Ohio State Univer., 1949.

Phillips, E. L. *Psychotherapy: a modern theory and practice.* Englewood Cliffs, N.J.: Prentice-Hall, 1956.

Rachman, S. Introduction to behavior therapy. *Behav. res. Ther.*, 1963, **1**, 3–15.

Raimy, V. (Ed.) *Training in clinical psychology.* Englewood Cliffs, N.J.: Prentice-Hall, 1950.

Rotter, J. B. *Social learning and clinical psychology.* Englewood Cliffs, N.J.: Prentice-Hall, 1954.

Winder, C. L. Psychotherapy. *Ann. Rev. Psychol.*, 1957, **8**, 309–330.

Wing, J. K. Institutionalism in mental hospitals. *Brit. J. soc. clin. Psychol.*, 1962, **1**, 38–51.

Wolpe, J. Reciprocal inhibition as the main basis of psychotherapeutic effects. *A. M. A. Arch. Neurol. Psychiat.*, 1954, **72**, 205–226.

Wolpe, J. *Psychotherapy by reciprocal inhibition.* Stanford, Calif.: Stanford Univer. Press, 1958.

Wolpe, J. The experimental foundations of some new psychotherapeutic methods. In A. J. Bachrach (Ed.), *Experimental foundations of clinical psychology.* New York: Basic Books, 1962.

BIOLOGICAL
METHODS OF
TREATMENT

In these closing chapters we have turned to examine some of the general techniques that have been developed to change the behavior of the patient in the direction of lowered pathology. Two overall classes of technique have been recognized: those that attempt to change the behavior of the patient by direct intervention in bodily processes which are believed to mediate the behavior in question, and those that seek to produce new learning by the manipulation of reinforcements. The former are generally termed the *somatic therapies,* while the application of the principles of learning (whether or not this is explicitly recognized) is termed *psychotherapy.* The latter were discussed in Chapter 16. Biological methods will be examined in this chapter.

Techniques of biological intervention have become very prominent in the past three or four decades. Three classes of technique may be identified:

1. Chemical intervention with bodily processes by the introduction of pharmacological material.
2. The induction of convulsions by electrical or chemical means.
3. Direct destruction of bodily tissue by surgical operation.

Under the general heading of somatic therapies, certain physical methods for producing temporary relaxation of the patient are also included. These will not be discussed here.

PSYCHOPHARMACOLOGY

The first problem in the study of psychopharmacology is that of classification. Several plausible ways may be advanced in which drugs might be classified. They may be grouped together on the basis of (1) similarity of *chemical structures;* (2) their action upon given *physiological systems,* for example, the conductivity of the nerve, or the parasympathetic-sympathetic balance in the autonomic system; (3) their effect upon *specific psychological functions,* such as the perceptual constancies; (4) their effect upon general *excitatory-inhibitory* aspects of behavior, as in the distinction between stimulants and depressants; (5) their effects in terms of *therapeutic* improvement in particular syndromes of behavior pathology.

Two major systems of classification are to be found in the current research literature. That used by the United States Public Health Service divides drugs into three broad groupings on the basis of their behavioral or psychological effects. This triple classification includes *tranquilizers, energizers,* and the *hallucinogens.* An alternative major classification scheme is that recommended by the World Health Organization (1958). It is a sevenfold classification and includes criteria from behavior, from the location of action of the drug and a "transitional" category. The categories are as follows:

1. The major tranquilizers
2. The minor tranquilizers
3. The sedatives
4. Centrally-acting anticholinergic drugs
5. Stimulant drugs
6. The psychotomimetic drugs
7. Transitional compounds

A summary account of these categories is given in Table 17-1. In the pages that follow, we shall consider only some of the major tranquilizers and the psychotomimetics that psychopharmacology has made available to us.

TRANQUILIZERS: THE PHENOTHIAZINES

The major tranquilizing drugs are so called because of the clinical observation that their use leads to a quieting of patients whose behavior is ordinarily marked by excitement and agitation. As this observation is made at a gross clinical level, it cannot be used as a serious basis for classifying the behavioral consequences of these compounds. However, it acts as a useful general label in a broad classification system at this point. The major tranquilizers include four classes of chemical compound.

Chemically speaking, the phenothiazines are classified in terms of the existence of the *phenothiazine nucleus* in the molecule of the drug. This nucleus is shown in Figure 17-1, together with the three side chains, the presence of which define the three types of phenothiazine compound in common use. One of the best known of these is *chlorpromazine,* shown as subtype a in Figure 17-1. Early work with this compound revealed that dosages of it had, among other effects, that of slowing down motor behavior. This effect was, of course, of considerable practical use in the management of agitated patients, and the drug has tended to be used for this purpose. However, a vast amount of experimentation has now been reported under controlled conditions, so that we are in some position to describe the effects of chlorpromazine with a fair amount of precision.

Chlorpromazine and Fear-induced Behavior

Numerous studies have been undertaken of the effect of chlorpromazine upon fear-induced behavior. The rationale for such studies comes in the first place from the clinical observation that administration of the drug is followed by quieting in distressed and anxious patients. We shall consider first a few experiments conducted on animals. Hunt (1956) reported the effect of dosages of chlorpromazine upon the conditioned

TABLE 17-1 A Provisional Grouping of Some Broad Pharmacological and Clinical Effects of Psychotropic Agents

Class	Broad pharmacological effects	Broad clinical effects	Some specific instances
The major tranquilizers or "neuroleptics"	Depression of autonomic centers (especially of the sympathetic system); reduction of motor activity and of conditioned avoidance responses. No anaesthesia, even in large doses.	Tranquilization of overactive psychotic syndromes. Indifference to endogenous or exogenous stimuli. Production of extrapyramidal syndrome in high doses.	Chlorpromazine Reserpine
The minor tranquilizers	Like the neuroleptic drugs, but effects less marked.	Lessened effect on psychotic syndromes Sedation in cases of anxiety No hypnotic effect	Hydroxyzine
The tranquilo-sedatives	Reduction of motor activity, ending in paralysis. Little autonomic effect. No anaesthesia, even in large doses.		Meprobamate
The hypno-sedatives	Reduction of spontaneous activity; ataxia leading to anaesthesia.	As above, but coupled with hypnotic effect	Pentobarbital Alcohol
Centrally acting antiacetylcholine drugs	A "normalizing" effect on certain experimentally induced behavioral states. No depression of motor activity. No central effect on autonomic centers.	Sedation in special instances of anxiety states. No hypnotic effect.	Benactyzine
The stimulant (psychotonic) drugs	Increased motor activity, alerting. Reduction of sleep and appetite. Central sympathetic effects.	Decrease of fatigue, stimulation. May increase symptoms in psychosis. Increase of anxiety, if present.	Amphetamine Piperadol Iproniazid
The psychotomimetic (hallucinogenic) agents	Marked effect on affect and perception. Increased motor activity. Catatonia. Fluctuating autonomic effects.	Marked effects on affect, perception, and thought process. Mimic acute psychotic disturbance.	Mescaline Lysergic acid diethylamide (LSD)

SOURCE: *World Health Organization.*

emotional response (CER) in rats. His findings indicated that when the animal was drugged (10 mg/kg subcutaneously), there was marked interference of acquisition of the CER, as judged by later ease of extinction under a nondrugged condition. Paradoxically, animals that acquired the CER under a nondrug condition were very slow to extinguish when extinction was carried out in a drugged condition. Thus in the latter case, the chlorpromazine did not eliminate the fearful behavior, provided that this had been acquired in a normal state.

However, we should note here the importance of dosage rate. Kinnard, Aceto, and Buckley (1962) repeated the procedure used by Hunt, but with smaller doses ranging from 0.5 to 3.0 mg/kg. Their findings indicated that doses of this kind did not eliminate the CER, and that the disappearance of anxiety "symptoms" with chlorpromazine administration seemed to be largely dependent upon giving a large enough dose to produce general depression of motor behavior.

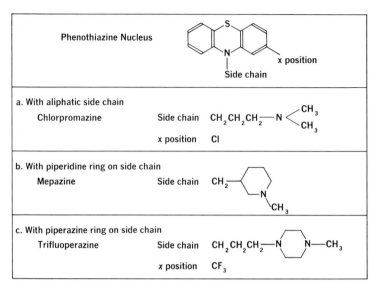

Figure 17-1.   Structure of major phenothiazine compounds.

Chlorpromazine and Conflict Behavior

Barry and Miller (1962) studied the effect of chlorpromazine upon rats that had been retrained to a condition of approach-avoidance conflict. These investigators used small doses (2 to 4 mg/kg) and found that this affected both approach and avoidance responses equally—suggesting that this drug has no selective effect upon the fear-motivated component of the conflict. Maher and Chapoton (1960) had studied an essentially similar problem. Animals were trained to an approach-avoidance conflict in an undrugged condition. They then received chlorpromazine (10 mg/kg) during subsequent trials when the animal was undergoing extinction of avoidance training. Here, the important problem was whether the drug would make the extinction of the avoidance behavior more rapid, and secondly, when this had been achieved under the drugged condition, whether it would remain as a permanent effect after the drug had been withdrawn. This study was intended as an analogue of the problem that arises in drug therapy, namely, whether the gains that might be made by the patient while under the drug will be permanent should the therapy be discontinued. In this study, the effects of the drug are shown in Table 17-2. As the data show, the drug slowed up the process of extinction, and the effects of this extinction were less efficient than those obtained

TABLE 17-2   Effects of Chlorpromazine upon Recovery from an Approach-Avoidance Conflict

	Trials to extinguish avoidance	Trials to produce three additional approach responses. No animals drugged.
Extinction under drug	23.92	11.51
Extinction under placebo	13.42	8.35

SOURCE: *Maher & Chapoton (1960)*.

by normal extinction procedures in an un-drugged control group. Similar effects were obtained in a study using the same method and apparatus by employing thiopropazate-dihydrochloride in lieu of chlorpromazine (Maher and Taylor, 1960).

There have been many studies of this kind dealing with varieties of experimentally produced anxiety in animals. The general tenor of the data suggest that we may reach certain conclusions about the action of this drug on such behavior. The first is that what-ever the action of chlorpromazine is, it does not appear to act as a specific fear reducer. In general, its action appears to lead to increasing depression of activity with in-creasing dosage. Thirdly, there is reason to suppose that excessive doses of chlorproma-zine may interfere with sensory input and perception generally, quite apart from the effect upon overt responses. Effects of this kind make it difficult to distinguish between behavior changes in which the drug may be disrupting the stimulus-response connec-tion, and changes in which the drug is effectively distorting the subject's perception of the stimulus.

Chlorpromazine and Patient Behavior

While the animal studies are suggestive of some issues in the understanding of the ac-tion of this drug, the central question is its effect upon the patient showing evidences of psychopathology. Carefully controlled studies have been rather lacking from the literature, but a good illustration of a comprehensive investigation is reported by Lasky (1960). In a large-scale investigation conducted by the Veterans Administration, the effects of chlorpromazine were compared with those of other drugs over a period of weeks. Following 12 weeks of treatment with chlorpromazine, 170 patients were compared with similar numbers treated with promazine, phenobarbitol, and lactose as a placebo. This study was conducted with careful control procedures. Double-blind assignment of drugs, restriction of other therapeutic measures during the period of

drug therapy, and assessment of improve-ment by many independent raters using several tests and scales, all contributed to an unusual degree of methodological preci-sion. The comparison between the effects of various compounds is shown in Figure 17-2. Inspection of this figure indicates that the reduction in severity of psychopathological behavior was most marked with chlorproma-zine and somewhat less so with promazine, while phenobarbitol and the placebo did not differ significantly.

While the clear superiority of chlorproma-zine seen in this study has not always been found by other investigators, there is gen-eral consensus among investigators that its

Figure 17-2. Effects of chlorpromazine and other drugs on clinical status over time. (Kornetsky, 1961.)

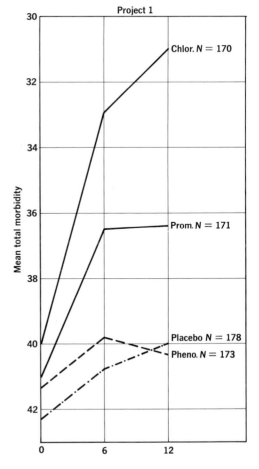

use is followed by an amelioration of behavior. We should note, however, that this change in behavior may involve aspects that do not in themselves reflect a return to normalcy of the patient's activities. Haase (1962) studied the effect of therapeutic doses of chlorpromazine (438 mg/day) upon overt activity levels in schizophrenic patients observed over long periods of time. Increases and decreases in walking and in speech activity were recorded and found to be significantly affected by chlorpromazine, as well as by other tranquilizing compounds. This agrees with the observations that were made above about the effects of chlorpromazine in depressing activity in animals. It points up again the need to distinguish between these effects and therapeutic changes in behavior that may exist above and beyond the sedative effect of the drug.

Chlorpromazine: Biological Aspects

We are far from a precise understanding of the manner in which chlorpromazine produces the bodily changes that mediate the alterations in behavior that have been reported. We are not clear what these bodily changes are, except in the grossest sense. Nevertheless, a tremendous research effort has been and is being made to uncover the answers to these questions. Two general classes of information are available; one of these relates to the physiological changes that have been observed to occur with the administration of the drug, and the other relates to the presumed manner in which the drug acts directly on various kinds of tissue.

Bodily Changes. Many types of bodily reaction have been noted with the use of chlorpromazine. Particular attention has been given to its effects upon the EEG.
EEG Effects. Chlorpromazine has been used with patients who suffer from intractable pain, and although the patient is still able to recognize the pain when drugged, the emotional reactions of fear and distress seem to be reduced or eliminated. Pain, as a

stimulus, appears to have lost its power to arouse the patient, and this is substantiated by examination of the effects of the drug upon the EEG of an experimental animal (the rabbit) as reported by Himwich (1955). In Figure 17-3 we see the arousal effect produced by pinching the rabbit's paw when not drugged, compared with the failure of this stimulus to block the alpha rhythm when the animal has received 5 mg/kg of chlorpromazine.
Sympathetic Effects. Coupled with this apparent diminution of the EEG alerting effect is general evidence of a reduction of sympathetic activity level of the human subject. A striking and reliable consequence of the administration of chlorpromazine is a drop in blood pressure, which occurs almost immediately when the drug is given intravenously and is delayed about 60 to 90 minutes when given orally. Although this effect is quite marked, it does not signal complete blocking of adrenergic activity. Norepinephrine, if given to the drugged patient, will lead to a rise in blood pressure. The amount of norepinephrine required to produce this rise is nearly twice the normal dosage. A small but measurable drop in body temperature is also common. Gastric motility is reduced, and the drug appears to have a direct inhibiting effect upon smooth muscle.

Hypotheses. One hypothesis that has been advanced to account for the action of chlorpromazine, and indeed of all the phenothiazines, is based upon the similarity of the structure of the side chains of adrenaline, noradrenaline, and serotonin to those of the phenothiazines. This similarity of structure leads to the application of what is sometimes called the "lock-and-key" hypothesis of drug action. If one substance is sufficiently like another that it can occupy the biological locations normally occupied by the other, then it may take up these sites to an extent that will exclude the normal candidate from occupancy. Metaphorically speaking, it is like a key that is shaped to fit into a certain lock, but is not the correct

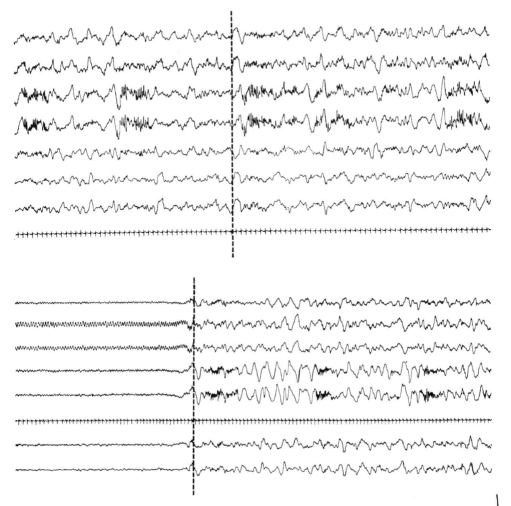

Figure 17-3. Electroencephalograms are used to show the effect of a drug on the brain's activity. In the two patterns shown here, each wavy line represents the electrical impulses recorded from distinct areas of a rabbit's brain. In the first record, the wave pattern at the left is the resting pattern. When a painful stimulus is applied, it changes the brain-wave pattern to that on the right side of the dashed line. The second record shows the effect of chlorpromazine: the pattern remains essentially unchanged after the stimulus. (Himwich, 1955.)

shape to turn it. Thus, for example, chlorpromazine might occupy the sites ordinarily occupied by adrenaline, thereby preventing the normal activity of adrenaline at those sites and serving to block adrenergic activity. As many of the observed effects of chlorpromazine are in line with the hypothesis of adrenergic blocking, it has the merit of accounting for certain elements of the data.

A second hypothesis has emphasized the action of chlorpromazine upon central structures in the brain and brainstem. We have already seen that there is a diminution in the alerting response of an animal that has received chlorpromazine when observed via an EEG trace. Himwich (1955) considers this phenomenon, together with the general data regarding the reduction in the distress produced by intractable pain, etc. He suggests that the mechanisms involved are the depression of reticular activity by chlorpromazine, and that this leads to the diminution of the arousal value of stimuli without preventing them from entering into consciousness by other routes—notably by way of the lemnisci (see Figure 17-4).

In addition to the reticular activating system, the hypothalamus has been considered a crucial site in the action of chlorpromazine. As we already know, this center is important in the organization of both sympathetic and parasympathetic activity. Coordination of emotional patterns of autonomic response is mediated by the hypothalamus, and research has indicated that its activity is depressed by chlorpromazine (Bein, Gross, Tripod, & Meier, 1953). The research data also suggested that chlorpromazine was specifically active in depressing

the sympathetic centers of the hypothalamus (the *posterior hypothalamic nuclei*), thus producing a shift toward parasympathetic dominance. Such a hypothesis is not incompatible with the notion that chlorpromazine blocks adrenergic activity; it simply tends to specify the site at which such blocking may take place.

Finally, we should note that several workers have been interested in the effect of chlorpromazine in raising the activity of the *amygdaloid complex*. With therapeutic dosages of chlorpromazine, the activity level of the amygdala has been seen to increase, while the accompanying motor behavior is tranquilized. Thus with a dose of 10 mg/kg of chlorpromazine, an experimental cat has been recorded refusing to attack a mouse, acting instead with apparent indifference. The same effect was created by Andy and Akert (1955) by producing hyperactivity in

Figure 17-4. Two pathways of stimulation in the human brain are shown in this diagram. Sensory impulses pass through the lemnisci to the specific relay nuclei of the thalamus in the center of the brain. From there they are relayed to the parts of the cerebral cortex concerned with the analysis of specific sensations. The system is shown by the dashed black arrows. The other set of pathways, called the activating system, begins with branches from the lemnisci. They carry impulses to the midbrain reticular formation, which in turn relays these impulses to the thalamus. From there the activating impulses are carried to the cerebral cortex by way of the diffuse projection system. These paths are indicated by black lines. The reticular formation also sends impulses to the hypothalamus. Secondary impulses from hypothalamus are suggested by dashed colored lines and from thalamus by solid colored lines paralleling the black. (Himwich, 1955.)

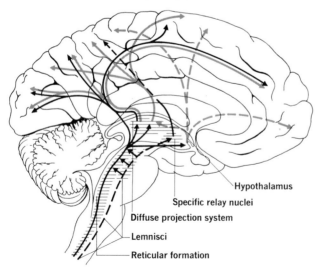

the amygdala with direct electrical stimulation. As soon as the stimulation ceased, there was a short period of continued amygdaloid hyperactivity, which then subsided. At this point the cat's apathy disappeared and it pounced upon the mouse.

The fact that the amygdala mediates "tranquil" behavior in this way has made it a possible candidate for the site of action of chlorpromazine and other compounds. However, some important drugs do not seem to produce activity in the amygdala but to generate their tranquilizing effects in some other way. Meprobamate, for example, depresses the activity of the thalamus but leaves that of the amygdala unchanged. Suffice it to say, at this point, that our knowledge of the processes by which chlorpromazine (and most other tranquilizers) exert their influence on behavior is very rudimentary.

TRANQUILIZERS: RESERPINE

Reserpine, another major tranquilizer, is an alkaloid extracted from the root of the plant *Rauwolfia serpentina*. Figure 17-5 presents the structure of reserpine together with some related compounds. Of central importance in the structure of this compound is the presence of the *indole nucleus*. This element of the structure is also found in serotonin, LSD 25, and a wide variety of derivatives found in body fluids. It is of importance in several current hypotheses regarding the etiology of certain patterns of psychopathology.

Reserpine and Fear-induced Behavior

As in the case of chlorpromazine, the effect of reserpine upon fear-induced behavior has been extensively studied in animals. The

Figure 17-5. Structure of indole substances.

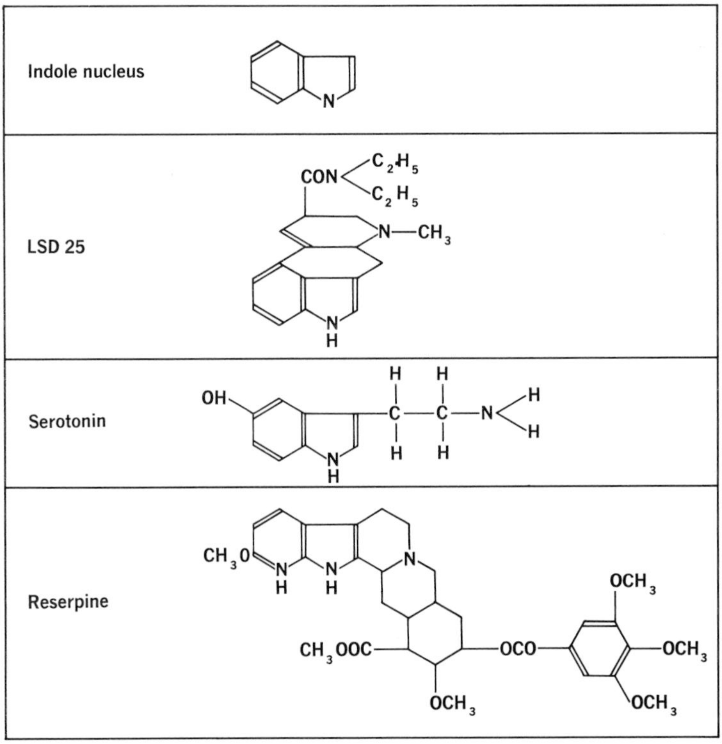

conditioned avoidance response and conditioned emotional responses have been the major foci of investigation. Weiskrantz and Wilson (1956) report that reserpine blocks the acquisition and the extinction of the conditioned emotion response in monkeys. They suggest that the drug affects both learning and performance in this way. However, subsequent investigation by Stein (1956) indicated that reserpine did not block the acquisition of the CER in rats, and raised the question of possible species differences here. Fink and Swinyard (1962) report blocking of the CAR in mice with reserpine. However, the study by Kinnard et al. (1962) cited in our previous discussion of chlorpromazine finds reserpine to be ineffective in blocking the CER except in doses large enough to generate motor paralysis. Hartry (1962) studied the effect of reserpine upon the incidence of psychogenic ulcers produced in laboratory rats. Ulcer-producing conditions were established by immobilizing rats under conditions of hunger and thirst. The presence or absence of reserpine dosage was irrelevant to the appearance of the ulcers. Hartry speculated to the effect that this kind of stress may produce the autonomic patterns of anger rather than anxiety. In general, we may say that the gross *behavioral* effects of reserpine are similar to those of chlorpromazine.

Reserpine and Antagonism to Psychotomimetic Agents

One method of studying the therapeutic effects of a procedure is to test its antagonism against abnormal behavior that has been induced experimentally. In the realm of psychopharmacology, this frequently takes the form of administering one of the compounds known to induce deviant behavior—the *psychotomimetic* drugs—and then administering the potential therapeutic compound. If the latter antagonizes the former, then it may provide us with some understanding of its therapeutic mechanism; this is dependent upon our existing knowledge of the manner in which the psychotomimetic produces the behavioral deviations.

An animal analogue of this method has been provided in a study reported by Keller and Umbreit (1956). They gave doses of LSD (lysergic acid diethylamide) to several varieties of fish and identified typical aberrations of behavior for each species. When this dosage was combined with the prior administration of either indole or tryptamine, these aberrations seemed to become permanent, persisting in some cases for months after the drug had been given. However, treatment of these fish with reserpine produced equally "permanent" cures in a large number of cases. Elder and Dille (1962) failed to find this elimination of LSD effects when they investigated reserpine-LSD antagonism in the behavior of cats. Careful studies of this kind of relationship in human subjects are, as yet, lacking. There are several reasons for this, some of which will be discussed later.

Reserpine and Patient Behavior

At this time, much the same situation prevails with reserpine as with chlorpromazine in regard to the availability of well-controlled studies of drug-produced changes in patient behavior. MacDonald, Ellsworth, and Enniss (1956) and Barrett, Ellsworth, Clark, and Ennis (1957) report systematic studies of the effects of reserpine upon the behavioral adjustment of inpatients in a Veterans' Administration Hospital. Their data suggest that reserpine produces significant improvements in ward behavior, which in turn is related to earlier discharge and better postrelease adjustment to society. An interesting additional outcome of these studies (Ellsworth and Clark, 1957) was that the improvement of the patient was significantly related to the variability of his palmar sweat readings. The "variable anxious" patient, defined by variability of palmar sweat readings, showed the most favorable response to reserpine, while the nonvariable patient responded poorly.

Pursuing this observation, the investigators then induced autonomic tension in a series of nonvariable patients by administration of *ephedrine,* followed by chlorpromazine. Other patients were retreated with chlorpromazine alone. Those treated with ephedrine followed by chlorpromazine now showed improvement; those treated with chlorpromazine alone did not. Inducing "tension" in this way, the authors conclude, enhances the effectiveness of chlorpromazine and supports the implications of the palmar sweat study.

Reserpine: Biological Aspects

Here again, we may consider first the physiological changes occurring with the administration of reserpine and secondly the hypotheses that have been advanced to account for both the biological and the behavioral phenomena.

Bodily Changes. Particular attention has been given, in the case of reserpine, to its effects upon serotonin and upon the catecholamines in the body of the patient. We shall examine these neurohormonal changes in some detail.

Neurohormonal Effects. Therapeutic doses of reserpine have been found to lead to striking decreases in the level of serotonin in the blood. Rodnight (1961), for example, finds decreases of as much as 90 per cent of the predrug level. Typical figures are given in Table 17-3. There is no doubt that these depletions do occur after administration of reserpine, but there are alternative mechanisms that might be adduced to account for them. At this point, suffice it to say that this serotonin depletion is found in assays of blood, brain tissue, and other organ storage sites.

Similar findings are reported for the levels of catecholamines in the human patient. Depletion of these amines has been found following reserpine dosage in the heart and adrenals of the rabbit, in the hypothalamus and adrenals of the cat, and in the sympathetic ganglia, adrenergic nerve trunks, and many other organ sites of rabbits, cats, and dogs. Different species show some striking differences in the sites that are affected in this way. Furthermore, not all

TABLE 17-3 Effect of Reserpine on Blood Serotonin Levels in Mentally Ill Subjects

Subject	Age (years)	Reserpine dosage (mg/day)	Period of administration (days)	Serotonin concentration ($m\mu g/ml$)
1. Psychotic illness	40	None		160
		5	1	15
		5	7	5
2. Neurotic disorder	36.	None		170
		1.5	7	<15
		1.5	14	<15
		1.5	63	<15
3. Schizophrenia	18	None		375
		10	1	<15
		5 to 7	7	<15
4. Senile dementia	68	None		350
		1	1	320
		1	5	About 15
		None	14	40

SOURCE: *Rodnight (1961).*

catecholamines are equally affected. Thus the loss of noradrenaline in the sympathetic ganglia is usually quite marked following reserpine, but the adrenaline assay may be relatively unchanged.

The mechanisms by which the content of an organ may be depleted following the administration of a drug are twofold. Either the drug produces a release in the stored amines so that these are secreted into the blood more rapidly than usual, or the drug acts to prevent the organ from taking up the amine for storage, while leaving it free to discharge it—thus resulting in a net loss of the amine content in the organ. Green (1962) has suggested that this may well be the case in the action of reserpine.

Nerve Transmission Effects. Because of its clear effects upon the adrenergic status of the body generally, much interest has been focused on the possibility that reserpine may achieve its tranquilizing effect by disrupting sympathetic nerve transmission. This possibility has been studied extensively in relation to the observed clinical consequences of the administration of the drug. These consequences are mainly parasympathomimetic and include a decrease in blood pressure, increased motility of the gut, and a fall in body temperature. Additional consequences are apathy and some sign of psychological depression.

Because the lowering of the blood pressure has been observed to occur in patients who are suffering from hypertension, the drug has seemed to hold some promise as a therapeutic agent in the treatment of high blood pressure. This, in turn, has inspired considerable study of the effects of reserpine upon the peripheral nerve endings responsible for the activation of the arteries, etc. Early studies performed by McQueen, Doyle, & Smirk (1954, 1955) demonstrated that the effect of reserpine was to inhibit the adrenergic control of peripheral circulation, while other experimenters have shown that reserpine blocks the effect of sympathetic nerve stimulation upon the appearance of the appropriate end organ.

All this suggests strongly that reserpine produces, in effect, deactivation of adrenergic (sympathetic) neurons with a concomitant imbalance of the organism toward parasympathetic dominance.

EEG Effects. Killam and Killam (1957) report that when reserpine is administered to the cat, seizurelike activity appears first in the amygdala and extends progressively to other parts of the rhinencephalon, including the septum. The activity does not appear to spread to the cortex. We may speculate that this seizure activity indicates that the rhinencephalon has been generally put out of action for the time being, and thus the intensity of emotional experience is temporarily diminished. A hypothesis along these lines has been advanced by Himwich (1960).

Side Effects. Motor symptoms have been reported as side effects with reserpine. Rigidity and tremor are especially frequent in these reports. Bodily retention of water, with edema and some concomitant weight gain, have been described. A reduction in sexual motivation in males has also been reported from several sources.

Hypotheses. While there are many variations on them, there are three major hypotheses current regarding the probable action of reserpine in producing behavioral changes. The first, the hypothesis of *adrenergic nerve blockage,* needs only a brief recapitulation here. Essentially, it holds that reserpine disrupts sympathetic nervous activity and hence antagonizes its appearance in stress, fear, anger, etc. Since the anxious patient is presumably overreacting to this kind of stimulation anyway, the shift to parasympathetic dominance brought about by the drug produces more tranquil behavior.

A second hypothesis notes the effects of reserpine upon the *rhinencephalon* and suggests that the hyperactivity produced in the amygdala and surrounding structures effectively disrupts their influence upon higher centers. Since the rhinencephalon is assumed to mediate emotional experience, it ceases to do so following reserpine medication, and there is a consequent diminution in the magnitude and frequency of emotional input to higher centers. This, in turn, produces tranquil behavior.

A third hypothesis relates to the action of reserpine upon *serotonin* levels in the brain. Briefly stated, the hypothesis supposes the destruction of serotonin by reserpine. Serotonin is assumed to be a transmitter substance at certain nerve endings, and the efficiency of this transmission is assumed to depend upon an adequate rate of disposal of the serotonin released at the nerve ending. Excessive serotonin is thus thought to lead to deactivation of the nerves that depend upon serotonin for transmission. As this hypothesis regards the serotonin-controlled nerves to be inhibitory in effect, then deactivation of them would lead to excited or overactive behavior. Restoration of proper serotonin activity would lead to a return of the behavior to normal activity levels. Reserpine is hypothesized to achieve this by its power to destroy serotonin, thus reducing excessive serotonin to normal levels.

All these hypotheses have weaknesses. Of the three, the third is perhaps the weakest because of the large number of assumptions that are required regarding the nerve-transmission functions of serotonin. From the standpoint of empirical evidence, the first hypothesis of adrenergic nerve blockage is perhaps in the strongest position at this time.

THE PSYCHOTOMIMETIC DRUGS

The class of compounds known as psychotomimetic is useful in the study of psychopathology chiefly because of the possible insights they may provide into various psychotic processes. They may also possess some utility in the testing of drug therapies where the psychotomimetic is used to induce a model psychosis first. However, some attention has been paid to these drugs as possibly having therapeutic value in themselves. Considerable controversy centers on this issue, and we should consider the evidence and problems here.

Three major compounds have been used: *mescaline, LSD,* and *psilocybin*. Both LSD and psilocybin possess the indole nucleus; mescaline does not. Mescaline is derived from the cactus peyote (*Lophophora Williamsii*). Certain parts of the spines are removed from the plant and dried to form "mescal buttons." The buttons themselves will produce hallucinatory experiences if ingested intact, but the major ingredient is the alkaloid *mescaline*. When used experimentally, mescaline is given in a pharmacological preparation.

Psilocybin is derived from the mushroom *Psilocybe mexicana*. There are several varieties of hallucination-producing mushrooms to be found in Mexico, most having been used in conjunction with religious ceremonies to induce "visions" which were assumed to have some mystic significance. An early description of the use of the mushroom by Mexican Indians comes to us from the writings of Motolinia (1941 edition):

They had another drunkenness which made them more cruel which was of small mushrooms, which are found here as in Castille; however the ones here are of such a nature that eaten raw and being sour, one drinks afterwards or eats with them a bit of honey; and after a little while they were seeing thousands of visions, expecially of snakes, and as they went completely out of their minds, it seemed to them that their legs and body were full of worms which were eating them alive. . . .

Hoffman, a Swiss chemist, produced the drug psilocybin from the Mexican mushroom in the late 1950s, and most of the research on this drug has been performed in the past five years.

LSD (lysergic acid diethylamide) is a synthetic derivative of ergot, a fungus growth found in cereals and grasses. Hoffman discovered its hallucinogenic characteristics in 1943, and a large body of research has been conducted into its psychological and biological effects. Inasmuch as LSD has generated the most research at this time, we shall consider it in detail as typifying the psychotomimetics in general.

LSD: Biological Effects

Within approximately 30 minutes of taking a dose of LSD, various bodily effects are reported by subjects. Palpitations, dryness of the throat, dizziness, tremulous breathing, nausea, headache, and difficulties in motor coordination are among them. Increased heart rate, raised blood pressure, lowered skin temperature, and pupillary dilation all indicate that the effects are those of sympathetic activity.

LSD: Psychological Effects

The psychological effects of LSD vary considerably from one person to another. Commonly reported among these are vivid visual hallucinations, often colorful in nature; distorted perception of shape and depth; changed perception of time; flight of ideas and associated difficulty in concentration. A brief extract from a description of a drug experience with LSD is given below from Bennett (1960).

Beginning with the physiological sensations, I was shortly flooded with a montage of ideas, images, and feelings that seemed to thrust themselves upon me unbidden. I had glimpses of very bright thoughts, like a fleeting insight into the psychotic process, which I wanted to write down or report to Dr. Krus. But they pushed each other aside. Once gone they could not be recaptured because the parade of new images could not be stopped. (p. 606–607.)

LSD: EEG Effects

The general effect of administration of LSD upon the EEG trace is that of increased arousal, together with a general decrease in the voltage output of cerebral electrical activity.

However, more careful measurement of psychological effects has been made. Animal studies have shown no decrement in operant conditioned performance (Berryman, Jarvik, & Nevin, 1962) in pigeons, but in sufficiently large doses Marrazzi (1962) reports that a conditioned approach response is eliminated, although the behavior of the animal is not generally depressed.

A dosage sufficient to produce this effect left *avoidance* behavior unaffected, however and led Marrazzi to point to the probable differences in the biological mechanisms mediating approach and avoidance behavior. At this juncture we need only note that the effects of LSD are not just those of depressing levels of response, but appear to be related selectively to different kinds of motivational or emotional process.

LSD and Therapy

There is no particular reason to suppose that a psychotomimetic drug will have any beneficial effects by virtue of the experiences that it produces. However, a minor movement has developed within the ranks of psychotherapists, one group claiming that the drug experience may produce insight on the part of individual patients and render hitherto "repressed" material accessible to consciousness—and hence to therapeutic discussion.

Smith (1959), for example, claims that psychotherapy coupled with LSD has had remarkable effects upon chronic alcoholics. The percentage of cures produced by this technique is a little unclear, however. An early report (Smith, 1958) indicated that 12 of 24 refractory alcoholics had "undergone substantial improvement in their drinking patterns after the treatment." However, one year later (Smith, 1959), the investigator commented that "not all of these patients subsequently remained abstinent. Many of the patients who later relapsed, however, had gone back to the most unfavorable environmental conditions" (p. 299). The net total of abstinent patients remaining from the original 24 is not stated, but it seems likely that no very impressive total of cures survived.

Investigators from the Alcoholism Research Clinic of the University of California at Los Angeles (Ditman, Hayman, & Whittesley, 1962) studied the long-term effects of LSD treatment of 74 subjects, including both normal controls and patients. With the passage of time, the number of claims of improvement fell so much that the authors were impelled to comment, "Perhaps LSD is unique in that it prompts so many claims, not only from the subjects and patients, but from the investigators themselves."

Freedman, Ebin, & Wilson (1962) administered LSD to 12 children diagnosed as "autistic schizophrenic." These children were all mute or nearly so. Roughly 20 minutes after ingestion and for 4 hours thereafter, the observers noted the usual somatic sequelae of facial flush, some ataxia, dilation of pupils, and many accompanying psychological phenomena of the usual kind. The hoped-for change from muteness to speech did not occur, and the drug was found to be therapeutically valueless.

There appears to be little or no reason to suppose that the administration of a hallucinogen such as LSD will have any favorable effect upon existing behavior pathology. We have no fundamental understanding of the manner in which these drugs operate, nor any rationale for supposing that temporary disorganization of perception should be of personal value to anyone.

ELECTROCONVULSIVE THERAPY

We may turn now from this brief consideration of the therapeutic use of drugs to the topic of convulsive therapy. While it is difficult to estimate the number of patients treated by any given technique from year to year, the popularity of a therapy may be reflected in the extent to which it is discussed or studied in professional and scientific journals. Wortis (1959) provides relevant data for the appearance of papers dealing with insulin coma, convulsive therapies, and drug therapies in world medical literature over the past 30 years. These are shown in Figure 17-6. It seems clear that drugs have become the major somatic therapy in psychiatric practice, but the use of convulsive treatment is still widespread and requires detailed discussion here.

The major type of convulsive treatment is that produced by passing an electric current

Figure 17-6. Number of articles published each year in the world's medical literature on insulin, convulsive, and drug treatment of psychoses. (Wortis, 1959.)

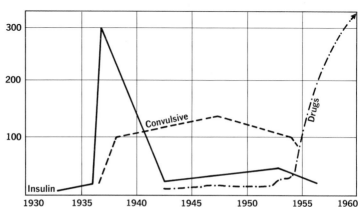

between electrodes placed on the patient's head. A current of sufficient magnitude produces responses reminiscent of a grand mal epileptic convulsion, and the patient passes into coma. Upon recovery of consciousness, there appears to be loss of memory, of greater or lesser degree, for the events prior to the treatment. As a method of treatment, the history of electroconvulsive therapy (ECT) is dated generally from its presentation by Cerletti and Bini at the First International Meeting on the Modern Treatment of Schizophrenia in 1937, although treatment by chemically induced convulsion had been announced some two years previously by Meduna in Hungary.

While there are many technical variants in the manner in which the convulsive shock is applied, the two main techniques involve *subconvulsive shock,* which induces unconsciousness without seizure, and *convulsive shock,* in which the complete seizure is present. Therapists who use ECT feel that the presence of the convulsion is necessary to the effectiveness of the treatment. When given at all, ECT is generally given in a series, sometimes as often as three or more times in a week.

A significant amount of research has been conducted into the effects of ECT both in animal experimental studies and in human clinical studies. For obvious reasons we have little or no data on the effect of ECT upon the responses of normal human controls, and thus the human studies are to a large extent confounded by the fact that the subject's performance is debilitated by the existing psychopathology.

Animal Studies on ECT

The bulk of animal studies has been directed at either of two main issues. The first of these is the memory loss or *retrograde amnesia* found to follow the convulsion; the second is the loss of conflict-induced responses. Investigation of the latter is predicated on the assumption that the therapeutic effects of ECT reported in human patients are analogous to the loss of "neu-

rotic" behaviors experimentally induced in animals.

Retrograde Amnesia.   When an animal has learned to respond to a stimulus in a particular fashion, the application of an electroconvulsive shock (ECS)[1] will lead, under some circumstances, to the seeming loss of the learned habit. This loss is regarded as an instance of retrograde amnesia and has been the subject of considerable study. The classic study was conducted by Duncan (1949). He trained rats to make an avoidance response in a two-compartment shuttle box and administered ECS at varying intervals after the daily trial. These intervals were of 20 seconds, 40 seconds, 4 minutes, 15 minutes, 1 hour, 4 hours, and 14 hours. From his data he noted that where the interval was 20 seconds there was no sign of any learning, while with intervals of 1 hour or more there was no loss. The intervening intervals showed progressive loss from 15 minutes to 40 seconds. Essentially similar findings were reported in comparable studies by Gerard (1955), Thompson and Dean (1955), and Heriot and Coleman (1962). From all these studies it is possible to generalize that intervals of less than 1 hour between the learning trial and ECS will produce some loss, while intervals of over 1 hour produce little or no loss.

Data of this kind have been widely interpreted in terms of what is called the *engram* or *stimulus-trace* hypothesis of learning. In essence, the hypothesis states that any stimulus event produces activity in the central nervous system of the subject, activity which must endure for some minimum period of time before it can be stored permanently. Disruption of the central nervous system during that period will effectively disrupt the storage of the event and thus eradicate it from the recall repertoire of the subject. Because ECS is presumed

---

[1] When referring to the use of electroconvulsive shock for nontherapeutic purposes (as in research), it is customary to use the term *ECS* rather than ECT.

to produce the necessary intensity of disruption, the retrograde amnesia phenomenon is usually interpreted in this light.

Unfortunately, the experimental evidence available to date has generated some difficulties for the stimulus-trace notion. Experiments by Poschel (1957) and by Adams and Lewis (1962) show that ECS has a detrimental effect upon learning even when it is given *before* training. Additional difficulty is created by the fact that many of the retrograde amnesaic results with animals seem to disappear with time. Clearly, the simple explanation that ECS disrupts the formation of a stimulus trace is inadequate to handle all the data.

Conditioned Emotional Responses. Hunt and Brady (1951) studied the effects of ECS upon an established conditioned emotional response (CER). The CER was defined in these studies as the suppression of a bar-pressing response in the presence of a condition stimulus previously paired with unavoidable shock. In these studies the ECS was given three or four days after the CER had first appeared and when it was still quite strong. At that time 21 shocks at the rate of three per day were given, and following this the CER was eliminated. Under some circumstances there was evidence that the CER reappeared after a 30-day rest interval. A major review of the literature is beyond the scope of this discussion, but the general tenor of the data is that ECS reliably attenuates responses based upon fear.

Conflict Responses. When an animal is trained to develop both an approach response and an avoidance response, the effect of ECS is to eliminate the avoidance response without influencing the approach response. Heistad (1955) trained animals to depress a lever for water and then superimposed a shock to the feet that produced conditioned crouching (CER). ECS abolished the crouching, and the animals returned to tilting the lever. Williams (1961) produced an approach-avoidance conflict of the standard Miller runway type. Animals who had been trained to run along an alley for food received noxious shock at the goal end, producing the usual behavioral oscillations in subsequent trials. The effect of subsequent ECS administration was to obliterate the avoidance component of the conflict, leaving the approach response unimpaired. From analogous experiments by Madsen and McGaugh (1961), Pearlman, Sharpless, & Jarvik (1961), and Heriot and Coleman (1962), the same picture emerges.

A Conditioned Inhibition Hypothesis. However, alternative explanations have been offered by Coons and Miller (1960) and by Lewis and Maher (1965), to the effect that the ECS is a stimulus of sufficient potency to elicit a response likely to compete successfully with almost any other response already conditioned to the same environmental stimuli.

The essence of the Lewis and Maher position is that ECS produces coma as an unconditioned response, and that this represents an extreme level of inhibition (Pavlovian "protective inhibition"). Consequently, any stimuli present in the sensory input of the subject at that time are likely to become conditioned stimuli for a response of conditioned inhibition. Conditioned responses are generally weakened versions of the unconditioned form of the response, and thus we should expect to find that the subject shows conditioned relaxation when returned to the environment in which it received the shock, this being an attenuated form of the coma that occurred in response to the shock itself.

Conditioned relaxation would be incompatible with any responses generally mediated by high states of arousal. Emotional or fear responses should be especially vulnerable to this kind of tension reduction, whereas responses mediated by hunger might be less disrupted, being normally performed under lower conditions of arousal than are avoidance responses.

Pertinent to this argument are comments made by Williams (1961). She noted that following ECS, the treated animals in their home cages "huddled in a ball in the rear corners of the cage or crouched on the food containers. They were hyperirritable when handled, and squealed, leaped, or froze when I attempted to lift them." However, when returned to the apparatus in which they had previously received ECS, "the animals behaved as if the grid were not emotion arousing," being markedly relaxed and easy to handle.

It is clearly difficult to generalize from animal to human behavior in the face of so complex and crude a procedure as the administering of a convulsive shock. Under the conditions in which this treatment is given to a human patient, it is especially difficult to discover the stimuli to which a conditioned inhibition might become attached—if this process should occur at all. Nevertheless, as we shall see shortly, the clinical efficacy of ECT in the human patient seems to be related significantly to the general dimension of arousal-inhibition—patients who show parasympathetic dominance producing somewhat more favorable results than do those with sympathetic tone.

General Conclusions from Animal Studies. Certain overall conclusions may be drawn from these animal experiments.

1. ECS seems to have a particularly attenuating effect upon learned emotional responses—both retroactively and proactively.

2. Disruption of learned responses is more marked the briefer the learning-shock interval.

3. The occurrence of the convulsion appears to be important in mediating the retrograde amnesia effect. This is congruent with the notion that ECS attenuates preshock learning by virtue of the prepotence of the response produced by the shock and its conditioning to surrounding stimuli.

4. Current hypotheses include disruption of consolidation of the stimulus trace, selective attenuation of emotional responses, and response competition, especially competition from conditioned inhibition.

Human Studies of ECT

By far the most systematic investigations of ECT upon human behavior have been performed by Cronholm and his associates. (Cronholm & Molander, 1957; Cronholm & Blomqvist, 1959; Cronholm & Ottosson, 1961; etc.). They have been largely concerned with the memory deficit following the convulsion, and have utilized highly controlled investigative techniques, in contrast to the loose clinical impressions reported by many other observers of these effects. In general, the technique has involved the patients' acquisition of standard learning material before the convulsive treatment. Measurements of retention are then made at varying intervals after the ECT has been administered.

In one of these investigations (Cronholm & Lagergren, 1959), a number was presented to the patient either 5, 15, or 60 seconds before ECT. Retention of this number was measured by testing recall at varying intervals after the convulsion. Data were obtained from several different patient groups; a typical outcome is presented in Figure 17-7. This curve shows the cumulative percentage of patients recalling the number up to 36 hours after ECT. As we see, the group receiving the shock 5 seconds after learning is perceptibly inferior in recall to those who received it 60 seconds after learning.

Armed with these data, the investigators considered the implications for the stimulus-trace hypothesis. In the first place, it is clear that considerable recall did occur, given enough time. Thus the ECT did not appear to destroy the trace completely. Mathematical analysis of the data for the two extreme groups (5 seconds and 60 seconds) made it possible to construct equations that described the rate of recovery in both of them. For a combination of patients diagnosed as suffering from "psychoneurosis" or "endogenous depression," the equations were:

$$Re_5 = -3.39 + 1.60 \log t$$
$$Re_{60} = -2.80 + 1.61 \log t$$

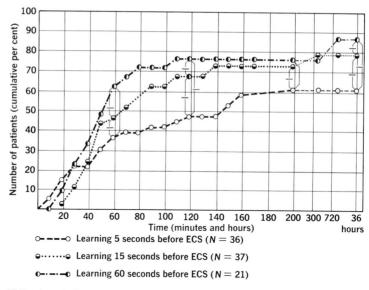

Figure 17-7. Cumulative percentages of patients having recalled the number learned before ECS relative to the time after ECS in the group of endogenous depression. (Cronholm & Lagergren, 1959.)

While we may not wish to attach any permanent validity to the quantities in these equations, the authors interpret them as indicating that a memory trace is weakened more when the learning-shock interval is short, that recovery takes place at the same *rate* independent of this interval over a total of about 160 minutes after ECT, and that the memory trace reaches a lower final level when the learning-shock interval is short than when it is long. The implications of these conclusions for a stimulus-trace position are a little more complicated than those that emerged from the animal studies already cited. Essentially, the implication is that ECT has two effects in retrograde amnesia. One is partial destruction of the trace, and the other is temporary disruption of the mechanisms of recall. The latter process dissipates with time, so that recall eventually becomes possible up to the limits permitted by the partial destruction of the trace.

All these effects diminished with the administration of subsequent ECT. Thus patients who were subject to the same procedures (number presentation, shock, and subsequent recall) showed progressively less retrograde amnesia after the second, third, and fourth ECT sessions. For the 5-second conditioning, this effect is shown in Figure 17-8. With regard to this finding, the investigators are more tentative in their interpretations but suggest that the reason could be improved learning because of practice in the situation, improvement in general mental status because of the therapeutic effects of ECT, or less effect of subsequent ECT convulsions because of some rising threshold caused by the series of treatments.

Maher, McIntire, & House (1962) studied the effects of ECT upon recognition of visual stimuli (colored slides of familiar objects) by patients where some of the material was presented 24 hours before ECT and the remainder within 1 hour before it. Retention was measured by presenting the slides mixed with an equal number of control stimuli that had not been included in the initial learning task and requiring the patient to identify those that he had seen before. In this study the recognition scores of the ECT group were significantly lower than those of the control group, with a nonsignificant

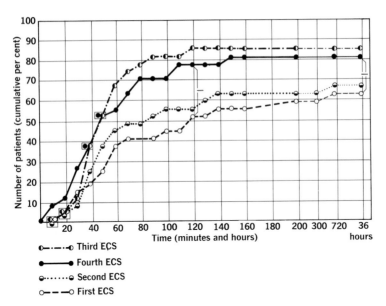

Figure 17-8. Cumulative percentages of patients in the combined group of psycho-neurosis and endogenous depression who recalled the number learned 5 seconds before ECS relative to the time after ECS at the first four treatments (*N* = 27). (Cronholm & Lagergren, 1959.)

Key:
- o—·—·—o Third ECS
- •——————• Fourth ECS
- o·······o Second ECS
- o— — —o First ECS

Y-axis: Number of patients (cumulative per cent)
X-axis: Time (minutes and hours)

tendency for the 1-hour material to be recognized less often than the 24-hour material. This is in agreement with earlier work of Zubin and Barrera (1941) and Mayer-Gross (1943). The latter found that the deficiency in recognition of pictures was considerably more marked when the post-shock test was conducted less than 24 hours after ECT.

Janis (1950) has reported that the retrograde amnesia following ECT is most pronounced for items of great personal significance associated with the patient's illness. A graphic illustration of these effects is given in Example 17-1, which presents transcripts of interviews held with a patient before and after ECT.

Further investigations by Janis produced evidence that under more controlled conditions (i.e., a word association test) there was difficulty in recall of previous responses attributable to deficiency in maintaining the "task-set" of the situation. From this, Janis offers the hypothesis that the posttreatment amnesias and related difficulties in producing personal memories following electric convulsive treatments "may arise from a basic disturbance in recall processes, consisting of an increased tendency to produce spurious, irrelevant associations which interfere with the production of the habitual associations necessary for evoking the recall of personal past experiences."

It is interesting at this point to return to the hypothesis of conditioned inhibition that was described earlier in our discussion of animal studies and retrograde amnesia. The personal memories that are difficult to recall in Janis's demonstration above are all rather traumatic memories, the recall of which is analogous to making a response that is highly arousing. Thus the selective loss of memory for personal items is rather heavily confounded here with a loss of memory for distressing items.

We may, therefore, consider his findings to be congruent with the more general hypothesis that ECS attenuates the production

EXAMPLE 17-1

Before ECT

The patient was a thirty-four-year-old male schizophrenic (paranoid) who had had 22 electroshocks.

Q. Has there been anything in particular that happened which disturbed you?

A. I tried to commit suicide. I thought I was losing my mind because I had a funny feeling in my head. A dull feeling all through my head. It wasn't painful but I felt I didn't care about anything because of that feeling. I tried to commit suicide because of that and because I thought I had syphilis. . . . I went to my room and got a scarf and put on a sweat shirt and blue work shirt. I had a few beers and at the bar I thought I heard a fellow say, "That smell sure is syphilis." I got a pint of whiskey after leaving my room and then I took a train. I don't know where I got off the train but I had drunk a lot. Then I saw my brother at a bar at S— and I drank some beer there. Then I went to a private driveway to an old mansion up on a hill and I put the scarf over the stone and I stepped off the stone. I tried to hang myself. I don't know what happened but I came to down at a gas station about a quarter mile from that driveway.

Q. What do you think happened?

A. Maybe the scarf broke. I don't remember how I got to the gas station. I accused a fellow at the gas station of taking my coat and hat—but he was right. I must have left it back where I tried to commit suicide.

Four Weeks after ECT: First Session

Q. Has there been anything in particular that happened which disturbed you?

A. I already told you all the things.

Q. Did you ever think about suicide?

A. No.

Second Session

Q. I believe you told me something about suicide several months ago when I talked with you.

A. About suicide? I don't remember anything about suicide. I can't recall ever thinking about suicide.

Q. Have you ever been drunk?

A. Yes.

Q. Did anything special ever happen when you were drunk?

A. Nothing much ever happened.

Q. Can you remember going to the town S— once when you were drinking?

A. I don't remember.

Q. Do you remember losing any clothing when you were drunk?

A. I remember I lost some clothes but I don't remember how. I lost a top coat through drinking—my brother told me it was in S— when he was here last week—but I can't remember anything about being in S—. My brother said I lost a hat and coat there.

Third Session

Q. When I talked with you several months ago you told me something about suicide thoughts you had before coming to the hospital.

A. I've been trying to remember that, but I can't.

Q. Do you think you might have tried to commit suicide?

A. I don't think I ever did. Did I? At Staff one of the doctors said that I tried to commit suicide but I don't think that's true.

Q. I'd like you to take a look at this list and see if one of these things applies to you. (The patient was shown the following list of 8 items, which were also read aloud to him, slowly.)

A   Took a big overdose of sleeping pills in your room in P.
B   Turned on the gas in a room with the windows shut.
C   Tied a scarf over a stone and stepped off of it, on a private driveway to an old mansion.
D   Started to slash your wrists while in a bathtub.
E   Stayed in a garage and breathed the exhaust of a car with its motor on.
F   Started to jump out of the window of a high building.
G   Got hold of a gun and started to use it when at your mother's house.
H   Took a bottle of iodine to drink when at your wife's room.

A. None of them means anything to me. Did I actually do one of those things?
Q. We'll talk about that later. Right now I want you to see if any of these seem familiar.
A. None of them do.
Q. Suppose that one of them did apply to you. Take a guess which one it might be.
A. I don't know. I'll guess H.

(Janis, 1950, p. 365–366.)

of responses that are mediated by or associated with high states of arousal, while leaving other responses relatively intact.

Therapeutic Effects of ECT

The scientific literature of psychopathology abounds with reports of investigations into the therapeutic efficiency of ECT. We shall consider the data as they refer to different diagnostic categories.

Schizophrenia. Early enthusiasts for the use of ECT reported remission rates as high as 55 to 60 per cent in hospitalized schizophrenic patients given shock treatment in the first year after admission. However, more prudent observations have been made by Kalinowsky and Worthing (1943) in their follow-up study of 200 patients who were given a complete series of ECT treatments. They found that the most important factor in predicting the remission of the symptoms was duration of illness—not treatment. Thus of the patients whose illness had a duration of less than 6 months, 67 per

cent improved, while for durations of 16 to 24 months and more than 24 months, the figures were 43.1 and 9.2 per cent, respectively. Even this study lacked a follow-up, so that we do not know how many of these patients ultimately relapsed. Rennie (1943) pursued this matter more closely and found that in a total of 43 patients treated with ECT, the remission rate of 55 per cent at the termination of treatment had fallen to 32 per cent when these persons were studied 3 years later. He concluded that the use of ECT was of doubtful value in patients diagnosed as schizophrenic—a conclusion that seems to be eminently justified.

Affective Disorders. Generally speaking, the results of ECT have been most encouraging in the treatment of depression. For example, Thomas (1954) studied the effects of ECT upon 307 cases of depression and reported 69 per cent recovered, 28 per cent improved, and only 3 per cent unchanged. Of the recovered group, only 23 per cent exhibited relapse. Kalinowsky and Hoch (1949) report other studies to the effect that remission rates of 80 per cent and higher are quite common when ECT is applied to depressed patients. Many of these studies are hampered by the lack of a control group of untreated patients, making it difficult to know whether the high success rates are due to the unusual efficacy of ECT or to the fact that depressions have a high probability of recovery anyway. One investigation by Huston and Locher (1948) reports figures bearing on this issue. They compared the remission rate of 74 depressive patients treated with ECT and a group of 80 controls. The results showed that 63 of the controls and 65 of the treated patients recovered, but the median recovery period for the latter was 9 months while that for the controls was 15 months. Otherwise the rates are not significantly different in the two groups.

In conclusion, it may be stated that there is little evidence of any kind to suggest the value of ECT except in cases of depression. Here, the general tenor of the evidence is that shock tends to hasten the recovery time, but that it is not essential to ultimate recovery. Any treatment that hastens the departure from hospital must be favorably regarded, however, and it is likely that ECT will be used for this purpose for some time to come.

Side Effects. Repeated assault upon the brain with electric shock sufficiently intense to produce a convulsion brings with it certain dangers. The most obvious of these is that the therapy will produce direct damage to central nervous tissue itself, substituting a brain-damage syndrome for some other form of psychopathology—or perhaps compounding the two. Additional complications arise with the possibility of heart failure or bone fracture during the administration of the ECT itself.

Brain Damage. During the early years of its application, the dangers of brain damage following ECT were minimized by its users. Jessner and Ryan (1941), for example,

quote the originators of the technique, stating, "Cerebral complications or mental sequelae have never been seen during or after the treatment with two years application of the method. That there are no anatomical reasons to expect such complication is shown by means of extensive investigations on shock-treated animals. They are never found in dogs treated with electric convulsive treatment; here only reversible changes such as Nissl's acute disease were seen."

Working with animals on this problem, Allen (1951) showed that changes are produced in the ganglion cells of the brain almost immediately, that they develop for a time, and that they then decrease. It has also been shown that hemorrhages occur in the substance of the brain, most often in one particular part, but also in a lesser degree elsewhere; that destruction of and damage to nerve cells occur in and about the areas affected by the hemorrhages; and that subsequent organization in those parts may be accompanied by further changes in nerve cells which are necessarily irreversible. Histological examination of the cerebral tissues of two patients who died following the application of ECT made it clear that those changes were produced in the brain, not as a result of the repeatedly induced convulsions, but as a result of the passage of the current itself.

Impressive evidence is presented in a histological study by Alpers and Hughes (1942) on the brains of two patients who died following termination of ECT. Case 1 had 62 electrical convulsions during 5 months and died 3 months after the last treatment; case 2 had 6 convulsive treatments, dying 5 months after the last treatment. The examinations showed that case 1 had fresh hemorrhages in the cerebral cortex, white matter, and brainstem, and that case 2 had old areas of perivascular damage chiefly in the white matter. In both instances the changes described appeared to be attributable to the convulsive treatment. The importance of case 1 lies in its demonstration of fresh and older hemorrhages, both being undoubtedly the result of the electrical convulsive treatment. The significance of case 2 is even greater than that of case 1, for it demonstrates that damage to the brain may result from relatively few treatments, and that such damage may persist for some time after the termination of treatment—5 months in this case.

Quite apart from these evidences of gross organic damage, there is the evidence that ECT produces impaired ability to acquire and retain new learning afterwards. Here again, the evidence is equivocal. Brengelmann (1959) reports impairment in visual learning appearing only when five or more shocks had been given. He attributes this deficit to an organic syndrome that develops only with repeated shock. Stone (1947) reported on the effects of a series of ECT treatments upon scores on a standard memory scale. He found that there was significant inferiority of performance on the part of the shock group and adduced this in support of the view that the effects of a *series* of ECT administrations is such as to bring about a gradual decline in intellectual efficiency.

Investigators who have studied the effects of a single shock upon later learning efficiency or intellectual performance have generally failed to find any stable significant loss. In some cases, there has been an improvement believed to be due to the clinical behavioral improvement in the patient attendant upon the treatment.

All in all, while the issue is still somewhat open, the best conclusion that we can draw at this time is that repeated ECT may produce perceptible damage to central nervous system structures and accompanying loss in behavioral efficiency.

Prognosis for Therapeutic Effectiveness. We have considered the effects of ECT largely in terms of classical diagnostic groups. Several investigators have been concerned with the identification of patients who might respond favorably to ECT by means of a quantitative test or criterion, regardless of the psychiatric syndrome. Five types of predictor have been used: the Funkenstein test, the *sedation threshold,* the amytal test, the EEG–delta wave test, and various verbal tests such as the MMPI. An excellent review of these tests has been provided by Thorpe (1962). We shall consider three of them here.

The Funkenstein Test. We have already discussed the essentials of this test in the section on the mecholyl test in Chapter 4. However, when using this procedure as a prognostic test for response to ECT, it is elaborated to include an intravenous injection of adrenalin together with the intramuscular injection of mecholyl. By measuring the subject's responses to both of these drugs, Funkenstein et al. (1952) developed seven categories or groups of response pattern. The major attributes of these groups are given in Table 17-4. Within this category, the patients in group VII showed 97 per cent improvement following ECT, while

TABLE 17-4 Grouping of Responses to Funkenstein Test

Injection	Systolic blood pressure response (mm Hg)						
	Group I	Groups II and III*	Group IV	Group V	Group VI	Group VII
Epinephrine	Rise of more than 50	Rise of more than 50	Rise of more than 50	Rise of 50 or less	Rise of more than 50	Rise of more than 50
Methacholine	Slight fall and early rise above preinjection level, but failure to return to preinjection level within 25 min.	Moderate or slight fall, with or without slight rise above preinjection level, but return to preinjection level	Moderate fall with marked compensatory delayed rise before return to preinjection level	Fall with failure to reach preinjection level within 25 min.	Fall with failure to reach preinjection level within 25 min.	Chill after injection; reliable readings not obtainable

* *Groups II and III have been amalgamated, as the differences between them are only slight.*
SOURCE: *Thorpe (1962).*

those in group I showed less than 10 per cent improvement. However, subsequent work by Alexander (1955), Sloane and Lewis (1956), and Lotsof and Yobst (1957) failed to confirm this; in fact, their findings tended to suggest that the reverse predictions would be correct. Bearing in mind data on the test-retest reliability and the relationship of the test response to the age of the patient, Thorpe (1962) concludes that while the Funkenstein test has some potential as a predictor, it requires further development before it can be regarded as useful clinically. For example, the reliance upon systolic blood pressure seems to be less justified than the use of several variables reflecting sympathetic activity.

The Sleep-threshold Test. Shagass, Naiman, and Mihalik (1956) reported that when ECT was given to patients with low sleep thresholds, the short-term response was more impressive than that of patients with high thresholds. In the sleep-threshold test, thiopental sodium is injected intravenously at the rate of 0.5 mg/kg body weight every 30 seconds until there is a failure of verbal or motor response to the calling of the patient's name. The lower the threshold for this response, the better the remission under ECT. The sleep threshold has been found to be highest for patients with anxiety state, and lowest for those diagnosed as hysteric (Shagass, 1957).

The Amytal Test. Much the same kind of finding has been reported with the use of sodium amytal. Kahn, Fink, and Weinstein (1956) administered the drug at a standard rate to patients about to undergo ECT and used their responses to a set of questions as evidence of the drug effect. Most of these questions are designed to elicit evidence of disorientation for time, place, and personal history. Here the patients with the lowest thresholds showed more favorable response to ECT than did those with high thresholds.

It seems clear that the common feature of the Funkenstein test, the sleep threshold test, and the amytal test is in their relevance to the question of sympathetic-parasympathetic dominance in the patient. The precise manner in which dominance may interact with the shock to produce good or poor results is far from clear, but may be considered as some indication of the importance of autonomic center activity in the mediation of ECT effects.

Theories of Therapeutic Effectiveness. In 1948, Gordon identified no fewer than fifty theories then current regarding the basis of the therapeutic effect in ECT. These ranged from metaphysical speculations that the patient experiences the physician as a mother because of his helplessness during the convulsion or that the patient experiences exhilaration at having overcome death and being reborn. Physiological theories included the belief that spasms are produced in brain capillaries and lead to the destruction of degenerate cells, as well as that structural changes in the hippocampus include the replacement of neurons by glial cells. However, throughout all the theorizing that has been reported in the literature, certain major hypotheses have been advanced.

Biological Hypotheses. The recurrent themes in biological explanations put forward to account for ECT effects are:

1. The shock acts as a stressor and thus triggers the alarm reactions described by Selyé in the general adaptation syndrome. Deficiency in the stress response is presumed to be at the root of the disordered behavior, and thus the patient is shocked into adequate functioning of the pituitary-adrenal axis.

2. Shock acts as a sympathetic stimulator in patients who are pathologically low in their arousability. Thus the ECT shifts them in the direction of sympathetic dominance and thus more effective responses to normal stimulation.

3. ECT destroys some unspecified pathological tissue.

Psychological Hypotheses. Here we find that the views put forward are either purely psychological, in the sense that the possible physiology of ECT is regarded as irrelevant, or psychobiological—i.e., concerned with the behavioral changes presumed to follow from the mediating physiological effects. Among the psychobiological explanations are:

1. The retrograde amnesia affects more recent habits, and as these are usually the pathological ones, they are eliminated to the benefit of the patient. Older, more adaptive patterns are not disrupted and now reappear.
2. ECT acts as a punishment, punishing the patient for symptomatic behavior—such as discussing his difficulties, for example. Thus, after ECT the patient represses the symptoms for which he was hospitalized and is unable to recall his earlier problems.
3. Avoidance behavior is selectively eliminated by ECT, and as anxiety is presumed to be basic to most disordered behavior, its elimination proves to be therapeutic.

Since the "psychological" explanations are largely literary, we shall simply mention that they involve the assertion that ECT has some unconscious meaning to the patient, either as a death threat or as guilt-relieving punishment and atonement.

Electroconvulsive therapy is a purely empirical technique. At this time there is no acceptable theoretical rationale for its use, little knowledge of its physical effects, considerable ambiguity in our understanding of its behavioral effects, and inadequate substantiation of its therapeutic efficiency. Nevertheless, the present and probable future use of ECT is well indicated by Kalinowsky's conclusion that "the place of ECT in the therapeutic armamentarium of the psychiatrist is definitely established in all mental institutions" (1959).

PSYCHOSURGERY

The third class of somatic therapies includes the use of surgical intervention to destroy tissue with the expectation that this will produce a desirable change in behavior. While there are several variants of technique, the main procedure that has been used is to sever the connections between certain areas of the frontal cortex and the rest of the central nervous system, but most specifically the thalamus. For this approach the general term "psychosurgery" has been used. Individual techniques have identifying names, hinging largely upon the specific procedure used to achieve the disruption of tracts connecting the frontal areas of the cortex and the thalamus. Among the major techniques are the following:

Prefrontal Leucotomy. Small holes are drilled in either side of the head, and a sharp cutting instrument (a *leucotome*) is used to cut the major neural pathways between the frontal areas and lower brain centers. This procedure was developed by Moniz (1937), one of the earliest workers in the field of psychosurgery.

Prefrontal Lobotomy. A modification of Moniz's procedure was developed in the United States by Freeman and Watts (cf. Freeman & Watts, 1948), the effect of which is much the same as the original, specifically, interrupting the larger part of the neural connections between the thalamic nuclei and the frontal areas.

Other variations of psychosurgery include *cerebral topectomy, transorbital lobotomy,* and *thermocoagulation.* Whatever the characteristics specific to the procedure, they all share the goal of reducing the emotional nucleus of the patient's behavior and hence of his psychopathology.

We shall postpone, for the moment, consideration of the theoretical justification for these procedures to treat some of the empirical findings. Partridge (1950) conducted a survey of the outcome of prefrontal leucotomy techniques on a group of 300 British patients. In this study the investigator, who had no preoperative contact with the patients, visited them personally to gain the data—to the extent of going to Africa to interview three of the sample.

Data was obtained in nonhospital surroundings, and for privacy interviews were sometimes conducted in a garden or in the interviewer's car. In one case where a female patient had suggested meeting in the lobby of a large London hotel, the interviewer found it necessary to "hire chairs in St. James's Park, where a reasonably complete examination (including retinoscopy) was possible, except that the number of evening strollers precluded elicitation of the abdominal reflexes."

In this group 23 patients died, 4 for reasons unrelated to the surgery. Of the remaining 19 deaths, 10 were attributed to the operation or to postoperative epilepsy. A wide range of side effects was reported, including increase in appetite, gains in weight, etc.

As the group of patients included a wide range of diagnoses, it is not surprising that a wide range of outcomes was reported. Because the investigation did not involve quantifiable measures of improvement, it is difficult to assess the general validity of the findings. By the same token, no comparison is provided with control patients bearing similar diagnoses but not operated on.

Intellectual Changes

Several investigators have studied the effects of psychosurgery upon cognitive behavior —specifically, upon intelligence and upon learning. A variety of these studies has been reviewed by Willett (1961). From his reviews emerges a predominant picture of "no change" in gross intelligence as measured by standard tests. Some investigators report particular deficits in the subtests of intelligence scales. For example, McCullough (1950) reports changes in the scores on the digit span, picture arrangement, and block design subtests of the Wechsler-Bellevue scale.

Many studies of learning and retention show no deficit postoperatively in the patient. However, a stimulating investigation was reported by Malmo and Amsel (1949), who argued that the frontal lobe lesions should lead to an increase in associative interference in performance. Associative interference, as we have seen in earlier discussions of schizophrenia, is evidenced by the making of strong competing responses to stimuli where these responses are inappropriate. Malmo and Amsel suggested that because this effect is usually found in the middle of a menial learning task— middle items typically being harder to learn —then the patient should be expected to show marked deterioration in performance in the middle of such a task. The data confirmed this effect, as Figure 17-9 shows.

In passing, we may note here a striking similarity to the effects found in a study reported by Carpenter (1952) of frontal lobe ablation in animals. He trained rats to a series discrimination task, hypothesizing that loss of frontal lobe function would be followed by interference of the last response in the series with those that should occur earlier. His data are shown in Figure 17-10.

Frontal Lobe Function and Inhibition

The study of cognitive deficit in psychosurgery may be aided by a consideration of general findings regarding the loss of inhibition in animals subjected to analogous operations. There are now reports of several investigations indicating clearly that with destruction of frontal cortical tissue, the responses of an experimental animal are likely to be marked by hyperactivity, much of which seems to consist of ready distractibility by any fluctuation in environmental stimulation. Hyperactivity and distractibility have been reported by Maher (1955), Maher and McIntire (1960), French (1959), and Maher, Elder, and Noblin (1962). In brief, it appears that performance on any task which requires concentrated and focused attention will be impaired when the frontal cortex is rendered nonfunctional. To the extent that the maintenance of attention is properly regarded as evidence of the ability to inhibit distracting stimuli, the loss of frontal function is accompanied by loss of inhibition.

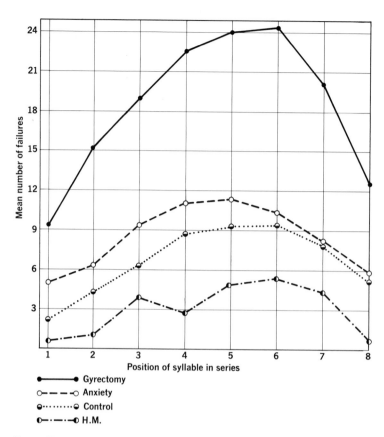

Figure 17-9. Composite curves showing mean number of failures at various syllables during learning by sixteen patients with "clinical anxiety," sixteen controls, five gyrectomy patients, and H.M. (one gyrectomy patient who appeared atypical). (Malmo & Amsel, 1949.)

Psychosurgery and Therapeutic Improvement

The difficulties in evaluating the therapeutic efficiency of psychosurgical procedures are, as the reader may well imagine, enormous. The selection of a patient for psychosurgery seems often to be a rather arbitrary decision based upon the failure of other less drastic techniques. Studies in which patients subjected to psychosurgical procedures are compared on follow-up with untreated matched control patients are relatively rare. However, some investigators (Jenkins, Holspopple, & Lorr, 1954) have achieved this kind of control and report significant improvement rates in the operated group.

Kalinowsky and Hoch (1961) citing British statistics reveal that 60 per cent of operated patients were able to leave the hospital and return to gainful occupations, while another 30 per cent were able to return home, although they did not become self-supporting. However, he goes on to point out: "These figures again are meaningless unless we realize that the selection of cases determines the outcome. Many of our hospitals have limited the operation to hopeless, deteriorated schizophrenics which naturally led to unsatisfactory results. Careful selec-

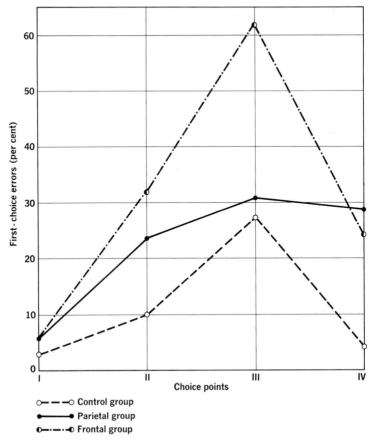

Figure 17-10. Error gradients for frontal ablation and control groups. (Carpenter, 1952.)

tion of cases obviously makes for favorable statistics" (p. 140).

Clearly it is difficult to make a generalization about the efficiency of psychosurgery. Many people, including professional workers in the field of psychosurgery, feel that a therapy which changes the patient in some irreversible fashion is necessarily questionable. Where the change is in the form of the destruction of a higher brain area, the doubts become strong indeed. With the advent of drug therapies, the use of psychosurgery to achieve quieting of agitated pa-

tients is less necessary, and there are signs that it is becoming a less popular therapeutic technique than was true a decade or so ago.

SUMMARY

We have now considered three of the major types of somatic therapy for the behavior disorders. The most striking feature of all these therapies—drug, electroconvulsive, and surgical—is that they were developed without benefit of theory. In fact, it is only a slight exaggeration to describe their development as largely accidental.

Because of this, we find that a considerable effort is going into the problem of developing adequate theories to account for the effects of these procedures. In every case, the problem faced in developing and testing hypotheses is exacerbated by the fact that the actual techniques are quite gross, while the bodily mechanisms with which they interfere are both complex and delicate.

Although the tranquilizers are more recent comers to the field of somatic therapy than either ECT or psychosurgery, the sophistication of psychopharmacological theory exceeds to a considerable degree that developed for the other two procedures. Although there has been much elaboration of the probable biochemical processes involved in the actions of tranquilizers, the relationship of these to pathological behavior remains the weakest link in the chain of theoretical reasoning.

When we turn to the problem of biology-behavior relationships as these are exemplified in the somatic therapies, we find that a common thread is discernible in the patterns of explanation for the three techniques under scrutiny. Data from the study of chlorpromazine, reserpine, ECT, and frontal lobe surgery tend to implicate the general dimension of activity level, with the concomitant notion of arousal and inhibition functions. In the case of psychosurgery, we find that the effects may be understood as shifts from inhibition to excitation, or at least as being the consequences of impairing the process that inhibits ordinary sensory input. The tranquilizers, on the other hand, seem to move the autonomic tonus of the patient toward a state of parasympathetic dominance, with accompanying diminution of alerting responses to external stimulation. Electroconvulsive shock effects are perhaps the most difficult to incorporate into any simple explanatory system. The data from human studies are quite unclear, and to a large extent unreliably quantified. Much of the animal data are amenable to a conditioned inhibition explanation, and this is the one that has been preferred in the earlier discussions in this chapter. However, the jump from animal to human behavior is a particularly hazardous one to make when the mediating mechanisms are so poorly understood. If the reader makes such a jump, it should be with caution.

Quite apart from the problems of theory are the equally pressing problems of the efficacy of these therapies and the limits within which such efficacy might be found. Treatment does not wait on the theoreticians. For the physician, the main questions are when to give the treatment and what to expect of it in the way of improvement in the patient's behavior. Much work is going on in the search for answers to these questions. Some of the tentative answers have been outlined in this chapter. The answers already achieved have begun to affect the use of these therapies. It is quite likely, for example, that the steady decline in enthusiasm for psychosurgical techniques will continue, giving way to the increasing interest in biochemical methods.

This is as it should be, of course. We must anticipate that techniques in the treatment of disordered behavior will rise and fall. Man's efforts to solve the problems that nature presents him provide us with a record of continual change. When methods become doctrines and practitioners become disciples, then our progress is delayed.

SUGGESTED READINGS

1. Campbell, D. *The psychological effects of cerebral electroshock.* In H. Eysenck (Ed.), *Handbook of abnormal psychology.* New York: Basic Books, 1961. A brief but thorough survey of the experimental research literature on ECS and behavior.

2. Partridge, N. *Prefrontal leucotomy.* Oxford: Blackwell, 1950. An account of the follow-up of 300 patients sub-

jected to psychosurgery. Written in a narrative style, it covers the outcome of treatment in chapters dealing with patients in various diagnostic categories.

3. Uhr, L., & Miller, J. G. *Drugs and behavior.* New York: Wiley, 1960. An excellent general survey of a variety of approaches to the study of drugs and psychological consequences of their administration. Particular attention is paid to issues of methodology and measurement.

4. Willett, R. A. The effects of psychosurgical procedures on behavior. In H. Eysenck (Ed.), *Handbook of abnormal psychology.* New York: Basic Books, 1961. A very thorough survey of the empirical data on the consequences of various psychosurgical procedures. Includes experimental studies and clinical outcome data.

REFERENCES

Adams, H. E., & Lewis, D. J. Retrograde amnesia and competing responses. *J. comp. physiol. Psychol.,* 1962, **55,** 302–305.

Alexander, L. Epinephrine-mecholyl test (Funkenstein test); its value in determining the recovery potential of patients with mental disease. *A.M.A. Arch. Neurol. Psychiat.,* 1955, **73,** 496–514.

Allen, I. M. Cerebral injury with shock treatment. *New Zealand med. J.,* 1951, **50,** 356–364.

Alpers, B. J., & Hughes, J. Changes in the brain after electrically induced convulsions in cats. *Arch. Neurol. Psychiat.,* 1942, **47,** 385–398.

Andy, O. J., & Akert, K. Seizure patterns induced by electrical stimulation of hippocampal formation in the cat. *J. Neuropath. exp. Neurol.,* 1955, **14,** 198–213.

Barrett, W. W., Ellsworth, R. B., Clark, L. D., & Ennis, June. Study of the differential behavioral effects of Reserpine, Chlorpromazine, and a combination of these drugs in chronic schizophrenic patients. *Dis. nerv. Sys.,* 1957, **18,** 1–7.

Barry, H., & Miller, N. E. Effects of drugs on approach-avoidance conflict tested repeatedly by means of a "telescope alley." *J. comp. physiol. Psychol.,* 1962, **55,** 201–210.

Bein, H. J., Gross, F., Tripod, J., & Meier, R. Experimentelle Untersuchungen über die Kreislaufwirkung der blutdrucksenkenden Hydrazinophthalazinederivate Apresalin und Nepresol. *Schweiz. med. Wschr.,* 1953, **83,** 1007–1022.

Bennett, C. The drugs and I. In L. Uhr & J. G. Miller (Eds.), *Drugs and behavior.* New York: Wiley, 1960.

Berryman, R., Jarvik, M., & Nevin, J. A. Effects of pentobarbital, lysergic acid, diethylamide and chlorpromazine on matching behavior in the pigeon. *Psychopharmacologia,* 1962, **3,** 60–65.

Brengelmann, J. C. *The effect of repeated electroshock on learning in depressives.* Munich: Springer, 1959.

Carpenter, A. J. Anticipatory behavior in the rat following frontal lesions. *J. comp. physiol. Psychol.,* 1952, **45,** 413–418.

Coons, E. E., & Miller, N. E. Conflict versus consolidation of memory traces to explain "retrograde amnesia" produced by E.C.S. *J. comp. physiol. Psychol.,* 1960, **53,** 524–531.

Cronholm, B., & Blomquist, C. Memory disturbances after electroconvulsive therapy. 2. Conditions one week after a series of treatments. *Acta Psychiat. Neurol. Scand.,* 1959, **34,** 18–25.

Cronholm, B., & Lagergren, A. Memory disturbances after electroconvulsive therapy. 3. An experimental study of retrograde amnesia after electroconvulsive shock. *Acta Psychiat. Neurol. Scand.,* 1959, **34,** 283–310.

Cronholm, B., & Molander, L. Memory disturbances after electroconvulsive therapy. 1. Conditions 6 hours after electroshock treatment. *Acta Psychiat. Neurol. Scand.,* 1957, **32,** 280–306.

Cronholm, B., & Ottosson, J. O. "Countershock" in electroconvulsive therapy. *Arch. gen. Psychiat.*, 1961, **4**, 254–258.

Ditman, K. S., Hayman, M., & Whittesley, J. Nature and frequency of claims following LSD. *J. nerv. ment. Dis.*, 1962, **134**, 346–352.

Duncan, C. P. The retroactive effect of electroshock on learning. *J. comp. physiol. Psychol.*, 1949, **42**, 32–44.

Elder, J. T., & Dille, J. M. An experimental study of the participation of the sympathetic nervous system in the lysergic acid diethylamide (LSD) reaction in cats. *J. pharmacol. exp. Therap.*, 1962, **136**, 162–168.

Ellsworth, R. B., & Clark, L. D. Prediction of the response of chronic schizophrenics to drug therapy, a preliminary report of the relationship between palmar sweat and the behavioral effects of tranquilizing drugs. *J. clin. Psychol.*, 1957, **13**, 59–61.

Fink, G. B., & Swinyard, E. A. Comparison of anticonvulsant and psychopharmacologic drugs. *J. pharm. Sci.*, 1962, **51**, 548–551.

Freedman, A. M., Ebin, Eva F., & Wilson, Ethel A. Autistic schizophrenic children. *Arch. gen. Psychiat.*, 1962, **6**, 203–215.

Freeman, W., & Watts, J. W. Pain mechanisms and frontal lobes: a study of prefontal lobotomy for intractable pain. *Ann. intern. Med.*, 1948, **28**, 747–754.

French, G. M. A. A deficit associated with hypermotility in monkeys with lesions of the dorsalateral frontal granular cortex. *J. comp. physiol. Psychol.*, 1959, **52**, 25–58.

Funkenstein, D. H., Greenblatt, M., & Solomon, H. C. An autonomic nervous system test of prognostic significance in relation to electroshock treatment. *Psychosom. Med.*, 1952, **14**, 347–362.

Gerard, R. W. Biological roots of psychiatry. *Science*, 1955, **122**, 225–230.

Gordon, H. L. Fifty shock therapy theories. *The Military Surgeon*, 1948, **3**, 397–401.

Green, A. F. Antihypertensive drugs. In S. Garattini & P. A. Shore (Eds.), *Advances in pharmacology*. Vol. 1. New York: Academic, 1962.

Haase, H. J. Die Beinflussung psychomotorischer Aktivität bei neuroleptischer und antidepressives Behandlung. *Nervenarzt*, March, 1962, **33(3)**, 116–124.

Hartry, Arlene L. The effects of reserpine on the psychogenic production of gastric ulcers in rats. *J. comp. physiol. Psychol.*, 1962, **55**, 719–721.

Heistad, G. T. An effect of electroconvulsive shock on a conditioned avoidance response. *J. comp. physiol. Psychol.*, 1955, **48**, 482–487.

Heriot, J. T., & Coleman, P. D. The effects of electroconvulsive shock on retention of a modified "one-trial" conditioned avoidance. *J. comp. physiol. Psychol.*, 1962, **55**, 1082–1084.

Himwich, H. E. The new psychiatric drugs. *Sci. Amer.*, Oct., 1955.

Himwich, H. Biochemical and neuropsychological action of psychoactive drugs. In L. Uhr & J. G. Miller (Eds.), *Drugs and behavior*. New York: Wiley, 1960.

Hunt, H. F. Some effects of drugs upon classical (Type S) conditioning. *Ann. N.Y. Acad. Sci.*, 1956, **65**, 258–267.

Hunt, H. F., & Brady, J. W. Some effects of electroconvulsive shock on a conditioned response ("anxiety"). *J. comp. physiol. Psychol.*, 1951, **44**, 88–98.

Huston, P. E., & Locher, L. M. Manic-depressive psychosis: course when treated and untreated with electric shock. *Arch. Neurol. Psychiat.*, 1948, **60**, 37–48.

Janis, I. L. Psychological effects of electric convulsive treatments. *J. nerv. ment. Dis.*, 1950, **3**, 359–397; 469–489.

Jenkins, R. L., Holsopple, J. Q., & Lorr, M. Effects of prefrontal lobotomy on patients with severe chronic schizophrenia. *Amer. J. Psychiat.*, 1954, **111**, 84–90.

Jessner, L., & Ryan, V. G. *Shock treatment in psychiatry*. New York: Grune & Stratton, 1941.

Kahn, R. L., Fink M., & Weinstein, E. A. Relation of amobarbitol test to clinical improvement in electric shock. *Arch. Neurol. Psychiat.*, 1956, **76**, 23–29.

Kalinowsky, L. B. Convulsive shock treatment. In S. Arieti (Ed.), *American handbook of psychiatry.* Vol. 2. New York: Basic Books, 1959.

Kalinowsky, L. B., & Hoch, P. H. *Shock treatment and other somatic procedures.* New York: Grune & Stratton, 1949.

Kalinowsky, L. B., & Hoch, P. H. *Somatic treatments in psychiatry; pharmacotherapy, convulsive, insulin, surgical and other methods.* New York: Grune & Stratton, 1961.

Kalinowsky, L. B., & Worthing, H. J. Results with electric convulsive therapy in 200 cases of schizophrenia. *Psychiat. Quart.*, 1943, **17**, 144–153.

Keller, D. L., & Umbreit, W. W. Chemically altered "permanent" behavior patterns in fish and their cure by reserpine. *Science,* 1956, **124** (3218), 407.

Killam, E. K., & Killam, K. F. Influence of drugs on central afferent pathways. In W. S. Fields (Ed.), *Brain mechanisms and drug action.* Springfield, Ill., Charles C Thomas, 1957.

Kinnard, W. J., Aceto, M. D. G., & Buckley, J. P. The effects of certain psychotropic agents on the conditioned emotional responses behavior of the albino rat. *Psychopharmacologia,* 1962, **3**, 227–230.

Lasky, J. J. Veterans administration cooperative chemotherapy projects and related studies. In L. Uhr & J. G. Miller (Eds.), *Drugs and behavior.* New York: Wiley, 1960.

Lewis, D. J., & Maher, B. A. Neural consolidation and electroconvulsive shock. *Psychol. Rev.,* 1965, **72**, 225–239.

Lotsof, E. J., & Yobst, J. The reliability of the mecholyl test. *Psychosom. Med.,* 1957, **19**, 370–373.

McCullough, M. W. Wechsler-Bellevue changes following prefrontal lobotomy. *J. clin. Psychol.,* 1950, **3**, 270–273.

McDonald, R. E., Ellsworth, R. B., & Enniss, June. Behavioral changes in chronic schizophrenics in response to reserpine. *Arch. Neurol. Psychiat.,* 1956, **75**, 575–578.

McQueen, E. G., Doyle, A. E., & Smirk, F. H. Mechanism of hypotensive action of reserpine, an alkaloid of *Rauwolfia Serpentia, Nature,* 1954, **174**, 1015.

McQueen, E. G., Doyle, A. E., & Smirk, F. H. The circulatory effects of reserpine. *Circulation,* 1955, **11**, 161.

Madsen, M. C., & McGaugh, J. L. The effect of ECS on one-trial avoidance learning. *J. comp. physiol. Psychol.,* 1961, **54**, 522–523.

Maher, B. A. Anticipatory and perseverative errors following frontal lesions in the rat. *J. comp. physiol. Psychol.,* 1955, **48**, 102–105.

Maher, B. A., & Chapoton, P. The comparative effects of chlorpromazine, restraint and displacement upon recovery from an approach-avoidance conflict. Paper presented to Southeast Psychol. Ass., Atlanta, Ga., 1960.

Maher, B. A., Elder, S. T., & Noblin, C. D. A differential investigation of avoidance reduction vs. hypermotility following frontal ablation. *J. comp. physiol. Psychol.,* 1962, **55**, 449–454.

Maher, B. A., & McIntire, R. W. The extinction of the CER following frontal ablation. *J. comp. physiol. Psychol.,* 1960, **53**, 549–552.

Maher, B. A., McIntire, R. W., & House, C. Retrograde amnesia following ECT. Paper presented to Southeast Psychol. Ass., Miami Beach, 1962.

Maher, B. A., & Taylor, J. A. The effects of thiopropazate-dihydrochloride upon recovery from an approach-avoidance conflict. Paper presented to Midwest Psychol. Ass., St. Louis, 1960.

Malmo, R. B., & Amsel, A. Anxiety produced interference in serial rote learning with observations on rote learning after partial frontal lobectomy. *J. exp. Psychol.,* 1949, **38**, 434–440.

Marrazzi, A. S. Synaptic and behavioral

correlates of psychotherapeutic and related drug actions. *Ann. N.Y. Acad. Sci.,* 1962, **96,** 211–226.

Mayer-Gross, W. Retrograde amnesia. *Lancet,* 1943, **2,** 603.

Moniz, E. Psycho-chirurgie. *Nervenarzt,* 1937, **10,** 113–118.

Motolinia's *Historia de los Indios de la Nuevo España.* Vol. 1. Mexico City: Chavez Hayhoe, 1941.

Partridge, N. *Prefrontal leucotomy.* Oxford: Blackwell, 1950.

Pearlman, C. S., Sharpless, S. K., & Jarvik, M. E. Retrograde amnesia produced by anesthetic and convulsant agents. *J. comp. physiol. Psychol.,* 1961, **54,** 109–112.

Poschel, B. P. H. Proactive and retroactive effects of electroconvulsive shock on approach-avoidance conflicts. *J. comp. physiol. Psychol.,* 1957, **50,** 392–396.

Rennie, T. Present status of shock therapy. *Psychiatry,* 1943, **6,** 127–137.

Rodnight, R. Body fluid indoles in mental illness. *Internat. Rev. of Neurobiol.* 1961, **3,**

Shagass, C. Neurophysiological studies of anxiety and depression. *Psychiat. Res. Rep.,* 1957, **8,** 100–117.

Shagass, C., Naiman, J., & Mihalik, J. An objective test which differentiates between neurotic and psychotic depression. *Arch. Neurol. Psychiat.,* 1956, **75,** 461–471.

Sloane, R. B., & Lewis, D. J. Prognostic value of adrenaline and mecholyl responses in electroconvulsive therapy. *J. psychosom. Res.,* 1956, **1,** 273–286.

Smith, C. M. A new adjunct to the treatment of alcoholism. *Quart. J. Stud. Alcohol,* 1958, **19,** 406–417.

Smith, C. M. Some reflections on the possible therapeutic effects of the hallucinogens—with special reference to alcoholism. *Quart. J. Stud. Alcohol,* 1959, **20**(2), 292–301.

Stein, L. Reserpine and the learning of fear. *Science,* 1956, **124** (3231), 1082–1083.

Stone, C. P. Losses and gains in cognitive functions as related to electroconvulsive shock. *J. abnorm. soc. Psychol.,* 1947, **42,** 206–214.

Thomas, D. Prognosis of depression with electric treatment. *Brit. med. J.,* 1954, **2,** 950–954.

Thompson, R., & Dean, W. A further study on the retroactive effects of ECS. *J. comp. physiol. Psychol.,* 1955, **48,** 488–491.

Thorpe, J. G. The current status of prognostic test indicators for electroconvulsive therapy. *Psychosom. Med.,* 1962, **24,** 554–567.

Uhr, L., & Miller, J. G. *Drugs and behavior.* New York: Wiley, 1960.

Weiskrantz, L., & Wilson, W. A. Effect of reserpine on learning and performance. *Science,* 1956, **123**(3208), 1110–1118.

Willett, R. A. The effects of psychosurgical procedures on behavior. In H. Eysenck (Ed.), *Handbook of abnormal psychology.* New York: Basic Books, 1961.

Williams, Gertrude J. The effect of electroconvulsive shock on an instrumental conditioned emotional response ("conflict"). *J. comp. physiol. Psychol.,* 1961, **54,** 633–637.

World Health Organization. Ataractic and hallucinogenic drugs in psychiatry. *Tech. Report Series,* 1958, **No. 152,** W.H.O. Geneva, 1958.

Wortis, J. *History of insulin shock.* New York: Philosophical Library, 1959.

Zubin, J., & Barrera, S. E. Effect of electroconvulsive therapy on memory. *Proc. Soc. exp. Biol. N.Y.,* 1941, **48,** 596–597.

NAME INDEX

Aborn, M., 394, 440
Aceto, M. D. G., 477, 484, 507
Achenbach, K., 90, 102
Adams, H. E., 166–168, 491, 505
Adams, J. K., 57, 71
Ader, R., 250, 271
Ades, H. W., 280, 298
Agarwal, P. S., 334, 355
Akert, K., 482, 505
Alexander, F., 242, 252, 256–258, 271
Alexander, L., 499, 505
Alfert, E., 195, 207
Allen, G., 352, 355
Allen, I. M., 497, 505
Allport, G. W., 110, 132
Allyon, T., 451, 452, 461, 464, 465, 467, 473
Alpero, B. J., 497, 505
Alzheimer, A., 275, 297
Ameen, L., 303, 327
Amsel, A., 181, 188, 501, 502, 507
Ancevich, S. S., 415, 440
Anderson, O. D., 136, 167
Anderson, W. W., 292, 297

Andy, O. J., 482, 505
Angel, C., 331, 356
Aprison, M. H., 333, 355
Apter, N. S., 336, 355
Arenberg, D., 198, 207
Arieti, S., 304, 318, 325, 326, 425, 437, 438
Arkoff, A., 323, 326
Arnhoff, F., 396, 439
Aronfreed, J., 203, 206
Atkinson, J. W., 66, 71, 198, 206
Atkinson, R., 387, 389
Ax, A., 85, 101, 183, 187
Axelrod, J., 330, 358

Babcock, H., 307, 326
Bacon, F., 473
Bahrick, H. P., 62, 71
Baker, A. A., 449, 473
Baker, S. J., 399, 400, 438
Balonov, L Ya., 341, 358
Bales, R. F., 401, 440
Balian, L., 318, 327
Balken, E. R., 401, 403, 410, 438

Baller, W. R., 292, 297
Balvin, R. S., 285, 286, 297
Bannerjee, S., 334, 355
Bannister, D., 422–424, 438
Bard, P., 291, 297
Barker, J. C., 463, 473
Baron, M. R., 179, 188
Barrera, S. E., 494, 508
Barrett, W. W., 484, 505
Barry, H., 478, 505
Bateman, D. E., 89, 90, 102
Bateman, J. F., 346, 347, 357
Bateson, G., 321, 325, 326
Baumeister, A. A., 295, 297
Beam, J. C., 185, 187
Beardslee, D. C., 71
Beck, E., 291, 298
Becker, W. C., 311, 326
Beckman, W. G., 121, 132
Beels, C. C., 250, 271
Bein, H. J., 482, 505
Belenkaya, N. Y., 342, 343, 355
Bell, N. W., 320, 326
Bender, L., 216, 236
Benjamin, J. D., 329, 355
Bennett, C., 448, 505
Berkowitz, L., 226, 236

509

Hull, C. L., 139, 168, 381, 382, 390
Hunt, H. F., 166, 168, 476, 477, 491, 506
Hunt, J. McV., 372, 377, 389, 390
Hunt, W. A., 396, 397, 439
Huston, P. E., 364, 372, 374–377, 386, 390, 392, 497, 506
Hyde, R. W., 336, 357

Inhelder, B., 9, 19
Inskip, W. M., 334, 356
Irvine, R., 365, 390
Isaac, W., 280, 298

Jackson, D. D., 321, 325, 326
Jackson, D. N., 179, 188
Jaco, E. G., 326
Janis, I. L., 494, 496, 506
Jarvik, M., 488, 491, 505, 508
Jasper, H. H., 92, 102
Jellinek, E., 27, 41
Jenkins, J. G., 55, 72
Jenkins, R. L., 502, 506
Jersild, A. T., 53, 72
Jessner, L., 497, 506
Jones, F. N., 74, 102
Jones, H. G., 278, 298
Jones, M., 29, 41
Jones, Mary, 474
Jones, Maxwell, 449, 462, 473
Jones, M. H., 74, 102
Jones, N. F., 396, 397, 439
Joy, V. L., 196, 207

Kaelbling, R., 89, 102
Kafka, A., 236
Kahn, R. L., 499, 506
Kalinowsky, L. B., 117, 132, 496, 500, 502, 507
Kalish, H., 47, 72, 163, 168
Kallman, F. J., 349, 353–354, 356
Kantor, R. E., 312, 326
Kaplan, B., 18, 326
Kardiner, A., 172, 188
Karlin, S. H., 330, 357
Karpman, B., 236
Kasanin, J., 430, 437, 439
Katkorsky, W., 460, 461, 474
Kauffman, D. A., 341, 358
Kawi, A. W., 122, 132
Keller, D. L., 484, 507
Kelly, G. A., 324, 327, 422–425, 439
Kelman, H., 471, 474
Kendig, I., 376, 390

Kennard, M. A., 345, 356
Kennedy, R. J. A., 292, 297
Kern, R., 78, 80, 101
Kesson, W., 175, 176, 188
Kety, S., 334, 356
Keynes, J. M., 108, 132
Killiam, E. K., 486, 507
Killiam, K. F., 486, 507
Kimble, G. A., 71
King, F. H., 90, 102
King, G. F., 311, 327, 381, 382, 391
King, S. H., 84, 102
Kinnard, W. J., 477, 484, 507
Kissen, D. M., 247, 268, 272
Klüver, H., 290, 291, 297
Knehr, C. A., 373, 391
Knott, J. R., 222, 236
Koffka, K., 431, 439
Kogan, N., 167
Kohn, M. L., 320, 327
Kopin, I. J., 334, 356
Korchin, S. J., 179, 188
Kornetsky, C., 122, 132, 479, 507
Kraepelin, E., 215, 236, 299, 327, 382, 391
Kräupl-Taylor, F., 449, 474
Kremen, I., 179, 188
Kringlen, E., 351, 356
Kubis, J., 180, 189
Kuntz, A., 82, 102
Kurland, A. A., 121, 132
Kutash, S. B., 206

Lacey, J. I., 48, 72, 89, 90, 102
Laffal, J., 284, 285, 297, 303, 327, 404, 407, 437, 439
Lagergren, A., 492–494, 505
Lane, J. E., 313, 327
Lane, R. C., 319, 327
Lang, P. J., 355, 389
Lasagna, L., 121, 132
Lasky, J. J., 479, 507
Lauer, J. W., 334, 356
Laverty, S. G., 415, 416, 440
Lavin, N. T., 463, 473
Lawlor, W. G., 374, 391
Lazarus, R. S., 194, 195, 207
Lea, A. J., 330, 357
Leach, B. E., 331, 356
Lehtinen, L. E., 282, 294, 298
Leifer, A. I., 330, 356
Lejeune, J., 125, 132, 294, 297
Lenkoski, D., 303, 327
Lennox, W. G., 95, 102, 289, 297
Leventhal, A. M., 385, 391
Levin, H., 204, 207, 218, 237
Levine, S., 79–81, 102

Levitt, E. E., 471, 474
Levy, S., 345, 356
Lewis, D. J., 166–168, 322, 327, 491, 499, 505, 507, 508
Lewis, E. D., 294, 297
Lewis, G. W., 79, 102
Lewis, J., 242, 243, 273
Lewis, W. C., 270–272
Lhamon, W. T., 371, 391
Lichtenheld, F. R., 330, 357
Lichtenstein, P. E., 136, 168
Liddell, D. W., 290, 297
Liddell, H. S., 136, 137, 168, 259, 272
Lidz, R. W., 317, 327
Lidz, T., 317, 318, 327
Lief, H. I., 468, 474
Lief, V. F., 468, 474
Lindemann, E., 121, 132
Lindsley, D. B., 97, 99, 102
Lindsley, O. R., 378–381, 391
Lipton, E. L., 265, 272, 273
Little, S. W., 261, 273
Locher, L. M., 479, 506
Longo, N., 194, 207
Loofbourrow, G. N., 84, 101, 102, 264, 271, 272
Lorenz, Maria, 399–401, 404, 410, 439
Lorenz, T. H., 270–272
Lorr, M., 502, 506
Lotsof, E. J., 499, 507
Lovinger, E., 369, 381, 382, 391
Lowinger, L., 345, 358
Lubin, A., 281, 298
Luchko, A. E. O., 341, 358
Luxenburger, H., 349, 357
Lykken, D. T., 179, 188, 221, 236
Lynn, R., 343, 357
Lyons, J. F., 292, 297

Mabry, M., 401, 439
McArthur, C., 268, 273
McClelland, D. C., 66, 71, 198, 206
Maccoby, E., 204, 207, 237
McCord, J., 226, 236
McCord, W., 226, 236
McCullough, M. W., 501, 507
MacDonald, N., 311, 325, 327, 415, 439
McDonald, R. E., 484, 507
McDonough, J. M., 365, 391
McGaugh, J. L., 491, 507
McGaughran, L. S., 420, 430, 439
McGuigan, F. J., 179, 188
McIntire, R. W., 164, 165, 168, 493, 501, 507

SUBJECT INDEX

Abstraction, brain-injury, 281
   schizophrenia, 419–421
   schizophrenic language, 396–397
Acetylcholine, 82–83, 333
ACTH (adrenocorticotropic hormone), function, 74–75
   LSD antagonism, 336
   schizophrenia, 336
Action, thought parameter in schizophrenia, 313–317
Activation (*see* Arousal)
Adjective-Verb Quotient (AVQ), 400, 401–403
Adrenal glands, in experimental hypertension, 255–256
   function, 74
   schizophrenia, 335–336
Adrenalectomy, 336
Adrenalin, 84–86, 329–330
Adrenochrome, 329, 330
Adrenolutin, 329
Agraphia, 284
Alcohol, 164
Alexia, 284
Alpha rhythm, attention, 92
   defined, 90–92

Alpha rhythm, feed-back circuit, 92–93
   mental deficiency, 295
   orienting response, 341
Alzheimer's disease, 275–276
American Psychiatric Association, diagnostic classification system, 23–25
Amobarbitol, 339
Amphetamine sulfate, 374
Amytal sodium, 374
Anger, autonomic patterns, 185–186
   mecholyl test, 84
Angst (*see* Anxiety)
Anxiety, angst, 177
   arousal, 176–177, 182
   autonomic measures, 184–186
   behavior rating scales, 185
   case example, 171–173
   clinical features, 171-173
   conditioned response to pain, 174–175
   definitions, 170–171, 178
   empirical aspects, 178–187
   existential, 177–178
   fundamental distress, 175–176

Anxiety, G.S.R. conditioning, 377
   Manifest Anxiety Scale, 178–179
   measurement, 178
   overarousal, 176–177
   questionnaires, 178–181
   rigidity, 181–182
   schizophrenia, 324–325
   semi-projective measures, 183–184
   subjective reports, 171
   symptoms, 171
   theoretical aspects, 173–178
   traumatic anxiety, 172–173
   verbal behavior measures, 185–187
   (*See also* Manifest Anxiety Scale)
Aphasia, 279, 284–285
Apparent movement, 365
Approach-avoidance conflict (*see* Conflict)
Arecoline, 399
Arousal, anxiety, 176–177, 182
   behavioral aspects, 97–99, 101
   caffein, 342